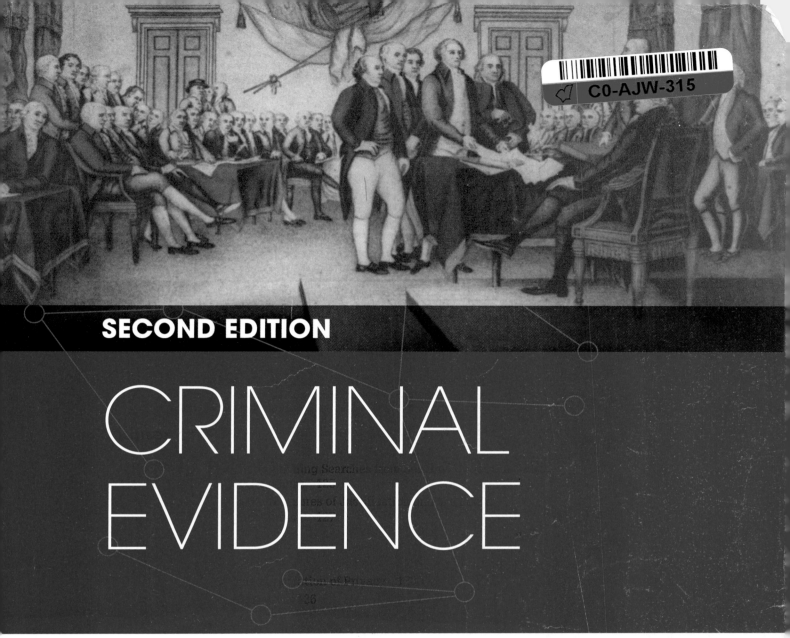

SECOND EDITION

CRIMINAL EVIDENCE

Marjie T. Britz, Ph.D.
Clemson University

PEARSON

Boston   Columbus   Indianapolis   New York   San Francisco   Amsterdam
Cape Town   Dubai   London   Madrid   Milan   Munich   Paris   Montréal   Toronto
Delhi   Mexico City   São Paulo   Sydney   Hong Kong   Seoul   Singapore   Taipei   Tokyo

Editorial Director: Andrew Gilfillin
Senior Acquisitions Editor: Gary Bauer
Editorial Assistant: Lynda Cramer
Program Manager: Tara Horton
Director of Marketing: Dave Gesell
Marketing Manager: Thomas Hayward
Marketing Assistant: Les Roberts
Project Manager Team Lead: Bryan Pirrmann
Project Manager: Susan Hannahs
Senior Operations Supervisor: Mary Fischer
Operations Specialist: Deidra Skahill
Senior Art Director: Diane Ernsberger
Cover Designer: Studio Montage
Cover Art: Gary S. Chapman/Getty Images
Full-Service Project Management: Sudip Sinha, Lumina Datamatics, Inc.
Composition: Lumina Datamatics, Inc.
Printer/Binder: Edwards Brothers Malloy Jackson Road
Cover Printer: Lehigh Phoenix Color
Text Font: 11/13 TimesLTPro Roman

Credits and acknowledgments borrowed from other sources and reproduced, with permission, in this textbook appear on the appropriate page within the text.

Library of Congress Cataloging-in-Publication Data

Britz, Marjie, author.
  Criminal evidence / Marjie T. Britz, Clemson University. — Second edition.
     pages cm
  Includes bibliographical references and index.
   ISBN 978-0-13-359833-9 — ISBN 0-13-359833-0   1. Evidence, Criminal—United States.
I. Title.
  KF9660.Z9B75 2015
  345.73'06—dc23

                                                                 2015029619

10 9 8 7 6 5 4 3 2

ISBN 10:   0-13-359833-0
ISBN 13: 978-0-13-359833-9

The book is dedicated to the memory of Joe W. Morgan, Jr. –
my mentor, my hero, my friend.

Contents

Contents   x
▼

Preface

Criminal Evidence is a comprehensive text that explores the laws of evidence in the United States. The text traces the historical evolution of American jurisprudence from inception to contemporary courts and is intended for both undergraduates and law students. The text is organized to reinforce foundational concepts (e.g., courtroom process and criminal procedure) discussed in introductory courses prior to the presentation of sophisticated legal constructs. Further, the text is designed to engage students through the application of real-world cases.

▶ New to This Edition

This edition has been completely updated and significantly expanded with nearly 40% more content, the introduction of five new pedagogical tools per chapter, and the complete text of the *Federal Rules of Evidence*, *Magna Carta*, and the *Bill of Rights*. Other overall changes include, but are not limited to:

- Inclusion of 42 additional cases
- Significant expansion of the Table of Contents
- Significant expansion of Chapter outlines at the beginning of each chapter
- Highlighting of Criminal Statutes, Rules of Criminal Procedure, & the Federal Rules of Evidence throughout the text
- Incorporation of charts, diagrams, textboxes, and photographs to demonstrate key concepts
- Significant expansion of pedagogical content per chapter
  - Chapter Outline
  - Learning Objectives
  - Key Terms
  - Discussion Questions
  - Recommended Resources
  - **New Pedagogical items**
    - Application of Law Textboxes – illustration of key concepts in American law through the discussion of interesting or highly publicized cases. For example, the author uses the case of New England Patriot Aaron Hernandez to demonstrate the exclusion of evidence
    - In Search of History Textboxes – exploration of important historical developments in the field
    - Clarification of Concepts Textboxes – more comprehensive discussion of similar or opposing legal concepts
    - Case Law Textboxes focusing on an appellate case, statute, or law
    - Margin Definitions – provides students with easy access to important definitions of concepts presented in each chapter

▶ Changes per Chapter

Chapter 1 – *The Evolution of the Law of Criminal Evidence* – Chapter 1 has been reorganized and significantly expanded both contextually and pedagogically. This includes the introduction of the five new learning tools incorporated into all chapters, and the addition of various sections. Generally speaking, all case law and federal statutes have been updated. Specifically, the following changes have been made.

- Significantly expanded upon section *The History of Law and Legal Process*, adding subsections: *Trials: The Jury System & Compulsory Testimony*, *Magna Carta*, and *Habeas Corpus*.

  - Includes Case Law Textbox: *Federal Suspension of Habeas Corpus* that comprehensively discusses the actions of Presidents Abraham Lincoln and George W. Bush, and the Supreme Court's interpretation of same.

- Significantly expanded upon the previous edition's discussion of probable cause, reasonable suspicion, and the Warrant and Reasonableness Clauses housed within the Fourth Amendment.

- Significantly expanded discussion of the Fifth Amendment, including the addition of subsections on the right to a grand jury, protection against double jeopardy, protection against self-incrimination, and the right to due process.

- Significantly expanded upon the previous edition's discussion of protections housed within the Sixth Amendment, including the addition of subsections on: speedy trials; jury impartiality; notification of charges; confrontation of witnesses; subpoena powers; and, effective counsel. This includes both a Case Law Textbox – *The Evolution of* Miranda and an Application of Law Textbox – *The Sixth Amendment and Jose Padilla.*

- Significantly expanded on discussions of the Eighth Amendment, including recent rulings by the Supreme Court and a Case Law Textbox – *Furman, Gregg, & the Eighth Amendment.*

- The author has added a section *Judicially Created Rights* which introduces students to rights that are fundamental to notions of due process, but which are not articulated in the Bill of Rights. This includes a discussion of the presumption of innocence and standards of proof.

- In addition to the new pedagogical tools included in each chapter, the author has added two sections *Finding Cases and Conducting Legal Research* and *Case Citations*. These sections are designed to assist undergraduate students in conducting legal research through the use of traditional published reports and/or digital sources.

- Among other topics, *In Search of History* boxes explore the evolution of the Fifth Amendment, the Magna Carta, England's Star Chamber.

Chapter 2 – *Federalism, Court Systems, and the Criminal Justice Process* – Like the preceding chapter, Chapter 2 has been reorganized and significantly expanded both contextually and pedagogically. This includes the introduction of the five new learning tools incorporated into all chapters, and the addition of various sections. Generally speaking, all case law and federal statutes have been updated. Specifically, the following changes have been made.

- Significantly expanded upon the discussion of the separation of powers, and includes a new section on *Federalism and Criminal Law*. This section discusses sovereignty and federalism. It further discusses federal enforcement agencies. It also includes a Clarification of Concepts Textboxes – *Limits of Federal Power* and *Federal Law Enforcement Under the Executive Branch*.

- Incorporated a Case Law Textbox – *Judicial Inconsistency: Warrantless Searches of Cell Phones Incident to Arrest*. It includes the 2014 Supreme Court rulings in *Riley v. California* and *U.S. v. Wurie*. This textbox demonstrates to undergraduates the lack of consistency in and between state and federal courts.

- Expanded on the discussion of courtroom actors and the American adversarial system, and included a Case Law Textbox – *Evaluating the Effectiveness of Counsel in Pretrial Proceedings*.

- Significantly expanded the previous discussion of affirmative defenses, including the addition of *duty to retreat clauses* in traditional self-defense statutes.

- Provided material on *Stand Your Ground Laws* that have been sensationalized by the media in recent years. Also added an Application of Law Textbox – *Stand Your Ground Laws and Trayvon Martin*.

- Added a new section on *Miscellaneous Affirmative Defenses* that explores non-traditional affirmative defenses, like the Twinkie, Nymphomaniac, and Sleepwalking defenses. Also includes a new Application of Law Textbox – *Teenagers, Entitlement, and the Affluenza Defense*.

- Added a Case Law Textbox – *Plea Bargaining Requirements* that delineates rules established by the Supreme Court.

- Significantly expanded on motions and disclosure, including an Application of Law Textbox – *A Brady Violation and a Wrongful Conviction* and a Case Law Textbox – *Prosecutorial Disclosure Obligations and the* Brady *Rule*.

Chapter 3 – *Forms of Evidence* – Like the other chapters in this edition, Chapter 3 has been completely updated and expanded upon both contextually and pedagogically. This includes the introduction of the five new learning tools incorporated into all chapters, and the addition of various sections. Generally speaking, all case law and federal statutes have been updated. Specifically, the following changes have been made:

- Significantly expanded sections of *Materiality*, *Competency*, and *Direct Versus Circumstantial Evidence*, and added Application of Law Textboxes – *He Said, She Said: The Jameis Winston Case Circumstantial Evidence, a Perfect Alibi, & a Motown Executive*; *Sex, Fraud, & Motive: The Preacher's Wife*; and, *The Carolina Panthers, a First Round Draft Pick, and Murder*.

- Significantly expanded discussion of *mens rea*, and added Case Law Text Box – *Inferences and Intent* and Clarification of Concepts Textbox – *Probable Cause vs. Beyond a Reasonable Doubt*.

Chapter 4 – *Search and Seizure and the Doctrine of Justification* – Like the other chapters in this edition, Chapter 4 has been completely updated and expanded upon both contextually and pedagogically. This includes the introduction of the five new learning tools incorporated into all chapters, and the addition of various sections. Generally speaking, all case law and federal statutes have been updated. Specifically, the following changes have been made:

- Significantly expanded upon discussion of all aspects of the Fourth Amendment

- Added section *Distinguishing Searches from Seizures Under the Fourth Amendment* that includes Case Law Textbox – *Traffic Stops, Drug Dogs, and the Fourth Amendment*

- Added section *Legal Measures of Justification and the Fourth Amendment* that discusses various standards and rationales for searches. The section also includes a Case Law Textbox – *Defining Probable Cause*, which looks at important cases that defined probable cause.

- Added section *Administrative Justifications* that explores searches not based on suspicious behavior or circumstances (e.g., health inspections, school searches, drug testing of student athletes, and searches of regulated businesses).

- Significantly expanded discussion of the expectation of privacy, including a Case Law Textbox that looks at important cases in the development of parameters. Also added Case Law Textbox *The Ortega Doctrine and Workplace Searches*.

Chapter 5 – *The Exclusionary Rule and the Fourth Amendment* – Like the other chapters in this edition, Chapter 5 has been completely updated and expanded upon both contextually and pedagogically. This includes the introduction of the five new learning tools incorporated into all chapters, and the addition of various sections. Generally speaking, all case law and federal statutes have been updated. Specifically, the following changes have been made:

- Expanded discussion on the Exclusionary Rule, and added a Case Law Textbox – *Wong Sun v. United States*

- Added Application of Law Textbox – *A New England Patriot and the Exclusionary Rule* that discusses the murder case of former NFL star Aaron Hernandez.

- Added Clarification of Concepts Textbox – *When the Fruits of the Poisonous Tree Doctrine Does Not Apply* that discusses when the protections extended in the Exclusionary Rule do not attach.

- Added Case Law Textbox – *Significant Cases Regarding the Exclusionary Rule* that summarizes important cases regarding the exclusionary rule beginning with *Weeks v. United States* (1914) through *Herring v. United States* (2009).

- Incorporated additional Case Law Textboxes that specifically addresses the expectation of privacy and overnight guests; containers, third parties, and the expectation of privacy; and, the totality of circumstances.

Chapter 6 – *Warrantless Searches* - Like the other chapters in this edition, Chapter 6 has been completely updated and expanded upon both contextually and pedagogically. This includes the introduction of the five new learning tools incorporated into all chapters, and the addition of various sections. Generally speaking, all case law and federal statutes have been updated. Specifically, the following changes have been made:

- Significantly expanded discussion of warrantless searches, including new sections on *Terry* Stops and Incident to Arrest.

- Added Case Law Textbox – *Important Post-*Terry *Decisions* that traces the evolution of stop-and-frisk searches permissible under the *Terry* Doctrine, including *Dickerson* and *Hiibel*.

- Added Case Law Textbox – *Evolution of Parameters Concerning Searching Incident to Arrest* that traces the evolution of Searches Incident to Arrest permissible since the first half of the twentieth century. This includes traditional provisions established in *Belton*, but which were overturned in *Arizona v. Gant*.

- Added Case Law Textbox – *Important Notes on Plain View Searches* that explores important cases regarding the requirements of inadvertent discovery and immediate apparency.

- Added Case Law Textbox – *Abandoning the Belton Rule: Arizona v. Gant* that discusses the Court's rationale under *Gant*.
- Added Case Law Textboxes that discuss automobile searches, parameters of consent, and non-vehicle inventory searches.

Chapter 7 – *Confessions* – Like the other chapters in this edition, Chapter 7 has been completely updated and expanded upon both contextually and pedagogically. This includes the introduction of the five new learning tools incorporated into all chapters, and the addition of various sections. Generally speaking, all case law and federal statutes have been updated. Specifically, the following changes have been made:

- Expanded discussion of the Fifth and Sixth Amendments and their application to courtroom testimony.
- Addition of Application of Law Textbox – *Unforeseen Developments and Mistrials*.
- Addition of Case Law Textbox – *The Confrontation Clause* that discusses significant cases in the clarification of the protections and boundaries of the Sixth Amendment.
- Addition of Clarification of Concepts Textbox – *Differentiating Confessions and Incriminating Statements*.
- Addition of Case Law Textboxes – *Situations in which* Miranda *Does Not Attach* and *Extending Self-Incrimination Protections to the Workplace* – which discuss situational characteristics that can expand or restrict protections within the Fifth and Sixth Amendments.
- Addition of Case Law Textbox – *The Right to Counsel* that discusses significant developments in jurisprudence regarding the right to counsel from the early twentieth century through the new millennium.
- Addition of Case Law Textbox – *Confessions* that explores case law regarding confessions .

Chapter 8 – *Qualifications of Witnesses* – Like the other chapters in this edition, Chapter 8 has been completely updated and expanded upon both contextually and pedagogically. This includes the introduction of the five new learning tools incorporated into all chapters, and the addition of various sections. Generally speaking, all case law and federal statutes have been updated. Specifically, the following changes have been made:

- Expanded on discussion of the Confrontation Clause and the competency and credibility of witnesses.
- Added Application of Law Textbox – *The Low Country Rapist – A Question of Competency* that illustrates the requirements for the demonstration of competency.
- Added Application of Law Textbox – *Hypnosis and Familial Bonds* that discusses the case of the South Hill rapist whose original conviction was reversed and remanded due to the introduction of post-hypnotic testimony.
- Expanded discussion of perjury and subpoenas, and added Application of Law – *Hillary Clinton and House Subpoenas*.

Chapter 9 – *Examination of Witnesses* – Like the other chapters in this edition, Chapter 9 has been completely updated and expanded upon both contextually and pedagogically. This includes the introduction of the five new learning tools incorporated into all chapters, and the addition of various sections. Generally speaking, all case law and federal statutes have been updated. Specifically, the following changes have been made:

- Provided additional clarification between lay and expert witnesses.

- Added Application of Law Textbox – *Expert Testimony in the Death of a Casino Mogul* that uses the case of Ted Binion to illustrate the fallibility of expert testimony.

- Added Application of Law Textbox – *The West Memphis Three and Witness Impeachment.*

- Expanded the discussion of standards for scientific testimony, and added Case Law Textbox – *Evidentiary Standards for the Admission of Expert Testimony*

Chapter 10 – *Hearsay* – Like the other chapters in this edition, Chapter 10 has been completely updated and expanded upon both contextually and pedagogically. Changes include the introduction of the five new learning tools incorporated into all chapters, and the addition of various sections. Generally speaking, all case law and federal statutes have been updated. Specifically, the following changes have been made:

- Significantly expanded the discussion of the history and rationale of the hearsay rule, and added an In Search of History Textbox – *Hearsay & Sir Walter Raleigh* that includes original statements.

- Added Application of Law textboxes: *Rae Carruth & Dying Declarations*
- Added Case Law Textbox – *Hearsay & Testimonial Statements* that specifically discusses the Court's rulings in *Crawford v. Washington* and *Davis v. Washington.*

Chapter 11 – *Privileged Communications* – Like the other chapters in this edition, Chapter 11 has been completely updated and expanded upon both contextually and pedagogically. This includes the introduction of the five new learning tools incorporated into all chapters, and the addition of various sections. Generally speaking, all case law and federal statutes have been updated. Specifically, the following changes have been made:

- Updated case law throughout the chapter, and included additional examples of state cases and codes California Evidence Code; examples of codified marital privileges, etc.)

- Added an Application of Law Textbox – *Wikileaks and Journalistic Freedom* that discusses the case of American Intelligence Analyst Bradley Manning.

Chapter 12 – *Documentary and Scientific Evidence* – Like the other chapters in this edition, Chapter 12 has been completely updated and expanded upon both contextually and pedagogically. This includes the introduction of the five new learning tools incorporated into all chapters, and the addition of various sections. Generally speaking, all case law and federal statutes have been updated. Specifically, the following changes have been made:

- Significantly expanded *Motions* section, including the addition of a Clarification of Concepts Textbox – *Common Motions Associated with Scientific Evidence* (e.g., Daubert motions, motions in limine, and motions to strike). In addition, I added a Case Law Textbox – *Prejudice & Change of Venue:*

Skilling v. United States, which involved Enron executives and which established a threshold for changing venue based on media-induced prejudice.

- Added assorted Case Law Textboxes – *Bank Deposits & Privacy: United States v. Miller*; *Contemporary Standard for Scientific Evidence: Daubert*; *The Fifth Amendment and Handwriting: Gilbert v. California*;

Chapter 13 – *Cyber Evidence and Demonstrative Evidence in the Pursuit of Justice* – Like the other chapters in this edition, Chapter 13 has been completely updated and expanded upon both contextually and pedagogically. This includes the introduction of the five new learning tools incorporated into all chapters, and the addition of various sections. Generally speaking, all case law and federal statutes have been updated. Specifically, the following changes have been made:

- Clarification of Concepts Textboxes have been incorporated throughout the chapter to illustrate important concepts for undergraduates. These include, but are not limited to: *Problems with Prosecuting Computer Crime*, *What Resources Are Lacking in Digital Evidence Analysis*; *Terms and Definitions of Computer Crime*; *Privacy in the Digital Age*; *When to Use Photographic Evidence*; *General Requirements for Admissibility of Photographs*, *Computer Graphics and Animations Versus Computer Simulations*.

- Application of Law Textboxes has also been used to apply legal concepts to interesting cases. These include but are not limited to the cases of the first online serial killer, Ed Robinson; and, Sharee Miller.

- Addition of a student exercise that requires students to identify relevant statutes and case law to address a series of questions regarding jurisdiction and the prosecution of online gambling.

► Instructor Supplements

Instructor's Manual with Test Bank. Includes content outlines for classroom discussion, teaching suggestions, and answers to selected end-of-chapter questions from the text. This also contains a Word document version of the test bank.

TestGen. This computerized test generation system gives you maximum flexibility in creating and administering tests on paper, electronically, or online. It provides state-of-the-art features for viewing and editing test bank questions, dragging a selected question into a test you are creating, and printing sleek, formatted tests in a variety of layouts. Select test items from test banks included with TestGen for quick test creation, or write your own questions from scratch. TestGen's random generator provides the option to display different text or calculated number values each time questions are used.

PowerPoint Presentations. Our presentations offer clear, straightforward outlines and notes to use for class lectures or study materials. Photos, illustrations, charts, and tables from the book are included in the presentations when applicable.

To access supplementary materials online, instructors need to request an instructor access code. Go to **www.pearsonhighered.com/irc**, where you can register for an instructor access code. Within 48 hours after registering, you will receive a confirming email, including an instructor access code. Once you have received your code, go to the site and log on for full instructions on downloading the materials you wish to use.

► Alternate Versions

EBooks This text is also available in multiple eBook formats. These are an exciting new choice for students looking to save money. As an alternative to purchasing the printed textbook, students can purchase an electronic version of the same content. With an eTextbook, students can search the text, make notes online, print out reading assignments that incorporate lecture notes, and bookmark important passages for later review. For more information, visit your favorite online eBook reseller or visit www.mypearsonstore.com.

► Acknowledgements

I wish to thank the reviewers of this book who provided many helpful comments and insights that have been incorporated into this edition; David A. Ferster, Edinboro University of Pennsylvania and Ian Moffett, Florida International University.

THE DECLARATION OF INDEPENDENCE.

1 The Evolution of the Law of Criminal Evidence

LEARNING OBJECTIVES

The learner will:

1 *Examine the history of law and the legal process*

2 *Identify and discuss the sources of the individual rights, including the U.S. Constitution and the Bill of Rights*

3 *Identify and discuss the implications of the Bill of Rights regarding evidence*

4 *Explain the concept of judicial review*

5 *Examine the history of the rules of evidence*

6 *Identify the federal sources of rules of evidence*

7 *Identify and discuss the role of the U.S. Constitution, Supreme Court, and the federal courts in evidence law*

8 *Examine the Uniform Rules of Evidence and the Federal Rules of Evidence*

9 *Examine the role of state constitutions, rules of evidence, and case law as they relate to evidence*

10 *Examine the content and quality of good evidence*

11 *Distinguish between the concepts of relevancy, materiality, and inadmissibility in evidence*

law the codification of social norms and expectations which are deemed necessary for the maintenance of a society.

substantive law law that defines the parameters of social behaviors.

procedural law the process of adjudicating social behaviors prohibited by substantive law.

mala in se criminal acts that are considered to be inherently wrong.

evidence the demonstration of truth or untruth of allegations in a court of law through the consideration of information that is relevant, competent, material, and probative.

Means for the control and regulation of human behavior exist in virtually every culture in the modern world. In fact, **law** in some form is noted in ancient civilization dating back thousands of years. Distinct from informal means of social control, laws provide formal guidelines and punishment for all members of society, irrespective of race, gender, age, ethnicity, or subculture. As such, they are deemed necessary for the maintenance of the particular society from which they derive. Indeed, the absence of such codification would result in a society in which conflict resolution could be achieved only through violence. Law, then, may be defined as the codification of social norms and expectations. This definition may be bifurcated further into laws of substance and laws of procedure. **Substantive law** defines the parameters of social behaviors, while **procedural law** defines the process of adjudicating those behaviors. Many similarities may be found cross-culturally within substantive laws, most particularly among crimes defined as inherently wrong. The ***mala in se*** crime of patricide, for example, is prohibited in virtually every civilized society. However, the procedure for the disposition of the same crime may be decidedly different across cultures. While some societies have large measures of both, Anglo-Saxon jurisprudence has been characterized mostly by procedural evolution.

Firmly situated within the framework of procedural law, **evidence** may be defined as the demonstration of truth or untruth of allegations in a court of law through the consideration of information that is relevant, competent, material, and probative. Unlike other areas of law, however, the rules of evidence are not universally regarded or considered. Although the introduction of evidence within the United States is heavily codified, many cultures approach the introduction of evidence in a haphazard manner at best. In order to come to a complete understanding of the American system, it is essential to explore the history of law and jurisprudence throughout the world.

MALA IN SE VERSUS *MALA PROHIBITA*

Mala in se crimes are defined as behaviors that are inherently wrong or immoral in and of themselves—irrespective of the prevailing law. The rape of a child or the eating of one's offspring would be examples of such in most societies.

Mala prohibita crimes, on the other hand, are behaviors that are not naturally immoral but whose wrongness lies in their legal prohibition. Such crimes in the United States might include: gambling, drug use, and vagrancy.

▶ The History of Law and Legal Process

Traditionally, legal systems—including the Egyptian, Mesopotamian, Hebrew, and Hindu—were based almost entirely on religious beliefs, grounded in assumptions that rulers were divinely guided in the development and application of justice. Secular systems emerged from the Greeks and, with few exceptions, contemporary systems have, as well.

mala prohibita
behaviors that are not inherently immoral but whose wrongness liesin their legal prohibition.

IN SEARCH OF HISTORY: SYSTEMS OF LAW ACCORDING TO WIGMORE

PRE-CHRISTIAN ERA

Egyptian (4000 B.C.–800 B.C.). This Egyptian era proved to be the most pervasive and foundational of all the legal systems identified by John Henry Wigmore, elements or characteristics of which are noted in virtually all the others. The codes of law consisted of some 40 scrolls in which self-representation was key. Interestingly, this system granted a level of equity and independence for females much greater than in subsequent laws. For example, under Egyptian law of this period, women held the right to divorce. In fact, it appears that subsequent Semitic codes gradually eroded all marital rights of women. Despite its sophistication, this system was characterized as nepotistic, with administrative and judicial responsibilities contained within a single office (i.e., the judge). In this system, petitioners represented themselves without the presence of advocates; Egyptians believed that other world systems were flawed in that an advocate's eloquence, or lack thereof, might unfairly influence the decision. The system was replaced by the Roman emperor Octavian after his defeat of Antony and Cleopatra.

Mesopotamian (4000 B.C.–100 B.C.). Best known for its development of a complex network of commercial custom and law, the Mesopotamian code is also one of the most preserved. The Code of Hammurabi, discovered in 1902 by the French explorer De Morgan, is an 8-foot pillar of 300 sections. It currently resides in the Louvre. For the most part, the Code of Hammurabi

included exhaustive provisions for marital relationships, with limited guidance for prosecution of crimes. It is characterized by the burden of proof resting solely with the accused and carried severe sanctions, including death, for failure to meet this burden.

Hebrew (1200 B.C.–Present). Still in existence, Hebrew law has evolved over a progression of five periods: Mosaic, Classic, Talmudic, Medieval, and Modern. Before 300 B.C., Hebrew law was consistent with others, then in existence in that laws were made by kings, judges, and prophets. Gradually, of course, church leaders became the legislators and arbiters of justice, and the "Scroll of the Law" (a.k.a. the Torah) resides in every synagogue in the world.

Chinese (Pre-2500 B.C.–1949). Unfortunately, Wigmore's conceptualization of the world's legal systems was created prior to the rise of Chinese communism. However, before 1949, the Chinese proved to be "the most law-abiding people on the face of the globe—but the laws by which they [abided] were laws of which they approved" (Wigmore, 1936, p. 148). This society was characterized by conciliation and mutual adjustments, which were characteristics essential to the driving force behind their judicial system.

Hindu (500 B.C.–Present). In the most basic sense, the Hindu Laws of Manu was a system of laws that rewarded some in society at the expense of others. Caste based in nature, the laws were required to be adhered to by all members, but obedience was much

(continued)

simpler for the Brahmins, whose lives were made much easier by the subjugation of the Sudras.

Greek (1200 B.C.–A.D. 300). Beginning in the Homeric period and ending with the Romans, the Greek system was the first to employ a jury system. During this period, citizens were ultimately responsible for interpreting the law, determining guilt, and administering punishment. During trial proceedings, magistrates acted merely as the chairperson of the assembly while average citizens, selected through the drawing of lots, served as judge, jury, and executioner. Many recognized the danger in such power, as Socrates cautioned, "The difficulty, my friends, is not in avoiding death, but in avoiding unrighteousness; for that pursues us faster than death."

Roman (400 B.C.–Fifth century A.D.). This period constituted the first comprehensive attempt at the incorporation of procedural law and produced a professional orator class (Cicero was considered the most successful orator of his time). During this period, a system that included a professional judge and jurists emerged, the jury-advocate system faded, and politics and law officially separated. According to Wigmore, the Roman system was characterized as such:

> *The praetor had become the typical judge of our modern ideals, the first of the kind—secular, not priestly; a lawyer, not a layman; an adjudicator, not an administrator ... professional jurists in copious treatises expounded legal principles in systematic forms ... schools of love-study arose and multiplied. (p. 420)*

CHRISTIAN ERA

Japanese (A.D. 500–Present). The legal system in Japan evolved over five distinct periods beginning before the advent of Christianity and continuing through the present day. Initially, the evolution was influenced heavily by Confucianism. By the third period, a sophisticated system emerged—one that included complex credit systems, commerce, legislation, and law. In keeping with Confucian principals, legal rulings were distributed only to fellow magistrates—assuming that competent rulers created a content society. Along with this concept of conciliation, a national law— similar to that developing in England—emerged. In fact, Western thought continued to influence the Japanese systems and resulted in a system remarkably similar to European law.

Mohammedan or Islamic (Seventh Century A.D.–Present). In contemporary society, Islam represents one of the three major world systems of law. According to Wigmore, the period between 800 and 1200 was marked by unrivaled advances in architecture, literacy, and education. As with early systems, Islamic laws were (and continue to be) religiously based—derived from three primary sources: the Koran, the word of God as written by Mohammed; Mohammed's teachings, as recorded through tradition; and emerging jurist opinions. Of the three extant systems, the Mohammedan system is the oldest.

Celtic (600 B.C.–A.D. 1400 to 1600). Characterized by three periods of extreme change, the Celtic system originally was based on mysticism and magic. Druids were considered to be both priests and jurists. It was believed that this was the perfect system, in that the Druids were actually bound by their own magic. Thus, unjust decisions resulted in actual physical harm to the practitioner. Only two of the protected areas of Gaul had any written legal procedure—Wales and Ireland. However, both of these were abolished through English conquest. Thus, their impact on contemporary legal thought is muted, at best.

Slavic. The Slavic culture was characterized by infighting and dissension, which ultimately resulted in a lack of a native legal system. Generally speaking, implementation of the Slavic "system" included areas as culturally diverse as Bohemia (now the Czech Republic), Poland, Yugoslavia, and Russia. Although the Bohemian and Russian systems never quite got off the ground because of the Parliament's and Tsar's refusal to give any ground to the peasants, the Poles and Slavs were more successful. However, both groups were influenced largely by other systems, including the Romanesque and Germanic.

Germanic (Early B.C.–Present). The emergence of this system was religious, based entirely on mythology, and spread throughout western Europe as the population fled the invading Asiatic tribes. The Anglican institution of trial by jury was implemented by Charlemagne in conjunction with a gradual nationalization of law. In addition, procedural guidelines for criminal trials evolved and the sixth century saw the implementation of the Imperial Chamber of Justice, a central court of appeal in which 8 of the 16 judges were Romanesque scholars.

Maritime. One of the oldest and most universal systems of law, the Maritime system dates back to the ancient Phoenicians (3000 B.C.). With the exception of a trend toward a nationalized system, Maritime law never changed, stretching across race, ethnicity, and religion.

Papal, or Canon, Law. Governed by the Pope, the Roman Catholic Church reigned supreme for twelve centuries over one of the most ceremonial of systems, and many of its traditional rituals are still observed. For example, the Sacra Romana Rota (Roman Holy Wheel), a civil tribunal to which kings once presented their cases, is still held. Although the Church has lost most of its authority over heads of state, it enjoyed periods of absolute authority in which kings, governments, and entire societies paid homage. Papal courts were responsible for the heresy trials of Galileo and Joan of Arc. Papal law has proved invaluable to contemporary proceedings. The Church forbade "trial by battle," for example, finding it to be irrational. It also revolutionized judicial procedure throughout western Europe and introduced the concept of equality under the law, erasing traditional distinctions between the rich and the poor. However, the temporal power of the Church was replaced by national courts beginning in the sixth century.

Romanesque (A.D. 1100–Present). Although its application is anything but universal, Romanesque law is currently the most common throughout the world. During the twelfth century, a resurrection of Justinian's law text in Italy resulted in an extensive period of philosophical study, while the fourteenth century witnessed the application of this Roman ideology to the extant Germanic and feudal customs in Italy. Gradually, such jurists branched out, bringing this application to Spain, England, France, the Netherlands, and Germany. However, the most notable event in this system's development was, of course, the Napoleonic Code. This code was the first of its kind to merge various extant codes and the Roman Common Law successfully into a national code.

Anglican (A.D. 1100–Present). Characterized by three distinct periods, the Anglican legal system is another of the legal systems currently spanning the globe. A code of common law began to evolve in early England, and Inns of Court were used to pass on such legal knowledge. Because of this unified legal code and entrenched legal profession (coupled with a heavy dose of nationalism), England did not fall to the Romanesque fever that was sweeping the Continent. As a result, the American system of justice was profoundly affected and many of the Framers of the Constitution were trained at the Inns of Court.

Secular systems began to emerge with the Romans. In approximately 450 B.C., the Twelve Tables were introduced as a means of satisfying both the patrician and plebian classes. Unlike the Ten Commandments, which delineated moral behavior, this particular code was primarily procedurally based. Although it provided for the form of presentation of a case, a formal jury system was not developed until much later. The tenets of the code, and the civil procedure included therein, spread to western Europe with the expansion of the Roman Empire. In fact, the pervasiveness of the Twelve Tables was such that much of it survived the fall of the Empire and was incorporated into the Napoleonic Code centuries later.

The Code of Hammurabi was not only the first legal code in the world to specifically define criminal behavior, but it also provided the framework for civil law, including product liability and medical malpractice.

229

If a builder build[s] a house for any one and do [*sic*] not build it solid; and the house, which he has built, fall [*sic*] down and kill[s] the owner; one shall put that builder to death.

220

If he opens an abscess with a bronze knife, and destroy [*sic*] the eye, he shall pay one-half what the slave was worth.

code of hammu-rabi oldest and best-preserved example of commercial custom and law. The Mesopotamian code, discovered in 1902, contains provisions for marital relationships and guidance for prosecution of crimes. Characterized by the burden of proof resting solely with the accused, the code carried severe sanctions, including death, for failure to meet this burden.

Preindustrial societies were characterized by strong tribal leadership that dispensed justice in the name of the tribe. Contemporary Western societies, however, may trace their roots to the **Code of Hammurabi** (circa 2270 **B.C.**), the oldest known legal code. The Code of Hammurabi was a study in complexity, with some of the laws being quite primitive and others quite sophisticated. Primitive ideals included retaliatory penalties such as "an eye for an eye and a tooth for a tooth," while sophisticated ideals included laws governing trade and commerce such as the beginning of concepts of product liability (229) and medical malpractice (220). As expected, early punishments were quite harsh. In the case of adultery (129), the Code provided that "if a man's wife be caught lying with another man, both shall be bound and thrown into the water." While such severity is not present in contemporary American law, it is important to note that the Code included foundations of criminal and civil codes. However, the European influence on American jurisprudence is both more apparent and direct.

Evolution and Impact of European Law

Before the Norman Conquest, English law was primarily created in an attempt to maintain social order. Most laws were class-based and included manor relationships such as that between vassal and the lord. Provisions for blood feuds were also included and were regulated by circumstances: Serfs avenging the murder of their lord, for example, could not be held liable by the kin of those slain in the lord's name. At the same time, serfs who killed others without legal justification could be held liable to the highest standard. However, the English government prior to Norman administration was largely decentralized, involving various officials and fiefdoms.

law of evidence the rules that dictate the admissibility of information into a court of law.

William of Normandy's conquest of England in 1066 signaled the beginning of the **law of evidence** and contemporary criminal procedure in the English system of justice. Although the Normans actually administered the cultural laws of the

CLARIFICATION OF CONCEPTS

COMMON LAW VERSUS CIVIL LAW

Common law refers to the system of law established in England that spread to much of the English-speaking world. Civil law developed during the Roman Empire and was modernized by the French in the nineteenth century under the direction of Napoleon Bonaparte.

John Billington, one of the original Pilgrims on the *Mayflower*, killed a neighbor in 1630. Because there was no statutory criminal law in place at the time, the court used the common-law crime of murder and the common-law rules of evidence. He was subsequently tried, convicted, and hanged.

land that had existed prior to their domination, they also developed entirely new systems of government and justice. While maintaining the traditional notions of a governing council, the English system was transformed into the precursor to the American bicameral legislature. One of the first initiatives involved the appointment of county sheriffs, who were puppets of the king, and the administrative council, who largely were responsible for taxation and financial considerations within their jurisdictions. Papal authority within the newly developed courts was denounced, theoretically separating the secular and ecclesiastical. However, the influence of the Church remained for several centuries, albeit in a less formal sense.[1] Continental feudalism, in which landowners were given responsibilities accompanied by privileges that allowed them to own lands in perpetuity rather than the length of time that their swords were needed, was created.

By the thirteenth century, the Norman courts and laws had been firmly established. Such entities, national (or common to all) in scope, came to be known as a system of **common law**. Proceedings and decisions of the courts were written down, summarized, and disseminated throughout Normandy so that consistency would be maintained. Ironically, this practice—undertaken to ensure consistency of application—resulted in a secondary source of law. As the practice took root, jurists increasingly justified their rulings on custom, tradition, and—most importantly—prior judicial decisions. This, in some cases, actually supplanted the legislation it was designed to uphold and became increasingly popular because of the infrequency of legislative meetings. Common law, then, is by definition a compilation of judge-made law.

common law a body of law based on the concept that legitimate legal authority derives from the consent of the people and is based on customs and traditions embodied in case law. It is also known as law of precedent.

Precedent and the Doctrine of *Stare Decisis*

Under the English common law system that emerged, decisions made by judges created **precedents**. Such rulings included justifications based on case characteristics, applicable law, and community standards. Rulings in seminal or unique cases proved especially valuable because jurists could substantiate their judicial opinion on previously published rulings. Such precedents, by nature, were binding on both the originating court and any lower court included within that jurisdiction. Theoretically, decisions of lower courts were not binding on higher courts, and in some cases, the higher courts did their own reasoning and concluding. This practice was brought to the United States with the colonists and continues to this day.

precedents prior judicial decisions that establish the legal authority or rule for future cases dealing with the same legal question.

Essentially the doctrine of precedent, ***stare decisis***, is a Latin phrase meaning "to stand by that which is decided." Theoretically, it requires courts to adhere to the law as decided by the highest court within a jurisdiction when such decision could be applied to the matter at hand and was reasonable in its inception. In fact, it "carries such persuasive force that the Court has always required a departure from precedent to be supported by some special justification."[2] In practice, this means that rulings from the U.S. Supreme Court are binding upon the entire federal court system, and rulings from state supreme courts are binding upon lower courts within the state. Precedents established in one state, however, are not binding upon bordering states. It is entirely possible, then, that a particular piece of

stare decisis literally "to stand by that which is decided"; the legal doctrine requiring courts to adhere to precedent law decided by an earlier high court and applicable when the same legal question is being considered.

exculpatory evidence introduced, for example, in an Alabama court may not be admitted in one in Georgia, even if it is critical to the defense. This style of law is quite different from the civil law system.

Civil Law

civil law   a legal system derived from Roman law; also the body of law of a state or nation based on legislation or legal authority which involves the rights of private citizens.

Civil law is a legal system derived from Roman law, especially the Corpus Juris Civilis (circa 529–534) of Emperor Justinian I. Although it evolved throughout the Middle Ages, it was changed most dramatically after the French Revolution with the introduction of the Napoleonic Code. Such codification had immeasurable impact upon areas around the globe, including Continental Europe, Japan, Latin America, and North America. Even in the United States, in which common law was well established, the Napoleonic Code would become the basis of the legal system in Louisiana before the Louisiana Purchase. Of course, this was entirely inconsistent with the legal principles espoused in the northeastern states colonized by English settlers. However, both currently are bound by the U.S. Constitution and Bill of Rights (Appendix A) and by subsequent interpretations by the Supreme Court. Thus, it can be argued that the primary distinction between common and civil law may be found in the methodological approach employed in their creation. Civil law systems, for example, are based primarily on legislation: Courts apply the provisions of statutes, thus creating a system of consistency through decisions based on principles. Case law, on the other hand, is a system in which cases are the primary source of law. In a system such as this, statutes are viewed as attacks on the system itself and thus are interpreted narrowly. This is not to suggest, however, that common law systems are completely implacable or that the doctrine of *stare decisis* prohibits reconsideration.

As a general rule, courts and jurists would prefer to not reverse previous decisions, because to do so would pronounce their own fallibility. However, reversals are not uncommon in American courtrooms. In a 2002 case, for example, the Supreme Court held that the execution of a mentally retarded person violated the Eighth Amendment's prohibition against cruel and unusual punishment, essentially reversing its opinion on the subject. Such reversals, though not uncommon, are usually couched in terms that negate the concept of partiality or hypocrisy on the part of the presiding jurists. Instead, courts attempt to justify their inconsistency by identifying or distinguishing the present case from earlier ones. As was evidenced in the justification supplied by the Court in *Atkins v. Virginia* (00-8452, 536 U.S. 304, 2002; 260 Va. 375, 534 S. E. 2d 312):

First, there is a serious question whether either justification underpinning the death penalty—retribution and deterrence of capital crimes—applies to mentally retarded

---

🔍 **CLARIFICATION OF CONCEPTS**

AMERICAN VERSUS ENGLISH LAW

American society currently relies upon common law and civil law. Theoretically, American courts attempt to apply statutes as intended by the legislature, while English courts do not make provisions or have consideration of legislative intent. Unlike English law, the American system provides for judicial review of legislation at all levels of the court structure. Although federal courts can strike down federal and state statutes that contravene the Constitution, state courts can nullify state statutes that they interpret as violating state or federal constitutions. Though not the norm, a handful of other countries provide for a limited amount of judicial review of legislation. These countries include Germany, Brazil, and Japan.

▼

offenders. As to retribution, the severity of the appropriate punishment necessarily depends on the offender's culpability. If the culpability of the average murderer is insufficient to justify imposition of death, see Godfrey v. Georgia, 446 U.S. 420, 433, the lesser culpability of the mentally retarded offender surely does not merit that form of retribution. As to deterrence, the same cognitive and behavioral impairments that make mentally retarded defendants less morally culpable also make it less likely that they can process the information of the possibility of execution as a penalty and, as a result, control their conduct based upon that information. Nor will exempting the mentally retarded from execution lessen the death penalty's deterrent effect with respect to offenders who are not mentally retarded. Second, mentally retarded defendants in the aggregate face a special risk of wrongful execution because of the possibility that they will unwittingly confess to crimes they did not commit, their lesser ability to give their counsel meaningful assistance, and the facts that they are typically poor witnesses and that their demeanor may create an unwarranted impression of lack of remorse for their crimes. (pp. 12–17)

Summarily, civil and common law systems provide for change. Common law systems originated in England and were transferred to various parts of the globe by conquest and custom. Initially, such law was largely unwritten because of the absence of statutory law, the infrequency of legislative meetings, and the lack of education among the general populace. Civil law, on the other hand, was a system of legislative codes of law, comprehensive in nature that delineated statutory-defined wrongs by private persons. Although previous cases are not necessarily ignored in this type of system, they are not afforded any level of binding authority.

Trials

Trials were first introduced in Western courts immediately following the Norman Conquest of 1066, when William the Conqueror introduced forms of trial to determine guilt or innocence. The first, **trial by battle**, was originally available to parties in private accusation of a felony and in land disputes. Private accusation cases occurred when a private party levied an accusation against another party for a crime committed against him or his family. Such procedures, supervised by a judge, were not available in cases in which the accused was indigent, a woman, an aged person, or anyone with an infirmity. Contested land disputes, quite common when no formal recording of deeds or titles was available, were adjudicated through the battle of hired champions. Depending on the particulars, these contests were fought either until one party surrendered or was killed. Generally speaking, only nobles could avail themselves of this avenue. In criminal cases, commoners were forced to endure trial by ordeal.

trial by battle an ancient dispute resolution method where those in dispute would fight one another until submission or death

Trial by ordeal originated as early as the sixth century and spread in pace with Christianity across Europe. Like trial by battle, **trial by ordeal** became popular after the Norman Conquest and was based on the notion that God, as the arbiter of justice, punishes the guilty and shields the innocent. In theory, the ordeal was not intended to produce the death of innocent and guilty parties alike; rather, it was designed to ascertain the truth by way of God personally revealing the party's guilt or innocence. In reality, however, all individuals were subject to torture. Common trials often included the handling of hot iron, the immersion of limbs in boiling water or fire, and the act of drowning. The ordeal reserved for those charged with more serious crimes was the Ordeal of Water, in which individuals were bound and cast into a body of water. If the persons floated, they were guilty; if they sank, they were innocent. Unfortunately, the outcome of such ordeals was necessarily death—those who floated were dispatched by other means; those who sank, drowned.

trial by ordeal medieval method of fact-finding, which involved torture and which was predicated on the notion that divine illumination would indicate guilt or innocence.

Criticisms of such practices existed throughout the tenure of the trial by ordeal, but not for reasons one might expect. The criticisms levied at the practice concerned the interpretation of the voice of God. Critics argued that the ordeals did not necessarily indicate a person's guilt or innocence of a particular crime, but rather his or her disfavor in the eyes of God. For example, God may wish to punish a person for something extraneous to the matter at hand. Although the Church spoke against such practices as early as the ninth century, political pressures largely kept them silent. In the late eleventh century, Pope Gregory VII initiated the concept of papal supremacy—a notion that eventually would lead to greater authority and autonomy for the Roman Church. In 1215, the Lateran Council formally banned the participation of priests in such ordeals.[3] As the absence of divine interpreters (i.e., the clergy) made it impossible to ascertain God's judgment, the practice became obsolete. However, the reliance on faith and religious principles was not limited to nor did it end with the cessation of ordeals.

The Jury System and Compulsory Testimony

wager of law or compurgation a medieval means of fact-finding in feudal courts in which the accused could choose to make a statement, take an oath, and provide individuals to swear to his veracity.

Another early attempt at fact-finding, a **wager of law or compurgation**, required the accused to swear an oath and produce "oath-helpers." These were individuals who would swear that the defendant was oath-worthy. Oath-helpers were not required to have knowledge of the particulars of the event in question and actually were discouraged from obtaining any. Quite simply, their role was to testify as to the trustworthiness of the defendant. This system was based on the concept that individuals would not imperil their soul to swear falsely for their neighbor. It must be noted that this system was heavily reliant upon sanctions of excommunication and would not have been possible in societies lacking such provisions. While excommunication resulting from either spiritual or social reasons was a real threat in small communities, population explosions and the onslaught of capitalism made this system of fact-finding obsolete. Indeed, this system was not as binding as those that evolved after its abolition. This method of fact-finding was rife with perjury, and proved to be as ineffective as trials by battle or ordeal. As such, it was largely discarded centuries prior to its formal abolition in 1833.

presentment juries precursors to American grand juries; panels of private citizens who were empowered by the Assize of Clarendon to report crime and criminals in their community at a ratio of 12 per 100 and 4 per township.

In 1166, Henry II developed the precursor to today's grand jury system. The series of ordinances known as the Assize of Clarendon ordained the selection and swearing of **presentment juries**. These bodies were tasked with informing the King's itinerant judges of crimes committed in their community and identifying any citizens suspected of criminal activity. Initially, these individuals were also tasked with investigating events and individuals in question; and, would decide whether the facts warranted a trial. Like other early methods of adjudication, this system was not effective as the accusatory jury (i.e., the grand jury) also rendered verdicts in cases proceeding to trial. As a result, the process of empanelling a separate body to determine fact and decide the guilt of the accused was established. The establishment of **petit juries** as fact finders proved foundational for contemporary due process and the rules of evidence.

petit jury a panel of individuals who are tasked with determination of fact and the rendering of a verdict in a trial.

Magna Carta

As noted previously, early methods of fact-finding were both ineffective and unfair. Prior to the first quarter of the thirteenth century, English citizens were routinely arrested solely on the basis of unsubstantiated, anonymous accusations or at the whim of the social elite. As a matter of fact, the monarchy and corresponding government were considered sacrosanct. Antigovernment sentiments were severely punished, and the monarchy was secured by the imprisonment of political dissidents. Such abuses coupled with King John's ongoing conflict with Pope Innocent III and higher taxes were vehemently rejected by the great barons of England who revolted against the Crown. In 1215, King John, wearied (and largely broken) by the ongoing conflict met with the barons on a field in Runnymede, England, and affixed his seal to an agreement that effectively ended the battle.[4]

▼

Although King John and the *Magna Carta* are largely credited with the introduction of contemporary notions of fair taxation, reasonable fines, and the protection of private property, such ideals were originally articulated by Henry I in the *Coronation Charter* (or *Charter of Liberties*) in 1100. However, it was promptly forgot-ten until Stephen Langton, Archbishop of Canterbury, reminded the Barons of the liberties that were guaranteed to them more than a century before. It was then that a new and expanded *Great Charter* (*Magna Carta*) was developed.

The **Magna Carta**, or *Great Charter*, included 63 chapters that guaranteed a variety of rights to the Church, the Barons, and private citizens including, but not limited to, the protection of private property and reasonable limits on taxation (see Appendix B). The document also included three chapters particular to the emerging notion of due process:

magna carta an agreement between King John and his Barons in 1215 that provided the foundations of due process and constitutional law in countries across the globe.

38. No bailiff, on his own simple assertion, shall henceforth put any one to his law, without producing faithful witnesses in evidence.

39. No freeman shall be taken, or imprisoned, or disseized, or outlawed, or exiled, or in any way harmed—nor will we go upon or send upon him, save by the lawful judgment of his peers or by the law of the land.

40. To none will we sell, to none deny or delay, right or justice.

Such unprecedented ideals denounced the notion that a mere accusation was sufficient grounds for a criminal proceeding, and represented the roots of probable cause found in the Fourth Amendment. In addition, it guaranteed all individuals due process.[5] The importance of the *Magna Carta* on the development of law in

The impact of the *Magna Carta* on American law can not be overstated as evidenced by the inclusion of the Great Seal on numerous historical documents.

the American colonies cannot be overstated. It was clearly paramount in the minds of the founding fathers who gathered in Philadelphia in 1774 in response to the *Coercive* or *Intolerable Acts* passed by Parliament. Indeed, the Great Seal of the *Magna Carta* was emblazoned on the resulting *Journal of the Proceedings of the First Continental Congress*.

Habeas Corpus

writ of habeas corpus an order in writing, issued in the name of the government by a judge of competent jurisdiction, and directed to a person who has another in his custody or detains him in confinement which commands him to bring such person so detained before the judge, at the time and place appointed, and to state the reasons for which he or she has imprisoned or otherwise deprived him/her of liberty.

The **writ of habeas corpus** is another imported legal concept that has a profound effect on American law, though its etymology is less clear.[6] Often traced back to English common law, the writ was described as the *glory of English law* by Sir William Blackstone.[7] The legal principle of *habeas corpus* continues to be a cornerstone of due process in the United States. It provides a guarantee against unlawful imprisonment, and is literally interpreted as *have the body*. In contemporary parlance, a *writ of habeas corpus* is

> an order in writing, issued in the name of the government by a judge of competent jurisdiction, and directed to a person who has another in his custody or detains him in confinement which commands him to bring such person so detained before the judge, at the time and place appointed, and to state the reasons for which he/she has imprisoned or otherwise deprived him/her of liberty.

Necessarily, in cases where such cause is either not present or proves insufficient, the detainee may be released. Like the *Magna Carta*, the *Writ of Habeas Corpus* has been found in societies around the world. While the first provided for the right to be free from incarceration without cause, the latter provided the mechanism through which those deprived of such could secure their release.

The right of citizens to demand review of their incarceration represented an essential protection against government abuse, which, as Blackstone famously noted, *does not always arise from the ill nature, but sometimes from the mere inattention, of government*.[8] Although the English Crown refused to recognize the right in the colonies, Americans were granted the right to *habeas corpus* in the U.S. Constitution, ARTICLE I, SECTION 9. To wit, "The privilege of the Writ of Habeas Corpus shall not be suspended, unless when in Cases of Rebellion or Invasion the public Safety may require it." The right was championed by all of the original colonies, and has found a place in the laws of virtually every state and American territory.

Traditionally, federal courts maintained jurisdiction over habeas corpus petitions from federal prisoners only. They could not interfere with state prisoners. During Reconstruction, however, Congress expanded federal judiciary powers at a level that remains unparalleled. Such expansion included their role in the federal system and their superiority over state courts.[9] Most importantly, the *Habeas Corpus Act of 1867* significantly expanded the authority of federal courts to issue writs of habeas corpus "in all cases where any person may be restrained of his or her liberty in violation of the constitution, or any treaty or law of the United States."[10] Since that time, state and federal prisoners have been able to petition federal courts for post-conviction relief.

⚖ **CASE LAW**

FEDERAL SUSPENSION OF HABEAS CORPUS

The right to the protection of physical liberty by *habeas corpus* is foundational to the U.S. Constitution, and virtually every other right enjoyed by American citizens. As Alexander Hamilton noted in *The Federalist* No. 84, stressed its necessity to protect against *the favorite and most formidable*

▼

instruments of tyranny. For many, it is unfathomable that such a guarantee could ever be revoked even temporarily, and yet, the Founding Fathers were cautious enough to recognize that some circumstances may require its suspension. Subsequently, *habeas corpus* in the United States was suspended in both the nineteenth and twenty-first centuries.

On April 27, 1861, President Abraham Lincoln took unilateral executive action and suspended habeas corpus. Three months later, the President, formally recognizing the lack of legal authority to do so, requested ratification from Congress. The eventual result was the *Habeas Corpus Suspension Act of 1863*. Among other things the Act authorized the President of the United States to suspend the guarantee of habeas corpus, and provided for the release of political prisoners. The suspension of habeas corpus in Union states was lifted by Andrew Johnson in 1865.

In the wake of the Terror Attacks of 2001, the immediate passage of the *Patriot Act*, and the Presidential Executive Order of November 13, 2001, foreign nationals identified as *enemy combatants* were indefinitely detained at military establishments, including the Charleston and Guantanamo Naval Bases. Several of these detainees sought relief through federal courts via habeas corpus. While initially unsuccessful in federal court, two cases, *Rasul v. Bush* (2004)[11] and *Hamdan v. Rumsfeld* (2006),[12] would ultimately bear fruit. In the former, the government's argument that federal courts lacked jurisdiction over Guantanamo detainees because they were neither citizens nor detained in the United States was rejected by the Court. In the latter, the government

argued that the President has the authority to convene military tribunals during times of war. While the Court failed to deny that this authority was within the President's purview, it found the commissions as constituted violated both the Geneva conventions and the United States Code of Military Justice (UCMJ).

As a result of these seminal rulings, the U.S. Congress passed the *Detainee Treatment Act of 2005* and the *Military Commissions Act of 2006*. It was signed into law by President George W. Bush on October 17, 2006. It reinstated the sovereignty of the U.S. military in cases involving detainees classified as enemy combatants—effectively suspending their right to challenge their detention via federal courts. However, the Court, once again, noted the centrality of the right. In *Boumediene et al. v. Bush* (2008),[13] the Court ruled that the MCA violated the *Suspension Clause*.[14] To wit:

> A brief account of the writ's history and origins shows that protection for the habeas privilege was one of the few safeguards of liberty specified in a Constitution that, at the outset, had no Bill of Rights; in the system the Framers conceived, the writ has a centrality that must inform proper interpretation of the Suspension Clause. That the Framers considered the writ a vital instrument for the protection of individual liberty is evident from the care taken in the Suspension Clause to specify the limited grounds for its suspension: The writ may be suspended only when public safety requires it in times of rebellion or invasion. The Clause is designed to protect against cyclical abuses of the writ by the Executive and Legislative Branches. It protects detainee rights by a means consistent with the Constitution's essential design, ensuring that, except during periods of formal suspension, the Judiciary will have a time-tested device, the writ, to maintain the "delicate balance of governance."

▶ Sources of Law in the American System

American jurisprudence may be divided into two distinct forms of law. The first, common law, is characterized by judge-made law and is based on the concept of *stare decisis*. The second, traditionally referred to as civil law but hereafter called legislative law, is composed of laws established by government entities. This second category includes constitutions, legislative acts, and administrative regulations from state and federal sources. It is the area of law characterized by codification and bears heaviest on criminal procedure. Unfortunately, it often is complicated by questions of jurisdictional sovereignty.

Since its inception, the American legal system has been one in which a strong central government provides a national infrastructure simultaneous to state governance of a judicial entity. To wit, as expressed in *Rochin v. California*[15]:

The power to define crimes belongs to Congress only as an appropriate means of carrying into execution its limited grant of legislative powers . . . broadly speaking, crimes . . . are what the laws of the individual States make them subject to the limitations . . . in the original Constitution, prohibiting bills of attainder and ex post facto laws, and of the Thirteenth and Fourteenth Amendments.

As such, most crimes are defined by state statute.

Theoretically speaking, each state is sovereign—having its own constitution, criminal code, and rules of procedure. As stated, most criminal offenses are violations of state codes not federal ones. In fact, there is no national police force, nor does the Constitution provide for one. Furthermore, there is not now, nor has there ever been, a federal common law. Indeed, all federal crimes are statutory crimes as defined and enacted by Congress—common law is reserved for the states. Criminal laws on the federal level may be enacted by Congress only in the following areas: the protection of Congress and its interests, including personnel, property, and information; the regulation of interstate and foreign commerce; the protection of civil rights; and the sovereignty of areas not otherwise claimed or accounted for, such as the District of Columbia, federal territories, and federal enclaves.

State and federal governments have the right (and responsibility) to pass laws to promote the health, safety, and welfare of their citizens, but states must conform to the requirements set forth in the U.S. Constitution. In other words, states may not abridge the rights guaranteed to individuals under the Constitution or the Bill of Rights. However, they may enhance or further protect those liberties at their discretion.

The U.S. Constitution and the Bill of Rights

bill of rights the first 10 amendments to the U.S. Constitution.

U.S. constitution the supreme law of the United of States of America; a document designed to create a strong central government while protecting the rights of individual citizens and sovereign states.

On July 4, 1776, the Declaration of Independence was issued by the Second Continental Congress. Divided into three parts, the Declaration negated the traditional notion of the divinity of rulers and argued that, irrespective of social class, all individuals were granted certain unalienable rights including life, liberty, and the pursuit of happiness. It included a preamble, a list of grievances, and the declaration itself. The grievances delineated those wrongs committed against the colonies by the king. This document was followed by the U.S. Constitution, which reiterated and expanded the fundamental rhetoric found within the Declaration of Independence. The Constitution was largely adopted by the new American republic in 1791, and after the addition of the **Bill of Rights**—the first 10 amendments. Without equivocation, this document represents the supreme law of the land in the United States. Designed to create a strong central government while protecting the individual rights of sovereign states, the **U.S. Constitution** represents the oldest codified national constitution in the contemporary world. In the purest sense, this document was intended to remedy past injustices and provide safeguards for the citizenry.

In the most basic sense, the U.S. Constitution provides for the development of a legal system in which the Supreme Court is the final arbiter and in which lower courts have varying jurisdictions. Although there are some exceptions, very little of the wording contained in the original Constitution directly addressed criminal law, in general, or criminal evidence, in particular. However, the first 10 amendments to the Constitution (Bill of Rights) began to correct this oversight and, coupled with case law, provided for the exclusion of evidence collected in violation of its tenets. In a nutshell, the Bill of Rights reiterated and expanded the fundamental rhetoric found within the Declaration of Independence.

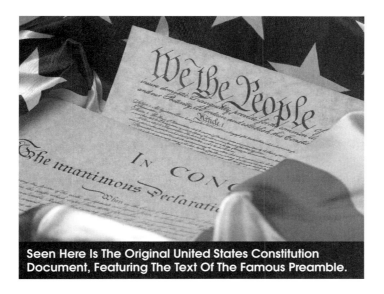
Seen Here Is The Original United States Constitution Document, Featuring The Text Of The Famous Preamble.

First Amendment

Congress shall make no law respecting an establishment of religion, or prohibiting the free exercise thereof; or abridging the freedom of speech, or of the press; or the right of the people peaceably to assemble, and to petition the Government for a redress of Grievances.

Commonly referred to as the Freedom of Speech and Religion clause, the First Amendment provides protection from persecution to individuals of different religions and ideologies and, through Supreme Court interpretation of the **establishment clause**, formally separates the church and state. In addition, it prevents government censorship of the media, allowing for public criticism of government entities—a practice long prohibited in England. Largely included because of past religious persecutions, the First Amendment allows a platform for free speech, assembly, and, of course, religious practice.

establishment clause as stated in the First Amendment: "Congress shall make no law respecting an establishment of religion," the clause formally separates the church and state and prevents the federal government from declaring or financially supporting a national religion. In addition, it prohibits preferential treatment by the government to any particular faith.

Second Amendment

A well-regulated militia, being necessary to the security of a free state, the right of the people to keep and bear arms shall not be infringed.

Although the Second Amendment has absolutely nothing to do with the laws of evidence, it has been hotly debated for several decades. Although many antigun lobbyists have argued that the right to bear arms does not include handgun ownership, opponents of the lobby wrap themselves in the verbiage, claiming that the Second Amendment specifically provides for private ownership of weapons. Historical analysis would suggest that the Amendment was directed at the creation of militias or citizen groups in the face of tyrannical government, but the Supreme Court has provided little guidance with the exception of allowing states to regulate gun ownership. Thus, the Second Amendment remains open to individual interpretation.

Third Amendment

No soldier shall, in time of peace, be quartered in any house without the consent of the owner, or in time of war, but in a manner to be prescribed by law.

Obsolete in contemporary society, the Third Amendment protected the rights of homeowners from governmental abuse of their property. Specifically prohibiting the involuntary occupation of residences by government officials or military personnel, the Third Amendment was another attempt to recognize the sanctity of homesteads.

Fourth Amendment

The right of the people to be secure in their persons, houses, papers, and effects, against unreasonable searches and seizures, shall not be violated, and no warrants shall issue but upon probable cause, supported by oath or affirmation, and particularly describing the place to be searched, and the persons or things to be seized.

Probable Cause

Arguably the most important provision contained within the Bill of Rights, the Fourth Amendment specifically precludes searches and seizures without probable cause. It was designed to halt the issuance of general warrants. In colonial times, such writs enabled British officers to search private residences, business locales, and public facilities at will. Such abuse by the government was thought to be one of the most important factors leading to the American Revolution. As such, the introduction of the Fourth Amendment was intended to provide security of citizens against tyrannical governments. The **probable cause** provision, in particular, required the state to demonstrate a level of certainty rising above mere suspicion. Not clearly articulated in the original verbiage of the Fourth Amendment, the standard has been consistently interpreted since by the courts. Discussed exhaustively in Chapter 4, it is sufficient to say here that the standard is established somewhere between "reasonable suspicion" and "beyond a reasonable doubt." For the most part, the standard is represented as a balancing act demonstrating that the probability of a crime having occurred is ascertained and that the evidence of such a crime is contained within the specified location.

> **probable cause**
> a legal concept established in the Fourth Amendment requiring the state to demonstrate a level of certainty rising above mere suspicion; or, information that would lead a reasonable person to conclude that the existence and discovery of contraband or other evidence is more probable than not.

As with other constitutional safeguards, the Court is consistently refining (and often redefining) the conceptual framework through the lens in which *probable cause* is viewed. While the Warren (1953–1969) and Burger (1969–1986) Courts seemed to lack a consistent interpretation, the Rehnquist (1986–2005) and Roberts (2005–present) Courts have been characterized as "originalists." Seeking to understand and appreciate the mindset of Constitutional Framers, these Courts have veered away from decisions passed on social expectations. However, actions undertaken by the NSA during the Obama Administration suggest an erosion of protections housed within the Fourth Amendment, and have alarmed both liberal and conservative leaning jurists.

🔍 CLARIFICATION OF CONCEPTS

THE WARRANT CLAUSE AND THE REASONABLENESS CLAUSE

It is important to note that there are two distinct clauses housed within the Fourth Amendment—the *Warrant Clause* and the *Reasonableness Clause*. As interpreted by the Court, the Fourth Amendment does NOT require a warrant for every search and seizure. While the Court has continued to recognize that warrants should accompany searches in most situations, they have also recognized a variety of broad categories of searches where warrants are not required

▼

if the circumstances are reasonable and *if* obtaining a warrant would be impractical. These include: automobiles, consensual searches, plain view doctrine, incident to arrest, and exigent circumstances. (These are thoroughly discussed in Chapters 4, 5, and 6.) In recent years, the Court has applied a *reasonableness standard* in which the public interest is balanced against an individual's privacy interest. As noted in *Rabinowitz*:

> it is unreasonable searches that are prohibited by the Fourth Amendment. It was recognized by the Framers of the Constitution that there were reasonable searches for which no warrant was required. *(United States v. Rabinowitz, 339 U.S. 56 (1950))*

The Emergence of Reasonable Suspicion as a Justification to Search

Although probable cause is guaranteed to American citizens as articulated in the Fourth Amendment, history has demonstrated a deliberate indifference to this standard by some government agencies and political administrations. From the 1940s through the 1960s, for example, J. Edgar Hoover directed surveillance on countless Americans and organizations who he suspected of subversive or radical behavior. These individuals included Martin Luther King, Jr., the Kennedy brothers, and Muhammad Ali. This practice and the Watergate scandal prompted a Senate Select Committee (chaired by Frank Church) to investigate government operations and domestic intelligence activities. Their mission was to set limits on domestic surveillance and provided strict guidelines and requirements for conducting foreign electronic surveillance. The products of their efforts were the *Guidelines on Domestic Surveillance of 1976* and *Foreign Intelligence Surveillance Act of 1978* (FISA). Both of these documents required probable cause, and both provided significant limitations on government agencies. However, the events of September 11, 2001, abruptly changed, perhaps forever, the boundaries and oversight that restricted the federal government.

Immediately following the terror attacks, Congress passed the *Uniting and Strengthening America by Providing Appropriate Tools Required to Intercept and Obstruct Terrorism* (USA Patriot Act). The legislation made significant changes to a number of Acts outlining limitations on government oversight, including: FISA, the *Electronic Communications Privacy Act of 1986* (ECPA), the *Money Laundering Control Act of 1986*, the *Immigration and Nationality Act*; and the *Bank Secrecy Act* (BSA). Among other things, the Act authorized: searches of homes and offices without prior notice, use of roving wiretaps for phones, and monitor of computers and e-mails.[16] Most importantly, the act lowered the quantum of cause necessary to conduct searches, seizures, and surveillance from probable cause to **reasonable suspicion**.

reasonable suspicion legal standard that is less than probable cause but more than an inchoate and unparticularized suspicion or "hunch."

 APPLICATION OF LAW

DOUBLE JEOPARDY AND MEL IGNATOW

On September 24, 1988, Brenda Sue Schaefer did not return home from a date with her fiance, Mel Ignatow. Known as scrupulously reliable, her family was immediately alarmed. By the time her car was discovered abandoned with a flat tire and broken window, authorities were already looking for the Louisville native. Their suspicion immediately focused on the last person to have seen her alive. Mel Ignatow was 14 years older than his beautiful fiancée, and was described as creepy by many in the community. Yet, his fancy sports car, expensive watches, and large boat must have made him more desirable to women as he maintained a long-term mistress in addition to Brenda Sue.

(continued)

Several weeks prior to her disappearance, Schaefer began to complain to her friends and family about Ignatow's weird sexual demands. She even related an incident where she had woken up on vacation to find Ignatow holding a chloroform-soaked cloth to her face. So when coworkers overheard a heated telephone argument in which she appeared to have broken off the relationship, many breathed a sigh of relief. Within days, Brenda Sue Schaefer vanished.

Once the criminal investigation identified Ignatow as the prime suspect, an FBI profiler noted that he exhibited the hallmarks of a criminal sexual sadist. He was also characterized as misogynistic, paranoid, and narcissistic. Several months after the investigation began, a court ordered the city to provide SWAT team protection to Ignatow after he received death threats. Dr. William Spalding, a Louisville doctor and former employer of Schaefer, was found guilty of making terroristic threats. In a twist of fate, Ignatow's statements made during Spalding's trial would prove pivotal in his future.

Although the prosecuting attorneys had a very weak case against Ignatow, they proceeded to the grand jury where they called Ignatow's longtime mistress, Mary Ann Shore, to the stand. During examination, Shore broke down and led authorities to a shallow grave behind her house containing the remains of Brenda Sue Schaefer. Due to the deterioration of the body, there was no physical evidence to demonstrate cause of death. However, Shore testified that several weeks prior to the murder, she assisted Ignatow in "scream proofing" her house and digging the grave. She further testified that Ignatow brought Schaefer to her house where she was bound to a coffee table, raped, and tortured prior to being killed by chloroform. Most importantly, Shore testified that she had taken pictures of all the activities that night, although she could not produce any evidence of such.

Although her statements seemed damning, she proved to be a poor witness. She wore inappropriate clothing and laughed throughout the proceedings. The defense argued that Shore was a scorned woman, and that she had killed Schaefer out of jealousy. The jury, eager to end deliberations before the impending Christmas holidays, acquitted Ignatow on all charges. The judge, reportedly embarrassed over the jury's decision, wrote a letter of apology to the Schaefer family.

Six months after Ignatow's acquittal, a workman discovered a plastic bag in Ignatow's old house which had been sold to fund his defense. The bag contained Schaefer's jewelry and three rolls of undeveloped film. Authorities developed the film which depicted Schaefer's rape, torture, and murder. They were unable to bring murder charges against Ignatow due to the Fifth Amendment's prohibition of double jeopardy. However, they were able to bring perjury charges against him with his previously sworn statements. Ignatow subsequently confessed in court. He served 5 years of an 8-year sentence for perjury to the grand jury, and several more for perjury in the trial of Dr. Spalding. Ironically, Ignatow died in 2008 after he struck his head on a coffee table.

Fifth Amendment

No person shall be held to answer for a capital, or otherwise infamous crime, unless on a presentment or indictment of a grand jury, except in cases arising in the land or naval forces, or in the militia, when in actual service in time of war or public danger; nor shall any person be subject for the same offense to be twice put in jeopardy of life or limb; nor shall be compelled in any criminal case to be a witness against himself, nor be deprived of life, liberty, or property, without due process of law; nor shall private property be taken for public use, without just compensation.

The Fifth Amendment contains several important provisions that act as safeguards against an oppressive government. These include the **right to a grand jury, freedom from double jeopardy, freedom from self-incrimination**, the **right to due process**, and the **right to just compensation for private property taken for public use**. The right to a grand jury and the right to due process were in direct response to the past abuses of the monarchies on private citizens—entities that used institutions such as the Star Chamber and the Spanish Inquisition. In both instances, sessions were held in secret, with no presentment of indictment, no right of appeal, no jurors, no witnesses, and no advocates. Such practices allowed officials to target political rivals and personal enemies, as well as create a system of bribery and extortion. Thus, the Fifth Amendment's requirements of due process and grand jury indictment are pivotal to the freedoms enjoyed in contemporary American society.

The Star Chamber was constructed under the reign of Edward II to house meetings of the King's Council. Although the etymology of the term *starred chambre* is unclear, it is alternatively thought to refer to either the shape or decoration of the room or its original purpose of hearing contracts between Jews and Christians. Theoretically, the Chamber was designed to allow for suits against the aristocracy by the lower class. In addition, it was originally created to serve in a supervisory capacity, and was the precursor to the appellate system. At the same time, sessions were held in private, and no provisions for the introduction of witnesses or evidence were available. This weakness was exploited under the House of Stuart, and the Chamber became synonymous with inequity and abuse of power during the reign of Charles I.

It had become a political court and a cruel court, a court in which divines sought to impose their dogmas and their ritual upon a recalcitrant nation by heavy sentences; in which a king, endeavouring to rule without a Parliament, tried to give the force of statutes to his proclamations, to exact compulsory loans, to gather taxes that the Commons had denied him; a whipping, nose-slitting, ear-cropping court; a court with a grim, unseemly humour of its own, which would condemn to an exclusive diet of pork the miserable puritan who took too seriously the Mosaic prohibition of swine's flesh.

The Star Chamber was formally abolished by Parliament in 1641. However, the term has lived in infamy, and is often used to refer to any system or judicial proceeding that lacks procedural safeguards.

Right to a Grand Jury

According to the Fifth Amendment, "no person shall be held to answer for a capital, or otherwise infamous crime, unless on a presentment or indictment of a grand jury, except in cases arising in the land or naval forces, or in the militia, when in actual service in time of war or public danger." Since inception, the Court has attempted to more clearly identify crimes of infamy. In *Ex Parte Wilson*,[17] the Court noted that:

> ... the competency of the defendant, if convicted, to be a witness in another case is not the true test; and that no person can be held to answer, without presentment or by a grand jury, for any crime for which an infamous punishment may be imposed by the court. The question is whether the crime is one for which the statutes authorize the court to award an infamous punishment not whether the punishment ultimately awarded is an infamous one. When the accused is in danger of being subjected to an infamous punishment if convicted, he has the right to insist that he shall not be put upon his trial, except on the accusation of a grand jury.

They also stressed that such guarantees were further strengthened by the separation of powers designed by the Framers, emphatically stating that "no declaration of congress is needed to secure or competent to defeat the constitutional safeguard."

Both the federal government and roughly half of all states still use grand jury systems in criminal cases. The remaining states have developed *preliminary hearings* for pretrial determination of probable cause (discussed in Chapter 2). In states that maintain both, preliminary hearings are most often utilized in felony cases. Unlike grand jury systems, preliminary hearing systems allow defendants to be both present and active during the proceeding.

Protection Against Double Jeopardy

The second protection contained within the Fifth Amendment is the prohibition of governmental persecution through repeated prosecution. In essence, it prohibits the repeated prosecution of an individual for the same crime in the same jurisdiction if they have formally been punished for or acquitted of the crime. However, various exceptions exist. The Fifth Amendment does not preclude, for example,

The Statute of Westminster I (1275) formally provided for the participation of the accused; compulsion of testimony and participation of the accused and allowed for the imprisonment, torture, or both of individuals who refused to cooperate. Initially, the statute intended to increase the level of cooperation by the accused. However, many individuals chose to die from torture rather than by government-sanctioned execution and they did this for a variety of reasons. Most importantly, the nature of the presenting jury selected and the inclusion of witnesses to the event in question, even the accuser, heightened the likelihood of conviction and the outcome was somewhat predetermined. Coupled with the provision of asset forfeiture of convicted felons, many individuals chose to die horrifically, while still innocent in the eyes of the law. The separation of the *presenting jury* and the trial jury in the twelfth century changed such practices and resulted in the first glimpse of contemporary juries (Wigmore, 1940).

retrying an individual whose original trial resulted in a mistrial or a hung jury. It does not preclude the retrying of an individual who has successfully secured a new trial through the appellate process nor does it preclude the prosecution of an individual for the same set of circumstances in multiple jurisdictions. For example, three of the four officers involved in the Rodney King beating were acquitted of all charges in their state trial. However, Officer Laurence Powell and Sergeant Stacey Koon were convicted of civil rights violations in federal court and sentenced to prison for the same incident. Such practice is made possible under the dual sovereignty doctrine.

dual sovereignty or separate sovereigns doctrine an exception to the double jeopardy clause of the Fifth Amendment; protects the interests of both state and federal authorities in cases in which a single act violates the laws of both sovereigns.

Under the **dual sovereignty or separate sovereigns doctrine**, individuals may be prosecuted for the same offense by two different government entities. Thus, individuals may be tried in state and federal courts for the same set of circumstances. However, they may not be charged in municipal and state courts, because the two are byproducts of the same government and derive their authority from the same body of law (i.e., the state constitution). Though such practice and ideology are hotly debated among legal scholars, the Supreme Court has continued to uphold the constitutionality of the doctrine.

Protection Against Self-Incrimination

In addition to the previous protections, the Fifth Amendment was also created to eliminate the barbarism of torture chambers. One of the most heinous of abuses in Europe throughout the Middle Ages and beyond, for example, included the practice of coercing testimony through torture. Both the rack and the "scavenger's daughter" involved the stretching and crushing of body parts, respectively, and were used routinely in England not as a form of punishment but as a mechanism to extract confessions. To prevent such atrocities in the United States, the Fifth Amendment prohibits compulsory testimony of defendants, specifically stating that a person "shall not be compelled in any criminal case to be a witness against himself." As noted by the Court, the protection against self-incrimination:

> Reflects many of our fundamental values and most noble aspirations: our unwillingness to subject those suspected of crime to the cruel trilemma of self-accusation, perjury or contempt; our preference for an accusatorial rather than an inquisitorial system of criminal justice; our fear that self-incriminating statements will be elicited by inhumane treatment and abuses; our sense of fair play which dictates a fair state-individual balance by requiring the government to leave the individual alone until good cause is show for disturbing him.

In *Brown v. Mississippi* (1936),[18] the Court prohibited states from using coerced confessions against defendants in criminal courts, but fell short of applying the amendment's protection against compulsory self-incrimination. However, the entirety of that protection was made binding on the states through the Fourteenth Amendment in *Malloy v. Hogan* (1964).[19]

In addition to protections recognized in *Brown* and *Malloy*, subsequent case law has barred the state from addressing the defendant's refusal to testify as indicative of his or her guilt. In fact, the Court has prohibited even the mention of the exercise of such right, asserting that such would negate the right itself. Such rights, unheard of in many regions of the world, are so well recognized by the average American that little consideration is given to their importance. The Fifth Amendment protection against self-incrimination, however, is not absolute. In fact, it only protects individuals from compulsory testimony. It does not protect them from being compelled to provide blood, urine, fingerprint, or DNA samples; nor does it extend to giving writing and voice samples needed for comparison. Finally, the privilege does not extend to police lineups or photographs.

The Right to Due Process

The final protection contained within the Fifth Amendment is the right to due process prior to the deprivation of life or liberty. This concept as applied in American Courts has its earliest roots in the *Magna Carta*.

> No freeman shall be taken, or imprisoned, or disseized, or outlawed, or exiled, or in any way harmed—nor will we go upon or send upon him—save by the lawful judgment of his peers or by the law of the land.[20]

In essence, the term *due process* means that individuals must be afforded equal access and exercise of the rules, procedures, and guarantees housed within American law. These include all those previously discussed, and those identified by the Supreme Court. The first case in the United States that evaluated the "Due Process Clause" was *Dred Scott v. Sandford* (1857). In that case, the Court ruled that a slave owner's due process rights would be violated if his property (i.e., the slave Dred Scott) was forfeited by the simple act of taking his property with him as he

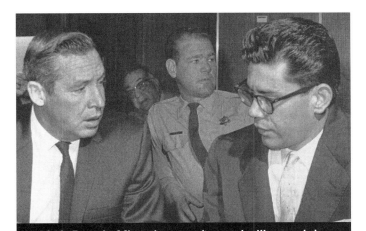

In 1963, Ernesto Miranda was charged with a variety of offenses including rape and kidnapping. While in police custody, Miranda, possessing only an elementary school education, confessed to the police. He was subsequently convicted and sentenced to a lengthy prison term. On appeal, the Supreme Court ruled that, prior to custodial interrogation, the police must notify an individual of his or her right to remain silent and right to an attorney. Today, these rights, commonly known as the Miranda Rights, are read to suspects in custody.

visited a nonslave state. (Due process rights were not extended to slaves until the ratification of the Thirteenth Amendment in 1865.)

Originally, the guarantee of due process was only binding on the federal government until the passage of the Fourteenth Amendment—one of three **Reconstruction Amendments**. This amendment was intended to secure the constitutional rights and protections for former slaves. The Amendment contains important clauses that are often litigated. These include: the *Citizenship Clause*, *Privileges or Immunities Clause*, *Due Process Clause*, and *Equal Protection Clause*. The Due Process Clause is the most important to criminal procedure and rules of evidence. It prohibits state and local governments from depriving individuals of life, liberty, or property without legislative authorization. Furthermore, it is an avenue through which the federal judiciary has applied the Bill of Rights to state law and actors.

The Supreme Court has consistently held that the Due Process Clause also provides that every criminal defendant is entitled to a fair trial. While the right to a trial resides in the Sixth Amendment, the Court has indicated that *fairness* in such proceedings is guaranteed by the Fifth and Fourteenth Amendments. The Bill of Rights, Supreme Court decisions, and rules of evidence and procedure have been created to ensure the right to a fair trial in criminal courts. Irrespective of these safeguards, mistakes occur in virtually every case brought to trial. On the appellate level, jurists must evaluate the magnitude of the error in question to determine if it constitutes **harmless** or **reversible error**. According to the U.S. Code, harmless error is an "error or defect which does not affect the substantial rights of the parties." While the Supreme Court has clarified the verbiage in criminal cases where they placed the dividing line between the two concepts at "whether there is a reasonable possibility that the evidence complained of might have contributed to the conviction."[21] Using this standard, the Court refused to adopt a rule that would automatically find any federal constitutional error harmful to the defendant. To wit,

> All 50 states have harmless error statutes or rules, and the United States long ago, through its Congress, established for its courts the rule that judgments shall not be reversed for "errors or defects which do not affect the substantial rights of the parties" . . . none of these rules, on its face, distinguishes between federal constitutional errors and errors of state law or federal statutes and rules. All of these rules, state or federal, serve a very useful purpose insofar as they block setting aside convictions for small errors or defects that have little, if any, likelihood of having changed the result of the trial. We conclude that there may be some constitutional errors which, in the setting of a particular case, are so unimportant and insignificant that they may, consistent with the Federal Constitution, be deemed harmless, not requiring the automatic reversal of the conviction.[22]

Sixth Amendment

In all criminal prosecutions, the accused shall enjoy the **right to a speedy and public trial**, by an **impartial jury of the State and district wherein the crime shall have been committed**, which district shall have been previously ascertained by law, and **to be informed of the nature and cause of the accusation; to be confronted with the witnesses against him; to have compulsory process for obtaining witnesses in his favor**, and to have **the assistance of counsel for his defense**.

The Sixth Amendment grants individuals the right to a speedy and public trial, the right to an impartial jury of one's peers, the right to be informed of the charges, the right to confront witnesses, the right to subpoena, and the right to counsel.

reconstruction amendments the Thirteenth, Fourteenth, and Fifteenth Amendments to the U.S. Constitution, which were ratified between 1865 and 1870 and which were intended to free and grant civil rights to former slaves.

harmless error an error which is not significantly related to the final disposition of the case.

reversible error an error of such magnitude that is related to the final disposition of the case.

Each of these rights represents essential threads in the fabric of the American criminal justice system. As stated previously, these rights trace their roots back to the *Magna Carta*. That document provided that there would be no criminal trial based on an unsubstantiated accusation, and perhaps more importantly, that "no freeman shall be taken, imprisoned ... except by lawful judgment of his peers or the law of the land."

 CASE LAW

THE EVOLUTION OF MIRANDA

In 1966, the Supreme Court responded to a variety of similar cases (i.e., *Westover v. U.S.*; *Vignera v. New York*; and *California v. Stewart*) that alleged that coercive interrogation tactics had resulted in confessions. Their consolidated ruling in *Miranda v. Arizona* [384 U.S. 436 (1986)] had a profound impact on police procedure. In essence, the ruling required law enforcement to inform custodial suspects of rights guaranteed to them in the Fifth, Sixth, and Fourteenth Amendments. It further ruled that in the absence of an express waiver of such rights, any statement made during police interrogation would be suppressed based on a presumption that they were the result of coercive tactics. Traditional *Miranda* warnings covering the minimum requirements set forth read as follows:

You have the right to remain silent. Anything you say can and will be used against you in a court of law. You have the right to an attorney, and to have an attorney present during interrogation. If you cannot afford an attorney, one will be appointed to you.

The Court cautioned that a *heavy burden* to demonstrate that a defendant knowingly and intelligently waived their rights would rest on the state in cases where an attorney was not present.

The ruling did not satisfy civil libertarians, who thought that it didn't go far enough, nor law enforcement, who thought that the requirement would result in a chilling effect on police interrogations. As expected, challenges to *Miranda* have been quite plentiful. In *Edwards*, police returned to question the suspect after he clearly indicated that he did not wish to make a statement without an attorney. He subsequently made an incriminating statement which resulted in his conviction. In evaluating the case, the Court pointed to earlier decisions (i.e., *Fare v. Michael C.* and *Rhode Island v. Innis*) and opined " ... we reconfirm these views and, to lend them substance,

emphasize that it is inconsistent with Miranda and its progeny for the authorities, at their instance, to reinterrogate an accused in custody if he has clearly asserted his right to counsel" [*Edwards v. Arizona*, 451 U.S. 477 (1981)].

Thirteen years later, the Court evaluated to what degree their "bright line" ruling in *Edwards* impacted cases where the invocation of the right to counsel was ambiguous or otherwise unclear. They reiterated that the previously established rule "serves the prophylactic purpose of preventing officers from badgering a suspect into waiving his previously asserted" rights. At the same time, the Court ruled that questioning may continue if the expressed desire is ambiguous or equivocal to a degree that a reasonable officer would have doubts as to whether the right was being requested. In their justification, the Court recognized that requiring officers to use their own judgment in ambiguous situations would "transform the Miranda safeguards into wholly irrational obstacles to legitimate investigative activity" by requiring the presence of an attorney even in situations where the suspect does not want one. In *Berghuis v. Thompkins* [560 U.S. 370 (2010)], the Court extended this to include the admission of voluntary statements made by an individual in custody who has been informed and understands his rights yet does not explicitly invoke or waive them. They ruled that a voluntary reply could be construed as implying a waiver even after a lengthy silence during interrogation (in this case more than three hours).

The erosion of Miranda was even more pronounced in *Salinas v. Texas* (2013).[23] In this case, the petitioner, who was not arrested and taken into custody, voluntarily answered questions regarding a murder, and only fell silent when investigators asked if shell casings found at the scene would match the gun in his possession. He subsequently answered further questions not involving

(*continued*)

▼

ballistics, but fled the area prior to the issuance of a warrant. Fourteen years later, he was arrested and convicted of the murder in question. During his trial, the prosecuting attorneys introduced his silence to that particular question as evidence of his guilt.

In evaluating whether the Fifth Amendment applied to pre-arrest statements or protected criminal defendants from inferences of guilt by remaining silent during questioning, the Court ruled:

(a) To prevent the privilege against self-incrimination from shielding information not properly within its scope, a witness who " 'desires the protection of the privilege ... must claim it' " at the time he relies on it ... This Court has recognized two exceptions to that requirement. First, a criminal defendant need not take the stand and assert the privilege at his own trial ... Petitioner's silence falls outside this exception because he had no comparable unqualified right not to speak during his police interview. Second, a witness' failure to invoke the privilege against self-incrimination must be excused where governmental coercion makes his forfeiture of the privilege involuntary ... Petitioner cannot benefit from this principle because it is undisputed that he agreed to accompany the officers to the station and was free to leave at any time.

(b) Petitioner seeks a third exception to the express invocation requirement for cases where the witness chooses to stand mute rather than give an answer that officials suspect would be incriminating, but this Court's cases all but foreclose that argument. A defendant normally does not invoke the privilege by remaining silent ... And the express invocation requirement applies even when an official has reason to suspect

that the answer to his question would incriminate the witness ... For the same reasons that neither a witness' silence nor official suspicion is sufficient by itself to relieve a witness of the obligation to expressly invoke the privilege, they do not do so together. The proposed exception also would be difficult to reconcile with Berghuis v. Thompkins, where this Court held in the closely related context of post-Miranda silence that a defendant failed to invoke his right to cut off police questioning when he remained silent for 2 hours and 45 minutes.

Petitioner claims that reliance on the Fifth Amendment privilege is the most likely explanation for silence in a case like his, but such silence is "insolubly ambiguous." ... To be sure, petitioner might have declined to answer the officer's question in reliance on his constitutional privilege. But he also might have done so because he was trying to think of a good lie, because he was embarrassed, or because he was protecting someone else. Not every such possible explanation for silence is probative of guilt, but neither is every possible explanation protected by the Fifth Amendment. Petitioner also suggests that it would be unfair to require a suspect unschooled in the particulars of legal doctrine to do anything more than remain silent in order to invoke his "right to remain silent." But the Fifth Amendment guarantees that no one may be "compelled in any criminal case to be a witness against himself," not an unqualified "right to remain silent." In any event, it is settled that forfeiture of the privilege against self-incrimination need not be knowing.

(c) Petitioner's argument that applying the express invocation requirement in this context will be unworkable is also unpersuasive. The Court has long required defendants to assert the privilege in order to subsequently benefit from it, and this rule has not proved difficult to apply in practice

The Right to a Speedy and Public Trial

The Sixth Amendment guarantees the right to both a speedy and public trial. The Court has ruled that with few exceptions, all proceedings must be open to the public. This avoids even the suggestion of underhandedness or persecution of the innocent. This right is not reserved simply for the trial phase. It has been extended to include *voir dire* of prospective jurors[24] and pretrial motion hearings.[25] At the same time, the Court has recognized that the right is not absolute[26] as special circumstances may occur that inhibit this guarantee. This could include, for example, cases receiving excess publicity that might interfere with a defendant's due process rights or cases involving highly sensitive information. However, the Court has also stressed that such cases would be rare and would require *special care*. Because the concept of secretive judicial proceedings is so abhorrent to the American conscience, courts must consider reasonable alternatives to closing the proceeding. The Court provided specific standards for courts to apply prior to excluding the public from any stage. To wit,

The party seeking to close the hearing must advance an overriding interest that is likely to be prejudiced, the closure must be no broader than necessary to protect that interest, the trial court must consider reasonable alternatives to closing the proceeding, and it must make findings adequate to support the closure.[27]

The right to a speedy trial may also trace its roots to the *Magna Carta*, and is guaranteed in the Sixth Amendment to the Constitution. This right, however, is "generically different from any of the other rights enshrined in the Constitution for the protection of the accused"[28] as there is a prevailing societal interest in a speedy trial that may run counter to the interests of the accused. As the Court noted in *Barker v. Wingo*, individuals released on bail may commit other crimes or may flee justice. To the defendant's detriment, lengthy delays may have a negative impact on potential rehabilitation, especially in cases where the defendant is confined to jail. On the other hand, the Court noted that a delay may actually be advantageous to an accused in cases where witnesses became unavailable. Finally, the Court considered the elusive nature of the concept itself noting that it is "impossible to determine with precision when the right has been denied . . . or . . . how long is too long in a system where justice is supposed to be swift but deliberate." In an attempt to more clearly delineate the concept, the Court established a four-part case-by-case balancing test that evaluated four factors: *length of delay*, *reason for the delay*, *time and manner in which the defendant assert his right*, and *degree of prejudice to the defendant which the delay caused.*

The federal government and many states have developed statutes that identify time limits. In 1974, for example, Congress passed the *Speedy Trial Act* that required a criminal defendant's trial to commence within 70 days of his indictment or initial appearance [18 U.S.C. § 3161 (a)(1)], and that entitled said defendant to dismissal of the charges if the deadline was not met [18 U.S.C. § 3161 (a)(2)]. The Act, however, specifically provides for the exclusion of days lost due to certain types of delays. In cases in state court where the right to a speedy trial was violated, then the indictment must be dismissed and/or the conviction overturned as no other remedy would be appropriate.

The Right to an Impartial Jury of Peers

A defendant's right to an impartial jury of his/her peers is contained within the Sixth Amendment. Simply put, all individuals have the right to a jury drawn from the community in which the offense was committed and who are not prejudiced in their examination of the offense. This does not suggest, however, that jurors must be completely ignorant of the crime or the defendant. It only requires that those selected are not predisposed to the defendant's guilt. Changes of venue are often granted in cases receiving significant media coverage to diminish the possibility of partiality. However, many cases are so notorious and so widely covered that changes of venue have little impact. In fact, the judge in the Scott Peterson case denied a change of venue for the sentencing of the man convicted of killing his wife and unborn child, arguing that the media coverage throughout the state of California had been so pervasive that a change of venue was a waste of time.

Another procedural mechanism to ensure impartiality may be found in the jury selection process (discussed in Chapter 2). In criminal cases, potential jurors are subjected to qualification by the state, the defense, and/or the court. During this process, known as *voir dire*, potential jurors may be excluded for a variety of reasons. Both sides are granted an unlimited number of **challenges for cause** and a specific number of **peremptory challenges**. The first of these, challenges for

voir dire the preliminary questioning of potential jurors or witnesses to ascertain competency to give or hear evidence

challenge for cause a request that a prospective juror be dismissed due to a specific and significant reason to believe that the individual is incapable of serving as a juror.

peremptory challenge challenge used by counsel to remove a potential juror without explanation.

cause, may include: relationship to a party to the case, mental infirmity, military obligations, undue hardship, predisposition or preconception of defendant's guilt or innocence, and any other obvious bias (e.g., membership in a hate group, victim of a similar crime). When potential jurors are challenged for cause, the requesting party must articulate the rationale. Peremptory challenges, on the other hand, do not require an explanation to the court. However, the Court has ruled that excluding jurors based on race violates the Sixth Amendment's guarantee of impartiality.

Traditionally, courts routinely excused potential jurors in capital cases who indicated that they were opposed to the death penalty. These dismissals were often predicated on the prosecutorial argument that such individuals would be unable to follow applicable law in the imposition of this lawful penalty. However, the Court in *Witherspoon v. Illinois* (1968) struck down an Illinois statute that provided for the removal of any individual through a challenge for cause who had *conscientious scruples against capital punishment* or who was opposed to it. They held:

1. Neither on the basis of the record in this case nor as a matter of judicial notice of presently available information can it be concluded that the exclusion of jurors opposed to capital punishment results in an unrepresentative jury on the issue of guilt or substantially increases the risk of conviction.

2. Although it has not been shown that this jury was biased with respect to guilt, it is self-evident that, in its distinct role as arbiter of the punishment to be imposed, this jury fell woefully short of that impartiality to which a defendant is entitled under the Sixth and Fourteenth Amendments.

3. A man who opposed the death penalty, no less than one who favors it, can make the discretionary choice of punishment entrusted to him by the State and can thus obey the oath he takes as a juror; but in a nation where so many have come to oppose capital punishment, a jury from which all such people have been excluded cannot perform the task demanded of it—that of expressing the conscience of the community on the ultimate question of life or death.

4. Just as a State may not entrust the determination of whether a man is innocent or guilty to a tribunal organized to convict, so it may not entrust the determination of whether a man should live or die to a tribunal organized to return a verdict of death; and no sentence of death can be carried out, regardless of when it was imposed or recommended that sentence was chosen by excluding venireman for cause simply because they voiced general objections to capital punishment or expressed conscientious or religious scruples against its infliction.[29]

The Court specifically excluded from consideration the prosecutorial right to challenge for cause those prospective jurors expressing reservations. However, after several iterations[30] in which the Court ruled that such challenges must demonstrate *substantial impairment* that issue was put to rest in *Uttecht v. Brown* (2007)[31] when the Court emphasized the *deference* appropriately afforded to the trial court. More succinctly,

The State may not infringe this right by eliminating from the venire those whose scruples against the death penalty would not substantially impair the performance of their duties. Courts reviewing claims ... owe deference to the trial court, which is in a superior position to determine the demeanor and qualifications of a potential juror.

The Right to Be Informed of Charges

Under the Sixth Amendment, individuals charged with a crime have the right "to be informed of the nature and cause of the accusation." Depending on jurisdiction and system in place, defendants are informed of the nature and cause of the charges against them during either the **initial appearance** or **arraignment**. The Court has recognized this right as "the first and most universally recognized requirement of due process,"[32] and has heard a variety of cases in which they evaluated whether guilty pleas made in the absence of notification are acceptable. The Court has held that only pleas considered to be both *voluntary* and *intelligent* are constitutionally valid,[33] and that a plea may not be considered intelligent unless a defendant first receives "real notice of the nature of the charge against him."[34]

The Right to Confront Witnesses

The **Confrontation Clause** is also firmly embedded in, and often considered to be the cornerstone of, the Sixth Amendment: "The accused shall enjoy the right … to be confronted with the witnesses against him." It is primarily an attempt to halt the British practice of using anonymity to mask unfounded or politicized charges, as in the case of Sir Walter Raleigh who was charged with treason after the death of his benefactor. Although his primary accuser was known to him and was his former friend and alleged co-conspirator, Lord Cobham, Raleigh was unable to mount a defense, because he was never granted the right to question Cobham. (His request was, however, duly noted: "Good my Lords, let my accuser come face to face, and be deposed. Were the case but for a small copyhold, you would have witnesses or good proof to lead the jury to a verdict; and I am here for my life!") Unfortunately for Raleigh, and for the interests of due process and fundamental rights, he was summarily convicted and executed.

The Confrontation Clause, then, is a clause embedded in the Sixth Amendment that provides that any criminal defendant has a right to confront any witness testifying against him/her (please see Chapter 7). It is the foundation for the *Hearsay Rule*. **Hearsay** *is defined as any statement, other than one made by the declarant while testifying at the current trial or hearing* which *a party offers in evidence to prove the truth of the matter asserted in the statement* (F.R.E. Rule 801). Generally speaking, the Hearsay Rule prohibits the introduction of any statement that matches the above definition. However, the Federal Rules of Evidence and the Supreme Court have delineated a variety of exceptions to the Rule. (Please see Chapter 10.)

The Power to Subpoena Witnesses

According to the Sixth Amendment, the defendant "shall enjoy the right … to have compulsory process for obtaining witnesses in his favor." Generally speaking, this means that a criminal defendant has the power to **subpoena** witnesses and force them to appear in court. This guarantee is strengthened by criminal penalties for failure to appear. This does not mean, however, that the witnesses will be cooperative. They may dodge service, fail to appear, "forget" information, or even refuse to testify per the Fifth Amendment's protection against self-incrimination.

The Right to an Attorney

Finally, the Sixth Amendment provides for the assistance of counsel. There are a variety of distinct rights recognized under the Assistance of Counsel Clause: the right to paid counsel of choice, the right to self-representation, the right to effective assistance of counsel, and the right to appoint counsel. The right to select an attorney of choice is necessarily limited to the rules of criminal procedure that require appropriate jurisdictional authorization to practice. It is also limited in cases where

initial appearance or arraignment the formal proceeding that follows the arrest of an accused in which: the accused is informed of the charges, bail is set, a plea is given, counsel is appointed, and the next court appearance is scheduled.

confrontation clause a clause embedded in the Sixth Amendment providing that any accused person has a right to confront any witness testifying against him or her. The clause is also used to refer to the common law rule preventing the admission of hearsay in a criminal trial.

hearsay any statement, other than one made by the declarant while testifying at the current trial or hearing that a party offers in evidence to prove the truth of the matter asserted in the statement.

subpoena a court summons which orders the named party to appear in court and produce documents or other tangible evidence if requested.

conflicts of interest or scheduling can be demonstrated. In *U.S. v. Gonzalez-Lopez* (2006), the Court reaffirmed previous rulings and held that "the Sixth Amendment violation is not subject to harmless-error analysis. Erroneous deprivation of the right to counsel of choice, 'with consequences that are necessarily unquantifiable and indeterminate, unquestionable qualifies as "structural error".' "[35]

While it is not generally advisable to represent oneself in a court of law, the right is an historic one, which may be found in the *Judiciary Act of 1789* enacted by the First Congress and signed by President George Washington. The right is currently codified in 28 U.S.C. § 1654. The vast majority of states have also explicitly conferred that right in their respective constitutions, and the Supreme Court has long upheld the sanctity of the provision.

> When the administration of the criminal law…is hedged about, as it is, by the Constitutional safeguards for the protection of an accused, to deny him in the exercise of his free choice the right to dispense with some of these safeguards…is to imprison a man in his privileges, and call it the Constitution.[36]

The Court has subsequently ruled that the Sixth and Fourteenth Amendments bar state courts from denying the right to self-representation.

The Sixth Amendment's Assistance of Counsel clause also ensures that individuals have the right to an attorney irrespective of financial situation. Thus, indigent defendants are entitled to a court-appointed or government-provided lawyer. This right was first recognized in the seminal case of *Powell v. Alabama* (1932)[37] where the Court ruled that the Sixth and Fourteenth Amendments required the appointment of counsel to any criminal defendant in a capital case. Approximately 30 years later in *Gideon v. Wainwright* (1963),[38] the Court extended the right to include any criminal defendant facing serious charges. Today, any indigent defendant who faces a possible sentence of six months or more has the right to appointed counsel. In addition, this right attaches in all critical stages in the criminal justice process, including but not limited to: custodial interrogation, post-indictment or post-arrest lineups, preliminary hearings, arraignments, trial, sentencing, and the first appeal post-conviction.

 APPLICATION OF LAW

THE SIXTH AMENDMENT AND JOSE PADILLA

In May of 2002, José Padilla, also known as Abdullah al-Muhajir, was arrested at Chicago's O'Hare International Airport upon his arrival from Pakistan. Suspected of scouting sites in which to detonate radioactive bombs and conspiring with senior Al-Qaeda officials, he was declared an enemy combatant and transferred to a military prison in Charleston, North Carolina, where he remained for more than three years. In February 2005, U.S. District Judge Henry F. Floyd ruled that the Sixth Amendment required the government to either charge him or release him. He was formally indicted by a grand jury in November 2005.

Of the original three charges, one was dismissed in whole, and another in part. Initially set for trial on January 22, 2007, a federal judge postponed the proceedings once again when Padilla's attorneys claimed that their client was suffering from Post-Traumatic

Stress Disorder as a result of his ordeal. On August 16, 2007, Padilla was found guilty on charges wholly unrelated to the original allegations that had been used to justify his military detention. Originally sentenced to 17 years, Padilla's sentence was overturned by the Eleventh Circuit as too lenient due to his lengthy criminal record and his Al-Qaeda training [*U.S. v. Jayyousi*, 657 F. 3d 1085, 1117-19 (11th Cir. 2011)]. Padilla's case represented one of the first contemporary cases in which legal questions arose regarding the confinement of "enemy combatants."

In 2008, Padilla filed suit against John Yoo, the Deputy Assistant Attorney General (USDOJ Office of Legal Counsel) from 2001 to 2003 seeking compensation for damages that he suffered from *unlawful actions*. However, the Ninth Circuit Court of Appeals ruled that questions concerning the legality of police actions and Yoo's judgments were irrelevant as the law in question was *not sufficiently clear that every reasonable official would have understood that what he was doing violated the plaintiff's rights* [*Padilla et al. v. Yoo* (11th Circuit, 2012) 09-16478].

Ironically, another case involving a man named Jose Padilla from Kentucky would significantly expand traditional protections provided in the Sixth Amendment. In this case, Padilla, a native of Honduras, had been a lawful permanent resident of the United States for more than 40 years. Additionally, Padilla had served honorably in the U.S. Armed Forces during the Vietnam War. In 2007, Padilla was arrested for the transportation of a large amount of marijuana in his tractor-trailer. Upon advice from counsel, who had assured him that his immigration status was not at issue as he had been a U.S. resident for a significant amount of time, Padilla pled guilty. His plea resulted in an order of mandatory deportation. Padilla subsequently appealed on the basis of ineffective counsel. In *Padilla v. Commonwealth of Kentucky*, 559 U.S. 356 (2010), the Supreme Court ruled that defense counsel must advise noncitizen defendants about the risk of deportation as a result of a guilty plea.

Finally, the Sixth Amendment guarantees the assistance of effective counsel. This right applies to all "critical stages of the criminal proceedings"[39] and to "plea offers that lapse or are rejected."[40] This does not suggest, however, that they are entitled to the best possible attorney, just a competent one. The Court has cautioned against *mechanical rules*, and established a significant bar that criminal defendants must reach to prove ineffectiveness. The *Strickland* test requires evaluation of the following:

(a) The proper standard for judging attorney performance is that of reasonably effective assistance ... the defendant must show that counsel's representation fell below an objective standard of reasonableness. Judicial scrutiny of counsel's performance must be highly deferential, and a fair assessment of attorney performance requires that every effort be made to eliminate the distorting effects of hindsight, to reconstruct the circumstances of counsel's challenged conduct, and to evaluate the conduct from counsel's perspective at the time. A court must indulge a strong presumption that counsel's conduct falls within the wide range of reasonable professional assistance. These standards require no special amplification in order to define counsel's duty to investigate, the duty at issue in this case.

(b) With regard to the required showing of prejudice, the proper standard requires the defendant to show that there is a reasonable probability that, but for counsel's unprofessional errors, the result of the proceeding would have been different. A reasonable probability is a probability sufficient to undermine confidence in the outcome. A court hearing an ineffectiveness claim must consider the totality of the evidence before the judge or jury

Seventh Amendment

In suits at common law, where the value in controversy shall exceed twenty dollars, the right of trial by jury shall be preserved, and no fact tried by a jury shall be otherwise re-examined in any court of the United States, than according to the rules of the common law.

The rights guaranteed under the Seventh Amendment have not been applied to the states via the Fourteenth Amendment. Thus, the right to a trial by jury in any civil trial is only applicable to federal courts.

Eighth Amendment

Excessive bail shall not be required, nor excessive fines imposed, nor cruel and unusual punishments inflicted.

The Eighth Amendment protects American citizens from imposition of excessive bail or fines and any punishment regarded as cruel and unusual. Although it specifically precludes excessive bail, the amendment does not mandate the establishment of bail for all defendants: "Where Congress has mandated detention on the basis of some other compelling interest ... the Eighth Amendment does not require release on bail" (*United States v. Salerno*, 481 U.S. 739, 1987). Indeed, the Supreme Court consistently has ruled that the government's "regulatory interest in community safety" can be more compelling than an individual's "liberty interest" (*United States v. Salerno*). However, some state statutes do include a provision for the establishment of bail for any defendant not charged with a capital offense. In Delaware, for example, "[a]ll prisoners shall be bailable by sufficient sureties, unless for capital offenses when the proof is positive or the presumption great" (Delaware Constitution, Article I, Section 12). For the most part, **excessive bail** is defined as any bail in excess of that which is necessary to ensure the appearance of the defendant at the action in question.

The Eighth Amendment also prohibits the imposition of **excessive fines**. Created to prevent prosecutorial misconduct, it does not apply to punitive damages awarded in cases between private parties, nor does it "constrain such an award when the government neither has prosecuted the action nor has any right to recover a share of the damages awarded."[41]

Finally, the Eighth Amendment prohibits the use of **cruel and unusual punishment**. Unfortunately, a definition of the phrase is not as obvious as might be expected. Ambiguity has existed since inception of the concept and was formally recognized by the Supreme Court as early as 1878. As Justice Clifford stated: "[D]ifficulty would attend the effort to define with exactness the extent of the constitution provision which provides that cruel and unusual punishments shall not be inflicted; but it is safe to affirm that punishments of torture are forbidden."[42]

excessive bail is defined as any bail in excess of that which is necessary to ensure the appearance of the defendant at the action in question.

excessive fine any monetary penalty that is disproportionate to the offense.

 CASE LAW

FURMAN, GREGG, AND THE EIGHTH AMENDMENT

Of the rights articulated in the Eighth Amendment, perhaps the most commonly cited regards the prohibition of cruel and unusual punishment. While courts have grappled with the issue for centuries, the imposition of the death penalty is the most controversial. Early courts upheld the use of the death penalty; *In Re Kemmler* (136 U.S. 436, 1890) stated that:

> Punishments are cruel when they involve torture or a lingering death; but the punishment of death is not cruel, within the meaning of that word as used in the Constitution. It implies there something inhuman and barbarous, and something more than the mere extinguishment of life.

This ideology went largely unchallenged until the latter part of the twentieth century. In a landmark decision in 1972, the Supreme Court ruled that the imposition of the death penalty violated both the Eighth and Fourteenth Amendments (*Furman v.*

Georgia).[43] The prohibition of cruel and unusual punishment was:

> ... not limited to torturous punishments or to punishments which were considered cruel and unusual at the time the Eighth Amendment was adopted; that a punishment was cruel and unusual if it did not comport with human dignity; and that since it was a denial of human dignity for a state arbitrarily to subject a person to an unusually severe punishment which society indicated that it did not regard as acceptable, and which could not be shown to serve any penal purpose more effectively than a significantly less drastic punishment, death was a cruel and unusual punishment.

Immediately following the edict, death sentences were converted to prison terms across the country, angering many legislators and private citizens alike. Many states scrambled to create statutes that would support government-sanctioned executions. Georgia's solution was to create a bifurcated trial process for capital cases in which judges (or juries) were provided the opportunity to hear mitigating and aggravating factors and in which defendants who were sentenced to death were afforded an automatic appeal. So, 4 years after declaring that the death penalty, on its face, constituted cruel and unusual punishment, the Supreme Court reversed itself. In *Gregg v. Georgia* (1976),[44] the Court declared that the imposition of the death penalty on murderers did not necessarily violate the Constitution.

To these ends, the Supreme Court has attempted to apply a formula in the assessment of punishment. Thus, in determining whether a particular punishment violates the Eighth Amendment's prohibition of cruel and unusual punishment, the Court has used a scale of measurement that includes:

> (i) [T]he gravity of the offense and the harshness of the penalty; (ii) the sentences imposed on other criminals in the same jurisdiction, that is, whether more serious crimes are subject to the same penalty or to less serious penalties; and (iii) the sentences imposed for commission of the same crime in other jurisdictions.[45]

Among other things, the Supreme Court has found that cruel and unusual punishments include the revocation of citizenship[46]; and terms of imprisonment disproportionate to the crime.[47] In addition, the Court has formally recognized that the cruel and unusual punishment clause of the Eighth Amendment has three distinct roles: the delineating of acceptable punishment, the balancing of punishment with the severity of the crime, and the limiting of criminalization of behavior.[48]

The Court has also continued to grapple with issues concerning the constitutionality of the death penalty. In recent years, the Court has forbidden the execution of mentally retarded citizens[49] and juveniles[50] on the grounds that those offenders had diminished personal responsibility for their crimes. In other cases involving questions of proportionality, the Court has looked to *evolving standards of decency*. For example, the Court in *Coker v. Georgia* ruled that the imposition of the death penalty as a punishment for the rape of an adult woman was *grossly disproportionate* and *excessive* as it was contrary to "present public judgment, as represented by the attitude of state legislatures and sentencing juries, concerning the acceptability of such a penalty."[51] In 2008, the Court expanded the prohibition of death sentences in cases involving child rape where the victim was not, nor intended to be, murdered. In their ruling, the Court continued to emphasize the importance of "objective indicia of society's standards, as expressed in legislative enactments and state practice with respect to executions."[52]

cruel and unusual punishment cruel and unusual punishment prohibited by the Eighth Amendment, the phrase is roughly defined as any punishment in excess of that which is fair and conscionable in contemporary society, such as torture, execution of mentally retarded or minor offenders, and disproportionate terms of imprisonment. Ambiguity regarding its definition continues to exist, with Justice Clifford defining only one specific example: "(D)ifficulty would attend the effort to define with exactness the extent of the constitution provision . . . but it is safe to affirm that punishments of torture are forbidden."

Ninth Amendment

> The enumeration in the Constitution, of certain rights, shall not be construed to deny or disparage others retained by the people.

The Ninth Amendment was intended to recognize that individuals held rights outside of those specifically mentioned in the Constitution, generally, and in the Bill of Rights, in particular. In fact, many of the Framers were concerned that such enumeration would significantly harness the rights of the people, in that the absence of specific verbiage addressing other areas would be tantamount to outright denial of their existence and that the articulation of specific limitations

▼

on governmental powers would fail to prevent abuses in areas outside of those written. More succinctly, as James Madison put it in 1789:

> [B]y enumerating particular exceptions to the grant of power, it would disparage those rights which were not placed in that enumeration; and it might follow, by implication, that those rights which were not singled out, were intended to be assigned into the hands of the General Government, and were consequently insecure.

Such rights, while sacrosanct, were simply too numerous to mention.

Largely overlooked since its inception, the Ninth Amendment has received much attention in recent years as individuals and institutions alike attempt to apply such reasoning to various issues including the right to life, the right to own handguns, the right to self-determination, the right to education, the right to an adequate standard of living, and the prohibition of genocide. Although not specifically articulated in the Constitution, the existence of certain fundamental civil liberties is argued for by many contemporary groups and protected by the language of the Ninth Amendment.

Tenth Amendment

> The powers not delegated to the United States by the Constitution, nor prohibited by it to the states, are reserved to the States respectively, or to the people.

As with the Ninth Amendment, the Tenth Amendment has been embraced by various groups to support controversial political agendas. Intended to ensure the rights of individual states and citizens, the Tenth Amendment was included by the

Basic American Rights in the Criminal Justice System

Right	Source
The freedom from unreasonable search and seizure	Fourth Amendment (Warrant Clause)
The right to a grand jury	Fifth Amendment
The protection against double jeopardy	Fifth Amendment
The protection against self-incrimination	Fifth Amendment
The right to due process	Fifth Amendment
The right to a speedy trial	Sixth Amendment
The right to a public trial	Sixth Amendment
The right to an impartial jury	Sixth Amendment
The right to be informed of charges	Sixth Amendment
The right to confront witnesses	Sixth Amendment (Confrontation Clause)
The right to compulsory process for obtaining favorable witnesses	Sixth Amendment
The right to counsel	Sixth Amendment
The freedom from excessive fines	Eighth Amendment
The freedom from cruel and unusual punishment	Eighth Amendment
The presumption of innocence and the standard of beyond a reasonable doubt	Supreme Court
The right to exclude evidence gathered unconstitutionally	Supreme Court (Exclusionary Rule)
The right to an expectation of privacy	Supreme Court

▼

Framers as a formal declaration of the limitations imposed upon the federal government. Basically, it prohibits an expansion of power by the federal government unless so authorized by the Constitution and provides for federal sovereignty only in the areas contained therein. With the exception of the time period surrounding the Civil War, the Tenth Amendment largely has been ignored by both the population and the courts. For whatever reason, Supreme Court rulings have recognized the rights of individual states but failed to address the merits of the Tenth Amendment (please see Chapter 2).

▶ Judicially Created Rights

Beyond a Reasonable Doubt and the Presumption of Innocence

In the United States, one of the most fundamental rights enjoyed by individuals charged with a criminal offense is the **presumption of innocence**. While it is clearly grounded in the Due Process Clause and can be traced to English common law, it was not formally articulated in the Constitution. Rather, it has been left to the courts to delineate both its construct and its breadth. Without exception, the Court has noted its centrality to the notion of Due Process.

> The principle that there is a presumption of innocence in favor of the accused is the undoubted law, axiomatic and elementary, and its enforcement lies at the foundation of the administration of our criminal law.[53]

In the eighteenth and nineteenth centuries, this presumption was so strong that it extended from the time of arrest to verdict (or case finality). As noted by Wigmore, it should "hover over the prisoner as a guardian angel from the moment of indictment until the verdict is determined."[54] Indeed, this philosophy was the foundation for the *Judiciary Act of 1789*, which guaranteed bail for all noncapital crimes. However, a series of cases in the twentieth century demonstrated the evolution of the concept that limited the protection to the trial process. For example, *Bell v. Wolfish* (1979) noted that the "principle has no application to a determination of the rights of a pretrial detainee during confinement before his trial has even begun."[55]

Today, the assurance of the presumption of innocence is largely found in the allocation of burden and high standard of proof required in criminal cases. Due Process requires that the **burden of proof** remains on the state throughout the proceedings. Describing it as one of our *most noble aspirations*, the Court clearly requires "the government to leave the individual alone until good cause is shown for disturbing him and by requiring the government in its contest with the individual to shoulder the entire load."[56]

As mentioned, the presumption also resides in the standard of proof which is required in criminal cases. This standard, **beyond a reasonable doubt** is the highest **standard of proof** that must be met in any trial, and dates at least from our early years as a nation.[57] Like other rights not formally articulated in the Constitution, the guarantee to such consideration was judicially determined to lie within the *Due Process Clause* of the Fifth Amendment. In 1970, the requirement that all criminal defendants were entitled to proof beyond a reasonable doubt was firmly established in the case *In re Winship*[58]:

> Lest there remain any doubt about the constitutional stature of the reasonable doubt standard, we explicitly hold that the Due Process Clause protects the accused against

presumption of innocence a rebuttable presumption required in criminal courts that the accused is innocent until evidence presented by the state sufficiently demonstrates guilt beyond a reasonable doubt.

burden of proof legal requirement referring to the affirmative duty of a party to establish that all elements of the issue in question are true and valid as alleged. In criminal trials, the burden of proof lies with the state.

beyond a reasonable doubt the highest legal standard of proof used in criminal courts and determined by the trier of fact. It requires a demonstration that no reasonable doubt exists.

standard of proof that quantum of evidence that is required to demonstrate the truth of the matter in a court of law.

▼

conviction except upon proof beyond a reasonable doubt of every fact necessary to constitute the crime with which he is charged.

Traditionally, *reasonable doubt* was defined as a state in which jurors "cannot say they feel an abiding conviction, to a moral certainty of the truth of the charge."[59]

▶ Rules of Evidence

The Constitution and the Bill of Rights are fundamental to the administration of justice and protection of individual rights, yet they do not provide rules pertaining to the law of evidence. In fact, the vast majority of evidence law has been founded upon common law principles, such as relevancy, competency, hearsay, and privileged communications. Subsequent case law has provided a clearer picture, but a formal codification of evidence law was not undertaken until the second half of the twentieth century.

Uniform Rules of Evidence

In 1974, the Uniform Rules of Evidence (URE) was created by the National Conference of Commissioners on Uniform State Law as a result of the arbitrary and capricious nature of laws among bordering states. American jurisprudence at the time was contingent largely upon prevailing community standards, which resulted in a patchwork of evidence law. The introduction of the Uniform Rules signaled an end to the common law of evidence.

Federal Rules of Evidence (see Appendix C)

Immediately after the passage of the Uniform Rules, the federal government introduced the Federal Rules of Evidence (FRE)—a code of law binding upon federal entities. In the most basic sense, the FRE was designed to ensure uniformity and consistency in judicial rulings, interpretations, and applications and to replace previous statutory and common law within the federal court system. The Federal Rules list is organized by article in the following manner (and will be discussed in detail in subsequent chapters):

ARTICLE I	General Provisions
ARTICLE II	Judicial Notice
ARTICLE III	Presumptions in Civil Actions and Proceedings
ARTICLE IV	Relevancy and Its Limits
ARTICLE V	Privileges
ARTICLE VI	Witnesses
ARTICLE VII	Opinions and Expert Testimony
ARTICLE VIII	Hearsay
ARTICLE IX	Authentication and Identification
ARTICLE X	Contents of Writings, Recordings, and Photographs
ARTICLE XI	Miscellaneous Rules

Most states have adopted the URE or the FRE with slight modification. While the URE initially unified many legal constructs, the Federal Rules halted the unification efforts, as states were provided a variety of choices. In recent years, the National Conference has attempted to bring the URE as close as possible to the rules enacted by Congress. By all accounts, the URE is far less vague than its counterpart.

It is important to note that federal law is also a product of legislation established by Congress and rulings issued by the Supreme Court. As a general rule, Congress has not attempted major revisions to the FRE. Throughout history, however, it has been quite active in the passage of legislation involving criminal law, criminal procedure, and the criminal justice system. Such acts include provisions for the custody of federal prisoners, surveillance limitations on federal agents, and the criminalization of specified behaviors. Congress has increasingly passed crime legislation, and a federalization of criminal law has emerged. In recent years, Congress has passed several different acts that specifically criminalize certain activities committed through the use of technology. For example, the passage of the Child Pornography Prevention Act trumpeted a federal commitment to penalize those who used the Internet to exploit children. In particular, the act criminalized the creation, possession, or distribution of computer-generated child pornography.

Attempts by Congress to legislate online behavior have not been entirely successful. In fact, the Child Pornography Prevention Act was struck down by the Supreme Court as being too vague and ambiguous. Such friction is necessarily a component of the American system of checks and balances. The Court's interpretation and application of the Constitution to congressional legislation is as important to evidence law as federal and state rules.

State Rules of Evidence

The issue of state sovereignty, alien to most cultures, is fundamental to the American system of criminal justice. Each state is sovereign—having its own constitution, criminal code, and rules of procedure. Such sovereignty is limited only by provisions of the U.S. Constitution that directly apply to the states. Although states may not abridge the rights guaranteed under the Constitution and the Bill of Rights, they may enhance or further protect those liberties at their discretion. Thus, with the exception of constitutional mainstays, states remain independent in their interpretation of evidentiary rules. This often results in inconsistency across state lines. For example, some states have recognized a limited media–informant privilege, but others have not.

Although all states have developed rules of evidence, most have modeled them after the FRE or the URE. However, some have developed a piecemeal approach in which case law has emerged as an important consideration.

▶ Defining Evidence

In law, evidence may be defined as "any matter of fact, the effect, tendency, or design of which, when presented to the mind, is to produce a persuasion concerning the existence of some other matter of fact; a persuasion either affirmative or disaffirmative of its existence" (Bentham, 1827, p. 17). More succinctly, it is the means of establishing the truth or untruth of a disputed fact. It may include all sorts of information introduced and accepted at trial, including physical objects, writings, scientific evaluation, and the like. Presented through the medium of witnesses, evidence is material that speaks to the issue at hand.

Historically, the introduction of evidence had to meet tests of **relevancy** and materiality. Relevant evidence refers to any material evidence having probative value regarding something at issue, with **probity** defined as evidence that has an impact upon the jury. **Materiality**, on the other hand, refers to evidence that is logically connected to a fact at issue. Contemporary courts have merged the two

relevancy refers to any material fact or information which tends to make the existence of any fact that is of consequence to the determination of the action more probable or less probable than it would be without the evidence.

probity evidence that has an impact upon the jury.

materiality a requirement for admissibility, it refers to evidence that is logically connected to a fact at issue and includes a consideration of the germaneness of information or testimony and a determination as to its impact on the trial.

concepts into the single issue of relevance. In order to determine the relevancy of an item in question, the court may employ deductive or inductive reasoning. Although the relevancy of a proffered item may appear to be obvious in nature, the judge may require an explanation of relevancy in his or her determination. However, not all relevant evidence is admissible. Relevant evidence may be excluded from presentment whenever it is unduly a prejudicial violation of the Hearsay Rule, privileged, or collected in violation of constitutional safeguards. It also may be excluded whenever it has only minimal relevance and is lengthy in its presentation or cumulative.

▶ Finding Cases and Conducting Legal Research

While jurists, prosecutors, and defense attorneys are well trained in the art of conducting legal research, other actors may not have received such instructions. Fortunately, there are a variety of methods and materials, both physical and virtual, which are readily available (and comprehensible) to even novices in the field. As with other areas of criminal justice and American law, there is no preferred or absolute procedure for conducting such inquiry.

Generally

Students or practitioners who want a general understanding of a particular area of law may choose to start with legal encyclopedias, textbooks, treatises, or law reviews. Encyclopedias, like *Corpus Juris Secundum*, provide a broad overview of American law at both federal and state levels, and are organized by topic. Available in print form from West Publishing, the volumes are accessible electronically via Westlaw. Criminal law or criminal evidence textbooks also present a broad overview of legal issues, and provide an historical and contextual framework from which specific or particular inquiries can be launched. On the other hand, foundational legal treatises—like those written by William Blackstone, John Henry Wigmore, or John Locke—supply philosophical and theoretical underpinnings of contemporary legal systems, illuminating legal rationale for case law development. Finally, articles contained in law reviews contain both an analysis of case law and the evolution of jurisprudential reasoning.

Specifically

Specific statutory, regulatory, or case law inquiries can be conducted in a variety of ways both physically and electronically. Today's practitioners or students may access a plethora of online repositories to browse or search topic areas or to locate a specific state or federal code or appellate case. These types of online resources are particularly advantageous, because they provide instant gratification and exponentially increase the speed of legal research. Resources that are free and available to all include, but are not limited to:

- FindLaw (www.lp.findlaw.com/)—FindLaw provides access to a wide variety of legal resources, including, but not limited to, state and federal codes, statutes, case law, legal news, legal articles, and career resources. While users do not need to register for a free account, doing so allows them to save preferences, access previous searches, and so on. Using the www.lp.findlaw.com address as opposed to the www.findlaw.com address takes users directly to the area where legal research is conducted.

- Legal Information Institute (www.law.cornell.edu)—Founded at Cornell University Law School in 1992, the Legal Information Institute publishes state and federal codes, statutes, and case law.
- U.S. Supreme Court (www.supremecourt.gov)—Homepage of the U.S. Supreme Court. It provides access to the latest docket and past decisions. However, it is not appropriate for general legal inquiries.
- Oyez Project (www.oyez.org)—Created in the 1980s and maintained at the Chicago-Kent College of Law, the Oyez Project was designed to be a multimedia archive and the authoritative source for all audio recorded in the U.S. Supreme Court.

Legal research may also be conducted through online campus libraries via LexisNexis and HeinOnline. Both allow users to access federal codes, Supreme Court decisions, and law reviews. LexisNexis additionally provides access to state cases and codes.

Case Citations

In order to conduct analysis and report findings of legal research, individuals must first understand the sometimes complex lexicon of the legal profession. While margin definitions and the glossary of this text will provide readers with legal descriptions, researchers must further familiarize themselves with the manner of **case citation** used in professional practice. In appellate cases, the citation will include the two main parties to a case (i.e., the *appellant* and *appellee* or *petitioner* and *respondent*), the date of the opinion, and the place where the opinion can be located. Opinions may be located in more than one source. For example, opinions of the U.S. Supreme Court can be found in three series of reports. To wit, *Dickerson v. United States*, 530 U.S. 428, 120 S. Ct. 2326, 147 L.Ed. 2d 405 (2000), was decided in 2000 and may be found:

case citation it is the unique identifier of a particular legal document that references where the full text of the opinion can be found.

- 530 U.S. 428—in the 530th volume of the *United States Reports* beginning on page 428.
- 120 S. Ct. 2326—in the 120th volume of the *Supreme Court Reporter* beginning on page 2326.
- 147 L.Ed. 2d 405—in the second series of books for the *United States Supreme Court, Lawyers Edition*, volume 147 beginning on page 405.

Decisions from the U.S. Court of Appeals are published in the Federal Reporter [F.; F.2d (second series—1924–1993); F.3d (third series—1993–present)] while those for the U.S. District Courts are in the Federal Supplement [(F.Supp.—1932–1997); F.Supp.2d —1997–present)]. The national reporter system publishes state court cases by geographical regions. For example, the Atlantic Reporter includes Connecticut, Delaware, District of Columbia, Maine, Maryland, New Hampshire, New Jersey, Pennsylvania, Rhode Island, and Vermont.

State courts also maintain their own individual citation style for appellate cases. While some states have a single-tiered appellate structure, others have a multilevel system. As a general rule, state appellate cases decided in the highest court end simply with the state name and date while lower appellate decisions include *App* in the citation. For example, the following cell phone privacy case, *Commonwealth v. Phifer*, 979 N.E.2d 210 (Mass. 2012) was heard by Massachusetts' court of last resort in 2012. The opinion may be found in the North Eastern Reporter, second series beginning on page 210.

► CONCLUSIONS

> In the respective jurisdictions of State, Federal, and Territorial Courts in the United States, each is governed in its own trials, independently of the others, by its own rules of Evidence, on the principle of Rule 7, except so far as the Federal Constitution compels or the respective State statutes permit a variation. (Wigmore, 1942: p. 13)

Without exception, all modern cultures have some mechanism for the administration of justice. While the processes and procedures are far from universal, grounded in cultural norms and mores, the notion of jurisprudence is worldwide. A combination of English and American traditions, jurisprudence is intended to eradicate abusive practices by government entities and to ensure equal protection under the law.

In the United States, the criminal process is designed to find fact—an adversarial system that protects the rights of the accused while finding the truth. Rules of evidence, however, may appear contrary to this notion, whenever pivotal information or product is excluded from trial.

The strength of American jurisprudence generally, and evidence law particularly, is that it is considered a living entity and continues to change. It is not developed in a vacuum—contemporary laws are a product of the intersection of social, legal, and historical beliefs with custom, culture, and nature happenings. In addition, all American rules are guided by community standards and current ideologies. Regarding technology, it is anticipated that the evolution of evidence law will increase exponentially as judges and legislators attempt to keep pace with a high-tech society.

Key Terms

Arraignment

Beyond a reasonable doubt

Bill of Rights

Burden of proof

Challenge for cause

Case citation

Civil law

Code of Hammurabi

Common law

Confrontation Clause

Cruel and unusual punishment

Dual sovereignty or separate sovereigns doctrine

Establishment clause

Evidence

Excessive bail

Excessive fines

Harmless error

Hearsay

Initial appearance

Law

Law of evidence

Magna Carta

Mala in se

Mala prohibita

Materiality

Petit jury

Precedents

Peremptory challenge

Presentment jury

Presumption of innocence

Probable cause

Probity

Procedural law

Reasonable suspicion

Reconstruction Amendments

Reversible error

Relevancy

Standard of proof

Stare decisis

Subpoena

Substantive law

Trial by battle

Trial by ordeal

U.S. Constitution

Voir dire

Wager of law or compurgation

Writ of Habeas Corpus

Discussion Questions

1. What is the importance of *Dickerson v. United States*?
2. What is the difference between common law and civil law? Where are these types of law practiced?
3. To what extent does the Fourth Amendment influence the American legal system?
4. How does the double jeopardy protection in the Fifth Amendment vary from the dual sovereignty doctrine? Give examples of the dual sovereignty doctrine.
5. According to the court, what are some of the provisions of the cruel and unusual punishment clause?
6. What are the sources of state evidence law?
7. What implications exist as a result of the varying state evidence laws?
8. What is the difference in relevant and material evidence?

Recommended Resources

Videos

A&E Television. Getting away with murder. *American justice*. How the double jeopardy prohibition allowed a murderer to go free. Available at: http://store.aetv.com.

A&E Television. Justice denied: Trial and error. *American justice*. Mishaps in the criminal justice system. Available at: http://store.aetv.com.

Insight Media. (1980). *Sources of law*. Available at: www.insight-media.com.

Insight Media. (1992). *Criminal trial procedure*. A full demonstration of the process, including preliminary instructions, opening statements, direct and cross examination, bench conferences, illness of actors, guilty pleas, jury instructions, and deliberations. Available at: www.insight-media.com.

Books

Friedman, Lawrence M. (2002). *American law in the 20th century*. New Haven, CT: Yale University Press.

Rehnquist, William H. (2002). *The Supreme Court*. New York: Alfred A. Knopf Publishing.

Strong, John W., Brown, Kenneth S., Dix, George E., Imwinkelried, Edward J., Kaye, D. H., Mosteller, Robert P., & Roberts, E. F. (1999). *McCormick on evidence*. St. Paul, MN: West Publishing.

Wigmore, John H. (1914). The code of Hammurabi, *Northwestern University Bulletin*. XIV (25).

Wigmore, John H. (1936). *Panorama of the world's legal system* (Library Edition). Washington, DC: Washington Law Book Company.

Wigmore, J. H. (1940). *A treatise on the Anglo-American system of evidence in trial at common law* (3rd ed.). Boston: Little, Brown and Company.

Wigmore, John H. (1942). *Wigmore's code of evidence*. Boston: Little, Brown and Company.

Online Sources

http://www.findlaw.com—A free legal search engine for both state and federal cases, codes, and regulations.

http://www.fclr.org—Home page of the Federal Courts Law Review, an electronic law review dedicated to legal scholarship relating to federal courts.

http://www.abanet.org/tech/ltrc/lawlink/home.html—Search engine sponsored by the American Bar Association. The site allows searches within publications of the ABA on a variety of topics.

http://www.abanet.org—Home page of the American Bar Association.

http://www.aallnet.org—Home page of the American Association of Law Libraries; includes a function that allows searches of its various publications on a variety of topics.

http://www.uscourts.gov—Official site of the federal judiciary. Search feature enables users to search for federal cases, constitutional evolutions, and judicial structure.

http://cafc.uscourts.gov/—U.S. Court of Appeals for the Federal Circuit Web site.

http://www.fjc.gov—Home page of the Federal Judicial Center, the education and research agency for the federal courts. The site contains the results of research sponsored by the Center, as well as educational materials.

Relevant Law

The Constitution of the United State of America The Bill of Rights

Magna Carta

References

Bentham, Jeremy (1827). *The Rationale of Judicial Evidence, Specifically Applied to English Practice* (edited by John Stuart Mill). London: Hunt & Clarke.

Madison, James (1789). *Annals of Congress* (439).

Maitland, Frederic W. and Montague, Francis C. (1915). *A sketch of English legal history*. London: G.P. Putnam's Sons.

Wigmore, John H. (1936). *Panorama of the world's legal system* (Library Edition). Washington, DC: Washington Law Book Company.

Wigmore, John H. (1942). *Wigmore's code of evidence*. Boston: Little, Brown, and Company.

Notes

1. Seizure of citizens without probable cause was also the basis for the writ of habeas corpus. Developed after the *Magna Carta* in the fourteenth century, it established the notion of corroboration while negating the possibility of seizing an individual based on "mere suspicion" (U.S. Constitution, Article 1, Section 9).

2. Many early systems of justice were patently unfair, operating on a system of bribes, or so-called "gifts"—seen in pockets across the world—including India in the seventeenth century and in Europe until the twentieth century.

1. Helmholz, R. H. (1983). Crime, compurgation and the courts of the medieval church. *Law and History Review, 1*(1), 1–26.

2. [*Dickerson v. United States*, 530 U.S. 428 (2000)]

3. Kempin, F. (1990). *Historical introduction to Anglo-American law* (3rd ed.). St. Paul, MN: West Publishing.

4. McIlwain, C. H. (1914). Due process of law in *magna carta*. *Columbia Law Review, 14*(1), 27–51.

5. It must be noted that the *Magna Carta* was promptly rejected by King John and Pope Innocent III who claimed that the document was signed under duress. However, the ideals that had been espoused were not as easily discarded, and the document was revived several times in England. More importantly, the spirit of the document permeated the ideals of individuals across the globe and its impact continues to this day.

6. The origins of the *writ of habeas corpus* are usually attributed to a time no earlier than the dawning of the fourteenth century. However, some scholars make a convincing argument that the writ is neither British nor Teutonic but Roman in origin. To wit, "In the condensation and codification of Roman court decisions known as the Pandects or the Digest which was compiled by order of Justinian, we find a writ so similar to habeas corpus that there can be no doubt that in Rome lies the true origin ... the writ is somewhat similar to the Praetorian Interdict of the Roman Civil Law 'de homine libero exhibendo,' in which the praetor ordered, when it was made to appear to him that a freeman was restrained of his liberty contrary to good faith, that he be liberated." [Glass, A. (1933). Historical aspects of habeas corpus. *St. John's Law Review, 9*, 55–70].

7. Blackstone, W. (1765–1769). *Commentaries on the laws of England*. Oxford: Clarendon Press.

8. Ibid.

9. Wiecek, W. M. (1970). The great writ and reconstruction: The habeas corpus act of 1867. *The Journal of Southern History, 36*(4), 530–548.

10. 14 Stat. 385

11. 542 U.S. 466 (2004)

12. 548 U.S. 557 (2006)

13. 553 U.S. 723 (2008)

14. [Art. I § 9, cl. 2]

15. (342 U.S. 165, 72 S.Ct. 205, 96 L.Ed. 183,1952)

16. Whitehead, J. W. & Aden, S. H. (2002). Forfeiting "enduring freedom" for "homeland security": A constitutional analysis of the USA Patriot Act and the justice department's anti-terrorism initiatives. *American University Law Review, 51*(6), 1080–1133.

17. [*Ex Parte Wilson*, 114 U.S. 417 (1885)]

18. [*Brown v. Mississippi*, 297 U.S. 278 (1936)]

19. 378 U.S. 1

20. *Magna Carta*

21. [*Fahy v. Connecticut*, 375 U.S. 85 (1963)]

22. [*Chapman v. California*, 386 U.S. 18 (1967)]

23. [*Salinas v. Texas*,

24. [*Presley v. Georgia*, 130 S. Ct. 721 (2010)]

25. [*Waller v. Georgia*, 467 U.S. 39 (2004)]

26. [*Sheppard v. Maxwell*, 384 U.S. 333 (1966)]

27. Ibid.

28. [*Barker v. Wingo*, 407 U.S. 514 (1972)]

29. [*Witherspoon v. Illinois*, 391 U.S. 510 (1968)]

30. [*Adams v. Texas*, 448 U.S. 38 (1980); *Wainwright v. Witt*, 469 U.S. 412 (1985)]

31. [*Uttecht v. Brown*, 551 U.S. 1 (2007)]

32. [*Smith v. O'Grady*, 312 U.S. 329 (1941)]

33. [*Brady v. U.S.*, 397 U.S. 742 (1970)]
34. [*Smith v. O'Grady*, 312 U.S. 329 (1941)]
35. [*U. S. v. Gonzalez-Lopez*, 548 U.S. 140 (2006)]
36. [*Adams v. U.S. ex rel. McCann*, 317 U.S. 269 (1942)]
37. [*Powell v. Alabama*, 287 U.S. 45 (1932)]
38. [*Gideon v. Wainwright*, 372 U.S. 335 (1963)]
39. [*Montejo v. Louisiana*, 556 U.S. 778 (2009)]
40. [*Missouri v. Frye*, 132 S. Ct. 1399, (2012)]
41. *Browning-Ferrs Industries v. Kelco Disposal*, 492 U.S. 257, (1989)
42. *Wilkerson v. Utah*, 99 U.S. 130 (1878[0])
43. 409 U.S. 902
44. 428 U.S. 153
45. [*Solem v. Helm*, 463 U.S. 277 (1983)]
46. [*Trop v. Dulles*, 356 U.S. 86 (1958)]
47. [*Solem v. Helm*, 463 U.S. 277 (1983)]
48. [*Ingraham v. Wright*, 430 U.S. 651, (1977)]
49. [*Atkins v. Virginia*, 536 U.S. 304 (2002)]
50. [(*Roper v. Simmons*, 541 U.S. 1040 (2005)]
51. [*Coker v. Georgia*, 433 U.S. 584 (1977)]
52. [*Kennedy v. Louisiana*, 554 U.S. 407 (2008)
53. [*Coffin v. United States*, 156 U.S. 432, 453 (1895)]
54. Wigmore, J. H. (1923). *A treatise on the Anglo-American system of evidence in trials at common law: Including the statutes and judicial decisions of all jurisdictions of the United States and Canada* (2nd ed.). Boston: Little, Brown and Company.
55. [*Bell v. Wolfish*, 441 U.S. 520 (1979)]
56. [*Murphy et al. v. The Waterfront Commission of New York Harbor*, 378 U.S. 52 (1964)]
57. [*In re Winship*, 397 U.S. 358 (1970)]
58. Ibid.
59. [*Commonwealth v. Webster*, 5 Cush. 295; 59 Mass. 295 (1850)]

THE DECLARATION OF INDEPENDENCE.

2 Federalism, Court Systems, and the Criminal Justice Process

The learner will:

❶ *Understand the meaning of federalism and how it applies to criminal law and criminal procedure*

❷ *Examine the concept of jurisdiction within the American criminal court system*

❸ *Explain the types and structures of the federal and state courts*

❹ *Delineate the responsibilities of the courtroom actors including the defense attorney, prosecuting attorney, and presiding judge*

❺ *Identify and discuss the components of the criminal process from initial complaint to appeals*

❻ *Explain the case-in-chief*

❼ *Explain the different pleas*

❽ *Examine the legal jargon of the criminal process*

❾ *Examine the various motions and their relevance to evidence*

❿ *Examine the presentation of evidence during the case-in-chief, rebuttal, and rejoinder*

⓫ *Discuss the factors that affect sentencing*

⓬ *Explain the appeals process as it relates to evidentiary matters*

▶ Jurisdiction, Federalism, and Sovereignty

The powers not delegated to the United States by the Constitution, nor prohibited by it to the States, are reserved to the States, respectively, or to the people. (U.S. Constitution, Tenth Amendment)

The Congress shall have Power To . . . make all Laws which shall be necessary and proper for carrying into Execution the foregoing Powers, and all other Powers vested by this Constitution in the Government of the United States, or in any Department or Officer thereof. (U.S. Constitution, Article 1, Section 8, Clause 18—the "Necessary and Proper Clause")

Because of past abuses by the Crown, the framers of the Constitution specifically precluded an autocratic system in which a federal government exercised complete control over the constituents of the nation. Indeed, the framers carefully crafted a document that would recognize state sovereignty. This form of government, unprecedented in concept, which divides power between sovereigns, is known as **federalism**. In the United States, distribution of powers in the federal system consist of several parts: *exclusive powers*, *shared powers*, *denied powers*, *enumerated powers*, and *implied powers*. **Exclusive powers** are those powers which belong exclusively to the specified sovereign which may not be infringed upon by another. **Shared powers** are those powers that are delegated to both sovereigns in a federalist system. **Denied powers** are those that are expressly forbidden. **Enumerated powers** are those areas of authority specifically articulated in Article I, Section 8 of the U.S. Constitution. Finally, **implied powers** are those powers exercised by Congress which are not explicitly defined in the Constitution, but are "necessary and proper" to execute the powers that are.

   While the founding fathers envisioned a system in which state sovereignty was both recognized and encouraged, the expansion of federal powers and the erosion of state's rights began in *McCulloch v. Maryland* (1819).[1] In *McCulloch*, the Court considered a case in which the General Assembly of Maryland imposed a tax on

federalism a system of government of constitutionally divided sovereignty in which power is vested in a central governing body constituent political units (such as states or provinces).

exclusive powers those powers that belong exclusively to the specified sovereign which may not be infringed upon by another.

shared powers those powers that are delegated to both sovereigns in a federalist system.

denied powers those powers that are expressly forbidden to a sovereign in a federalist system.

enumerated powers those areas of authority specifically articulated in Article I, Section 8 of the U.S. Constitution.

implied powers those powers exercised by Congress which are not explicitly defined in the Constitution, but are "necessary and proper" to execute the powers that are.

LIMITS OF FEDERAL POWERS

EXCLUSIVE POWERS	SHARED POWERS	DENIED POWERS
Print money	Courts	Violation of Bill of Rights
Establish post office and postage	Collect taxes	Imposition of export taxes among states
Regulate commerce between states and international trade	Build highways	Use of money from the Treasury without passage and approval of appropriations bill
Borrow money on the credit of the United States	Borrow money	Change state boundaries
Enter treaties with foreign governments	Create and enforce laws	Deny citizens the right to vote (15th and 19th Amendments)
Conduct a census	Charter banks and corporations	Permit slavery (13th Amendment)
Declare war	Condemn private property with compensation	Grant titles of nobility
Mediate disputes between two or more states and a state and citizen of another state		
Establish laws of citizenship		
Pay the federal debt		
Establish bankruptcy laws		
Establish laws to enforce the Constitution		
Establish federal courts lower than the Supreme Court		
Limit appellate jurisdiction of federal Courts		

all banks or branches not chartered by the Maryland legislature. In this case, the bank in question was one created by the federal government. Although not a question of law posed in the case, the Court deviated from the original thrust of the suit and examined whether the state had the authority to incorporate a bank as it was not expressly enumerated in the Constitution. Chief Justice Marshall pointed to the historical presumption in his opinion:

> The first congress created and incorporated a bank . . . nearly each succeeding congress . . . has acted and legislated on the presumption of the legal existence of such a power in the government. Individuals, it is true, have doubted, or thought otherwise; but it cannot be shown, that either branch of the legislature has, at any time, expressed an opinion against the existence of the power . . . when all branches of the government have thus been acting on the existence of this power, nearly thirty years, it would seem almost too late to call it in question, uncles its repugnancy with the constitution were plain and manifest.

Thus, the Court opined that the historical or operational reality could imply a power not otherwise stated. In clarifying, the "necessary and proper" clause of Article I, the Court ignored the provisions housed within the Tenth Amendment, stating that

> Congress, by the constitution, is invested with certain powers; and as to the objects, and within the scope of these powers, it is sovereign. Even without the aid of the general clause in the constitution empowering congress to pass all **necessary and proper** laws for carrying its powers into execution, the grant of powers itself necessarily implies the grant of all usual and suitable means for the execution of the powers granted.

The Court went further, suggesting that the framers did not *intend* to *enumerate particulars*, and that if "it be a fit instrument to an authorized purpose, it may be used, not being specially prohibited." Such reasoning exponentially expanded the powers of the federal government.

For most of the nation's history, challenges to federalism via the Tenth Amendment have been largely unsuccessful. In fact, in one of the earliest cases, the Court specifically noted that the Tenth Amendment "added nothing to the instrument as originally ratified and has no limited and special operations."[2] Yet, more recent cases have acknowledged the importance of the Amendment in the granting of both state and individual rights. To wit:

> Federalism has more than one dynamic. In allocating powers between the States and National Government, federalism 'secures to citizens the liberties that derive from the diffusion of sovereign power.' It enables States to enact positive law in response to the initiative of those who seek a voice in shaping the destiny of their own times, and it protects the liberty of all persons within a State by ensuring that law enacted in excess of delegated governmental power cannot direct or control their actions. Federalism's limitations are not therefore a matter of rights belonging only to the States. In a proper case, a litigant may challenge a law as enacted in contravention of federalism, just as injured individuals may challenge actions that transgress . . . The claim need not depend on the vicarious assertion of a State's constitutional interests, even if those interests are also implicated.[3]

► Federalism and Criminal Law

As stated previously, each state has exclusive jurisdiction in the areas of codification of civil and criminal law, judicial procedures, and legislative responsibility, inasmuch as such does not violate the Constitution. States may extend additional rights to their citizenry but may not abridge those guaranteed by the federal government. While many states have borrowed generously from the Federal Rules of Evidence, the Federal Rules of Criminal Procedure, and the U.S. Code, others have done less so. As a result, courtroom procedures, rules of evidence, and even judiciary structures vary widely across the United States.

It is important to note that the vast majority of criminal acts in the United States are a violation of state statutes while only a minority constitutes federal crimes. In some cases, a particular act in question may violate both state and federal criminal codes. Due to the **separate sovereigns exception** to the Fifth Amendment, a perpetrator may be charged and tried in both jurisdictions for the same act. For example, kidnapping an individual and transporting them or their body across state lines could result in criminal proceedings in both state and federal court.

Contrary to popular belief, the United States does not maintain a national police force nor does the Constitution provide for one. While there are federal law enforcement agencies, their creation and purview is limited to the statutory authority granted to them by Congress. Such authority necessarily relies upon the criminalization of conduct under federal law. There are four broad areas in which criminal laws may be enacted by the federal government: regulation of interstate and foreign commerce; protection of civil rights; protection of the federal government itself, federal employees, and administration of federal functions; and the enactment of laws for nonstate jurisdictions (i.e., territories, military bases, etc.). Due to the absence of enforcement, investigation, and prosecution powers in the Constitution, defendants in federal court often challenge the authority of the U.S. government to govern their behavior within state jurisdiction. However, the Court has historically expanded federal authority via the "Necessary and Proper Clause" (U.S. Constitution, Article I, Section 8, Clause 18).

separate sovereigns exception an exception to the double jeopardy clause of the Fifth Amendment which protects the interests of both state and federal authorities in cases in which a single act violates the laws of both sovereigns.

SEPARATE SOVEREIGNS

Some actions constitute a violation of both state and federal laws. Drug trafficking, for example, is illegal in all states and within the boundaries of the United States. Kidnapping is also a violation of both state and federal laws, but federal statutes require a demonstration of federal interest, like conveyance across state lines. In the following text, kidnapping is defined by the State of South Carolina and by the United States.

South Carolina Code 16-3-910

Whoever shall unlawfully seize, confine, inveigle, decoy, kidnap, abduct or carry away any other person by any means whatsoever without authority of law, except when a minor is seized or taken by his parent, is guilty of a felony, and, upon conviction, must be imprisoned for a period not to exceed thirty years unless sentenced for murder as provided in Section 16-3-20.

18 U.S. Code 1201

(a) *Whoever unlawfully seizes, confines, inveigles, decoys, kidnaps, abducts, or carries away and holds for ransom or reward or otherwise any person, except in the case of a minor by the parent thereof, when—*

   (1) the person is willfully transported in interstate or foreign commerce, regardless of whether the person was alive when transported across a State boundary, or the offender travels in interstate or foreign commerce or uses the mail or any means, facility, or instrumentality of interstate or foreign commerce in committing or in furtherance of the commission of the offense;

(2) any such act against the person is done within the special maritime and territorial jurisdiction of the United States;

(3) any such act against the person is done within the special aircraft jurisdiction of the United States as defined in section 46501 of title 49;

(4) the person is a foreign official, an internationally protected person, or an official guest as those terms are defined in section 1116 (b) of this title; or

(5) the person is among those officers and employees described in section 1114 of this title and any such act against the person is done while the person is engaged in, or on account of, the performance of official duties shall be punished by imprisonment for any term of years or for life and, if the death of any person results, shall be punished by death or life imprisonment.

ARTICLE I, SECTION 8, CLAUSE 18

Necessary and Proper Clause

The Congress shall have Power To . . . make all Laws which shall be necessary and proper for carrying into Execution the foregoing Powers, and all other Powers vested by this Constitution in the Government of the United States, or in any Department or Officer thereof.

▶ Law Enforcement in the United States

According to the most recent information from the Uniform Crime Reports, there are more than 18,000 law enforcement agencies in the United States. These include municipal, county, state, tribal, university, and federal agencies. By far, the vast majority of these agencies are local in nature and enforce state statutes and local ordinances. They include municipal (cities, towns, townships, etc.), county, and university/college departments. Depending on the particular needs of their respective jurisdictions, many officers employed in these locales may spend as much time in municipal courts on traffic and ordinance violations as they do in state courts on felony charges.

State agencies, on the other hand, are tasked exclusively with enforcement of state codes. They are created by state law and involve prosecution of criminal violations and enforcement of fire, health, sanitation, hunting/fishing, tax, and other regulations. State police organizations may be categorized in one of three ways: patrol or traffic enforcement, multiservice or general powers, or investigative. Patrol/traffic systems include those agencies that exclusively enforce traffic, motor vehicles, and commercial carriers. The South Carolina Highway Patrol is an example. Multiservice state agencies are those organizations that are involved with the statewide enforcement of criminal laws, the prevention of crime, the pursuit and apprehension of offenders, and the collection of evidence (e.g., New Jersey State Police, Michigan State Police, etc.). Finally, some state police agencies are purely investigative by design. Examples include: The Georgia Bureau of Investigation, South Carolina's State Law Enforcement Division (SLED), and North Carolina's State Bureau of Investigation.

Federal law enforcement agencies enforce federal law. They are created and empowered by Congress. The first federal agency, the U.S. Marshals Service (USMS), was created in the *Judiciary Act of 1789*—the same legislation that established the federal judiciary.

> That a marshal shall be appointed in and for each district for the term of four years, but shall be removable from office at pleasure, whose duty it shall be to attend the district and circuit courts when sitting therein, and also the Supreme Court in the District in which that court shall sit. And to execute throughout the district, all lawful precepts directed to him, and issued under the authority of the United States, and he shall have power to command all necessary assistance in the execution of his duty, and to appoint as there shall be occasion, one or more deputies, who shall be removable from office by the judge of the district court, or the circuit court sitting within the district, at the pleasure of either . . .

Today, the USMS continues to support the federal court system. They are tasked with the service of subpoenas, writs, and warrants. They are also responsible for the protection of federal judges, the security of federal courtrooms, the transportation of federal prisoners, the apprehension of federal fugitives, and the protection of federal witnesses.

Helped greatly by the Congressional creation of the Department of Justice in 1870, the number of federal agencies has expanded exponentially. They may be found in all three branches of the federal government, and vary in their scope, structure, and authority. Current agencies include, but are not limited to: the Federal Bureau of Investigation (FBI); the Bureau of Alcohol, Tobacco, and Firearms (BATF); U.S. Secret Service (USSS); the Drug Enforcement Administration (DEA); and Immigration and Customs Enforcement (ICE). These agencies are limited in authority and jurisdiction to those areas articulated by Congress, and are bound by federal law. The majority of these agencies may be found under the Executive Branch (as illustrated next). The results of their investigations are forwarded to federal prosecutors (i.e., U.S. attorneys) and adjudicated in federal court.

▶ The Federal Courts

> The judicial Power of the United States shall be vested in one Supreme Court, and in such inferior Courts as the Congress may from time to time ordain and establish. The Judges, both of the supreme and inferior Courts, shall hold their Offices during

FEDERAL LAW ENFORCEMENT UNDER THE EXECUTIVE BRANCH

Federal law enforcement powers may be found within each of the three federal branches: Executive, Judicial, and Legislative. They vary in scope, structure, and authority. By far, federal police powers are housed within the executive branch.

Department of Agriculture

- U.S. Forest Service

Department of Commerce

- Bureau of Industry and Security
- National Institute of Standards and Technology
- National Oceanic and Atmospheric Administration
- Office of Security

Department of Defense

- Pentagon Force Protection Agency
- DOD Police
- Defense Logistics Agency Police
- National Security Agency
- Defense Intelligence Agency
- National Geospatial-Intelligence Agency

Department of the Army

- USA Criminal Investigation Command
- USA Military Police Corps
- Department of the Army Police
- USA Corrections Command

Department of the Navy

- Naval Criminal Investigative Service (NCIS)
- USMC Criminal Investigative Division (MC CID)
- Department of the Navy Police
- Marine Corps Provost Marshal's Office
- USMC Police

Department of the Air Force

- Air Force Office of Special Investigations
- Air Force Security Forces Center
- Department of the Air Force Police

Department of Energy

- Office of Health, Safety, Security
- Office of Secure Transportation

Department of Health and Human Services

- USDA Office of Criminal Investigations
- NIH Police

Department of Homeland Security (DHS)

- Federal Protective Service
- U.S. Coast Guard Investigative Service
- U.S. Customs and Border Protection (CBP)
- U.S. Immigration and Customs Enforcement (ICE)
- U.S. Citizenship and Immigration Services
- U.S. Secret Service (USSS)
- Transportation Security Administration (TSA)
- Federal Air Marshal Service (FAMS)

Department of Housing and Urban Development (HUD)

- Protective Service Division

Department of the Interior (DOI)

- Bureau of Indian Affairs Police
- Bureau of Land Management Office of Law Enforcement
- Bureau of Reclamation Office of Law Enforcement
- National Park Service
- Division of Law Enforcement, Security, and Emergency Services
- U.S. Park Police
- U.S. Fish and Wildlife Service
- Office of Law Enforcement
- Division of Refuge Law Enforcement

Department of Justice (DOJ)

- Bureau of Alcohol Tobacco, Firearms, and Explosives (BATF)
- U.S. Drug Enforcement Administration (DEA)
- Federal Bureau of Investigation (FBI)
- Federal Bureau of Prison (BOP)
- U.S. Marshals Service (USMS)

Department of State (DoS)

- U.S. Diplomatic Security Service

Department of Transportation

- Federal Aviation Administration (FAA)
- Office of Odometer Fraud Investigation

Department of the Treasury

- Bureau of Engraving and Printing Police
- Financial Crimes Enforcement Network (FINCEN)
- Internal Revenue Service Criminal Investigation Division

- United States Mint Police
- Special Inspector General for the *Troubled Asset Relief Program*

Department of Veterans Affairs

- Veterans Affairs Police

In addition to the law enforcement agencies listed, all departments have Inspector Generals that have general investigative powers.

---

good Behavior, and shall, at stated Times, receive for their Services a Compensation which shall not be diminished during their Continuance in Office. (U.S. Constitution, Article III, Section 1)

To the colonies, the signing of the U.S. Constitution signaled a new beginning in many ways. Among other things, it guaranteed fundamental rights that had been denied previously; it provided for the election of public officials; it recognized state sovereignty; and it empowered Congress to develop a judiciary as deemed appropriate. Unfortunately, it provided little guidance regarding the specifics of this last proviso. Thus, the newly elected Congress found it necessary to develop a more comprehensive schematic for the federal judiciary. This was accomplished through the passage of the *Judiciary Act of 1789.*

Creating a federal court system that recognized state sovereignty was not an easy task. The **Judiciary Act of 1789** was an attempt to establish a strong federal court system that could evaluate the constitutionality of state statutes, doctrines, and judicial rulings when appropriate and dispense justice in matters of federal law. It established a Supreme Court with 6 justices, 13 district courts (one in each state), and 3 circuit courts (Eastern, Middle, and Southern). It also provided for federal subpoena power, outlined jurisdictional responsibilities and granted citizens the right to be heard in federal court when issues of constitutional concern were raised and rejected by the highest state appellate court. It is doubtful that the framers could have foreseen the tremendous growth that the country would experience. Currently, 13 circuit courts and 94 district courts exist, and the Supreme Court has grown from 6 justices to 9.

To ensure that the federal court system and its officers remained free from corruption or coercion, the Constitution extended two pivotal assurances to the federal judiciary. First, irrespective of jurisdiction, all federal judges were to be appointed for life and could only be removed through impeachment or through conviction by Congress for treason, bribery, or other high crimes. Second, compensation of the judiciary could not be diminished "during their Continuance in Office." Thus, neither the president nor the Congress could reduce the salaries of the federal judiciary.

District Courts

Federal district courts are federal **courts of general jurisdiction** that have the authority to hear most categories of federal cases, whether civil or criminal in nature. Currently, 94 federal judicial districts exist (with at least one per state), including Puerto Rico and the District of Columbia. The largest states, including California, Texas, and New York, have four or more. In addition, the

Judiciary Act of 1789 legislation establishing the U.S. Marshals Service, the office of Attorney General, a strong federal court system, a Supreme Court, and jurisdictional responsibilities granting citizens the right to be heard in federal court when issues of constitutional concern were rejected by the highest state appellate court.

federal district courts federal trial courts or courts of general jurisdiction.

courts of general jurisdiction a court that has legal authority to hear cases involving civil and criminal matters within the geographical area over which it presides. (Depending on jurisdiction, such courts may also be known as trial courts, district courts, circuit courts, or superior courts.)

▼

Table 2-1

U.S. District Courts—Criminal Defendants Commenced, by Offense, During the 12-Month Periods Ending March 31, 2009 Through 2013

Offense	2009	2010	2011	2012	2013	Percent Change 2012–2013[1]
TOTAL	95,272	98,365	103,274	98,845	91,678	−7.3
Violent Offenses, Total	**2,935**	**2,875**	**2,911**	**2,665**	**2,843**	**6.7**
Homicide	167	142	130	149	147	−1.3
Robbery, Total	**1,086**	**1,005**	**929**	871	**799**	**−8.3**
Bank	1,022	941	887	833	769	−7.7
Other Robbery Offenses	64	64	42	38	30	−21.1
Assault	859	877	915	880	1,004	14.1
Kidnapping	164	140	159	122	107	−12.3
Racketeering	387	413	467	372	398	7.0
Carjacking	152	148	131	112	233	108.0
Terrorism	38	66	68	57	47	−17.5
Other Violent Offenses	82	84	112	102	108	5.9
Property Offenses, Total	**15,759**	**16,638**	**17,997**	**16,432**	**14,962**	**−8.9**
Burglary	**49**	**57**	**62**	**56**	**61**	**8.9**
Larceny and Theft, Total	**2,696**	**2,815**	**2,819**	**2,677**	**2,861**	**6.9**
Bank	76	69	49	37	48	29.7
Postal Service	293	272	298	227	202	−11.0
Interstate Shipments	28	47	25	10	22	120.0
Theft of U.S. Property	1,890	1,953	1,979	1,973	2,161	9.5
Theft Within Maritime Jurisdiction	126	207	192	189	193	2.1
Transportation of Stolen Property	157	153	184	154	164	6.5
Other Larceny and Theft Offenses	126	114	92	87	71	−18.4
Embezzlement, Total	**715**	**640**	**616**	**568**	**508**	**−10.6**
Bank	193	159	137	126	105	−16.7
Postal Service	262	237	215	180	154	−14.4
Financial Institutions	36	22	17	18	17	−5.6
Other Embezzlement Offenses	224	222	247	244	232	−4.9
Fraud, Total	**11,074**	**11,777**	**13,214**	**11,938**	**10,517**	**−11.9**
Tax	594	641	590	526	580	10.3
Financial Institutions	699	846	751	596	485	−18.6
Securities and Exchange	81	125	119	98	100	2.0
Mail	661	604	638	477	434	−9.0
Wire, Radio, or Television	499	549	770	607	618	1.8
Bankruptcy	59	74	71	64	63	−1.6

Table 2-1 Continued

Offense	2009	2010	2011	2012	2013	Percent Change 2012–2013[1]
Social Security	844	511	546	518	425	−18.0
False Personation	52	48	51	33	31	−6.1
Citizenship and Naturalization	294	302	230	226	221	−2.2
Passport	445	692	855	632	621	−1.7
Identification Documents and Information	2,124	2,432	2,780	2,528	1,388	−45.1
False Claims of Government Services	243	228	265	400	432	8.0
False Statements	900	642	629	632	601	−4.9
Conspiracy to Defraud the United States	1,096	1,042	1,086	1,236	1,165	−5.7
Unauthorized Access Devices	903	853	797	826	756	−8.5
Computer	110	120	95	116	93	−19.8
Health Care	468	575	560	465	609	31.0
Attempt and Conspiracy to Defraud	881	1,403	2,280	1,876	1,812	−3.4
Other Fraud Offenses	121	90	101	82	83	1.2
Forgery and Counterfeiting	**1,018**	**1,127**	**1,091**	**1,023**	**861**	**−15.8**
Auto Theft	**60**	**64**	**34**	**35**	**40**	**14.3**
Other Property Offenses	**147**	**158**	**161**	**135**	**114**	**−15.6**
Drug Offenses, Total	**29,419**	**29,759**	**30,795**	**31,739**	**29,190**	**−8.0**
Marijuana, Total	**6,674**	**7,879**	**7,788**	**8,193**	**7,119**	**−13.1**
Sell, Distribute, or Dispense	3,826	4,888	5,280	5,590	3,792	−32.2
Import/Export	1,596	1,394	934	1,022	678	−33.7
Manufacture	366	360	362	402	402	0.0
Possession	886	1,237	1,212	1,179	2,247	90.6
All Other Drugs, Total	**22,674**	**21,759**	**22,893**	**23,451**	**21,970**	**−6.3**
Sell, Distribute, or Dispense	20,539	19,500	20,336	20,519	19,231	−6.3
Import/Export	1,116	1,164	1,572	1,959	1,761	−10.1
Manufacture	680	730	651	634	646	1.9
Possession	339	365	334	339	332	−2.1
Other Drug Offenses	**71**	**121**	**114**	**95**	**101**	**6.3**
Firearms and Explosives Offenses, Total	**9,020**	**8,585**	**8,531**	**8,814**	**8,356**	**−5.2**
Firearms, Total	**8,829**	**8,363**	**8,307**	**8,645**	**8,169**	**−5.5**
Possession by Prohibited Persons	5,285	4,946	4,786	5,062	4,747	−6.2
Furtherance of Violent/ Drug-Trafficking Crimes	2,231	2,087	1,994	1,971	1,898	−3.7

(continued)

Table 2-1 Continued

Offense	2009	2010	2011	2012	2013	Percent Change 2012–2013[1]
Other Firearms Offenses	1,313	1,330	1,527	1,612	1,524	−5.5
Explosives	**191**	**222**	**224**	**169**	**187**	**10.7**
Sex Offenses, Total	**2,828**	**2,875**	**3,237**	**3,479**	**3,335**	**−4.1**
Sexual Abuse of Adults	94	115	118	125	135	8.0
Sexual Abuse of Minors	422	579	657	692	735	6.2
Sexually Explicit Material	1,790	1,752	1,779	1,789	1,668	−6.8
Transportation for Illegal Sexual Activity	229	145	205	217	234	7.8
Sex Offender Registry	286	279	466	650	560	−13.8
Other Sex Offenses	7	5	12	6	3	−
Justice System Offenses, Total	**1,103**	**1,015**	**988**	**935**	**927**	**−0.9**
Aiding, Abetting, or Accessory	205	177	178	143	189	32.2
Obstruction of Justice	310	310	308	338	278	−17.8
Escape from Custody	287	266	290	236	272	15.3
Failure to Appear	213	186	157	131	131	0.0
Perjury	43	33	26	36	22	−38.9
Contempt	45	43	29	51	35	−31.4
Immigration Offenses, Total	**25,581**	**28,055**	**29,530**	**26,572**	**24,483**	**−7.9**
Alien Smuggling	3,746	3,039	2,986	2,733	2,658	−2.7
Improper Entry by Alien	2,052	1,447	1,158	517	266	−48.5
Improper Reentry by Alien	18,322	22,063	23,927	22,157	20,494	−7.5
Fraud and Misuse of Visa/Permits	1,405	1,443	1,383	1,078	982	−8.9
Other Immigration Offenses	56	63	76	87	83	−4.6
General Offenses, Total	**2,298**	**2,224**	**2,580**	**2,326**	**2,293**	**−1.4**
Bribery	169	150	165	137	161	17.5
Money Laundering	965	955	1,044	1,108	1,111	0.3
RICO[2]	114	138	189	221	132	−40.3
Racketeering	46	61	48	40	45	12.5
Extortion and Threats	165	148	160	152	142	−6.6
Gambling and Lottery	41	59	58	60	90	50.0
Failure to Pay Child Support	94	71	64	59	59	0.0
Other General Offenses	704	642	852	549	553	0.7
Regulatory Offenses, Total	**2,044**	**2,041**	**2,169**	**2,204**	**1,952**	**−11.4**
Civil Rights	123	113	118	126	151	19.8
Copyright	64	60	61	54	53	−1.9
Food and Drug	40	65	49	76	64	−15.8
Hazardous Waste Treatment, Disposal, and Storage	32	43	32	38	31	−18.4

Table 2-1 Continued

Offense	2009	2010	2011	2012	2013	Percent Change 2012–2013[1]
Telegraph, Telephone, and Radiograph	2	7	7	10	8	−20.0
National Defense	42	34	82	59	82	39.0
Antitrust	45	20	54	48	28	−41.7
Labor	82	88	78	87	50	−42.5
Game and Conservation	285	258	227	262	288	9.9
National Parks/Recreation	125	151	160	112	121	8.0
Customs	123	116	196	215	181	−15.8
Postal Service	112	98	125	74	55	−25.7
Reporting of Monetary Transactions	209	301	368	315	316	0.3
Migratory Bird	103	132	112	227	59	−74.0
Maritime and Shipping	122	119	107	95	95	0.0
Aircraft Regulations	75	67	47	75	64	−14.7
Other Regulatory Offenses	460	369	346	331	306	−7.6
Traffic Offenses, Total	**4,285**	**4,298**	**4,536**	**3,679**	**3,337**	**−9.3**
Drunk Driving	1,511	1,558	1,493	1,204	1,324	10.0
Other Traffic Offenses	2,774	2,740	3,043	2,475	2,013	−18.7

NOTE: This table includes defendants in all cases filed as felonies or Class A misdemeanors, but includes only those defendants in cases filed as petty offenses that were assigned to district judges rather than magistrate judges.
[1] Percent change not computed when fewer than 10 defendants reported for the previous period.
[2] RICO = Racketeer Influenced and Corrupt Organizations Act.
Source: www.uscourts.gov. Administrative Office of the U.S. Courts

Virgin Islands, Guam, and the Northern Mariana Islands—territories of the United States—maintain district courts that hear most federal cases, including bankruptcy cases. Finally, two special trial courts exist that maintain nationwide jurisdiction over special cases. The Court of International Trade, for example, hears cases in which international trade and customs issues arise; while the U.S. Court of Federal Claims hears claims against the United States including, but not limited to, illegal seizures of private property by the federal government, federal contractual disputes, and other cases involving monetary damages against the United States.

Each of the 94 federal judicial districts maintains a U.S. District Court. The size of the judiciary ranges from 2 to 32, depending on the size of the district's population. Regardless of the number of judges in any particular district, only one presides over a particular trial. The size of the entire district court judiciary constantly changes in response to population growth and caseload.

In the latter half of the twentieth century, federal court judges were given the power to appoint **magistrates**, or junior judicial officers, for fixed terms ranging from 4 years for part-time officers to 8 years for full-time magistrates. To alleviate the caseloads placed upon district judges, federal magistrates now handle arraignments, preliminary matters, certain types of civil cases, and lesser criminal cases. For the most part, district judges handle felony cases and civil jury trials. While rulings by magistrate judges are binding, most are subject to review, modification, and reversal by a district judge of that court. The sole exception to this

magistrate a lower court judge or judicial official who has restricted authority generally limited to preliminary proceedings or lesser criminal cases.

rule involves civil cases in which all parties have agreed to the jurisdiction of the magistrate judge before final disposition.

Federal district courts serve as trial courts in the federal system. Maintaining original jurisdiction over federal criminal and civil cases, district courts serve as the gatekeepers of the federal system, and are one example of **courts of original jurisdiction**. They are empowered to hear all cases involving violations of federal statutes and civil disputes between citizens from different states. Traditionally, dockets of district courts were primarily comprised of civil cases. However, additions to Title 18 of the U.S. Code in areas involving computer crime, terrorism, and narcotics have exponentially increased the criminal caseload of federal district judges. Although Congress has significantly increased the federal judiciary to accommodate the increase in dockets, many federal civil cases remain delayed.

court of original jurisdiction the court that has the authority to hear a case first. In criminal cases, trial courts have original jurisdiction.

Appellate Courts

federal circuit court an intermediate appellate court of the U.S. federal court system that decides appeals from the district court within its particular judicial circuit.

The number of appellate courts, or **federal circuit courts**, in the federal system has increased considerably from the three originally provided for in Article III. Currently, a total of 13 circuit courts exist—11 regional courts, plus 1 for the District of Columbia and 1 for the Court of Appeals for the Federal Circuit. The latter maintains nationwide jurisdiction over appeals of special cases, such as cases involving patents and cases decided by the Courts of International Trade and Federal Claims. The federal appeals court in the District of Columbia only hears cases from that jurisdiction.

The regional circuit courts are organized by territory (see Figure 2-1). All 13 courts and their jurisdictions are listed here:

FIRST CIRCUIT
—Maine, Massachusetts, New Hampshire, Rhode Island, and Puerto Rico

SECOND CIRCUIT
—New York, Vermont, and Connecticut

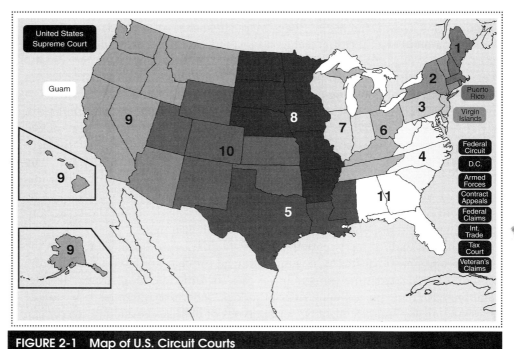

FIGURE 2-1 Map of U.S. Circuit Courts

Source: Pearson Education, Inc., Hoboken, NJ.

THIRD CIRCUIT
—Pennsylvania, New Jersey, Delaware, and the U.S. Virgin Islands

FOURTH CIRCUIT
—Maryland, North Carolina, South Carolina, Virginia, and West Virginia

FIFTH CIRCUIT
—Louisiana, Texas, and Mississippi

SIXTH CIRCUIT
—Michigan, Ohio, Kentucky, and Tennessee

SEVENTH CIRCUIT
—Illinois, Indiana, and Wisconsin

EIGHTH CIRCUIT
—North Dakota, South Dakota, Minnesota, Nebraska, Iowa, Missouri, and Arkansas

NINTH CIRCUIT
—California, Oregon, Washington, Arizona, Montana, Idaho, Nevada, Alaska, and Hawaii

TENTH CIRCUIT
—Colorado, Kansas, New Mexico, Oklahoma, Utah, and Wyoming

ELEVENTH CIRCUIT
—Alabama, Georgia, and Florida

DISTRICT OF COLUMBIA
—Washington DC, Tax Court, and Federal Administrative Agencies

FEDERAL
—Patent, International Trade, Claims Court, and Veterans' Appeals

The number of the federal judiciary within circuits varies greatly, from 6 in the First Circuit to 32 in the Ninth. As a rule, hearings are presented before a three-judge panel. This system leaves much to be desired, and has resulted in numerous contradictory rulings both intra-court and inter-court. The Fourth Circuit, for example, often is characterized as conservative, while the Ninth is anything but. In addition, matters involving the same legal question may be answered quite differently from within the same circuit. In such cases, the circuit may sit ***en banc*** (literally, "by the full court" or "full bench") to reconcile the issue. In large circuits, such as the Ninth, as few as 11 judges may qualify to be *en banc* under federal law.

en banc a session where the entire membership of the court participates in the decision as opposed to the regular quorum.

Bankruptcy Court

The federal court system is also solely responsible for the hearing of bankruptcy cases. Bankruptcy, then, is under the exclusive jurisdiction of the federal court system and may not be filed in state court, as originally established in Article 1 of the Constitution. Each of the 94 federal judicial districts has independent bankruptcy courts attached to them per order of the Bankruptcy Reform Act of 1978. Currently, there are 324 bankruptcy judges in the United States, and each was appointed by the Court of Appeals for 14-year terms per order of the Bankruptcy Amendments and Federal Judgeship Act of 1984.

Supreme Court

As with the lower tiers of the federal judiciary, the creation of the U.S. Supreme Court was provided for in Article III, Section 1, of the Constitution: "The judicial Power of the United States, shall be vested in one supreme Court, and in such

JUDICIAL INCONSISTENCY—WARRANTLESS SEARCHES OF CELL PHONES INCIDENT TO ARREST

As noted, one of the greatest strengths of the American legal system is the recognition of both federal and state interests. However, the fragmented court system can also result in contrary decisions in which Constitutional rights and legal protections are inconsistently extended in the absence of a ruling by the U.S. Supreme Court. Such is the case with the application of the Fourth Amendment to the warrantless search of cell phones incident to arrest. In 2007, a criminal defendant in the U.S. District Court for the District of Massachusetts was found guilty of felonious possession of a firearm [18 U.S.C. 922(g)]; possession of crack cocaine with intent to distribute [21 U.S.C. 841 (a)]; and, distribution of a controlled substance [21 U.S.C. 841]. He was sentenced to more than 20 years in prison. His convictions were largely predicated on evidence uncovered at the defendant's private residence after officers opened a flip phone found in his possession to review the call log and retrieve the phone number identified as "my house." Armed with that information and a screensaver of a woman holding a child, the officers went to the physical address of the phone number and observed the woman from the photograph in the residence. Execution of the subsequent search warrant revealed weapons, drugs, and cash. On appeal, the First Circuit vacated two of his convictions rejecting the government's argument that the container rule established in *U.S. v. Robinson* provided for the search of the cell phone incident to arrest. They ruled:

> This "literal reading of the Robinson decision," fails to account for the fact that the Supreme Court has determined that there are categories of searches undertaken following an arrest that are inherently unreasonable because they are never justified by one of the Chimel rationales: protecting arresting officers or preserving destructible evidence . . . we believe that warrantless cell phone data searches are categorically unlawful under the search-incident-to-arrest exception, given the government's failure to demonstrate that they are ever necessary to promote officer safety or prevent the destruction of evidence. We read Robinson as compatible with such a

> finding ... Instead, warrantless cell phone data searches strike us as a convenient way for the police to obtain information related to a defendant's crime of arrest – without having to secure a warrant.

This ruling is inherently inconsistent with decisions in a number of other federal circuits, including the 4th, 5th, and 7th. In *U.S. v. Murphy*, the 4th Circuit reviewed a case in which a defendant challenged his conviction on drug offenses and possession of counterfeit currency. He argued that the evidence that was contained on his cell phone was improperly admitted as: 1) the phone was not located on his person at the time of his arrest; and 2) retrieval of data from a cell phone requires a warrant as the large storage capacity of his phone heightened his expectation of privacy. The court rejected his argument for a number of reasons noting that his assumption that data on small devices is more volatile was unfounded. Further, they noted that requiring

> police officers to ascertain the storage capacity of a cell phone before conducting a search would simply be an unworkable and unreasonable rule. It is unlikely that police officers would have any way of knowing whether the text messages and other information stored on a cell phone will be preserved or be automatically deleted simply by looking at the cell phone . . . Rather, it is very likely that in the time it takes for officers to ascertain a cell phone's particular capacity, the information stored therein could be permanently lost.

Due to the plethora of cases in both federal circuit courts and state appellate courts, the U.S. Supreme Court granted certiorari in *Riley v. California* and *U.S. v. Wurie* on January 17, 2014.

In *Riley*, the Court considered a case in which police had seized a cell phone from Petitioner incident to his arrest for a weapons charge deriving from a routine traffic search. Officers on the scene accessed information contained on the phone and noted repeated use of a term associated with street gangs. An additional warrantless search of the contents of the phone was undertaken hours later by a gang investigator who uncovered photographs and videos indicating Riley's involvement in a previous shooting. He was consequently convicted and given an enhanced sentence due to his gang membership.

In *Wurie*, the Court considered a case in which officers accessed the call log of a cell phone seized in the lawful arrest to identify the phone number associated with the label "my house." Officers subsequently traced that number to what they suspected was the suspect's address, and secured a search warrant for the premises. During the search, officers found drugs, cash, ammunition, and a firearm. The trial court denied his motion to suppress the items found in the search of his residence, and he was convicted.

The Court held that the police are generally prohibited from searching digital information stored on a cell phone seized from an individual who has been arrested. The Court specifically referred to the rationale in the *Chimel* decision that provided for the search of the area in the immediate control of an individual incident to arrest.

> *. . . a search of digital information on a cell phone does not further the government interests identified in Chimel, and implicates substantially greater individual privacy interests than a brief physical search . . . digital data stored on a cell phone cannot itself be used as a weapon to harm an arresting officer or to effectuate the arrestee's escape. Officers may examine the phone's physical aspects to ensure that it will not be used as a weapon, but the data on the phone can endanger no one. To the extent that a search of cell phone data might warn officers of an impending danger, e.g., that the arrestee's confederates are headed to the scene, such a concern is better addressed through consideration of case-specific exceptions to the warrant requirement, such as exigent circumstances.*

inferior Courts as the Congress may from time to time ordain and establish." Officially unveiled in 1790 after the passage of the Judiciary Act of 1789, this legislation provided for justices to be nominated by the President and approved by the Senate for lifetime appointments. Originally, the Supreme Court comprised one chief justice and five associates. However, Congress has gradually increased its size over the past two centuries. Currently, one chief justice and eight associates (28 U.S.C. { 1) preside over the Court, including: Chief Justice John G. Roberts, Jr. (George W. Bush nominee, 2005); Antonin Scalia (Ronald Reagan nominee, 1986); Anthony M. Kennedy (Ronald Reagan nominee, 1988); Clarence Thomas (George Bush nominee, 1991); Ruth Bader Ginsburg (Bill Clinton nominee, 1993); Stephen G. Breyer (Bill Clinton nominee, 1994); Samuel Anthony Alito Jr. (George W. Bush nominee, 2006); Sonia Sotomayor (Barack Obama nominee, 2009); and Elena Kagan (Barack Obama nominee, 2010). It is estimated that the Court receives more than 7,000 **writs of certiorari** (i.e., petitions for hearing) each year.

writ of certiorari a formal request to a superior court for legal review of potential legal error regarding a lower court's decision.

The Supreme Court has original jurisdiction only in cases involving suits between states, suits involving a foreign citizen, and suits between the federal government and a state. The Supreme Court is considered "the **court of last resort**" for cases in the federal system and for state cases that involve constitutional issues. Thus, the Court's caseload consists primarily of appeals. In that way, its docket is almost entirely discretionary—developing out of a review process initiated by the filing of a writ of certiorari. A petition for such a writ is defined as an appeal from a party to an appellate court to order the forwarding of court documents regarding a particular case to the higher court for review. Such petitions, numbering in the thousands annually, are originally reviewed by a staff of law clerks that selects only those cases deemed meritorious in some aspect. Those cases then are forwarded to the Supreme Court for review. (See Figure 2-2 (a) for a typical state court structure, and 2-2 (b) for the federal structure.)

court of last resort a court from which there is no further appeal of a judgment rendered by it in review of a decision by a lower court.

Once the cases are forwarded from the clerks to the Court, the Chief Justice leads the Court in discussions concerning the individual cases. Notes from such deliberations are recorded by the most junior justice, and oral voting commences

▼

Pennsylvania
(Court structure as of Calendar Year 2010)

Supreme Court   COLR
7 justices sit en banc   S

CSP Case Types:
- Appeal by right criminal, civil, administrative agency. Interlocutory appeals in criminal, civil, administrative agency
- Appeal by permission criminal, civil, administrative agency. Interlocutory appeals in criminal, civil, administrative agency.
- Exclusive death penalty.
- Original proceeding application for writ. Exclusive bar/judiciary, certified question.   link

Commonwealth Court*   IAC   **Superior Court**   IAC
9 judges sit in 3-judge panels and en banc   A   *15 judges sit in 3- judge panels and en banc*   S
                                    S
CSP Case Types: CSP Case Types:
- Appeal by right criminal, civil, administrative   - Appeal by right criminal, civil, Interlocutory
  agency. Interlocutory appeals in criminal, civil,   appeal in criminal, civil.
  administrative agency.   - Appeal by permission criminal, civil,
- Appeal by permission criminal, civil, limited   Interlocutory appeal in criminal, civil.
  administrative agency. Interlocutory appeals in   - Original proceeding application for writ.
  criminal, civil, administrative agency.
- Original proceeding application for writ   link   link

Court of Common Pleas (60 districts in 67 counties)   GJC
450 judges   A
Jury trials in most cases   M

CSP Case Types:
- Tort, contract, real property, probate/ estate, administrative agency appeals, miscellaneous civil.
- Domestic relations.
- Felony, miscellaneous criminal.
- Exclusive juvenile.   link

Philadelphia Municipal Court LJC   **Philadelphia Traffic Court** LJC   **Magisterial District Judge** LJC
25 judges   M   *7 judges*   M   **Court*** (544 courts)   M
No jury trials   *No jury trials*   *544 judges*
                                                                              No jury trials
CSP Case Types: CSP Case Types:
- Landlord/tenant, real property ($0   - Traffic infraction, parking   CSP Case Types:
  - $15,000), small claims (up to   violation.   - Small claims (up to $8,000).
  $10,000), miscellaneous civil.   - Felony, preliminary hearings,
- Felony, preliminary hearings,   misdemeanor.
  misdemeanor.   - Traffic/other violations.
- Ordinance violations.   link   link   link

*Commonwealth Court hears cases brought by and against the Commonwealth.
**Effective January 1, 2005, the Pittsburgh Municipal Court merged with the Allegheny County Magisterial District Judge Court.

Legend

☐ = Appellate level   COLR = Court of Last Resort   A = Appeal from Admin. Agency
                         IAC = Intermediate Appellate Court   S = State funded
☐ = Trial level   GJC = General Jurisdiction Court   L = Locally funded
                         LJC = Limited Jurisdiction Court   M = Mixed: state and locally funded
↑ = Route of appeal

AOC Web site:
www.pacourts.us

FIGURE 2-2   (a, b) –Generic state court structure

---

rule of four   to be placed on the docket, a case must receive at least four affirmative votes from Supreme Court justices for certiorari (in which the Supreme Court agrees to hear the case).

according to seniority. To be placed on the docket, the case must receive at least four affirmative votes. This is known as the **rule of four**. If the rule of four is not satisfied, then the petition is denied and the ruling of the lower court is left intact. Denial of certiorari (also cert) is not an acceptance or agreement of the legal reasoning or verdict by the lower court nor does it establish a precedent or have any other binding power. It simply means that the requisite four votes to hear the case were not obtained.

Selection of a particular case by the Supreme Court may at times appear to be random, and it is always subjective. Such capriciousness has been recognized by Chief Justice William Rehnquist.[4] Theoretically, the Supreme Court hears cases in which it has original jurisdiction; in which there is a constitutional issue in question; and in which there are diverse rulings among lower courts (either within the federal system itself or among state and federal courts). The Supreme Court's rulings are binding on all federal courts and can be binding on state courts when the Fourteenth Amendment is made applicable.

▶ The State Courts

Although the Supreme Court of the United States often issues rulings that are binding on the states, most criminal cases (and civil cases, for that matter) are heard and ruled upon in state courts. In 2006, for example, more than 102 million cases were filed in state courts).[5] Without question, state courts have more impact on the lives of average citizens and laws often are based on the prevailing standards of the community in which they were developed. As such, laws, judicial process, caseloads, and government structure vary widely across jurisdictions. However, all states have a structured appellate system in which due process is pursued. Some states achieve this goal more effectively than others, as some state systems are more organized than others. North Dakota and the District of Columbia, for example, are streamlined—having a unified trial system and single court of last resort; while the court system in Georgia is more complex—having nine different trial courts and numerous layers of appellate courts. Caseloads also vary widely, with the state of California serving a population greater than some entire countries. Thus, the effectiveness and efficiency of court systems varies widely. However, there are generally four types of state courts: courts of limited jurisdiction, courts of general jurisdiction, intermediate appellate courts, and courts of last resort.

Courts of limited jurisdiction (also known as magistrate court, municipal court, county court, and justice of the peace court) are specialty courts that, by definition, are limited in the scope of cases in which they have jurisdiction. According to the National Center for State Courts, more than two-thirds of all cases filed in state courts are heard in courts of limited jurisdiction. These courts are reserved largely for traffic cases, small claims cases, misdemeanor filings, and preliminary hearings in felony cases.[6] Also, these courts are used for the issuance of search and arrest warrants, and in some jurisdictions, they are used for family law and probate. Unlike other courts, there is no absolute right to a jury trial in most of these courts. In fact, such a right would significantly hamper, if not entirely obliterate, timely adjudication of the tens of millions of cases filed in these courts per year. Losing parties may seek a **trial de novo**. Unlike traditional appeals in which the trial record is reviewed for legal errors, a trial de novo is an entirely new trial—separate and independent from the original. By far, these courts represent the largest body of the state judiciary. In 2010, for example, there were approximately 30,000 limited jurisdiction judicial officers compared to roughly 12,000 judicial officers in courts of general jurisdiction.[7] This number, however, is constantly subject to change because courts open and close based on need and changes in court system classification.

Courts of general jurisdiction (also known as trial courts, district courts, circuit courts, or superior courts) represent the next tier of court in many state systems. Less than 20 percent of all state cases are filed in courts of general jurisdiction. Hearing criminal and civil matters, these courts are known as trial courts because individuals before them possess the right to a jury trial. The courts are primarily considered courts of original jurisdiction for felony trials, although only 20 percent of their caseload involves criminal cases.[8] Also, they are responsible for all other matters not reserved for courts of limited jurisdiction and, sometimes, they serve as the appellate court in a trial de novo originating in a lower court. Caseloads vary greatly by jurisdiction. In 2010, for example, 855,720 cases were filed in Florida's courts of general jurisdiction, while Wyoming had 8,139.[9]

trial de novo a form of appeal in which an appellate court conducts an entirely new trial of a matter. Unlike traditional appeals that review the court record for legal error, a trial de novo is a completely separate and independent hearing.

intermediate appellate courts or courts of appeals found throughout the federal system and within the majority of state systems, these courts are the court of first review.

HABEAS CORPUS

In addition to the Magna Carta, the writ of habeas corpus is considered a significant development in the march toward democracy. Literally, "possession of the body," a petition for a writ of habeas corpus pleads release from unlawful imprisonment. Successful petitions require the release of a prisoner to a judicial officer who may determine the legality of imprisonment. Considered so vital to concepts of freedom, it is included in Article 1, Section 9 of the U.S. Constitution. To wit, "the privilege of the Writ of Habeas Corpus shall not be suspended, unless when in Cases of Rebellion or Invasion the public Safety may require it." Petitions are most often filed by individuals who are currently incarcerated.

writ of habeas corpus an order in writing, issued in the name of the government by a judge of competent jurisdiction, and directed to a person who has another in his custody or detains him in confinement that commands him to bring such person so detained before the judge, at the time and place appointed, and to state the reasons for which he/she has imprisoned or otherwise deprived him/her of liberty.

Because of rising caseloads, **intermediate appellate courts** (also known as **courts of appeals**) have significantly increased in volume since the founding of most states. Only 11 states and the District of Columbia function without 1, with some states having more than 1. For the most part, intermediate appellate courts are the courts of first review. Consequently, their caseload is significantly higher than courts of last resort.

Courts of last resort are referred to most often as state supreme courts, except in New York where it is known as the court of appeals. Like the U.S. Supreme Court, much of the docket in state supreme courts is discretionary, in that the court decides which cases to hear. This is particularly true in states that do not maintain intermediate appellate cases. Irrespective of appellate structure, many state supreme courts are also obligated to hear automatic appeals stemming from death penalty cases. For the most part, however, their involvement in cases is highly discretionary—reserved for cases with significant legal issues. Their rulings are the final word on issues involving state law. As such, the only available option for unsuccessful parties in criminal matters is to identify a Constitutional issue or to file a **writ of habeas corpus** in a federal district court. Many death row inmates, for example, have argued that the imposition of capital punishment represents cruel and unusual punishment and violates the Eighth Amendment. While some have appealed directly to the U.S. Supreme Court, many others have filed writs in district courts.

Table 2-2 Court Structure by State

A complete discussion of all differences in state law is outside the scope of this book, but a brief organizational structure of state courts vs. federal courts is illustrated in the following tables.

State	Court of First Instance (General Jurisdiction)	Intermediate Appellate Court	Court of Last Resort
Alabama	(District) Circuit Court (41 judicial districts)	Court of Civil Appeals* Court of Criminal* Appeals (1969—single Court of Appeals)	Supreme Court
Alaska	(District) Superior Court (4 districts)	Court of Appeals	Supreme Court
Arizona	(County) Superior Court (15 counties)	(Division) Court of Appeals (2 divisions)	Supreme Court
Arkansas	Circuit Court (23 judicial circuits)	Court of Appeals	Supreme Court

Table 2-2 Continued

State	Court of First Instance (General Jurisdiction)	Intermediate Appellate Court	Court of Last Resort
California	(County) Superior Court (58 counties)	(District) Court of Appeals (6 appellate districts)	Supreme Court
Colorado	District Court (22 judicial districts)	Court of Appeals	Supreme Court
Connecticut	District Court (13 judicial districts)	Appellate Court	Supreme Court (previously Supreme Court of Errors)
District of Columbia	Superior Court	(None)	Court of Appeals (previously Municipal Court of Appeals)
Delaware	Superior Court* (previously Superior Court and Orphans' Court)Court of Chancery*	(None)	Supreme Court (previously Court of Errors and Appeals)
Florida	Circuit Court (20 judicial circuits)	District Court of Appeal (5 districts)	Supreme Court
Georgia	Superior Court (49 judicial circuits)	Court of Appeals	Supreme Court
Hawaii	Circuit Court (4 circuits: First, Second, Third, Fifth)	Intermediate Court of Appeals	Supreme Court
Idaho	District Court (7 judicial districts)	Court of Appeals	Supreme Court
Illinois	Circuit Court (22 judicial circuits)	(District) Appellate Court (5 districts)	Supreme Court
Indiana	County Circuit Court (90 counties)	(District) Court of Appeals (5 districts) (previously Appellate Court)	Supreme Court
Iowa	District Court (8 districts)	Court of Appeals	Supreme Court
Kansas	District Court (31 districts)	Court of Appeals	Supreme Court
Kentucky	Circuit Court (57 circuits)	Court of Appeals	Supreme Court (1976—Court of Appeals)
Louisiana	District Court (40 districts)	(Circuit) Court of Appeals (5 circuits)	Supreme Court (1813—Superior Court)
Maine	Superior Court	(None)	Supreme Judicial Court
Maryland	Circuit Court (8 judicial circuits)	Court of Special Appeals	Court of Appeals
Massachusetts	Trial Court of the Commonwealth (7 departments: Superior Court,* District Court,* Boston Municipal Court,* Juvenile Court,* Housing Court,* Land Court,* Probate and Family Court*	Appeals Court	Supreme Judicial Court
Michigan	Circuit Court (57 circuits) Court of Claims	Court of Appeals	Supreme Court
Minnesota	District Court (10 districts)	Court of Appeals	Supreme Court

(continued)

Table 2-2 Continued

State	Court of First Instance (General Jurisdiction)	Intermediate Appellate Court	Court of Last Resort
Mississippi	District Circuit Court (22 districts)	Court of Appeals	Supreme Court
Missouri	Circuit Court (45 circuits)	(District) Court of Appeals (3 districts)	Supreme Court
Montana	District Court (22 judicial districts)	(None)	Supreme Court
Nebraska	District Court (12 districts)	Court of Appeals	Supreme Court
Nevada	District Court (9 judicial districts)	(None)	Supreme Court
New Hampshire	Superior Court	(None)	Supreme Court
New Jersey	(Vicinage) Superior Court (15 vicinages)	Superior Court, Appellate Division (previously Court of Chancery, Supreme Court, and Prerogative Court)	Supreme Court (previously Court of Errors and Appeals)
New Mexico	District Court (13 judicial districts)	Court of Appeals	Supreme Court
New York	(District) Supreme Court* (12 judicial districts) County Court* (57 counties)	Supreme Court,* Appellate Term (3 judicial departments) Supreme Court,* Appellate Division (4 departments)	Court of Appeals (1848—Court for the Correction of Errors, Supreme Court of Judicature, and Court of Chancery)
North Carolina	(District) Superior Court (46 districts)	Court of Appeals	Supreme Court
North Dakota	District Court (7 judicial districts)	Court of Appeals	Supreme Court
Ohio	(County) Court of Common Pleas (88 counties)	(District) Court of Appeals (12 districts)	Supreme Court
Oklahoma	District Court (26 judicial districts)	Court of Civil Appeals	Supreme Court* Court of Criminal Appeals* (1959—Criminal Court of Appeals)
Oregon	(District) Circuit Court (27 judicial districts)	Court of Appeals	Supreme Court
Pennsylvania	District Court of Common Pleas (60 judicial districts)	(District) Superior Court* (3 districts) Commonwealth Court*	(District) Supreme Court (3 districts)
Rhode Island	Superior Court	(None)	Supreme Court
South Carolina	(Circuit) Court of Common Pleas* (16 circuits) (Circuit) Court of General Sessions* (16 circuits)	Court of Appeals	Supreme Court
South Dakota	Circuit Court (7 circuits)	(None)	Supreme Court
Tennessee	(District) Circuit Court* (31 judicial districts) (District) Criminal Court* (31 judicial districts) (District) Chancery Court* (31 judicial districts)	(Grand Division) Court of Appeals* (3 grand divisions) (Grand Division) Court of Criminal Appeals* (3 grand divisions)	Supreme Court

Table 2-2 Continued

State	Court of First Instance (General Jurisdiction)	Intermediate Appellate Court	Court of Last Resort
Texas	District Court (420 districts)	(District) Court of Appeals (14 districts)	Supreme Court* Court of Criminal Appeals*
Utah	District Court (8 districts)	Court of Appeals	Supreme Court
Virginia	Circuit Court (31 judicial circuits)	Court of Appeals	Supreme Court (previously Supreme Court of Appeals)
Vermont	Superior Court* District Court* Family Court*	(None)	Supreme Court
Washington	(County) Superior Court (39 counties)	(Division) Court of Appeals (3 divisions)	Supreme Court
West Virginia	Circuit Court (31 judicial circuits)	(None)	Supreme Court of Appeals
Wisconsin	(District) Circuit Court (10 judicial administrative districts)	(District) Court of Appeals (4 districts)	Supreme Court
Wyoming	District Court (9 districts)	(None)	Supreme Court
American Samoa	High Court, Trial Division	(None)	High Court, Appellate Division
Guam	Superior Court	(None)	Supreme Court
Puerto Rico	Superior Court (13)Municipal Court (13)	Court of Appeals	Supreme Court
U.S. Virgin Islands	(Division) Territorial Court (2 divisions)	(None)	(None)

▶ Courtroom Actors and the American Adversarial System

Theoretically, the American system of criminal justice is based on the concept of advocacy, adversary, and justice. Under common law and the English system, the process of justice was designed to be a fact-finding process—an inquisitorial system similar to those found in civilized and developed countries across the globe.[10] In these types of systems, the judge plays both an active and predominant role—leading the search for truth. In the United States, however, the presumption of innocence necessarily results in an accusatorial model which has been recognized by the Court. In their ruling which applied the Fifth Amendment's protection against self-incrimination to state actors, the Court ruled that "the shift reflects recognition that the American system of criminal prosecution is accusatorial, not inquisitorial, and that the Fifth Amendment privilege is its essential mainstay … governments, state and federal, are thus constitutionally compelled to establish guilt by evidence independently and freely secured, and may not by coercion prove a charge against an accused out of his own mouth."[11]

While the contemporary system is legally accusatorial, it is also overwhelmingly adversarial by nature. Unlike inquisitorial systems in which judges actively participate in fact-finding, judges in adversarial systems are neutral participants who referee or moderate faithful (and often zealous) advocacy by prosecution and defense representatives. Thus, the American adversarial system is designed to protect citizens from persecution by the government. Theoretically, the judge is to be a neutral participant, the police are to be fair and impartial, and the prosecutor and the police are to be separate entities. In this system, the primary players are the government's representative and the defense attorney. However, law enforcement officers, community spokespersons, and judges often become intimately involved in the eventual outcome. While some may argue that the truth may be obfuscated in these systems as victory rather than truth becomes the objective, others see the strength in a system which guarantees advocacy for the defense.

Prosecutors

There are three main categories of courtroom actors: prosecutors, defense attorneys, and judges. While all maintain law degrees, their respective roles in court vary dramatically. Like judges, prosecutors receive their mission and their authority from legislation. The Judiciary Act of 1789, for example, provided for the presidential appointment of federal prosecutors (i.e., U.S. attorneys) in each court district and the Office of the Attorney General. The Attorney General's primary responsibility "shall be to prosecute and conduct all suits in the Supreme Court in which the United States shall be concerned, and to give his advice and opinion upon questions of law when required by the President of the United States, or when requested by the heads of any of the departments."[12] The office was soon overburdened, and several assistants and private attorneys were retained. After the Civil War, the office received greater power and autonomy and became the Department of Justice (DOJ). This 1870 Act also established the Office of the Solicitor General and granted the DOJ control over federal law enforcement. Currently, the Attorney General presides over one of the world's largest law firms and oversees the enforcement of federal laws. State prosecutors, on the other hand, are largely elected officials. Known as district attorneys, solicitors, state's attorneys, and commonwealth attorneys, state prosecutors maintain a largely discretionary caseload and are not bound by law to pursue any particular case.

According to standards adopted by the American Bar Association, **prosecutors** are ministers of justice and not solely advocates for the government. Theoretically, this includes assurances of procedural justice and findings of guilt only in cases in which sufficient evidence exists. Prosecutors are ethically bound to exercise restraint in cases in which charges are not supported by probable cause; to cease practices that encourage the waiver of pretrial rights by defendants who are not represented by counsel; to ensure timely disclosure of exculpatory evidence and/or mitigating factors; to make reasonable efforts to ensure that the defendant has been advised of his right to counsel; and to refrain from making extrajudicial statements that have a substantial likelihood of heightening public condemnation of the accused.

Defense Attorneys

Although they wear assorted hats, criminal **defense attorneys** have the primary responsibility of effectively and conscientiously serving as counselor and advocate to the accused. Every felony defendant is entitled to an attorney as provided by case law and the Sixth Amendment to the Constitution. Thus, many defendants retain their own counsel, and indigent defendants are represented by either a public defender or appointed counsel. Government compensation is provided for the defense of the indigent. Public defenders are salaried government employees whose caseload is entirely composed of individuals in economic need, whereas appointed counsel involves attorneys with private practices who are compensated by the state on a case-by-case basis when they are appointed by the judge to

prosecutor adversarial counterpart to the defense attorney whose responsibility is to serve not only as an advocate for the government but to pursue procedural justice and a finding of guilt in cases in which sufficient evidence exists. In criminal cases, the prosecuting attorney has the burden of proof for demonstrating guilt beyond a reasonable doubt.

defense attorney adversarial counterpart to the prosecutor whose responsibility is to serve as counsel and advocate for the accused. In criminal cases, the defense attorney attempts to create reasonable doubt in the minds of the jury.

COURTROOM ACTORS AT A GLANCE

The American criminal justice system is designed to be adversarial, not inquisitorial. Ostensibly designed to be a fact-finding process, the system provides for two opposing advocates to present all relevant information to a jury and function within legal boundaries as an unbiased legal expert.

The defense attorney has the responsibility to:

- Serve the interests of his or her client
- Engage in an adversarial system to zealously protect clients' rights and attempt to create reasonable doubt in the minds of the jury

The prosecuting attorney has the responsibility to:

- Seek justice (The system emphasizes the seeking of truth, not simply a conviction.)
- Attempt to demonstrate to a fair and impartial jury that the defendant is guilty beyond a reasonable doubt

The presiding judge has the responsibility to:

- Protect the rights of the accused
- Protect the public interest
- Interpret applicable law
- Instruct the jury

represent an indigent person. While systems for appointment vary by state, states require all sitting members of the bar to participate in a rotating system or to have attorneys volunteer for appointment on a **pro bono** (i.e., for the public good) basis. Regardless of the selection procedures and criteria, indigent defendants are only entitled to the counsel appointed to them by the court. They are not entitled to a selection nor are there any provisions for preference.

Defense attorneys have various roles in the American system of criminal justice. Their primary role, as stated earlier, involves the advocacy and counsel of the defendant, with all the duty, diligence, and fortitude these entail. Defense attorneys are ethically bound to avoid delays by all legal means available, including the maintenance of a workable caseload, and should diligently meet all deadlines established by applicable rules so as not to harm their clients' interests. They should continue their education and training so as to best serve their clients. They are expected to develop a relationship of trust and confidence with the accused and to further this by keeping the defendant fully apprised of all aspects of the case. They are expected to discuss all possible outcomes of a case frankly, including giving a candid assessment of the expectations. They are obligated to enter into plea negotiations on behalf of their client while protecting the defendant's rights. They must also protect the legal interest of their client even in cases in which the defendant is adverse to such. This includes strategic and tactical decisions of the trial process. Before trial initiation, they are expected to conduct a complete investigation of the facts of the case, applicable laws, and any appropriate issues requiring expert assistance. During sentencing, the defense should attempt to secure the lowest possible sentence for the accused. Often, this is accomplished through an examination of current sentencing guidelines, an understanding of relevant past cases, and a presentation of mitigating factors. Defense counsel is also responsible for presenting appropriate posttrial motions to secure the right of appeal, irrespective of a continuing contractual relationship. Defense attorneys also are responsible for informing the defendant of appellate options, potential outcomes, and important deadlines.

Although often demonized by the media, defense attorneys are essential to the American system of criminal justice. Without them, the process and all premises

pro bono literally "for the public good," legal work performed by defense attorneys generally without pay to assist the indigent or others with legal problems and limited funds; also may involve legal work performed for charities and social causes.

EVALUATING THE EFFECTIVENESS OF COUNSEL IN PRETRIAL PROCEEDINGS

The Sixth Amendment to the Constitution establishes the rights of the accused as related to criminal prosecutions. One of the most important of these is the assistance of counsel. This right extends to all 'critical' stages of the criminal proceedings [*Montejo v. Louisiana*, 556 U.S. 778 (2009)]. These *critical stages* include: arraignments [*Hamilton v. Alabama*, 368 U.S. 218 (1961)]; postindictment interrogations [*Massiah v. United States*, 377 U.S. 201 (1964)]; and the entry of a guilty plea [*Argersinger v. Hamlini*, 407 U.S. 25 (1975)]. Although the Court has not interpreted this to mean that criminal defendants are entitled to perfect representation, they have established that "the Sixth Amendment right to counsel is the right to the effective assistance of counsel, and the benchmark for judging any claim of ineffectiveness must be whether counsel's conduct so undermined the proper functioning of the adversarial process that the trial cannot be relied on as having produced a just result." [*Strickland v. Washington*, 466 U.S. 668 (1984)]

The resulting standard for challenging effectiveness is known as the *Strickland Rule*, and requires a demonstration that counsel's performance: 1) fell below an objective standard of reasonableness; and 2) raises a reasonable probability that the result would have been different but for his/her ineffectiveness. While this typically establishes a high threshold for criminal defendants seeking relief, the Court has recently ruled that codified standards of professional practice may be considered as important guides in ineffective claims.

In *Missouri v. Frye* (2009), defense counsel failed to communicate two possible plea offers from the prosecuting attorney, one of which included an offer to reduce the charge to a misdemeanor and a 90-day sentence. As a result, the offers expired. One week prior to his preliminary hearing, Frye was arrested again for driving with a revoked license. He subsequently pled guilty and received a three year sentence. On appeal, he argued that his counsel's failure to communicate the earlier plea offers violated his Sixth Amendment right to effective counsel. While recognizing that a defendant does not have a right to be offered a plea, the Court recognized that defense counsel "has the duty to communicate formal prosecution offers to accept a plea on terms and conditions that may be favorable to the accused."

In the same session, the Court also considered the case of *Lafler v. Cooper* (2009). In this case, defense counsel presented a plea offer to the defendant but advised him to reject it. At the subsequent trial, the defendant was convicted and sentenced to a term which exceeded that which was originally offered. Restating their earlier position in *Frye*, the Court noted that "the reality that criminal justice today is for the most part a system of pleas, not a systems of trials . . . [and that] it is insufficient simply to point to the guarantee of a fair trial as a backstop that inoculates any errors in the pretrial process." In addition, the Court considered the question as to what would constitute an appropriate remedy in this particular case. They ordered the State to reoffer the plea agreement.

---

judge adversarial referee between prosecutors and defense attorneys whose responsibilities are to ensure fairness, adherence to the rule of law, and good sportsmanship between the parties during a trial.

in the Constitution and Bill of Rights would be null and void. Their presence is necessary for advocacy. It is important to note that defense attorneys ethically are prohibited from avoiding participation in controversial or otherwise unpopular cases—except in the case of good cause. Thus, their representation of an individual accused of a particularly heinous crime is not indicative of their personal assessment of the case or of the defendant. Zealously defending clients in a court of law is their ethical duty.

Judges

Like prosecutors and defense attorneys, **judges** perform various roles during the administration of justice. At its core, the judge's role may be characterized as a referee—serving to ensure fairness and good sportsmanship between the parties.

Judges are expected to be impartial and to fulfill three primary responsibilities during the trial process: comply with the rules, instruct the jury, and make appropriate legal determinations. Unlike the jury, which is responsible for evaluating the weight of the evidence, the judge is responsible for evaluating the admissibility of the evidence. His or her job, for example, is to ensure that evidence collected illegally, evidence that is unduly prejudicial, or evidence that is irrelevant to the facts of the case is excluded from presentment. The judge is an interpreter of the law and must rule on motions and objections. In addition, the judge is responsible for maintaining decorum in the courtroom and for appropriately applying the rules of evidence. This includes ruling on questions of relevancy, **vicinage**, and materiality. Also, the judge is tasked with determining the competence of witnesses and assessing the qualification of expert witnesses. Finally, the judge is responsible for instructing the jury on the law or laws applicable to the case. These **jury instructions** include, but are not limited to: the elements of the crime, the burden of proof, the standard of proof, and admonitions against external influences. Proper instruction of the jury is extremely important. Failure to do so can constitute an error of such magnitude that the decision gets reversed on appeal. This is known as **reversible error**. Other areas ripe for challenges of reversible error include, but are not limited to: improper admission of evidence; improper exclusion of evidence; *Brady* violations; denial of self-representation; judicial bias; and, conflicts of interest.

The federal rules of evidence, and some state rules, also allow judges to independently call and question witnesses.

vicinage the statutory jurisdiction of a particular court.

jury instructions instructions given to the jury by the presiding judge concerning the elements of the crime, the burden of proof, the standard of proof, admonitions to avoid external influences, and other items pertinent to the particular case.

reversible error an error of such magnitude that is related to the final disposition of the case.

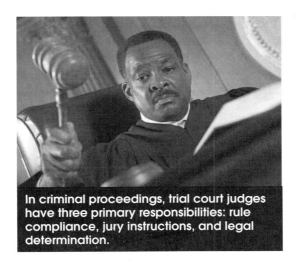
In criminal proceedings, trial court judges have three primary responsibilities: rule compliance, jury instructions, and legal determination.

FEDERAL RULES OF EVIDENCE

ARTICLE VI—WITNESSES

Rule 614—calling and interrogation of witnesses by court

(a) Calling. The court may call a witness on its own or at a party's request. Each party is entitled to cross-examine the witness.

(b) Examining. The court may examine a witness regardless of who calls the witness.

(c) Objections. A party may object to the court's calling or examining a witness either at that time or at the next opportunity when the jury is not present.

Selection of Federal and State Judges

Judges are selected in a variety of ways. As stated previously, all federal judges are appointed for life terms with the exception of bankruptcy judges who are appointed for terms of 14 years. Appointments are made in many states—a historical artifact of the Judiciary Act of 1789 in the federal system. In state and federal systems, appointments are made by the chief executive officer of the jurisdiction.

Another method of selecting state judges is through popular election. This approach gained popularity in the mid-nineteenth century, immediately before the Civil War, when many states revitalized their state constitutions. The judicial revision movement was especially strong in the free and slave states, in response to the fact that judgeships were awarded based not on competence but on patronage dawned.[13] Such realization, coupled with the strength of Jacksonian Democrats, significantly altered the method of judicial selection in many states. In 1832, Mississippi became the first state to formally change its constitution to allow for the popular election of judges. Most states admitted to the Union later adopted a system of popular elections for judicial officers. Currently, nine states use partisan ballots and 13 use nonpartisan ballots to elect judges.

IN SEARCH OF HISTORY: DIVINITY AND JUSTICE

Historically, judges have been assumed to be just. One notable example was the Irish judge, Morann: ". . . who wore a gold collar; for when his judgment was just, the collar grew larger and fell to his waist, but if it should be unjust, the collar would grow smaller about his neck and choke him." (Wigmore, 1928: 668)

The third method of selection is commonly known as the Missouri plan. This approach can be characterized as a hybrid—an appointed-elective system. Originally created by the American Judicature Society in 1909, the final method of selecting judges is through the merit system, which includes three primary steps:

1. Development of a list of qualified candidates from a nonpartisan judicial nominating committee
2. Appointment by the chief executive officer in a jurisdiction (i.e., governor)
3. Periodic submission to the electorate for retention or removal

Each approach was designed to provide for heightened levels of accountability, independence, and impartiality by the judiciary, but all have faced significant criticism. Not surprisingly, the most heavily criticized are systems of appointment and merit. Proponents of the appointed system, for example, argue that lifetime appointments are necessary to negate external influences thereby increasing assurances of impartiality. At the same time, opponents argue that appointed positions are inherently political and can pervert the notions of justice and fair play. Proponents of the merit process argue that the periodic election component ensures judicial accountability, while opponents argue that the modified system is nothing more than a smokescreen designed to obscure political connections. Examination of all reveals one thing—continuing controversy surrounds the selection of judiciary within state systems. Regardless of the controversy, the merit system for judicial selection is gaining in popularity.

▶ The Criminal Justice Process

The parameters of this book preclude an exhaustive discussion of the criminal justice process, but highlights of the trial process are discussed next.

Supreme Court members (first row L-R) Associate Justice Clarence Thomas, Associate Justice Antonin Scalia, Chief Justice John Roberts, Associate Justice Anthony Kennedy, Associate Justice Ruth Bader Ginsburg, (back row L-R) Associate Justice Sonia Sotomayor, Associate Justice Stephen Breyer, Associate Justice Samuel Alito and Associate Justice Elena Kagan pose for photographs in the East Conference Room at the Supreme Court building.

Pretrial Proceedings

Although much attention is garnered by the actual trial of a defendant, especially in high-profile cases, much activity occurs before the trial even begins. A great deal of work is completed by actors outside the physical courtroom, and each actor has an essential role to play in the American criminal justice system.

Complaints

In most states, several avenues exist for the processing of criminal complaints. By definition, a **criminal complaint** is a legal document, filed with the appropriate judicial authority that initiates prosecution of an alleged offense. Most often, a local magistrate or court official files the complaints, but private citizens, prosecuting attorneys, and law enforcement officials can file them as well. Criminal complaints must include the specifics of the incident in question, including, but not limited to the offense charged; the time, date, and place of occurrence; and the name of the suspected offender. While specificity is important in a general sense, it is especially important in terms of date and place. The date of the offense in question is important to ensure that the **statute of limitations** has not expired. Specifying jurisdiction will ensure legal authority, or the statutory jurisdiction of a particular court. In most states, the criminal complaint also serves as the charging document for preliminary hearings. The filing of the complaint is the delivery of a complaint to the court clerk for placement on the docket. In addition, many arrest and search **warrants** are predicated on information contained within criminal complaints. As established in the Bill of Rights, search and arrest warrants must be based on probable cause. In particular, they must describe the items in question and their probable location. Warrants are issued singularly to law enforcement personnel upon sworn affidavit.

criminal complaint
a legal document, filed with the appropriate judicial authority, that initiates prosecution of an alleged offense.

statute of limitations
a type of federal or state law that restricts the time within which legal proceedings may be brought or offenses charged.

warrants legal directives showing probable cause that are issued by magistrates or judicial officials authorizing law enforcement officers to conduct arrests, seizures, or searches of persons or specified items at particular times and places.

arraignment or initial appearance
The formal proceeding which follows booking in state systems or the indictment or information in the federal system. During this time, the accused is informed of the charges, bail is set, a plea is given, and the next court appearance is scheduled. Also, the judge ensures that the accused is aware of his or her right to an attorney and, in the case of an indigent defendant, appointment of counsel is made.

Arraignment or Initial Appearance

booking administrative procedure during which a suspect is formally entered into the criminal justice system through the process of photographing, fingerprinting, and documenting the offense charged.

Upon arrest, a suspect is taken to a public law enforcement establishment for **booking**. This process, administrative in nature, involves the entry into the police ledger of the charge, suspect's name, and time of arrest. During this process, the jurisdictional agency may also obtain identification information, such as fingerprints and photographs. As expeditiously as possible thereafter, the defendant is brought before the judge for the first time. During this **arraignment, or initial appearance**, the suspect is informed of the charges, bail is set, and the next court appearance is scheduled. Also, the judge ensures that the accused is aware of his or her right to an attorney, and in the case of an indigent defendant, an appointment of counsel is made. In cases where an arrest has been made without a warrant, the arraignment also serves as a probable cause hearing and must be held within 48 hours absent extraordinary circumstances.[14] Such probable cause determination is not necessary in cases in which a judicial official previously had signed an arrest warrant or whenever the defendant will not be held in custody.

APPLICATION OF LAW

CELEBRITIES, WEST MEMPHIS THREE, AND THE ALFORD PLEA

The West Memphis Three: A Case for Reasonable Doubt?—On May 5, 1993, three children vanished while riding their bikes in the rural community of West Memphis, Arkansas. Their bodies were discovered alongside a ditch the following day. They had been stripped naked, hogtied, molested, and murdered. One of the children had been emasculated. From the onset, the case proved troublesome to the small community. Shortly thereafter, West Memphis police arrested three teenagers who did not quite fit into the culture of rural Arkansas. They proved to be fans of heavy metal music and black clothing and were shown not to be admirers of sports or church. A break was made in the case when Jessie Misskelley, an individual who fell below the standard for mental retardation, confessed to the crime, and implicated Damien Echols and Jason Baldwin. During both subsequent trials, it became evident that the prosecution had an absolute lack of direct evidence. Tried separately from the other two, Jessie Misskelley was convicted primarily on his confession. He was sentenced to life plus 40 years.

During the trial of Jason Baldwin and Damien Echols, the prosecuting attorneys emphasized the secondary transference of a few fibers, and a knife found in a lake behind Jason Baldwin's house six months after the murder. They also presented evidence which purported to demonstrate Damien Echols' involvement in satanic worship. However, there was no direct evidence placing any of the boys at the scene. In fact, the trial was characterized by inconsistencies and unanswered questions, including, but not limited to:

- A "satanic expert" who held a mail-order PhD (discussed in Chapter 9)
- Testimony by the police that they "lost" potentially exculpatory evidence

- Testimony regarding a stranger who, on the night of the incident, was found bleeding in the bathroom of a local chicken franchise
- The absence of blood or semen at the crime scene
- The introduction of a knife owned by one of the victims' fathers, which had human DNA consistent with his stepson

Despite the lack of evidence, both boys were subsequently convicted. Jason Balwin received life in prison without parole. Damien Echols received a death sentence.

The case attracted the attention of filmmakers, authors, and celebrities. Footage from both trials was included in a documentary by HBO films, and author Mara Leveritt wrote a book about the case, *Devil's Knot*, which is now a major motion picture starring Reese Witherspoon and Colin Firth. In addition, various celebrities, including Eddie Vedder (Pearl Jam), Natalie Maines (Dixie Chicks), and Johnny Depp, were quite vocal in their support of the trio, and were largely responsible for keeping attention (and money) focused on the case.

Despite monumental support and countless appeals, the trio remained incarcerated for over 18 years steadfastly protesting their innocence. During this period, new DNA evidence and witness statements emerged, which suggested that Terry Hobbs, the stepfather of one of the victims, may have been responsible for the boys' deaths. In 2011, a deal between the defense and the prosecution vacated the earlier convictions, and allowed Echols, Baldwin, and Misskelley to enter an Alford plea. The judge then imposed a sentence of time served, and they were released. The deal prohibits them from seeking redress in a civil court.

Pleas and Plea Bargaining

Defendants must enter a **plea** during the arraignment. The range of pleas includes guilty, not guilty, not guilty by reason of affirmative defense, or nolo contendere (no contest). Individuals who plead guilty fully admit their culpability. Such a plea is made in open court and must be accompanied by a showing that such a plea is entered knowingly, intelligently, and voluntarily since "a plea of guilty is more than a confession which admits that the accused did various acts; it is itself a conviction."[15] Thus, certain rights are waived upon the introduction of a guilty plea, including Fifth Amendment protection against self-incrimination, the Sixth Amendment right to trial by jury, and the Sixth Amendment right to confront one's accusers. Because of the gravity of a guilty plea, it traditionally has required an admission by the defendant of the particular act. In contemporary courts, this requirement is no longer present. In establishing the **Alford plea**, the Court held that:

> . . . while most pleas of guilty consist of both a waiver of trial and an express admission of guilt, the latter element is not a constitutional requisite to the imposition of criminal penalty. An individual accused of crime may voluntarily, knowingly, and understandingly consent to the imposition of a prison sentence even if he is unwilling or unable to admit his participation in the acts constituting the crime.[16]

Thus, the Alford plea is an attractive alternative to individuals facing substantial incriminating evidence because it allows them to plead guilty while maintaining their innocence. Judges are not obligated to accept Alford pleas.

In some states, conditional pleas are increasing in number. Because the Supreme Court has consistently ruled that a plea of guilty negates traditional constitutional guarantees before the plea, many defendants now choose to enter conditional pleas, allowing them to appeal a certain issue on the record.[17] The likelihood of a guilty plea varies by case characteristics, including, but not limited to, severity of the offense, weight of the evidence, likelihood of conviction, and length of sentence. Guilty pleas, for example, are most common in misdemeanor cases. In fact, some jurisdictions have actually streamlined the plea process for certain charges, such as DUI, to allow defendants to plead guilty to the charge with a standardized sentence.

Another alternative for many defendants is to plead **nolo contendere**, or "no contest." Simply put, a plea of nolo contendere means that the defendant neither admits nor disputes the charge levied against him or her. The term literally translates from Latin as "I do not wish to argue." The introduction of such a plea allows the court to find the individual guilty without the person admitting to the facts of the case. As with Alford pleas, courts are not legally bound to accept them. In addition, both pleas present philosophical conundrums. They provide ways for the wrongfully accused to assert his or her innocence (while acknowledging the likelihood of a conviction), but they also allow guilty defendants to avoid personal accountability.

plea a claim of guilty, not guilty, not guilty by reason of affirmative defense, or nolo contendere (no contest) made by an individual in response to charges against him or her.

Alford Plea a plea in criminal court that allows a defendant to assert his or her innocence but admit or acknowledge the existence of sufficient evidence to find the person guilty. Judges may then find the person guilty or put aside a finding for a later dismissal—the prospect of a later dismissal engenders interest in this type of plea.

nolo contendere a plea accepting charges without admitting or denying guilt which subjects the defendant to punishment while allowing denial of the alleged facts in other proceedings.

 CLARIFICATION OF CONCEPTS

AFFIRMATIVE DEFENSES

Throughout American history, individuals have attempted to justify the actions they commit in particular situations, especially those that are criminal in nature. An affirmative defense is a legal justification for an individual's actions. Those asserting affirmative defense do not deny the action in question, just the culpability associated with it. Common affirmative defenses include, but are not limited to, insanity, entrapment, coercion or duress, necessity, and self-defense.

► Affirmative Defenses

affirmative defense a legal justification for an individual's actions, such as insanity, entrapment, coercion or duress, necessity, and self-defense. Those asserting affirmative defense do not deny the action in question, just the culpability associated with it.

Perhaps the most common plea entered by individuals seeking trial is a plea of not guilty, in which the accused denies the performance or commission of the offense charged. A plea of not guilty by reason of **affirmative defense**, however, is decidedly different. Individuals pleading not guilty by reason of affirmative defense admit to the performance of the act, but deny the illegality of their own actions. For example, a defendant might make a plea admitting to his or her participation in the event in question, but denying personal culpability to avoid civil or criminal responsibility. This is accomplished by introducing mitigating or extenuating circumstances, such as insanity, self-defense, entrapment, or coercion or duress. Traditionally, the burden of proof for affirmative defenses has rested on the government—the State was required to disprove such a charge. Most states recognized the futility of such requirements and modified their statutes to shift the burden to the defendant. However, the federal government maintained that burden until the attempted assassination of Ronald Reagan in 1981.

Insanity

M'Naghten standard the "right/wrong test" used to determine whether an individual did not know the nature of an act or that it was wrong and thus may employ the insanity defense.

After John Hinckley, Jr. was found not guilty by reason of insanity, most government judiciaries revamped insanity statutes. For example, the federal government increased the level of mental disease or defect necessary to successfully use the defense to "severe." In addition, it squarely placed the burden of proof for an insanity claim on the defense.

The insanity defense was recognized in the United States for the first time during the mid-nineteenth century soon after it was developed in England. The M'Naghten standard was soon the preeminent method for determinations of insanity. Known as the "right/wrong test," the **M'Naghten standard** referred to individuals who did not know the nature of the act or that it was wrong. This proved to be quite beneficial to prosecutors who simply had to demonstrate that the person engaging in the behavior knew that the behavior was wrong. Thus,

Andrea Yates (C) and her attorneys George Parnham (L) and Wendell Odom (R)react after the verdict in her murder retrial is read. Yates was found not guilty by reason of insanity for the 2001 drowning deaths of her five children. Yates was subsequently be committed to a state mental hospital, with periodic hearings before a judge to determine whether she should be released. Yates' 2002 conviction had been overturned on appeal due to erroneous testimony by forensic psychiatrist, Park Dietz.

INSANITY DEFENSE

(a) **Affirmative Defense**

It is an affirmative defense to a prosecution under any federal statute that, at the time of the commission of the acts constituting the offense, the defendant, as a result of a severe mental disease or defect, was unable to appreciate the nature and quality or the wrongfulness of his acts. Mental disease or defect does not otherwise constitute a defense.

(b) **Burden of Proof**

The defendant has the burden of proving the defense of insanity by clear and convincing evidence.

the irresistible impulse test was developed, which provided for the acquittal of individuals who simply could not control their behavior irrespective of recognition of rightness or wrongness. However, this test proved problematic because civilized society depends on the proper control of its members' impulses, and the test offered no way to determine which impulses could or could not be resisted. Despite its imperfections, this standard had been adopted by nearly one-half of the United States by the dawn of the twentieth century.

During the 1950s, an increase in the visibility of the field of psychology led to the use of psychological testimony in American courtrooms. As a result, the Durham Test emerged. This test evaluated whether a defendant had a mental disease or a defect and whether such a defect could result in the commission of a criminal act. It never gained popularity and was largely abandoned by the 1960s. Around the same time, another test emerged that would be broadly embraced across the United States. This test, known as the Model Penal Code Test, was the most comprehensive attempt to remedy concerns and criticisms levied against traditional tests. First, it lowered M'Naghten's requirement from absolute knowledge of right and wrong to a substantial incapacity to appreciate the difference. In addition, it combined elements from the irresistible impulse test in which ability to control behavior was considered. By the early 1980s, every federal court except the District of Columbia and First Circuits had adopted the Model Penal Code's Substantial Capacity Test.

In 1981, John Hinckley, Jr. fired six shots at President Ronald Reagan as he walked toward his waiting limousine. The bullets struck White House Press Secretary James Brady in the head, a District of Columbia police officer, a U.S. Secret Service agent, and President Reagan. Apprehended at the scene, Hinckley would later claim that his desire to impress actress Jodie Foster was the motivation for the shooting. (He was mimicking De Niro's Travis Bickle from *Taxi Driver.*) In 1982, Hinckley was found *not guilty by reason of insanity*. He remains confined at St. Elizabeth's Hospital in Washington, D.C. However, he currently is permitted extensive absences from the facility.

In the wake of the outcry after Hinckley's trial, Congress passed the *Insanity Defense Reform Act of 1984*. The Act was more restrictive than traditional standards for insanity. Under 18 U.S.C. 17(a), individuals are only considered insane when they can demonstrate through *clear and convincing evidence* that they are unable to appreciate the nature and quality or wrongfulness of their acts. In addition, the act established a comprehensive civil commitment procedure, with the result that those found not guilty would still be remanded into the custody of mental health professionals. The court then has 40 days to hold a hearing to determine the person's future (i.e., release or commitment). The Supreme Court upheld the constitutionality of the act in *Shannon v. United States* (1994). The act also provides for the release of individuals who are deemed to no longer pose a risk to others.

Necessity

According to the Supreme Court, a necessity defense "traditionally covered the situation where physical forces beyond the actor's control rendered illegal conduct the lesser of two evils."[18] Recognition of this defense has not been as pronounced as in other areas such as self-defense and insanity. The first real example of its use involved the rather infamous case of *Regina v. Dudley and Stephens*.[19] In Dudley, the first mate and the captain of a capsized ship were charged with and convicted of the murder of their cabin boy after they killed him so they could eat him. During the trial, the pair argued that it was an act borne of necessity and that they committed to act to save their own lives. The high court initially convicted them and sentenced them to death. However, their sentence was quickly commuted to six months in prison. One conclusion, then, is that although necessity normally is not accepted as an affirmative defense in murder cases, it is often treated as a mitigating factor. In a nutshell, the affirmative defense of necessity may be characterized as a balancing act between society's interests and one's personal gain. A contemporary example might include a situation in which someone who is legally intoxicated drives their child who is having an asthma attack to the emergency room.

Duress

duress an affirmative defense at common law, duress is now largely considered a mitigating factor that may justify the actions of an individual claiming to have been forced to commit a crime, such as murder, against his or her will.

A third type of affirmative defense is duress. As its name implies, **duress** simply means that an individual has been forced to do something against his or her will. Evidence of duress, when presented in court, may serve to mitigate or entirely excuse an individual's actions. While courts tend to allow the defense of duress in many types of cases, some jurisdictions specifically preclude it in homicide cases. When Patty Hearst, heiress to the William Randolph Hearst publishing empire and member of the Symbionese Liberation Army (SLA), was arrested in 1975, she claimed to have been brainwashed and forced to engage in bank robberies and assorted other criminal activities out of fear. Although the jury found her guilty, her sentence was commuted by President Jimmy Carter and she served only 2 years of a 7-year sentence. Duress has been employed in numerous cases in which families, friends, or loved ones were threatened.

Self-Defense

Unlike the other affirmative defenses discussed earlier, valid claims of self-defense often are considered justifiable—with acquittal as a result. Traditionally, the requirements for successful claims of self-defense included: (1) an honest and reliable belief that the use of force; (2) was necessary to repel; (3) *imminent* and *unlawful* force; and (4) the force exerted was not in excess of that which was necessary. In every case, such beliefs or perceptions were required to be reasonable, but they did not necessarily have to be right. To justify the use of deadly force in self-defense, defendants had to prove that the force used was proportionate to the initial force, and that the force was necessary to protect life, to escape serious bodily harm or rape or, in some states, to halt a robbery. In addition, the courts consistently ruled that the threat precipitating the force must have been immediate. For this reason, courts generally rejected battered woman's syndrome as an affirmative defense in cases where the alleged abuser was killed while sleeping. Most state statutes expressly prohibited the use of deadly force in the protection of property, and only permitted the use of force in cases in which the force used against the individual was unlawful. Thus, it could not be used against officers making a lawful arrest. For this reason, arguments of self-defense made by the surviving Branch Davidians after the killing of four

ATF agents at the Waco compound was rejected by the court. Finally, most traditional statutes included **duty to retreat clauses** that attached in any area outside of an individual's home. For example, the New Jersey Code of Criminal Justice, Section 2C: 3-4 provides:

> (b) The actor knows that he can avoid the necessity of using such force with complete safety by retreating or by surrendering possession of a thing to a person asserting a claim of right thereto or by complying with a demand that he abstain from any action which he has no duty to take, except that: (1) The actor is not obliged to retreat from his dwelling, unless he was the initial aggressor . . .

In such statutes, individuals in their domiciles are exempt from any legal duty to retreat. Such exemptions are known as **Castle Laws**. Most duty to retreat states and the federal government (through the Model Penal Code) adopted the Castle Doctrine.

In contemporary times, many states have greatly expanded the exemption traditionally reserved for private homes. In 2005, Florida enacted a **Stand Your Ground Law** which authorized the use of force by citizens when they were presented with force in any area outside the home where they had the legal authority to be. More specifically, Florida Statute, Title XLVI, Chapter 776.012 & 776.013 protected an individual from both civil liability and criminal penalty in cases in which deadly force was used in self-defense and, in some circumstances, granted him/her the presumption of reasonable fear—an element which traditionally would have been decided by a jury. Numerous states soon followed suit—greatly strengthening legal protections for those who use deadly force. Though controversial, states are increasingly recognizing an individual's right to protect themselves both inside and outside his/her home.

Miscellaneous Affirmative Defenses

While the previously discussed defenses have found some standing in criminal courts, others are little more than fantastical inventions by defense attorneys created in the face of seemingly insurmountable evidence. Most have attempted to demonstrate a "diminished capacity" at the time of the crime due to an external factor. Some of the more unique have included, but are not limited to:

- **The "Twinkie Defense"**—On November 27, 1978, Dan White, a conservative city supervisor, laid in wait for San Francisco Mayor George Moscone and Supervisor Harvey Milk. White was angered by the pair after Milk convinced Muscone to refuse to reinstate him as City Supervisor, a post he had resigned from just days earlier. He was particularly angry at Milk, who was appointed as chairman of the Streets and Transportation Committee upon White's request. When they arrived at work, White entered Moscone's office and shot him several times. He then entered Milk's office and dispatched him in the same fashion. Both victims suffered two gunshot wounds to the head at point blank range. During his trial, his defense team pointed to White's long career of service as a sergeant in the 101st Airborne, a police officer, and a fireman with the San Francisco Fire Department. Arguing that the act was completely uncharacteristic of his past behavior, the defense argued that White was suffering from a diminished capacity due to depression exacerbated by hid diet of junk foods and sugary drinks. The jury acquitted him on first-degree murder and convicted him of the lesser charge of voluntary manslaughter. As a result of the public outrage created by the lesser verdict and sentence

duty to retreat clause portion of a self-defense statute which requires individuals to retreat, if possible, from

Castle Laws or the Castle Doctrine portion of a self-defense statute which removes the duty to retreat before employing deadly force when one is in their home.

Stand Your Ground Law laws which authorize the use of force by citizens when they are presented with force in any area outside the home where they have the legal authority to be. Such laws are generally accompanied with a legal presumption of reasonable fear which must be overcome in legal proceedings.

STAND YOUR GROUND LAWS AND TRAYVON MARTIN

On February 26, 2012, a neighborhood watch captain, George Zimmerman, calls 911 to report a "suspicious person." Disregarding the instructions provided by the dispatcher, Zimmerman exits his vehicle and approaches Trayvon Martin. Soon thereafter, the pair struggle and shots are fired. Responding officers note that Zimmerman is bleeding from the nose and the back of the head and that Zimmerman admits to shooting Martin in self-defense. Medical reports received by investigators two weeks later confirm a laceration of the scalp and a fractured nose.

Initially, Sanford Police Department did not charge Zimmerman in connection with the death of Trayvon Martin stating that there was no evidence to suggest that Zimmerman's account of events was incorrect. Grassroots efforts at high schools and colleges coupled with actions by political groups, like the NAACP, result in heightened tensions in South Florida and beyond. The United States Justice Department and the FBI are directed to look into the matter as a civil rights case, and President Obama joins the fray stating "If I had a son he would look like Trayvon." Under intense pressure from various corners, Florida Governor Rick Scott appoints Angela B. Corey as the state attorney responsible for the investigation. In an unusual move, Corey bypasses the grand jury and Zimmerman is charged with second-degree murder nearly two months after the shooting.

Race was a central theme throughout the trial prosecutors (and protestors) painting Zimmerman and the community as racists who devalue African-American life. Circumstantial evidence presented against Zimmerman included, but was not limited to: testimony from Martin's parents; cell phone records for Zimmerman, Martin, and Martin's girlfriend; Zimmerman's college transcripts; testimony from a former college professor (via Skype); and, regarding Zimmerman's knowledge of Stand Your Ground laws. Direct evidence against Zimmerman was often conflicting with some witnesses claiming that Trayvon was the aggressor. The prosecution's star witness, Trayvon Martin, who was on the phone with him when Zimmerman

approached him, testified that Trayvon told her that "a creepy ass cracker" was following him, that she heard a man ask him what he was doing, that she instructed him to run, and that she heard a "hard-breathing man" in the background before getting cut off. She testified that when she called him back, he told her that he was back at his father's fiancee's house and that he thought that he had lost the man. Unfortunately for the prosecution, she proved to be a poor witness as her accounts varied. Her credibility took a further hit, after it was revealed that she had lied to the authorities about her whereabouts on the day of Martin's funeral.

Legally speaking, the prosecution had a very difficult standard to prove as Zimmerman's medical records noted both a fractured nose and lacerations of the scalp. In the absence of conclusive evidence as to who started the physical altercation, the jury of six women was forced to acquit him of second-degree murder. Their verdict was immediately greeted with outrage across the country.

The case remains controversial. Many public interest groups and law enforcement agencies continue to urge legislatures to remove Stand Your Ground Laws from state law, and Reverend Al Sharpton and Trayvon's parents have vowed to keep fighting until all officials supporting the law are removed. President Obama has even called on states to review their statutes. Currently, there are two dozen states with Stand Your Ground laws.

of 7 years, White committed suicide less than 2 years after serving his sentence. California eventually abandoned its "diminished capacity" law.

- **The "Nymphomaniac Defense"**—In the 1990s, housewife Kathy Willets and her husband, a Broward County Sheriff's Deputy, were charged with various charges of prostitution after it was discovered that Mrs. Willets was accepting money for sexual activities while her husband took notes (and sometimes video recordings) from the closet. The charges worried many prominent men in the Florida town as the pair

TEENAGERS, ENTITLEMENT, AND THE *AFFLUENZA* DEFENSE

As evidenced by the discussion, some affirmative defenses, like self-defense, have solid, logical foundations, while others appear to strain the boundaries of judicial incredulity. In most cases, fantastical explanations have been firmly rejected by judges and jurors alike. However, a recent case in Texas sent shockwaves across the nation as the public wondered if application of entitlement expectations had gone too far.

In 2013, youth minister Brian Jennings was driving home from his son's graduation party when he spotted Breanna Mitchell stranded on the side of the road with a flat tire. Stopping to help, he was soon joined by a woman and her daughter who had walked over from their home to assist. All four of them were struck and killed by a Ford F350 driven by Ethan Couch, a 16 year old whose blood alcohol was more than three times the legal limit. Nine other individuals were injured in the crash, including some of the seven passengers in Couch's truck.

During the criminal trial, testimony indicated that Couch and his passengers had been drinking at an unsupervised party at one of his family's homes. A psychologist for the defense argued that Couch suffered from poor parenting whose lack of restrictions or punishments had resulted in perceptions of entitlement and impunity. He argued that his parents' habit of using their power, influence, and money to extricate him from previous legal troubles had mentally handicapped Couch. The defense asked the judge to consider Texas statutes, which allowed her to consider diminished culpability and the prospects for reform in juvenile cases. The prosecuting attorney, on the other hand, asked the judge to end the cycle of entitlement, and sentence the 16 year old to prison. He warned that continuing to allow the family's wealth to insulate the teen from punishment would result in heightened perceptions of impunity and encourage future criminal behavior.

Couch faced a maximum sentence of 20 years for killing four people and injuring nine. Judge Jean Boyd accepted his guilty plea, and sentenced him to 10 years of probation. As a condition of his probation, Couch must complete a rehabilitation program at a private facility in California that offers equine sports, yoga, and massages. His family will pay for the treatment. Judge Jean Boyd will not be seeking reelection.

---

kept a "little black book" (aka The List) of both financial transactions and sexual performance. Among a moral crusader, the luminary was Fort Lauderdale Vice Mayor John Danziger, who had been successful in temporarily closing the city's strip clubs. The couple's attorney, Ellis Rubin, claimed that Kathy was suffering from nymphomania, and that the encounters were nothing more than "surrogate sex." The revelation that the Willets' had contacted various tabloid news programs to sell a videotaped liaison with Danziger suggested that the pair had other motives. Kathy eventually spent 8 months in prison for violating the conditions of her probation, and the couple enjoyed some brief celebrity on the stripper circuit after she posed for *Playboy*. Publication of "the list" occurred years after the courtroom drama.

- **The "Sleepwalking Defense"**—In 1997, Phoenix police responded to a 9-1-1 call from an individual that stated that he thought his neighbor, Scott Falater, was trying to drown his wife. Clad in pajamas with damp hair, Falater, a prominent member of his church, seemed confused when police knocked on his door shortly thereafter. A videotaped interview later taken in an interrogation room reveals a soft-spoken man who appears to have no explanation, or even knowledge, of the night's events. In his subsequent trial, Falater's defense team argued that Falater was sleepwalking when he stabbed his wife of 20 years more than 40 times and drowned her in the family pool. The defense presented evidence that Falater had a history of sleepwalking and that stress at work had resulted in serious sleep deprivation. Experts testified that violent acts, even those resulting in death, could be committed by sleepwalkers without their awareness. However, Falater's actions after the crime seemed to point to a degree of consciousness that belied this argument. He had removed his bloody clothes and placed them and the murder weapon in a plastic container before hiding them in the wheel well of his car. He had also bandaged his hand and quieted the family dog. He was convicted of first-degree murder. (It is important to note that other defendant's have achieved some success with the sleepwalking defense.)

▶ Plea Bargaining

plea bargaining
process by which a defendant pleads guilty or no contest in a criminal case in exchange for some agreement with the prosecutor as to the punishment generally, the prospect of a lighter sentence for the defendant and avoidance of a trial for the prosecutor engenders mutual interest in such bargaining.

No clear estimate of the frequency or effectiveness of plea bargaining in criminal cases exists, rather there are disparate findings in the numerous studies currently available. However, one common theme weaves through such studies: The likelihood of a plea is affected by various factors, including, but not limited to, jurisdiction, crime charged, corroborating evidence, number of defendants, victim characteristics, and nature of offense. **Plea bargaining** is a term used to describe the process through which an individual pleads guilty or no contest to a particular offense with some understanding of probable sentence. Numerous reasons are often present regarding why defendants enter into such plea agreements. First, plea bargaining is most likely to happen in instances in which the state's case is particularly strong, in which there are multiple counts, in which charges may be reduced, in which punishment might be diminished, and in which prosecutors agree not to charge others. On April 10, 2003, for example, Vincent "the Chin" Gigante finally dropped the crazy act he had adopted decades ago and pleaded guilty to various counts of racketeering. As part of his plea agreement, the government promised not to pursue charges against his family who had been assisting him in the obstruction of justice for years.[20]

Plea bargaining can happen at any stage of the court process, but judges are not bound by law or procedure to accept any particular plea. Prosecutors often engage in plea bargaining when their cases are not particularly strong or their caseload is overwhelming. Plea bargaining is beneficial to them because it assures them of adjudication, it allows them to clear multiple cases simultaneously, and it all but eliminates appeals. In any event, all pleas must be voluntary and intelligent,[21] and

---

⚖ CASE LAW

PLEA BARGAINING REQUIREMENTS

Although criminal defendants do not have the right to be offered a plea [*Weatherford v. Bursey*, 429 U.S. 545 (1977)] nor a federal right that a judge accepts it [*Santobello v. New York*, 404 U.S. 257 (1971)], the following rules apply regarding pleas and plea bargaining:

- Criminal defendants have the right to an attorney during the plea bargaining process if they would have been entitled to one during a trial on the same charges.
- Criminal defendants have the right to know the immigration consequences that result

from a guilty plea. [*Padilla v. Kentucky*, 130 S.Ct. 1473 (2010)]

- Criminal defendants have the right to effective counsel as measured by the *Strickland test*. [*Hill v. Lockhart*, 474 U.S. 52 (1985)]
- Criminal defendants have the right to know the charges and the elements of such. [*Henderson v. Morgan*, 426 U.S. 637 (1976)]
- Guilty pleas must be made knowingly and voluntarily. [*Boykin v. Alabama*, 395 U.S. 238 (1969)]

may be considered intelligent only when the accused first receives real notice of the nature of the charges against him.[22] Prior to accepting a guilty plea, the judge must first establish that the defendant is fully aware of the constitutional rights that are being waived. These include the privilege against self-incrimination; the right to a trial by jury; and the right to confront one's accuser. This is known as a **Boykin waiver**.[23] Some of the most notorious criminals in the United States have plea bargained, including Spiro Agnew, James Earl Ray, Jeffrey Dahmer, and Salvatore "Sammy the Bull" Gravano.

▶ Motions and Duties to Disclose

Like plea bargains, motions may be submitted by either party at any time during the criminal justice process after indictment. A **motion** is a formal request to the court to perform a certain action or make a ruling in a particular matter. Various motions are available to counsel. Too many exist for a complete accounting here, but they include: requests for physical or mental examinations, summary judgment, change of venue, and dismissal. However, some of the most common, and controversial, involve the suppression or discovery of evidence.

Motions to Suppress

Motions to suppress are requests by counsel to prevent the introduction of a specific piece of evidence. These motions often are grounded in the exclusionary rule and typically involve allegations of impropriety on the part of law enforcement. (The exclusionary rule will be discussed in detail in the next chapter.) However, such motions are not limited to this application. Under the Federal Rules of Criminal Procedure (Rule 12), there are two general categories of pretrial motions:

- Title IV, Rule 12(b)2—***Motions That May Be Made Before Trial***—*A party may raise by pretrial motion any defense, objection, or request that the court can determine without a trial of the general issue.*

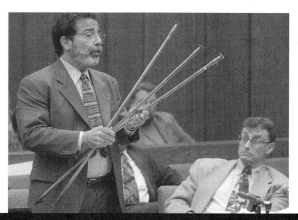

During the murder trial of Michael Peterson, testimony from a medical examiner was introduced which involved the death of Elizabeth Ratliff, the mother of Peterson's adopted daughters and Peterson's former neighbor in Germany. Although her death was originally ruled an accident by a German court, exhumation and subsequent examination of her remains implicated Peterson who had been both the last person seen with her and the person who discovered her body. Prosecutors alleged that Peterson murdered her in the same manner of his wife as both women were found at the bottom of a staircase. A motion to suppress the evidence was unsuccessful, and Peterson was convicted of bludgeoning his wife to death with a fireplace poker.

Boykin waiver a waiver required of all criminal defendants entering guilty pleas in which it must be demonstrated that they are intelligently and voluntarily waiving three important Constitutional rights: the privilege against self incrimination; the right to a trial by jury; and, the right to confront one's accuser.

motions a formal request submitted to the court that a specific judgment or order be made.

motion to suppress requests by counsel to prevent the introduction of a specific piece of evidence.

- Title IV, Rule 12(b)3—***Motions That Must Be Made Before Trial***—*The following must be raised before trial:*

  (A) *a motion alleging a defect in instituting the prosecution;*

  (B) *a motion alleging a defect in the indictment or information—but at any time while the case is pending, the court may hear a claim that the indictment or information fails to invoke the court's jurisdiction or to state an offense;*

  (C) *a motion to suppress evidence;*

  (D) *a Rule 14 motion to sever charges or defendants; and,*

  (E) *a Rule 16 motion for discovery.*

The Federal Rules and most states also allow defendant's to request notice of the government's intent to use any evidence that the defendant would be entitled to discover under law immediately after the arraignment or preliminary hearing. In state cases, suppression hearings are held after the preliminary hearing for two primary reasons: (1) Because not all preliminary hearings result in a trial, the state saves administrative costs when cases are not bound over for trial; and (2) motions to suppress are often filed in response to information revealed during the preliminary hearing.

Motions to suppress may be filed in cases in which a particular piece of evidence is considered unduly prejudicial. This is not uncommon in cases involving uncharged crimes. The 2003 North Carolina case of William Peterson is an example. Peterson,

 APPLICATION OF LAW

A BRADY VIOLATION AND A WRONGFUL CONVICTION

On June 30, 1995, arson investigators in Indiana arrived at the trailer home of Kristine Bunch. Inside the home they found the body of her 3-year-old child. Almost immediately, the state arson investigator concluded that the fire had started in two separate locations and had been intentionally set with a liquid accelerant. He later testified that one of the fires started by the front door and the other in the child's bedroom. His testimony was corroborated by a forensic analyst with the U.S. Bureau of Alcohol, Tobacco, and Firearms (ATF) who testified that he had identified a "heavy petroleum distillate" in flooring samples taken from both areas. The defense countered with their own arson expert who testified that the cause of the fire should be classified "as undetermined" as there was a "probability" that it was accidental.

On March 4, 1996, the jury found the 22-year-old pregnant woman guilty of murder and arson. She was subsequently sentenced to concurrent terms of incarceration of 60 years for the murder and 50 years for the arson. In 1998, her murder conviction was affirmed by the Indiana Supreme Court who noted the presence of a heavy petroleum distillate in several locations. However, the court vacated her arson conviction as it violated the double jeopardy protections in the Fifth Amendment.

In 2006, Bunch's case was brought to the attention of the Center on Wrongful Convictions who contacted three fire forensic experts who concurred that the prosecution's witnesses in the case were probably incorrect. Subpoenaing ATF files from the original investigation,

the Center received previously undisclosed documents showing that "no heavy petroleum distillate had been found anywhere in the trailer." In fact, the only accelerant found in the home was kerosene in the living room carpet where the family used a kerosene heater in the winter. All samples taken from the child's bedroom were completely negative. Such information was highly exculpatory, and had been withheld from Bunch's trial counsel. Bunch's appellate team immediately filed an amended petition for post-conviction relief. The request was granted, and Decatur County Circuit Court Judge, who had presided over the original trial, agreed to hold an evidentiary hearing.

In 2009, Judge Westhafer reviewed the new evidence in the case, including the ATF documents that clearly represented a Brady violation. After 9 months, Westhafer denied post-conviction relief stating that while Bunch "had new resources available to her at the post-conviction hearing, new experts do not create new evidence. The issues raised and the conclusions reached—while packaged differently—remain basically the same." He concluded by saying that he did not believe that the ATF documents would have altered the jury's verdict. Appealing the decision, Bunch's team presented the case to the Court of Appeals of Indiana who ultimately reversed. This reversal was upheld by the Indiana Supreme Court. Kristine Bunch was released from prison 17 years, 1 month, and 16 days after she was arrested for the fire that killed her child.

charged in the bludgeoning death of his wife, argued that his wife sustained her injuries by falling down the stairs. Unfortunately for him, he had made a similar claim in the death of the mother of two of his adopted children years earlier. Although he filed a motion to suppress testimony regarding the earlier incident, the judge permitted said evidence. Peterson was summarily convicted. (On December 20, 2013, the North Carolina Supreme Court granted Peterson a new trial based on the fact that SBI blood analyst Duane Deaver gave false and misleading testimony at Peterson's original trial).

Motions to Discover

Motions to discover are common in criminal cases, although they are often pro forma—when both sides understand the obligation to disclose information. These motions become necessary: (1) when the rules are not clearly established; (2) when one side believes that the information is privileged; or (3) when attorneys have an antagonistic relationship. In the most general sense, **discovery** refers to the pretrial process during which information is exchanged between opposing parties. This process allows the parties to identify potential witnesses, evidence, and strategies. Traditionally, the duty of discovery rested solely on the side of the prosecution.

The Federal Rules of Evidence and the Supreme Court require prosecuting attorneys to share evidence to be presented upon request by the defense. Such responsibility includes disclosure of evidence contained within the defendant's case file and any information held in police files.[24] It is important to note that prosecuting attorneys must share their information, including information and evidence favorable to the defendant, regardless of the presence or absence of defense requests for such. The duty to share exculpatory evidence is known as the **Brady rule**. However, the Court has ruled that such prosecutorial responsibility does not extend to the introduction of exculpatory evidence during grand jury proceedings. In that,

> . . . requiring the prosecutor to present exculpatory as well as inculpatory evidence would alter the grand jury's historical role, transforming it from an accusatory body that sits to assess whether there is adequate basis for bringing a criminal charge into an adjudicatory body that sits to determine guilt or innocence. Because it has always been thought sufficient for the grand jury to hear only the prosecutor's side, and, consequently that the suspect has no right to present, and the grand jury no obligation to consider, exculpatory evidence, it would be incompatible with the traditional system to impose upon the prosecutor a legal obligation to prevent such evidence.[25]

In addition, the Court has ruled that there is no fundamental right to production of written statements, memorandums, and personal recollections of opposing counsel. This mandate, known as the **work-product doctrine**, was initially recognized by the Court in *Hickman v. Taylor*.[26]

motion to discover a request to the court to order the opposing party to produce.

discovery the pretrial process during which information is exchanged between opposing parties.

Brady rule judicial ruling requiring prosecutors to share all exculpatory evidence with the defense, including any information that may tend to lessen culpability or mitigate subsequent punishment.

work-product doctrine protects materials prepared in anticipation of a legal proceeding. Rooted in *Hickman v. Taylor*, 329 U.S. 495 (1947).

 CLARIFICATION OF CONCEPTS

COMMON ITEMS IN DISCOVERY

While state statutes vary, the following items are usually included in disclosure of information in a criminal case.

- Witness lists identifying all witnesses to be called with the exception of the defendant
- Results of laboratory or scientific testing to be introduced in court

- Statements of co-conspirators
- Recorded statements of witnesses to be called
- Itemized list of physical evidence
- Expert witness reports

PROSECUTORIAL DISCLOSURE OBLIGATIONS AND THE *BRADY* RULE

In *Brady v. Maryland* [373 U.S. 83 (1963)], the Court evaluated whether a prosecutor has a duty to disclose exculpatory evidence upon request. In this case, Brady and an accomplice were convicted of first-degree murder and sentenced to death. In preparation for the trial, Brady's attorney requested all extrajudicial statements made by his accomplice. The pair were tried separately with Brady's trial occurring first. During his trial, Brady took the stand and admitted his participation in the crime but claimed that his companion did the actual killing. During his closing arguments, Brady's attorney conceded that his client was guilty of first-degree murder, but asked the jury to render a verdict *without capital punishment*. He was subsequently convicted and sentenced to death. After an appeal to the Maryland Court of Appeals was denied, it was revealed that the prosecution had withheld a confession from Brady's companion in which he expressly admitted being responsible for the killing.

The Court ruled that suppression of evidence favorable to an accused who has requested it violates the Constitutional right to due process "where the evidence is material either to guilt or to punishment, irrespective of the good faith or bad faith of the prosecution." In their opinion, the Court relied upon *Mooney v. Holohan* [294 U.S. 103 (1935)] and *Pyle v. Kansas* [317 U.S. 213 (1942)]—both of which involved the deliberate introduction of perjured testimony by the prosecution.

> *The principle of Mooney v. Holohan is not punishment of society for misdeeds of a prosecutor but avoidance of an unfair trial to the accused. Society wins not only when the guilty are convicted by when criminal trials are fair; our system of the administration of justice suffers when any accused in treated unfairly ... a prosecution that withholds evidence on demand of an accused which, if made available, would tend to exculpate hi or reduce the penalty helps shape a trial that bears heavily on the defendant. That casts the prosecutor in the role of an architect of a proceeding that does not comport with standards of justice . . .*

While *Brady* only extended the right to exculpatory evidence upon request of the defense, subsequent case law has clarified the contours of the state's disclosure obligations. In *Giglio v. United States* [405 U.S. 150 (1972)], the Court ruled that in cases where the reliability of a witness may determine guilt or innocence, the suppression of evidence which impugned his/her credibility constitutes a due process violation. Thus, *Giglio* extended the Rule to include impeachment, as well as exculpatory, evidence. In *Unites States v. Agurs* [427 U.S. 97 (1976)], the Court shifted the Court's focus from prosecutorial misconduct or misrepresentation to injury suffered by the defendant as a result of material exculpatory evidence.[27] As a result, the basis for evaluating the injury suffered and the materiality of the evidence came to the forefront of *Brady* cases. In *Agurs*, the Court found that "implicit in the requirement of materiality is a concern that the suppressed evidence might have affected the outcome of the trial." Thus, a due process violation would occur in cases where prosecutors failed to disclose material evidence that could have altered the verdict whether or not such evidence was requested by the defense. The standard of materiality to be applied in appeals based on nondisclosure was established in *United States v. Bagley* [473 U.S. 667 (1985)]. The *Bagley standard* of *reasonable probability* has been applied to other areas of legal inquiry.

Summarily, there are three primary requirements for successful *Brady* challenges. (1) There is a prosecutorial obligation of disclosure which exists irrespective of a request by the defendant; (2) which includes all impeachment and exculpatory evidence; (3) provided that there is a *reasonable probability* that the result of the proceeding would have been different had it been disclosed to the defense.

Historically, a lawyer is an officer of the court and is bound to work for the advancement of justice while faithfully protecting the rightful interests of his clients. In performing his various duties, however, it is essential that a lawyer work with a certain degree of privacy, free from unnecessary intrusion by opposing parties and their counsel [329 U.S. 495, 511]. Proper preparation of a client's case demands that he assemble information, sift what he considers to be the relevant from the irrelevant facts, prepare his legal theories and plan his strategy without undue and needless interference. That is the historical and the necessary way in which lawyers act within the framework of our system of jurisprudence to promote justice and to protect their clients' interests. This work is reflected, of course, in interviews, statements, memoranda, correspondence, briefs, mental impressions, personal beliefs, and countless other tangible and intangible ways— aptly though roughly termed by the Circuit Court of Appeals in this case (153 F.2d 212, 223) as the "Work product of the lawyer." Were such materials open to opposing counsel on mere demand, much of what is now put down in writing would remain unwritten. An attorney's thoughts, heretofore inviolate, would not be his own. Inefficiency, unfairness, and sharp practices would inevitably develop in the giving of legal advice and in the preparation of cases for trial. The effect on the legal profession would be demoralizing. And the interests of the clients and the cause of justice would be poorly served.

Although many states have established parameters for the disclosure of evidence by the prosecutor, the Supreme Court has ruled that the name of an informant must be disclosed when the true identity of the person is necessary for the defendant's case even if a risk exists of harm to the informant. As stated, the burden of disclosure traditionally rested on the shoulders of the prosecutor. However, the contemporary trend is toward a system of reciprocal discovery, in which both sides must share information. In some jurisdictions, for example, a defendant must disclose any alibi witness that they intend to call.

grand jury an investigative body of impartial citizens selected to hear evidence of criminal allegations presented by the state to determine whether sufficient probable cause exists to pursue trial. Grand juries may compel witnesses to appear at the hearings, which may be held in secret and generally are not attended by the defendant.

true bill a grand jury finding that sufficient evidence exists to support the claim that a person more likely than not committed a crime and should be indicted and prosecuted.

▶ Preliminary Hearings and Grand Juries

The Fifth Amendment to the Constitution provides that "no person shall be held to answer for a capital, or otherwise infamous crime, unless on a presentment or indictment of a Grand Jury." In **grand jury** systems, a panel of citizens is selected to hear evidence of criminal allegations presented by the state to determine whether sufficient probable cause exists to return a **true bill**, a finding of truth to the allegations. Upon such a finding, the grand jury then issues a formal charge against

 CASE LAW

THE RIGHT TO A GRAND JURY AND *HURTADO V. CALIFORNIA* [110 U.S. 516 (1884)]

A little more than a century after the signing of the U.S. Constitution, the Supreme Court refused to extend the guarantee of a grand jury to state courts. Instead, the Court held that states could develop their own preliminary proceedings. To wit,

No individual or body of men has a discretionary or arbitrary power to commit any person to prison; no man can be restrained of his liberty, be prevented from removing himself from place to place as he chooses, be compelled to go to a place contrary to his inclination, or be in any way imprisoned or confined, unless by virtue of the expressed laws of the land.' *Tried by these principles, we are unable to say that the substitution for a presentment or indictment by a grand jury of the proceeding

by information after examination and commitment by a magistrate, certifying to the probable guilt of the defendant, with the right on his part to the aid of counsel, and to the cross-examination of the witnesses produced for the prosecution, is not due process of law. It is, as we have seen, an ancient proceeding at common law, which might include every case of an offense of less grade than a felony, except misprision of treason; and in every circumstance of its administration, as authorized by the statute of California, it carefully considers and guards the substantial interest of the prisoner. It is merely a preliminary proceeding, and can result in no final judgment, except as the consequence of a regular judicial trial, conducted precisely as in cases of indictments.

indictment a formal charge against a defendant that initiates a criminal proceeding based upon a formal, written accusation of a criminal offense presented to a judicial official upon affirmation of a grand jury.

information a formal accusation of a criminal offense made by a public official following a demonstration of probable cause in a preliminary hearing.

the defendant in the form of an **indictment**. This is similar to the issuance of an **information** immediately following a finding of probable cause in a preliminary hearing. (Grand juries may also issue presentments, in which they make criminal allegations on their own.) Grand juries can be held before or after a suspect is taken into custody. While grand juries are required in federal court, the Supreme Court has ruled that the Fifth Amendment does not require the same of states.

In most states, a preliminary hearing is conducted soon after the arraignment or initial appearance (terminology varies by state). Preliminary hearings are often reserved for felony cases only. In the most general sense, this hearing is often a mini-trial in which a judge determines whether sufficient evidence exists to proceed to trial. Such determination uses a probable cause standard, evaluating whether there is probable cause to believe that a crime has been committed and that the defendant committed the crime. Both sides have the right to present their cases during this phase, but many defense attorneys will simply cross-examine the witnesses and any evidence presented by the prosecutor. The rules of evidence are not as strict during this phase. Both preliminary hearings and grand juries may be characterized as probable cause hearings.

Jury

petit jury body of dispassionate citizens that determines guilt in a criminal trial (a "small" jury, as opposed to a "grand" jury). In civil cases, the petit jury helps determine fiduciary responsibility.

The Sixth Amendment to the U.S. Constitution provides that all criminal defendants in the United States shall have the right to a ". . . speedy and public trial, by an impartial jury. . . ." Such a jury is known as a **petit jury**, and it may be used in criminal and civil cases. In criminal cases, the petit jury is the body that determines guilt. Although not common in criminal cases, such right may be waived. Unlike grand juries that may convene in private and are largely accusatory in nature, the petit jury is a public institution that determines guilt after a full and impartial view of the evidence.

A jury may be characterized as a trier of fact. Before the mid-nineteenth century, American juries were responsible for both fact-finding and for the application of law (early American jurists were laypersons). As a matter of fact, formal legal education in the United States did not begin until the late eighteenth century. Thus, only the privileged few who had been fortunate enough to attend the English Inns of Court had specialized knowledge. Consequently, the notion abounded during colonial times that jurors could set aside or otherwise disregard a judge's direction. During this period, directed verdicts were common. Today, juries are simply tasked with evaluating the believability of evidence, applying the law that the judge has provided, and determining whether the prosecution has met its burden of proof.

▨ IN SEARCH OF HISTORY: THE TRIAL OF WILLIAM PENN

In 1670, William Penn was formally charged in London for preaching to an unlawful assembly. By all accounts, such charges were levied at Penn because he failed to practice the same faith as the King of England. Although they had been instructed by the court to find Penn and his co-defendant guilty as charged, the jury returned with a verdict of not guilty. The court refused to accept their verdict and demanded that they return to deliberations. This process was repeated numerous times with the same result. During this process, the court punished the jury who were sequestered and deprived of food, water, and the basic necessities of life. And, yet, the jury refused to render the verdict that the court demanded. Finally, the jury refused to deliberate any further. The court fined each of them and ordered them imprisoned until the fine was paid. In the United States, the Sixth Amendment guarantees that jurors cannot be punished for failing to render a verdict desirable to the court.

Although most contemporary juries consist of twelve jurors, the Supreme Court has ruled that six is sufficient.[28] Jury selection is initiated by the composition of a Master List, which includes registered voters within a jurisdiction. Individuals may be excused legally before the trial begins for various reasons, including, but not limited to, disability, loss of wages, and military service. However, individuals who are not excused in this manner are subjected to qualification by the state and the defense. This process, known as **voir dire**, involves the questioning of potential jurors and assurance of legal standards. For example, potential jurors must be at least 18 years of age, must be jurisdictional residents, etc. In federal court (and in some states), the judge conducts this qualifying and questioning. Most often, this process consists primarily of questioning by counsel, and jurors may be excused from participation for a variety of reasons during this period. Both sides are granted an unlimited number of challenges for cause. Such challenges include any reasonable demonstration of bias, and both sides can excuse potential jurors because of this. For example, a defense attorney might excuse a member of the Ku Klux Klan for cause if the accused is African American. Challenges also may be used when it is demonstrated that a potential juror has a preconceived perception of guilt. Such challenges are limitless because the Sixth Amendment guarantees the right to an impartial jury for all. Conversely, whenever the rationale for excusal is not articulated, counsel must use a peremptory challenge. Although the exact number of peremptory challenges varies by state, the federal and state courts have established a finite number in all jurisdictions. In criminal cases, however, counsel must demonstrate that the issuance of such challenges is not based on race.[29]

voir dire the preliminary questioning of potential jurors or witnesses to ascertain competency to give or hear evidence.

 CASE LAW

PEREMPTORY CHALLENGES AND DISCRIMINATION

The Fourteenth Amendment to the Constitution was ratified on July 9, 1868. Among other protections, the Amendment granted citizenship to "all persons born or naturalized in the United States," forbade states from denying any individual "life, liberty, or property without due process of law," and required states to provide all persons "within its jurisdiction the equal protection of the laws." Theoretically, the Amendment immediately extended the protection of civil rights to all Americans. However, a study of case law indicates a pattern of inconsistency of application in criminal courts. The practice of excluding African Americans from jury panels is illustrative of same.

Eleven years after ratification of the Fourteenth Amendment, the Supreme Court struck down a West Virginia statute that only allowed white males to serve as jurors. In their decision, the Court firmly denounced the law stating:

The very fact that colored people are singled out and expressly denied by a statute all rights to participate in the administration of the law . . . is practically a brand upon them, affixed by the law, an assertion of their inferiority, and a stimulant to that race prejudice which is an impediment to securing to individual of the race that equal justice which the law aims to secure to all others. [*Strauder v. West Virginia*, 100 U.S. 303 (1879)

In the 1960s the Court appeared to have lost its fervor in this regard when they considered the case of an African-American male who was sentenced to death for rape in a County which had not had an African-American juror in more than a decade. In *Swain v. Alabama* [380 U.S. 202 (1965)], a case in which all six of the potential jurors who were African American were peremptorily struck by the prosecutor, the Court ruled that "the prosecutor's striking . . . under the peremptory challenge system, which permits a challenge without a reason stated, does not constitute denial of equal protection of the laws." They further ruled that a defendant is "not constitutionally entitled to a proportionate number of his race on the trial jury or jury panel."

(continued)

More than 100 years after the *Strauder* decision, the Court returned to its underlying rationale in *Batson v. Kentucky* [476 U.S. 79 (1986)] noting that "the Equal Protection Clause forbids the prosecutor to challenge potential jurors solely on account of their race or on the assumption that black jurors as a group" will be unable to be impartial. Furthermore, the Court held that in cases where the defendant may make a prima facie case demonstrating exclusion based on race, prosecutors must provide *race-neutral* reasons justifying the challenge. *Batson* emphasized the role of the trial court in identifying purposeful discrimination. In further rulings, the Court has held that the reasons articulated by the state are subject to federal review [*Miller-El v. Dretke*, 545 U.S. 231 (2005)] and the standard for review is substantial. [*Snyder v. Louisiana*, 552 U.S. 472 (2008)]

sequestration the isolation of a jury from the public or the separation of witnesses to ensure the integrity of testimony.

Once a jury is impaneled, the trial court judge may decide that the case characteristics are such that it is necessary to isolate the jury. **Sequestration** means that the jury is physically separated from the public for a specified proceeding or period of time. For example, jurors may be sequestered during the sentencing phase, deliberations, meal breaks, or the duration of the trial. Although not uncommon, jury sequestration for the length of a trial is not the norm because of the hardships associated with the physical separation of spouses, families, work, and the like—jurors in the 1994 O. J. Simpson murder trial, for example, were sequestered for more than 9 months. Sequestration is most often employed in high-profile cases in which the media has displayed a heightened interest in the people, events, and proceedings of the case. It has been used in organized crime cases as well, to protect witnesses from corruption or harm. Despite these instances, sequestration is rarely necessary, and admonitions from judges regarding the sanctity of the process and the responsibility of jurors to remain free from prejudice and persuasion usually considered to be sufficient precautions by judicial officials. During the trial of Jodi Arias, the judge denied a defense motion to sequester jurors for the remainder of the trial even after a juror was removed and videos emerged online which showed her parents telling authorities that she had mental problems.

opening statements initial presentation made by counsel in a criminal trial regarding material things that will be introduced during the trial. Such statements do not constitute evidence, and conjecture is generally not allowed.

case-in-chief portion of a trial in which the party with the burden of proof presents its case by calling witnesses and presenting all manner of evidence to prove its case, including direct (eye witness testimony), circumstantial, demonstrative, real, testimonial, and scientific (expert).

Opening Statements

After jury selection has been completed, counsel for both sides will formally introduce their respective cases to the panel. In the most general sense, **opening statements** are a presentation of what the particular side will prove during the trial. They do not constitute evidence. Technically, opening statements are not considered an argument. Rather, they are an attempt by counsel to completely summarize the evidence that is to be introduced. In reality, however, opening statements are often used to craft a story and garner sympathy for either side's cause. Because the process does not include the actual proffer of evidence, extraneous facts and circumstances that would be considered irrelevant during the **case-in-chief** (the portion of the trial whereby the party with the burden of proof presents its case) would be admissible. Such information might be included by the prosecution to humanize the victim or by the defense to humanize the defendant. For example, a prosecutor might describe Ms. Jones as a widow with four children who volunteered at the burn unit at the local hospital, but this information would not be necessarily relevant to the case (unless such circumstances precipitated her specific victimization, such as if she had been murdered in front of her four children in the hospital parking lot). The inclusion of these details is often designed to evoke sympathy from the jury. Because the burden of proof remains on the state, the prosecution is required to present its case first, and this order remains throughout the trial.

Although no evidence is introduced during this period, the importance of opening statements cannot be overstated. It is the first chance for counsel to capture the attention and sympathy of the jury, and a measure of oratory skill is often a prerequisite to success in many cases. Individuals who have honed this courtroom skill are often characterized as performers or entertainers. Some are considered legendary, including F. Lee Bailey, Johnnie Cochran, Gerry Spence, and Richard "Racehorse" Haynes. Indeed, many argue that such skill obscures the truth and often leads to an outcome inconsistent with the realities of the evidence.

Presentation of Evidence

Just as prosecutors are legally bound to issue the initial salvo in opening statements, they are similarly obligated throughout the trial. As such, they initiate the presentment of evidence. Presentment begins when the first witness is called and ends when the prosecution rests. Evidence presented speaks to the "truth" of the calling party's argument and can range from eyewitness testimony to scientific tests. All manner of evidence may be contained within the case-in-chief, including, but not limited to, direct, circumstantial, demonstrative, real, testimonial, and scientific. As such, the presentation of the case-in-chief can be an arduous process, especially when the case involves contradictory stories, numerous witnesses, complicated legal issues, or complex scientific analysis. In the O. J. Simpson trial, for example, the prosecution's case-in-chief took more than 5 months to present. Upon conclusion of its case-in-chief, the prosecution rests. At that time, the defense has the opportunity to present its case-in-chief. Technically speaking, the defense does not have the obligation to present evidence because the defendant is considered innocent until proven guilty. While defense counsel may rest without calling a single witness or argue that the prosecution failed to meet its burden of proof, this is an exceptionally rare approach and, generally, is not considered good practice.

Once the defense has rested, the prosecution is permitted to call witnesses or introduce evidence to rebut material presented by the defense. This is called **rebuttal** or case-in-rebuttal. For the purposes of fairness, the defense is given a similar opportunity to refute or disprove evidence presented by the prosecution during rebuttal. This is called **rejoinder** or case-in-rejoinder. This process continues until both sides are satisfied or until the court concludes that the proof and counterproof is redundant, immaterial, or irrelevant. Evidence contained within the rebuttal-rejoinder period is narrower in scope than that presented during the case-in-chief, because it must be directed at information presented by the adverse party during the most recent proffering. As such, each subsequent rebuttal-rejoinder period should be shorter than the last.

In all of the above processes, the questioning of witnesses is further guided by procedural rules. During the case-in-chief, counsel engages in the direct examination of those witnesses it has called. **Direct examination** is the questioning of a witness by the calling party. Leading questions, or those that suggest a preferred response, are not allowed during this period. Answers to questions posed during direct are often narrative in nature. An example of a proper question might be: "Where were you on the night of August 25, 2013?"; as opposed to "What happened on August 25, 2013 after the defendant shot the victim?" that may be intended to elicit the same information but would be considered improper.

The process of **cross-examination**, on the other hand, involves the questioning of a witness by opposing counsel and commences immediately after the direct examination of said witness. Cross-examination is the cornerstone of the Sixth Amendment and has a long history. John Henry Wigmore, the preeminent

rebuttal an attempt to disprove or contradict other evidence or presumptions through the offering of countervailing proof or argument.

rejoinder a defendant's response to a prosecution claim during rebuttal.

direct examination interrogation of a witness by attorneys by the side that called him or her to testify during which witnesses are asked open ended questions designed to elicit a narrative response in which the witness competently recounts the events in question, such as "Where were you on the night of August 25, 2012?".

cross-examination questioning of a witness by opposing counsel; occurs after direct examination and is designed to ensure the veracity of testifying witnesses, to show the facts in the most favorable light to the cross-examiner's side, and sometimes, to impeach the witness.

scholar on evidence, has credited the practice of cross-examination to Socrates. To wit,

> . . . even during those thirty days of imprisonment that elapsed before the fatal cup of hemlock was handed to him, and while he sat in chains, conversing with his disciples in those masterpieces of dialogue transmitted to us by Plato, we find him still shrewdly and genially wielding that wonderful weapon of cross-examination, in discussing the immortality of the human soul.[30]

Questions asked during cross-examination are limited to the scope of the direct examination. Thus, only questions directed at issues that were introduced during direct examination are admissible. Although often coached by the calling party before the trial itself, witnesses sometimes "open the door" for opposing counsel, which means that the witness reveals something that allows opposing counsel to pursue an avenue of questioning that would have not been available but for the witness's testimony. While leading questions may be asked during this period, argumentative questions, or questions that are harassing in nature, may not. In any event, the judge plays an important role in the questioning of witnesses. However, it is the responsibility of counsel to raise objections where necessary, thereby preserving the record for appeal. Without the objection of counsel, appellate issues regarding said questioning will not be considered. This is known as the **contemporaneous objection rule**.

The impeachment of witnesses (discussed in greater detail in Chapter 8) may occur during cross-examination. This is an attempt by opposing counsel to lessen the witness's credibility. Various strategies for impeachment exist, including, but not limited to, showing that the witness is lying, demonstrating that the witness is a felon, and disclosing that the witness is being rewarded or being allowed to avoid punishment for his or her testimony.

Like the period of rebuttal-rejoinder discussed previously, each side has the right to continue questioning witnesses until satisfied or until the court determines that the testimony is redundant, immaterial, or irrelevant. Thus, the calling party may engage in a redirect examination of the witness immediately following cross, and so on. Redirect is often necessary to repair the credibility of the witness.

Closing Arguments

At the conclusion of the presentation of evidence, both sides offer closing arguments. In the most general sense, a **closing argument** is a summary of the case that was presented. During the process, both sides summarize the case and the evidence in a way that best serves their client. No new evidence may be introduced during closing arguments, and objections may be raised whenever counsel misstates the evidence. It is the responsibility of the prosecution to overcome all reasonable doubt—by restating the evidence and disproving alternative scenarios introduced by the defense. Conversely, the defense seeks to establish reasonable doubt. Defense counsel does not have the responsibility to prove reasonable doubt because the defendant is cloaked in the presumption of innocence, but most defendants will aggressively attack the prosecution's case during closing arguments. Because the prosecution has the burden of proof, it is given the opportunity to offer additional closing arguments after the defense has concluded. Thus, the prosecution goes first and last during closing arguments.

Instructions to the Jury

Immediately preceding deliberations by the jury and immediately following closing arguments, the judge will offer instructions to the jury. Essentially, the

contemporaneous objection rule
legal requirement that motions to suppress evidence be presented simultaneous to the question asked, the answer give, or the admission of evidence.

closing argument
the concluding statement of each party's counsel which reiterates the important arguments and evidence most favorable to their case. Occurring after the presentment of evidence, closing arguments may not contain new information.

judge arms the jury with the information necessary to evaluate the unlawfulness of the behavior in question and the culpability of the accused. While instructions will vary based on case characteristics, some general principals apply in all cases. The judge must include all applicable substantive principles of law, definitions of standards of proof, and allocation of burden. In addition, jury instructions typically include standard admonitions regarding the process and conduct of deliberations and the definition of evidence. The judge may further instruct the jury to disregard particular pieces of evidence that were arbitrated during the trial and dismissed from consideration. Finally, the judge may issue limiting instructions to define the parameters in which some evidence may be considered. In most cases, both the state and defense counsel are permitted to submit potential jury instructions to the judge and to opposing counsel before the conclusion of the presentation of evidence. The issuance of instructions to the jury by judges is extremely important because mistakes may constitute reversible error. Capital cases require instructions that emphasize the gravity of the crime.

Deliberations

After the evidence has been presented and the judge has issued instructions, the jury is transformed from a passive observer to an active participant in the criminal justice process. Before this time, jurors are not permitted to discuss the case, either among themselves or with others. However, this changes once jurors are given the case by the judge and retire to a private area. Their first action as a group is to elect a jury foreperson. This person is responsible for maintaining control during the deliberations, which are held in secrecy, and for either announcing the verdict or delivering it to the judge. The assurance of confidentiality is necessary for impartiality because it encourages the free flow of information in a democratic society. Questions that arise during deliberations may be submitted to the judge for consideration. When this occurs, the judge will summon both sides for a reading of the question. In most instances, questions are addressed through the rereading of the jury instructions or portions of the transcript.

In the federal system (and in most states), felony verdicts are required to be unanimous, although the Court has upheld the right of the states to determine level of consensus in noncapital cases.[31] If deliberations stall or reach an impasse, the court and counsel shall be informed. At this time, the judge may issue a dynamite charge. Such a charge is issued usually in the form of an admonition from the judge that encourages the jury to continue their work and reminds them of the time and expense already expended in this endeavor. In addition, the admonition speaks directly to those individuals who hold the minority opinion and encourages them to consider their position and that of their fellow jurors and to entertain the notion that their position might be in error. Many defendants object to such a charge, arguing that it violates due process and unfairly disadvantages them. Indeed, some studies on hung juries indicate that the majority of them favored conviction. Regardless, dynamite charges are used most often in criminal courtrooms. Juries that remain deadlocked and are incapable of rendering a final verdict are declared hung. A hung jury, one that fails to reach a verdict, results in a mistrial.

A **mistrial** occurs when a final disposition of guilt has not been established. Although mistrials are often caused by hung juries, other reasons and circumstances occur to cause one to be declared, including, but not limited to, prosecutorial misconduct, corruption of the actors, juror impropriety, or other actions that might unfairly disadvantage the accused.

mistrial a trial that ends without a final disposition of guilt being established.

directed verdict
a verdict of acquittal which results in cases where a judge instructs the jury to acquit the defendant due to the prosecution's failure to meet the required standard of proof.

mitigating factors
case characteristics that tend to reduce the culpability of the defendant and the applicable sentence. Some common mitigating factors include, but are not limited to, age of the defendant, intoxication level, absence of criminal history, childhood victimization, and cooperation with authorities.

aggravating factors   case characteristics that tend to increase the defendant's culpability and subsequent sentence. They include, but are not limited to, past criminal history, dismemberment of body, and flight from prosecution.

In cases in which the jury has achieved the requisite consensus, the verdict is then read in open court by the court clerk, the judge, or the jury foreperson. A polling of the jury is often requested, and jurors may be required to announce their individual verdict. This assures that the process was fair and that due process was conducted. In criminal cases, possible verdicts are limited to guilty, not guilty, or not guilty by reason of affirmative defense.

Findings of guilty may result in a direct appeal. Unlike traditional types of appeals (discussed later in the chapter), a direct appeal is made by the defense attorney to the trial judge. In essence, a direct appeal is a request by the defense to set aside or reverse the jury's verdict. Although some direct appeals have worked in the past, it is rare for a trial judge to set aside the jury's verdict. Indeed, it happens only when the judge believes that the jury was unreasonable or that reversible legal error occurred during the trial. A direct appeal is separate from a **directed verdict** in which the judge instructs the jury to render a verdict of acquittal due to the prosecution's failure to meet the required standard of proof. It may be done independently by a trial court judge or could be prompted by a motion filed by the defense.

Sentencing

Upon the pronouncement of a "not guilty" verdict, the court will enter a judgment of acquittal and the defendant will be released immediately from custody. A "guilty" verdict, however, will result in the imposition of sentencing. Sentences for felonious conduct range from probation to execution. In noncapital cases, the court will often impose sentencing immediately. Capital cases often have a secondary process or sentencing phase in which mitigating and aggravating factors are presented to the jury. **Mitigating factors** are those case characteristics that tend to reduce the culpability of the defendant and the applicable sentence. Some common mitigating factors include, but are not limited to, age of the defendant, intoxication level, absence of criminal history, childhood victimization, and cooperation with authorities. Conversely, **aggravating factors** are those case characteristics that tend to increase the defendant's culpability and subsequent sentence. They include, but are not limited to, past criminal history, dismemberment of body, and flight from prosecution. Judges may not impose any punishment they desire. The imposition of punishment must fall within the parameters of that jurisdiction and the U.S. Constitution. Most states have adopted or modified the Federal Sentencing Guidelines, which carefully delineates the range of sanctions available and justifications for departure.

 APPLICATION OF LAW

JUDICIAL DISCRETION, DIRECTED VERDICTS, AND A MURDERING AU PAIR

Louise Woodward, a young nanny from England, was convicted of second-degree murder in the shaking death of Matthew Eappen, the infant son of a pair of New England doctors. The case evoked strong feelings across the country and led to heated debates about the role of working women. Initially, Judge Hiller B. Zobel imposed the mandatory sentence of life in prison. Weeks later, the same judge set aside the jury's verdict at the request of the defense, reducing the charge from second-degree murder to involuntary manslaughter. He also reduced her sentence from life in prison to time served, which outraged many individuals across the country. His justification was that the jury's verdict was inconsistent with the facts. He argued that Woodward lacked the requisite malice necessary for the finding of second-degree murder. Woodward immediately returned to England, where she was embraced by her community and treated as a survivor.

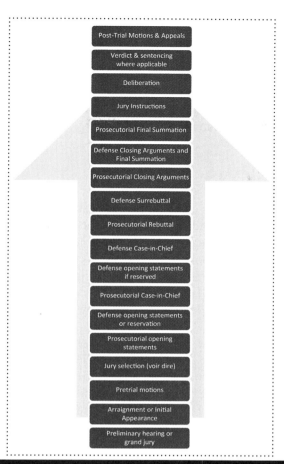

Post-Trial Motions & Appeals

Verdict & sentencing where applicable

Deliberation

Jury Instructions

Prosecutorial Final Summation

Defense Closing Arguments and Final Summation

Prosecutorial Closing Arguments

Defense Surrebuttal

Prosecutorial Rebuttal

Defense Case-in-Chief

Defense opening statements if reserved

Prosecutorial Case-in-Chief

Defense opening statements or reservation

Prosecutorial opening statements

Jury selection (voir dire)

Pretrial motions

Arraignment or Initial Appearance

Preliminary hearing or grand jury

FIGURE 2-3   Criminal case flowchart

▶ Posttrial Motions and Appeals

The contemporary criminal court system in the United States is bifurcated into a two-tiered entity consisting of trial and appellate courts. Unlike trial courts that hear evidence and determine guilt or innocence, appellate courts are singularly tasked with the evaluation of process. Composed of a panel of judges, appellate courts must evaluate whether or not the trial court erred in the application of law. Unfortunately, the fragmentation of the American judicial process often results in inconsistency, in that only cases decided in the court immediately superior are binding in the absence of a ruling by the highest court. Thus, the "dying declaration" of a suspect who implicates his brother may be admissible in one county, but not in another.

Individuals convicted by a trial court may appeal such conviction for a variety of reasons. However, only appeals that are timely and proper may be considered. The entry of judgment initiates the appellate clock, and briefs must be submitted within the parameters established by law. In addition, appeals in state courts must delineate within the procedural documents some deviation from due process. Such documents may include a clerk's transcript of the case documentation or the reporter's transcript of all that was said during trial. Appeals on evidentiary matters may be heard if the groundwork was laid at the original trial. As stated previously, attorneys have the responsibility of objecting to evidence that they consider being inadmissible under the rules.

brief a written legal argument that summarizes the case and includes a statement of relevant facts and issues of law.

Appeals are initiated upon the filing of a brief. An appellate **brief** is a summary of the case, and it includes a statement of relevant facts and issues of law and a rationale for appeal. The issues of law that are raised must be documented properly, and the rationale for appeal must be supported by case law or statute. Only the defense may appeal a verdict, because the prosecution's appeal following a verdict of "not guilty" would constitute double jeopardy. Posttrial motions and appeals are the last avenue for convicted offenders.

▶ CONCLUSIONS

The structure of the American criminal justice system can be described best as a model of interrelated, independent agencies at the state and federal level. Many crimes occur as violations of state criminal codes and are investigated at the state and local level under general police powers. Some criminal offenses are violations of federal law and some are offenses that violate state and federal codes. Without general police powers, federal law enforcement agencies are charged with investigating violations of specific federal laws (passed by Congress) that are assigned to their respective agencies.

State and federal governments are sovereign, but they must maintain codes and procedures that uphold the U.S. Constitution. These include rules of evidence. Since 1975, when Congress enacted the Federal Rules of Evidence, most states have elected to adopt them but retain the right to modify and interpret the rules as deemed necessary. Therefore, rules of evidence can still differ from state to state, as well as between state and federal courts.

Another important aspect of our criminal justice system relevant to the rules of evidence is its adversarial nature, which provides the framework for the main courtroom actors: the prosecutor, the defense attorney, and the judge. The prosecutor and defense attorney are adversaries attempting to present facts that are most favorable to their case. The adversaries combat with one another by petitioning the judge to exclude or admit evidence. The behavior of the actors is governed further by the fact that the United States employs an accusatorial system. Unlike the inquisitorial system of many European countries, an accusatorial system allows the defendant the absolute right to remain silent. Under an inquisitorial system, defendants do not have an absolute right to remain silent, and judges, in some special circumstances, can conduct investigations. In the American accusatorial system, information collected by the police in violation of a defendant's right to remain silent often can be ruled inadmissible.

The criminal court process can be lengthy and usually is initiated by the filing of a criminal complaint, the outcome of which may be a verdict or plea bargain. The duration of the process varies based on the applicable procedural rules. Irrespective of jurisdiction, the court process is guided by provisions firmly embedded in the U.S. Constitution, Rules of Criminal Procedure, and case law.

Key Terms

Affirmative defense	Boykin waiver	Circuit courts
Aggravating factors	Brady rule	Closing arguments
Alford plea	Brief	Contemporaneous objection rule
Arraignment	Case-in-chief	Courts of general jurisdiction
Booking	Castle Law or Castle Doctrine	Court of last resort

Courts of original jurisdiction
Criminal complaint
Cross-examination
Defense attorneys
Denied powers
Direct examination
Directed verdict
Discovery
Duress
Duty to retreat clause
En banc
Enumerated powers
Exclusive powers
Federal circuit courts
Federal district courts
Federalism
Grand jury
Indictment
Information

Intermediate appellate courts
Implied powers
Judges
Judiciary Act of 1789
Jury instructions
Magistrates
M'Naghten standard
Mistrial
Mitigating factors
Motions
Motion to discover
Motion to suppress
Nolo contendere
Opening statements
Petit jury
Plea
Plea bargaining
Pro bono
Prosecutors

Rebuttal
Rejoinder
Reversible error
Rule of four
Separate sovereigns exception
Sequestration
Shared powers
Stand Your Ground laws
Statute of limitations
Trial de novo
True bill
Vicinage
Voir dire
Warrants
Work-product doctrine
Writ of certiorari
Writ of habeas corpus

Discussion Questions

1. Discuss the methods of appointing judges and advantages and disadvantages of each.
2. What problems are associated with Alford and nolo contendere pleas?
3. What is the difference between exculpatory and inculpatory evidence?
4. How does a plea of not guilty differ from a plea of not guilty by reason of affirmative defense?
5. What are some examples of the use of a plea of not guilty by reason of affirmative defense?
6. Briefly list and describe the elements of the criminal justice process.
7. What is the difference between challenges for cause and peremptory challenges?

Recommended Resources

Videos

A&E Television. It's not my fault: Strange defenses. American justice. Famed attorney Alan Dershowitz examines three bizarre cases that demonstrate potential problems with unconventional legal strategies. Available at: http://store.aetv.com.

A&E Television. Child's play, deadly play. American justice. This is the story of Lionel Tate, the youngest person ever to receive a sentence of life without parole. Available at: http://store.aetv.com.

Books

Breyer, Stephen. *Active liberty: Interpreting our democratic constitution.* New York: Vintage.

Dressler, Joshua and Thomas, George C. (2003). *Criminal procedure: Principles, policies, and perspectives* (2nd ed.). Minnesota: Thomson-West Publishing.

Fallon, Richard H., Meltzer, Daniel J., and Shapiro, David, L. (2004). *Hart and Weschler's the federal courts and the federal system 2004 supplement* (5th ed.). New York: Foundation Press.

Hall, Kermit L., Ely, James W., and Grossman, Joel B. (2005). *The Oxford companion to the Supreme Court of the United States.* UK: Oxford University Press.

Rehnquist, William H. (2002). *The supreme court.* New York: Alfred A. Knopf Publishing.

Scalia, Antonin (1997). *A matter of interpretation: Federal courts and the law.* Princeton, NJ: Princeton University Press.

Wigmore, John H. (1914). *The code of Hammurabi.* Northwestern University Bulletin. XIV (25).

Wigmore, John H. (1928). *Panorama of the world's legal system* (Library Edition). Washington, DC: Washington Law Book Company.

Wigmore, J. H. (1940). *A treatise on the Anglo-American system of evidence in trial at common law* (3rd ed.). Boston: Little, Brown and Company.

Wigmore, John H. (1942). *Wigmore's code of evidence.* Boston: Little, Brown and Company.

Online Sources

http://www.law.umich.edu/special/exoneration—link to The National Registry of Exonerations which is sponsored by the University of Michigan Law School. Provides detailed information about all known exonerations in the United States since 1989.

http://www.ncsc.org—National Center for State Courts Web site.

http://uscfc.uscourts.gov—United States Court of Federal Claims Web site.

http://www.law.cornell.edu—Official Web site of Cornell Law School's Legal Information Institute (LII) listing court decisions, structure, and law reviews.

http://www.ussc.gov—United States Sentencing Commission Web site; includes sentencing guidelines, crime statistics, reports to Congress, and federal judiciary links.

http://www.ojp.usdoj.gov/bjs/—United States of Department of Justice/Bureau of Justice Statistics Web site that includes sentencing statistics, offender characteristics, conviction rates, and juvenile justice reports.

http://www.washlaw.edu—Free legal search engine that includes links to state and federal courts, decisions, statutes, and even international codes of law.

Society publications, historical data, and links to related sites provide for case searching (maintained by The Supreme Court Historical Society).

Relevant Cases Cited

Apodaca v. Oregon, 406 U.S. 404 (1972)

Batson v. Kentucky, 476 U.S. 79 (1986)

Bond v. United States, 131 S. Ct. 2355 (2011)

Boykin v. Alabama, 395 U.S. 238 (1969)

Brady v. Maryland, 373 U.S. 83 (1963)

County of Riverside v. McLaughlin, 500 U.S. 44 (1991)

Georgia v. McCollum, 505 U.S. 42 (1992)

Hickman v. Taylor, 329 U.S. 495 (1947)

Iowa v. Tovar, 541 U.S. 77 (2004)

Johnson v. Louisiana, 406 U.S. 356 (1972)

Kyles v. Whitley, 514 U.S. 419 (1995)

Malloy v. Hogan, 378 U.S. 1 (1964)

McCulloch v. Maryland, 17 U.S. 316 (1819)

Miller-El v. Dretke, 545 U.S. 231 (2005)

North Carolina v. Alford, 400 U.S. 25 (1970)

Rogers v. Richmond, 365 U.S. 534 (1961)

Smith v. O'Grady, 312 U.S. 329 (1941)

Snyder v. Louisiana, 552 U.S. 472 (2008)

Strauder v. West Virginia, 100 U.S. 303 (1879)

Swain v. Alabama [380 U.S. 202 (1965)

Teban v. United States, 382 U.S. 406 (1966)

United States v. Sprague et al., 282 U.S. 716 (1931)

United States v. Williams, 504 U.S. 36 (1992)

Williams v. Florida, 399 U.S. 78 (1970)

Notes

1. [*McCulloch v. Maryland*, 17 U.S. 316 (1819)]
2. [*United States v. Sprague* et al., 282 U.S. 716 (1931)]
3. *Bond v. United States*, 131 S. Ct. 2355 (2011)
4. Rehnquist, W. H. (2002). *The supreme court.* New York: Alfred A. Knopf Publishing.
5. CSP (2012). *Examining the work of state courts: An analysis of 2010 court caseloads.* Grant No. 2011-BJ-CX-K062. Courts Statistics Project: Washington, D.C.
6. Ibid.
7. Ibid.
8. Ibid.
9. Ibid.
10. [*Teban v. United States*, 382 U.S. 406 (1966)]
11. [*Rogers v. Richmond*, 365 U.S.534 (1961) reaffirmed in [*Malloy v. Hogan*, 378 U.S. 1 (1964)]
12. (Chapter 20, Section 35, 1 Stat. 73, 92–93)
13. Hall, K. (1983). The judiciary on trial: State constitutional reform and the rise of an elected judiciary 1846-1860. *The Historian*, 46, 337-354.
14. [*County of Riverside v. McLaughlin*, 500 U.S. 44 (1991)]
15. [*Boykin v. Alabama*, 395 U.S. 238 (1969)]
16. [*North Carolina v. Alford*, 400 U.S. 25 (1970)]
17. [*Iowa v. Tovar*, 541 U.S. 77 (2004)]; [*Boykin v. Alabama*, 395 U.S. 238 (1969)]
18. Wigmore (1940)

19. 14 QBD 273 (1884)
20. Grennan, S. and Britz, M. (2006). *Organized crime: A worldwide perspective*. New York: Prentice-Hall.
21. [*Boykin v. Alabama*, 395 U.S. 238 (1969)
22. [*Smith v. O'Grady*, 312 U.S. 329 (1941)]
23. [*Boykin v. Alabama*, 395 U.S. 238 (1969)
24. [*Kyles v. Whitley*, 514 U.S. 419 (1995)]
25. [*United States v. Williams*, 504 U.S. 36 (1992)]
26. [*Hickman v. Taylor*, 329 U.S. 495 (1947)]
27. Petegorsky, M. N. (2013). Plea bargaining in the dark: The duty to disclose exculpatory Brady evidence during plea bargaining. *Fordham Law Review*, 81(6), 3598–3650.
28. [*Williams v. Florida*, 399 U.S. 78 (1970)]
29. [*Batson v. Kentucky*, 476 U.S. 79, (1986)]; [*Georgia v. McCollum*, 505 U.S. 42 (1992)]
30. Wigmore (1936: 293)
31. [*Johnson v. Louisiana*, 406 U.S. 356 (1972)]; [*Apodaca v. Oregon*, 406 U.S. 404 (1972)]

THE DECLARATION OF INDEPENDENCE.

3 Forms of Evidence

LEARNING OBJECTIVES

The learner will:

1 *Explain the different types of evidence*

2 *Examine what comprises circumstantial versus direct evidence*

3 *Explain the difference between "guilty actions" and "guilty minds"*

4 *Explain the role the character plays in the admissibility of evidence*

In the most general sense, the term **evidence** refers to any means by which the veracity of a fact in question can be established or proved. More specifically, it is the demonstration of truth or untruth of allegations in a court of law through the consideration of information that is relevant, material, and competent. It is available in many forms and may be represented by material objects, scientific analysis, or eyewitness accounts. Evidence can address the tangible—such as the murder weapon, photographs, documents, records—and the intangible—such as motive, demonstration of means, and eyewitness accounts. As defined by Wigmore, evidence is:

> . . . any knowable fact or group of facts offered to or considered by a legal tribunal for the purpose of producing a persuasion, affirmative or negative, on the part of the tribunal, as to a proposition of fact (not of law or of logic) on which the determination of the tribunal is to be given. (Wigmore, 1942: 1)

Thus, evidence is matter that illuminates the truth. However, not all such material may be admitted into court. Information that does not satisfy constitutional requirements, for example, may be excluded (discussed in Chapter 5). The nature of the American adversarial system also requires that the proponent of a proffered piece of evidence must demonstrate the item's relevance, materiality, and competency. Such characteristics are often hotly contested by opposing counsel who seeks to reject items or information counter to their position.

evidence relevant, competent, material, and probative information or other matter that demonstrates truth. In American jurisprudence, all evidence is introduced through witness testimony.

FEDERAL RULES OF EVIDENCE

ARTICLE IV—RELEVANCY AND ITS LIMITS

Rule 401—Definition of "Relevant Evidence"

"Relevant Evidence" means evidence having any tendency to make the existence of any fact that is of consequence to the determination of the action more probable or less probable than it would be without the evidence.

Rule 402—Relevant Evidence Generally Admissible: Irrelevant Evidence Inadmissible

All relevant evidence is admissible, except as otherwise provided by the Constitution of the United States, by Act of Congress, by these rules or by other rules prescribed by the Supreme Court pursuant to statutory authority. Evidence which is not relevant is not admissible.

Rule 403—Excluding Relevant Evidence for Prejudice, Confusion, Waste of Time, or Other Reasons

The court may exclude relevant evidence if its probative value is substantially outweighed by a danger of one or more of the following: unfair prejudice, confusing the issues, misleading the jury, undue delay, wasting time, or needlessly presenting cumulative evidence.

▶ Relevance

The determination of **relevancy** is the cornerstone of evidence admissibility. Such evaluation must weigh the probative value of an item carefully, considering whether the introduction of such best serves the interest of justice. States vary in their interpretation of the relevance of an item in question. According to Mueller and Kirkpatrick,[1] four evaluative schemes are in place today. The first only establishes the relevance of material that makes the point in question more probable than not. This system is clearly not workable, because evidence tends to be cumulative in nature. Thus, the exclusion of preliminary evidence would result in a silencing of argument.

The second system of inquiry holds that relevance may be established only in cases in which the inference—a deduction that may be drawn from evidence—is more probable than others. Unfortunately, this system is no more feasible than the former, because it requires a hearing of all of the scenarios before introduction. Thus, evidence presented near the beginning of a proceeding would be far more scrutinized than that introduced later. The third system, championed by the pre-eminent scholar John Henry Wigmore, relied on an evaluation of the "plus value" of the item in question. More succinctly, evidence was deemed relevant only in situations in which the probative value of an item was greater than minimal. The final standard, and by far the most common, is the introduction of evidence that tends to demonstrate the truth of the point in question more than its absence.[2] This final standard of admissibility is most consistent with the Federal Rule 401. By far the most lenient, Rule 401 is more likely to result in the admissibility of an item than not.

 APPLICATION OF LAW

CIRCUMSTANTIAL EVIDENCE AND JURY NULLIFICATION: THE CASE OF T. CULLEN DAVIS

Hours after a divorce judge had proved sympathetic to Priscilla Davis' petition, shots rang out at the Texas mansion of her estranged husband, T. Cullen Davis, heir to one of the nation's largest oil fortunes. Among the victims were his ex-wife Priscilla; her 12-year-old daughter, Andrea Wilborn; Priscilla's boyfriend, Stan Farr; and a friend of Andrea's, Gus "Bubba" Gavrel Jr. All had been shot at close range, and young Andrea Wilborn and Priscilla's boyfriend, Stan Farr, were dead at the scene. Wilborn had been shot execution style in the back of her head while in a kneeling position on the basement floor, apparently just as the assailant attempted to ambush the others. Priscilla Davis, with her bleached blonde hair and flashy clothes, survived. She would later testify that the shooter was her estranged husband. Other evidence included:

- Testimony of Beverly Bass (the only visitor to the mansion that night who remained unscathed) that Cullen Davis did the shooting
- Bass' corroborating testimony that Priscilla told the gunman that she "loved him"

- Priscilla's testimony to a neighbor immediately following the incident that Cullen was up there "shooting her children" and "killing everybody"
- Testimony by Cullen's brother that he did not appear surprised at the shootings
- Photo identification of Cullen by Gus "Bubba" Gavrel Jr., who survived a gunshot wound to the chest that night
- Other circumstantial evidence regarding the rancorous divorce proceedings and prior threats by the defendant

Despite the overwhelming evidence, T. Cullen Davis was found not guilty, largely because of his wealth and his choice of counsel, the infamous Richard "Racehorse" Haines, who portrayed Priscilla as a gold-digging woman of ill repute. Post-trial interviews revealed that many jurors felt that the notion of a man as wealthy as Davis murdering his wife was absurd. Rich men hire people for that sort of thing.

Famed defense attorneys Phil Burleson (L) and Richard "Racehorse" Haynes flank multimillionaire T. Cullen Davis on the opening day of his murder trial. Davis was prosecuted for the murder of his stepdaughter and his estranged wife's boyfriend, as well as for the attempted murder of Priscilla Davis, his estranged wife. Davis was subsequently found "not guilty" on these charges.

Irrespective of standard, questions that might be asked about the relevance of evidence include, but are not limited to: What is the offered evidence being used to show or demonstrate? What is the material issue in the case at hand? Does the offered evidence establish or tend to establish the issues before the court? The answers to these questions and the weight afforded them may change over time, as relevancy is not a static concept. In fact, definitions of relevancy may be based on judicial precedent or community standards. Thus, while it is clear that irrelevant evidence is not admissible, FRE. Rule 402 also provides that even evidence deemed relevant is not necessarily admissible. This includes information that is gathered in violation of the Bill of Rights, or that violates established state or federal rules of criminal procedure or evidence, or that violates jurisdictional case law. Although Rule 402 makes no attempt to provide parameters for exclusion, additional rules have provided some clarification. For example, Rule 403 provides for the exclusion of **relevant evidence** when the probative value is "substantially outweighed by the danger of unfair prejudice, confusion of the issues, or misleading the jury, or by considerations of undue delay, waste of time, or needless presentation of cumulative evidence."

relevant evidence any material fact or information which tends to make the existence of any fact that is of consequence to the determination of the action more probable or less probable than it would be without the evidence.

▶ Materiality

For admissibility purposes, information or matter must also be material and competent. Generally speaking **materiality** refers to evidence that is logically connected to a fact at issue and includes a consideration of the germaneness of information or testimony and a determination as to its impact on the trial at hand. As noted by various courts, the *materiality* and the *relevancy* of an object or statement are inherently separate concepts. To wit,

materiality a requirement for admissibility, it refers to evidence that is logically connected to a fact at issue and includes a consideration of the germaneness of information or testimony and a determination as to its impact on the trial.

> "Material" when used in respect to evidence is often confused with "relevant," but the two terms have wholly different meanings. To be "relevant" means to relate to the issue. To be "material" means to have probative weight, i.e., reasonably likely to influence the tribunal in making a determination required to be made. A statement may be relevant but not material[3] . . . and . . . the issue to which the false statement is material need not be the main issue; it may be a collateral issue. And it need not bear directly upon the issue but may merely augment or diminish the evidence upon some point. But it must have some weight in the process of reaching a decision.[4]

EXAMPLES OF RELEVANT EVIDENCE IN THE TRIAL OF T. CULLEN DAVIS

- Forensic evidence that matched the gun used in the killing of his 12-year-old stepdaughter to the one used to shoot the others.

- Eyewitness testimony of individuals (including surviving victims) who witnessed Davis shooting his estranged wife and her boyfriend.

- Testimony that Davis was arrested at the airport as he was preparing to leave the country.

- Evidence that the divorce proceedings between the two had greatly angered Davis.

Traditionally, the issue of materiality was to be measured by the trier of law (i.e., the judge) as opposed to the trier of fact (i.e., the jury). More recently, the Supreme Court recognized that both state and federal courts lacked consistency. In *United States v. Gaudin* [515 U.S. 506 (1995)], they noted that "though uniform post-ratification practice can shed light upon the meaning of an ambiguous constitutional provision, the practice here is not uniform, and the core meaning of the guarantee is ambiguous." As such, the Court ruled that in cases where the materiality of a statement is an element of the offense charged, the jury, not the judge, must apply the law to the facts of the case.

► Competency

competent evidence that evidence which is both relevant and material which has no impediment to its admissibility.

The last requirement of criminal evidence is competency. **Competent evidence** is that evidence which is both relevant and material which has no impediment to its admissibility. (The competency of witnesses is discussed fully in Chapter 9.) For example, hearsay statements that do not fall within one of the varied exceptions or a confidential communication about defense strategy between an attorney and his or her client would be incompetent. The Supreme Court has expressed caution in applying other blanket rules of admissibility to state courts. However, they clarified that rules limiting the admissibility of evidence for a specific purpose do not necessarily render such evidence inadmissible for others.

GANG AFFILIATION, PREJUDICE, AND *UNITED STATES V. ABEL* [469 U.S. 54 (1984)]

In *United States v. Abel* [469 U.S. 54 (1984)], the Court considered a case where a witness had testified that the defendant belonged to a prison gang which swore to perjure themselves whenever it was necessary to assist fellow gang members. The Court ruled that evidence that is probative to the bias of a witness in a criminal case can be admissible even if such evidence is prejudicial to the defendant. To wit:

It seems clear to us that the proffered testimony with respect to Mills' membership in the Aryan Brotherhood sufficed to show potential bias in favor of respondent; because of the tenets of the organization described, it might also impeach his veracity directly. But there is no rule of evidence which provides that testimony admissible for one purpose and inadmissible for another purpose is thereby rendered inadmissible; quite the contrary is the case. It would be a strange rule of law which held that relevant, competent evidence which tended to show bias on the part of a witness was nonetheless inadmissible because it also tended to show that the witness was a liar.

ARTICLE VI, WITNESSES

Rule 602—Need for Personal Knowledge

A witness may testify to a matter only if evidence is introduced sufficient to support a finding that the witness has personal knowledge of the matter. Evidence to prove personal knowledge may consist of the witness's own testimony. This rule does not apply to a witness's expert testimony under Rule 703.

Competency is a demonstration that the witness had personal knowledge required by Rule 602 of the Federal Rules of Evidence.

▶ Real Evidence

All evidence admissible in court must be relevant, material, and competent, but it may be further distinguished by the type of evidence it represents. **Real evidence** is any evidence that can be perceived with one of the five senses. It is the object itself, not a representation, testimonial impression, viewpoint, or expert opinion. It includes, but is not limited to, physical items, pictures, trial exhibits, and witness testimony. It may be direct or circumstantial in nature, but it is always the object itself. Real evidence is almost always deemed relevant, irrespective of individual characteristics; however, it must be reinforced with secondary or corroborative evidence. As with all other forms of evidence, real evidence must be introduced by a witness.

real evidence any evidence that may be experienced through one of the five senses. The object itself, not a representation, testimonial impression, viewpoint, or expert opinion.

▶ Direct Versus Circumstantial Evidence

The U.S. Constitution requires the prosecution to produce sufficient credible evidence to establish proof of guilt beyond a reasonable doubt. This may be accomplished through the introduction of direct evidence and/or circumstantial evidence. In most cases, both are presented to the jury and used to prove guilt, clarify disputed facts, or establish specific elements. Ideally, direct evidence outweighs the amount of circumstantial evidence submitted, but this is

APPLICATION OF LAW

DIRECT EVIDENCE AND T. CULLEN DAVIS

Much of the evidence in the 1977 murder trial of T. Cullen Davis was testimonial and circumstantial, but the evidence in his next go-round was not. Approximately a year after the initiation of the first proceedings, T. Cullen Davis was arrested for the solicitation of murder of the judge in his divorce proceedings. This time, Davis had been videotaped meeting with an FBI informant who displayed for him a photograph of the judge covered in blood in the trunk of a car. Upon hearing that the hit man had "gotten the judge dead" for him, Davis paid him $25,000. The informant, a private investigator Cullen Davis had hired for the first trial, was also supposed to kill at least a dozen other people, including Priscilla Davis and two witnesses from the earlier trial. Finally, it appeared that Davis would be convicted of a serious offense. Despite the videotape evidence, the jury found him not guilty. Years later, a member of the defense team would reveal numerous improper actions on the part of the defense in both trials, including jury tampering and paying off government investigators.

circumstantial evidence matter, material, or information that requires an inference; or, evidence that indirectly proves or disproves a fact.

inference a logical conclusion that the jury may or may not make.

direct evidence information, material, or matter that proves or disproves a fact without the need for inference or presumption.

not always the case. In fact, circumstantial evidence is perhaps the best known (and certainly the most exploited) form of criminal evidence. By definition, **circumstantial evidence** is matter, material, or information that requires an inference—a logical conclusion that the jury may or may not make. Conversely, **direct evidence**, traditionally referred to as testimonial evidence, is information, material, or matter that proves or disproves a fact without the need for inference or presumption. Witness testimony may fall into either category. For example, testimony by an eyewitness who saw a blue sedan leave the bank around the time of the robbery would be circumstantial; while a statement by an individual who actually witnessed the crime and the escape in the blue sedan would be direct. Inarguably, the latter type of testimony would be preferred in a criminal case.

Although early common law considered circumstantial evidence to be inferior to direct, allowing it only under exceptional circumstances, its usage gained general acceptance in the nineteenth century with one important caveat.[5] As noted by William Wells in 1853, "in order to justify the inference of legal guilt from circumstantial evidence, the existence of the inculpatory facts must be absolutely incompatible with the innocence of the accused, and incapable of explanation upon any other reasonable hypothesis of his guilt."[6] This standard, however, does not exist in contemporary courts, and many cases are built almost exclusively on a foundation of circumstantial evidence. Indeed, the Court has ruled that a guilty verdict based solely on circumstantial evidence is constitutional as there is no intrinsic difference between the two. To wit:

> Circumstantial evidence . . . is intrinsically no different from testimonial evidence. Admittedly, circumstantial evidence may in some cases point to a wholly incorrect result. Yet this is equally true of testimonial evidence. In both instances, a jury is asked to weigh the chances that the evidence correctly points to guilt against the possibility of inaccuracy or ambiguous inference . . . the jury must use its experience with people and events in weighing the probabilities. If the jury is convinced beyond a reasonable doubt, we can require no more.[7]

Thus, direct evidence and circumstantial evidence may both be used to demonstrate guilt, and to prove the statutory elements of a behavior in question. They may also be used to prove mental state, intent, and motive. For example, most states that enforce capital punishment require a demonstration of specific intent in the charged murder. For example, one eyewitness may provide direct evidence by testifying that he or she witnessed the stabbing death of the victim—thereby proving the actual killing. However, another may provide circumstantial evidence in the form of testimony by stating that the accused had discussed killing the victim two weeks before the event.

Prima facie evidence is evidence that "stands on its face," stands alone, or speaks for itself. More specifically, it refers to the strongest evidence in the case. With rare exceptions, prima facie is defined as direct evidence. An example of a prima facie case is that of Charles Ng and Leonard Lake, in which dozens of videotapes recovered from a property owned by Lake's ex-wife revealed taped torture sessions of various individuals in which Ng and Lake played a prominent role.

Scientific evidence may be either direct or circumstantial but is generally classified as circumstantial evidence, because it requires an inference of culpability. The presence of a defendant's DNA on a vaginal swab obtained from a victim of sexual assault, for example, may directly prove that sexual contact had occurred but fails to demonstrate that the contact was nonconsensual.

prima facie evidence in a criminal case that "stands on its face," stands alone, or speaks for itself, such as a videotape showing the criminal act being committed and the person or persons involved; sufficient enough to prove the case in the absence of substantial evidence to the contrary.

HE SAID, SHE SAID: THE JAMEIS WINSTON CASE

On December 7, 2012, a Florida State University coed filed a sexual battery incident report with the Tallahassee Police Department after reporting the incident to representatives of the university police department. She claimed that she had been drinking at a local establishment, and that she couldn't remember what happened after drinking a shot from someone who was unknown to her. She further stated that she became aware that she was riding in a taxi and that "there was another person in the taxi. We went to an apartment, I don't know where it was. I kept telling him to stop but he took all my clothes off. He started having sex with me and then his roommate came in and told him to stop. He moved us to the bathroom 'because the door locked' and I'm not 100% sure how everything in there happened."[8] Although she initially reported that she did not know the identity of her attacker, the victim contacted authorities on January 10, 2013, indicating that the rapist was Jameis Winston, a classmate and quarterback for the Florida State Seminoles. Police notes from that time indicate that her attorney advised her to hesitate to pursue charges against the athlete due to potential repercussions for fingering the Heisman trophy hopeful. In

February of the same year, Jameis Winston's attorney informed authorities that he would not consent to an interview and the case became "inactive."

In November of 2013, the media exposed the case to the public. As a result, DNA samples were ordered for Winston and three others. Jameis Winston's attorney subsequently reported that Winston had consensual sex with the victim—an account that was collaborated by two witnesses to the event 11 months after the attack was reported to police. During the same month, Tallahassee police chief Tim Coe stated that the victim had stopped cooperating and had decided not to press charges, a charge which is vehemently denied by the victim, her family, and her attorney. On December 5, 2013, Florida State Attorney William "Willie" Meggs announced that no charges would be filed in the case due to a lack of evidence and that the case was closed, clearing the way for Winston's Heisman hopes. He was awarded the coveted trophy 11 days later. Since that time, Winston has remained in the news for bad behavior, including but not limited to shoplifting and shouting obscene lyrics derogatory to women from atop a table in a campus building.

► Circumstantial Inferences of Guilt

As stated, circumstantial evidence is evidence that requires an inference or presumption by the fact finder. There are many areas in which circumstantial evidence may be used to establish the guilt of the accused including, but not limited to: proof of intent, proof of motive, proof of means, modus operandi, flight to avoid prosecution, and concealment. Conversely, the defense may use the absence of circumstantial evidence to demonstrate its innocence.

Means, Motive, and Opportunity

Under the law, prosecutors bear no obligation or responsibility to prove **means** (ability to commit the offense), **motive** (reason or circumstance that compels an individual to act), or **opportunity** (a set of circumstances which make the offense possible) in a criminal case. However, the proof of these things can strengthen the government's case immeasurably and the absence of them can be used by the defense as illustrative of innocence. For example, prosecutors in the O. J. Simpson case suggested that only a person of great strength and speed could have performed the grisly stabbings of two grown adults. They pointed to Simpson's athletic skill, arguing that the strength, speed, and aggression necessary to succeed in the NFL clearly demonstrated his ability (i.e., *means*) to commit the murders. The defense, on the other hand, portrayed O. J. Simpson as a victim of gridiron abuse, incapable of even raising a golf club at times. They argued that Simpson was physically incapable of perpetrating the incident in question. Thus, both sides introduced circumstantial evidence to prove or disprove means.

means the ability to commit the offense that is often demonstrated through evidence of special knowledge, physical prowess, or the like.

motive reason or circumstance that compels an individual to act. In a criminal case, it is the primary reason or rationale for a defendant's criminal actions (e.g., revenge, jealousy, or the need for money).

opportunity a set of circumstances that make the offense possible. In a criminal case, this is demonstrated through time that is unaccounted for during the period that the offense occurred.

Although questions remained, Florida State Attorney William Meggs announced that no charges would be filed against Jameis Winston for sexual assault less than one week before Heisman Trophy ballots were due.

Means may also be established through the demonstration of special knowledge, intelligence, possession of similar instrument, or access to weapon. Take the case of John Orr, a fire department captain and arson investigator, who was charged and convicted of numerous arsons including one that killed four people in a hardware store. Circumstantial evidence presented against Orr included a manuscript he authored that was eerily similar to the cases under investigation and testimony regarding his intensive training history in arson investigation. Subsequently, Orr was convicted and is serving a life sentence at Lompoc Penitentiary in California. On the flip side, the defense could argue that the characteristics or sophistication of the action in question are such that the accused could not have possibly accomplished the action. In the West Memphis Three case, for example, defense attorneys for Jason Baldwin and Damien Echols argued that the absence of blood at the disposal site and the removal of skin from one of the victim's genitalia required a level of sophistication and precision that the defendants did not possess.

In homicide cases, weapons are often introduced as circumstantial evidence to demonstrate the defendant's guilt. Prosecuting attorneys may demonstrate, for example, that the bullets lodged within the deceased's skull match those fired from the defendant's weapon in a forensic laboratory. Coupled with evidence that the defendant inherited $3 million from the death, a jury might find the defendant guilty even without corroborating direct evidence. In the absence of a murder weapon, the prosecution may also present circumstantial evidence to indicate the defendant's possession of a similar instrument. In murder cases, particularly ones in which a murder weapon has not been found, it is often sufficient to prove that the accused owned a similar weapon but is unable or unwilling to produce it. Even in cases where no scientific evidence exists to tie a suspect weapon with the actual incident, the presence of such is often enough to sway a jury. In the trial of

During his trial for the murder of his ex-wife and Ron Goldman, O.J. Simpson claimed that injuries sustained during his football career had rendered him physically incapable of inflicting the grievous wounds.

the Kennedy cousin, Michael Skakel, for example, the fact that a broken Toney Penna 6 iron had been used to murder Martha Moxley was used as circumstantial evidence against him, as his Toney Penna club was missing mysteriously from his own set. Another example can be found in the West Memphis Three case, in which a knife found several months after the defendants were indicted was introduced even though no evidence indicated that it was the actual murder weapon.

In the absence of an eyewitness, jurors expect to hear testimony regarding the defendant's opportunity to commit the crime in question. In this regard, the presence or absence of an **alibi**, often becomes critical in a criminal proceeding. In many cases, criminal defendants establish reasonable doubt by demonstrating their whereabouts during the time the crime was committed. For example, defendants may provide time cards, cash register receipts, ticket stubs, or photographs of themselves at another location. They might also call witnesses who will testify that they were with the defendant during the period in question. In other cases, establishing an alibi or proof of their whereabouts may not be a simple task. For example, they may have been alone or otherwise unable to remember the exact circumstances of the time in question. How many people would be able to provide an alibi witness for their whereabouts one year ago? Who could remember where they were between the hours of 6:00 p.m. and 7:00 p.m. on that particular day? As with evidence entered to counter testimony regarding the means, alibis can be of significant service to the defendant. In many cases, their presence alone may result in an acquittal.

In addition to alibis, the Perry Mason public demands to hear some discussion of motive. Motive may be defined as the reason or circumstance that compels an individual to act. In a criminal case, it is the primary reason or rationale for a defendant's criminal action. This is not to be confused with **criminal intent**, a necessary element of a crime involving a conscious decision on the part of an individual to engage in an unlawful act. While a demonstration of intent is required across criminal statutes, a similar requirement for motive is less common, particularly in state statutes. Federal statutes that require a demonstration of motive include those

alibi proof of whereabouts; literally, *another place.*

criminal intent a necessary element of a crime involving a conscious decision on the part of an individual to engage in an unlawful act.

CIRCUMSTANTIAL EVIDENCE, A PERFECT ALIBI, AND MURDER-FOR-HIRE

Perhaps the most bizarre case of an alibi offered by a criminal defendant occurred in Silver Spring, Maryland. As a young man, Lawrence Horn seemed to live a charmed life. A successful musician, record producer, and engineer for Motown Records, Horn lived large during the heyday of the R&B giant, but was living a shadow of his former life by the time he orchestrated the murder of his son, ex-wife, and medical aide. Ironically, the man who was instrumental in creating the culture, legacy, and myth of superstars like Smokey Robinson, Marvin Gaye, and the Supremes secured his own place in history not for his skill within the recording studio, but for his audacious attempt to thwart justice in a triple homicide case.

While it is impossible to determine the moment that Lawrence Horn began to think of the economic benefits of his own son's death, it could have begun when the child was only thirteen months old. It was then that the child had suffered catastrophic brain damage due to hospital negligence. Rendered a quadriplegic due to the mistake, Trevor was given the bleakest of prognoses—expected to die within a short period of time. But, Trevor surprised the medical community. With the constant care of his mother and a full time nurse, his condition stabilized. Eventually, his mother secured a significant settlement from the hospital which would guarantee a lifetime of medical care for the child. Never one to miss an opportunity and dissatisfied with the $125K awarded specifically to him, Lawrence Horn petitioned the court for a larger share of the financial settlement. The judge subsequently denied Horn's request, noting that he had not been a part of Trevor's life prior to the accidence; and, more importantly, that the money was specifically intended to provide for the boy's medical care. He did allow, however, that Horn

would be entitled to the remainder of the initial settlement if he was preceded in death by both Trevor and his former wife. Perhaps this was the precise moment when Horn began to consider the unthinkable?

On a blustery March day, investigators were called to the scene of a triple homicide in Silver Spring, Maryland. Upon arrival, they found the bodies of Mildred and Trevor Horn and Janice Saunders, the night nurse. Both women suffered gunshot wounds to the face and appeared to have been surprised by the attack. The eight year old was found suffocated in his crib. Within days, investigators identified Lawrence Horn as the primary suspect in the slayings, as he stood to inherit the child's trust fund. When investigators in Los Angeles reported to Horn's Hollywood residence, he claimed that he had been home the night of the homicides and could provide indisputable verification of his whereabouts. Towards that end, he provided investigators with a home video that he had recorded of himself WATCHING TELEVISION. He was quick to point out the program that he was watching had the running time and date on the screen! Thus, he argued, it was impossible that he participated in the killings that had happened over 3,000 miles away. The jury found the alibi implausible.

Unfortunately for him, Horn was not as discriminate in his choice of a hitman as he was in his television program. Apparently, the storefront minister (and former inmate) that he selected was not as practiced in the art of murder as he proclaimed—relying instead on a book he ordered from Paladin Press, *Hit Man: A Technical Manual for Independent Contractor*. Both men were convicted in the slayings. Surviving members of the victims' families were awarded several million dollars from Paladin's insurance company after filing suit against the publisher.

criminal acts that interfere with constitutionally protected rights or are directed at protected classes. For example, 18 U.S.C. 249, provides for the criminal prosecution of an individual who causes "bodily injury to any person, **because of** the actual or perceived race, color, religion, or natural origin (emphasis added)." Thus, federal prosecution of hate crime requires a demonstration of prejudice on the part of the offender. Circumstantial evidence that might satisfy this requirement could include, but is not limited to: defendant's membership in a federally recognized hate group; racist or separatist rhetoric expressed by the defendant before, during, or after the attack; or previous attacks motivated by prejudice.

As stated, a demonstration of motive is not a legal requirement in the majority of criminal cases. However, it is always relevant in a criminal case as it provides an explanation as to the reason that a particular act happened. Circumstantial evidence demonstrating motive in spousal killings, for example, may include, but is not limited to: extramarital affairs, jealousy, life insurance policies, and other financial gain. Motives for infanticide might include: life insurance, anger at spouse, anger at child, or post-partum depression. Motives for other homicides might include: financial gain (as in a robbery resulting in a homicide), rage, disputes between neighbors, racial hatred, revenge, and so forth. In fact, motives run the gamut from the commonplace, like financial gain, to the bizarre, like killing a rival to secure a spot on the high school cheerleading squad. Motives are limited only by imagination, but jurors often place great importance on them. In cases where competing motives are presented, justice is not always clear.

Guilty Actions and Consciousness of Guilt

Just as jurors expect to hear evidence of motive, they are also likely to prefer some **consciousness of guilt** on the part of the defendant. For the most part, this includes a demonstration of post-event behavior that is uncharacteristic of the accused. This may come in many different shapes and sizes. For example, a sudden change in appearance, like a change in hairstyle, facial hair, or body art might indicate that a criminal defendant is attempting to thwart identification by potential eyewitnesses. In other cases, the sudden sale of a prized automobile might suggest that the accused in a murder case worried that forensic analysis of the car might reveal scientific evidence linking the victim to the defendant. Other broad categories in which consciousness of guilt might be inferred include: the concealment or destruction of evidence, sudden wealth, flight to avoid prosecution, and the threatening of witnesses.

consciousness of guilt inferred through the introduction of circumstantial evidence, which demonstrates uncustomary behavior, statements, or demeanor by the defendant.

APPLICATION OF LAW

SEX, FRAUD, AND MOTIVE—THE PREACHER'S WIFE

Although a demonstration of motive is not required under traditional homicide statutes, prosecutors often strengthen their case by explaining the reason that a criminal defendant murdered their victim. Sometimes, straightforward explanations are accepted by juries and criminal convictions result. In cases where defendants admit their act but offer a different explanation, however, juries may reject the prosecution's assertions.

On March 22, 2006, church members in a small town in Tennessee entered the residence of their pastor, Matthew Winkler, after he failed to show up for that evening's service. They discovered his dead body on the floor of his bedroom. He had been shot in the back at close range with a 12-gauge shotgun. His wife, Mary, their three children, and the family van were noticeably absent from the residence. Immediately issuing an Amber Alert, authorities originally feared that the family had been taken against their will. They were subsequently located in the beach town of Orange Beach, Alabama. Under questioning by authorities, the soft spoken woman indicated that she had shot her husband after they argued about money.

During the trial, prosecuting attorneys produced evidence, which demonstrated that Mary Winkler had engaged in a Nigerian check kiting fraud, which included a variety of fraudulent check deposited in domestic and international financial institutions. They argued that Mary Winkler had killed her husband after he had discovered her crimes. Winkler's defense team countered that her motives for killing her husband were markedly different. They argued that she committed the execution murder of her sleeping husband out of shame and fear. On the stand, Winkler testified that the much-loved preacher was a sexual deviant who forced her to perform demeaning sexual acts, including sodomy. To support her claims, the defense introduced high heel shoes and a wig that she said she was forced to wear by the victim. Throughout her testimony (and courtroom attendance), Winkler looked at the floor and spoke in hushed tones. Reporters contrasted her diminutive stature with that of her victim. However, church members refused to believe her story, claiming that the preacher was incapable of the acts that she described.

Indicted on a charge of first-degree murder, Winkler was ultimately found guilty of voluntary manslaughter by a jury of ten women and two men. She was caught on camera smirking as the verdict was pronounced. She was sentenced to 210 days in prison minus the 143 days that she had spent in jail prior to posting bail. Of the 67 days remaining, the judge allowed her to spend 60 of those in a mental health facility. Upon release, Mary successfully gained custody of her three children.

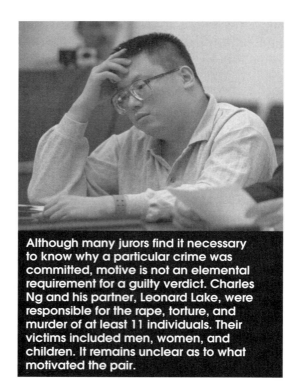

Although many jurors find it necessary to know why a particular crime was committed, motive is not an elemental requirement for a guilty verdict. Charles Ng and his partner, Leonard Lake, were responsible for the rape, torture, and murder of at least 11 individuals. Their victims included men, women, and children. It remains unclear as to what motivated the pair.

concealment concealment fraudulent commission or omission of relevant facts, such as disposing of the murder weapon, hiding stolen property, or burning incriminating statements.

sudden wealth the sudden and uncharacteristic purchasing of expensive items, such as the paying off of bills and the giving of charitable donations, which may indicate that a defendant has experienced a financial windfall and, in the absence of a reasonable explanation regarding the source of such sudden wealth, juries tend to consider it a motive.

Concealment

Concealment is one of the most common actions after the commission of the act and may be introduced into the record as circumstantial evidence against the defendant. Concealment might include disposing of the murder weapon, hiding stolen property, or burning incriminating statements. Such activities are consistent with a consciousness, or acknowledgment, of guilt—and this fact is often noted by juries. Concealment may also include the interference with or the intimidation of witnesses to the event in question. One of the most interesting cases in which concealment as circumstantial evidence was used successfully by the prosecution involved an Arizona man charged in the stabbing and drowning death of his wife of 20 years.

Sudden Wealth

The **sudden wealth** of an individual may prove to be equally compelling to a jury. The purchase of expensive items, the paying off of bills, and the uncharacteristic

 APPLICATION OF LAW

CONCEALMENT, SLEEPWALKING, AND MURDER

Scott Falater claimed that he had no recollection of stabbing his wife more than 40 times, dragging her to the family pool, and holding her head underwater. He claimed that he had a history of sleepwalking and that the crime occurred while he was asleep. However, prosecutors introduced evidence that demonstrated that Falater had a consciousness of guilt, in that he hid the murder weapon in the wheel well of his Volvo and changed into his pajamas before the arrival of law enforcement officials. The jury considered the concealment of evidence as indicative of consciousness of guilt and found Falater guilty of murder. He was sentenced to life imprisonment without the possibility of parole.

FOUND MONEY AND SUDDEN WEALTH IN PHILADELPHIA

When Joey Coyle recovered a bag of money that had fallen from an armored truck in Philadelphia, he thought that he had hit the jackpot. More than one million dollars had fallen from the vehicle headed for the famed casinos of Atlantic City. Within hours, the press was reporting that the police intended to charge the individual(s) who found the money with theft if it was not returned. Coyle, who was a down-on-his-luck neighborhood kid, failed to heed the warning. Instead, he went on a weeklong shopping binge—purchasing expensive goods, picking up bar tabs for neighborhood locals, and booking an exotic vacation with his newly returned ex-girlfriend.

Unfortunately for Coyle, his largesse proved to his downfall. When he was arrested at the airport, police discovered more than $100k strapped to his body, and arrested him for theft. A jury later acquitted Coyle based on his defense of temporary insanity, but many in the neighborhood and the media chastised him for the way he had responded to his good fortune. In the minds of many in his working class neighborhood, he should have kept his mouth shut and the money close—at least until the media spotlight dimmed. Joey Coyle later hanged himself. He was just 40 years old.

giving of charitable donations are indicators that a defendant has experienced a financial windfall. In the absence of a reasonable explanation for such sudden wealth, juries are likely to consider such information carefully during their deliberations. Although the burden of proof remains with the state, testimony and other evidence of sudden wealth often results in a decision that is not advantageous to the defendant.

Flight to Avoid Prosecution and Threatening of Witnesses

Some jurors will perceive the flight to avoid prosecution and threatening witnesses as indicative of guilt. There is a resounding perception that truly innocent individuals will seek justice by cooperating with the authorities. Indeed, individuals who refuse to cooperate with the authorities by fleeing prosecution all but proclaim their culpability in the minds of many American jurors. This includes cases in which suspects either flee from the crime scene or flee when arrest is imminent. In the case of a fatal shooting, for example, testimony that the defendant ran from the scene might be indicative of his or her involvement in the assault. On the other hand, an individual who flees the area once he is identified as a suspect may seem equally guilty.

THE PANTHER, AN UNPLANNED PREGNANCY, AND MURDER

When Cherica Adams met Rae Carruth, a wide receiver for the Carolina Panthers, she was instantly smitten. Despite knowing that the first round draft pick was a player both on and off the field, Adams continued an on-again/off-again relationship with the athlete. Becoming pregnant by the athlete, Adams looked forward to a more permanent place in his life. Unfortunately for her, Rae Carruth had no intention of adding another child to either his life or his financial obligations. Strongly advising her to have an abortion, Carruth repeatedly informed her that pregnant women were at elevated risk of dying from unnatural causes. Despite his threats (and

abandonment), Cherica Adams continued the pregnancy, and the pair appeared to reconcile in her final trimester.

On November 16, 1999, the pair planned to go to a movie. Carruth told Adams that they should both take their cars to the theater so that they could spend the night together at his place. He told her that he would lead the way. Approaching an intersection, Carruth stopped in the middle of an intersection—effectively blocking Adams' escape route. A car pulled up alongside her and the occupants fired several rounds into her vehicle before speeding away. Struck four times, Adams managed to drive into a nearby yard and call

(continued)

911. She gave authorities a detailed account of the night's events. Upon arrival at the hospital, doctors performed an emergency C-section, and Adams soon lapsed into a coma.

Indicted for the attempted murder of Cherica Adams, Carruth told authorities that she would clear him upon recovery. Unfortunately for him, Adams succumbed to her injuries the following month. Instead of turning himself into authorities as required by his $3 million bail, Carruth fled. He was later found in the trunk of another girlfriend's car with food, water, and bottle for personal needs. His flight from prosecution was introduced in his trial as circumstantial evidence of his guilt. Carruth was subsequently convicted of conspiracy to commit the murder after the prosecution successfully argued that he wanted her dead to avoid paying child support.

Admissions by Conduct

Jurors will often consider the flight to avoid prosecution as circumstantial evidence of an individual's guilt. However, numerous other behaviors also might be circumstantially indicative of guilt. These actions, generally known as admissions by conduct (discussed in greater detail in Chapter 10), are generally admissible under Federal Rule of Evidence 801, which governs the admissibility of hearsay evidence. They include:

• Adoptive admissions

• Admissions by silence

• Failure or refusal to call witnesses, produce evidence, or submit to physical examinations

• Actions taken to obstruct justice

• Plea negotiations

• Payment of medical expenses

MODEL PENAL CODE

MENS REA

There are four general categories of intent under the Model Penal Code.

(a) Purposely. A person acts purposely with respect to a material element of an offense when:

   i. if the element involves the nature of his conduct or a result thereof, it is his conscious object to engage in conduct of that nature or to cause such a result; and

   ii. if the element involves the attendant circumstances, he is aware of the existence of such circumstances or he believes or hopes that they exist.

(b) Knowingly. A person acts knowingly with respect to a material element of an offense when:

   i. if the element involves the nature of his conduct or the attendant circumstances, he is aware that his conduct is of that nature or that such circumstances exist; and

   ii. if the element involves a result of his conduct, he is aware that it is practically certain that his conduct will cause such a result.

(c) Recklessly. A person acts recklessly with respect to a material element of an offense when he consciously disregards a substantial and unjustifiable risk that the material element exists or will result from his conduct. The risk must be of such a nature and degree that, considering the nature and purpose of the actor's conduct and the circumstances known to him, its disregard involves a gross deviation from the standard of conduct that a law-abiding person would observe in the actor's situation.

(d) Negligently. A person acts negligently with respect to a material element of an offense when he should be aware of a substantial and unjustifiable risk that the material element exists or will result from his conduct. The risk must be of such a nature and degree that the actor's failure to perceive it, considering the nature and purpose of his conduct and the circumstances known to him, involves a gross deviation from the standard of care that a reasonable person would observe in the actor's situation.

Guilty Mind

In order to sustain a guilty verdict, the state must demonstrate that the accused possessed **mens rea** or criminal intent. Standards for *mens rea* (Latin for "guilty mind") vary by state. However, there are four general categories of *mens rea* that are incorporated into criminal codes. These categories are: intentionally (or purposely), knowingly, recklessly, and negligently. Each of these designations evaluates the level of foresight and willfulness. Methods of proof vary by categorization, but are demonstrated through circumstantial evidence.

Generally speaking, the law provides for the inference that individuals intend to affect the foreseeable consequences of their deliberate acts. Such statutory declarations may, for example, allow jurors to conclude that an individual who fires a gun in a crowded elevator intended to cause harm to one or more of the occupants. In attempted murder cases, such an inference may be made if a weapon capable of causing death is utilized in a manner consistent with that end.

> **mens rea** literally from the Latin for "guilty mind," the term refers to the criminal intent that is necessary as an element to sustain a guilty verdict in a criminal case. There are four general categories of *mens rea* that are incorporated into criminal codes. These categories are intentionally (or purposely), knowingly, recklessly, and negligently.

CASE LAW

INFERENCES AND INTENT

As stated throughout the text, American due process requires the demonstration of proof to each and every material element of a criminal offense beyond a reasonable doubt. Towards that end, prosecuting attorneys may use direct or circumstantial evidence or a combination thereof. This evidence can include, and may even rely upon, permissive inferences. In *Barnes v. United States* [412 U.S. 837 (1973)], the Court consider a case in which an individual was convicted of possessing U.S. Treasury checks stolen from the mail, forgery, and check fraud. Among other issues, he appealed on the grounds that there was insufficient evidence that he knew that the checks were stolen from the mail—a material element of 18 U.S.C. § 1708. In answering this and other questions raised in the appeal, the Court held:

a) If a statutory inference submitted to the jury as sufficient to support conviction satisfies the reasonable doubt standard (i.e., the evidence necessary to invoke the inference is sufficient for a rational juror to find the inferred fact beyond a reasonable doubt) as well as the more-likely-than-not standard, then it clearly accords with due process.

b) Here, where the evidence established that petitioner possessed recently stolen Treasury checks payable to persons he did not know and it provided no plausible explanation for such possession consistent with innocence, the traditional common law inference satisfies the reasonable doubt standard, the most stringent standard applied by the Court in judging permissive criminal law inferences, and, therefore, comports with due process.

c) Although the introduction of any evidence, direct or circumstantial, tending to implicate the defendant in the alleged crime increases the pressure on him to testify, the mere massing of evidence against him cannot be regarded as a violation of his privilege against self-incrimination.

d) In light of its legislative history and consistent judicial construction, 18 U.S.C. § 1708 requires only knowledge that the checks were stolen, and not knowledge that they were stolen from the mails.

Modus Operandi

modus operandi
the "way of operating" used to prove that a defendant has exhibited a pattern in behavior or methodology during the commission of criminal acts.

In addition to demonstrating consciousness of guilt or guilty actions after the fact, the prosecution may present circumstantial evidence of a guilty mind. This type of evidence can include the modus operandi, habit, uncharged crimes, or bad character. **Modus operandi** refers to the "method of operation." Thus, prosecutors may present evidence showing that the defendant routinely perpetrates the same crime in the same manner. This is especially true in serial or signature crimes. As with other areas of criminal evidence, the trial judge is singularly responsible for the admission or exclusion of such evidence. For example, the trial judge in the 1982 Atlanta trial of Wayne Williams—convicted of the murders of two African-American youths—allowed testimony that the modus operandi of the perpetrator was to routinely throw the bodies of his victims into the river. The judge in the trial of serial killer John Norman Collins, on the other hand, would not admit such evidence. As a result, the number of charges levied against Collins was lessened significantly, although the brutality of his crimes was such that Collins received the maximum penalty under the law. Habit and routine are admissible under the Federal Rules of Evidence.

Theoretically speaking, the American system of criminal justice is such that only those crimes charged in the matter at hand are relevant in the trying of said crimes. The introduction of evidence of past behaviors or uncharged crimes that has not been properly adjudicated and held to the legal standard of "beyond a reasonable doubt" would certainly disadvantage the accused by prejudicing the jurors. Thus, introducing such evidence is extremely limited in most cases. However, there are provisions in the law [FRE 404(b), 413, 414, 415] that allow this type of information to be introduced by the prosecution to infer motive, opportunity, intent, preparation, plan, knowledge, identity, or absence of mistake or accident. In addressing past actions that may be admissible under the rule, courts have ruled that:

> . . . the court may admit the evidence so long as it is satisfied that the evidence is relevant, with relevancy determined by whether a jury could reasonably conclude by a preponderance of the evidence that the past act was a sexual assault and that it was committed by the defendant. (*Johnson v. Elk Lake School District, et. al.*, 3rd District [2002])

For the most part, states have developed rules similar to those articulated in F.R.E. Rule 404 as opposed to those articulated in Rule 413. In Florida, for example, it is known as the Williams Rule and it allows the admission of uncharged crimes and bad acts for the purposes of inferring motive, intent, preparation, or method of operations. However, it specifically precludes testimony or evidence that seeks solely to prove the propensity to commit a particular crime or to prove bad character. This rule received much attention in the rape trial of William Kennedy Smith (nephew of Senator Edward M. Kennedy, President John F. Kennedy, and Attorney General Robert Kennedy) when the presiding judge refused to admit the testimony of three other women who claimed that Smith had either attempted to or actually had raped them in the 1980s. Smith was found not guilty of the rape in Palm Beach. However, the outcome might have been decidedly different had the testimony of his former alleged victims been admissible.

Character

Per Rule 404 of the Federal Rules of Evidence, character evidence generally is not admissible for the demonstration of guilt. Theoretically, the character of the defendant is considered sacrosanct unless the defendant himself or herself places it into question. For example, if a parade of defense witnesses testifies that the accused is

ARTICLE IV: RELEVANCE AND ITS LIMITS

Rule 404—Character Evidence: Crimes or Other Acts

(a) Character Evidence.

(1) *Prohibited Uses.* Evidence of a person's character or character trait is not admissible to prove that on a particular occasion the person acted in accordance with the character or trait.

(2) *Exceptions for a Defendant or Victim in a Criminal Case.* The following exceptions apply in a criminal case:

(A) a defendant may offer evidence of the defendant's pertinent trait, and if the evidence is admitted, the prosecutor may offer evidence to rebut it;

(B) subject to the limitations in Rule 412, a defendant may offer evidence of an alleged victim's pertinent trait, and if the evidence is admitted, the prosecutor may:

(i) offer evidence to rebut it; and

(ii) offer evidence of the defendant's same trait; and

(C) in a homicide case, the prosecutor may offer evidence of the alleged victim's trait of peacefulness to rebut evidence that the victim was the first aggressor.

(3) *Exceptions for a Witness.* Evidence of a witness's character may be admitted under Rules 607, 608, and 609 aq.

(b) Crimes, Wrongs, or Other Acts.

(1) *Prohibited Uses.* Evidence of a crime, wrong, or other act is not admissible to prove a person's character in order to show that on a particular occasion the person acted in accordance with the character.

(2) *Permitted Uses; Notice in a Criminal Case.* This evidence may be admissible for another purpose, such as proving motive, opportunity, intent, preparation, plan, knowledge, identity, absence of mistake, or lack of accident. On request by a defendant in a criminal case, the prosecutor must:

(A) provide reasonable notice of the general nature of any such evidence that the prosecutor intends to offer at trial; and

(B) do so before trial—or during trial if the court, for good cause, excuses lack of pretrial notice.

Rule 406—Habit; Routine Practice

Evidence of the habit of a person or the routine practice of an organization, whether corroborated or not and regardless of the presence of eyewitnesses, is relevant to prove that the conduct of the person or organization on a particular occasion was in conformity with the habit or routine practice.

Rule 413—Similar Crimes in Sexual-Assault Cases

(a) Permitted Uses. In a criminal case in which a defendant is accused of a sexual assault, the court may admit evidence that the defendant committed any other sexual assault. The evidence may be considered on any matter to which it is relevant.

(b) Disclosure to the Defendant. If the prosecutor intends to offer this evidence, the prosecutor must disclose it to the defendant, including witnesses' statements or a summary of the expected testimony. The prosecutor must do so at least 15 days before trial or at a later time that the court allows for good cause.

(c) Effect on Other Rules. This rule does not limit the admission or consideration of evidence under any other rule.

the most honest man in the county, then the prosecution may present witnesses to counter such claims. The inadmissibility of character evidence cements the notion of judicial fairness. For the most part, evidence of an individual's character lacks probity and is far outweighed by the potential for the interjection of prejudice into the proceedings at hand. Such evidence, in fact, could distract the triers of fact from the immediate matter, so that an arbitrary system of reward and punishment

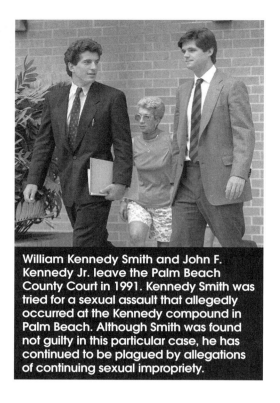

William Kennedy Smith and John F. Kennedy Jr. leave the Palm Beach County Court in 1991. Kennedy Smith was tried for a sexual assault that allegedly occurred at the Kennedy compound in Palm Beach. Although Smith was found not guilty in this particular case, he has continued to be plagued by allegations of continuing sexual impropriety.

could be employed. The "good guys" would be exonerated irrespective of the facts, just as the "bad guys" would be convicted. Thus, the defendant's character is largely off-limits for the prosecution. The victim's character, on the other hand, is fair game.

The character of the victim may be admitted in cases where questions of that character are relevant to the proceedings at hand. Thus, evidence that the alleged victim had a history of violence would be admissible in a case in which he claims to have been attacked by a fellow bar patron. The issue becomes a little more complicated in sexual assault cases where rape shield laws might be in effect.

Rape shield laws were largely created in the 1980s to protect victims of sexual assault from the humiliation often heaped upon them by defense attorneys. In the most general sense, they were intended to eliminate questions that were irrelevant to the current proceedings and that tended to portray the victim in an unflattering light. Until the passage of rape shield laws, victims could be asked questions regarding their sexual history, sexual preferences, and even, sexual activity with their spouses. However, the laws have proved largely ineffectual because of the various exceptions that exist. For example, in the Kobe Bryant case, the defense clearly intended to question the alleged victim's sexual past. Even before the case had been placed on the docket, media stories vilified the woman by painting her as promiscuous. As a general rule, defense attorneys may question the victim's sexual history whenever they can demonstrate its relevance to the current proceedings. Because sexual assault cases hinge on the question of consent, the defense may argue that the victim's sexual history is relevant to prove that the victim routinely engaged in such activity.

Prior Molestation

Another area in which the Federal Rules (414[a]) allow for the introduction of bad acts or uncharged crimes lies in the area of child molestation. Very similar to the provisions provided in Rule 413, this rule allows for the introduction of evidence of child molestation in cases where the defendant is being charged with

ARTICLE IV: RELEVANCE AND ITS LIMITS

Rule 412—Sex Offenses Cases: Relevance of Victim's Past Behavior or Alleged Sexual Predisposition

(a) Evidence generally inadmissible.

The following evidence is not admissible in any civil or criminal proceeding involving alleged sexual misconduct except as provided in subdivisions (b) and (c):

1. Evidence offered to prove that any alleged victim engaged in other sexual behavior

2. Evidence offered to prove any alleged victim's sexual predisposition

(b) Exceptions.

1. In a criminal case, the following evidence is admissible, if otherwise admissible under these rules:

    (a) evidence of specific instances of sexual behavior by the alleged victim offered to prove that a person other than the accused was the source of semen, injury or other physical evidence;

    (b) evidence of specific instances of sexual behavior by the alleged victim with respect to the person accused of the sexual misconduct offered by the accused to prove consent or by the prosecution; and

    (c) evidence the exclusion of which would violate the constitutional rights of the defendant.

2. In a civil case, evidence offered to prove the sexual behavior or sexual predisposition of any alleged victim is admissible if it is otherwise admissible under these rules and its probative value substantially outweighs the danger of harm to any victim and of unfair prejudice to any party. Evidence of an alleged victim's reputation is admissible only if it has been placed in controversy by the alleged victim.

child molestation. Under federal law, only individuals under the age of 14 are considered children.

Prior Abuse

Battered child syndrome or the past abuse of a child may be introduced as circumstantial evidence in the murder of a child in that:

> The demonstration of battered child syndrome "simply indicates that a child found with [serious, repeated injuries] has not suffered those injuries by accidental means" (Id., at 507, 95 Cal.Rptr., at 921). Thus, evidence demonstrating battered child syndrome helps to prove that the child died at the hands of another, and not by falling off a couch, for example; it also tends to establish that the "other," whoever it may be, inflicted the injuries intentionally. When offered to show that certain injuries are a product of child abuse, rather than accident, evidence of prior injuries is relevant, even though it does not purport to prove the identity of the person who might have inflicted those injuries.[9]

Some states have adopted battered woman syndrome as a form of limited affirmative defense in cases where women are accused of the murder or attempted murder of their spouses. Unlike the forms of circumstantial evidence discussed previously, the battered woman syndrome is most often offered by the defense, as opposed to the prosecution. The Supreme Court has recognized that:

> Descriptions of this syndrome emphasize the husband's repeated and violent beatings and the wife's dependency—economic and emotional—that make it practically impossible for her to leave. When faced with an immediate threat, victims may be driven to take the lives of their mates as the only possible method of escaping the threat. Although traditional self-defense theory may seem to fit the situation only imperfectly . . . the battered woman's syndrome as a self-defense theory has gained increasing support over recent years.[10]

In 2004, sexual assault charges against Los Angeles Lakers' star Kobe Bryant were dropped after the victim refused to cooperate further. Her lack of cooperation in the criminal case followed a decision by the court to allow questions regarding her sexual history despite of Colorado's rape shield laws. In March 2005, Kobe Bryant settled the lawsuit for an undisclosed amount. The treatment of the victim throughout the criminal process angered many victims' advocate groups.

Thus, evidence of past abuse may be introduced as circumstantial evidence by the defense to prove the affirmative defense of self-defense. However, such information may also be used against the interest of the accused when the prosecution tries to demonstrate that the woman's life was never in danger because the past beatings were never fatal.

▶ Other Uses of Circumstantial Evidence

As the preceding discussions demonstrate, the use of circumstantial evidence to infer the guilt of a defendant is more than common in criminal cases.

Inference of Possession

Physical possession of an item has always carried great weight in American courtrooms. Whether the case involved a property dispute or a burglary, the sheer control of an item inferred ownership. This reasoning has carried over to other areas in the criminal justice system. The possession of a certain weight of a particular controlled substance, for example, calls for the legal inference of distributional intent even before trial begins. In fact, this very wording is in virtually every criminal code. Other inferences occur within the confines of the courthouse.

> To sustain a conviction for possession of cocaine with intent to distribute, the government must prove beyond a reasonable doubt that the defendant knowingly possessed the cocaine and that he intended to distribute it. Id. To prove conspiracy to possess cocaine with intent to distribute, the government must establish three elements: (1) that a conspiracy to possess cocaine existed; (2) that the defendant knew of the goal of the conspiracy; and (3) that the defendant, with knowledge, voluntarily joined it. . . .

Where the government's case is circumstantial, "reasonable inferences, and not mere speculation, must support the jury's verdict." . . . To sustain a conviction for possession with intent to distribute a controlled substance, the government need not prove that a defendant had knowledge of the particular drug involved, but the government did need to prove that he knew he was dealing with a controlled substance . . . "all of the circuits, including this one, require something more than mere presence in [a car in which drugs are hidden] to sustain a [drug possession] conviction." (*United States v. Stanley*, 24 F.3d 1314, 1320 [11th Cir.1994]). But we have upheld convictions when presence is combined with other evidence from which guilt can be inferred. . . . Although the government presented no evidence that Mejia was involved in or present for any negotiations for the purchase of cocaine, Mejia's extensive presence, combined with the other evidence of guilt, was [sic] support a conclusion that he participated in a conspiracy to possess cocaine with intent to distribute.[11]

Automobiles

Millions of drivers in the United States rely on their driver's licenses for their livelihood, entertainment, and other needs. Unlike other countries where automobiles are considered a luxury, most Americans treat them as a basic necessity of life. However, many of those same individuals labor under the misconception that driving is a fundamental right. It is not a right guaranteed to citizens by the Constitution or by any statutory act. It is in fact, a privilege. As such, provisions enable the seizure of one's driver's license for noncompliance of traffic laws. For example, most states have implied consent statutes that allow the immediate suspension of driving privileges for individuals who refuse to submit to blood–alcohol content (BAC) testing or road sobriety tests. The Supreme Court has consistently ruled that such action does not violate due process of law because the issuance of licenses is controlled by the states and is extended to their constituents as a privilege. Subsequently, the Court has also ruled that the refusal to submit to such tests could be used as an inference of guilt. Lower courts have also ruled that the inference that an intoxicated person seated behind the wheel of a parked car with the keys in the ignition has operated the vehicle. Hence, some jurisdictions provide for the prosecution of such an individual for drunk driving. In addition, inferences may be drawn regarding possession of contraband found within the confines of a personally operated vehicle. When found upon an individual, possession is clear. In cases in which criminal evidence or contraband is found in the general area around the individual, it may be inferred that the item, claimed or not, is the property of the driver.

Prior False Claims and Lack of Accident

In some cases involving fraud, evidence may be submitted that demonstrates that the accused had previously filed false claims or that the complainant had previously filed claims against others that were later found to be unsubstantiated. In a criminal case in which a defendant acknowledges the incident but issues the affirmative defense of accident, the prosecution may introduce or demonstrate patterns of criminal activity. Such circumstantial evidence, for example, may be introduced in a case where an individual claims to have mistakenly grabbed the wrong purse or briefcase.

▶ Inferences That May Not Be Drawn

Circumstantial evidence may be used to infer guilt in many different situations, but it may not be used in those situations in which an individual invokes a right that is guaranteed by the Constitution, extended by a state, or upheld by the Supreme Court.

Refusal to Testify

As discussed, the cornerstone of American democracy is the ability to embrace our rights as citizens without fear of reprisal from the state. For the most part, these are situated firmly in the Bill of Rights. The right to remain silent is one universally known right, forever immortalized in the 1966 Miranda warnings. However, the perception that an innocent person has nothing to hide runs nearly as deep. Such rights were originally addressed by the Court in *United States v. Hale*, 422 U.S. 171 (1975), in which the Court ruled that the use of post-arrest, post-Miranda warnings silence was not admissible in federal cases. Since that time, this right has been solidified further, and the Court has even expanded it to include the responsibility of a jurist to protect said rights of the defendant and to minimize all erroneous perceptions. The Court held that:

> Petitioner had a right to the requested instruction under the privilege against compulsory self-incrimination of the Fifth Amendment as made applicable to the States by the Fourteenth Amendment, a state trial judge having a constitutional obligation, upon proper request, to minimize the danger that the jury will give evidentiary weight to a defendant's failure to testify. (pp. 295–305)
>
> (a) The penalty imposed upon a defendant for the exercise of his constitutional privilege not to testify is severe when there is an adverse comment on his silence, *Griffin v. California*, 380 U.S. 609, but even without adverse comment, a jury, unless instructed otherwise, may well draw adverse inferences from a defendant's silence. Instructions to the jury on the law are perhaps nowhere more important than in the context of the Fifth Amendment privilege against compulsory self-incrimination. While no judge can prevent jurors from speculating about why a defendant stands mute in the face of a criminal accusation, a judge can, and must, if requested to do so, use the unique power of the jury instruction to reduce that speculation to a minimum.[12]

Exercise of Right to Counsel

An additional area in which the state is prohibited from venturing is the invocation of the right to an attorney as guaranteed by the Sixth Amendment. The Court has consistently ruled that no implication of guilt may be inferred when a defendant exercises his right to counsel. Their justifications have varied, but the consensus has been that the right is so fundamental and so widely recognized by individuals in society that its implementation lacks any probative value. In *Wainwright v. Greenfield*, 474 U.S. 284 (1986), the Court addressed the introduction of testimony that the defendant had requested an attorney and had refused to answer the questions of officers. It ruled that:

> . . . while it is true that the Miranda warnings contain no express assurance that silence will carry no penalty, such assurance is implicit to any person who receives the warnings. In such circumstances, it would be fundamentally unfair and a deprivation of due process to allow the arrested person's silence to be used to impeach an explanation subsequently offered at trial. Mr. JUSTICE WHITE, concurring in the judgment in *United States v. Hale*, [422 U.S.], at 182–183, put it very well:" '[W] hen a person under arrest is informed, as Miranda requires, that he may remain silent, that anything he says may be used against him, and that he may have an attorney if he wishes, it seems to me that it does not comport with due process to permit the prosecution during the trial to call attention to his silence at the time of arrest and to insist that because he did not speak about the facts of the case at that time, as he was told he need not do, an unfavorable inference might be drawn as to the truth of his trial testimony. . . .

► Substitutions for Evidence

Irrespective of type or form, some situations arise in American criminal courts when the jury is instructed on what to believe and is not free to draw independent inferences. Each has been determined to be necessary to expedite the criminal justice process because many questions or issues are not in debate and do not require arbitration. These situations, including presumptions, stipulations, and judicial notice, are such that jurors must adopt the statement or evidence as fact.

Stipulations

Of these three types of situations involving mandatory compliance, the simplest is stipulations. A **stipulation**, simply put, is a product of an agreement between opposing counsels regarding specific facts of the case. Such agreements usually are reached only when they are mutually beneficial to counsels' case. When stipulations are presented to the fact finder, their nature necessarily precludes further testimony or evidence concerning the facts as stipulated. However, in many cases, the stipulation of a fact is more advantageous to one side and may be rejected by opposing counsel.

stipulation a product of an agreement between opposing counsels regarding specific facts of the case.

Presumptions

The next type of situation in which the jury or fact finder is bound to accept a particular fact or truth involves legal presumptions. By definition, a **presumption** is a conclusion or deduction that is required by law. Unlike an inference—a deduction that may be drawn—a presumption may be overcome only with a showing of sufficient evidence. Under law, presumptions must be based on logical assumptions, and when presented by the prosecution, must be established beyond a reasonable doubt. For example, the presumption of innocence, a mainstay in American jurisprudence, requires a finding of not guilty in cases in which a conclusion of guilt was not demonstrated beyond a reasonable doubt.

presumption a conclusion or deduction that is required by law.

 CLARIFICATION OF CONCEPTS

PRESUMPTIONS VERSUS INFERENCES

A *presumption* is a conclusion made as to the existence or nonexistence of a fact that must be drawn from other evidence that is admitted and proven to be true. Conclusive presumptions are irrefutable; rebuttable presumptions may be challenged to disprove presumed fact. For example, most states presume that children under the age of 10 are not competent to serve as witnesses. Such a presumption is rebuttable. Thus, trial judges may admit the testimony of individual children on a case-by-case basis after the child's competency has been evaluated outside the presence of the jury.

An *inference*, on the other hand, is a logical or deductive conclusion drawn from evidence, generally the conclusion that something is more probable than not. The New England case of Dirk Greineder, a renowned allergist, accused of killing his wife in a public park provides an example. Although the physician testified that he had attempted to resuscitate his wife after finding her dead, the lack of blood on the good doctor's hands suggested that he was lying. After finding him guilty, many jurors claimed that this inference overcame the presumption of innocence afforded him.

In the most general sense, two types of presumptions exist. The first are **conclusive presumptions**, which are irrefutable. The second are **rebuttable presumptions**, which opposing counsel may challenge and overcome by presenting strong evidence to disprove presumed fact. Before DNA testing, for example, many states maintained a conclusive presumption of paternity in cases in which a child was born during a marriage. Such presumptions could not be challenged even in the face of irrefutable evidence available during that time, such as sterility. Such social policy was representative of a culture that presumed that marital partners remained faithful and that challenges of paternity were attempts to circumvent fiduciary responsibility. With advances in paternity testing, however, many states have now established rebuttable presumptions, in which challenges of paternity may be issued and won. This is not true in every state, and some men may find themselves legally and financially responsible for a child who is not biologically their own.

conclusive presumptions an irrefutable conclusion that must be drawn by a fact-finder.

rebuttable presumptions a legal conclusion that may be challenged and overcome by the presentment of strong evidence by opposing counsel.

Judicial Notice

judicial notice an action taken by the court to make a determination of fact without the formality or examination by a jury.

Judicial notice is the term used to denote an action taken by the court to make a determination of fact without the formality of examination by a jury. To wit, the court makes an irrefutable statement of fact to the jury. As noted in *Palmer v. Mitchell*[13]

> . . . The doctrine of judicial notice operates to admit into evidence, without formal proof, those facts which are a matter of common and general knowledge and which are established and known within the limits of the jurisdiction of the court.

(Legally speaking, civil juries are required to accept such facts as true. Although criminal juries are not bound as tightly to this standard, most fail to recognize the subtlety.) This practice is all but mandatory in American courts of law as elevated caseloads encourage any action that would streamline the criminal justice process. Imagine a system in which the smallest, least significant fact had to be formally proven, such as the current year, existence of the solar system, or number of tires on a standard automobile. This is not to suggest, however, that unclear circumstances are routinely determined at the discretion of the presiding

---

FEDERAL RULES OF EVIDENCE

ARTICLE II. JUDICIAL NOTICE

Rule 201—Judicial Notice of Adjudicative Facts

(a) Scope. This rule governs judicial notice of an adjudicative fact only, not a legislative fact.

(b) Kinds of Facts That May Be Judicially Noticed. The court may judicially notice a fact that is not subject to reasonable dispute because it:

(1) is generally known within the trial court's territorial jurisdiction; or

(2) can be accurately and readily determined from sources whose accuracy cannot reasonably be questioned.

(c) Taking Notice. The court:

(1) may take judicial notice on its own; or

(2) must take judicial notice if a party requests it and the court is supplied with the necessary information.

(d) Timing. The court may take judicial notice at any stage of the proceeding.

(e) Opportunity to Be Heard. On timely request, a party is entitled to be heard on the propriety of taking judicial notice and the nature of the fact to be noticed. If the court takes judicial notice before notifying a party, the party, on request, is still entitled to be heard.

(f) Instructing the Jury. In a civil case, the court must instruct the jury to accept the noticed fact as conclusive. In a criminal case, the court must instruct the jury that it may or may not accept the noticed fact as conclusive.

judge. In fact, judicial notice exists in a climate in which procedural safeguards attempt to ensure fundamental fairness to criminal defendants.

Judicial notice, then, is limited to things recognized as fact. In a nonjury trial, the presiding judge simply issues a statement of fact that is introduced into the official record—the term judicial notice is often not uttered in these situations. However, in a jury trial, the judge is required to formally instruct the jury as to the rationale and definition of judicial notice. Because of the lack of evidentiary proof offered, judicially noticed facts are also known as nonevidence facts.

There are four general areas of judicial notice: legislative facts, adjudicative facts, political facts, and matters of law. Although **legislative facts** may be subdivided into three areas, the term generally refers to facts that might include the interpretation of a statute or constitutional provision or the creation or modification of a common law rule. Legislative facts might also include the legislative history of a relevant statute, interpretation of nonlegal facts used in a relevant legislative process, and information about the impact of extant law.

Although not specifically defined in F.R.E 201, **adjudicative facts** normally are facts that would require proof if not judicially noticed. Thus, they may be characterized as substitutes for evidence. Adjudicative facts include, but are not limited to, common definitions, pronunciations, idioms, slang, and body language. They also include demographic, historical, and (limited) scientific facts, such as chemical symbols. For example, a judge might take judicial notice of a common intersection, the distance between landmarks, or the general acceptance of fingerprinting. In other cases, the ratification of legal documents, major historical discoveries, and documented historical facts, such as D-Day or Pearl Harbor day, might also be noticed. All of these facts, which are known throughout the community, are considered adjudicative or evaluative facts.

As in other areas of evidence law, the Federal Rules of Evidence are largely vague and inconclusive in this area. Greater guidance is found in the Uniform Rules of Evidence (U.R.E.).

legislative facts
factual information regarding the interpretation of a statute or constitutional provision, creation or modification of a common law rule, legislative history of a relevant statute, or information about the impact of extant law.

adjudicative facts
facts that would require proof if not judicially noticed, such as chemical symbols and common definitions and pronunciations.

▶ CONCLUSIONS

All evidence admissible in courts of the United States must be relevant, material, and competent. The U.S. Constitution requires each element of a crime to be proved beyond a reasonable doubt. To prove these elements, direct evidence or circumstantial (indirect) evidence can be employed. In most criminal cases, both types are used, but a conviction can stand on circumstantial evidence alone. Direct evidence proves a fact without the need for inference or presumption. Circumstantial evidence, on the other hand, does require a presumption that indirectly proves a fact. Circumstantial evidence, nonetheless, can be extremely powerful. For instance, even scientific evidence such as DNA is classified as circumstantial evidence. The introduction of DNA evidence requires the jury to make the inference that the DNA was left by the defendant.

Sometimes a situation will arise in which juries are not free to draw their own conclusions or inferences and are instructed on how to interpret a particular piece of evidence. These situations are considered substitutions for evidence, and they include presumptions, stipulations, and judicial notice. Stipulations are often facts that both parties have either agreed upon or have facts that have been unsuccessfully challenged. A presumption differs from an inference in that a certain conclusion must be drawn, while a conclusion by inference may be drawn. Judicial notice refers to items that are commonly recognized as fact by the court (nonevidence facts) and are introduced in jury trials through judicial instruction.

Key Terms

Adjudicative facts

Alibi

Circumstantial evidence

Competent evidence

Concealment

Conclusive presumptions

Consciousness of guilt

Criminal intent

Direct evidence

Evidence

Inferences

Judicial notice

Legislative facts

Materiality

Means

Mens rea

Modus operandi

Motive

Opportunity

Presumption

Prima facie

Real evidence

Rebuttable presumptions

Relevancy

Relevant evidence

Stipulation

Sudden wealth

Discussion Questions

1. What factors determine the admissibility and relevancy of evidence?
2. Discuss the evidence issues in the two cases of T. Cullen Davis.
3. What are the main differences between circumstantial evidence and direct evidence?
4. What can be inferred from circumstantial evidence?
5. What inferences cannot be drawn from circumstantial evidence?
6. What are common examples of consciousness of guilt?
7. What are the differences between presumptions and inferences?
8. What is the function of judicial notice?
9. How do presumptions, inferences, and judicial notice function as substitutes for evidence? Are these constitutional? In what circumstances are these substitutes used?

Recommended Resources

Videos

A&E Television. Oil, money . . . murder. *American justice.* This is the case of T. Cullen Davis. Available at: http://store.aetv.com.

CourtTV. Oil, money, and mystery. *Dominick Dunne's power, privilege, and justice.* This includes the case of T. Cullen Davis as covered in Dominick Dunne's book *Power, Privilege, and Justice.* Available at http://www.courttv.com/store/dvds/dunne/CT1420.html.

A&E Television. The California killing field. *American justice.* This video covers the Charles Ng and Leonard Lake murders and the expensive prosecution of Ng. Available at: http://store.aetv.com.

A&E Television. When a child kills. *American justice.* This is the story of the youngest person to ever be tried as an adult for murder. It also illustrates concepts of *mens rea* and legal maturity. Available at: http://store.aetv.com.

HBO Productions. *Paradise lost: The child murders at Robin Hood Hills.* This documentary aptly illustrates various legal concepts, including reasonable doubt and impeachment of witnesses. Widely available.

HBO Productions. *Paradise lost: Revelations.* Widely available.

Books

Lasseter, Don. (2000). *Die for me: The terrifying true story of the Charles Ng/Leonard Lake torture murders.* New York: Pinnacle.

Leveritt, Mara. (2002). *Devil's knot: The true story of the West Memphis Three.* New York: Atria Books.

Sizer, Mona D. (2000). *Texas justice, bought and paid for.* Texas: Republic of Texas.

Online Sources

http://www.findlaw.com—Search state and federal case law, statutes, and federal and state constitutions.

http://www.law.cornell.edu/—Official Web site of Cornell Law School's Legal Information Institute for court decisions, structure, law reviews, and more.

http://www.aetv.com—Online informational Web site for the A&E network. Includes program listings and access to an online store for various programs, such as Investigative Reports, City Confidential, American Justice, and others.

http://www.supremecourtus.gov/—Official Web site of the U.S. Supreme Court for access to rules, procedures, and opinions of the Court.

http://www.law.cornell.edu/rules/fre/—Search the Federal Rules of Evidence here. Web site contains a powerful search engine to help you locate information using key terms and phrases.

Relevant Cases Cited

Barnes v. United States 412 U.S. 837 (1973)

Carter v. Kentucky, 450 U.S. 288 (1981)

Griffin v. California, 380 U.S. 609 (1965)

Estelle v. Mcguire, 502 U.S. 62 (1991)

Henry v. United States, 361 U.S. 98 (1959)

Holland v. United States, 348 U.S. 121, (1954)

Johnson v. Elk Lake School District, et. al., 3rd District (2002) – F.R.E. 404

Moran v. Ohio, 469 U.S. 948 (1984)

Rice v. Paladin Enterprises, Inc., 128.3d 233 (4th Cir. 11/10/1997)

Sandstrom v. Montana, 442 U.S. 510 (1979)

Ulster County Court v. Allen, 442 U.S. 140 (1978)

United States v. Abel 469 U.S. 54 (1984)

United States v. Gaudin 515 U.S. 506 (1995)

United States v. Hale, 422 U.S. 171 (1975)

United States v. Mejia, 97 F.3d 1391, 1392 (11th Cir.1996)

United States v. Weinstock, 231 F.2d 699 (D.C. Cir. 1956)

Wainwright v. Greenfield, 474 U.S. 284 (1986)

Notes

1. Mueller, C. B. and Kirkpatrick, L. C. (2004). *Evidence under the rules* (4th Edition). Aspen Law: New York.
2. Ibid.
3. [*United States v. Weinstock*, 231 F.2d 699 (D.C. Cir. 1956)]
4. 231 F.2d at 703.
5. Rosenberg, I. M. and Rosenberg, Y. L. (1995). Perhaps what ye say is based only on conjecture: Circumstantial evidence, then and now. *Houston Law Review*, *31*, 1391–1427.
6. Wills, W. (1853). *An essay on the principles of circumstantial evidence.* Philadelphia: T. & J.W. Johnson Publishing
7. *Holland v. United States*, 348 U.S. 121 (1954)
8. Victim's Statement as released to the public by the Tallahassee Police Department.
9. *Estelle v. Mcguire*, 502 U.S. 62 (1991)
10. *Moran v. Ohio*, 469 U.S. 948 (1984)
11. *United States v. Mejia*, 97 F.3d 1391, 1392 (11th Cir. 1996)
12. *Carter v. Kentucky*, 450 U.S. 288 (1981)
13. 206 N.E. 2d 775 (Ill. App. 1965)

THE DECLARATION OF INDEPENDENCE.

4 Search and Seizure and the Doctrine of Justification

LEARNING OBJECTIVES

The learner will:

1 *Discern the differences between probable cause and reasonable suspicion*

2 *Explain probable cause as it relates to search warrants*

3 *Explain the inception of the right to privacy*

4 *Explain the inclusions and exceptions to the right of privacy*

⑤ *Examine the right of privacy as it relates and does not relate to technology*

⑥ *Discuss the issue of privacy versus governmental invasion as it relates to the U.S. Constitution*

⑦ *Explain the considerations for determination of probable cause in the case of a warrant*

⑧ *Examine the parameters of staleness, vicinage, and particularity in search warrants*

⑨ *Explain the types of warrants*

The passage of the Magna Carta in 1215 signaled the beginning of an evolutionary process, the product of which was the due process of law. Before the passage, citizens could be questioned, detained, and arrested at the whim of the government. The Magna Carta forbade such incidents, and introduced the notion of "reasonable grounds"—the precursor to the American concept of probable cause. With the Magna Carta and traditional atrocities committed by the British Crown in mind, the framers of the U.S. Constitution took pains to safeguard the rights of individuals to be secure in their persons and property by articulating standards of cause and providing legal mechanisms for assurances of such rights. The standards and processes articulated in the first 10 amendments of the Constitution are commonly known as the Bill of Rights. For American citizens, the protection from unlawful detainment, inquiry, and searches resides firmly within the Fourth Amendment. Ratified in 1791, the Fourth Amendment provides:

> The right of the people to be secure in their persons, houses, papers, and effects, against unreasonable searches and seizures, shall not be violated, and no warrants shall issue, but upon probable cause, supported by oath or affirmation, and particularly describing the place to be searched, and the persons or things to be seized.

Since its ratification, the Court has consistently been called upon to interpret the parameter and meaning of the Amendment. Indeed, it may be argued that the Fourth Amendment has received more judicial attention than all the others. Areas of clarification posed to the Court have included, but have not been limited to: distinguishing searches from seizures, doctrines of justification, the expectation of privacy, the Warrant Clause, and remedies for violation.

▶ Distinguishing Searches from Seizures Under the Fourth Amendment

Katz vs United States — Telephone booth case

Although often overlooked, the first measure of consideration in a Fourth Amendment analysis involves the question as to when it attaches. It is important to note that the Amendment's protections only apply to: (1) government actions in (2) private areas. They do not apply to investigations conducted by nongovernment entities *unless* those investigations are initiated by, or under the supervision of, state actors; nor do they apply to areas lacking an expectation of privacy. Traditionally, protections were limited to the physical intrusion into an individual's home or other area in which he or she had a property interest. Thus, traditional definitions of searches were closely tied to property rights. However, the Court greatly extended the Amendment's reach in *Katz v. United States* (1967)[1] when it considered whether an expectation of privacy existed in a public telephone booth. The Court clarified that the protections of the Fourth Amendment were not as limited as previously thought. In fact, the Court recognized that both intangible items and areas accessed without a physical intrusion may be protected within its parameters.

> . . . the Fourth Amendment protects people, not places. What a person knowingly exposes to the public, even in his own home or office, is not a subject of Fourth Amendment protection . . . but what he seeks to preserve as private, even in an area accessible to the public, may be constitutionally protected . . . it is true that the absence of such penetration was at one time thought to foreclose further Fourth Amendment inquiry . . . for that Amendment was thought to limit only searches and seizures of tangible property. But "(t)he premise that property interests control the right of the Government to search and seize has been discredited . . . Indeed, we have expressly held that the Fourth Amendment governs not only the seizure of tangible items, but extends as well to the recording of oral statements, overheard without any "technical trespass under . . . local property law."

The implications of *Katz* were immediate and long reaching. First, the ruling extended constitutional protections to intangibles, including conversations. Second, the Court specifically tied the rights to an individual's expectation of privacy. Thus, a **search** in contemporary parlance may be defined as an examination of an individual's person, property, or other area in which they have a reasonable expectation of privacy by law enforcement.

It is important to note that while the terms "search" and "seizure" are often treated synonymously, the concepts are both legally and practically disparate. Depending on case characteristics, investigators may be authorized to search but not seize or vice versa. The Court has distinguished the terms thusly

> The first Clause of the Fourth Amendment provides that the "right of the people to be secure in their persons, houses, papers, and effects, against unreasonable searches and seizures, shall not be violated" . . . this text protects two types of expectations, one involving "searches," the other "seizures." A "search" occurs when an expectation of privacy that society is prepared to consider reasonable is infringed. A "seizure" of property occurs when there is some meaningful interference with an individual's possessory interests in that property.[2]

So, a **seizure** may be defined as a government action which meaningfully interferes with an individual's possessory interests in that property. Such interest may be *actual* or *constructive*. Individuals have **actual possession** of property if they are physically holding or grasping it. They have **constructive possession** of property if they possess it but are not physically touching it. For example, individuals have actual possession of drugs concealed in their mouth; and constructive possession of the drugs found in their closet.

Like searches, questions as to the legality of a particular seizure hinge upon the reasonableness of the action from inception to conclusion. For the most part, seizures of persons or property occur after a search. However, the Court has recognized a compelling government interest in the pre-search seizure of individuals in a number of cases. For example, officers may seize individuals toward:

- . . . effective crime prevention and detection; it is this interest which underlies the recognition that a police officer may in appropriate circumstances and in an appropriate manner approach a person for purposes of investigating possibly criminal behavior even though there is no probable cause to make an arrest. *Terry v. Ohio* [392 U.S. 1 (1968)]
- . . . preventing flight in the event that incriminating evidence is found, "minimizing the risk of harm" both to the officers and the occupants, and "orderly completion of the search" Michigan v. Summers [452 U.S. 692 (1981)]

search an examination of an individual's person, property or other area in which they have a reasonable expectation of privacy by law enforcement.

seizure a government action that meaningfully interferes with an individual's possessory interests in that property.

actual possession a consideration in the evaluation of an individual's possessory interest in an object which is demonstrated when that individual is physically holding or grasping the object.

constructive possession a consideration in the evaluation of an individual's possessory interest in an object which is demonstrated when that individual possesses it but is not physically touching it, such as when the item is located in the individual's car.

TRAFFIC STOPS, DRUG DOGS, AND THE FOURTH AMENDMENT

In *Illinois v. Caballes* (2005),[3] the Court considered whether the Fourth Amendment required "*reasonable*, articulable suspicion to justify using a drug-detection dog to sniff a vehicle during a legitimate traffic stop." In this case, Respondent was stopped by an Illinois state trooper for speeding. A second trooper, a member of the Illinois State Police Drug Interdiction Team, responded to the scene after hearing the first trooper's report to dispatch. Upon arrival, he observed the respondent in the trooper's car awaiting a warning citation to be issued. He then walked his narcotics canine around respondent's car. The dog alerted, and a subsequent search of the vehicle revealed marijuana concealed in the trunk. The entire incident lasted less than 10 minutes. During his trial, respondent moved to suppress the evidence and quash the arrest arguing that the use of the dog improperly prolonged the arrest. More specifically, he argued that the search of his car and the seizure of his person was unconstitutional as it was not based on "specific and articulable facts" and that the use of the dog "unjustifiably enlarged the scope of a routine traffic stop into a drug investigation." The trial court disagreed and the respondent was convicted and sentenced to 12 years imprisonment.

The Illinois Supreme Court overturned the lower court's decision ruling that the initially lawful traffic stop became an unlawful seizure as a result of the canine sniff that occurred outside the respondent's stopped car. Granting certiorari, the Court held that:

> . . . conducting a dog sniff would not change the character of a traffic stop that is lawful at its inception and otherwise executed in a reasonable manner, unless the dog sniff itself infringed respondent's constitutionally protected interest in privacy. Our cases hold that it did not . . . Official conduct that does not "compromise any legitimate interest in privacy" is not a search subject to the Fourth Amendment. . . . We have held that any interest in possessing contraband cannot be deemed "legitimate," and thus, governmental conduct that only reveals the possession of contraband "compromises no legitimate privacy interest" . . . accordingly, the use of a well-trained narcotics-detection dog—one that "does not expose noncontraband items that otherwise would remain hidden from public view," during a lawful traffic stop, generally does not implicate legitimate privacy interests. In this case, the dog sniff was performed on the exterior of respondent's car while he was lawfully seized for a traffic violation.

▶ Legal Measures of Justification and the Fourth Amendment

In the United States, individuals are protected from government tyranny by the Constitution and the Bill of Rights. Among other guarantees housed within, the pair entitles all Americans to due process, freedom of movement, and limited government intrusion. The Fourth Amendment specifically ensures the right of individuals to be secure in their persons, houses, papers, and effects. It is predicated on the elusive construct of probable cause and may be characterized as a careful balance between individual rights and community interests. Since its inception, the Court has sought to clarify the parameters of the Amendment while also recognizing other legal measures of justification. Thus, the evolution of Fourth Amendment jurisprudence seeks to secure the fundamental privileges associated with American citizenry, but also seeks to provide for the protection of the society that spawned them. Toward this end, the next issue in any Fourth Amendment analysis is to determine whether the standard of justification has been satisfied.

LEGAL MEASURES OF JUSTIFICATION

- **Administrative justification**—a judicially created measure of justification that provides for the limited search of an area in cases where the safety of society outweighs an individual's interest in privacy. Most often used to justify health inspections, intrusions into government workers involved with mass transportation, or school searches.

- **Reasonable suspicion**—the lowest of all legal standards of justification is less than probable cause but is that which is necessary to authorize an investigative detention. It requires a demonstration that a reasonable perception exists that a crime has been, is being, or will be committed.

- **Probable cause**—situated between reasonable suspicion and beyond a reasonable doubt is the standard required for an arrest, issuance of a warrant, and affectation of physical detainment. It requires a demonstration that a reasonable person could conclude that the accused has committed a crime or that evidence of such crime exists.

---

administrative justification a judicially created measure of justification that provides for the limited search of an area in cases where the safety of society outweighs an individual's interest in privacy. Most often used to justify health inspections, intrusions into government workers involved with mass transportation, or school searches.

Traditionally, the standard of justification for all government searches and seizures of private areas was probable cause. As the Court noted in *Brinegar*,

> . . . These long-prevailing standards seek to safeguard citizens from rash and unreasonable interferences with privacy and from unfounded charges of crime. They also seek to give fair leeway for enforcing the law in the community's protection. Because many situations which confront officers in the course of executing their duties are more or less ambiguous, room must be allowed for some mistakes on their part. But the mistakes must be those of reasonable men, acting on facts leading sensibly to their conclusions of probability. The rule of probable cause is a practical, nontechnical conception affording the best compromise that has been found for accommodating these often opposing interests. Requiring more would unduly hamper law enforcement. To allow less would be to leave law abiding citizens at the mercy of the officers' whim or caprice.[4]

Since that time, however, the Court has recognized a variety of areas and situations in which probable cause is not required. These exceptions to the probable cause requirement of the Fourth Amendment allow officers to conduct searches and seizures with a lower degree of certainty. Generally, exceptions to the requirement involve areas less intrusive than those permitted with probable cause. In all cases, the justification must precede government action, and cannot be applied after the fact. The Court has recognized three levels of justification consistent with the principles of the Fourth Amendment. From highest to lowest, they are: (1) probable cause, (2) reasonable suspicion, and (3) administrative justification. Such degrees are based on the general premise that the measure of intrusion is directly related to the level of justification required—as intrusion increases so does the level of justification.

Probable Cause

probable cause situated between reasonable suspicion and beyond a reasonable doubt, it is the standard required for an arrest, issuance of a warrant, and affectation of physical detainment. It requires a demonstration that a reasonable person could conclude that the accused has committed a crime or that evidence of such crime exists.

Probable cause may be defined as the standard of justification necessary to affect the arrest of an individual or that induces the belief in the minds of a "reasonable" officer that the accused probably committed a crime. While it does not demand the same level of certainty as that which is necessary to sustain a criminal conviction in court, it does require a showing that rises above mere suspicion. It is a balancing act to ascertain that the issue in question is more probable than not. As the Supreme Court articulated in *Carrol v. United States*, probable cause exists when

DEFINING PROBABLE CAUSE

The substance of all the definitions of "probable cause" is a reasonable ground for belief of guilt. And this "means less than evidence which would justify condemnation" or convictions. It has come to mean more than bare suspicion; Probable cause exists where "the facts and circumstances within their (the officers') knowledge and of which they had reasonably trustworthy information (are) sufficient in themselves to warrant a man of reasonable caution in the belief that" an offense has been or is being committed (*Carroll v. United States*, 267 U.S. 132, 162, 288, 39 A.L.R. 790 15. [*Brinegar v. United States*, 338 U.S. 160, 60 S. Ct. 1302 (1949)]).

Since that time, the Court has attempted to clarify the standard in a number of cases:

- *BRINEGAR V. UNITED STATES*, 338 U.S. 160, 60 S. Ct. 1302 (1949)

  In dealing with probable cause . . . as the very name implies, we deal with probabilities. These are not technical: they are the factual and practical considerations of everyday life on which reasonable and prudent men, not legal technicians, act.

- *DRAPER V. UNITED STATES* (QUOTING BRINEGAR), 358 U.S. 307 (1959)

  . . . the so-called distinction places a wholly unwarranted emphasis upon the criterion of admissibility in evidence,

to prove the accused's guilt, of the facts relied upon to show probable cause. That emphasis, we think, goes much too far in confusing and disregarding the difference between what is required to prove guilt in a criminal case and what is required to show probable cause for arrest or search. It approaches requiring (if it does not in practical effect require) proof sufficient to establish guilt in order to substantiate the existence of probable cause.

- *ILLINOIS V. GATES*, 462 U.S. 213, 103 S. Ct. 2317, 76 L.Ed.2d 527 (1983)

  An informant's "veracity," "reliability," and "basis of knowledge" are all highly relevant in determining the value of his report . . . they should be understood simply as closely intertwined issues that may usefully illuminate the commonsense, practical question whether there is "probable cause" to believe that contraband or evidence is located in a particular place. . . . The totality-of-the-circumstances approach is far more consistent with our prior treatment of probable cause than is any rigid demand that specific "tests" be satisfied by every informant's tip . . . probable cause does not demand the certainty we associate with formal trials.

> . . . "the facts and circumstances within their (the officers') knowledge and of which they had reasonably trustworthy information (are) sufficient in themselves to warrant a man of reasonable caution in the belief that" an offense has been or is being committed.[5]

Thus, the question involves a weighing of probabilities, much akin to those demonstrated by the commerce of gambling. Although the possibility of beating the house exists, the probability of losing is significantly higher. So, law enforcement officers and judicial officials carefully evaluate whether the evidence or situation is merely a possibility or one that has a high probability. However, this is not now nor can it ever be an exact science, a fact that the Court has recognized in numerous cases. To wit,

> *The process does not deal with hard certainties, but with probabilities. Long before the law of probabilities was articulated as such, practical people formulated certain common-sense conclusions about human behavior; jurors as fact finders are permitted to do the same—and so are law enforcement officers. Finally, the evidence thus collected must be seen and weighed not in terms of library analysis by scholars, but as understood by those versed in the field of law enforcement.[6]*
>
> *Probable cause is a fluid concept—turning on the assessment of probabilities in particular factual contexts—not readily, or even usefully, reduced to a neat set of legal rules.[7]*

Probable cause stance

▼

Probable cause is required for all arrests, searches, and/or seizures made with warrants. It is also required in all warrantless arrests. However, it is not required in all warrantless searches as the Court has recognized several broad categories of warrantless searches not predicated on probable cause. Most notably, warrantless searches are permitted in the absence of probable cause to secure officer safety or to prevent the destruction of criminal evidence. They are also permitted if items are in plain view or if consent is provided by a legally competent person with a possessory interest in the area under consideration. (Please see Chapter 6 for a comprehensive discussion of warrantless searches.)

Like other standards of justification, grounds for probable cause require an analysis of the totality of the circumstances. While it may be established by a single fact in some cases, others may require a combination of factors to satisfy the requirement. For example, the discovery of a communication between two individuals that outlines a plot to kill a third person may be sufficient in and of itself. However, a statement made by an individual who claims to have overheard a conversation detailing said plot may not. The latter may require a determination of the veracity or credibility of the witness.

Reasonable Suspicion

reasonable suspicion the lowest of all legal standards of evidence, it is less than probable cause but is that which is necessary to authorize an investigative detention. It requires a demonstration that a reasonable perception exists that a crime has been, is being, or will be committed.

As with probable cause, the concept of reasonable suspicion has not been entirely achieved, comprehensively defined, or fully encapsulated in law. Originally articulated in *Terry v. Ohio*, reasonable suspicion is a standard that is less than probable cause but one sufficient to authorize an investigative detention. It is often cited by law enforcement officers as justification for the questioning and temporary detention of private citizens without a demonstration of probable cause. Without question, the efficacy of American law enforcement would be curtailed significantly without such utilization, as it is grounded in historical practices both American and English and is necessary to the law enforcement function. The Supreme Court has formally recognized such and has declared the practice of field interrogation as constitutional when "specific and articulable facts, which, taken together with rational inferences from those facts, reasonably warrant that intrusion", or "particularized, objective facts which, taken together with rational inferences from those facts, reasonably warrant[ed] suspicion that a crime [was] being committed."[11] Thus, officers do maintain the right to temporarily detain private citizens, but only when reasonable suspicion may be found. The Court has recognized the difficulty, however, in defining the concept and specifically articulating the parameters associated with it, declaring in *Ornelas v. United States*:

> Articulating precisely what "reasonable suspicion" and "probable cause" mean is not possible. They are commonsense, nontechnical conceptions that deal with "the factual and practical considerations of everyday life on which reasonable and prudent men, not legal technicians, act. (*Illinois v. Gates*, 462 U.S. 213, 231 [1983]) (quoting *Brinegar v. United States*, 338 U.S. 160, 175 (1949). . . . As such, the standards are "not readily, or even usefully, reduced to a neat set of legal rules." (Gates, supra, at 232). . . . We have cautioned that these two legal principles are not "finely-tuned standards," comparable to the standards of proof beyond a reasonable doubt or of proof by a preponderance of the evidence. (Gates, supra, at 235) They are instead fluid concepts that take their substantive content from the particular contexts in which the standards are being assessed.[12]

In reality, such lack of specificity has resulted in myriad legal challenges of searches and seizures, as will be seen in later chapters.

PROBABLE CAUSE VERSUS BEYOND A REASONABLE DOUBT

Unlike the concepts of reasonable suspicion and probable cause, which are specifically designed to establish the parameters of searches, seizures, and detainments by law enforcement authority, the phrase **beyond a reasonable doubt** refers to a legal standard by which a determination of guilt is established by the trier of fact. Affirmative conclusions of the standard are such that the repercussions to the accused may be of a permanent nature. Satisfaction of said standard is determined independently by the trier of fact (whether judge or jury) and are evaluated and scrutinized by the appropriate judicial authority within the confines of a criminal court. As such, application and oversight are at a much higher level than those decisions made on the street. In addition, such a standard is only applied to those individuals who exercise their right for judicial adjudication, and such determination is made by a judge or jury upon the conclusion of a fair trial.

As with the former standards, the concept of "beyond a reasonable doubt" has a long history in the United States. Originally enunciated in the 1970 case of *In re Winship*,[8] the Court noted that:

> The "demand for a higher degree of persuasion in criminal cases was recurrently expressed from ancient times, [though] its crystallization into the formula 'beyond a reasonable doubt' seems to have occurred as late as 1798. It is now accepted in common law jurisdictions as the measure of persuasion by which the prosecution must convince the trier of all the essential elements of guilt." . . . although virtually unanimous

adherence to the reasonable doubt standard in common-law jurisdictions may not conclusively establish it as a requirement of due process, such adherence does "reflect a profound judgment about the way in which law should be enforced and justice administered."[9]

A finding of guilt may be predicated on an assortment of evidence, including both direct and circumstantial. However, the Court notes that each element of the crime charged must be demonstrated at this level. Both juveniles and adults are afforded the standard during criminal proceedings.

As a further clarification, the Court has clearly distinguished between the standard of proof at a criminal trial (i.e., beyond a reasonable doubt) and the law enforcement standard authorizing searches, arrests, and other police actions.

> The so-called distinction places a wholly unwarranted emphasis upon the criterion of admissibility in evidence, to prove the accused's guilt, of the facts relied upon to show probable cause. That emphasis, we think, goes much too far in confusing and disregarding the difference between what is required to prove guilt in a criminal case and what is required to show probable cause for arrest or search. It approaches requiring (if it does not in practical effect require) proof sufficient to establish guilt in order to substantiate the existence of probable cause. There is a large difference between the two things to be proved, as well as between the tribunals which determine them and therefore a like difference in the quanta and modes of proof required to establish them.[10]

Administrative Justifications

The final standard of justification that has been recognized by the Court is, perhaps, the most difficult to encapsulate. Searches justified by administrative rationales vary widely by both government actors and areas searched. Authority to conduct such searches weighs the interests of public safety against the privacy right of an individual. The Supreme Court has recognized a variety of situations where limited searches may be conducted for administrative purposes. These include, but are not limited to: enforcement of health codes, searches of heavily regulated businesses, school searches, drug testing of special populations, and searches necessary to ensure public safety.

beyond a reasonable doubt the highest legal standard of proof, it is the standard that demonstrates a finding of guilt or proof by triers of fact (jurors or judges) in a criminal proceeding. Reasonable doubt requires a demonstration that no reasonable doubt exists.

Canines are often employed by law enforcement to detect the presence of illegal narcotics in a variety of situations, including vehicle stops. The Court has recognized that automobiles have a reduced expectation of privacy.

In 1959, the Court in *Frank v. Maryland* upheld the conviction of an individual who was charged with a violation of the Baltimore City Code, which required residents to submit to an inspection of their residence if health inspectors determined that it was necessary for public health. The Court recognized that

> . . . inspection without a warrant, as an adjunct to a regulatory scheme for the general welfare of the community and not as a means of enforcing the criminal law, has antecedents deep in our history . . . if a search warrant be constitutionally required, the requirement cannot be flexibly interpreted to dispense with the rigorous constitutional restrictions for its issue. A loose basis for granting a search warrant for the situation before us is to enter by way of the back door to a recognition of the fact that by reason of their intrinsic elements, their historic sanctions, and their safeguards, the Maryland proceedings requesting permission to make a search without intruding when permission is denied, do not offend the protection of the Fourteenth Amendment.[13]

The Court reiterated their earlier rationale in *Frank* in later cases involving health inspections arguing that such are only minimally invasive as they are not directed at the identification of evidence for a criminal case. In addition, the Court has recognized other administrative justifications since *Frank*.

Though the Court has recognized a variety of situations in which administrative justifications may provide a reasonable grounds for a warrantless search of private property, they have consistently held that they must be conducted for purposes other than the discovery of criminal evidence. In addition, such searches are limited in scope to the public interest which they address, and that they are governed by a standard of reasonableness from inception to conclusion.

ADMINISTRATIVE JUSTIFICATIONS

Although the Fourth Amendment clearly established probable cause as the standard of justification for law enforcement searches, the Court has recognized that lesser justifications may reasonably justify limited intrusions into individual privacy rights.

- **Health Inspections**—*Camara v. Municipal Court* (1967)—upheld health code inspections on the grounds that the interests of public health outweighed the limited invasion of an individual's privacy. The Court also noted that such inspections should be conducted in a routine and consistent manner to avoid the appearance of selective enforcement.

- **School Searches**—*New Jersey v. T.L.O.* (1985)—the Court upheld the search of a student's purse by a high school principle. The Court recognized that the warrant requirement was "unsuited to the school environment; requiring a teacher to obtain a warrant before searching a child suspected of an infraction of school rules would unduly interfere with the maintenance of the swift and informal disciplinary procedures needed in the schools." In addition, the Court recognized that the school setting "requires some modification of the level of suspicion of illicit activity needed to justify a search."

- **Drug Testing of Student Athletes**—*Veronia School District v. Acton* (1995)—the Court upheld a school board policy that required student athletes to submit to random urinalysis. In their decision, the Court noted that participation in school athletics resulted in a reduced expectation of privacy due to the imposition of rules and restrictions placed upon them as a requirement of continued participation. As such, random drug screening not directed toward a particular individual was constitutional as the government had a compelling interest in reducing drug use by juveniles.

- **Searches of Regulated Businesses**—the Court has consistently recognized a reduced expectation of privacy in businesses that are highly regulated. As a result, the Court has upheld the warrantless search of a gun dealership [*United States v. Biswell* (1972)—*Gun Control Act of 1968*—]; of a mine [*Donovan v. Dewey* (1981)—*Federal Mine Safety and Health Act of 1977*]; and a junkyard [*New York v. Burger* (1987)—*New York Vehicle and Traffic Law {415}*] to ensure compliance with government regulations designed to promote public safety.

▶ The Expectation of Privacy

The next important consideration in any Fourth Amendment analysis is the determination of the corresponding **expectation of privacy** afforded to an individual in a particular case. Although not specifically discussed in the Constitution, inferences contained therein coupled with federal and state statutes, state constitutions, and, most importantly, case law have emerged to create a legally sacrosanct concept that is now a cornerstone of the Fourth Amendment's prohibition of unreasonable search and seizure. Traditionally, an individual's expectation of privacy was limited to an individual's private residence. The case of *Olmstead v. United States* in 1928 is illustrative of this strict interpretation. The case, which involved a large-scale conspiracy to distribute alcohol in violation of the Volstead Act, focused on the question of whether electronic eavesdropping was permissible under the Fourth Amendment if no physical trespass onto private property occurred. The Court ruled that it was, arguing that:

> . . . [t]he language of the amendment cannot be extended and expanded to include telephone wires, reaching to the whole world from the defendant's house or office. The intervening wires are not part of his house or office, any more than are the highways along which they are stretched.[14]

expectation of privacy protection against government-sponsored searches, seizures, and unlawful entry (including unauthorized disclosure of personal belongings) without probable cause and due process into areas deemed private. Although not specifically discussed in the Constitution, the "right to be left alone" (Justice Louis Brandeis) has developed into a liberty of personal autonomy valued by all Americans. It is protected by (and narrowly defined in) the First, Fourth, Fifth, and Fourteenth Amendments.

THE SUPREME COURT AND THE EXPECTATION OF PRIVACY

***Hoffa v. United States*, 385 U.S. 293 (1966)—** upheld the use of confidential informants

. . . no rights under the Fourth Amendment were violated by the failure of Partin to disclose his role as a government informer. When Hoffa made incriminating statements to or in the presence of Partin, his invitee, he relied not on the security of the hotel room, but on his misplaced confidence that Partin would not reveal his wrongdoing.

***Smith v. Maryland*, 442 U.S. 735 (1979)—**upheld the warrantless installation of a pen register capable of capturing dialed numbers from a suspect telephone.

. . . we doubt that people in general entertain any actual expectation of privacy in the numbers they dial. . . Telephone users, in sum, typically know that they must convey numerical information to the phone company; that the phone company has facilities for recording this information; and that the phone company does in fact record this information for a variety of legitimate business purposes. Although subjective expectations cannot be scientifically gauged, it is too much to believe that telephone subscribers. . . harbor any general expectations that the numbers they dial will remain secret.

***Payton v. New York*, 445 U.S. 573 (1980)—**struck down a New York statute that authorized police officers to enter a private residence without a warrant (and, if necessary, with force) to make a felony arrest; held that:

. . . the physical entry of the home is the chief evil against which the wording of the Fourth Amendment is directed. To be arrested in the home involves not only the invasion attendant to all arrests, but also an invasion of the sanctity of the home, which is too substantial an invasion to allow without a warrant, in the absence of exigent circumstances, even when it is accomplished under statutory authority and when probable cause is present. In terms that apply equally to seizures of property and to seizures of persons, the Fourth Amendment has drawn a firm line at the entrance to the house. Absent exigent circumstances, that threshold may not reasonably be crossed without a warrant.

***California v. Greenwood*, 486 U.S. 35 (1988)—** upheld the warrantless search and seizure of garbage left outside the curtilage of a home.

. . . the warrantless search and seizure of the garbage bags left at the curb. . . would violate the Fourth Amendment only if respondents manifested a subjective expectation of privacy in their garbage that society accepts as objectively reasonable. . . it is common knowledge that plastic garbage bags left on or at the side of a public street are readily accessible to animals, children, scavengers, snoops, and other members of the public. Moreover, respondents placed it for the express purpose of conveying it to a third party.

***Kyllo v. United States*, 533 U.S. 27 (2001)—**ruled that the use of a thermal imaging device to detect the growth of marijuana in a home constituted an unlawful search as the device was also capable of detecting lawful activities including intimate details.

. . . where the Government uses a device that is not in general public use, to explore details of the home that would previously have been unknowable without physical intrusion, the surveillance is a "search" and is presumptively unreasonable without a warrant. . .

Thus, the Court distinguished between searches that involved a physical trespass of a private residence and those that did not. In 1967, however, the Court reversed this ruling, arguing that an expectation of privacy may exist even in areas outside the home.[15] In *Katz* (1967), the Court stated that:

. . . the Fourth Amendment protects people, not places. What a person knowingly exposes to the public, even in his own home or office, is not a subject of Fourth Amendment protection. . . but what he seeks to preserve as private, even in an area accessible to the public, may be constitutionally protected.

Summarily, they ruled that an expectation of privacy may be created in situations in which individuals take affirmative action to make it such. Thus, communications held on public telephones may be granted protection if individuals have a reasonable expectation of privacy or take measures to make their communication private. Consequently, all federal, state, and domestic wiretaps now require a court order predicated on probable cause.

Since the reversal of *Olmstead*, the Court has been tasked with numerous circumstances far removed from questions of telephonic communications. Under current law, the legal establishment of a reasonable expectation of privacy requires a demonstration that: (1) the individual had a subjective expectation of privacy; and, (2) that the subjective expectation of privacy is one that society is prepared to recognize as reasonable. As neither of these are present in garbage, abandoned property, or open fields, the Court has refused to extend Fourth Amendment protections to these areas.

> The test of legitimacy is not whether the individual chooses to conceal assertedly "private" activity, but whether the government's intrusion infringes upon the personal and societal values protected by the Amendment. The fact that the government's intrusion upon an open field is a trespass at common law does not make it a "search" in the constitutional sense. In the case of open fields, the general rights of property protected by the common law of trespass have little or no relevance to the applicability of the Fourth Amendment.[16] Nor have they extended a protection to fenced backyards that are visible to the naked eye from airplanes.[17]

Although the Court has provided continual clarification of the reasonable expectation of privacy in many areas, it has not provided much guidance in the area of technological developments. Such advances include, but are not limited to, electronic mail, cellular telephones, and GPS tracking systems. To further complicate things, lower courts have issued inconsistent rulings, and a patchwork of legal precedent has emerged. These courts have not agreed on the level of privacy afforded to individual files, workplace computers, or administrative networks. In addition, inconsistent interpretations have emerged as to expectations of privacy and the use of passwords, encryption, and steganography. Thus, no clear demarcation of reasonable privacy expectations has emerged.

Expectations of privacy vary based on situational characteristics. As a general rule, individuals in their home enjoy a higher expectation of privacy than at their workplace, and public employees are afforded higher levels than are their private counterparts. However, all considerations of such expectations hinge on the reasonableness of the expectation when balanced against governmental interest, whether the expectation was consistent with the operational realities of the area and whether the search was reasonable in scope and practice.

THE *ORTEGA* DOCTRINE AND WORKPLACE SEARCHES

The application of the elusive concept of a right to privacy is further bifurcated in private and public workplaces. Generally speaking, public employers are much more limited in their actions than are their private counterparts. Purely personal items that have no connection to the employment relationship are not subject to standards for a workplace search.

Factors that may be considered in both types of cases include whether the items or areas to be searched have been set aside for the employee's exclusive or personal use; whether the employee has been given permission to store personal information within the area; whether the employee has been advised that the system may be accessed by others; whether there has been a history of searches or inspections of the area; and whether there is a clearly articulated policy that identifies common areas and private ones.

Public employees are bound by rulings articulated in *O'Connor v. Ortega* [480 U.S. 709 (1987)]. The *Ortega* doctrine specifically evaluates:

- whether the employee's expectation of privacy was consistent with the operational realities of the workplace (i.e., the exclusivity of the workspace, accessibility to workplace by others, nature of employee's duties, knowledge of search procedures or practices, and reason for search

- whether the invasion of the employee's Fourth Amendment protections was reasonable when balanced against governmental interest in the intrusion (reasonable suspicion is sufficient in investigations involving work-related employee misconduct)

- whether the search was reasonable at inception and was the subsequent scope of the search related to the original justification of the search

---

Summarily, an unalienable right to privacy is not specifically articulated in the Constitution, and case law reveals that the Court has not generalized a constitutional right to privacy. It has noted that other provisions of the Constitution protect privacy from other forms of governmental invasion, such as the First Amendment's imposing limitation upon governmental abridgment of freedom to associate and privacy in one's association, or the Third Amendment's prohibiting the nonconsensual peacetime quartering of soldiers. Thus, the right to privacy is moderated only by the expectation of such privacy, which is not a generalized notion, but based on case characteristics, including those things knowingly divulged to third parties.[18] At the current time, no benchmark for privacy and the use of technological devices has been developed.

▶ Warrants

As mentioned previously, the Fourth Amendment specifically provides that ". . . no Warrants shall issue, but upon probable cause, supported by Oath or affirmation, and particularly describing the place to be searched, and persons or things to be seized." Thus, the law specifically provides for the preparation, documentation, and execution of a physical search warrant. The Amendment, as with most of the Bill of Rights, was related directly to past injustices experienced by colonials and their ancestors. More succinctly, it was a direct response to the use of strong-arm tactics by British soldiers armed with "writs of assistance."

Before the ratification of the U.S. Constitution and the Bill of Rights, colonists routinely were harassed for arbitrary reasons by capricious British soldiers. To prevent a furtherance or continuation of such abuses in the newly independent territory, the framers of the Constitution and the Bill of Rights specifically precluded

THE U.S. SECRET SERVICE, GAMING, AND PRIVACY

Perhaps the most notorious of all court cases regarding privacy involved a small company in Texas, Steve Jackson Games, Inc., that produced and published game-playing software and manuals. It also ran a bulletin board system (BBS) in which members posted messages and sent and received electronic mail. SJG came to the attention of the Secret Service when it became known that an SJG co-systems operator had illegally downloaded a sensitive 911 document by hacking into a Bell South Computer. Arguing that the ease of accessibility threatened emergency communications, the Secret Service in 1990 raided SJG and seized 3 computers, 300 disks, and a variety of other equipment.

The Illuminati BBS, owned by SJG, was effectively shut down. The Secret Service then read messages stored on the board and deleted others at will. SJG argued that the government had violated provisions in the Federal Wiretap Act and Title I of the ECPA. In a seminal ruling, the court ruled that e-mails are only subject to interception during actual transmission and the Federal Wiretap Act did not apply to e-mails in electronic storage. In addition, the court ruled that Title I of the ECPA is not applicable to the unauthorized access of electronic messages stored in a service provider computer. However, the court did find that the Secret Service had violated the requirements of Title II of the ECPA ([18 U.S.C.] 2703). The court also declined to extend a "good faith" defense for the agents' reliance on the warrants. This case proved to be a public relations disaster for the U.S. Secret Service. Having long been characterized as the most professional of the federal agencies, the Secret Service had enjoyed immunity from the scandals that had plagued other agencies. But, the fallout of the SJG case included an increasingly suspicious and hostile audience of computer users toward the government in general and the Secret Service in particular.

Steve Jackson Games, Inc. v. United States Secret Service, 816 F. Supp. 432 (W.D. Tex., 1993)

and disallowed such behavior. When speaking of the origination of the Warrant Clause contained within the Fourth Amendment, the Court stated:

> Against this background two protections emerge from the broad constitutional proscription of official invasion. The first of these is the right to be secure from intrusion into personal privacy, the right to shut the door on officials of the state unless their entry is under proper authority of law. The second, and intimately related protection, is self-protection: the right to resist unauthorized entry which has as its design the securing of information to fortify the coercive power of the state against the individual, information which may be used to effect a further deprivation of life or liberty or property. Thus, evidence of criminal action may not, save in very limited and closely confined situations, be seized without a judicially issued search warrant. It is this aspect of the constitutional protection to which the quoted passages from *Entick v. Carrington* and *Boyd v. United States* refer. Certainly it is not necessary to accept any particular theory of the interrelationship of the Fourth and Fifth Amendments to realize what history makes plain, that it was on the issue of the right to be secure from searches for evidence to be used in criminal prosecutions or for forfeitures that the great battle for fundamental liberty was fought. While these concerns for individual rights were the historic impulses behind the Fourth Amendment and its analogues in state constitutions, the application [359 U.S. 360, 366] of the Fourth Amendment and the extent to which the essential right of privacy is protected by the Due Process Clause of the Fourteenth Amendment are of course not restricted within these historic bounds.[19]

[handwritten margin note: warrant clause]

Probable Cause and the Warrant Clause

To protect against egregious offenses by the government, procedures ensuring due process were enacted. In the newly formed territory and in the contemporary American system, warrants—documents that authorize officers to conduct arrests, seizures, or searches—can be issued only by a judge or magistrate upon a showing of probable cause. Such warrants must specifically articulate person(s), place(s), and object(s) to be seized and be accompanied by an affidavit. As a binder on the

warrant a legal directive showing probable cause that is issued by magistrates or judicial officials authorizing law enforcement officers to conduct arrests, seizures, or searches of persons or specified items at particular times and places.

power of governmental intrusion, warrants typically are required before the arrest, search, or seizure takes place except in very limited cases, such as observation of a crime or exigent circumstances. In addition, the preparation and execution of warrants cannot go beyond the "four corners" of the application and affidavit. This **"four corners" rule** means (1) that judges may not seek probable cause beyond the information contained within the "four corners" of the supporting affidavit and (2) that law enforcement officers cannot go beyond the "four corners" of the warrant itself.

As stated earlier, probable cause is an elusive concept and the application of it often appears arbitrary and capricious. In the law, no magical measure of probable cause exists. Rather, magistrates must make their determinations by weighing the individual right to privacy against society's right to gather evidence of criminal behavior. To provide some guidance, the Supreme Court has consistently evaluated standards of probable cause. The initial standard, Aguilar-Spinelli test, involved a rigid two-pronged examination of the case. The first prong, or basis of knowledge prong, evaluated the origination of the informant's knowledge. While the second prong, or veracity prong, which needed to be satisfied, evaluated the truthfulness and reliability of the originating informant.

The rigidity of Aguilar-Spinelli test proved too cumbersome to officers and jurists alike, and the Court abandoned the test in favor of a totality of the circumstances test. This more flexible standard, set forth in *Illinois v. Gates*, stated that:

> . . . the task of the issuing magistrate is simply to make a practical, common sense decision, whether, given all the circumstances set forth in the affidavit before him, including the "veracity" and "basis of knowledge" of persons supping hearsay information, there is a fair probability that contraband or evidence of a crime will be found in a particular place. And the duty of a reviewing court is simply to ensure that the magistrate has a "substantial basis for . . . concluding" that probable cause existed.[20]

Although the Court allowed for independent evaluation of the two, evidence that did not meet both could be admissible if corroboration was present. Thus, the totality of the circumstances test allowed for the establishment of probable cause even in cases in which the informant did not observe the actual criminal activity. Rather, the new test allows magistrates to evaluate various factors to determine reliability. These include, but are not limited to, past reliability of the source, identification of source as a victim or eyewitness to the crime, appearance of source before a magistrate, and the revelation that the source is a police officer.

"four corners" rule
legal requirement preventing judges from seeking probable cause beyond the information contained within the specific parameters ("four corners") of the supporting affidavit and preventing law enforcement officers from going beyond the "four corners" of the warrant itself.

Probable cause has been defined by the court in numerous ways. In determining whether probable cause is present, magistrates consider the totality of the circumstances. Based on the situation displayed in the photograph, a magistrate would probably find probable cause to believe that the vendor was selling stolen or otherwise illegal software.

Staleness, Particularity, and Vicinage

As stated, probable cause is established through the evaluation of two sets of facts: (1) facts that logically indicate the presence of objects to be seized and (2) facts that indicate the reliability of the first set of facts. However, these are not the only factors that magistrates must evaluate. Magistrates must also consider and establish parameters for the age of information, vicinity of criminal activity, and the particularity and the breadth of the proposed search.

Staleness

A further important consideration in the issuance of a search warrant involves a determination of **staleness**—the timeliness of the probable cause or the period between the precipitating factor and the execution of the warrant. Although the Supreme Court has not specifically delineated appropriate guidelines, many lower courts have recognized that the concept is complex and may be influenced by numerous factors, including "the nature of the criminal activity, the length of the activity, and the nature of the property to be seized."[21] In child pornography cases, for example, the government successfully argued that because collectors of child pornography tend to keep images for extended periods of time, it was reasonable to believe that images transferred 10 months prior were still there.[22] Thus, magistrates must evaluate many factors to ensure that probable cause exists at the time of the issuance of the warrant.

staleness the timeliness of the probable cause or the period between the precipitating factor and the execution of the warrant.

Particularity

The Fourth Amendment's requirement that a warrant "particularly" describes "the places to be searched, [and] the persons or things to be seized" clearly lacks ambiguity and uncertainty. To the contrary, it is immediately apparent that the framers of the Constitution intended the highest level of protection from abusive governments. All warrants are required to identify, with specificity and particularity, the place to be searched, the items to be seized, and the criminal behavior in question for two reasons. In 2004, the Court in *Groh v. Ramirez* noted that:

> . . . the particularity requirement's purpose is not limited to preventing general searches; it also assures the individual whose property is searched and seized of the executing officer's legal authority, his need to search, and the limits of his power to do so.[23]

particularity it refers to a requirement housed within the Fourth Amendment that mandates specificity of place, time, and actual items to be searched or seized. With particularity, items unrelated to the specific boundaries remain immune from scrutiny.

Thus, the Court has consistently ruled that warrants must be adequately narrow so that individual officers may reasonably infer the limits of the search. In addition, this particularity must be so specified that unrelated items remain immune from search or seizure. Unfortunately, the Court has not issued opinions on forensic analysis of computer documents and lower courts have not been consistent in their interpretation of the particularity and specificity necessary in computer cases.

Vicinage

Although James Madison's efforts to formally recognize a vicinage provision in the U.S. Constitution were rebuffed, Article III, Section 2 does provide that:

> The Trial of all Crimes, except in Cases of Impeachment, shall be by Jury; and such Trial shall be held in the State where the said Crimes shall have been committed; but when not committed within any State, the Trial shall be at such Place or Places as the Congress may by Law have directed.

Many states have adopted similar language, and individuals retain the right to be charged and tried in the geographic location of original jurisdiction. Subsequently, warrants may be issued only by judicial officials who bear authority over the location in question.

UNITED STATES DISTRICT COURT

District of _____

In the Matter of the Search of
(Name, address or brief description of person or property to be searched)

SEARCH WARRANT UPON ORAL TESTIMONY

Case Number: _____

TO: _____ and any Authorized Officer of the United States

Sworn oral testimony has been communicated to me by _____
Affiant

that ☐ on the person of, or ☐ on the premises known as (name, description and/or location)

in the _____ District of _____ there is now
concealed a certain person or property, namely (describe the person or property)

I am satisfied that the circumstances are such as to make it reasonable to dispense with a written affidavit and that there is probable cause to believe that the property or person so described is concealed on the person or premises above described and that grounds for application for issuance of the search warrant exist as communicated orally to me in a sworn statement which has been recorded electronically, stenographically, or in long-hand and upon the return of the warrant, will be transcribed, certified as accurate and attached hereto.

YOU ARE HEREBY COMMANDED to search on or before _____
Date

the person or place named above for the person or property specified, serving this warrant and making the search ☐ in the day-time — 6:00 AM to 10:00 PM ☐ at anytime in the day or night as I find reasonable cause has been established and if the person or property be found there to seize same, leaving a copy of this warrant and receipt for the person or property taken, and prepare a written inventory of the person or property seized and promptly return this warrant to _____
U.S. Magistrate Judge (Rule 41(f)(4))
as required by law.

_____ at _____
Date and Time Issued   City and State

_____ _____
Name and Title of Judge   Signature of Judge

I certify that on _____ at _____
Date   Time

_____ orally authorized the
Judge

issuance and execution of a search warrant conforming to all the foregoing terms.

_____ _____ _____
Name of affiant   Signature of affiant   Exact time warrant

EXAMPLE OF FEDERAL SEARCH WARRANT APPLICATION BASED ON ORAL TESTIMONY.

▶ Types of Warrants

As provided for under the Fourth Amendment, search warrants are issued based on probable cause on a regular basis across the nation. As stated previously, such warrants must be accompanied by affidavits and must specifically identify time, place, and items in question. However, not all warrants are the same. In fact, individual case characteristics establish the parameters.

Anticipatory Search Warrants

Anticipatory search warrants are extremely unique in that they are issued before the arrival of the evidence in a particular location. Often used in narcotics cases, they provide the opportunity for law enforcement officers to secure a search warrant before the delivery of a large shipment of narcotics. Anticipatory warrants are fairly recent developments, and not all state legislatures have recognized their utility and constitutionality. However, other states have established definitive parameters for the issuance of such warrants:

> (1) The anticipatory warrant must set out, on its face, explicit, clear, and narrowly drawn triggering events which must occur before execution may take place; (2) Those triggering events, from which probable cause arises, must be (a) ascertainable and (b) preordained, meaning that the property is on a sure and irreversible course to its destination; and finally, (3) No search may occur unless and until the property does, in fact, arrive at that destination.[24]

Sneak-and-Peak Warrants

Sneak-and-peak warrants are issued in many different situations in which law enforcement officers gain surreptitious entry into premises or areas where a reasonable expectation of privacy exists, including, but not limited to, residences and offices. Significantly criticized by privacy advocates, they are championed by law enforcement officials who argue that such warrants are less intrusive than seizures

anticipatory search warrants legal documentation giving search and seizure authority before the evidence has arrived, such as a large shipment of narcotics.

sneak-and-peak warrants legal authorization for law enforcement officials to gain surreptitious entry into premises or areas, such as residences and offices, upon determination that evidence is likely to be present. Significantly criticized by privacy advocates, the constitutionality of these warrants has been upheld by the Supreme Court as early as 1979.

ALABAMA RULES OF CRIMINAL PROCEDURE

RULE 3.8—GROUNDS FOR ISSUANCE OF A SEARCH WARRANT

a. Issuance. A search warrant authorized by this rule may be issued if there is probable cause to believe that the property sought:
1. was, or is expected to be, unlawfully obtained;
2. was or is expected to be, used as the means of committing or attempting to commit any offense under the laws of the State of Alabama or any political subdivision thereof;
3. is, or is expected to be, in the possession of any person with intent to use it as a means of committing a criminal offense, or is, or is expected to be, in the possession of another to whom that person may have delivered it for the purpose of concealing it or preventing its discovery; or,
4. constitutes, or is expected to constitute, evidence of a criminal offense under the laws of the state of Alabama or any political subdivision thereof.

as no items are removed. The Supreme Court upheld their constitutionality as early as 1979 when it ruled that:

> Nothing in the language of the Constitution or in this Court's decisions interpreting that language suggests that, in addition to these requirements, search warrants also must include a specification of the precise manner in which they are to be executed. On the contrary, it is generally left to the discretion of the executing officers to determine the details of how best to proceed with the performance of a search authorized by warrant—subject to the general Fourth Amendment protection "against unreasonable searches and seizures."[25]

Sneak-and-peak warrants have been involved in cases in which electronic surveillance equipment was installed or removed; photographs of suspected methamphetamine labs were taken, and GPS systems were established. Two recent cases in which sneak-and-peak warrants proved invaluable to law enforcement were at the Branch Davidian compound in Waco, Texas, in the early 1990s and the 1994 case of Aldrich Ames, the CIA official who spied on the United States for the Soviets. Although use of such warrants in the past has been relatively limited, the passage and implementation of the 2001 Patriot Act (and its subsequent revisions) have increased the application of them.

No-Knock Warrants

no-knock warrant
a legal authorization issued by a judicial officer that grants law enforcement permission to enter premises without first notifying the occupants or owners. Such warrants are issued only in cases in which there exists a risk of harm to evidence, officers, or the community.

Historically, law enforcement officers were required to provide notice to the occupants of a premise that a warrant was about to be served. The principle is deeply rooted in the Fourth Amendment and serves as protection against unreasonable searches and seizures. In addition, the law exists for practical reasons because it "reduces the likelihood of injury to police officers who might be mistaken, upon an unannounced intrusion into a home, for someone with no right to be there."[26] In practice, it requires officers to announce their presence or risk the dismissal of criminal evidence. Once the announcement has been issued, case characteristics will dictate the amount of time necessary to establish reasonableness before forced entry. Not all cases, however, require "knock and announce." Some cases ". . . countervailing law enforcement interests—including, e.g., the threat of physical harm to police, the fact that an officer is pursuing a recently escaped arrestee, and the existence of reason to believe that evidence would likely destroyed if advance notice were given—may establish the reasonableness . . . of an unannounced entry."[27] Thus, officers may obtain a no-knock warrant when demonstration is made of the existence of potentiality for circumvention of justice or threat to human life. Unlike traditional warrants, **no-knock warrants** are those that do not require an announcement prior to entry.

Nighttime Search Warrants

nighttime search warrant a legal authorization issued by a judicial officer which grants law enforcement to enter premises at night.

As with no-knock and sneak-and-peak warrants, **nighttime search warrants** are the exception rather than the rule. Most warrants are executed during daylight hours for several reasons, not the least of which are officer safety and cost efficiency, and are not precluded by law. As the Court in *Gooding v. United States* noted:

> A search warrant could be served at any time of the day or night so long as the issuing officer was "satisfied that there is probable cause to believe that the grounds for the application exist. . . ." Case law had uniformly interpreted the language to mean that

As a general rule, search warrants are executed during daylight hours upon notification to the individuals affected. However, in some cases, circumstances might dictate the need for forced entry, the presence of tactical units. or nighttime execution. For practical reasons, many states have developed specific statutes delineating restrictions on nighttime warrants.

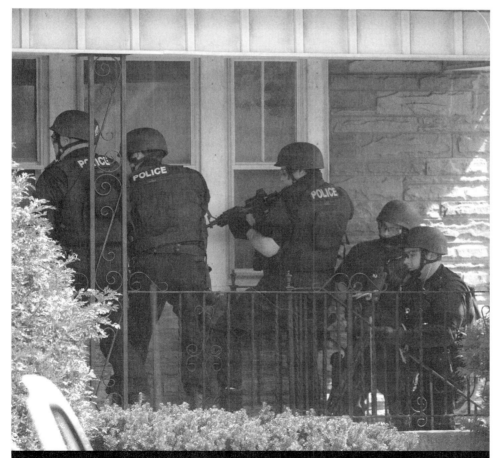

Special Weapons and Tactics (SWAT) teams were initially developed for riot situations and confrontations with armed suspects. While they are still deployed in such situations, the majority of their time is devoted to serving high-risk search warrants, particularly in cases involving narcotics or weapons.

probable cause for the warrant itself was all that was necessary for a nighttime search. The officers or agents simply had to establish probable cause for believing that the sought-after property would be found in the place to be searched.[28]

▶ Warrantless Searches (Discussed in Chapter 6)

Strictly interpreted, the Fourth Amendment to the Constitution prohibits the search and seizure of property or persons in the absence of probable cause. However, criminal justice policy and interpretations of the Constitution and case law are rarely concrete. In fact, questions of legality or the parameters of police authority are best answered with "it depends." The Warrant Clause of the Fourth Amendment is illustrative of this. The Court recognized this in *Katz v. United States* (1967)[29] where it noted that

> . . . searches conducted outside the judicial process, without prior approval by judge or magistrate, are per se unreasonable under the Fourth Amendment—subject only to a few specifically established and well delineated exceptions.

So, while the Court emphasized that the interposition of a judicial official was a Constitutional requirement under the Warrant Clause, it also recognized that exceptions to the clause's requirement existed. Today, the Supreme Court recognizes six broad categories of searches which do not necessitate a warrant. These are known as **warrantless searches**. (Please see Chapter 6 for a complete discussion of warrantless searches.)

warrantless search a law enforcement search of a person or a place conducted in the absence of a warrant; or a category of search in which the U.S. Supreme Court has recognized an exception to the Warrant Clause of the Fourth Amendment.

1. Field interrogations or *Terry* stops
2. Incident to arrest
3. Consent
4. Plain view
5. Automobiles
6. Exigent circumstances

▶ Conclusions

The Fourth Amendment to the Constitution provides that no search or seizure may be affected in the absence of probable cause. Visited by the Court in numerous cases, probable cause is generally defined as facts and circumstances that would lead a reasonable person to conclude that the discovery of contraband or evidence is more probable than not. Such determination is not absolute, nor is it without judicial scrutiny. In fact, the Court has ruled on numerous cases in an attempt to clarify the somewhat elusive concept. In their quest, the Court has also evaluated the appropriate level of an expectation of privacy enjoyed by American citizens; and, while such a notion is not articulated in the verbiage of the Amendment, the concept of an expectation of privacy is intrinsic to considerations of probable cause.

Since its inception, the Fourth Amendment has protected the right of Americans to be free from a capricious government. The requirement of a judicially approved warrant before the search or seizure of an area is the cornerstone of liberty in a democratic society. At the same time, the Court has recognized that some situations exist in which the interest of society is best served in the absence of a warrant. However, in all such cases, the requirement of probable cause is absolute.

The Fourth Amendment establishes parameters for government action and protects the privacy of its citizenry. However, its evolution has not been without controversy. The development of technology and the changing face of crime have solidified the notion of evolutionary lawmaking that began with the passage of the Magna Carta, and the application of traditional parameters of the Fourth Amendment has proved difficult at times.

Key Terms

Actual possession

Administrative justification

Anticipatory search warrants

Beyond a reasonable doubt

Constructive possession

Expectation of privacy

"Four corners" rule

Nighttime search warrants

No-knock warrant

Particularity

Probable cause

Reasonable suspicion

Search

Seizure

Sneak-and-peak warrants

Staleness

Warrantless search

Warrants

Discussion Questions

1. Discuss the differences between the legal measures of perception.
2. Why do officers have the right to temporarily detain private citizens? In your opinion, should the officers have this right? Use cases and court proceedings to support your opinion.
3. What is the role of probable cause in searches and seizures?
4. To what extent does the right to privacy protect technological advances? In your opinion, to what extent should the right to privacy protect technological advances?
5. Is probable cause enough to justify a search warrant?
6. What issues must be considered when a search warrant is being issued?
7. What is the difference between a sneak-and-peak search warrant and a no-knock search warrant? Give examples of the use of each in recent cases.
8. What is the significance of *Brinegar v. United States* (1949) regarding probable cause?

Recommended Resources

Videos

North Coast Polytechnic Institute. Search and Seizure/ Search Warrant (12 individual tapes). This series provides information to law enforcement officers concerning Search and Seizure and Search Warrants with emphasis upon conducting warrantless searches. Available at: http://www.ncpi-ohio.com/videos.htm.

Insight Media. Constitutional Law: The USA Patriot Act. Available at: http://www.insight-media.com.

A&E Television. Why O. J. Simpson Lost: The Civil Trial. *American justice.* Presentation demonstrates the differences in standards and burdens of proof between civil and criminal courts. Available at: http://store.aetv.com.

Insight Media. Probable Cause and Reasonable Suspicion. Presentation explores the difference between probable cause and reasonable suspicion and highlights issues such as curfew laws, profiling, hearsay, and dealing with suspects with criminal records. Available at: www.insight-media.com.

as well as general legal topics such as law enforcement, terrorism, and cyber crime.

Books

Amar, Akhil Reed (2000). *The bill of rights: Creation and reconstruction.* New Haven, CT: Yale University Press.

Amar, Akhil Reed (2005). *America's constitution: A biography.* New York: Random House.

Breyer, Stephen (2005). *Active liberty: Interpreting our democratic constitution.* New York: Alfred A. Knopf Publishing.

Dressler, Joshua and Thomas, George C. (2003). *Criminal procedure: Principles, policies, and perspectives* (2nd ed.). Minnesota: Thomson-West Publishing.

Wetterer, Charles M. (1998). *The fourth amendment: Search and seizure.* New Jersey: Enslow Publishers.

Zotti, Priscilla Machado (2005). *Injustice for all: Mapp vs. Ohio and the Fourth Amendment.* New York: Peter Lang Publishing.

Online Sources

http://www.findlaw.com—Search state and federal case law, statutes, and federal and state constitutions to identify issues pertaining to the Fourth Amendment.

http://www.aclu.com—Home page of the American Civil Liberties Union Web site with links and information on emerging case law, including issues involving the Fourth Amendment and technology.

http://harvardlawreview.org/category/leading-case/ - Listings and links to leading court cases on various issue.

http://www.megalaw.com—Searchable legal database to search state and federal sources of law and evidence,

Relevant Cases Cited

Adams v. Williams, 407 U.S. 143 (1972)

Brinegar v. United States, 338 U.S. 160 (1949)

California v. Ciraolo, 476 U.S. 207 (1986)

California v. Greenwood, 486 U.S. 35 (1988)

Carroll v. United States, 267 U.S. 132 (1925)

Chimel v. California, 395 U.S. 752 (1969)

Dalia v. United States, 441 U.S. 238, (1979)

Draper v. United States, 358 U.S. 307 (1959)

Duncan v. Louisiana, 391 U.S. 145 (1968)

Frank v. Maryland, 359 U.S. 360 (1959)

Gooding v. United States, 416 U.S. 430 (1974)

Hiibel v. Sixth Judicial District Court of Nevada, 542 U.S. 177 (2004)

Illinois v. Caballes, 543 U.S. 405 (2005)

Illinois v. Gates, 462 U.S. 213 (1983)

In re Winship, 397 U.S. 358 (1970)

Katz v. United States, 389 U.S. 347 (1967)

Lewis v. United States, 385 U.S. 206 (1966)

Michigan v. Long, 463 U.S. 1032 (1983)

Minnesota v. Dickerson, 508 U.S. 366 (1993)

Oliver v. United States, 466 U.S. 170 (1984)

Olmstead v. United States, 277 U.S. 438 (1928)

Ornelas v. United States, 517 U.S. 690 (1996)

Pennsylvania v. Mimms, 434 U.S. 106 (1977)

Terry v. Ohio, 392 U.S. 1 (1968)

United States v. Cortez, 339 U.S. 411 (1981)

United States v. Jacobsen, 466 U.S. 109 (1984)

United States v. Rabinowitz, 339 U.S. 56 (1950)

Wilson v. Arkansas, 514 U.S. 927 (1995)

Notes

1. *Katz v. United States*, 389 U.S. 347 (1967)
2. *United States v. Jacobsen*, 466 U.S. 109 (1984)
3. *Illinois v. Caballes*, 543 U.S. 405 (2005)
4. *Brinegar v. United States*, 338 U.S. 160 (1949)
5. *Carroll v. United States*, 267 U.S. 132 (1925)
6. *United States v. Cortez*, 339 U.S. 411 (1981)
7. Ibid.
8. *In re Winship*, 397 U.S. 358 (1970)
9. *Duncan v. Louisiana*, 391 U.S. 145 (1968)
10. *Brinegar v. United States*, 338 U.S. 160 (1949)
11. *Terry v. Ohio*, 392 U.S. 1 (1968)
12. *Ornelas v. United States*, 517 U.S. 690 (1996)
13. *Frank v. Maryland*, 359 U.S. 347 (1959)
14. *Olmstead v. United States*, 277 U.S. 438 (1928)
15. *Katz v. United States*, 389 U.S. 347 (1967)
16. *Oliver v. United States*, 466 U.S. 170 (1984)
17. *California v. Ciraolo*, 476 U.S. 207 (1986)
18. *Lewis v. United States*, 385 U.S. 206 (1966)

19. *Frank v. Maryland*, 359 U.S. 360 (1959)
20. *Illinois v. Gates*, 462 U.S. 213 (1983)
21. *United States v. Snow*, 919 F. 2d 1458 (10th Cir. 1990)
22. *United States v. Lacy*, 119 F. 3d 742 (9th Cir. 1997)
23. 298 F. 3d 1022 (9th Cir. 2003)
24. *State of North Carolina v. Dionne Terrell Phillips*, #COA02-1509 (2003)
25. *Dalia v. United States*, 441 U.S. 238 (1979)
26. *United States v. Nolan*, 718 F.2d 589, 596 (3rd Cir. 1983)
27. *Wilson v. Arkansas*, 514 U.S. 927 (1995)
28. *Gooding v. United States*, 416 U.S. 430 (1974)
29. *Katz v. United States*, 389 U.S. 347 (1967)

THE DECLARATION OF INDEPENDENCE.

5 The Exclusionary Rule and the Fourth Amendment

LEARNING OBJECTIVES

The learner will:

1 *Explain the origins of the exclusionary rule*

2 *Explain the cases relevant to the exclusion of evidence*

3 *Discuss the importance of the "fruits of the poisonous tree" doctrine as it relates to the exclusion of evidence*

4 *Explain the exceptions to the exclusionary rule*

5 *Examine areas that are unprotected by the exclusionary rule*

6 *Identify the role of private searches and third-party organizations in relation to the exclusionary rule*

7 *Explain how the right of privacy relates to the exclusionary rule*

8 *Explain the different applications of the exclusionary rule in criminal versus civil cases*

9 *Examine how abandoned property relates to the exclusionary rule*

10 *Explain the factors that distinguish curtilage from open fields*

11 *Explain the application of the exclusionary rule to curtilage and open fields*

▶ The Exclusionary Rule

Before the formal recognition of civil liberties and due process requirements, American courts were rife with cases in which evidence collected in an illegal manner was introduced against a defendant. Such cases involved law enforcement officers and government agents unlawfully or clandestinely entering private residences or businesses to collect incriminating material. Improper on its face, such information was used routinely against defendants in criminal cases. Although affected individuals could seek relief in civil courts or by petitioning solicitors to press criminal charges against the agents, the damage done by the illegally seized evidence in the criminal case was often insurmountable. To discourage such practices, the Supreme Court created the exclusionary rule.

The **exclusionary rule** is a legal principle in which the introduction of criminal evidence collected or analyzed in violation of the Constitution is forbidden. The rule is designed to discourage police from circumventing protections housed within the Fourth and Fifth Amendments and to prevent prosecutorial misconduct including violations of the statutory rights of defendants or violations of court rules. Because it is a judge-made rule, as opposed to one designed by statute or legislation, its validity and authority have been consistently arbitrated in the appellate process. Many individuals have questioned the deterrent effect of the rule, arguing that no empirical link between exclusion and illegal practices has been uncovered.

Origins

As stated, the exclusionary rule is one of the most controversial legal issues in criminal justice. Unlike other similar rules, it is not grounded in the U.S. Constitution but simply is a judicial remedy for violations involving the Fourth Amendment. Although it has remained largely intact since its inception, the exclusionary rule has undergone significant revisions by the Court and various exceptions now exist.

In the 1914 case of *Weeks v. United States*,[1] the Supreme Court created a law excluding any evidence collected in violation of statute or procedure. The case involved an individual who had been convicted of using the mail to conduct an illegal gambling enterprise. The defendant was convicted largely based on testimony and evidence derived from the forcible, warrantless search of his private residence. The Supreme Court reversed the decision, arguing that evidence collected in such a manner by federal agents was inadmissible in a criminal courtroom. Their rationale was eloquently put:

> The effect of the Fourth Amendment is to put the courts of the United States and Federal officials, in the exercise of their power and authority, under limitations and restraints as to the exercise of such power and authority, and to forever secure the

exclusionary rule
legal mandate requiring the exclusion of any evidence collected by law enforcement personnel in a manner that violates any provision in the Bill of Rights. This judge-made rule is designed to discourage law enforcement from circumventing the protections offered in the Fourth and Fifth Amendments.

people, their persons, houses, papers and effects against all unreasonable searches and seizures under the guise of law. This protection reaches all alike, whether accused of crime or not, and the duty of giving to it force and effect is obligatory upon all entrusted under our Federal system with the enforcement of the laws. The tendency of those who execute the criminal laws of the country to obtain conviction by means of unlawful seizures and enforced confessions, the latter often obtained after subjecting accused persons to unwarranted practices destructive of rights secured by the Federal Constitution, should find no sanction in the judgments of the courts which are charged at all times with the support of the Constitution and to which people of all conditions have a right to appeal for the maintenance of such fundamental rights.

… If letters and private documents can thus be seized and held and used in evidence against a citizen accused of an offense, the protection of the Fourth Amendment declaring his right to be secure against such searches and seizures is of no value, and, so far as those thus placed are concerned, might as well be stricken from the Constitution. The efforts [364 U.S. 206, 210] of the courts and their officials to bring the guilty to punishment, praiseworthy as they are, are not to be aided by the sacrifice of those great principles established by years of endeavor and suffering which have resulted in their embodiment in the fundamental law of the land. (*Weeks v. United States*, 232 U.S. 383, 391)

However, the Court did not extend such a prohibition on state officers. Thus, illegally obtained evidence by state and local law enforcement officers was still admissible in state and federal courts. This **silver platter doctrine** allowed state authorities to serve up illegally obtained evidence to federal agents. Although clearly in violation of the spirit of the law, the practice was largely routine until 1960, when the Court ruled that:

Evidence obtained by state officers during a search which, if conducted by federal officers, would have violated the defendant's immunity from unreasonable searches and seizures under the Fourth Amendment is inadmissible over the defendant's timely objection in a federal criminal trial, even when there was no participation by federal officers in the search and seizure.[2]

Although the Supreme Court applied the Fourth Amendment to the states via the due process clause of the Fourteenth Amendment in the 1949 case of *Wolf v. Colorado*,[3] it did not require the implementation of the exclusionary rule. This was partially remedied by its decision in *Rochin v. California*,[4] in which the Court considered whether evidence of narcotics that had been obtained through the involuntary stomach pumping of the defendant should be admissible. Likening the morphine capsules to a coerced confession, the Court stated:

… we are compelled to conclude that the proceedings by which this conviction was obtained do more than offend some fastidious squeamishness or private sentimentalism about combating crime too energetically. This is conduct that shocks the conscience. Illegally breaking into the privacy of the petitioner, the struggle to open his mouth and remove what was there, the forcible extraction of his stomach's contents—this course of proceeding by agents of government to obtain evidence is bound to offend even hardened sensibilities. They are methods too close to the rack and the screw to permit of constitutional differentiation.

It has long since ceased to be true that due process of law is heedless of the means by which otherwise relevant and credible evidence is obtained. This was not true even before the series of recent cases enforced the constitutional principle that the States may not base convictions upon [342 U.S. 165, 173] confessions, however much verified, obtained by coercion. These decisions are not arbitrary exceptions to the comprehensive right of States to fashion their own rules of evidence for criminal trials. They are not sports in our constitutional law but applications of a general principle. They are only instances of the general requirement that States in their prosecutions respect

silver platter doctrine the doctrine that allows state authorities to serve up illegally obtained evidence to federal agents to be used in federal court. The practice was ruled unconstitutional in *Elkins v. United States.*

▼

certain decencies of civilized conduct. Due process of law, as a historic and generative principle, precludes defining, and thereby confining, these standards of conduct more precisely than to say that convictions cannot be brought about by methods that offend "a sense of justice." See Mr. Chief Justice Hughes, speaking for a unanimous Court in *Brown v. Mississippi*, 298 U.S. 278, 285–286. It would be a stultification of the responsibility which the course of constitutional history has cast upon this Court to hold that in order to convict a man the police cannot extract by force what is in his mind but can extract what is in his stomach.

To attempt in this case to distinguish what lawyers call "real evidence" from verbal evidence is to ignore the reasons for excluding coerced confessions. Use of involuntary verbal confessions in State criminal trials is constitutionally obnoxious not only because of their unreliability. They are inadmissible under the Due Process Clause even though statements contained in them may be independently established as true. Coerced confessions offend the community's sense of fair play and decency. So here, to sanction the brutal conduct which naturally enough was condemned by the court whose judgment is before us, would be to afford brutality the cloak of law. Nothing [342 U.S. 165, 174] would be more calculated to discredit law and thereby to brutalize the temper of a society.

However, the Supreme Court did not apply the exclusionary rule to the states at this time. Instead, they relied upon the Due Process Clause of the Fourteenth Amendment. Application of the exclusionary rule by the states was mandated in *Mapp v. Ohio*.[5]

Application to the States: *Mapp v. Ohio*

On May 23, 1957, Cleveland police officers kicked open the front door of Dollree Mapp's residence. Upon her request to provide a "warrant," the officers showed her a piece of paper they indicated was said warrant. Miss Mapp placed the paper in the top of her shirt, at which point, the officers proceeded to forcibly recover the paper from her dress, arrest her, and search the premises where they uncovered obscene materials. Upon her conviction, Mapp appealed the introduction of such evidence claiming that the seized items were introduced improperly and no warrant was ever produced.

Since the Fourth Amendment's right of privacy has been declared enforceable against the States through the Due Process Clause of the Fourteenth, it is enforceable against them by the same sanction of exclusion as is used against the Federal Government. Were it otherwise, then just as without the Weeks rule the assurance against unreasonable federal searches and seizures would be "a form of words," valueless and undeserving of mention in a perpetual charter of inestimable human liberties, so too, without that rule the freedom from state invasions of privacy would be so ephemeral and so neatly severed from its conceptual nexus with the freedom from all brutish means of coercing evidence as not to merit this Court's high regard as a freedom "implicit in the concept of ordered liberty."[6]

The ignoble shortcut to conviction left open to the State tends to destroy the entire system of constitutional restraints on which the liberties of the people rest. Having once recognized that the right to privacy embodied in the Fourth Amendment is enforceable against the States, and that the right to be secure against rude invasions of privacy by state officers is, therefore, constitutional in origin, we can no longer permit that right to remain an empty promise. Because it is enforceable in the same manner and to like effect as other basic rights secured by the Due Process Clause, we can no longer permit it to be revocable at the whim of any police officer who, in the name of law enforcement itself, chooses to suspend its enjoyment. Our decision, founded on reason and truth, gives to the individual no more than that which the Constitution guarantees him, to the police officer no less than that to which honest law enforcement is entitled, and, to the courts, that judicial integrity so necessary in the true administration of justice.[7]

▼

Thus, the Court applied the exclusionary rule to the states through application of the Fourteenth Amendment. Their rationale was one of deterrence. As such, the rule was applied to the states to prevent future misconduct by state law enforcement officials.

Derivative Evidence Rule or Fruits of the Poisonous Tree Doctrine

derivative evidence rule or "fruits of the poisonous tree" an extension of the exclusionary rule. Suppresses any evidence that was predicated or derived from evidence deemed inadmissible due to unconstitutional actions by the state. Also known as the Fruits of the Poisonous Tree Doctrine, it includes the suppression of evidence in the following areas: additional evidence that would not have been discovered; witnesses who might have remained unknown; and, confessions or admissions made under the presentment of illegally obtained evidence.

Just 2 years after the Mapp decision, the Court ruled that evidence derived directly or indirectly from the illegal action of the police was inadmissible. The **derivative evidence rule** states that **"fruits of the poisonous tree"** were equivalent to the root action of the police itself. In a landmark decision, the Court considered compulsory statements issued by an individual after an illegal search by law enforcement officers. It argued that the issuance of the compulsory statements was directly related to the original illegal action on part of the law enforcement officers. To wit,

> The essence of the constitutional provision prohibiting unreasonable searches and seizures is not merely that evidence so acquired shall not be used before a court but that it shall not be used at all; while facts thus obtained may be proved like any others if knowledge of them is gained from an independent source, nevertheless the knowledge gained by the government's own wrongs cannot be used by it in a criminal prosecution.... In order to make effective the fundamental constitutional guarantees of sanctity of the home and inviolability of the person, *Boyd v. United States*, 116 U.S. 616, this Court held nearly half a century ago that evidence seized during an unlawful search could not constitute proof against the victim of the search. *Weeks v. United States*, 232 U.S. 383. The exclusionary prohibition extends as well to the indirect as the direct products of such invasions.[8]

The Court has also ruled that evidence or confessions elicited through coercive tactics in which authorities demonstrate the weight of the evidence obtained from

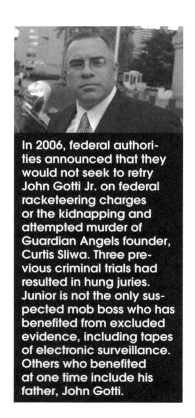

In 2006, federal authorities announced that they would not seek to retry John Gotti Jr. on federal racketeering charges or the kidnapping and attempted murder of Guardian Angels founder, Curtis Sliwa. Three previous criminal trials had resulted in hung juries. Junior is not the only suspected mob boss who has benefited from excluded evidence, including tapes of electronic surveillance. Others who benefited at one time include his father, John Gotti.

their unlawful actions is not admissible. In *Fahy v. Connecticut*,[9] for example, the Court overturned the conviction of a man charged with painting swastikas on Jewish synagogues. For the most part, the Court recognized the cumulative effect of the introduction of the paintbrush and the paint against petitioner that had been obtained unlawfully. It noted that the cumulative effect of such introduction was inseparable from the court's determination of guilt in that the derivative effects permeated all areas of the evidence, including the defendant's confession at the police station and his decision to testify on his own behalf. The Court overturned the conviction, finding that:

> … petitioner should have had a chance to show that his admissions were induced by being confronted with the illegally seized evidence. . . . Nor can we ignore the cumulative prejudicial effect of this evidence upon the conduct of the defense at trial. It was only after admission of the paint and brush and only after their subsequent use to corroborate other state's evidence and only after introduction of the confession that the defendants took the stand, admitted their acts, and tried to establish that the nature of those acts was not within the scope of the felony statute under which the defendants had been charged. We do not mean to suggest that petitioner has presented any valid claim based on the privilege against self-incrimination. We merely note this course of events as another indication of the prejudicial effect of the erroneously admitted evidence.[10]

Thus, the derivative evidence rule is applicable in a variety of situations, including, but not limited to, the suppression of evidence involving additional evidence that would not have been discovered; witnesses who might have remained

---

 CASE LAW

WONG SUN V. UNITED STATES, 371 U.S. 471 (1963)

In 1963, federal agents in San Francisco lawfully arrested Hom Way. Subsequently, they found heroin in his possession, and he indicated that he had purchased the substance from "Blackie Toy." Acting on that information, and in the absence of probable cause, agents made an unlawful entry to the laundry owned by the suspect. Although no heroin was found in his possession, Mr. Toy was arrested. Upon his arrest, Toy made incriminating statements against himself and a third individual, Johnny Yee. As a result, agents proceeded to the home of Johnny Yee—who subsequently surrendered the heroin in question and incriminated a fourth suspect, Wong Sun. Following the pattern, Wong Sun was arrested. All were summarily found guilty.

Upon review, the Supreme Court considered several issues raised by appellants Sun and Toy and ruled:

1. On the record in this case, there was neither reasonable grounds nor probable cause for Toy's arrest, since the information upon which it was based was too vague and came from too untested a source to accept it as probable cause for the issuance of an arrest warrant; and this defect was not cured by the fact that Toy fled when a supposed customer at his door early in the morning revealed that he was a narcotics agent.

2. On the record in this case, the statements made by Toy in his bedroom at the time of his unlawful arrest were the fruits of the agents' unlawful action, and they should have been excluded from evidence.

3. The narcotics taken from a third party as a result of statements made by Toy at the time of his arrest were likewise fruits of the unlawful arrest, and they should not have been admitted as evidence against Toy.

4. After exclusion of the foregoing items of improperly admitted evidence, the only proofs remaining to sustain Toy's conviction are his and his codefendant's unsigned statements; any admissions of guilt in Toy's statement require corroboration; no reference to Toy in his codefendant's statement constitutes admissible evidence corroborating any admission by

(continued)

Toy; and Toy's conviction must be set aside for lack of competent evidence to support it.

5. In view of the fact that, after his unlawful arrest, petitioner Wong Sun had been lawfully arraigned and released on his own recognizance and had returned voluntarily several days later when he made his unsigned statement, the connection between his unlawful arrest and the making of that statement was so attenuated that the unsigned statement was not the fruit of the unlawful arrest and, therefore, it was properly admitted in evidence.

6. The seizure of the narcotics admitted in evidence invaded no right of privacy of person or premises which would entitle Wong Sun to object to its use at his trial.

7. Any references to Wong Sun in his codefendant's statement were incompetent to corroborate Wong Sun's admissions, and Wong Sun is entitled to a new trial, because it is not clear from the record whether or not the trial court relied upon his codefendant's statement as a source of corroboration of Wong Sun's confession.

unknown; and confessions or admissions made under the presentment of illegally obtained evidence. Thus, the exclusionary rule and its application have had a significant impact upon the administration of justice within American boundaries through the suppression of evidence. Indeed, it is likely that many individuals who were factually guilty were acquitted or had their convictions overturned because of it. At the same time, the decades since *Mapp* and *Wong Sun* have seen a comparable increase in modifications that provide for the admittance of some information or evidence obtained unlawfully.

► Exceptions to the Exclusionary Rule

As stated, the exclusionary rule is a legal principle found in constitutional law that prohibits the introduction of evidence in a criminal trial that has been collected or analyzed in violation of protections guaranteed by the U.S. Constitution. In the most basic sense, the rule serves as both a remedy and a disincentive for law enforcement authorities and prosecutors who collect evidence in violations of the Fourth and Fifth Amendments. Thus, it further protects individuals from unreasonable searches and seizures and compulsory self-incrimination. However, it is not a blanket for all evidence that has been obtained illegally. The Court has emphasized that the rule is restricted in its applicability to those cases in which suppression of evidence is necessary to discourage unlawful practices by authorities and to those proceedings in a criminal court. The exclusionary rule is often cited in criminal appeals, and the Court has continued to clarify both its original meaning and scope. In 2006, the Court provided a synopsis of the evolution of the rule when they opined:

> Suppression of evidence, however, has always been our last resort, not our first impulse. The exclusionary rule generates "substantial social costs," ... which sometimes include setting the guilty free and the dangerous at large. We have therefore been "cautio[us] against expanding" it and "have repeatedly emphasized that the rule's 'costly toll' upon truth-seeking and law enforcement objectives presents a high obstacle for those urging [its] application," ... We have rejected "[i]ndiscriminate application" of the rule ... and have held it to be applicable only "where its remedial objectives are thought most efficaciously served," ... that is, "where its deterrence benefits outweigh its 'substantial social costs,' " ...
>
> We did not always speak so guardedly. Expansive dicta in Mapp, for example, suggested wide scope for the exclusionary rule ... ("[A]ll evidence obtained by searches and seizures in violation of the Constitution is, by that same authority, inadmissible

in a state court") … "was to the same effect. But we have long since rejected that approach … " [w]hether the exclusionary sanction is appropriately imposed in a particular case, … is 'an issue separate from the question whether the Fourth Amendment rights of the party seeking to invoke the rule were violated by police conduct.' " …

Even in the early days of the exclusionary rule, we declined to "hold that all evidence is 'fruit of the poisonous tree' simply because it would not have come to light but for the illegal actions of the police. Rather, the more apt question in such a case is 'whether, granting establishment of the primary illegality, the evidence to which instant objection is made has been come at by exploitation of that illegality or instead by means sufficiently distinguishable to be purged of the primary taint.' "[11]

Purged Taint or Attenuation Exception

As stated, various exceptions to the exclusionary rule have been enacted since its inception. The first of these actually was considered in *Wong Sun* and was a direct result of the fruits of the poisonous tree doctrine. This exception, often known as the attenuation or purged taint exception evaluates whether the causal connection between the illegal action and the seizure of evidence is sufficiently attenuated. In that, documentation that the evidence was obtained in a manner unrelated to the illegal activity may be sufficient for admissibility. The three-pronged test for evaluation of attenuation was established in *Brown v. Illinois*.[12] Factors considered included: (1) elapsed time between the illegal action and the acquisition of evidence; (2) presence of intervening circumstances; and (3) purpose and flagrancy of misconduct. In addition, the Court held that Miranda warnings, in and of themselves, may not prove sufficient to dissipate the taint of an illegal arrest. Courts have used this exception in various cases, but most particularly in those in which the testimony of witnesses whose identities were discovered through illegal actions are admitted. In *United States v. Ceccolini*, the Court ruled:

> The exclusionary rule concerning illegally obtained evidence should be invoked with much greater reluctance where the claim for exclusion is based on a causal relationship between a constitutional violation and the discovery of a live witness than when a similar claim is advanced to support suppression of an inanimate object.[13]

APPLICATION OF LAW

A NEW ENGLAND PATRIOT AND THE EXCLUSIONARY RULE

According to prosecutors in Bristol County, Massachusetts, Aaron Hernandez—a star tight end for the New England Patriots—was responsible for at least three murders in and around the Boston area during his career. They alleged that on the night of June 16, 2013, Hernandez summoned two associates from Connecticut to his home in Attleboro, Massachusetts. The trio then picked up Odin Lloyd—the boyfriend of the athlete's fiancee—and took him to a remote area and shot him execution trial. They argued that the act was in retaliation for Lloyd's association with individuals disliked by Hernandez. During the trial, prosecutors also argued that Hernandez had a history of violent behavior, and was known to carry multiple weapons. Evidence in the case included text messages between the alleged co-conspirators and the victim; testimony by witnesses that the victim was afraid of Hernandez; a weapon belonging to a Hernandez associate which was found near the death scene; physical evidence which placed all of the evidence in a car seen on the night of the murder; digital evidence from his personal cell phone; recordings from a home surveillance system; and assorted other items. Evidence that was tossed out by the trial court judge included: the testimony of Alexander Bradley, a former victim of Hernandez who is currently suing the athlete for shooting him in the face; public photographs of Hernandez holding a firearm; testimony regarding additional homicide charges; and digital evidence from two cell phones and three tablets seized from the athlete's home.

Fortunately for prosecutors, sufficient evidence remained. Aaron Hernandez was convicted of capital murder and sentenced to life in prison without the possibility of parole.

The Court rationalized its decision by arguing that the exclusion of the testimony of same would not serve the interest of justice. Rather,

> … exclusion of the witness' testimony would perpetually disable the witness from testifying about relevant and material facts regardless of how unrelated such testimony might be to the purpose of the originally illegal search or the evidence discovered thereby.[14]

Good Faith Exception

good faith exception an exception to the exclusionary rule that permits the admission of evidence that was collected in an unconstitutional manner if the law enforcement officers involved in the collection reasonably believed that their actions were legally permissible, as in cases in which officers were executing a warrant later found to be defective.

The attenuation exception is just one of many exceptions that the Court has recognized to the exclusionary rule. Most have been rationalized or evaluated on the deterrent effect that might be realized by the exclusion of such testimony or evidence. One such exception is the **good faith exception**. Established in *United States v. Leon*,[15] the good faith exception argues that: (1) the exclusionary rule was designed to deter police misconduct rather than to punish the errors of judges and magistrates; (2) no evidence existed to suggest that judges and magistrates are inclined to ignore or subvert the Fourth Amendment or that lawlessness among these actors requires the application of the extreme sanction of exclusion; and (3) no evidence existed to show that the exclusion of materials gathered would have a significant deterrent effect on the issuing judicial official. Of the three, the most important factor was the deterrent effect that would result on future actions. Thus, the Court made it clear that if the officer's actions were objectively reasonable that exclusion would have no deterrent effect on future behavior in that his or her actions were reasonable at their inception. To wit,

> The wrong condemned by the Amendment is "fully accomplished" by the unlawful search or seizure itself … and the exclusionary rule is neither intended nor able to "cure the invasion of the defendant's rights which he has already suffered." *Stone v. Powell*, supra, at 540 (White J., dissenting). The rule thus operates as "a judicially created remedy designed to safeguard Fourth Amendment rights generally through its deterrent effect, rather than a personal constitutional right of the party suffered. (*United States v. Calandra*, supra, at 348) … But the balancing approach that has evolved during the years of experience with the rule provides strong support for the modification currently urged upon us … our evaluation of the costs and benefits of suppressing reliable physical evidence seized by officers reasonably relying on a warrant issued by a detached and neutral magistrate leads to the conclusion that such evidence should be admissible in the prosecution's case in chief … we discern no basis, and are offered none, for believing that exclusion of evidence seized pursuant to a warrant will have a significant deterrent effect on the issuing judge or magistrate … judges and magistrates are not adjuncts to the law enforcement team; as neutral judicial officers, they have no stake in the outcome of particular criminal prosecutions. The threat of exclusion thus cannot be expected significantly to deter them. Imposition of the exclusionary sanction is not necessary meaningfully to inform judicial officers of their errors, and we cannot conclude that admitting evidence obtained pursuant to a warrant while at the same time declaring that the warrant was somehow defective will in any way reduce judicial officers' professional incentives to comply with the Fourth Amendment, encourage them to repeat their mistakes, or lead to the granting of all colorable warrant requests.[16]

However, the Court did make clear the instances in which the exception would not apply. Cases in which the magistrate or judicial official was deceived by information in the affidavit or by the affiant himself or herself that was false or should have been known to be false; in which the magistrate or judicial official "totally abandoned" his or her judicial role; the basis for the warrant was "so lacking in indicia of probable cause" as to render its existence unreasonable; or where the warrant was facially deficient to such an extent that an executing officer could not have reasonably assumed its validity.

▼

WHEN THE FRUITS OF THE POISONOUS TREE DOCTRINE DOES NOT APPLY

The exclusionary rule, a cornerstone in contemporary jurisprudence, suppresses evidence collected through an illegal police action. The rule is designed to deter future police misconduct, and it is this rationale through which exceptions are considered. Since its origination in *Weeks v. United States*, some instances exist in which the Court has allowed the introduction of such evidence.

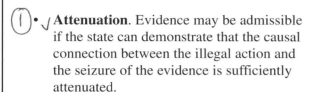

- **Attenuation**. Evidence may be admissible if the state can demonstrate that the causal connection between the illegal action and the seizure of the evidence is sufficiently attenuated.

- **Independent Act**. Evidence may be admissible if the state can demonstrate that

an independent act by an individual other than law enforcement severed the causal chain of illegality and evidence.

- **Independent Source**. Evidence may be admissible if the state can demonstrate that the evidence could have derived from a source removed from the causal link.

- **Inevitable Discovery**. Evidence may be admissible if the state can demonstrate that the evidence would have been discovered without the illegal act.

- **Good Faith**. Evidence may be admissible if the state can demonstrate that the evidence was discovered while the officers were acting with reasonable assurance of the validity of their action.

In addition, the Court has repeatedly ruled that the exception could not be used to introduce evidence collected through error by law enforcement officials, even if the error was inadvertent. Indeed, the exception may only be applied in cases in which the police relied upon others who had committed error. The Court reiterated both the purpose of the exclusionary rule and the justification of inclusion in *Massachusetts v. Sheppard*[17] when it evaluated the admission of evidence collected at a scene by officers operating under a defective warrant. The blame, they argued, was squarely outside the parameters of the investigating officers' reasonable assurance of the validity of said warrant.

> … the police conduct in this case clearly was objectively reasonable and largely error-free. An error of constitutional dimensions may have been committed with respect to the issuance of the warrant, but it was the judge, not the police officers, who made the critical mistake. "[T]he exclusionary rule was adopted to deter unlawful searches by police, not to punish the errors of magistrates and judges." *Illinois v. Gates*, 462 U.S. 213, 263 (1983) (White, J., concurring in judgment). Suppressing evidence because the [468 U.S. 981, 991] judge failed to make all the necessary clerical corrections despite his assurances that such changes would be made will not serve the deterrent function that the exclusionary rule was designed to achieve.[18]

The Court has also grappled with the issue of clerical error, a wholly independent concept from that of irresponsibility by judicial authorities. In *Arizona v. Evans*,[19] the Court considered the introduction of evidence obtained after a search of a suspect's car was undertaken based on erroneous information within a computer database. Once again reiterating the rationale for the creation of the exclusionary rule, the Court found that the exclusion of evidence derived from a clerical error would have no deterrent effect on future actions by the police. In fact, the primary significance of the case involved the refusal of the Court to extend the rule beyond its original parameters of police conduct, and it ruled:

> If court employees were responsible for the erroneous computer record, the exclusion of evidence at trial would not sufficiently deter future errors so as to warrant such

a severe sanction. First, as we noted in Leon, the exclusionary rule was historically designed as a means of deterring police misconduct, not mistakes by court employees. See Leon, supra, at 916; [*Arizona v. Evans*, 514 U.S. 1 (1995), 13] see also Krull, supra, at 350. Second, respondent offers no evidence that court employees are inclined to ignore or subvert the Fourth Amendment or that lawlessness among these actors requires application of the extreme sanction of exclusion. See Leon, supra, at 916, and n. 14; see also Krull, supra, at 350–351. To the contrary, the Chief Clerk of the Justice Court testified at the suppression hearing that this type of error occurred once every three or four years.

… there is no basis for believing that application of the exclusionary rule in these circumstances will have a significant effect on court employees responsible for informing the police that a warrant has been quashed. Because court clerks are not adjuncts to the law enforcement team engaged in the often competitive enterprise of ferreting out crime, see *Johnson v. United States*, 333 U.S. 10, 14 (1948), they have no stake in the outcome of particular criminal prosecutions. Cf. Leon, supra, at 917; Krull, supra, at 352. The threat of exclusion of evidence could not be expected to deter such individuals from failing to inform police officials that a warrant had been quashed.[20]

Thus, the Court has consistently ruled that information or evidence gathered by the police who are acting in good faith on a warrant later found to be defective may be introduced at trial. Their rationale has remained consistent throughout the passage of decades since the inception of the exclusionary rule.

Finally, the Court has upheld the admissibility of evidence collected by an officer in objectively reasonable reliance on the constitutionality of a statute that is subsequently declared unconstitutional. Once again, the Court reiterated the rationale for the creation of the exclusionary rule, arguing that the exclusion of evidence in such a case "would have little deterrent effect on future police misconduct, which is the basic purpose of the rule. Officers conducting such searches are simply fulfilling their responsibility to enforce the statute as written. If a statute is not clearly unconstitutional, officers cannot be expected to question the judgment of the legislature that passed the law."[21]

Independent Source and Inevitability of Discovery Exception

independent source legal concept that permits the introduction of evidence that initially was discovered during, or as a consequence of, an unlawful search but later obtained independently from lawful activities untainted by the initial illegality.

inevitability of discovery exception an exception to the exclusionary rule that allows for the admissibility of evidence collected in an unconstitutional manner if the prosecution can show that the evidence would have been inevitably discovered, through other means.

As with the "good faith" exception to the exclusionary rule, the Court has found that information or evidence collected independent of the illegal police action is admissible. In the most basic sense, the Court recognized that while the government should not profit or benefit from illegal practices, it should also not be worse off than it would have been had the misconduct not occurred. Thus, evidence that derives from an **independent source** may be admissible in court even if it had been collected on some level via illegal police actions.

The Court has ruled that evidence that normally would be suppressible because of unwarranted or unlawful government action may be introduced if the discovery of such would have occurred anyway. This **inevitability of discovery exception** was first articulated in *Nix v. Williams*.[22] In this case, officers questioned a suspect in the disappearance of a child after assuring his counsel that they would not. As a result, the defendant, Williams, made several incriminating statements including the location of the child's body. During the trial, Williams moved to block the introduction of the body as "fruits" of the illegal questioning by the police. However, the Court ruled that such evidence was not suppressible because the body would have been discovered anyway as a result of the large search that had been undertaken. More specifically, the Court reiterated the rationale for the existence of the exclusionary rule and cautioned against creating a disadvantage for the prosecution in a manner inconsistent with notions of fair play.

▼

SIGNIFICANT CASES REGARDING THE EXCLUSIONARY RULE

Weeks v. United States, 232 U.S. 383 (1914). This case established the exclusionary rule, applying it to illegal actions committed by federal law enforcement authorities. However, it did not apply the rule to state authorities because the Fourth Amendment had not yet been incorporated into the due process clause.

> *... the tendency of those who execute the criminal laws of the country to obtain convictions by means of unlawful seizures and enforced confessions, the latter often obtained after subjecting accused persons to unwarranted practices destructive of rights secured by the Federal Constitution, should find no sanction in the judgments of the courts, which are charged at all times with the support of the Constitution, and to which people of all conditions have a right to appeal for the maintenance of such fundamental rights.*

Rochin v. California, 342 U.S. 165 (1952). This case introduced the concept that evidence obtained illegally could be excluded via the Due Process Clause of the Fourteenth Amendment.

> *... use of involuntary verbal confessions in State criminal trials is constitutionally obnoxious not only because of their unreliability. They are inadmissible under the Due Process Clause even though statements contained in them may be independently established as true. Coerced confessions offend the community's sense of fair play and decency. So here, to sanction the brutal conduct which, naturally enough, was condemned by the court whose judgment is before us would be to afford brutality the cloak of law.*

Mapp v. Ohio, 367 U.S. 643 (1961). This case explicitly applied the exclusionary rule to state authorities and decided that all evidence collected in violation of the U.S. Constitution is inadmissible in court.

> *... the ignoble shortcut to conviction left open to the State tends to destroy the entire system of constitutional restraints on which the liberties of the people rest. Having once recognized that the right to privacy embodied in the Fourth Amendment is enforceable against the States, and that the right to be secure against rude invasions of privacy by state officers is, therefore, constitutional in original, we can no longer permit that right to remain an empty promise.*

Wong Sun v. United States, 371 U.S. 471 (1963). This case introduced the notion of the "fruits of the poisonous tree." To wit, evidence indirectly tied to the unlawful action of officers is inadmissible.

> *... we need not hold that all evidence is "fruits of the poisonous tree" simply because it would not have come to light but for the illegal actions of the police. Rather, the more apt question in such a case is "whether, granting establishment of the primary illegality, the evidence to which instant objection is made has been come at by exploitation of that illegality or instead by means sufficiently distinguishable to be purged of the primary taint.*

United States v. Crews, 445 U.S. 463 (1980). This case introduced the "independent source" exception to the exclusionary rule and decided that evidence collected through unlawful behavior may still be introduced if it can be demonstrated that the evidence could have been obtained through an independent source.

> *... the pretrial identification obtained through use of the photograph taken during respondent's illegal detention cannot be introduced; but the in-court identification is admissible ... because the police's knowledge of respondent's identity and victim's independent recollections of him both antedated the unlawful arrest, and were thus untainted by the constitutional violation.*

Nix v. Williams, 467 U.S. 431 (1984). This case introduced the "inevitability of discovery" exception to the exclusionary rule. It provided for the introduction of illegally obtained evidence if it could be demonstrated that the discovery of such evidence was inevitable.

> *... the core rationale for extending the exclusionary rule to evidence that is the fruit of unlawful police conduct is that such course is need to deter police from violations of constitutional and statutory protections notwithstanding the high social cost of letting obviously guilty persons go unpunished. On this rationale, the prosecution is not to be put in a better position than it would have been if no legalillegality had transpired. By contrast, the independent source doctrine— allowing admission of evidence that has been discovered by means wholly independent of any constitutional violation—rests on the rationale*

(continued)

that society's interest in deterring unlawful police conduct and the public interest in having juries receive all probative evidence of a crime are properly balanced by putting the police in the same, not a worse, position that they would have been in if no police error or misconduct had occurred. Although the independent source doctrine does not apply here, its rationale is wholly consistent with, and justifies adoption of, the ultimate or inevitable discovery exception to the exclusionary rule.

United States v. Leon, 468 U.S. 897 (1984). This case introduced the "good faith" exception to the exclusionary rule. To wit, evidence collected by officers who were relying upon a warrant issued by a detached and neutral magistrate may be introduced even if the warrant later proves defective.

... whether the exclusionary sanction is appropriately imposed in a particular case, our decisions make clear, is "an issue separate from the question whether the Fourth Amendment rights of the party seeking to invoke the rule were violated by police conduct" ... only the former question is currently before us, and it must be resolved by weighing the costs and benefits of preventing the use in the prosecution's case in chief of inherently trustworthy tangible evidence obtained in reliance on a search warrant issued by a detached and neutral magistrate that ultimately is found to be defective ... the substantial social costs exacted by the exclusionary rule ... have long been a source of concern ... an objectionable collateral consequence of this interference ... is that some guilty defendants may go free or receive reduced sentences. Particularly when law enforcement officers have acted in objective good faith or their transgressions have been minor, the magnitude of the benefit conferred on such guilty defendants offends basic concepts of the criminal justice system.

Massachusetts v. Sheppard, 468 U.S. 981 (1984). This case reiterated that which was articulated in Leon—evidence collected by officers acting in good faith is admissible even when another party has made an error.

... the police conduct in this case clearly was objectively reasonable and largely error-free. An error of constitutional dimensions may have been committed with respect to the issuance of the warrant, but it was the judge, not the police officers, who made the critical mistake... . "the exclusionary rule was adopted to deter unlawful searches by police, not to punish the errors of magistrates and judges" ... suppressing evidence because the judge failed to make all the necessary clerical corrections despite his assurances that such changes would be made will not serve the deterrent function that the exclusionary rule was designed to achieve.

Arizona v. Evans, 514 U.S. 1 (1995). This case extended the "good faith" exception to errors made by court employees.

If court employees were responsible for the erroneous computer record, the exclusion of evidence at trial would not sufficiently deter future errors so as to warrant such a severe sanction. First ... the exclusionary rule was historically designed as a means of deterring police misconduct, not mistakes by court employees ... Second, respondent offers no evidence that court employees are inclined to ignore or subvert the Fourth Amendment or that lawlessness among these actors requires application of the extreme sanction of exclusion ... Finally, and most important, there is no basis for believing that application of the exclusionary rule in these circumstances will have a significant effect on court employees responsible for informing the police that a warrant has been quashed. Because court clerks are not adjuncts to the law enforcement team engaged in the often competitive enterprise of ferreting out crime, they have no stake in the outcome of particular criminal prosecutions.

Minnesota v. Olson, 495 U.S. 91 (1990). This case explicitly provided for a reasonable expectation of privacy for overnight guests, which provided for the exclusion of evidence collected in the absence of constitutional standing.

... hosts will more likely than not respect the privacy interests of their guests, who are entitled to a legitimate expectation of privacy despite the fact that they have no legal interest in the premises and do not have the legal authority to determine who may or may not enter the household. If the untrammeled power to admit and exclude were essential to Fourth Amendment protection, an adult daughter temporarily living in the home of her parents would have no legitimate expectation of privacy, because her right to admit or exclude would be subject to her parents' veto ... because respondent's expectation of privacy was rooted in "understandings that are recognized and permitted by society" ... it was legitimate, and respondent can claim the protection of the Fourth Amendment.

Hudson v. Michigan, 547 U.S. 586(2006). This case provides an historical analysis of both the rational and scope of the rule, and clearly delineates those instances where it is applicable. More specifically, the Court refused to extend the protections of the exclusionary rule for a violation of the "knock and announce rule."

> *This Court has rejected "[i]ndiscriminate application" of the exclusionary rule ... holding it applicable only "where its deterrence benefits outweigh its 'substantial social costs,' ... Exclusion may not be premised on the mere fact that a constitutional violation was a "but-for" cause of obtaining the evidence. The illegal entry here was not the but-for cause, but even if it were, but-for causation can be too attenuated to justify exclusion. Attenuation can occur not only when the causal connection is remote, but also when suppression would not serve the interest protected by the constitutional guarantee violated. The interests protected by the knock-and-announce rule include human life and limb ... , and property ... and privacy and dignity of the sort that can be offended by a sudden entrance. But the rule has never protected one's interest in preventing the government from seeing or taking evidence described in a warrant. Since the interests violated here have nothing to do with the seizure of the evidence, the exclusionary rule is inapplicable.*

Groh v. Ramirez, 540 U.S. 551 (2004). This case evaluated whether an officer was entitled to qualified immunity after conducting a search in which a magistrate issued a search warrant that relied on an affidavit that particularly described the items in question, but which failed to specifically identify those items on the warrant itself. The Court ruled that evidence collected in a search conducted with a warrant lacking sufficient particularity was inadmissible.

> *... the fact that the application adequately described the "things to be seized" does not save the warrant from its facial invalidity. The Fourth Amendment ... requires particularity in the warrant, not in the supporting documents ... we do not say that the Fourth Amendment forbids a warrant from cross-referencing other documents. Indeed, most Courts of Appeals have held that a court may construe a warrant with reference to a supporting application or affidavit if the warrant uses appropriate words of incorporation, and if the supporting document accompanies the warrant ... But in this case, the warrant did not incorporate other documents by reference, nor did either the affidavit or the application ... accompany the warrant ... In this respect the warrant was so obviously deficient that we must regard the search as "warrantless" within the meaning of our case law.*

Herring v. United States, 555 U.S. 135 (2009). This case was the first to extend a good faith exception to a search that was conducted after officers arrested an individual based on erroneous information (i.e., the presence of an outstanding arrest warrant) relayed to them by another police agency.

> *... our cases establish that such suppression is not an automatic consequence of a Fourth Amendment violation. Instead, the question turns on the culpability of the police and the potential of exclusion to deter wrongful police conduct. Here the error was the result of isolated negligence attenuated from the arrest. We hold that in these circumstances the jury should not be barred from considering all the evidence.*

The core rationale for extending the exclusionary rule to evidence that is the fruit of unlawful police conduct is that such course is needed to deter police from violations of constitutional and statutory protections notwithstanding the high social cost of letting obviously guilty persons go unpunished. On this rationale, the prosecution is not to be put in a better position than it would have been in if no illegality had transpired. By contrast, the independent source doctrine—allowing admission of evidence that has been discovered by means wholly independent of any constitutional violation—rests on the rationale that society's interest in deterring unlawful police conduct and the public interest in having juries receive all probative evidence of a crime are properly balanced by putting the police in the same, not a worse, position than they would have been in if no police error or misconduct had occurred. Although the independent source doctrine does not apply here, its rationale is wholly consistent with and justifies adoption of the ultimate or inevitable discovery exception to the exclusionary rule. If the prosecution can establish by a preponderance of the evidence that the information ultimately or inevitably would have been discovered by lawful means—here the volunteers' search—then the deterrence rationale has so little basis that the evidence should be received.[23]

► Areas Unprotected by the Exclusionary Rule

As discussed previously, the exclusionary rule was created judicially. As such, it has been attacked by privacy advocates and law enforcement personnel alike. It has also been attacked by civil libertarians who argue that it would be more effective if it had been created legislatively. Without exception, all sides argue that its application has been arbitrary, capricious, and inconsistent at best. The modifications and alterations, at worst, have circumvented the spirit of justice in the United States. However, the Court continues to struggle with the appropriateness of its existence and the parameters of its application. As such, a second body of law has developed in which clarification is attempted. Such jurisprudential content has focused on areas in which the application of the rule is not in question—areas in which no respite from inclusion of evidence is available.

Private Searches, Private Persons, and Third-Party Origination

As with the remainder of the Bill of Rights, the Fourth Amendment's prohibition of unreasonable searches and seizures applies only to government agents and officials. It does not preclude the behavior or actions of a private person unless said person is operating as a government entity. In the case of *Burdeau v. McDowell*,[24] the Court ruled that evidence that had been stolen from the defendant's office by private persons in the employ of the bank for which petitioner worked could be used in a criminal trial. The Court rationalized its decision by reiterating the purpose of the Constitution, in general, and the Bill of Rights, in particular.

> The Fourth Amendment gives protection against unlawful searches and seizures, and as shown in the previous cases, its protection applies to governmental action. Its origin and history clearly show that it was intended as a restraint upon the activities of sovereign authority, and was not intended to be a limitation upon other than governmental agencies; as against such authority it was the purpose of the Fourth Amendment to secure the citizen in the right of unmolested occupation of his dwelling and the possession of his property, subject to the right of seizure by process duly issued.[25]

Thus, no protection exists under the Fourth Amendment for those searches conducted by third parties acting independently absent all direction and supervision from the government. This issue is increasingly common in the courts as more and more cases are brought to the attention of law enforcement via computer repair technicians, network administrators, and systems analysts.

In *United States v. Pervaz*,[26] the court evaluated the admissibility of information gathered by a cellular telephone company after being alerted by authorities that it was being victimized. The court ruled that the application of the Fourth Amendment in third-party origination cases hinges on a variety of factors, including, "the extent of the government's role in instigating or participating in the search, its intent and the degree of control it exercises over the search and the private party, and the extent to which the private party aims primarily to help the government or to serve its own interests" (at 6). In this case, the court ruled that the company's actions were primarily motivated by its wish to identify those individuals guilty of defrauding their consumers, as opposed to helping the government. In addition, the fact that the government was not informed of the company's intention to undertake action to ascertain the culprit's identities was indicative of the lack of control exercised by the government in this situation. Clearly, this case involved individuals or entities acting independently of government instruction. Such was not the case, however, in *United States v. Hall*,[27] when a computer technician copied files from a computer he was repairing under the direction of law enforcement. In this particular case, the technician inadvertently discovered several images of child pornography, phoned the authorities, and copied the files that they specified. Although the court recognized that the authorities acted inappropriately, they upheld the conviction on the grounds that the actual warrant was predicated on items found before law enforcement instruction. In this case, the court also evaluated the argument that the rule to allow time for warrant preparation perpetrated by said repairman under the direction of law enforcement was violative of the Fourth Amendment. Citing *United States v. Mayomi*,[28] the court ruled that the one-day delay was not unreasonable because it was brief and based on adequate suspicion (at 994).

 CASE LAW

CONTAINERS, EXPECTATIONS OF PRIVACY, AND THIRD PARTIES— *UNITED STATES V. JACOBSEN*

Early in the morning of May 1, 1981, a supervisor for Federal Express asked the office manager to evaluate a package that had been damaged by a company forklift. In keeping with written policy, the pair then opened the package to examine its contents for insurance purposes. Inside the cardboard box wrapped in brown paper, they discovered five or six pieces of crumpled newspaper covering a 10-inch tube made of silver insulation tape. Cutting open the tube, the employees found four zip-lock plastic bags—the innermost of which contained white powder. They then alerted DEA, and replaced the plastic bags in the tube and put the tube and newspapers back in the box. Upon arrival, the responding DEA agent noted that one end of the tube had been slit open. He then removed the bags, saw the white powder, and removed a trace of the white powder. After a field test revealed the substance as cocaine, he, along with other responding agents, then obtained and executed a warrant on the address to which the package was addressed.

On appeal, respondent argued that the introduction of the drug evidence was unconstitutional as he had an expectation of privacy in a sealed package. While the Court recognized a de facto expectation of privacy necessitating a warrant to search the contents, they noted that

> the fact that agents of the private carrier independently opened the package and made an examination that might have been impermissible for a government agent cannot render otherwise reasonable official conduct unreasonable. The reasonableness of an official invasion of the citizen's privacy must be appraised on the basis of

the facts as they existed at the time that invasion occurred.

The Court did recognize that the agent's actions constituted both a search and a seizure under the Fourth Amendment. However, they determined both to be reasonable.

> … The fact that, prior to the field test, respondents' privacy interest in the contents of the package had been largely compromised is highly relevant to the reasonableness of the agents' conduct in this respect. The agents had already learned a great deal about the contents of the package from … employees … The package itself, which had previously been opened, remained unsealed, and the Federal Express employees had invited the agents to examine its content. Under these circumstances, the package could no longer support any expectation of privacy … such containers may be seized, at least temporarily, without a warrant … since it was apparent that the tube and plastic bags contained contraband and little else, this warrantless seizure was reasonable for it is well settled that it is constitutionally reasonable for law enforcement officials to seize "effects" that cannot support a justifiable expectation of privacy without a warrant based on probable cause to believe they contain contraband.

The Court then considered whether the additional intrusion brought about by the field test constituted an unlawful search and seizure. The Court held that it did not, stating that

> … to the extent that a protected possessory interest was infringed, the infringement was de minimis and constitutionally reasonable.

▼

Lack of Standing and Absence of an Expectation of Privacy Violation

Evidence seized in an unlawful manner may also be admissible if the defendant lacks the legal standing to move to suppress it. Such movement, known as a motion to suppress, is only applicable in cases in which the defendant can demonstrate that an illegal action was taken against him or her personally or that his or her expectation of privacy was violated. Violation of the rights of a third party may not be considered as part and parcel of such legal posturing. Cases in which incriminating evidence against the defendant is collected while in residence of another's control may be introduced against the defendant irrespective of the legality of said seizure because that individual lacks standing.

> Originally adjudicated in the case of *Jones v. United States*,[29] the Court ruled that: In order to qualify as a "person aggrieved by an unlawful search and seizure," one must have been a victim of a search or seizure, one against whom the search was directed, as distinguished from one who claims prejudice only through the use of evidence gathered as a consequence of a search or seizure directed at someone else... . Ordinarily, then, it is entirely proper to require of one who seeks to challenge the legality of a search as the basis for suppressing relevant evidence that he allege, and if the allegation be disputed that he establish, that he himself was the victim of an invasion of privacy.

The Court has continued to reiterate that the expectation of privacy of one is not violated if committed against another. In *Rakas v. Illinois*,[30] for example, the Court refused to extend an expectation of privacy to passengers in an automobile. They argued that challenges to evidence issued in such cases lacked the legal standing to merit suppression of evidence. In their determination of standing, the Court ruled that the issue involved two independent inquires. First, "whether the proponent of a particular legal right has alleged "injury in fact"; and, second,

---

 CASE LAW

OVERNIGHT GUESTS AND THE EXPECTATION OF PRIVACY

As stated, the Court in Olson ruled that an overnight guest at a residence may be afforded an expectation of privacy regarding their belongings. However, the issue may not be so easily defined as whether they actually sleep in the residence, and not all guests are afforded the same expectation. In making their determinations, courts have identified the following as factors that might be considered:

1. The visitor has some property rights in the dwelling;
2. The visitor is related by blood or marriage to the owner or lessor of the dwelling;
3. The visitor receives mail at the dwelling or has his or her name on the door;
4. The visitor has a key to the dwelling;
5. The visitor maintains regular or continuous presence in the dwelling, especially sleeping there regularly;
6. The visitor contributes to the upkeep of the dwelling, either monetarily or otherwise;
7. The visitor has been present at the dwelling for a substantial length of time before the arrest;
8. The visitor stores his or her clothes or other possessions in the dwelling;
9. The visitor has been granted by the owner exclusive use of a particular area of the dwelling;
10. The visitor has the right to exclude other persons from the dwelling;
11. The visitor is allowed to remain in the dwelling when the owner is absent;
12. The visitor has taken precautions to develop and maintain his privacy in the dwelling.

RAWLINGS V. KENTUCKY, 448 U.S. 98 (1980)

On October 18, 1976, police officers in Bowling Green, Kentucky, went with an arrest warrant to the home of an individual to arrest him. Although unsuccessful in their endeavor, the officers conducting the search observed affirmative evidence of narcotics. Obtaining a search warrant for the premises, the officers then searched those individuals present. Such search resulted in the discovery of drugs and an excessive amount of cash within one of the occupant's purses.

Rawlings immediately claimed possession of both, was arrested, and subsequently, filed a motion to suppress claiming that he had an expectation of privacy in the contents of the purse. However, the Court's decision ran contrary to such assertion. In its ruling, the Court considered the "totality of the circumstances" and the ownership interest of the purse in ascertaining that the defendant did not have a reasonable expectation of privacy therein.

whether the proponent is asserting his own legal rights and interests rather than basing his claim for relief upon the rights of third parties."

Subsequent decisions by the Court have recognized other areas in which an expectation of privacy does exist. In *Minnesota v. Olson*,[31] the Court recognized an expectation of privacy for overnight guests. In its determination, the Court considered "that hosts will more likely than not respect their guests' privacy interests even if the guests have no legal interest in the premises and do not have the legal authority to determine who may enter the household." However, the Court has clearly delineated factors that may be considered in the determination of the expectation of privacy an individual guest may be afforded. For example, In *Minnesota v. Carter*,[32] the Court held that "while an overnight guest may have a legitimate expectation of privacy in someone else's home . . . one who is merely present with the consent of the householder may not. . . . And, an expectation of privacy in commercial property is different from, and less than, a similar expectation at home." Thus, the Court consistently evaluates the expectation of privacy afforded to individuals.

Abandoned Property

Issuing a formal claim under the exclusionary rule most often involves the expectation of privacy. The Court has repeatedly protected those areas in which individuals have a constitutionally protected expectation. The Amendment does not protect the merely subjective expectation of privacy, but only those "expectation[s] that society is prepared to recognize as 'reasonable.'"[33] Thus, the Court has denoted that only those areas in which: (1) an individual expects privacy and (2) society recognizes same as reasonable are afforded an expectation of privacy protected via the Fourth Amendment. Over the years, the Court also has delineated certain areas in which the same expectation is not recognized. One such area is abandoned property.

Discarded Items

Often, individuals intentionally will discard criminal evidence or contraband to circumvent justice. This occurs in many different cases, such as when a murder suspect disposes of the weapon in a community dumpster or remote location. It is also quite common in narcotics or criminal contraband cases. In each of these scenarios, the Court has ruled that the voluntary abandonment of an item negates any expectation of privacy that an individual may claim to it in the future. However, if the abandonment is a result of an illegal action on the part of the police, it may be introduced.

"throw-away" evidence items collected by the police that have been discarded, thrown down, or similarly abandoned by an individual.

The first case in which **"throw-away" evidence** was considered was that of *Hester v. United States*,[34] in which the Court considered whether the alcoholic contents of containers that had been thrown down by suspected moonshiners during a police chase were admissible. The Court ruled that indeed they were and refused to suppress the evidence. Subsequent cases have extended the same exception to thrown down or otherwise discarded narcotics (e.g., *Michigan v. Chesternut*).[35] In addition, courts across the country have refused to extend an expectation of privacy to individuals who deny the ownership of an item in question and to abandoned motor vehicles.

Curtilage and Open Fields

open fields doctrine refers to the legal concept in which the courts have consistently ruled that no expectation of privacy can be created in an open field. Thus, the Fourth Amendment does not apply to such areas.

The Court has continued to grapple with the parameters of privacy expectations. Although it has consistently protected private residences, personal belongings, and electronic communications, it has not extended protection to include all areas that are privately owned. In fact, it has consistently ruled that open fields do not enjoy Fourth Amendment protection. This ideology, known as the **open fields doctrine**, was first enunciated in the case of *Hester v. United States*.[36] To wit, " … the special protection accorded by the Fourth Amendment to the people in their 'persons, houses, papers and effects,' is not extended to the open fields. The distinction between the latter and the house is as old as the common law." Their rationale largely lay in the accessibility of fields to the general public and to law enforcement officials. The Court, however, has recognized that some areas attached to a private residence, known as **curtilage**, may be afforded protection under the Bill of Rights.

curtilage the enclosed area of land surrounding a dwelling, distinct from the residence itself (because no roof exists over it).

The distinction between curtilage and open fields is not necessarily an easy one. The courts have delineated four factors that may be considered: (1) the proximity of the area in question to the house; (2) whether the area is enclosed in some way through the use of fences or other enclosures; (3) the nature and use of the property in question; and, of course (4) the affirmative actions undertaken by the owner to ensure privacy.[37] Thus, a locked storage shed located in a fenced-in yard approximately 10 yards from the back door would certainly enjoy an expectation of privacy by its owner. At the same time, front yard areas visible from the street in a well-lit community probably would not. The Court has repeatedly held that warrantless aerial observation of a home's curtilage is not to be afforded an expectation of privacy. To wit,

(a) The touchstone of Fourth Amendment analysis is whether a person has a constitutionally protected reasonable expectation of privacy, which involves the two inquiries of whether the individual manifested a subjective expectation of privacy in the object of the challenged search, and whether society is willing to recognize that expectation as reasonable. *Katz v. United States*, 389 U.S. 347. In pursuing the second inquiry, the test of legitimacy is not whether the individual chooses to conceal assertedly "private activity," but whether the government's intrusion infringes upon the personal and societal values protected by the Fourth Amendment. (pp. 211–212)

(b) On the record here, respondent's expectation of privacy from all observations of his backyard was unreasonable. That the backyard and its crop were within the "curtilage" of respondent's home did not itself bar all police observation. The mere fact that an individual has taken measures to restrict some views of his activities does not preclude an officer's observation from a public vantage point where he has a right to be and which renders the activities clearly visible. The police observations here took place within public navigable airspace, in a

It is well recognized that the Supreme Court has consistently extended the protections of the Fourth Amendment to private residences. In addition, it has recognized some areas connected or in close proximity to the main residence. Generally speaking, these areas known as "curtilage" are either inherently private or have been made so through individual actions. Front yards are typically not granted protection.

physically nonintrusive manner. The police were able to observe the [476 U.S. 207, 208] plants readily discernible to the naked eye as marijuana, and it was irrelevant that the observation from the airplane was directed at identifying the plants and that the officers were trained to recognize marijuana. Any member of the public flying in this airspace who cared to glance down could have seen everything that the officers observed. The Fourth Amendment simply does not require police traveling in the public airways at 1,000 feet to obtain a warrant in order to observe what is visible to the naked eye.[38]

The Court has also ruled that garbage left on the curb for trash removal is also absent an expectation of privacy because it is readily accessible to animals, children, scavengers, snoops, and other members of the public.

▶ Criminal Versus Civil Cases

Unlike civil cases in which liberty is not at stake, negative repercussions in criminal cases most often include incarceration as a possibility. In addition, the civil process does not include a presumption of innocence such as that included in criminal cases. As such, civil courts have traditionally been less restrictive on the types of evidence that might be introduced. In particular, the exclusionary rule does not apply to civil cases. Thus, evidence that might not be admissible in a criminal proceeding may be introduced in a civil case. Just months after actor Robert Blake was acquitted of all charges stemming from the execution-style murder of his wife, jury selection began for the wrongful death case filed by her family. Evidence that had been suppressed during the criminal proceedings, including items seized from the actor's home, was introduced during the civil action.

The Court specifically addressed the application of the exclusionary rule to civil cases in *United States v. Janis*,[39] and rationalized that:

> The debate within the Court on the exclusionary rule has always been a warm one. It has been unaided, unhappily, by any convincing empirical evidence on the effects of the rule. The Court, however, has established that the "prime purpose" of the rule, if not the sole one, "is to deter future unlawful police conduct." ... In the complex and turbulent history of the rule, the Court never has applied it to exclude evidence from a civil proceeding, federal or state.

In addition, the Court reiterated its early positions regarding the deterrent effect of the exclusionary rule, stating that:

> ... we conclude that exclusion from federal civil proceedings of evidence unlawfully seized by a state criminal enforcement officer has not been shown to have a sufficient likelihood of deterring the conduct of the state police so that it outweighs the societal costs imposed by the exclusion.[40]

▶ Conclusions

Although the Fourth Amendment to the Constitution specifically forbids unreasonable searches and seizures, it does not specifically preclude the introduction of evidence obtained through violation of same. As a result, American citizens historically have been convicted on illegally seized evidence. In the 1914 case of *Weeks v. United States*, the Court introduced the Exclusionary Rule. This judicially created concept prohibited the admission of any and all evidence obtained by or derived from federal agents in violation of constitutional provisions. Subsequently, the prohibition was applied to the actions of state officers in *Mapp v. Ohio*. In its justification, the Court opined that the exclusion of such evidence would deter future police misconduct.

The original prohibitions housed within the exclusionary rule have been eroded significantly since its inception. The Court has consistently limited the initial parameters and has recognized a significant number of exceptions based primarily on the deterrent effect of exclusion. For example, evidence obtained by an officer who is acting in good faith is admissible in court, because no misconduct existed upon seizure. At the same time, the Court has also refused to exclude evidence that would have been otherwise discovered; or that resided in nonprivate areas; or that had been collected by nonpublic personnel.

Neither the U.S. Constitution nor the Bill of Rights specifically delineate an expectation of privacy afforded the citizenry, but the Supreme Court has elucidated certain situations that increase freedom from state scrutiny. More succinctly, efforts taken by individual citizens to enhance privacy in personal effects, residences, and communications may decrease governmental intrusion if society determines those actions and areas are reasonable in scope. Accordingly discarded or abandoned property is afforded no such protection.

Key Terms

Curtilage	Good faith exception	Silver platter doctrine
Derivative evidence rule	Independent source	"Throw-away" evidence
Exclusionary rule	Inevitability of discovery exception	
"Fruits of the poisonous tree"	Open fields doctrine	

Discussion Questions

1. What is the significance of *Mapp v. Ohio* (1961)?
2. Discuss the importance of the "fruits of the poisonous tree" doctrine as it relates to the exclusion of evidence.
3. Discuss when the "fruits of the poisonous tree" doctrine does not apply.
4. What is the significance of *United States v. Pervaz* (1997)?
5. How does the expectation of privacy apply to overnight guests?
6. How does the right of privacy relate to the exclusionary rule?
7. What are some exceptions to the right of privacy?
8. Should open fields have Fourth Amendment protection?

Recommended Resources

Videos

Exceptions to the search warrant requirement—Part 1: LETN #532-0099. Available at http://www.filmo.com/letn.htm.

Exceptions to the search warrant requirement—Part 2: LETN #532-0100. Available at http://www.filmo.com/letn.htm.

Insight Media. Legal limbo: The war on terror and the judicial process. Available at: http://www.insight-media.com.

Books

Hermann, Michele G. (2003). *Search and seizure checklists*. St. Paul, MN: Thomson/West Publishing.

Kasimar, Yale. (2003). *In defense of the search and seizure exclusionary rule*. Harvard Journal of Law and Public Policy, *26*(1). Retrieved December 20, 2006 from http://www.law.harvard.edu/students/orgs/jlpp.

LaFave, Wayne R. (2004). *Search and seizure*, Criminal Practice Series (4th ed.). New York: Thomson/West Publishing.

McInnis, Thomas. (2000). *The Christian burial case: An introduction to criminal and judicial procedure*. Connecticut: Praeger Publishing.

Online Sources

http://www.law.cornell.edu/wex/index.php/Evidence— Online informational Web site for sources and links to traditional and emerging cases and issues in criminal evidence.

http://www.landmarkcases.org/—Legal search engine for direct links to landmark cases in constitutional law and relevant issues, such as the "exclusionary rule."

http://caselaw.lp.findlaw.com/data/constitution/amendment04/06.html—Informational Web site for comprehensive analysis of the exclusionary rule from inception to today.

http://law.richmond.edu/jolt/—Informational Web site with links to the Journal of Law and Technology at the University of Richmond.

http://www.findlaw.com—Free legal search engine for state and federal case law, statutes, codes, and regulations (also accessible are state and federal constitutions).

Relevant Cases Cited

Arizona v. Evans, 514 U.S. 1 (1995)

Brown v. Illinois, 467 U.S. 431 (1984)

Burdeau v. McDowell, 256 U.S. 465 (1921)

California v. Ciraolo, 476 U.S. 207 (1986)

Elkins v. United States, 364 U.S. 206 (1960)

Fahy v. Connecticut, 375 U.S. 85 (1963)

Groh v. Ramirez, 540 U.S. 551 (2004)

Herring v. United States, 555 U.S. 135 (2009)

Hester v. United States, 265 U.S. 57 (1924)

Hudson v. Michigan, 547 U.S. 586(2006)

Illinois v. Gates, 462 U.S. 213 (1987)

Illinois v. Krull, 480 U.S. 340 (1987)

Katz v. United States, 389 U.S. 347 (1967)

Mapp v. Ohio, 367 U.S. 643 (1961)

Massachusetts v. Sheppard, 468 U.S. 981 (1984)

Michigan v. Chesternut, 486 U.S. 567 (1988)

Minnesota v. Carter, 525 U.S. 23 (1998)

Minnesota v. Olson, 495 U.S. 91 (1990)

Murray v. United States, 487 U.S. 533 (1988)

Nix v. Williams, 467 U.S. 431 (1984)

Rakas v. Illinois, 439 U.S. 128 (1978)

Rawlings v. Kentucky, 448 U.S. 98 (1980)

Rochin v. California, 22 U.S. 383 (1952)

Silverthorne Lumber Co. v. United States, 251 U.S. 385 (1952)

United States. v. Ceccolini, 435 U.S. 268 (1978)

United States v. Crews, 445 U.S. 463 (1980)

United States v. Dunn, 480 U.S. 294 (1987)

United States v. Hall 142 F. 3d 988 (7th Circuit, 1998)

United States v. Jacobsen, 466 U.S. 109 (1984)

United States v. Leon, 468 U.S. 897 (1984)

United States v. Mayomi, 873 F. 2d 1049 (7th Circuit, 1989)

United States v. Pervaz, 118 F.3d 1 (1st Cir. 1997)

Weeks v. United States, 232 U.S. 383 (1914)

Wolf v. Colorado, 338 U.S. 25 (1949)

Wong Sun v. United States, 371 U.S. 471 (1963)

Notes

1. 22 U.S. 383 (1914)
2. *Elkins v. United States*, 364 U.S.206 (1960)
3. 338 U.S. 25 (1949)
4. 342 U.S. 165 (1952)
5. 367 U.S. 643 (1961)
6. Ibid.
7. Ibid.
8. *Silverthorne Lumber Co. v. United States*, 251 U.S. 385 (1952)
9. 375 U.S. 85 (1963)
10. *Fahy v. Connecticut*, 375 U.S. 85 (1963)
11. *Hudson v. Michigan*, 547 U.S. 586 (2006)
12. 422 U.S. 590 (1975)
13. *United States. v. Ceccolini*, 435 U.S. 268 (1978)
14. Ibid.
15. 468 U.S. 897 (1984)
16. Ibid.
17. 468 U.S. 981 (1984)
18. Ibid.
19. 514 U.S. 1 (1995)
20. Ibid.
21. *Illinois v. Krull*, 480 U.S. 340 (1987)
22. 467 U.S. 431 (1984)
23. Ibid.
24. 256 U.S. 465 (1921)
25. Ibid.
26. 118 F.3d 1 (1st Cir. 1997)
27. 142 F. 3d 988 (7th Circuit, 1998)
28. 873 F. 2d 1049 (7th Circuit, 1989)
29. 362 U.S. 257 (1960)
30. 439 U.S. 128 (1978)
31. 495 U.S. 91 (1990)
32. 525 U.S. 83 (1998)
33. *Oliver v. U.S.*, 466 U.S. 170 (1984)
34. 265 U.S. 57 (1924)
35. 486 U.S. 567 (1988)
36. 265 U.S. 57 (1924)
37. *United States v. Dunn*, 480 U.S. 294 (1987)
38. *California v. Ciraolo*, 476 U.S. 207 (1986)
39. 428 U.S. 433 (1976)
40. Ibid.

THE DECLARATION OF INDEPENDENCE.

6 Warrantless Searches

CHAPTER OUTLINE

Investigative Detention
Seizures and Investigative Detentions
Stop-and-Frisks or *Terry* Stops
Incident to Arrest
"Plain View" Doctrine
"Plain Feel" Doctrine
Automobile Searches
    Automobile Inventory Searches
    Closed Containers in Automobile
      Searches
    Other Issues with Searches of
      Automobiles

Consent
    Voluntariness of Consent
    Scope of Consent
    Third-Party Consent
Administrative Justifications
  and the Special Needs
  of Government
    Inventory Searches
    Building, Home, and Business
      Inspections
    Checkpoints
    School and Workplace Searches
Conclusions

LEARNING OBJECTIVES

The learner will:

1 *Understand the principles of probable cause and reasonable suspicion as they relate to warrantless searches*

2 *Be knowledgeable of admissibility of* Terry *stops*

3 *Be familiar with "plain view" and "plain feel" doctrine*

4 *Be able to discuss the justifications for warrantless searches of automobiles*

5 *Be knowledgeable of the justifications for inventory searches*

6 *Be able to discuss the considerations for admissibility of searches*

7 *Possess knowledge of the types of special needs searches*

warrant requirement
a provision found
within the Fourth
Amendment that
mandates the
attainment of a
warrant by police prior
to the execution of a
search or an arrest.

**probable cause
requirement** a pro-
vision housed within
the Fourth Amend-
ment, which limits
the attainment of
warrants to situations
in which probable
cause is established.

**warrantless
searches** a law
enforcement search
of a person or a
place conducted
in the absence of
a warrant; or, a
category of search
in which the U.S.
Supreme Court
has recognized an
exception to the
Warrant Clause of the
Fourth Amendment in
situations where the
interests of society
outweigh the inva-
siveness of govern-
ment action.

***terry* stops** legal
authority for a law
enforcement official
to conduct a "pat-
down" or search
of a person's outer
clothing or visual
search of a vehicle
for contraband.
Although the *Terry*
stop is not an arrest,
the person is not free
to leave; also called
a "stop-and-frisk."

As discussed previously, Fourth Amendment jurisprudence is primarily concentrated in four areas: (1) distinguishing and defining searches and seizures; (2) the **Warrant Requirement**, in which warrantless searches are semantically precluded except in specific and tightly constricted situations; (3) the **probable cause requirement**, whose exclusive provisions are closely associated with the Warrant Requirement's proscription of police inquiries into probable cause; and, (4) the exclusionary rule, which presumptively excludes any information or evidence gathered in violation of the preceding two. However, the Supreme Court has continued to delineate areas that fall outside the parameters of the restrictions placed upon government officials through the Fourth Amendment. In fact, various situations exist in which the Court has excepted the exclusionary rule to include information that was gathered through illegal means. In addition, it has created generalized circumstances in which warrants themselves are not necessitated at all.

As stated, probative information or evidence may be excluded from trial in various situations. A murder weapon may be inadmissible, for example, in a case in which the police engaged in a nonconsensual search of the suspect's personal things. At the same time, the Court has continued to recognize exceptions to the exclusionary rule and has refused to suppress evidence when such suppression had no deterrent effect on future police misconduct. In addition, the Court recognized special situations in which warrants were not required, including:

- Border searches[1]
- Consent searches[2]
- Container searches[3]
- Exigent circumstances[4]
- Searches incident to a lawful arrest[5]
- "Plain view"[6]
- Special needs[7]
- Stop-and-frisks[8]
- Inventory searches[9]

In each of these, the Court has indicated that privacy, liberty, property, dignity, and security must be carefully considered in the application of the Fourth Amendment.[10] It has ruled that the areas carved out that include exceptions to the basic tenets of the Fourth Amendment, commonly known as **warrantless searches**, may be conducted when circumstances are such that the interests of society outweigh the invasiveness of the action.

▶ Investigative Detention

In the United States, investigative inquiries take one of three forms: (1) encounters that are entirely voluntary; (2) arrests in which probable cause of criminal activity has been demonstrated; and (3) investigative stops, or ***Terry* stops**, in which a law enforcement officer has a reasonable suspicion to believe that the individual has either committed, is committing, or will commit a crime. Throughout the nation's history, one of the most prized fundamental rights is the right to be free from government interference without clear and unquestionable authority of law. For the most part, this fact, so fundamental to American concepts of liberty, does not interfere with the interest of justice. Most citizens will voluntarily speak to law enforcement authorities upon request. Those who do not, however, continue to enjoy the absolute freedom to be unresponsive, uncommunicative, and uncooperative to police representatives without fear of reprisal or seizure. Thus, the Court

According to the *Terry* decision, officers may stop and frisk an individual for their personal safety. However, such exploration is limited to the outside clothing of the individual. Officers may only exceed that scope when they feel an identifiable weapon.

recognized the need for investigative stops and did not forbid them entirely. Traditionally, those that were conducted without reasonable suspicion were necessarily dependent upon the voluntary cooperation of the private citizen.

> The person [460 U.S. 491, 498] approached, however, need not answer any question put to him; indeed, he may decline to listen to the questions at all and may go on his way. . . . He may not be detained even momentarily without reasonable, objective grounds for doing so; and his refusal to listen or answer does not, without more, furnish those grounds. . . . If there is no detention—no seizure within the meaning of the Fourth Amendment—then no constitutional rights have been infringed.[11]

However, recent rulings by the Court have troubled some privacy advocates. Their fear is that the Fourth and Fifth Amendments have come under attack since the tragic events at the World Trade Center on September 11, 2001. They point to the recent decision in *Hiibel v. Sixth Judicial District Court of Nevada, Humboldt County*,[12] in which the Court ruled that compulsory self-identification to law enforcement personnel was not unconstitutional and was not a violation of the Fourth Amendment's prohibitions against unreasonable searches and seizures nor was it a violation of the Fifth Amendment's protection from self-incrimination. In a nutshell, the Court ruled that compulsory disclosure of identification did not violate the Fourth Amendment because (1) it served an important government interest; (2) it was immediately relevant to the original purpose of a *Terry* stop; (3) the threat of criminal sanction was necessary for compliance; and (4) such a request would not alter the nature of the stop itself. In addition, the Court ruled that such compulsion did not violate the Fifth Amendment because the disclosure of identity, in and of itself, did not reasonably pose a danger of the self-incrimination forbidden by the statute. Thus, the Court ruled that in temporary investigative detentions, state statutes that require self-identification by private citizens are constitutional.

▶ Seizures and Investigative Detentions

Defining the parameters that necessarily indicate a seizure during an investigative detention, the Court held that a person:

> . . . has been "seized" within the meaning of the Fourth Amendment only if, in view of all of the circumstances surrounding the incident, a reasonable person would have

believed that he was not free to leave. Examples of circumstances that might indicate a seizure, even where the person did not attempt to leave, would be the threatening presence of several officers, the display of a weapon by an officer, some physical touching of the person of the citizen, or the use of language or tone of voice indicating that compliance with the officer's request might be compelled . . . In the absence of some such evidence, otherwise inoffensive contact between a member of the public and the police cannot, as a matter of law, amount to a seizure of that person.[13]

Thus, this free-to-leave test includes consideration of the circumstances particular to the event in question and must be evaluated on a case-by-case basis.

Reasonable suspicion, the quantum of evidence necessary for an investigative detention, may be demonstrated in various ways. As discussed in the previous chapter, reasonable suspicion is firmly situated between individual perception and probable cause. Thus, it is more than a hunch, but less than the quantum necessary to effect an arrest. The Supreme Court has grappled with the definition for decades and has continued to reiterate the difficulty associated with such, arguing that all determinations should be made on an individual basis. While it has described reasonable suspicion as a "particularized and objective basis" for suspecting the person stopped of criminal activity,[14] the Court has noted that:

. . . the principal components of a determination of reasonable suspicion or probable cause will be the events which occurred leading up to the stop or search, and then the decision whether these historical facts, viewed from the standpoint of an objectively reasonable police officer, amount to reasonable suspicion or to probable cause.[15]

Thus, reasonable suspicion is the level of evidence that would lead a reasonable person to believe that a crime has been committed, is being committed, or is about to be committed. As with numerous situations in criminal justice, the totality of the circumstances must be considered in such determinations.

▶ Stop-and-Frisk or *Terry* Stops

In the United States, individual citizens are entitled to unfettered movement within domestic borders. Government interference with such guarantee is generally restricted to special situations. In 1891, the Court noted the importance of this stating:

No right is held more sacred, or is more carefully guarded, by the common law, than the right of every individual to the possession and control of his own person, free from all restraint or interference of others, unless by clear and unquestionable authority of law . . . the right to one's person may be said to be a right of complete immunity; to be let alone.[16]

Prior to the 1960s, the inviolability of the Fourth Amendment was absolute. Searches and seizures of both persons and property were limited to those situations where a warrant predicated on probable cause was granted by the appropriate judicial official.

In 1968, the Court heard the case of *Terry v. Ohio*,[17] and the first broad category of warrantless searches emerged. The facts of the case as laid out before the Court were relatively simple. A seasoned detective stopped and frisked three men who appeared to be casing a store. He subsequently arrested the trio after a pat down on the outside of two of the suspects' clothing revealed that they were carrying handguns. During the resulting trial, the defense moved to suppress the weapons as they were discovered in the absence of a warrant. The trial court allowed the weapons to be introduced stating that the officer's actions were reasonable as they were not intrusive and were conducted out of concern for his own safety. The Court considered whether evidence seized in the absence of probable cause was admissible. Toward that end, they balanced an individual's right to be secure in their person against the government's interest in officer safety. Differentiating a brief investigative detention and an arrest, the Court noted that the officer's action did not require a demonstration of probable cause. The Court affirmed the ruling of the trial court stating:

> . . . where a police officer observes unusual conduct which leads him reasonably to conclude in light of his experience that criminal activity may be afoot and that the persons with whom he is dealing may be armed and presently dangerous, where in the course of investigating this behavior he identifies himself as a policeman and makes reasonable inquiries, and where nothing in the initial stages of the encounter serves to dispel his reasonable fear for his own or others' safety, he is entitled for the protection of himself and others in the area to conduct a carefully limited search of the outer clothing of such persons in an attempt to discover weapons which might be used to assault him. Such a search is a reasonable search under the Fourth Amendment, and any weapons seized may properly be introduced in evidence against the person from whom they were taken.

Since *Terry*, the Court has heard various cases testing the parameters established herein. In particular, the Court has repeatedly heard cases in which the immediacy and apparency of the suspected danger were at issue. The Court, for example, has consistently ruled that cases in which a search of interior pockets was conducted outside the scope of safety concerns was unconstitutional.[18] The Court has continued to delineate the constraints of protective searches during investigative detentions, reiterating earlier decisions predicated on the safety concerns of law enforcement personnel. In *Minnesota v. Dickerson*,[19] for example, the Court held that protective searches are limited in scope to those areas, places, and objects that reasonably may conceal items dangerous to the police. Searches are further limited to those objects, revealed through exterior searches and the sense of touch, that are immediately identifiable as weapons. Items may not be seized (or even revealed) in the absence of specific information leading to a reasonable belief that the suspect object was an identifiable weapon. The *Terry* doctrine has been further expanded in recent years to include limited inspections of passenger compartments of vehicles if an officer possesses reasonable, articulable suspicion that a suspect is armed and dangerous. In explaining its ruling, the Court held that *Terry* "did not restrict the preventive search to the person of the detained suspect." It reiterated earlier rulings, arguing that the:

> . . . protection of police and others can justify protective searches when police have a reasonable belief that the suspect poses a danger. Roadside encounters between police and suspects are especially hazardous, and danger may arise from the possible presence of weapons in the area surrounding a suspect.[20]

As in other areas of criminal law, any evidence or criminal contraband found during a legitimate search under the doctrine is admissible. However, the Court has cautioned that such searches, conducted in the absence of probable cause, must be limited in scope and duration.

▶ Incident to Arrest

Just as the Court has recognized a compelling government interest in the prevention of crime and the protection of police officers during brief investigative detentions, the Court has recognized a similar need immediately prior to

IMPORTANT POST-*TERRY* DECISIONS

Terry v. Ohio represented the first time that the Court balanced the interests of an individual's security against the government's interest in crime prevention and officer safety when suspending the Warrant Clause of the Fourth Amendment in brief investigative detentions. Since 1968, the Court has recognized a number of general categories of searches in which warrants are not required. In addition, they have expanded the initial parameters established by the *Terry* Court.

- *Adams v. Williams*, 407 U.S. 143 (1972)—four years after establishing the constitutionality of a *Terry* stop. The Court considered whether a tip from a previously reliable informant was sufficient indicia to justify the officer reaching through an automobile's open window and removing a gun from the Petitioner's waistband. In upholding the constitutionality of the actions, the Court noted:

  . . . we reject respondent's argument that reasonable cause for a stop and frisk can only be based on the officer's personal observation, rather than on information applied by another person. Informants' tips, like all other clues and evidence coming to a policeman on the scene, may vary greatly in their value and reliability. One simple rule will not cover every situation. Some tips, completely lacking in indicia of reliability, would either warrant no police response or require further investigation before a forcible stop of a suspect would be authorized. But in some situations—for example, when the victim of a street crime seeks immediate police aid and gives a description of his assailant, or when a credible informant warns of a specific impending crime—the subtleties of the hearsay rule should not thwart an appropriate police response.

- *Pennsylvania v. Mimms*, 434 U.S. 106 (1977)—in this case, officers stopped Petitioner Mimms for driving with an expired plate. Upon exiting the vehicle at their request, police noted a large "bulge" under his jacket and subsequently discovered an illegal firearm. On appeal, Mimms sought to have the weapon ruled unconstitutional arguing that the order to exit the vehicle was an improper seizure. The Court rejected that argument noting that the

. . . intrusion can only be described as de minimis. The driver is being asked to expose to view very little more of his person than is already exposed. The police have already lawfully decided that the driver shall be briefly detained; the only question is whether he shall spend that period sitting in the driver's seat of his car or standing alongside it. Not only is the insistence of the police on the latter choice not a "serious intrusion upon the sanctity of the person,'" but it hardly rises to the level of a "petty indignity" . . . what is, at most, a mere inconvenience cannot prevail when balanced against legitimate concerns for the officer's safety.

- *Michigan v. Long*, 463 U.S. 1032 (1983)—Two Michigan officers observed a car traveling erratically before finally landing in a ditch. Approaching the vehicle, the officers encountered the defendant outside of the vehicle. When the driver approached the vehicle to retrieve his registration, officers saw a hunting knife in the driver's floorboard. The officers then frisked the defendant and conducted a search of the car's interior where they discovered a bag of marijuana. During the postarrest impoundment, more marijuana was found in the trunk. On appeal, the Petitioner argued that the search of the passenger compartment was unconstitutional and the subsequent search of the trunk represented a *fruit of the poisonous tree*. The Court rejected both arguments and extended *Terry* to include the search of the passenger compartment of a vehicle if there is a reasonable belief that it is necessary to protect officer safety. The Court stated:

  The protective search of the passenger compartment of respondent's car was reasonable under the principles articulated in Terry and other decisions of this Court. Although Terry involved the stop and subsequent patdown search for weapons of a person suspected of criminal activity, it did not restrict the preventive search to the person of the detained suspect. Protection of police and others can justify protective searches when police have a reasonable belief that the suspect poses a danger. Roadside encounters between police and suspects are especially hazardous, and danger may arise from the possible presence of weapons in the area surrounding a suspect. Thus, the search of the passenger compartment of an automobile, limited to those areas in which a weapon may be placed or hidden, is permissible if the police officer possesses a reasonable belief based on specific and articulable facts which, taken together with the rational inferences from those facts, reasonably warrant the officer to believe that the suspect is dangerous and the suspect may gain immediate control of weapons. If, while conducting a legitimate Terry search of an automobile's interior, the officer discovers contraband other than weapons, he cannot be required to ignore the contraband, and the Fourth Amendment does not require its suppression in such circumstances. The circumstances of this case justified the officers in their reasonable belief that respondent posed a danger if he were permitted to reenter his vehicle. Nor did they act unreasonably in taking preventive measures to ensure that there were no other weapons within respondent's immediate grasp before permitting him to reenter his automobile. The fact that respondent was under the officers' control during the investigative stop does not render unreasonable their belief that he could injure them.

- *Minnesota v. Dickerson*, 508 U.S. 366 (1993)—in this case, officers conducted a patdown search of an individual who was acting suspiciously after leaving a house known for drug activity. Although the officers did not find a weapon, one officer testified that he felt "a lump of crack cocaine in cellophane." Analogizing the case to those considered in the *plain view doctrine*, the Court ruled:

    . . . although the officer was lawfully in a position to feel the lump in respondent's pocket, because Terry entitled him to place his hands upon respondent's jacket, the court below determined that the incriminating character of the object was not immediately apparent to him. Rather, the officer determined that the item was contraband only after conducting a further search, one not authorized by Terry or by any other exception to the warrant requirement. Because this further search of respondent's pocket was constitutionally invalid, the seizure of the cocaine that followed is likewise unconstitutional.

It is important to note, however, that the Court did recognize the admissibility of criminal contraband seized within the confines of a *Terry* stop.

- *Hiibel v. Sixth Judicial District Court of Nevada*, 542 U.S. 177 (2004)—a deputy sheriff responding to a report of a man assaulting a woman in a red and silver GMC truck observed the suspect vehicle on the side of the road. The suspect was standing next to the truck and the victim was inside. The defendant refused to comply with repeated orders to produce identification in compliance with Nevada's "Stop and Identify" statute. He was subsequently arrested and charged with *willfully resisting, delaying, or obstructing a public officer in discharging or attempting to discharge any legal duty of his office.* The Court considered whether an arrest resulting from mandatory disclosure of identity was violative of the Fourth and Fifth Amendments. In their ruling the Court noted that such laws were grounded in early English vagrancy laws, and that they had recently found constitutional infirmity in such statutes. The Court also noted that they had recognized similar constitutional limitations of the scope and operation of stop and identify statutes. At the same time, the Court recognized the government interest in investigating potential criminal activity and protecting officer safety. In upholding the arrest and the Nevada statute, the Court opined:

    . . . the principles of Terry permit a state to require a suspect to disclose his name in the course of a Terry stop. The reasonableness of a seizure under the Fourteenth Amendment is determined "by balancing its intrusion on the individual's Fourth Amendment interests against its promotion of legitimate government interests. . . The Nevada statute satisfies that standard. The request for identity has an immediate relation to the purpose, rationale, and practical demands of a Terry stop. The threat of criminal sanction helps ensure that the request for identity does not become a legal nullity. On the other hand, the Nevada statute does not alter the nature of the stop itself . . . a state law requiring a suspect to disclose his name in the course of a valid Terry stop is consistent with Fourth Amendment prohibitions against unreasonable searches and seizures.

search incident to arrest a search of a criminal suspect and his/her immediate area prior to or following an arrest, conducted for the purpose of securing officer safety, preventing the destruction of criminal evidence, and/or discovering criminal contraband.

and immediately following the arrest of a criminal suspect. This has resulted in an additional exception to the Warrant Clause of the Fourth Amendment commonly referred to as a **search incident to arrest**. This type of search is permissible only in cases where officers are making a lawful arrest, and generally limited to the area in the immediate control of the arrestee. In a residence, or building, this would generally be limited to their person and the location immediately within their control (including boxes or other containers). In an automobile, this would be limited to the passenger compartment of the vehicle (including boxes or other containers). Officers may also search areas necessary to secure their safety. For example, they may look into rooms where a person may be hiding.

In *Chimel v. California*,[21] the Court evaluated whether law enforcement authorities could search the area surrounding an arrestee incident to a lawful arrest. In keeping with the general conservatism of the Court at the time, the Court ruled that:

> A similar analysis underlies the "search incident to arrest" principle, and marks its proper extent. When an [395 U.S. 752, 763] arrest is made, it is reasonable for the arresting officer to search the person arrested in order to remove any weapons that the latter might seek to use in order to resist arrest or effect his escape. Otherwise, the officer's safety might well be endangered, and the arrest itself frustrated. In addition, it is entirely reasonable for the arresting officer to search for and seize any evidence on the arrestee's person in order to prevent its concealment or destruction. And the area into which an arrestee might reach in order to grab a weapon or evidentiary items must, of course, be governed by a like rule. A gun on a table or in a drawer in front of one who is arrested can be as dangerous to the arresting officer as one concealed in the clothing of the person arrested. There is ample justification, therefore, for a search of the arrestee's person and the area "within his immediate control"—construing that phrase to mean the area from within which he might gain possession of a weapon or destructible evidence.

However, the Court clearly did not extend such searches to areas outside the arrestee's immediate control. To the contrary, the Court specifically addressed the issue in its ruling:

> There is no comparable justification, however, for routinely searching any room other than that in which an arrest occurs—or, for that matter, for searching through all the desk drawers or other closed or concealed areas in that room itself. Such searches, in the absence of well-recognized exceptions, may be made only under the authority of a search warrant. The "adherence to judicial processes" mandated by the Fourth Amendment requires no less.[22]

Four years later, the Court reiterated the need to secure officer safety. However, the Court also recognized that an incident to arrest search was much broader than traditional strictures imposed under the *Terry* doctrine, not restricted to any "probable fruits" or "further evidence" of that particular crime, and that the preservation of evidence was a legitimate police concern. Indeed, the Court held that a search incident to arrest was a legal certainty, not inconsistent with the Fourth Amendment. Thus, officers were not legally bound to articulate either threat of harm to human life or destruction of evidence as justification of said searches. In its ruling, which specifically overturned some of the original principles as established in *Weeks*, it ruled:

> The justification or reason for the authority to search incident to a lawful arrest rests quite as much on the need to disarm the suspect in order to take him into custody as it does on the need to preserve evidence on his person for later use at trial . . . the

standards traditionally governing a search incident to lawful arrest are not, therefore, commuted to the stricter Terry standards by the absence of probable fruits or further evidence of the particular crime for which the arrest is made.[23]

In recent years, the Court has continued to expand areas that might be searched incident to a lawful arrest. Building on the principal originally established in *Chimel*, the Court has struggled to create a divining rod for officers who must weigh the protections articulated in the Fourth Amendment and officer safety and the preservation of evidence.

One area of searches incident to arrest that has been scrutinized consistently by the Court involves automobiles. Such evaluation is above and beyond that which has been arbitrated in the search of automobiles themselves, which will be discussed next. More succinctly, the Court has upheld the warrantless search of an automobile's interior incident to lawful arrest, even when said interior was not immediately accessible to the occupant. Reiterating its rulings in *Chimel* and *Robinson*, the Court ruled that:

> Not only may the police search the passenger compartment of the car in such circumstances, they may also examine the contents of any containers found in the passenger compartment. And such a container may be searched whether it is open or closed, since the justification for the search is not that the arrestee has no privacy interest in the container but that the lawful custodial arrest justifies the infringement of any privacy interest the arrestee may have.[24]

In its justification, the Court recognized the necessity for creating a working definition with established parameters for the officer in the field. In addition, the Court, citing concerns for officer safety, has expanded the right to search from contemporaneous to "recent occupants."[25] However, it has steadfastly refused to extend such permissions to occasions in which citations (such as traffic tickets) are issued in lieu of a "custodial arrest."[26]

 CASE LAW

EVOLUTION OF PARAMETERS CONCERNING SEARCHES INCIDENT TO ARREST

In *Johnson v. United States*, 333 U.S. 10 (1948), the Court considered a case in which police officers, acting on a tip from a confidential informant, responded to an address where a strong odor of opium emanated. Upon entering the apartment after the occupant opened the door, the officers searched the room and seized evidence of opium and smoking paraphernalia. On appeal, the Petitioner argued that the search was unlawful in the absence of a warrant. The Supreme Court agreed noting that the officers possessed sufficient probable cause to secure a warrant prior to entry. They opined:

> . . . The point of the Fourth Amendment which often is not grasped by zealous officers is not that it denies law enforcement the support of the usual inferences which reasonable men draw

from evidence. Its protection consists in requiring that those inferences be drawn by a neutral and detached magistrate, instead of being judged by the officer engaged in the often competitive enterprise of ferreting out crime. Any assumption that evidence sufficient to support a magistrate's disinterested determination to issue a search warrant will justify the officers in making a search without a warrant would reduce the Amendment to a nullity, and leave the people's homes secure only in the discretion of police officers.

In *Trupiano v. United States*, 334 U.S. 699 (1948), the Court considered a case in which federal agents performed a warrantless, nighttime raid on an illegal distillery three weeks after they determined that the Petitioner was involved in criminal activity. The arrest, search, and seizure

(continued)

were a result of a three-week investigation in which an undercover informant provided samples of alcohol, sugar bags, yeast wrappers, and a five-gallon can taken from the still. On the night of the raid, agents looking through a back door observed a still in operation. They entered the building, seized the still and arrested the sole occupant. A second suspect was arrested within minutes outside the building. Petitioners Trupiano and Riccardelli were arrested later that night. Petitioners moved to suppress the evidence on the grounds that it was illegally obtained. The Government argued that the arrest was authorized as felonious activity happened in their presence and that the evidence was lawfully seized incident to a lawful arrest. While the Court upheld the constitutionality of the arrest, it did not uphold the seizure of the still. Reiterating the ruling in *Johnson*, the Court ruled:

> . . . no reason is offered for not obtaining a search warrant except the inconvenience to the officers and some slight delay necessary to prepare papers and present the evidence to a magistrate. These are never very convincing reasons, and, in these circumstances, certainly are not enough to bypass the constitutional requirement.

In *United States v. Rabinowitz* (1950),[27] the Court considered a case in which officers conducted a search of a desk, safe, and filing cabinets after executing an arrest warrant on an individual who had sold forged postage stamps to an undercover agent. During the search, officers recovered 573 forged stamps. Rabinowitz was subsequently indicted for possessing and concealing the stamps seized during the search in addition to the original charges. On appeal, the Petitioner argued that the evidence should have been suppressed as the search of the room, desk, and filing cabinets exceeded that area permissible incident to a lawful arrest. The Court disagreed on five counts: (1) the search and seizure were incident to a valid arrest; (2) the search was limited to a business room which was accessible to the public and the officers; (3) the room was small and under the immediate and complete control of Rabinowitz; (4) the search did not extend beyond the room that was used for unlawful purposes; and (5) the possession of the forged and altered stamps was a crime. Most importantly, the Court overturned *Trupiano*,

. . . to the extent that Trupiano v. United States requires a search warrant solely upon the basis of the practicability of procuring it, rather than upon the reasonableness of the search after a lawful arrest, that case is overruled. The relevant test is not whether it is reasonable to procure a search warrant, but whether the search was reasonable. That criterion, in turn, depends upon the facts and circumstances—the total atmosphere of the case. It is a sufficient precaution that law officers must justify their conduct before courts which have always been, and must be, jealous of the individual's right of privacy within the broad sweep of the Fourth Amendment.

In *Chimel v. California*, 395 U.S. 752 (1969), the Court considered a case in which officers, armed with an arrest warrant, searched the entire house of an individual. The search included the attic, the garage, and a small workshop. It also included searches in drawers. Evidence seized in the hour long search included medals, tokens, and other objects. On appeal, Petitioner argued that the evidence was the result of an unlawful search. The Government contended that the search was permissible as it was "incident to arrest." The Court rejected that argument, and clearly delineated parameters for searches incident to a lawful arrest. They ruled that a warrantless search incident to arrest was limited to the suspect's immediate control except in cases where there existed a clear and present danger to police officers or, the destruction or concealment of criminal evidence.

In a landmark decision in 1981, the Court extended the search-incident-to-arrest provisions established in *Chimel* to the passenger compartment of an automobile. In *New York v. Belton* [453 U.S. 454 (1981)], the Court recognized the confusion that may result for line officers in *case-by-case adjudication* versus *standardized procedures* in the application of *Chimel* to automobiles.

> . . . no straightforward rule has emerged from the litigated cases respecting . . . the question of the proper scope of a search of the interior of an automobile incident to a lawful custodial arrest of its occupants. . . . When a person cannot know how a court will apply a settled principle to a recurring factual situation, that person cannot know the scope of his constitutional protection, nor can a policeman know the

scope of his authority. . . . Accordingly, we hold that, when a policeman has made a lawful custodial arrest of the occupant of an automobile, he may, as a contemporaneous incident of that arrest, search the passenger compartment of that automobile.

This ruling governed the actions of police officers for nearly three decades and was known as the *Belton* Rule. Both federal and state courts routinely admitted evidence that was located in a vehicle's passenger compartment incident to a lawful arrest. In 2009, the Court abandoned the **Belton Rule** completely. In *Arizona v. Gant*, the Court recognized that the original rationale for the rule failed to consider the lack of danger that an arrestee posed to either safety or evidence in an area that was no longer in his or her immediate control.

▶ "Plain View" Doctrine

In addition to concerns regarding the safety of police personnel, the Court has also recognized the preservation of evidence as a legitimate law enforcement mission. In *Coolidge v. New Hampshire*,[28] for example, the Court specifically ruled that evidence that was in plain view may be admissible in court if the officer was in a lawful position, the discovery was inadvertent, and the evidentiary value of the item was immediately apparent. Relying on previous case law in the area of warrantless searches, the Court ruled that the **"plain view" doctrine**:

> . . . serves to supplement the prior justification—whether it be a warrant for another object, hot pursuit, search incident to lawful arrest, or some other legitimate reason for being present unconnected with a search directed against the accused—and permits the warrantless seizure.

However, the Court cautioned against a loose interpretation of this approach, stating that the "plain view" doctrine may be used only:

> . . . where it is immediately apparent to the police that they have evidence before them; the "plain view" doctrine may not be used to extend a general exploratory search from one object to another until something incriminating at last emerges.[29]

The emergence of the "plain view" doctrine was not without criticisms, and challenges soon emerged regarding to the wording of the initial ruling. In particular, the question as to the **immediate apparency** of criminal evidence was at issue. In *Arizona v. Hicks*,[30] the Court evaluated whether law enforcement personnel could invoke the "plain view" doctrine when the circumstances did not reach the level of probable cause. In *Hicks*, police lawfully entered an apartment where shots had been fired through the floor, injuring an individual below. While there, the officers seized an assortment of weapons and noticed expensive stereo equipment that, in their estimation, was suspicious. Upon moving the equipment to access serial numbers, they phoned the station that identified them as stolen property. The Court rejected the government's contention that the items should be admissible under the "plain view" doctrine, stating that:

> The policeman's actions come within the purview of the Fourth Amendment. The mere recording of the serial numbers did not constitute a "seizure" since it did not meaningfully interfere with respondent's possessory interest in either the numbers or the stereo equipment. However, the moving of the equipment was a "search" separate and apart from the search that was the lawful objective of entering the apartment.[31]

Thus, the Court reiterated earlier rulings in which both the immediate apparency of an item and the legality of police presence were deemed necessary for doctrinal application.

belton rule evidence rule established by the U.S. Supreme Court that permitted officers to make a contemporaneous search of a passenger compartment of an automobile incident to a lawful arrest. (It was overturned in *Arizona v. Gant* (2009).

"plain view" doctrine legal authority allowing collection of criminal evidence when the item in question is unobstructed, the officer or authority is in a lawful position, and the evidentiary value of the item is immediately apparent.

immediate apparency a term used exclusively in consideration of the constitutionality of a particular "plain view" search. The term refers to the instant recognizability of a particular item's evidentiary value.

CASE LAW

IMPORTANT NOTES ON PLAIN VIEW SEARCHES

In *Coolidge v. New Hampshire*, 403 U.S. 443 (1971), the Court formally delineated three requirements for a warrantless *plain view search* was permissible. In summarizing a collection of cases previously decided by the Court, they noted:

> . . . what the "plain view" cases have in common is that the police officer in each of them had a prior justification for an intrusion in the course of which he came inadvertently across a piece of evidence incriminating the accused. The doctrine serves to supplement the prior justification—whether it be a warrant for another object, hot pursuit, search incident to lawful arrest, or some other legitimate reason for being present unconnected with a search directed against the accused—and permits the warrantless seizure. Of course, the extension of the original justification is legitimate only where it is immediately apart to the police that they have evidence before them; the "plain view" doctrine may not be used to extend a general exploratory search from one object to another until something incriminating at least emerges.
>
> . . . the limits on the doctrine are implicit in the statement of its rationale. The first of these is that plain view, alone, is never enough to justify the warrantless seizure of evidence . . . the second limitation is that the discovery of evidence in plain view must be inadvertent. . .

Since that time, the Court has revisited the original requirements: (1) a lawful position of officer; (2) inadvertency of discovery; and (3) immediate apparency.

Inadvertent discovery. *Horton v. California*, 496 U.S. 128 (1990)—the Court rejected the immediate apparency requirement established in *Coolidge* noting that:

> . . . the seizure of an object in plain view does not involve an intrusion on privacy. If the interest in privacy has been invaded, the violation must have occurred before the object came into plain view and there is no need for an inadvertence limitation on seizures to condemn it. The prohibition against general searches and general warrants serves primarily as a protection against unjustified intrusions on privacy. But reliance on privacy concerns that support that prohibition is misplaced when the inquiry concerns the scope of an exception that

merely authorizes an officer with a lawful right of access to an item to seize it without a warrant.

Immediate apparency. *Texas v. Brown*, 460 U.S. 730 (1983)—the Court rejected the absolute knowledge of an item's evidentiary value replacing it with a reasonableness standard.

> The "immediately apparent" language in Coolidge, supra, does not establish a requirement that a police officer "know" that certain items are contraband or evidence of a crime. " The seizure of property in plain view involves no invasion of privacy, and is presumptively reasonable, assuming that there is probable cause to associate the property with criminal activity." . . . Probable cause is a flexible, common-sense standard, merely requiring that the facts available to the officer would warrant a man of reasonable caution to believe that certain items may be contraband or stolen property or useful as evidence of a crime; it does not demand any showing that such a belief be correct or more likely true than false.

Immediate apparency. *Arizona v. Hicks*, 480 U.S. 321 (1987)—the Court rejected a search where stereo equipment found by police executing a lawful search for evidence unrelated to the stereo was moved to retrieve the serial number. They held that the moving of the equipment and the retrieval did not satisfy the *immediate apparency* requirement established in *Coolidge*.

> . . . the search was invalid because, as the State concedes, the policeman had only a "reasonable suspicion"—*i.e.,* less than probable cause to believe—that the stereo equipment was stolen. Probable cause is required to invoke the "plain view" doctrine as it applies to seizures. It would be illogical to hold that an object is seizable on lesser grounds, during an unrelated search and seizure, than would have been needed to obtain a warrant for it if it had been known to be on the premises. Probable cause to believe the equipment was stolen was also necessary to support the search here, whether legal authority to move the equipment could be found only as the inevitable concomitant of the authority to seize it or also as a consequence of some independent power to search objects in plain view.

▶ "Plain Feel" Doctrine

inadvertent discovery an accidental or unplanned detection. The term is usually restricted to discussions or considerations of "plain view" searches.

"plain feel" doctrine legal authority that provides for the collection of items when such items are inadvertently discovered on an individual's person during legitimate police actions.

In recent years, the courts have revisited the "plain view" doctrine with a view toward clarifying whether objects seized on reasonable suspicion through a sense outside of sight might be eligible for the "plain view" exception. Often called **"plain feel" doctrine**, the courts have appeared arbitrary and capricious in their interpretation and application. In *State v. Washington*,[32] for example, a court upheld the admissibility of three watches discovered during a pat down of a suspect who met the description of an individual who had participated recently in the robbery of a jewelry store. In this particular case, the appellate court held that plain view included all senses, including smell, sight, touch, hearing, and taste. In a similar vein, the United States Court of Appeals for the District of Columbia upheld the introduction of bags of heroin discovered during a stop-and-frisk of a defendant and his property. The court rejected the notion that the "plain feel" recognition of drugs by a veteran officer should be ignored simply because the items posed no immediate risk to the officer's safety.[33] In addition, the Court has upheld the admissibility of items seized in circumstances in which other senses were the basis of reasonable suspicion, including that of smell and touch. In *Illinois v. Caballes*,[34] for example, the Court upheld the constitutionality of drug sniffing dogs in the absence of specific probable cause. In their evaluation, the Court considered whether indicia of probable cause was necessary in cases in which a legitimate government interest (in this case, a traffic stop) was sufficient justification for narcotics-sniffing dogs. In a nutshell, the Court rejected the notion that individuals have an expectation of privacy in criminal contraband that is secreted away. To wit,

> . . . any interest in possessing contraband cannot be deemed "legitimate," and thus, governmental conduct that only reveals the possession of contraband "compromises no legitimate privacy interest." . . . This is because the expectation "that certain facts will not come to the attention of the authorities" is not the same as an interest in "privacy that society is prepared to consider reasonable." . . . In *United States v. Place*, 462 U.S. 696 (1983), we treated a canine sniff by a well-trained narcotics-detection dog as "*sui generis*" because it "discloses only the presence or absence of narcotics, a contraband item."

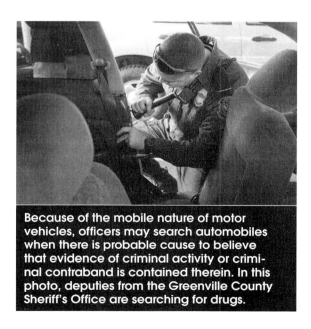

Because of the mobile nature of motor vehicles, officers may search automobiles when there is probable cause to believe that evidence of criminal activity or criminal contraband is contained therein. In this photo, deputies from the Greenville County Sheriff's Office are searching for drugs.

Accordingly, the use of a well-trained narcotics-detection dog—one that "does not expose noncontraband items that otherwise would remain hidden from public view," Place, 462 U.S. (at 707), during a lawful traffic stop, generally does not implicate legitimate privacy interests. In this case, the dog sniff was performed on the exterior of respondent's car while he was lawfully seized for a traffic violation. Any intrusion on respondent's privacy expectations does not rise to the level of a constitutionally cognizable infringement.[35]

Thus, the Court has explicitly recognized some exceptions to the Warrant Requirement as specified in the Fourth Amendment. Many of these areas have resided in areas where there is a reduced expectation of privacy, while others have recognized areas in which privacy concerns are not at issue. Such areas include those that are subject to police scrutiny during lawful detainment and arrest, including those that reasonably might impact officer safety. However, it must be noted that the Court has resisted lower court attempts to analogize "plain touch" and "plain feel," consistently arguing that the sense of touch is more invasive and less reliable than that of sight.

▶ Automobile Searches

As stated in the preceding section, the Court has continued to expand areas that previously had been inviolable under the Fourth Amendment. The authority of police personnel to undertake a warrantless roadside search of an automobile was first established in *Carroll v. United States*.[36] In that case, the Court evaluated whether the warrantless search of suspected bootleggers' car was reasonable. In an interesting juxtaposition of the Fourth Amendment and the asset forfeiture provision contained within the National Prohibition Act, the Court allowed the introduction of evidence seized during a roadside stop. In its justification, the Court specifically articulated provisos within the Act that permitted the seizure and destruction of any intoxicating liquor and the potential for the destruction of criminal evidence of same. However, the rubric has been applied to various other cases in which the Act does not apply. In the most general sense, the Court's decision permitted the warrantless, roadside search of a motor vehicle if there was probable cause to believe that evidence of criminal activity or criminal contraband was contained therein. In later cases, the Court reiterated the original argument that the securing of a warrant in automobile cases in which probable cause exists may lead to the destruction of evidence and serve to circumvent vested societal interests.

> . . . [T]hose lawfully within the country, entitled to use the public highways, have a right to free passage without interruption or search unless there is known to a competent official, authorized to search, probable cause for believing that their vehicles are carrying contraband or illegal merchandise.[37]

In the decades since *Carroll*, the Court has continued to evaluate the situations in which officers may conduct a warrantless search of automobiles and the parameters to which they must abide. In 1970, the Court in *Chambers v. Maroney*[38] considered whether the warrantless search of a vehicle that had been moved from the roadside to the police department was constitutional within the boundaries of the Fourth Amendment. In this case, the Court argued that such searches were permissible outside the scope of the incident to arrest exception, noting that:

> . . . the circumstances that furnish probable cause to search a particular auto for particular articles are most often unforeseeable; moreover, the opportunity to search is fleeting since a car is readily movable. Where this is true, as in Carroll and the case before

us now, if an effective search is to be made at any time, either the search must be made immediately without a warrant or the car itself must be seized and held without a warrant for whatever period is necessary to obtain a warrant for the search.

In its justification, the Court recognized that the standard of probable cause necessary to effect a warrantless search was sufficient to substantiate the search of a vehicle in a location other than that of origination due primarily to the historical distinction between private residences and automobiles traveling on public thoroughfares. To wit,

> For constitutional purposes, we see no difference between on the one hand seizing and holding a car before presenting the probable cause issue to a magistrate and on the other hand carrying out an immediate search without a warrant. Given probable cause to search, either course is reasonable under the Fourth Amendment . . . there is little to choose in terms of practical consequences between an immediate search without a warrant and the car's immobilization until a warrant is obtained. The same consequences may not follow where there is unforeseeable cause to search a house. . . . But . . . there is a constitutional difference between houses and cars.[39]

Thus, officers may undertake the search of a car in said circumstances even though time permitted them to seek a warrant for the search. This exigency requirement was also evaluated nearly three decades after *Chambers v. Maroney*. Once again, the Court ruled that the securing of a warrant was not necessary to search automobiles when probable cause—that the vehicle contained criminal evidence or contraband—existed. In *Pennsylvania v. Labron*,[40] the Court explicitly stated that the sheer mobility of an automobile created the exigency necessary for a warrantless search.

In 1985, the Court extended a consistent rationale to the warrantless roadside search to a motor home being operated on public roadways. In the case of *California v. Carney*,[41] the Court considered whether a motor home capable of

---

 CASE LAW

ABANDONING THE *BELTON* RULE: *ARIZONA V. GANT*, 556 U.S. 332 (2009)

In 2009, the Court considered whether the *search incident to arrest exception* as defined in *Chimel* and applied to the vehicle searches under the *Belton* Rule could justify the warrantless search of the contents of an individual's car who had been arrested for driving with a suspended license and handcuffed in the back of a patrol car prior to the search. In a departure from *Belton*, the Court refused to extend the parameters of a search incident to arrest to the contents of a vehicle once it was out of the arrestee's immediate control.

> . . . *The experience of the 28 years since we decided Belton has shown that the generalization underpinning the broad reading of that decision is unfounded. We now know that articles inside the passenger compartment are rarely "within the area into which an arrestee might reach" . . . and blind adherence to Belton's faulty assumption*

would authorize myriad unconstitutional searches. The doctrine of stare decisis does not require us to approve routine constitutional violations. . . . Police may search a vehicle incident to a recent occupant's arrest only if the arrestee is within reaching distance of the passenger compartment at the time of the search or it is reasonable to believe the vehicle contains evidence of the offense of arrest. When these justifications are absent, a search of an arrestee's vehicle will be unreasonable unless police obtain a warrant or show that another exception to the warrant requirement applies.

As a result of the *Gant* decision, officers are prohibited from conducting a warrantless search of the passenger compartment of a motor vehicle incident to a lawful arrest: (1) the arrestee may still access the vehicle; or (2) the vehicle contains evidence of the offense leading to the arrest.

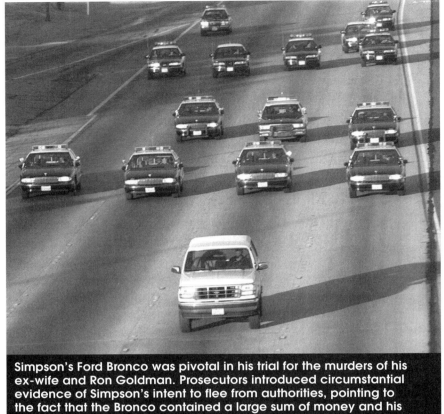

Simpson's Ford Bronco was pivotal in his trial for the murders of his ex-wife and Ron Goldman. Prosecutors introduced circumstantial evidence of Simpson's intent to flee from authorities, pointing to the fact that the Bronco contained a large sum of money and his Heisman trophy. Investigators recovered the items when Simpson surrendered to the police. (Other evidentiary items contained within or upon the Bronco included: blood, a shovel, a towel, and a heavy-duty plastic bag.)

being used as a means of transportation was more appropriately considered a "residence" or an "automobile." In its ruling, the Court dismissed the notion that some vehicles were more sacrosanct than others simply based on size or "quality of its appointments." In addition, the Court ruled that any vehicle that is either being or has the capability of a mode of transportation squarely fits under the automobile exception to the Warrant Clause of the Fourth Amendment. In its decision, the Court reiterated its findings in earlier cases in which it bifurcated justifications for said exceptions, in that vehicles are mobile; and that, "there is a reduced expectation of privacy stemming from the pervasive regulation of vehicles capable of traveling on highways."

Automobile Inventory Searches

inventory searches
legal term referring to the warrantless search of a person or physical object by law enforcement authorities conducted upon the arrest of an individual or impoundment of property which documents all items contained within.

Unlike individuals who may be "seized" only through lawful arrest, automobiles may be seized by law enforcement in many different situations, including, but not limited to, suspicion of DUI and improper registration. As such, the Court has created case law in which the issue of inventory searches has been evaluated. **Inventory searches** by definition are searches that are conducted by law enforcement personnel of an individual's personal belongings. They are conducted in various situations and include those in which a suspect is taken into custody or a car is impounded. Theoretically, these searches are designed to protect the individual by documenting all items in his or her personal possession before arrest or seizure. In automobiles, searches are conducted on all vehicles that come into the custody of police personnel whether through the arrest of a suspect, the abandonment of property, or other means.

In the 1976 case of *South Dakota v. Opperman*,[42] the Court evaluated whether evidence of narcotics contained within a backpack in an automobile impounded on suspicion of DUI obtained through the inventory search of the impounded car was admissible. The Court upheld such inclusion stating that:

> . . . the decisions of this Court point unmistakably to the conclusion reached by both federal and state courts that inventories pursuant to standard police procedures are reasonable. . . . In applying the reasonableness standard adopted by the Framers, this Court has consistently sustained police intrusions into automobiles impounded or otherwise in lawful police custody where the process is aimed at securing or protecting the car and its contents.

The Court has continued to reiterate the tenets of inventory searches originally espoused in *Lafayette* and *Opperman*, arguing that there is a vested government interest in the protection of an owner's personal belongings and any unwarranted accusations of theft or damage to law enforcement personnel as long as the police follow standardized caretaking procedures in good faith. However, the Court did preclude any "inventory" search that was undertaken in an investigative vein.

> Police, before inventorying a container, are not required to weigh the strength of the individual's privacy interest in the container against the possibility that the container might serve as a repository for dangerous or valuable items. There is no merit to the contention that the search of respondent's van was unconstitutional because departmental regulations gave the police discretion to choose between impounding the van and [479 U.S. 367, 368] parking and locking it in a public parking place. The exercise of police discretion is not prohibited so long as that discretion is exercised—as was done here—according to standard criteria and on the basis of something other than suspicion of evidence of criminal activity.[43]

Closed Containers in Automobile Searches

Just as the Court has had to establish parameters associated with inventory searches of automobiles, it has also had to grapple with the boundaries associated with closed containers located within a vehicle that has been lawfully stopped. The first case that evaluated whether the "automobile exception" permitted the search of a locked container housed within a motor vehicle was *United States v. Chadwick*.[44] In this case, the Court had to evaluate whether the search of a double-locked footlocker in the trunk of a car owned by a suspected drug dealer was permissible under the "automobile exception" to the Warrant Requirement. In their justification, the Court ruled that the introduction of evidence discovered through the search and seizure of the footlocker violated the Fourth Amendment, as "person's expectations of privacy in personal luggage are substantially greater than in an automobile." Although apparently contrary to previous rulings, the Court explained that the exigency of said search was all but eliminated upon seizure of the item in question and that attainment of a warrant in such a situation was necessary to halt inquiries of government intrusiveness. This preliminary ruling was upheld in the later case of *Arkansas v. Sanders*, in which the Court ruled the "automobile exception" from the Warrant Requirement and its progeny "will not be extended to the warrantless search of one's personal luggage merely because it was located in an automobile lawfully stopped by the police"; and again in *Florida v. Wells*[45] that cautioned against "general rummaging."

NON-VEHICLE INVENTORY SEARCHES, *ILLINOIS V. LAFAYETTE*, 462 U.S. 640 (1983)

Consistent with the Fourth Amendment, it is reasonable for police to search the personal effects of a person under lawful arrest as part of the routine administrative procedure at a police station incident to booking and jailing the suspect. The justification for such searches does not rest on probable cause, and hence the absence of a warrant is immaterial to the reasonableness of the search. Here, every consideration of orderly police administration—protection of a suspect's property, deterrence of false claims of theft against the police, security, and identification of the suspect—benefiting both the police and the public points toward the appropriateness of the examination of respondent's shoulder bag [*Illinois v. Lafayette*, 462 U.S. 640 (1983)].

Irrespective of the rulings in *Chadwick* and *Sanders*, the Court has recognized some areas in which personal luggage and closed containers may be searched under the "automobile exception" to the Warrant Requirement. The Court has specifically held, for example, that personal luggage and closed containers may be searched if probable cause exists to suspect that those containers or personal belongings contain criminal evidence or contraband.[46] However, the Court did limit the scope of such a search to those areas in which items reasonably suspected might reside.

In *Florida v. Wells*,[47] the Court evaluated whether an "all or nothing" policy violated the Fourth Amendment. In the case, the Court evaluated whether an inventory search of a closed container not narrowly guided by departmental policy was constitutional. Before said ruling, the Court had narrowly defined same. In *Wells*, however, the Court attempted to clarify apparent contradictions in *Carroll*, *Chadwick*, and *Sanders*:

> But in forbidding uncanalized discretion to police officers conducting inventory searches, there is no reason to insist that they be conducted in a totally mechanical "all or nothing" fashion." [I]nventory procedures serve to protect an owner's property while it is in the custody of the police, to insure against claims of lost, stolen, or vandalized property, and to guard the police from danger." . . . A police officer may be allowed sufficient latitude to determine whether a particular container should or should not be opened in light of the nature of the search and characteristics of the container itself. Thus, while policies of opening all containers or of opening no containers are unquestionably permissible, it would be equally permissible, for example, to allow the opening of closed containers whose contents officers determine they are unable to ascertain from examining the containers' exteriors. The allowance of the exercise of judgment based on concerns related to the purposes of an inventory search does not violate the Fourth Amendment.[48]

Thus, the Court deviated from the course originally delineated in *Bertine*, in which specific parameters were established for standardized police procedures. In fact, the *Wells* court specifically permitted a level of law enforcement discretion that had been lacking in previous decisions.

Other Issues with Searches of Automobiles

Since the invention of motor vehicles and the explosion of interstate commerce, the Supreme Court has been inundated with cases involving automobiles. Although many of these cases have focused exclusively on the parameters of content searches, others have focused on the circumstances in which traffic stops may occur. The Court originally articulated said standards in *United States v. Cortez*.[49]

In determining what cause is sufficient to authorize police to stop a person, the totality of the circumstances—the whole picture—must be taken into account. Based upon that whole picture the detaining [449 U.S. 411, 412] officers must have a particularized and objective basis for suspecting the particular person stopped of criminal activity. The process of assessing all of the circumstances does not deal with hard certainties, but with probabilities, and the evidence collected must be weighed as understood by those versed in the field of law enforcement. Also, the process must raise a suspicion that the particular individual being stopped is engaged in wrongdoing.

The concepts originally articulated in *Cortez* were tested again some 15 years later, when the Court evaluated whether the pretextual traffic stop of a motorist based solely on probable cause that a violation of traffic laws had been committed was reasonable under the parameters established by the Fourth Amendment even in cases in which said probable cause was not the motivating factor behind said stop. To wit, "subjective intentions play no role in ordinary, probable-cause Fourth Amendment analysis."[50] (However, the Court has been adamantly opposed to law enforcement stops that are not predicated on articulable probable cause.) Finally, the Court has ruled that law enforcement authorities do not have the absolute responsibility or bear the burden of informing suspects of their right to leave during an automobile search. To the contrary, the Court has ruled that:

> The Fourth Amendment does not require that a lawfully seized defendant be advised that he is "free to go" before his consent to search will be recognized as voluntary. The Amendment's touchstone is reasonableness, which is measured in objective terms by examining the totality of the circumstances. In applying this test, the Court has consistently eschewed bright-line rules, instead emphasizing the fact-specific nature of the reasonableness inquiry.[51]

▶ Consent

Of all the warrantless searches that have been discussed, **consent searches** are the only ones in which probable cause, reasonable suspicion, or an articulable justification is not required. In fact, demonstration of the voluntary nature of said search is usually all that is required to uphold evidence that is introduced in the absence of a search warrant. Although they are still bound by the tenets contained within the Fourth Amendment, an individual's waiver of same is sufficient to permit the introduction of evidence collected as a result of such relinquishment. However, parameters of consent searches are limited to the duration of the original assent. Withdrawal of same reduces all expectation of permission by law enforcement and immediately ceases any search activities. In the most general sense, the concept of consent as adjudicated by the Court may be divided into three broad concerns: scope, voluntary, and third party.

consent searches
searches conducted in the absence of a warrant, which are predicated on the permission of the homeowner or other competent party but which are limited to the scope of said permission. Original assent is where withdrawal of same reduces all expectation of permission by law enforcement, and immediately ceases any search activities. In the most general sense, the concept of consent as adjudicated by the Court may be divided into three broad concerns: scope, voluntary, and third party.

🔍 CLARIFICATION OF CONCEPTS

CLOSED CONTAINERS AND AUTOMOBILES

In *United States v. Chadwick* the Court ruled that the "automobile exception" to the Warrant Requirement did not extend to the search of a double-locked footlocker found in the trunk of a car as a "person's expectations of privacy in personal luggage are substantially greater than in an automobile." The ruling was upheld in subsequent rulings, which prohibited general rummaging. However, the Court does permit searches of closed containers and locked compartments located within an automobile IF probable cause exists to believe that they contain criminal contraband or evidence.

Voluntariness of Consent

By far, the most common area evaluated by the Court in consent searches involves the question of voluntary cooperation. As stated, consent obtained validly negates the requirement of a warrant or probable cause. However, the voluntary nature of the consent is often the crux of admissibility. Jurists must evaluate, for example, whether the cooperation or willingness of the grantor was entirely voluntary or predicated on the actions or words of another. Information or evidence collected as a result of consent may be deemed inadmissible whenever it is determined that the actor was acting under duress or was coerced in any way. For example, consent to search that is extended only after authorities lie about the existence of a search warrant is invalid.[52] Determination of voluntariness is accomplished through a careful consideration of the totality of circumstances. Even so, the Court has recognized the difficulty in creating comprehensive definitions, conceding that there is:

> . . . no talismanic definition of "voluntariness," mechanically applicable to the host of situations where the question has arisen. "The notion of 'voluntariness' . . . is itself an amphibian." It cannot be taken literally to mean a "knowing" choice. "Except where a person is unconscious or drugged or otherwise lacks capacity for conscious choice, all incriminating statements—even those made under brutal treatment—are 'voluntary' in the sense of representing a choice of alternatives. On the other hand, if 'voluntariness' incorporates notions of 'but-for' cause, the question should be whether the statement would have been made even absent inquiry or other official action. Under such a test, virtually no statement would be voluntary because very few people give incriminating statements in the absence of official action of some kind." It is thus evident that neither linguistics nor epistemology will provide a ready definition of the meaning of "voluntariness."[53]

In determining whether a defendant's will was overborne in the case at hand, the Court-mandated standard of the "totality of the circumstances" has included numerous characteristics. Such factors have included characteristics of the accused and the details of the interrogation or search itself. Factors that may lessen or negate the certainty of voluntary consent or confessions have included:

- The age (youthfulness) of the accused [*Haley v. Ohio*, 332 U.S. 596 (1948)]
- Low level of education [*Payne v. Arkansas*, 356 U.S. 560 (1958)]
- Low intelligence [*Fikes v. Alabama*, 352 U.S. 191 (1957)]
- Lack of any advice to the accused of his or her constitutional rights [*Davis v. North Carolina*, 384 U.S. 737 (1966)]
- Length of detention [*Chambers v. Florida*, 309 U.S. 227 (1940)]
- The repeated and prolonged nature of the questioning [*Ashcraft v. Tennessee*, 322 U.S. 143 (1944)]
- The use of physical punishment such as the deprivation of food or sleep [*Reck v. Pate*, 367 U.S. 433 (1961)]

In each of these cases, the Court ruled that ". . . none of them turned on the presence or absence of a single controlling criterion; each reflected a careful scrutiny of all the surrounding circumstances."[54] In addition, the Court ruled that the failure to advise an individual of his or her right to refuse said search was not a necessary component in obtaining consent. To wit: ". . . while the subject's knowledge of a right to refuse is a factor to be taken into account, the prosecution is not required to demonstrate such knowledge as a prerequisite to establishing a voluntary consent." This ruling has been affirmed in numerous recent cases and

POLICE AUTHORITY AND PERSONAL LUGGAGE

Do police have the authority to request a search of personal luggage in the absence of reasonable suspicion?

Yes. In *United States v. Drayton et al.* ([2002], 536 U.S. 194), police officers conducted a bus sweep as part of a routine narcotics and firearms interdiction effort. They asked and received consent to search both the personal luggage and the persons of Drayton and a friend. Subsequently, they found drugs on both parties and summarily arrested them for narcotics trafficking. In appealing their conviction, the parties argued that the search was unconstitutional because the contraband was uncovered as a direct result of coercive police conduct. The Supreme Court disagreed, ruling:

. . . the Fourth Amendment permits officers to approach bus passengers at random to ask questions and request their consent to searches, provided a reasonable person would feel free to decline the requests or otherwise terminate the encounter. . . . The Court identified as "particularly worth noting" the factors that the officer, although obviously armed, did not unholster his gun or use it in a threatening way, and that he advised respondent passenger that he could refuse consent to a search. Relying on this last factor, the Eleventh Circuit erroneously adopted what is in effect a per se rule that evidence obtained during suspicionless drug interdictions on buses must be suppressed unless the officers have advised passengers of their right not to cooperate and to refuse consent to a search.

has even been expanded to consensual searches in which no suspicion of criminal activity is present.[55]

This is not to suggest, however, that all consensual searches that appear voluntary are admissible. To the contrary, whenever said consent is obtained as a result of an illegal seizure, then the fruits of such will be deemed inadmissible [*Florida v. Royer*, 460 U.S. 491 (1983)].

Thus, the voluntariness of a confession includes the traditional considerations of age, education, intelligence, and the physical and mental conditions of the person granting consent. However, evaluation of the admissibility of evidence obtained through a consensual search must also include an evaluation of the scope of said consent and the legitimacy of the individual grantor (please see Chapter 7 for the exclusion of confession and a complete discussion of *Miranda*).

Scope of Consent

In the most general sense, the parameters of a particular consensual search are limited to the terms of the consent. More specifically, the individual grantor retains the right to limit, guide, or otherwise terminate the resulting search throughout its duration. As the Court ruled in *Florida v. Jimeno*,[56] "(t)he standard for measuring the scope of a suspect's consent under the Fourth Amendment is that of 'objective' reasonableness—[that is] what would the typical reasonable person have understood by the exchange between the officer and the suspect." As always, the Court's decision may be applied only on a case-by-case basis and does not provide practitioners with a blanket, workable definition.

Third-Party Consent

The final consideration in the evaluation of the admissibility of particular consensual searches involves the legitimacy of the person extending such permission. Although it is clear that a mentally competent individual of legal age may grant consent to search his or her personal belongings, situations in which **third-party consent**—where third parties extend permission—are more ambiguous. In a

third-party consent
usually used to refer to permission to search an area, granted by a nonowner or an individual without a proprietary interest of said area. Determinations of the admissibility of items collected in such searches involves consideration of common authority and competency.

REASONABLENESS AND THE SCOPE OF CONSENT: *UNITED STATES V. TURNER*, 169 F.3D 84 (1ST CIR. 1999)

In the early morning hours of July 28, 1997, a young woman was awakened in her apartment by a knife-wielding masked intruder. She fought off her attacker, cutting her hands in the process. Turner, her next-door neighbor, notified the authorities, claiming that he had observed the suspect's flight while sitting upstairs at his computer. While investigating the attack, detectives noticed smeared blood on both the victim and Turner's window sills—which were ajar. Upon his consent to search his apartment for signs of an intruder, officers discovered blood inside the apartment. They also accessed his computer files without his knowledge after noticing photos of female bondage. Subsequently, they discovered images of child pornography. The First Circuit, in excluding the images, ruled that the search of the computer could not be construed as being within the scope of the consent given.

. . . The objective reasonableness of this understanding becomes even more clear when one considers the fruits of the consensual search that had taken place just before Turner signed the written consent; that is, the concrete physical evidence associated with the assault itself, including scattered blood stains and a knife that fit the description given by the victim. Moreover, when the detectives later announced their intention to search for "evidence of the assault itself," an objectively reasonable person likely would infer that they intended to search for evidence of the same ilk; that is, for incriminating objects directly linked to the nearby crime scene, not for documentary or photographic evidence. See United States v. Gutierrez-Hermosillo, *142 F.3d 1225, 1231 (10th Cir.), cert. denied, 119 S.Ct. 230 (1998) (courts must examine totality of circumstances in determining scope of consent);* United States v. Torres, *32 F.3d 225, 231 (7th Cir. 1994) (same);* United States v. Huffhines, *967 F.2d 314, 319 (9th Cir. 1992) (same).*

general sense, the Court has recognized the legitimacy of a marital partner's interest in the spouse's property and, accordingly, may extend consent to search said items. The Court has recognized a similar interest in a parent-child relationship and recognized the authority of a parent's consent. However, the Court has not recognized the reverse and has even negated the notion that children may grant law enforcement authorities legitimate access to their parent's belongings.

Although the Court has upheld third-party consent in these cases, the emerging landscape of interpersonal relationships and nontraditional cohabitation situations has clouded the issue significantly. In *United States v. Matlock*,[57] the Court reiterated earlier rulings that upheld the constitutional validity of "third-party consent" searches, ruling that:

> These cases at least make clear that when the prosecution seeks to justify a warrantless search by proof of voluntary consent, it is not limited to proof that consent was given by the defendant, but may show that permission to search was obtained from a third party who possessed common authority over or other sufficient relationship to the premises or effects sought to be inspected.

Thus, determination of the legitimacy of the authority of a third party hinges on an evaluation of "common authority" that the person possessed over a given property or area.

The issue of common authority is further complicated in unclear ownership of property cases. Although the Court has refused to acknowledge the authority of a landlord to grant consent over a property rented to another,[58] it has extended a limited authority to others, including roommates, former intimates, friends, and extended family members in specific cases. In most cases, such authority can be exercised only when (1) there exists "mutual use of the property by persons generally having joint access or control for most purposes"; and (2) the nonconsenting party is not present.[59]

As stated, officers are often confronted with situations in which it is unclear as to the extent of common authority exercised over a particular location. Thus, later cases have permitted the admissibility of evidence collected during a search of premises even when it was later demonstrated that the grantor did not enjoy the "common authority" originally required by *Matlock*. In applying various decisions unrelated to questions of "common authority," the Court concluded that:

> As with the many other factual determinations that must regularly be made by government agents in the Fourth Amendment context, the "reasonableness" of a police determination of consent to enter must be judged not by whether the police were correct in their assessment, but by the objective [497 U.S. 177, 178] standard of whether the facts available at the moment would warrant a person of reasonable caution in the belief that the consenting party had authority over the premises. If not, then warrantless entry without further inquiry is unlawful unless authority actually exists. But if so, the search is valid.[60]

Thus, third-party consent to search is limited to those areas for which a reasonable officer would conclude that such a party enjoyed common authority. Known as the "apparent authority" rule, this decision allows officers to search areas without ascertaining the property interest of the person issuing consent.

▶ Administrative Justifications and the Special Needs of Government

As with other aspects of the Fourth Amendment that have evolved since the document's inception, the Supreme Court has recognized the administrative justification exception to the probable cause and warrant requirements originally articulated therein, which have been alternatively called "special needs" or "regulatory" searches. Irrespective of verbiage, such situations allow authorities to conduct warrantless searches in various situations, including, but not limited to, inventory searches, inspections, checkpoints, school disciplinary searches, and government searches. (Although other administrative searches are permissible under the Court's interpretation of the Fourth Amendment, they are largely irrelevant to the laws of evidence and will not be discussed here.)

Inventory Searches

Inventory searches, as discussed, may be conducted on automobiles and individuals under arrest and are theoretically designed to protect the owner from loss or theft while the property is under the control of law enforcement authorities. In practice, however, these searches often are used to search for criminal evidence or contraband. Motivation notwithstanding, automobile inventories are only permissible when they: (1) follow a legal impoundment; (2) are of a routine nature, adhering to the standard operating procedures of the jurisdictional authority; and (3) do not intend to conceal an investigatory police motive outside the parameters of the inventory itself.[61] To wit,

> . . . the expectation of privacy in one's automobile is significantly less than that relating to one's home or office. . . . When vehicles are impounded, police routinely follow caretaking procedures by securing and inventorying the cars' contents. These procedures have been widely sustained as reasonable under the Fourth Amendment.[62]

Personal inventories—inventories of an individual's personal effects upon arrest—often are called **arrest inventories** and are conducted during routine booking procedures. Such searches are permissible to safeguard personal possessions but are also permissible because of the security and safety concerns associated with custodial arrests. For the most part, all items may be searched, including containers found within the possession of the arrestee. In its ruling, the Court pointed out that "the justification for such searches does not rest on probable cause, and hence the absence of a warrant is immaterial to the reasonableness of the search."[63]

Building, Home, and Business Inspections

Traditionally, health, wellness, and structural inspections of private residences were permitted because it was rationalized that such inspections were necessary for the betterment of the community. However, the Court in *Camara v. Municipal Court* explicitly prohibited them, ruling that "with certain carefully defined exceptions, an unconsented warrantless search of private property is 'unreasonable.'"[64] In making its determination, the Court recognized that whenever factors such as time, age, and condition of a building are such that inspection is necessitated, the issuance of a search warrant predicated on probable cause may be obtained. In addition, the Court articulated its expectation that such probable cause would be generalized (i.e., focusing on buildings and not individuals). However, the Court has recognized that a welfare inspection of a private residence is permissible under the Fourth Amendment because it serves:

> . . . the paramount needs of the dependent child; enables the State to determine that the intended objects of its assistance benefit from its aid and that state funds are being properly used; helps attain parallel federal relief objectives; stresses privacy by not unnecessarily intruding on the beneficiary's rights in her home; provides essential information not obtainable through secondary sources; is conducted, not by a law enforcement [400 U.S. 309, 310] officer, but by a caseworker; is not a criminal investigation; and (unlike the warrant procedure, which necessarily implies criminal conduct) comports with the objectives of welfare administration.[65]

In its ruling, the Court explicitly recognized that case or social workers did not fall under the law enforcement umbrella that governs application of the Fourth Amendment. As such, investigative searches may not be undertaken under the guise of welfare inspection.

As in other areas of criminal jurisprudence, the Court has differentiated inspections of private residences from business establishments. In fact, the Court has consistently upheld the right of sovereigns to implement and enforce regulatory legislation that includes provisions for warrantless searches. In *Colonnade Corp. v. United States*,[66] for example, the Court upheld the warrantless search of a liquor store. In its justification, the Court cited the long history of government regulation of the liquor industry and society's need for strict regulation of same. In a similar vein, the Court in *United States v. Biswell*[67] evaluated warrantless searches (i.e., inspections) of gun dealerships as provided for by statute. In reaching its conclusion, the Court weighed reasonable expectations of privacy and government interests, ruling that:

> It is also plain that inspections for compliance with the Gun Control Act pose only limited threats to the dealer's justifiable expectations of privacy. When a dealer chooses to engage in this pervasively regulated business and to accept a federal license, he does so with the knowledge that his business records, firearms, and ammunition will be subject to effective inspection. Each licensee is annually furnished with a revised compilation of ordinances that describe his obligations and define the inspector's authority . . . We

Although the Supreme Court has consistently recognized an automobile exception to the Warrant Requirement of the 4th Amendment, they have not extended that exception to the search of personal luggage within an automobile. Generally speaking, officers must have a warrant or the consent of the owner to conduct a roadside search of suitcases.

have little difficulty in concluding that where, as here, regulatory inspections further urgent federal interest, and the possibilities of abuse and the threat to privacy are not of impressive dimensions, the inspection may proceed without a warrant where specifically authorized by statute.[68]

Since *Biswell*, the Court has modified the "regulated business" exception. Indeed, the Court in *Donovan v. Dewey*,[69] explicitly rejected the notion that all closely regulated businesses are subject to imposition of warrantless inspections. Instead, the Court identified three mandatory criteria for such searches: (1) that the government has a substantial government interest in the questioned activity; (2) that warrantless searches are necessary for the effective enforcement of the law; and, most importantly, (3) that the inspection protocol must provide "a constitutionally adequate substitute for a warrant."

Checkpoints

Since the inception of the Fourth Amendment, the Court has evaluated the constitutionality of warrantless searches conducted at checkpoints. Such considerations have included border, drunk driving, and drug interdiction. One of the first cases to examine the notion of checkpoint searches was *United States v. Martinez-Fuerte*.[70] In *Martinez-Fuerte*, the Court considered whether the Immigration and Naturalization Service (INS) could constitutionally establish permanent checkpoints on major highways away from the Mexican border for brief questioning. In its ruling, the Court upheld such practices ruling that checkpoint searches did not have to be predicated on "any individualized suspicion that the particular vehicle contains illegal aliens." In its justification, the Court evaluated various issues and concluded that: (1) the intrusion occasioned by a brief investigative stop to ascertain residence could not be equated to the search of a private residence; (2) motorists could choose to avoid such checkpoints because of their permanency; (3) individualized suspicion was not possible because of the heavy traffic flow surrounding border areas; (4) officer discretion was not to be considered because supervisors controlled the location and administration of checkpoints; and (5) that a requirement of probable cause would largely eliminate any deterrent effect on smuggling operations.

In a similar ruling, the Court in *Michigan Department of State Police v. Sitz*[71] evaluated whether warrantless, suspicionless checkpoints designed to identify drunk drivers was consistent with the reasonableness requirement of the Fourth Amendment. In this case, the Court examined a practice of the state police in which all drivers were detained for approximately 25 seconds while officers looked for signs of intoxication. In those cases in which such evidence was apparent, drivers were tested for sobriety and subsequently were arrested or released upon conclusion of the evaluation period. In a ruling consistent with principles originally articulated in *Martinez-Fuerte*, the Court held that the practice was constitutional because: (1) government interest in eradicating the drunk-driving problem far outweighed the minor inconvenience of a brief investigative detention; (2) impartiality and equity were assured because locations were selected in strict compliance with departmental policy, and randomization of selection was negated by a questioning of all motorists; and consequently, (3) discretionary practices of individual officers were absent.

The Court has also upheld the practice of roadblocks to verify licensing and registration, recognizing that such a practice upholds a valid public safety interest.[72] However, it has failed to recognize those checkpoint programs whose primary purpose was the identification of ordinary criminal activity. For example, in *City of Indianapolis v. Edmond*,[73] the Court refused to uphold the constitutionality of narcotics checkpoints. In its justification, the Court ruled that:

> We have never approved a checkpoint program whose primary purpose was to detect evidence of ordinary criminal wrongdoing. Rather, our checkpoint cases have recognized only limited exceptions to the general rule that a seizure must be accompanied by some measure of individualized suspicion. We suggested in Prouse that we would not credit the "general interest in crime control" as justification for a regime of suspicionless stops. . . . Consistent with this suggestion, each of the checkpoint programs that we have approved was designed primarily to serve purposes closely related to the problems of policing the border or the necessity of ensuring roadway safety. Because the primary purpose of the Indianapolis narcotics checkpoint program is to uncover evidence of ordinary criminal wrongdoing, the program contravenes the Fourth Amendment.[74]

Thus, the Court is not prepared to recognize all types of warrantless checkpoints as developed under jurisdictional policy or legislation.

School and Workplace Searches

In terms of the parameters established by the Court in administrative or regulatory searches of private individuals, it is apparent that public school administrators and public employers may conduct searches for disciplinary purposes even when probable cause is lacking. In a very unique ruling, the Court in *New Jersey v. T.L.O.*[75]

Entrance into the United States requires questioning and inspection. Agents with the U.S. Customs and Border Protection of the Department for Homeland Security routinely search individuals and their belongings as they enter the country

recognized that said administrators were to be considered representatives of the state, indistinguishable from law enforcement officers, but permitted the warrant-less search of individual property for disciplinary purposes. In its rationale, the Court recognized that schoolchildren enjoyed legitimate expectations of privacy and the need to provide a safe, disciplined environment conducive to learning.

> But striking the balance between school children's legitimate expectations of privacy and the school's equally legitimate need to maintain an environment in which learning can take place requires some easing of the restrictions to which searches by public authorities are ordinarily subject. Thus, school officials need not obtain a warrant before searching a student who is under their authority. Moreover, school officials need not be held subject to the requirement that searches be based on probable cause to believe that the subject of the search has violated or is violating the law. Rather, the legality of a search of a student should depend simply on the reasonableness, under all the circum-stances, of the search. Determining the reasonableness of any search involves a determi-nation of whether the search was justified at its inception and whether, as conducted, it was reasonably related in scope to the circumstances that justified the interference in the first place. Under ordinary circumstances the search of a student by a school official will be justified at its inception where there are reasonable grounds for suspecting that the search will turn up evidence that the student has violated or is violating either the law or the rules of the school. And such a search will be permissible in its scope when the mea-sures adopted are reasonably related to the objectives of the search and not excessively intrusive in light of the student's age and sex and the nature of the infraction.[76]

In a case remarkably similar to *T.L.O.*, the Court evaluated whether searches of government workplaces by public employers were constitutional under the Fourth Amendment. In *O'Connor v. Ortega*,[77] the Court recognized a legitimate public inter-est in the search of public workplaces for work-related employee malfeasance. In justifying such warrantless searches, the Court ruled that any delay in correcting the employee misconduct caused by the delay in the development of probable cause to satisfy warrant requirements might result in "tangible and often irreparable" damage to the agency's work and to the public interest. As such, the Court upheld the right of public employers to search for evidence of such misconduct. However, the Court applied a strict scrutiny standard in which only those searches initiated for miscon-duct were covered. The Court specifically precluded any searches intended to inves-tigate criminal activity or other "nonwork-related statutory or regulatory standards."

► CONCLUSIONS

The Fourth Amendment protects citizens from unreasonable searches and seizures, and the exclusionary rule suppresses evidence that has been obtained in violation of constitutional rights afforded by the Fourth Amendment. However, the Supreme Court has continued to define areas where the exclusionary rule does not apply. Furthermore, not only has the Court outlined exceptions to the exclusionary rule, it has created generalized situations in which warrants are not necessary at all, including: border searches, consent searches, container searches, exigent circumstances, searches incident to a lawful, plain view, special needs, stop-and-frisks, and inventory searches.

The Court has consistently recognized that not everything carries the same expectation of privacy. For example, the Court does not recognize the same expectation of privacy for a vehicle as it does for a dwelling: if the driver or passenger of an automobile is arrested, the entire passenger compartment can be searched, but a warrant must be obtained to search a building or a dwelling unless consent is given. The Court basically has refused to suppress evidence whenever such suppression has no deterrent effect on future police misconduct. Another element of the Court's reasoning regarding situations in which warrants are not necessary is the safety of law enforcement personnel. In all of the circumstances outlined by the Court, the overreaching argument is that searches may occur when the benefit to society is greater than the invasiveness of the action. Summarily, the Court has demonstrated a tendency to permit evidence that is collected in the absence of a warrant whenever the actions of the police are reasonable in their inception and their execution. This includes actions that are necessary for either the safety of the officer and the public or the preservation of evidence. Also, the Court has consistently upheld the admissibility of evidence that is discovered inadvertently or within the boundaries of a consensual search.

Key Terms

Arrest inventories

Belton Rule

Consent searches

Immediate apparency

Inadvertent discovery

Inventory searches

"Plain feel" doctrine

"Plain view" doctrine

Probable cause requirement

Protective searches

Search incident to arrest

Stop-and-frisks

Terry stops

Third-party consent

Warrant Requirement

Warrantless searches

Discussion Questions

1. For what reasons may a warrantless search be conducted?
2. How does *Minnesota v. Dickerson* (1993) relate to the *Terry* doctrine?
3. According to the U.S. Supreme Court, how is compulsory self-identification not a violation of the Fourth and Fifth Amendments?
4. What are the parameters of a search incident to arrest?
5. How does the individual's right to privacy and the court's application of warrantless searches relate to stop and frisks? To personal luggage?
6. What factors may lessen the certainty of voluntariness?
7. In your opinion, should third-party consent be allowed in warrantless searches?

Recommended Resources

Videos

Insight Media. *Florida v. J.L.* This video investigates the Supreme Court ruling that an anonymous tip indicating that a person is carrying a gun is insufficient reason to justify a warrantless search. Available at: http://www.insight-media.com.

Insight Media. *Kyllo v. United States.* This video investigates the Supreme Court ruling that a thermal imaging device aimed at a private home from a public street constitutes a search and requires a warrant. Available at: http://www.insight-media.com.

Books and Journals

Bradley, Craig M. (2006). A sensible emergency doctrine: Probable cause and warrantless entry. *Trial, 42*(8).

Fisanick, Christian A. (2003). *Vehicle search law deskbook.* St. Paul, MN: Thomson/West Publishing.

Hendrie, Edward (2002). Inferring probable cause: Obtaining a search warrant for a suspect's home without direct information that evidence is inside. *FBI Law Enforcement Bulletin, 71*(2), 23–32.

Joseph, Paul R. (2002). *Warrantless search law deskbook.* St. Paul, MN: Thomson/West Publishing.

Lerner, Craig S. (2003). The reasonableness of probable cause. *Texas Law Review, 81*(4), 951–1029.

Tetu, Philip Raoul (1995). *Probable cause: Between the police officer and the magistrate.* Illinois: Charles C. Thomas.

Online Sources

http://www.findlaw.com—Search state and federal case law, statutes, codes, regulations, and federal and state constitutions.

http://law.onecle.com/—Free legal search engine for state and federal cases, codes, and regulations; provides enhanced searching features, including those for searching state criminal procedures.

http://www.washlaw.edu/—Free legal search engine that includes links to state and federal courts, decisions, statutes, and even international codes of law.

http://www.supremecourthistory.org/—This Web site lists relevant publications and provides for case searching and links to other relevant pages (maintained by The Supreme Court Historical Society).

http://www.ndaa.org/—Home page of the National District Attorney Association; includes links to research publications and topics such as criminal procedure.

Relevant Cases Cited

Adams v. Williams, 407 U.S. 143 (1972)

Arizona v. Gant, 556 U.S. 332 (2009)

Arizona v. Hicks, 480 U.S. 321 (1987)

Arkansas v. Sanders, 442 U.S. 753 (1979)

Ashcraft v. Tennessee, 322 U.S. 143 (1944)

Bumper v. North Carolina, 391 U.S. 543 (1968)

California v. Carney, 471 U.S. 386 (1985)

California v. Acevedo, 500 U.S. 565 (1991)

Camara v. Municipal Court, 387 U.S. 523 (1967)

Carroll v. United States, 267 U.S. 132 (1925)

Chambers v. Florida, 309 U.S. 227 (1940)

Chambers v. Maroney, 399 U.S. 42 (1970)

Chimel v. California, 395 U.S. 752 (1969)

City of Indianapolis v. Edmond, 531 U.S. 32 (2000)

Colonnade Corp. v. United States, 397 U.S. 72 (1970)

Colorado v. Bertine, 479 U.S. 367 (1987)

Coolidge v. New Hampshire, 403 U.S. 443 (1971)

Davis v. North Carolina, 384 U.S. 737 (1966)

Delaware v. Prouse, 440 U.S. 648 (1979)

Donovan v. Dewey, 452 U.S. 494 (1981)

Fikes v. Alabama, 352 U.S. 191 (1957)

Florida v. Jimeno, 500 U.S. 248 (1991)

Florida v. Royer, 460 U.S. 491 (1983)

Florida v. Wells, 495 U.S. 1 (1990)

Griffin v. Wisconsin, 483 U.S. 868 (1987)

Haley v. Ohio, 332 U.S. 596 (1948)

Hiibel v. Sixth Judicial District Court of Nevada, Humboldt County, 542 U.S. 177 (2004)

Horton v. California, 496 U.S. 128 (1990)

Illinois v. Caballes, 543 U.S. 405 (2005)

Illinois v. Lafayette, 462 U.S. 640 (1983)

Johnson v. United States, 333 U.S. 10 (1948)

Knowles v. Iowa, 525 U.S. 113 (1998)

Maryland v. Buie, 494 U.S. 325 (1990)

Michigan Department of State Police v. Sitz, 496 U.S. 444 (1990)

Michigan v. Long, 463 U.S. 1032 (1983)

Minnesota v. Dickerson, 508 U.S. 366 (1993)

National Treasury Employee's Union. v. Von Raab, 489 U.S. 656 (1990)

New Jersey v. T.L.O., 469 U.S. 325 (1985)

New York v. Belton, 453 U.S. 454 (1981)

O'Conner v. Ortega, 480 U.S. 709 (1987)

Ohio v. Robinette, 519 U.S. 33 (1996)

Ornelas v. United States, 517 U.S. 690 (1996)

Payne v. Arkansas, 356 U.S. 560 (1956)

Pennsylvania v. Labron, 518 U.S. 938 (1996)

Pennsylvania v. Mimms, 434 U.S. 106 (1977)

Reck v. Pate, 367 U.S. 433 (1961)

Schneckloth v. Bustamonte, 412 U.S. 218 (1973)

Sibron v. New York, 392 U.S. 40 (1968)

Skinner v. Railway Labor Executives Association, 109 S.Ct. 1384 (1990)

South Dakota v. Opperman, 428 U.S. 364 (1976)

State v. Washington, 396 N.W.2d 156 (1986)

Stoner v. California, 376 U.S. 483 (1964)

Terry v. Ohio, 392 U.S. 1 (1968)

Thornton v. United States, 124 S. Ct. 2127 (2004)

Torres v. Puerto Rico, 442 U.S. 465 (1979)

Trupiano v. United States, 334 U.S. 699 (1948)

Union Pacific Railroad Company v. Botsford, 141 U.S. 250 (1891)

United States v Chadwick, 433 U.S. 1 (1977)

United States v. Biswell, 406 U.S. 311 (1972)

United States v. Cortez, 449 U.S. 411 (1981)

United States v. Drayton et al., 536 U.S. 194 (2002)

United States v. Martinez-Fuerte, 428 U.S. 543 (1976)

United States v. Matlock, 415 U.S. 164 (1974)

United States v. Mendenhall, 446 U.S. 544 (1980)

United States v. Montoya de Hernandez, 473 U.S. 531 (1985)

United States v. Place, 462 U.S. 696 (1983)

United States v. Rabinowitz, 339 U.S. 56 (1950)

United States v. Robinson, 414 U.S. 218 (1973)

United States v. Ross, 456 U.S. 798 (1982)

United States v. Turner, 169 F.3d 84 (1st Cir. 1999)

United States v. Villamonte-Marques, 462 U.S. 579 (1983)

United States v. Williams, 822 F.2d 1174, 1184 (D.C. Cir. 1987)

Warden v. Hayden, 387 U.S. 294 (1967)

Whren v. United States, 517 U.S. 806 (1996)

Wyman v. James, 400 U.S. 309 (1971)

Notes

1. *United States v. Montoya de Hernandez*, 473 U.S. 531 (1985); *United States v. Villamonte-Marques*, 462 U.S. 579 (1983); *Torres v. Puerto Rico*, 442 U.S. 465 (1979)
2. *United States v. Matlock*, 415 U.S. 164 (1974); *Schneckloth v. Bustamonte*, 412 U.S. 218 (1973)
3. *California v. Acevedo*, 500 U.S. 565 (1991); *United States v. Ross*, 456 U.S. 798 (1982); *Arkansas v. Sanders*, 442 U.S. 753 (1979); *United States v. Chadwick*, 433 U.S. 1 (1977)
4. *Warden v. Hayden*, 387 U.S. 294 (1967)
5. *Maryland v. Buie*, 494 U.S. 325 (1990); *New York v. Belton*, 453 U.S. 454 (1981); *United States v. Robinson*, 414 U.S. 218 (1973); *Chimel v. California*, 395 U.S. 752 (1969)
6. *Horton v. California*, 496 U.S. 128 (1990); *Arizona v. Hicks*, 480 U.S. 321 (1987); *Coolidge v. New Hampshire*, 403 U.S. 443 (1971)
7. *Skinner v. Railway Labor Executives Association*, 109 S.Ct. 1384 (1990); *National Treasury Employee's Union. v. Von Raab*, 489 U.S. 656 (1990); *Griffin v. Wisconsin*, 483 U.S. 868 (1987); *O'Connor v. Ortega*, 480 U.S. 709 (1987); *New Jersey v. T.L.O.*, 469 U.S. 325 (1985)
8. *Michigan v. Long*, 463 U.S. 1032 (1983); *Terry v. Ohio*, 392 U.S. 1 (1968)
9. *Colorado v. Bertine*, 479 U.S. 367 (1987); *Illinois v. Lafayette*, 462 U.S. 640 (1983); *South Dakota v. Opperman*, 428 U.S. 364 (1976)
10. Rickles, 2005
11. *Florida v. Royer*, 460 U.S. 491 (1983)
12. 542 U.S. 177 (2004)
13. *United States v. Mendenhall*, 446 U.S. 544 (1980)
14. *United States v. Cortez*, 449 U.S. 411 (1981)
15. *Ornelas v. United States*, 517 U.S. 690 (1996)
16. *Union Pacific Railroad Company v. Botsford*, 141 U.S. 250 (1891)
17. *Terry v. Ohio*, 392 U.S. 1 (1968)
18. *Sibron v. New York*, 392 U.S. 40 (1968)
19. 508 U.S. 366 (1993)
20. *Michigan v. Long*, 463 U.S. 1032 (1983)
21. 395 U.S. 752 (1969)
22. Ibid.
23. *United States v. Robinson*, 414 U.S. 218 (1973)
24. *New York v. Belton*, 453 U.S. 454 (1981)
25. *Thornton v. United States*, 124 S. Ct. 2127 (2004)
26. *Knowles v. Iowa*, 525 U.S. 113 (1998)
27. *United States v. Rabinowitz*, 339 U.S. 56 (1950)
28. 403 U.S. 443 (1991)
29. *Coolidge v. New Hampshire*, 403 U.S. 443 (1971)
30. 480 U.S. 321 (1987)
31. Ibid.
32. 396 N.W.2d 156, 158 (Wis. 1986)
33. *United States v. Williams*, 822 F.2d 1174, 1184 (D.C. Cir. 1987)
34. 543 U.S. 405 (2005)
35. Ibid.
36. 267 U.S. 132 (1925)

37. Ibid.
38. (1970) 399 U.S. 42
39. Ibid.
40. 518 U.S. 938 (1996)
41. 471 U.S. 386 (1985)
42. 428 U.S. 364 (1976)
43. Ibid.
44. 433 U.S. 1 (1977)
45. 495 U.S. 1 (1990)
46. *United States v. Ross*, 456 U.S. 798 (1982); *California v. Acevedo*, 500 U.S. 565 (1991)
47. 495 U.S. 1 (1990)
48. Ibid.
49. 449 U.S. 411 (1981)
50. *Whren v. United States*, 517 U.S. 806 (1996)
51. *Ohio v. Robinette*, 519 U.S. 33 (1996)
52. *Bumper v. North Carolina*, 391 U.S. 543 (1968)
53. *Schneckloth v. Bustamonte*, 412 U.S. 218 (1973)
54. Ibid.
55. *United States v. Drayton*, 536 U.S. 194 (2002)
56. 500 U.S. 248 (1991)
57. 415 U.S. 164 (1974)
58. *Stoner v. California*, 376 U.S. 483 (1964)
59. *United States v. Matlock*, 415 U.S. 164 (1974)
60. *South Dakota v. Opperman*, 428 U.S. 364 (1976)
61. Ibid.
62. Ibid.
63. *Illinois v. Lafayette*, 462 U.S. 640 (1983)
64. 387 U.S. 523 (1967)
65. *Wyman v. James* (1971) 400 U.S. 309
66. 397 U.S. 72 (1970)
67. 406 U.S. 311 (1972)
68. Ibid.
69. 452 U.S. 494 (1981)
70. 428 U.S. 543 (1976)
71. 496 U.S. 444 (1990)
72. *Delaware v. Prouse*, 440 U.S. 648 (1979)
73. 531 U.S. 32 (2000)
74. Ibid.
75. 469 U.S. 325 (1985)
76. Ibid.
77. 480 U.S. 709 (1987)

THE DECLARATION OF INDEPENDENCE.

7 Confessions

LEARNING OBJECTIVES

The learner will:

1 *Examine the provisions of the Fifth Amendment*

2 *Discuss the protections and exceptions of the double jeopardy clause*

3 *Examine the case law regarding self-incrimination*

4 *Explain the protections provided by the* Miranda *warnings*

5 *Explore the parameters of* Miranda

6 *Examine the role of confessions by co-conspirators and
co-defendants in conjunction with the Sixth Amendment*

No person shall be held to answer for a capital, or otherwise infamous crime, unless on a presentment or indictment of a Grand Jury . . . nor shall any person be subject for the same offence to be twice put in jeopardy of life or limb; nor shall be compelled in any criminal case to be a witness against himself, nor be deprived of life, liberty, or property without due process of law; nor shall private property be taken for public use, without just compensation (Fifth Amendment, U.S. Constitution)

▶ The Fifth Amendment

The **Fifth Amendment** to the U.S. Constitution includes provisions and prohibitions regarding the grand jury system, double jeopardy, self-incrimination, due process, and impressment of private property. As discussed in Chapter 2, the **grand jury system** is one in which private citizens serve as criminal justice gatekeepers, advancing only those cases in which sufficient evidence is available. The **double jeopardy** provision contained therein, in the most basic sense, prohibits trying of an individual more than once for the same crime. Such prohibitions originally were made available under common law in the form of a **procedural defense**, such as *autrefois acquit* or *autrefois convict.*[1] Such defenses asserted that the defendant previously had been acquitted or convicted, respectively, and were incorporated into the Fifth Amendment as an attempt to limit prosecutorial abuse by the government through the use of repeat prosecutions designed primarily to harass or oppress individual citizens. In criminal jury trials, jeopardy attaches upon the impaneling and swearing in of the jury (and its alternates); in a nonjury trial, it is attached after the initial witness is called upon and sworn in. More specifically, the double jeopardy clause of the Fifth Amendment includes three essential protections for American citizens against: (1) a second prosecution for the same offense after acquittal; (2) a second prosecution for the same offense after conviction; and (3) multiple punishments for the same offense.[2] Thus, individuals may not be tried again for the same crime even in cases in which new evidence conclusively proves their guilt.[3]

Several exceptions to the double jeopardy clause, however, do exist. Double jeopardy does not attach in cases that do not achieve legal finality or conclusion. Thus, cases in which a trial is cancelled prior to the return of a verdict (i.e., **mistrial**) may face further adjudication or arbitration by the court. In most cases involving a mistrial, the court will hold a retrial of the same. According to the Fifth Amendment prohibition against double jeopardy, however, mistrials may not result in future criminal proceedings of the same case if: (1) the court's declaration was erroneous; or, (2) the defendant's motion for mistrial was a result of prosecutorial misconduct. Mistrials are most often granted in cases in which: (1) judicial processes were deficient or were violated; (2) evidence was improperly admitted; (3) unfair influence over decision-making might result because of factors external to the courtroom; (4) the court determines that it lacks jurisdiction over a particular case; and (5) jury attrition (whether through illness or death or juror misconduct) occurs. In a similar vein, a **hung jury** is a jury that becomes unable to reach a verdict with the requisite degree of unanimity, the result of which may be the declaration of a mistrial—and a new trial may be ordered. (As a general rule, cases dismissed by a judge because of insufficient evidence are not retried, although some state and federal laws allow for limited pursuit.) Interestingly,

fifth amendment no person shall be held to answer for a capital, or otherwise infamous crime, unless on a presentment or indictment of a Grand Jury, except in cases arising in the land or naval forces, or in the Militia, when in actual service in time of War or public danger; nor shall any person be subject for the same offence to be twice put in jeopardy of life or limb; nor shall be compelled in any criminal case to be a witness against himself, nor be deprived of life, liberty, or property, without due process of law; nor shall private property be taken for public use, without just compensation.

grand jury system an alternative to the preliminary hearing system. The system is characterized as a panel of citizens selected to hear evidence of criminal allegations presented by the state to determine whether sufficient probable cause exists to return a true bill (i.e., finding of truth in the allegations).

double jeopardy fifth amendment protection against an individual being tried for a criminal offense more than once in the same jurisdiction. Double jeopardy protection does not preclude prosecution of individuals for the same set of circumstances in different jurisdictions, which explains why some individuals have been acquitted in a federal court but found at fault in a state court.

UNFORESEEN DEVELOPMENTS AND MISTRIALS

Mistrials may be declared for a variety of reasons. Deadlocked (i.e., hung) juries, prosecutorial misconduct, and procedural violations are but a few examples. Some non-case-specific situations can result in the declaration of a mistrial as well.

In late 2005, Pamela Vitale—the wife of prominent defense attorney Daniel Horowitz—was found at their home bludgeoned to death. The case generated national attention, in part because of the gruesome details of the crime, including satanic and Goth symbolism carved into

the body. Another major factor was the notoriety associated with Horowitz and his high-profile clients. In a separate murder trial, a California judge declared a mistrial citing as a direct reason the excessive media attention of Vitale's murder. The mistrial occurred in the highly publicized trial of Susan Polk, a California woman charged with stabbing to death her millionaire husband, Frank "Felix" Polk, a therapist 23 years her senior whom she had met as a 16-year-old patient. Daniel Horowitz was defending Mrs. Polk at the time of his wife's murder.

---

procedural defense an argument that seeks to negate the criminal charges through the assertion that the criminal justice process in the specific case was violated.

mistrial a trial that ends without a final disposition of guilt being established.

hung jury a jury that is unable to reach a verdict with the requisite degree of unanimity, the result of which may be the declaration of a mistrial.

separate sovereigns or dual sovereignty exception an exception to the double jeopardy clause of the Fifth Amendment that protects the interests of both state and federal authorities in which a single act violates the laws of both sovereigns.

cases in which a mistrial was erroneously declared by the court or when prosecutorial misconduct resulted in a defense request for a mistrial may not be retried, because the Supreme Court has ruled that such situations are protected under the double jeopardy clause.

In yet another exception, retrials resulting from successful postconviction appeals are also permissible, because the original judgment is invalidated upon reversal. (Ironically, the previous trial is not completely erased, and testimony recorded may be introduced at subsequent proceedings. See Chapter 10.) In an important distinction, the double jeopardy clause does not apply to separate offenses or in separate jurisdictions involving the same set of circumstances. For example, individuals may be charged with the offense itself and the conspiracy to commit such offense at the same time.[4]

> A substantive crime and a conspiracy to commit that crime are not the "same offense" for double jeopardy purposes . . . even if they are based on the same underlying incidents, because the "essence" of a conspiracy offense "is in the agreement or confederation to commit a crime.[5]

Also, the Supreme Court repeatedly has upheld a **separate sovereigns exception** to the double jeopardy clause, recognizing the duality of interests of federal and state governments. Thusly, the Court upheld prosecutions in which individuals were tried in both systems for the same set of circumstances, reiterating that the protections of the double jeopardy clause only attach to prosecutions for the same criminal act in the same jurisdiction and do not negate the right of prosecution by separate sovereigns. In the case of Timothy McVeigh, for example, state and federal officials could have filed charges against him for the bombing of the Alfred P. Murrah federal building in Oklahoma City that killed 167 people, including 19 children. McVeigh, executed by the federal government in 2001, was convicted of the bombing in federal court but could have faced multiple charges stemming from the same incident had the state of Oklahoma chosen to pursue charges.

Finally, the double jeopardy clause of the Fifth Amendment does not attach in cases in which different standards of proof apply. Thus, it does not attach in civil cases irrespective of adjudication in criminal courts. Because the standard of proof in civil cases is much less than the traditional criminal standard, it is entirely possible that an individual acquitted in a criminal court may be found liable in a civil one. Such was the case of O. J. Simpson, who was acquitted of the savage slayings of his wife, Nicole Brown Simpson, and her friend, Ron Goldman. In that case, the estates of the slain couple successfully filed a wrongful death suit in which they were

Timothy McVeigh was executed by the federal government in 2001 following a sentence of death for the murders of 167 people in the bombing of the Alfred P. Murrah federal building in Oklahoma City. Although entitled to try McVeigh in state court for the same murders, the state of Oklahoma was satisfied with the federal prosecution and sentencing. The Separate Sovereigns exception to the 5th Amendment allows both state and federal authorities to pursue prosecution in crimes which violate both state and federal law.

awarded more than 33 million dollars. In addition, double jeopardy does not apply in parole violation hearings in which criminal acts by an individual may be part and parcel of such proceedings, even in those acts for which he or she has been acquitted.

Other protections afforded to American citizens under the Fifth Amendment include the right to due process, the freedom from impressment of private property, and the prohibition against self-incrimination. The right to **due process,** as guaranteed by the Fifth Amendment, generally protects citizens from the possibility of an oppressive federal government and secures the right to procedural certainty. Traditionally, such protections granted individuals the assurance that safeguards, as provided in the remaining amendments of the Bill of Rights, would be adhered to in federal courts. Currently, the right to due process is guaranteed to all citizens in all courts through the incorporation of the Fourteenth Amendment. Thus, all citizens enjoy the certainty of procedural adherence to state and federal laws. This includes the totality of the Bill of Rights, including the protection from **impressment of private property**.

The right to freedom from arbitrary seizures of personal property stems from practices in England in which supplies, equipment, and land routinely were taken from citizens for governmental use. Such capricious heavy-handedness was recognized by the framers and incorporated into the Fourth and Fifth Amendments. Although the Fourth Amendment protected citizens from general rummaging and looting, the Fifth safeguarded the property of individuals from governmental abuse. And, although these protections are important to the daily lives of Americans, they are not often cited in criminal court. The prohibition against self-incrimination, on the other hand, is one of the cornerstones of criminal jurisprudence.

due process a highly valued guarantee of the Fifth Amendment that protects citizens from the potential of an oppressive government and grants them equal protection and judicial fairness under the law (and explicitly prohibits deprivation of life, liberty, property, and other rights granted by statute).

impressment of private property the confiscation and utilization of privately owned property for state use.

THE CONFRONTATION CLAUSE

Although the Fifth Amendment to the U.S. Constitution protects defendants from compulsory testimony in a criminal proceeding, the Sixth Amendment's Confrontation Clause allows courts to compel individuals to testify when they are not a party to the current proceeding with assurances that such statements may not be used against them in a subsequent criminal case. More importantly, the Confrontation Clause prohibits the introduction of testimony not subjected to cross-examination by the defense. (As with most areas of criminal law, the Court has recognized limited exceptions. These hearsay exceptions are discussed in Chapter 10.) Such requirements have been formalized and reiterated in a number of Supreme Court decisions.

- *Alford v. United States*, 282 U.S. 687 (1931)—the Court held that it is not within a trial court's purview to stop cross-examination of a state witness simply to protect him/her from being discredited.

  . . . the extent of cross-examination with respect to an appropriate subject of inquiry is within the sound discretion of the trial court. It may exercise a reasonable judgment in determining when the subject is exhausted . . . but no obligation is imposed on the court . . . to protect a witness from being discredited on cross-examination, short of an attempted invasion of his constitutional protection from self-incrimination, properly invoked. There is a duty to protect him from questions which go beyond the bonds of proper cross-examination merely to harass, annoy, or humiliate him . . . but no such case is presented here. The trial court cut off *in limine* all inquiry on a subject with respect to which the defense was entitled to a reasonable cross-examination. This was an abuse of discretion and prejudicial error.

- *Pointer v. Texas*, 380 U.S. 400 (1965)—the Court held that a transcript of witness testimony recorded in an earlier proceeding is inadmissible at trial if that witness is not available for cross-examination at trial. More importantly, the Court recognized the Sixth Amendment's Confrontation Clause was a fundamental constitutional right and was applicable to the states via the Fourteenth Amendment.

  . . . the introduction of the transcript in a federal criminal case would have been a clear denial of the right of confrontation, since the statement was made without an adequate opportunity for cross-examination, and the right must be determined by the same standards in a state proceeding.

- *Smith v. Illinois*, 390 U.S. 129 (1968)—the Court held that the failure to disclose a police informant's true identity violated the Confrontation Clause. Reiterating their earlier decision in *Alford*, the Court noted:

  . . . in Alford . . . this Court unanimously reversed a federal conviction because the trial judge had sustained objections to questions by the defense seeking to elicit the "place of residence" of a prosecution witness over the insistence of defense counsel that "the jury was entitled to know who the witness is, where he lives and what his business is" . . . what the Court said in reversing that conviction is fully applicable here.

- *Bruton v. United States*, 391 US 123 (1968)—a pivotal case in delineation of the protections of the Confrontation Clause, *Bruton* held that the statements of one co-conspirator may not be introduced against another co-conspirator unless the declarant took the stand and was subject to cross-examination. They held:

  . . . the introduction of Evans' confession posed a substantial threat to petitioner's right to confront the witnesses against him, and this is a hazard we cannot ignore. Despite the concededly clear instructions to the jury to disregard Evans' inadmissible hearsay evidence inculpating petitioner, in the context of a joint trial we cannot accept limiting instructions as an adequate substitute for petitioner's constitutional right of cross-examination. The effect is the same as if there had been no instruction at all.

▶ Self-Incrimination

Acts or declarations either as testimony at trial or prior to trial by which one implicates himself in a crime. The Fifth Amendment, the United States Constitution, as well as provisions in many state constitutions and laws, prohibit the government from requiring a person to be a witness against himself involuntarily or to furnish evidence against himself. (*Black's Law Dictionary*, 2004)

Of the many protections extended under the Fifth Amendment, perhaps the most commonly known is the prohibition against compulsory testimony. Generally speaking, the freedom from **self-incrimination** protects defendants from compulsory testimony. As such, individuals may **"take the Fifth"** and refuse to answer questions or to issue statements with the assurance that such refusal may not be introduced in court.[6] The Court has evaluated the parameters of this privilege in several different cases and has found that such protection:

> . . . not only protects the individual against being involuntarily called as a witness against himself in a criminal prosecution but also privileges him not to answer official questions put to him in any other proceeding, civil or criminal, formal or informal, where the answers might incriminate him in future criminal proceedings.[7]

In addition to the protection against self-incrimination specifically articulated in the Fifth Amendment, Federal Rules of Evidence (FRE) 104 and 410 prohibit the

self-incrimination statements or communications that may expose the declarant to criminal prosecution.

"take the fifth" an invocation of the Fifth Amendment protection against compulsory testimony against oneself in which a defendant may refuse to testify against his or her interests on the grounds that the information may be incriminating.

FEDERAL RULES OF EVIDENCE

Rule 104. Preliminary Questions

(a) **In General**. The court must decide any preliminary question about whether a witness is qualified, a privilege exists, or evidence is admissible. In so deciding, the court is not bound by evidence rules, except those on privilege.

(b) **Relevance That Depends on a Fact**. When the relevance of evidence depends on whether a fact exists, proof must be introduced sufficient to support a finding that the fact does exist. The court may admit the proposed evidence on the condition that the proof be introduced later.

(c) **Conducting a Hearing So That the Jury Cannot Hear It**. The court must conduct any hearing on a preliminary question so that the jury cannot hear it if

  (1) the hearing involves the admissibility of a confession;

  (2) a defendant in a criminal case is a witness and so requests; or

  (3) justice so requires.

(d) **Cross-Examining a Defendant in a Criminal Case**. By testifying on a preliminary question, a defendant in a criminal case does not become subject to cross-examination on other issues in the case.

(e) **Evidence Relevant to Weight and Credibility**. This rule does not limit a party's right to introduce before the jury evidence that is relevant to the weight or credibility of other evidence.

Rule 410. Pleas, Plea Discussions, and Related Statements

(a) **Prohibited Uses.** In a civil or criminal case, evidence of the following is not admissible against the defendant who made the plea or participated in the plea discussions:

  (1) a guilty plea that was later withdrawn;

  (2) a nolo contendere plea;

  (3) a statement made during a proceeding on either of those pleas under Federal Rule of Criminal Procedure 11 or a comparable state procedure; or

  (4) a statement made during plea discussions with an attorney for the prosecuting authority if the discussions did not result in a guilty plea or they resulted in a later-withdrawn guilty plea.

(b) **Exceptions.** The court may admit a statement described in Rule 410(a)(3) or (4):

  (1) in any proceeding in which another statement made during the same plea or plea discussions has been introduced, if in fairness the statements ought to be considered together; or

  (2) in a criminal proceeding for perjury or false statement, if the defendant made the statement under oath, on the record, and with counsel present.

introduction of statements made during plea bargaining and require *in camera* hearings prior to the introduction of a confession, respectively.

Historical Case Law Developments

The prohibition against self-incrimination was articulated as early as 1897, when the Supreme Court heard the case of *Bram v. United States*[8] and ruled that an involuntary statement made by a defendant in custody is entirely inadmissible. Taking great care to trace the history and rationale of the prohibition, the Court reasoned that:

> While the admissions or confessions of the prisoner, when voluntarily and freely made, have always ranked high in the scale of incriminating evidence, if an accused person be asked to explain his apparent connection with a crime under investigation, the ease with which the questions put to him may assume an inquisitorial character, the temptation to press the witness unduly, to browbeat him if he be timid or reluctant, to push him into a corner, and to entrap him into fatal contradictions, which is so painfully evident in many of the earlier state trials, notably in those of Sir Nicholas Throckmorton and Udal, the Puritan minister, made the system so odious as to give rise to a demand for its total abolition. The change in the English criminal procedure in that particular seems to be founded upon no statute and no judicial opinion, but upon a general and silent acquiescence of the courts in a popular demand. But, however adopted, it has become firmly imbedded in English as well as in American jurisprudence. So deeply did the iniquities of the ancient system impress themselves upon the minds of the American colonists that the states, with one accord, made a denial of the right to question an accused person a part of their fundamental law; so that [168 U.S. 532, 545] a maxim, which in England was a mere rule of evidence, became clothed in this country with the impregnability of a constitutional enactment.[9]

Traditionally, this ruling was only binding on the actions of federal authorities in federal courtrooms. However, the Fifth Amendment and all of the provisions contained therein were applied in 1964 to state courts through the Fourteenth Amendment.[10] This included the extension of the self-incrimination protection to statutory inquiries as well as trials. This decision overturned original rulings by the Court, including those that were originally articulated in *Adamson v. California*,[11] in which the Court ruled that prosecutors were permitted to comment on a defendant's silence. In *Adamson*, the Court recognized the untenable situation of the accused that might result *and* the state's right to use the defendant's failure to speak against him or her. To wit,

> . . . this forces an accused who is a repeated offender to choose between the risk of having his prior offenses disclosed to the jury or of having it draw harmful inferences from uncontradicted evidence that can only be denied or explained by the defendant.[12]

At the same time, the Court refused to extend the protections of the Fifth Amendment to state courts, ruling that:

> . . . the due process clause does not protect, by virtue of its mere existence, the accused's freedom from giving testimony by compulsion in state trials that is secured to him against federal interference by the Fifth Amendment.[13]

However, the Court reversed *Adamson* in 1964 and made the protections in the Fifth Amendment applicable in state courts.[14]

Just two years later, the Court heard the seminal case of *Miranda v. Arizona*,[15] which created a comprehensive framework for custodial interrogations and introduced perhaps the most repeated phrase in the popular media. (Indeed, *Miranda*'s

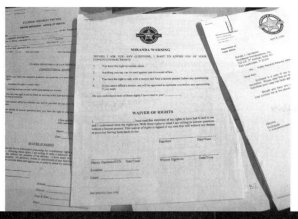

Beginning in 1966, law enforcement officers have been required to inform suspects in custody of their right to remain silent and their right to an attorney. The above photo depicts a standard *Miranda* form which documents that the suspect has been notified of their rights as evidenced by the signature of the issuing officer, the criminal suspect, and a witness.

admonition of the right to remain silent has become so commonplace that it has been argued that such recitation is no longer necessary in that every American citizen fundamentally understands his or her rights.) In *Miranda*, the Court evaluated four separate cases in which verbal and written **confessions**—voluntary, self-incriminating statements of events made to the police by an individual who admits agency or participation in a criminal offense—were obtained through methods of interrogations that were characterized by isolation and coercion. The Court demonstrably abhorred and condemned traditional "incommunicado" interrogations and ruled that no statement, whether exculpatory or inculpatory, stemming from the custodial questioning of a suspect by law enforcement officials could be introduced *unless* the state demonstrated that it had taken procedural safeguards to secure the rights guaranteed by the Fifth and Sixth Amendments.

> . . . the atmosphere and environment of incommunicado interrogation as it exists today is inherently intimidating and works to undermine the privilege against self-incrimination. Unless adequate preventive measures are taken to dispel the compulsion inherent in custodial surroundings, no statement obtained from the defendant can truly be the product of his free choice.[16]

In a deviation from traditional rulings, the Court also clearly identified mandatory measures to be employed by police personnel to secure such rights. These requirements have subsequently been encapsulated into what are now known as *Miranda* **warnings** and are limited to informing accused persons that:

1. they have the right to remain silent;
2. anything they say may be used against them;
3. they have the right to an attorney during the interrogation process; and
4. an attorney will be appointed to them if they cannot afford to hire one.

In addition, the Court clearly indicated that all interrogation must cease once a defendant expresses his or her desire to remain silent, and, if a request for an attorney is made, then the interrogation may not continue until such time that an attorney is present. The Court also reiterated that the invocation of the privilege may occur at any time and is not negated if an accused who has previously volunteered information expresses a desire to quit the communication. The Court has expanded this provision since their original decision in *Miranda*.

confessions a voluntary, self-incriminating statement of events made to the police by an individual who admits agency or participation in a criminal offense.

miranda **warnings** legally required warnings issued by law enforcement officials to individuals taken into custody. Warnings involve notification that (1) they have the right to remain silent, (2) that anything they say may be used against them, (3) they have the right to an attorney during the interrogation process, and (4) that an attorney will be appointed if they cannot afford to hire one.

Frank Costello was the first of many mobsters to invoke his Fifth Amendment rights when forced to testify. Since the Kefauver hearings, the list of mobsters taking the Fifth includes most current and past crime bosses.

interrogation as interpreted by the Court, the term for purposes of *Miranda* refers not only to express questioning by the police, but also to any words or actions on the part of the police which are likely to elicit an incriminating response.

bright-line rule a rule established by the Court in *Edwards v. Arizona* which states that individuals invoking their rights may not be subjected to further interrogation in the absence of counsel unless the suspect initiates the dialogue with the authorities.

At the present time, individuals invoking their rights may not be subjected to further **interrogation** until counsel is provided ". . . unless the suspect himself initiates the dialogue with the authorities."[17] This "**bright-line rule**" established in *Edwards v. Arizona* specifically forbade future questioning so that the authorities were not able to "wear down the accused and persuade him to incriminate himself notwithstanding his earlier request for counsel's assistance."[18] In an attempt to clarify the parameters of "interrogation" and determine the attachment of *Miranda*, especially in cases in which invocation of rights has occurred, the Court has ruled that:

> We conclude that the Miranda safeguards come into play whenever a person in custody is subjected to either express . . . questioning or its functional equivalent. That is to say, the term "interrogation" under Miranda refers not only to express questioning, but also to any words or actions on the part of the police (other than those normally attendant to arrest and custody) that the police should know are reasonably likely to elicit an incriminating response from the suspect. The latter portion of this definition focuses primarily upon the perceptions of the suspect, rather than the intent of the police. This focus reflects the fact that the Miranda safeguards were designed to vest a suspect in custody with an added measure of protection against coercive police practices, without regard to objective proof of the underlying intent of the police. A practice that the police should know is reasonably likely to evoke an incriminating response from a suspect thus amounts to interrogation. But, since the police surely cannot be held accountable for the unforeseeable results of their words or actions, the definition of interrogation can extend only to words or actions on the part of police officers that they should have known were reasonably likely to elicit an incriminating response.[19]

Thus, the Court has recognized limited situations in which an accused's postinvocation statements are admissible. Such cases are to be evaluated on a case-by-case basis, and no blanket rule exists. At the same time, the Court expressly excluded voluntary statements as a group from those that are protected under the Fifth Amendment, stating that " . . . there is no requirement that police stop a person who enters a police station and states that he wishes to confess to a crime, or a person who calls the police to offer a confession or any other statement he desires to make. Volunteered statements of any kind are not barred by the Fifth Amendment."[20] In more recent cases, the Court repeatedly has upheld the original ruling issued in *Miranda*.

In a departure from other rulings that differentiated the handling of mentally incompetent defendants, the Court has not extended any additional *Miranda* protections for those individuals lacking the mental acumen to knowingly waive same.

> Coercive police activity is a necessary predicate to finding that a confession is not "voluntary" within the meaning of the Due Process Clause. . . . While a defendant's mental condition may be a "significant" factor in the [479 U.S. 157, 158] "voluntariness" calculus, this does not justify a conclusion that his mental condition, by itself and apart from its relation to official coercion, should ever dispose of the inquiry into constitutional "voluntariness."[21]

Thus, the Court reiterated that the singular, original purpose of *Miranda* was to prevent coercive statements and to eliminate confessions obtained through torture. This was not the only case in that the protections originally enunciated in *Miranda* faced erosion. In fact, other situations have emerged that are more obvious in their implications.

Parameters of *Miranda*

As expansive as the *Miranda* ruling was, it did not attach to all investigations or interrogations by law enforcement authorities. In fact, *Miranda* was limited to those situations in which an individual was in custody and being interrogated about specific criminal conduct. Thus, *Miranda* warnings were not considered necessary in noncustodial interrogations or prior to interrogations of the defendant in custody. In defining custodial interrogation, the Court ruled that ". . . we mean questioning initiated by law enforcement officers after a person has been taken into custody or otherwise deprived of his freedom of action in a significant way."[22] Subsequent definitions have further clarified the term, relying upon the "reasonable man" standard as found in other areas of criminal jurisprudence.[23] Summarily, prosecutors seeking to introduce **incriminating statements**— statements made by a person in police custody that do not necessarily acknowledge guilt but tend to implicate the accused—must demonstrate that such statements were voluntarily given after said suspect was informed of his or her rights, that the rights were understood, and that the accused voluntarily waived these rights.

incriminating statements statements made by a person in police custody that do not necessarily acknowledge guilt but tend to implicate the accused.

 CLARIFICATION OF CONCEPTS

DIFFERENTIATING CONFESSIONS AND INCRIMINATING STATEMENTS

- Confessions acknowledge guilt and include information regarding each essential element of the criminal offense. Confessions are considered direct evidence. For example, John D. is arrested by the police on sexual assault charges following an attack on his neighbor. During questioning, John D. tells them that he had entered her apartment through an unlocked basement window at approximately 12:30. He reports that he tied her to a chair and penetrated her vaginally, and then took a shower before leaving the premises through the front door. He states that she deserved it as she would tease him by lying out topless.

- Incriminating statements do not necessarily acknowledge guilt, but they tend to implicate the defendant's culpability in one or more areas. Unlike confessions, incriminating statements are considered circumstantial evidence. For example, when questioned by police about his involvement in the Martha Moxley murder, Michael Skakel told police that he had been with her shortly before she was murdered. When the police asked him if his DNA would be present near the scene, Skakel again denied his involvement in her murder but admitted that he had fondled himself in a tree outside her window late that night.

SITUATIONS IN WHICH *MIRANDA* DOES NOT ATTACH

- Routine traffic stops (*Berkemer v. McCarty*, 468 U.S. 442)

- *Terry* stops or brief investigative detentions [*Terry v. Ohio*, 392 U.S. 1 (1968)]

- Voluntary statements made by suspect [*Miranda v. Arizona*, 384 U.S. 436 (1966)]

- Noncustodial situations [*Miranda v. Arizona*, 384 U.S. 436 (1966)]

- Routine booking questions [*Pennsylvania v. Muniz*, 496 U.S. 582 (1990)]

- Questioning by non-law-enforcement personnel

- Information gathered by undercover operatives [*Hoffa v. United States*, 385 U.S. 293 (1966)]

The importance of *Miranda* cannot be overstated, but it does not attach in all situations. In fact, it only applies to cases in which custodial interrogations of criminal activity occur. Consequently, it does not apply to the actions of private citizens, including store clerks and private security officers. It does not apply to routine booking questions, such as age, height, weight, and the like.[24] It also does not apply to investigative detentions based on reasonable suspicion (i.e., *Terry* stops). The Court has made a distinction between nonthreatening (or noninvasive) questioning and that which occurs during custodial questioning. Such justification was explained best by the Court in reference to traffic stops:

> . . . Two features of an ordinary traffic stop mitigate the danger that a person questioned will be induced "to speak where he would not otherwise do so freely". . . . First, detention of a motorist pursuant to a traffic stop is presumptively temporary and brief . . . questioning incident to an ordinary traffic stop is quite different from stationhouse interrogation, which frequently is prolonged, and in which the detainee often is aware that questioning will continue until he provides his interrogators the answers they seek. . . . Second, circumstances associated with the typical traffic stop are not such that the motorist feels completely at the mercy of the police . . . the typical traffic stop is public, at least to some degree. Passersby[sic], on foot or in other cars, witness the interaction of officer and motorist. This exposure to public view both reduces the ability of an unscrupulous policeman to use illegitimate means to elicit self-incriminating statements and diminishes the motorist's fear that, if he does not cooperate, he will be subjected to abuse. The fact that the detained motorist typically is confronted by only one or at most two policemen further mutes his sense of vulnerability. In short, the atmosphere surrounding an ordinary traffic stop is substantially less "police dominated."[25]

Miranda warnings are also not required in general *on-the-scene* questioning in fact-finding inquiries regarding specific crimes; nor are they required in the general questioning of residents because cooperating in police investigations or operations is an act of responsible citizenship. Although it is possible that such questioning inadvertently might include the questioning of the actual perpetrator, *Miranda* only attaches in cases in which a suspect is in custody and being interrogated. In addition, *Miranda* warnings are not necessary in investigative detentions based on reasonable suspicion. In the case of automobile stops in search of evidence concerning illegal immigration, the Court has ruled that:

> . . . when an officer's observations lead him reasonably to suspect that a particular vehicle may contain aliens who are illegally in the country, he may stop the car briefly and investigate the circumstances that provoke suspicion. As in Terry, the stop and inquiry must be "reasonably related in scope to the justification for their initiation.[26]

EXTENDING SELF-INCRIMINATION PROTECTIONS TO THE WORKPLACE

The Court has recognized a variety of situations outside an actual criminal proceeding in which the Constitution protects individuals from self-incrimination. Interestingly, many have to do with professional situations and focus on the fear or threat of loss of employment. Specifically, the Court recognized the rights of attorneys [*Spevack v. Klein*, 385 U.S. 511 (1967)], school teachers [*Slochower v. Board of Higher Education of New York City*, 350 U.S. 551 (1956)], and police officers. The Court's justification was articulated best in *Garrity v. New Jersey*, 385 U.S. 493 (1967) when it considered whether statements compelled through the threat by police officers of termination of employment during a state investigation into officer misconduct were admissible in court. It ruled that:

. . . the option to lose their means of livelihood or to pay the penalty of self-incrimination is the antithesis of free choice to speak out or to remain silent. That practice, like interrogation practices we reviewed in Miranda . . . is "likely to exert such pressure upon an individual as to disable him from making a free and rational choice." We think the statements were infected by the coercion inherent in this scheme of questioning and cannot be sustained as voluntary under our prior decisions . . . we conclude that policemen, like teachers and lawyers, are not relegated to a watered-down version of constitutional rights. . . . We now hold the protection of the individual under the Fourteenth Amendment against coerced statements prohibits use in subsequent criminal proceedings of statements obtained under threat of removal from office, and that it extends to all whether they are policemen or other members of our body politic.

For the most part then, *Miranda* warnings are mandatory in those custodial situations in which interrogation is initiated. However, the Court has recognized some exceptions.

Public Safety Exception and the Rescue Doctrine

Generally speaking, *Miranda* warnings are necessary at some point in most criminal cases. The Court has long cautioned against involuntary statements obtained through coercion and has traditionally prohibited the use of non-Mirandized statements. At the same time, the Court has recognized certain limited situations in which such statements may be admissible. One such situation, known as the **public safety exception**, was first articulated in the 1984 case of *New York v. Quarles*[27] in which a young woman approached police and informed them that she had been sexually assaulted at gunpoint. Locating the suspect in the local grocery store, the officers asked the individual the location of his weapon and he identified the area of the store where he had discarded it. During investigation, the police located the weapons. The Court ruled that the officers' actions did not violate the Fifth Amendment because "an answer was needed to insure [sic] that future danger to the public did not result from the concealment of the gun in a public area."[28] In clarifying its opinion, the Court indicated that:

> The doctrinal underpinnings of *Miranda* do not require that it be applied in all its rigor to a situation in which police officers ask questions reasonably prompted by a concern for the public safety. In this case, so long as the gun was concealed somewhere in the supermarket, it posed more than one danger to the public safety: an accomplice might make use of it, or a customer or employee might later come upon it.[29]

Similar justifications have been found in state courts, when the government has argued that the non-Mirandized questioning of a suspect in cases in which the potentiality of victim rescue is present. In *People v. Riddle*, the California court

public safety exception one of several exceptions to the Exclusionary Rule that provides for the admission of illegally collected evidence if the items were collected in a situation where the interests of community safety outweighed the interests of personal liberty.

THE RIGHT TO COUNSEL

The right to counsel is an essential foundation of due process guaranteed to Americans via the Sixth and Fourteenth Amendments. However, it was not always available to all criminal defendants in the United States. In fact, these rights were not guaranteed to any criminal defendant in state courts until 1932 when it was extended to include defendants in capital cases; nor were they guaranteed to juveniles until 1967. At the current time, the right to counsel is afforded to all criminal defendants facing incarceration. This includes the right to counsel in parole hearings [*Morissey v. Brewer*, 408 U.S. 471 (1972)] and probation revocation hearings [*Gagnon v. Scarpelli*, 411 U.S. 778, (1973)].

- *Powell v. Alabama*, 287 U.S. 45 (1932)—one of the seminal cases securing the right to assistance of counsel rights guaranteed by the Sixth Amendment, *Powell* held that a defendant in a capital case was entitled to counsel whether retained or appointed. However, the Court failed to extend this right to non-capital cases.

  . . . whether this would be so in other criminal prosecutions, or under other circumstances, we need not determine. All that is necessary now to decide, as we do decide, is that in a capital case, where the defendant is unable to employ counsel, and is incapable adequately of making his own defense because of ignorance, feeble-mindedness, illiteracy, or the like, it is the duty of the curt, whether requested or not, to assign counsel for him as a necessary requisite of due process of law; and that duty is not discharged by an assignment at such a time or under such circumstances as to preclude the giving of effective aid in the preparation and trial of the case . . . In a case such as this, whatever may be the rule in other cases, the right to have counsel appointed, when necessary, is a logical corollary from the constitutional right be heard by counsel.

- *Johnson v. Zerbst*, 304 U.S. 458 (1938)—the Court extended the protections recognized in *Powell* to non-capital, felony cases in federal courts. Quite simply, the Court held that

. . . Since the Sixth Amendment constitutionally entitles one charged with crime to the assistance of counsel, compliance with this constitutional mandate is an essential jurisdictional prerequisite to a federal court's authority to deprive an accused of his life or liberty. When this right is properly waived, the assistance of counsel is no longer a necessary element of the court's jurisdiction to proceed to conviction and sentence. If the accused, however, is not represented by counsel and has not competently and intelligently waived his constitutional right, the Sixth Amendment stands as a jurisdictional bar to a valid conviction and sentence depriving him of his life or his liberty. A court's jurisdiction at the beginning of trial may be lost "in the course of the proceedings" due to failure to complete the court—as the Sixth Amendment requires—by providing counsel for an accused who is unable to obtain counsel, who has not intelligently waived this constitutional guaranty, and whose life or liberty is at stake. If this requirement of the Sixth Amendment is not complied with, the court no longer has jurisdiction to proceed. The judgment of conviction pronounced by a court without jurisdiction is void,

- *Gideon v. Wainwright*, 372 U.S. 335 (1963)—the Court held that every person accused of a crime, whether state or federal, is entitled to an attorney at trial even if they could not afford one. This case was a direct extension of their earlier ruling in *Powell*, and provided for the appointment of counsel to indigent defendants in non-capital cases. In *Gideon*, the Court recognized that both state and federal governments spend *vast sums of money* to prosecute criminal defendants—a strong indicator that attorneys are necessities and not luxuries.

  . . . The right of one charged with crime to counsel may be deemed fundamental and essential to fair trials in some countries, but it is in ours. From the very beginning, our state and national constitutions and laws have laid great emphasis on procedural and substantive safeguards designed to assure fair trials before impartial tribunals in which every defendant stands equal before the law. This noble ideal cannot be realized if the poor man charged with crime has to face his accusers without a lawyer to assist him.

- *Escobedo v. Illinois*, 378 U.S. 478 (1964)—although the precursor to *Miranda*, *Escobedo* is often overlooked. In a further extension of *Gideon*, the Court ruled that once a police investigation graduates from a general inquiry into an unsolved crime to a focus on a particular suspect in custody, that person has the right to counsel and the right to be notified of his/her right to silence.

  . . . we hold, therefore, that where, as here, the investigation is no longer a general inquiry into an unsolved crime, but has begun to focus on a particular suspect, the suspect has been taken into police custody, the police carry out a process of interrogations that lends itself to eliciting incriminating statements, the suspect has requested and been denied an opportunity to consult with his lawyer, and the police have not effectively warned him of his absolute constitutional right to remain silent, the accused has been denied "the Assistance of Counsel" in violation of the Sixth Amendment to the Constitution as "made obligatory upon the States by the Fourteenth Amendment" . . . and that no statement elicited by the police during the interrogation may be used against him at a criminal trial.

- *In re Gault*, 387 U.S. 1 (1967)—the Court held that constitutional protections against self-incrimination and the right to counsel applied in juvenile delinquency hearings. Noting that the outcome of such proceedings may result in incarceration, the Court held that

  . . . it would be extraordinary if our Constitution did not require the procedural regularity and the exercise of care implied in the phrase "due process." Under our Constitution, the condition of being a boy does not justify a kangaroo court . . the points to which the judge directed his attention were little different from those that would be involved in determining any charge of violation of a penal statute. The essential difference between Gerald's case and a normal

criminal case is that safeguards available to adults were discarded in Gerald's case . . so wide a gulf between the State's treatment of the adult and of the child requires a bridge sturdier than mere verbiage, and reasons more persuasive than cliché can provide. . . . The juvenile needs the assistance of counsel to cope with problems of law, to make skilled inquiry into the facts, to insist upon regularity of the proceedings, and to ascertain whether he has a defense and to prepare and submit it. The child "requires the guiding hand of counsel at every step in the proceedings against him."

- *Argersinger v. Hamlin*, 407 U.S. 25 (1972)—the Court held that the provisions of *Gideon* are applicable to any criminal prosecution regardless of classification if a sentence of imprisonment is possible. Thus, state and federal courts must provide counsel for any indigent defendants charged with a felony or misdemeanor in which jail or prison time could result.

  . . . we are by no means convinced that legal and constitutional questions involved in a case that actually leads to imprisonment even for a brief period are any less complex than when a person can be sent off for six months or more.

- *Scott v. Illinois*, 440 U.S. 367 (1979)—the Court held that indigent criminal defendants cannot be sentenced to a term of imprisonment if the state had not afforded him/her the assistance of appointed counsel. However, the guarantee does not extend to a statutory offense for which imprisonment is authorized by not imposed. is not necessary.

  . . . Although the intentions of the *Argersinger* Court are not unmistakably clear from its opinion, we conclude that *Argersinger* did indeed delimit the constitutional right to appointed counsel in state criminal proceedings . . . *Argersinger* has proved reasonably workable, whereas any extension would create confusion and impose unpredictable, but necessarily substantial, costs on 50 quite diverse States.

- *Alabama v. Shelton*, 535 U.S. 654 (2002)—the Court held that a suspended sentence that may *end up in the actual*

(continued)

deprivation of a person's liberty may not be imposed unless the defendant had been afforded the assistance of counsel in the prosecution of the crime charged. To wit,

The Sixth Amendment does not permit activation of a suspended sentence upon an indigent defendant's violation of the terms of his probation where the State did not provide him counsel during the prosecution of the offense for which he is imprisoned.

A suspended sentence is a prison term imposed for the offense of conviction. Once the prison term is triggered, the defendant is incarcerated not for the probation violation, but for the underlying offense. The uncounseled conviction at that point "result[s] in imprisonment," . . . it "end[s] up in the actual deprivation of a person's liberty." This is precisely what the Sixth Amendment, as interpreted in *Argersinger* and *Scott*, does not allow.

ruled that *Miranda* warnings are not necessary when three characteristics are present: (1) an urgent need exists and no other possibility abounds; (2) there is a possibility to save human life; and (3) the primary motive of the interrogator is rescue (Gardner, et al., 2004).

Sequential Interrogations

Just as *Miranda* attaches to all custodial situations in which special circumstances are not present, it also applies to all interrogations, partial or comprehensive, that are attempted during the custodial period. Although *Miranda* warnings do not have to be recited continuously during such period, any interrogation subsequent to the invocation of rights must adhere to the protections contained within the original ruling. For example, in *Edwards v. Arizona*,[30] the Court considered a case in which a suspect had requested the assistance of counsel, but was questioned on the following day by detectives after informing him again of his *Miranda* rights. In reversing his conviction, the Court ruled that subsequent interrogation may not be initiated by the government, stating that:

> When an accused has invoked his right to have counsel present during custodial interrogation, a valid waiver of that right cannot be established by showing only that he responded to police-initiated interrogation after being again advised of his rights. An accused, such as petitioner, having expressed his desire to deal with the police only through counsel, is not subject to further interrogation until counsel has been made available to him, unless the accused has himself initiated further communication, exchanges, or conversations with the police. Here, the [subsequent interrogation] was at the instance . . . of the authorities, and his confession, made without having had access to counsel, did not amount to a valid waiver and hence was inadmissible.[31]

In a subsequent ruling, the Court reiterated its earlier position and expanded such protections to include situations in which the invocation of *Miranda* rights occurred during arraignment. In *Michigan v. Jackson*,[32] the Court considered the question as to whether the protection extended under *Edwards* applied to suspects requesting the assistance of counsel during their arraignment. In its ruling, the Court unequivocally included the protections afforded to those individuals by *Miranda* and *Edwards*, even when the subsequent interrogation was undertaken with no knowledge of the defendant's invocation of rights. Although the ruling addressed protections found in the Sixth—as opposed to the Fifth—Amendment, the expansion of *Miranda* had profound effects on law enforcement practices.

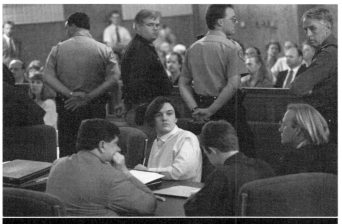

In 1994, three teenage boys were convicted of mutilating, raping, and murdering three 8-year-old boys in Arkansas. One of the suspects, Jesse Misskelley, confessed to the police and implicated his two friends. Tried separately, Misskelley was convicted and sentenced to life plus 40 years. His refusal to take the stand against his friends, Jason Baldwin and Damien Echols, prevented his confession from being introduced. However, both were convicted, and Damien Echols was sentenced to death.

▶ The Confrontation Clause of the Sixth Amendment

Co-Conspirator's and Co-Defendant's Confessions

The Confrontation Clause of the Sixth Amendment provides for the cross-examination of all individuals and entities providing evidence against an accused (discussed in greater detail in Chapter 8). As such, the Court has ruled that the introduction of statements made by co-conspirators and co-defendants is permissible only in special situations. In each of the situations, independent corroboration is required. Such corroboration is necessary because of the presumption that co-defendants or individuals receiving some consideration by the government are deemed untrustworthy—such as when individuals are receiving compensation, whether monetary or otherwise—*and* because the testimony of said accomplice is highly incriminating. When corroboration is present, statements or confessions by co-defendants are only admissible against the defendant when: (1) he or she takes the stand during the trial; (2) the two parties are tried separately; (3) references to the defendant are omitted from the testimony; and (4) the charges against the defendant are dropped.[33] In justifying its ruling, the Court recognized the unreliability of such statements, stating that:

> Not only are the incriminations devastating to the defendant but their credibility is inevitably suspect, a fact recognized when accomplices do take the stand and the jury is instructed to weigh their testimony carefully given the recognized motivation to shift blame onto others. The unreliability of such evidence is intolerably compounded when the alleged accomplice, as here, does not testify and cannot be tested by cross-examination. It was against such threats to a fair trial that the Confrontation Clause was directed.[34]

CONFESSIONS

Case law in regards to the admissibility of confessions in criminal cases hinges upon evaluations of the voluntariness of the statement in question. The Court has recognized several factors to consider in determining whether a defendant's will was overborne in a particular case. These characteristics have included, but have not been limited to, the age of the accused, level of education, level of intelligence, ignorance of constitutional rights, length of detention, nature of questioning, and physical circumstances of questioning and detention, such as lack of food, sleep deprivation, and the like.

- *Brown v. Mississippi*, 297 U.S. 278, 56 S. Ct. 461 (1936)—the Court held that in cases where a conviction rests solely on a confession that was extorted through physical violence or torture violated the Fourteenth Amendment. While the Court refused to overturn their earlier rulings in *Twining v. New Jersey* and *Snyder v. Massachusetts* which held that the freedom from the compulsory testimony of a defendant could be suspended by the state, they held that

  . . . compulsion by torture to extort a confession is a different matter. The State is free to regulate the procedure of its courts in accordance with its own conception of policy unless, in so doing, if "offends some principle of justice so rooted in the traditions and conscience of our people as to be ranked as fundamental" . . . the State may abolish trial by jury. It may dispense with indictment by a grand jury and substitute complaint or information . . . but the freedom of the State in establishing its policy is the freedom of constitutional government and is limited by the requirement of due process of law. Because a State may dispense with a jury trial, it does not follow that it may substitute trial by ordeal. The rack and torture chamber may not be substituted for the witness stand.

- *Blackburn v. Alabama*, 361 U.S. 199 (1960)—the Court ruled that a defendant is deprived of due process if at any stage of a trial, the involuntariness of a confession is conclusively demonstrated. The Court overturned the conviction of a defendant with a documented history of mental illness who had confessed to a robbery.

In the case at bar, the evidence indisputably establishes the strongest probability that Blackburn was insane and incompetent at the time he allegedly confessed. Surely, in the present stage of our civilization, a most basic sense of justice is affronted by the spectacle of incarcerating a human being upon the basis of a statement he made while insane; and this judgment can without difficulty be articulated in terms of the unreliability of the confession, the lack of rational choice of the accused, or simply a strong conviction that our system of law enforcement should not operate so as to take advantage of a person in this fashion. And when the other pertinent circumstances are considered—the eight to nine-hour sustained interrogation in a tiny room which was upon occasion literally filled with police officers; the absence of Blackburn's friends, relatives, or legal counsel; the composition of the confession by the Deputy Sheriff, rather than by Blackburn—the chances of the confession's having been the product of a rational intellect and a free will become even more remote, and the denial of due process even more egregious.

- *Rogers v. Richmond*, 365 U.S. 534, 81 S. Ct. 735 (1961)—the Court held that confessions must be carefully screened by the trial court for verification of its voluntary nature prior to its introduction into court.

The employment instead, by the trial judge and the Supreme Court of Errors, of a standard infected by the inclusion of references to probable reliability resulted in a constitutionally invalid conviction, pursuant to which Rogers is now detained "in violation of the Constitution." A defendant has the right to be tried according to the substantive and procedural due process requirements of the Fourteenth Amendment. This means that a vital confession, such as is involved in this case, may go to the jury only if it is subjected to screening in accordance with correct constitutional standards. To the extent that, in the trial of Rogers, evidence was allowed to go to the jury on the basis of standards that departed from constitutional requirements—to that extent, he was unconstitutionally tried, and the conviction was vitiated by error of constitutional dimension.

- *Culombe v. Connecticut*, 367 U.S. 568 (1961)—the Court held that any evaluation as to the voluntariness of a confession should involve a three-phased process.

. . . The inquiry whether, in a particular case, a confession was voluntarily or involuntarily made involves, at the least, a three-phased process. First, there is the business of finding the crude historical facts, the external, "phenomenological" occurrences and events surrounding the confession. Second, because the concept of "voluntariness" is one which concerns a mental state, there is the imaginative recreation, largely inferential, of internal, "psychological" fact. Third, there is the application to this psychological fact of standards for judgment informed by the larger legal conceptions ordinarily characterized as rules of law but which also comprehend both induction from, and anticipation of, factual circumstances.

No more restricted scope of review would suffice adequately to protect federal constitutional rights. For the mental state of involuntariness upon which the due process question turns can never be affirmatively established other than circumstantially—that is, by inference; and it cannot be competent to the trier of fact to preclude our review simply by declining to draw inferences which the historical facts compel. Great weight, of course, is to be accorded to the inferences which are drawn by the state courts. In a dubious case, it is appropriate, with due regard to federal-state relations, that the state court's determination should control. But where, on the uncontested external happenings, coercive forces set in motion by state law enforcement officials are unmistakably in action; where these forces, under all the prevailing states of stress, are powerful enough to draw forth a confession; where, in fact, the confession does come forth and is claimed by the defendant to have been extorted from him; and where he has acted as a man would act who is subjected to such an extracting process—where this is all that appears in the record—a State's judgment that the confession was voluntary cannot stand.

- *Arizona v. Fulminate*, 499 U.S. 279 (1991)—the introduction of a coerced confession cannot sustain a guilty verdict unless the state proves that it constitutes *harmless error* beyond a reasonable doubt. In reaching their decision, the Court emphasized the evidentiary weight that jurors may attribute to confessions.

A confession is like no other evidence. Indeed, "the defendant's own confession is probably the most probative and damaging evidence that can be admitted against him. . . . [T]he admissions of a defendant come from the actor himself, the most knowledgeable and unimpeachable source of information about his past conduct. Certainly, confessions have profound impact on the jury, so much so that we may justifiably doubt its ability to put them out of mind even if told to do so." . . . In the case of a coerced confession such as that given by *Fulminate* to *Sarivola*, the risk that the confession is unreliable, coupled with the profound impact that the confession has upon the jury, requires a reviewing court to exercise extreme caution before determining that the admission of the confession at trial was harmless . . . under harmless error analysis, which the Court has determined applies to the admission of coerced confessions, the State has failed to meet its burden of establishing, beyond a reasonable doubt, that the admission of . . . confession was harmless.

The *Bruton* Rule

Violations of the **Bruton** rule—that confessions identifying the defendant can be used only when the individual who confesses takes the witness stand—are called *Bruton* violations. However, prosecutors routinely attempt to circumvent the spirit of the Court's ruling by encouraging co-defendants to become witnesses for the prosecution in exchange for a reduction of charges. In other instances, prosecutors may choose to edit the original statement carefully and remove all references to co-defendants or co-conspirators.

bruton rule a legal ruling establishing that the confession of a co-conspirator that identifies or otherwise implicates the defendant can only be used when the individual who confesses takes the witness stand and is subject to cross-examination.

► Constraints on Law Enforcement

As stated, confessions or incriminating statements are often regarded as compelling indicators of the guilt of the accused. However, the framers of the U.S. Constitution and the Court have recognized the prohibition against compulsory testimony by the defendant and the introduction of coerced confessions. Firmly rooted in the Bill of Rights and broadly interpreted by the Court, such protections are designed to prevent egregious behavior by law enforcement authorities and limit the possibility of false confessions. As such, police officers and government agents are restricted in their methods of interrogation. The rack and the screw have been cast aside, and any form of physical or emotional torture is strictly forbidden.

Promises, Threats, Physical Coercion, and Lies

Although contemporary law enforcement officers in the United States are prohibited from extracting confessions through the use of physical torture, they are not entirely forbidden from collecting such information through deceptive strategies, including the issuance of promises, threats, and lies. Promises, for example, include assurances to tell the court about the suspect's cooperation and assurances of leniency for him or her, for suspect's family, or for others. However, the level of deception, trickery, and promises that can legally be utilized by law enforcement is not clear. The Supreme Court has attempted to clarify the parameters in several cases and has consistently ruled that the threat of physical violence or similar acts necessarily negates confessions because case law had:

> ". . . made clear that a finding of coercion need not depend upon actual violence by a government agent"; a 'credible' threat is sufficient. . . . As we have said . . . coercion can be mental as well as physical, and the blood of the accused is not the only hallmark of an unconstitutional inquisition [*Blackburn v. Alabama*, (1960), 361 U.S. 199] . . . ." Thus, cases hinge upon the totality of the circumstances surrounding their acquiescence especially the question 'whether the defendant's will was overborne at the time he confessed.'" [*Lynumn v. Illinois* (1963), 372 U.S. 528]

In essence, the Supreme Court has traditionally disallowed testimony that was extracted through the use of physical coercion. In its justification, the Court has continued to reiterate two reasons. To wit,

> The abhorrence of society to the use of involuntary confessions does not turn alone on their inherent untrustworthiness. It also turns on the deep-rooted feeling that the police must obey the law while enforcing the law; that in the end life and liberty can be as much endangered from illegal methods used to convict those thought to be criminals as from the actual criminals themselves. [*Spano v. New York*, 360 U.S. 315, 79 S.Ct. 1202, 3 L.Ed.2d 1265 (1959)]

Thus, the Court has recognized both that involuntary confessions lack veracity and that the American system of criminal justice should be one of fairness and due process.

► When the Self-Incrimination Protection of the Fifth Amendment Does Not Apply

The Constitutional prohibition against self-incrimination does not apply to all actions by a defendant. Rather, the protections housed within the Fifth Amendment only apply to evidence of a communicative or testimonial nature. The Amendment does not attach to statements that might incriminate a third party, nor does it apply to physical evidence—the Fourth Amendment addresses issues of physical evidence. In addition, the freedom from self-incrimination and compulsory testimony is applicable only to individuals and does not apply to corporations, businesses, labor unions, and other organizations. Finally, it does not apply in noncriminal cases in which a state's public interest is unrelated to the enforcement of its criminal laws. To wit,

> The possibility that a production order will compel testimonial assertions that may prove incriminating does not, in all contexts, justify invoking the privilege to resist production. . . . Even assuming that this limited testimonial assertion is sufficiently incriminating and "sufficiently testimonial for purposes of the privilege," . . . . Bouknight may not invoke the privilege to resist the production order because she has assumed custodial duties related . . . to production and because production is required as part of a noncriminal regulatory regime. . . . The Court has on several occasions recognized that the Fifth Amendment privilege may not be invoked to resist compliance with a regulatory regime constructed to effect the State's public purposes unrelated to the enforcement of its criminal laws.[35]

Field Sobriety Tests and Blood Testing

In recent years, there has been a marked increase in the number of community activist groups focusing on drunk driving. Initiating with Mothers Against Drunk Driving (MADD), the media, politicians, and the public have focused increasingly on the dangers posed by intoxicated drivers. As such, many communities aggressively enforce zero-tolerance policies. The standard of measure in the evaluation of proper police strategy and constitutional protections against self-incrimination was formally recognized by the Supreme Court as early as 1957, when it ruled on a case in which an auto accident claimed the lives of three people. In *Breithaupt v. Abram*,[36] the Court considered whether the drawing of a sample of blood from an unconscious driver who smelled of alcohol violated the Fifth Amendment's protection against compulsory testimony or the Fourteenth Amendment's guarantee of due process. In its evaluation, the Court formally recognized the public interest in preventing drunk driving, while carefully measuring the level of intrusiveness on the part of the government. Regarding the due process challenge, the Court ruled that:

> Basically the distinction rests on the fact that there is nothing "brutal" or "offensive" in the taking of a sample of blood when done, as in this case, under the protective eye of a physician. To be sure, the driver here was unconscious when the blood was taken, but the absence of conscious consent, without more, does not necessarily render the taking a violation of a constitutional right; . . . and certainly the test as administered here would not be considered offensive by even the most delicate. Furthermore, due process is not measured by the yardstick of personal reaction or the sphygmogram of the most sensitive person, but by that whole community sense of "decency and fairness" that has been woven by common experience into the fabric of acceptable conduct. It is on this bedrock that this Court has established the concept of due process. . . . We therefore conclude [352 U.S. 432, 437] that a blood test taken by a skilled technician is not such "conduct that shocks the conscience," . . . nor such a method of obtaining evidence that it offends a "sense of justice," . . . . This is not to say that the . . . indiscriminate taking of blood under different conditions or by those not competent to do so may not amount to such "brutality" as would come under the *Rochin* rule.[37]

At the same time, the Court considered whether the introduction of said evidence at trial would reach the level of compulsory testimony as prohibited by the Fifth Amendment. In a rather dismissive way, the Court ruled that previous case

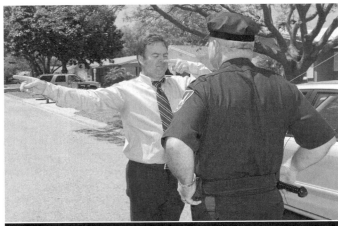

Drunk driving has been a concern of the public and the police for many years. The Court has upheld the constitutionality of field sobriety tests and blood testing in the detection of drivers who are suspected of driving a motor vehicle while intoxicated.

law had established that only testimonial or communicative evidence is protected. This reasoning was later reaffirmed by the Court in *Schmerber v. California*,[38] when the Court upheld the involuntary taking of blood from a conscious individual who had been advised by counsel not to submit to such testing.

Compulsory Participation

Although the Fifth Amendment protects individuals from compulsory testimony in a criminal proceeding, it generally does not prohibit the introduction of all activities, behaviors, or demeanors of criminal defendants. In fact, the Court has largely deemed those nonverbal statements or evidence that may be self-incriminating as unworthy of such protection. As discussed above, medical evaluations that are nonintrusive in nature are routinely admitted into evidence. Just as the Court has ruled that the compulsion of involuntary breath, blood, and DNA samples do not violate due process or the Fifth Amendment, so too they have recognized the legal appropriateness of compulsory participation in identification procedures and videotaped bookings.

Identification Procedures

Just as the Court has refused to recognize any Fifth Amendment protection in the drawing of blood and breathalyzer analysis, it has also refused to extend the umbrella of the Fifth to pretrial and posttrial identification procedures. In *United States v. Wade*,[39] the Court evaluated a range of issues, including the application of Fifth Amendment protections to a postindictment lineup for identification purposes, application of the Sixth Amendment's right to counsel during lineups, and whether an identification arising from said lineups (conducted without the assistance of counsel) was admissible. Its ruling was a mixed bag in which neither civil libertarians nor crime control advocates found total solace. Regarding the Sixth Amendment questions, the Court clearly indicated that postindictment identification procedures must be conducted with the assistance of counsel. At the same time, the Court refused to recognize a Fifth Amendment prohibition against compulsory lineups when it ruled that:

> Neither the lineup itself nor anything required therein violated respondent's Fifth Amendment privilege against self-incrimination since merely exhibiting his person for

observation by witnesses and using his voice as an identifying physical characteristic involved no compulsion of the accused to give evidence of a testimonial nature against himself which is prohibited by that Amendment.[40]

Reiterating its earlier ruling in *Schmerber*, the Court held that the freedom from self-incrimination "offers no protection against compulsion to submit to fingerprinting, photography, or measurements, to write or speak for identification, to appear in court, to stand, to assume a stance, to walk, or to make a particular gesture."[41] This is not to suggest that all lineups are admissible in court. Only those that are fair and equitable may be introduced. Those that are prejudiced or suggestive to such an extent that the resulting identification is all but inevitable may not be introduced[42] because they clearly are in violation of the Fifth Amendment's due process clause.[43]

Videotaped Bookings

The Court has also considered whether *Miranda* warnings were necessary before videotaping a suspect during the booking procedure. In *Pennsylvania v. Muniz*,[44] the Court ruled that videotaping suspects during routine booking procedures in DUI cases violated a suspect's right to be free from self-incrimination. The Court disallowed portions of the videotape in which questioning of the suspect was recorded, but it did allow the remainder. Reiterating several previous rulings, the Court pointed out that Fifth Amendment protection extended only to evidence that was communicative or testimonial in nature. It did not include a generalized depiction of the suspect's slurred speech, his apparent lack of muscular coordination, or the sobriety test administered by the police. In addition, the Court admitted the suspect's statements made during the sobriety test and his refusal to participate in breath analysis, as they were voluntary and not elicited during a custodial interrogation.

Polygraph Examinations

Contrary to depictions in the popular media, polygraph examinations and hypnosis are not nearly so legally robust. Some states do allow the admission of polygraphs when both sides agree to and stipulate to their use before the administration of said test, but others forbid their introduction entirely. In fact, the Court has formally recognized the dissension in the scientific community regarding their reliability and has upheld the rights of states to disregard them completely. Just as the Court protects defendants from compulsory submission to such examinations, it has also precluded defendants from introducing the results of same to prove their innocence.[45] It is important to remember that statements made before, during, or after a polygraph examination are not privileged. Polygraph examiners, assistants, detectives, and other witnesses may testify to statements made by individuals during the process as long as the examinations were voluntary and as long as the individual had been properly Mirandized.

Congressional legislation has also mirrored the Court's position through enactment of the *Employee Polygraph Protection Act* that protects employees of interstate commerce businesses from most preemployment screening and on-the-job polygraphs. As in other areas of the law, however, numerous exceptions exist, including occupations and positions that may affect public safety, such as transportation. In addition, some government agencies and officials have employed the use of testing for specific reasons. In 1992, Roger Keith Coleman, an inmate on death row in Virginia, took a polygraph examination at the request of then-governor Mark Wilder to demonstrate his innocence in support of his clemency petition. He subsequently failed and was summarily executed.

► CONCLUSIONS

The Fifth Amendment to the Constitution provides a range of protections for American citizens. It contains provisions and prohibitions regarding the grand jury system, double jeopardy, due process, the impressment of private property, and self-incrimination. The Supreme Court has repeatedly held that individuals may not be tried twice for the same offense in the same jurisdiction. In addition, the Court has repeatedly evaluated the prohibition against self-incrimination, and its rulings have addressed various issues, such as custody, coercion, and voluntariness.

By far the most commonly known right afforded by the Fifth Amendment is the protection against self-incrimination. Self-incrimination can transpire through confessions or incrimination statements. Confessions acknowledge guilt, contain information regarding each essential element of the crime, and are considered *direct* evidence. Incriminating statements implicate a defendant's culpability and are classified as *circumstantial* evidence. The law extended protection against self-incrimination as early as the late nineteenth century, but it culminated with *Miranda v. Arizona* in 1966.

The *Miranda* case outlined the requirement that law enforcement personnel must inform defendants of their rights at the time of arrest. These rights include the right to remain silent, the right to an attorney, and the warning that anything defendants may say can be used against them in court. While *Miranda* warnings do not have to be continuously recited, they do extend to situations such as custodial questioning. Also, the rights afforded under *Miranda* can be invoked at any point (for example, a suspect may stop answering questions or request an attorney at any time after arrest). However, some situations exist in which *Miranda* does not attach. These situations include but are not limited to routine traffic stops, non-custodial questioning, voluntary statements, routine booking questions, and questioning by non-law-enforcement personnel.

The protection against self-incrimination also extends to co-defendants under circumstances in which the only evidence to implicate the defendant in question is the confession of an accomplice. Because of the Sixth Amendment right of the accused to confront his or her accusers, the information in the confession identifying the defendant can be used only when the individual who confesses takes the witness stand. This protection is known as the *Bruton* rule.

There exists a perception in the United States that innocent people do not confess to crimes they did not commit. However, confessions are often repudiated, denied, or otherwise recanted—a fact that the Supreme Court has recognized in numerous cases. As such, the Court has ruled that confessions in and of themselves are not sufficient to indicate the guilt of a defendant. In several rulings, the Court has ruled that the U.S. Constitution requires that "the government seeking to punish an individual produce the evidence against him by its own independent labor rather than by the cruel, simple, expedient of compelling it from his own mouth."[46] To further protect defendants from self-incrimination, the Court has continued to uphold the ruling that the government must inform defendants of their constitutionally guaranteed rights. In addition, the F.R.E. 104 (c) provides that the introduction of all confessions be preceded by an evaluation of same by the judge outside the presence of a jury.

Also, the Court has recognized that confessions may be introduced only after the voluntariness of the confessions has been established. Factors that are evaluated in the determination of such include, but are not limited to, physical coercion, length of questioning, age and mental ability of defendant, and situational characteristics. For example, the Court has ruled that public employees may not be compelled to issue statements that may be used against them in a court of law, because the fear of employment loss is "likely to exert such pressure upon an individual as to disable him from making a free and rational choice."[47] Thus, a careful evaluation of the *totality of the circumstances* accompanies each and every confession prior to rulings on admissibility. Such a requirement has been included in F.R.E. 410.

Finally, the Court has ruled that the Fifth Amendment, as applied through the Fourteenth Amendment, prohibits the government and the court from commenting on a defendant's invocation of the right to remain silent. Thus, no inferences may be drawn by state actors in open court.

Key Terms

Bright-line rule

Bruton rule

Confessions

Double jeopardy

Due process

Fifth Amendment

Grand jury system

Hung jury

Impressment of private property

Incriminating statements

Interrogation

Miranda warnings

Mistrial

Procedural defense

Public safety exception

Self-incrimination

Separate sovereigns exception

"Take the Fifth"

Discussion Questions

1. How does the double jeopardy clause apply to mistrials?
2. Give two examples of the exceptions to the double jeopardy clause.
3. What is the difference between a confession and an incriminating statement? How do these relate to the *Miranda* ruling?
4. Give two examples of exceptions to *Miranda* warnings.
5. In your opinion, should the Fifth Amendment apply to blood testing and field sobriety tests?

How has the Court ruled regarding the admissibility of such tests?

6. In your opinion, should the Fifth Amendment apply to compulsory lineups? How has the Court ruled regarding the admissibility of these lineups?
7. Should refusal to participate in breath analysis be protected under the Fifth Amendment? Why or why not?

Recommended Resources

Videos

CourtTV. The interrogation of Michael Crowe. *Mugshots*. This documentary highlights the mistakes made in the interrogation of Michael Crowe that resulted in the false confessions of three teenagers. Available at: http://www.courttv.com.

Insight Media. An overview of investigative interviewing. Available at: http://www.insight-media.com.

A&E Television. Shamed into confession. *American justice*. This video highlights the case of a man who falsely confessed to the murder of a priest because of feelings of guilt associated with his sexual relationship with the priest. Available at: http://store.aetv.com.

Insight Media. Miranda considerations. This video identifies the factors that necessitate a *Miranda* warning for police questioning. Available at: http://www.insight-media.com.

A&E Television. Getting away with murder. *American justice*. This documentary discusses the Mel Ignatow case and potential problems with double jeopardy. Available at: http://store.aetv.com.

Books

Dershowitz, Alan M. (2004). *America on trial: Inside the legal battles that transformed our nation—From the Salem witches to the Guantanamo detainees*. New York: Time Warner Book Group.

Lewis, Anthony (1989). *Gideon's trumpet*. Vintage: New York.

Hagen, Ed and Nissman, David M. (1994). *Law of confessions* (2nd ed.). St. Paul, MN: Thomson/West Publishing.

DeClue, Gregory. (2005). *Interrogations and disputed confessions*. Florida: Professional Resource Press.

Levy, Leonard W. (1999). *Origins of the fifth amendment*. New York: Ivan R. Dee Publishing.

Alschuler, Albert. (1994). A peculiar privilege in historical perspective: The right to remain silent. *Michigan Law Review*, 94(8): 2625–2673.

Conti, Richard P. (1999). The psychology of false confessions. *Journal of Credibility Assessment and Witness Psychology*, 2(1): 14–36.

Online Sources

http://www.findlaw.com—A free legal search engine for state and federal cases, codes, regulations, and federal and state constitutions.

http://www.iacp.org—Official home page of the International Association of Chiefs of Police; searchable Web site with links to publications and various professional organizations. It also has a research component and information regarding best practices.

http://www.innocenceproject.org—Official home page of an anti-death penalty group that highlights cases in which criminals were wrongly convicted; also links to research on false confessions and the impact of confessions on the minds of jurors.

http://rcarterpittman.org/essays/Bill_of_Rights/Fifth_Amendment.html—Includes R. Carter Pittman's essay on the evolution of the Fifth Amendment and other essays by the eminent constitutional scholar.

http://www.fclr.org—Official home page of the Federal Courts Law Review, an electronic law review dedicated to legal scholarship relating to federal courts.

http://www.abanet.org/tech/ltrc/lawlink/home.html—A search engine sponsored by the American Bar Association, which allows users to search various ABA publications and topics.

http://www.aallnet.org—Official home page of the American Association of Law Libraries; provides a search function allowing users to search its various publications and topics.

http://www.uscourts.gov—Official Web site of the federal judiciary; use the search feature to locate federal cases, constitutional evolutions, and judicial structure.

Relevant Cases Cited

Adamson v. California, 332 U.S. 46 (1947)

Alabama v. Shelton, 535 U.S. 654 (2002)

Alford v. United States, 282 U.S. 687 (1931)

Argersinger v. Hamlin, 407 U.S. 25 (1972)

Arizona v. Fulminate, 499 U.S. 279 (1991)

Baltimore Department of Social Services v. Bouknight, 493 U.S. 549 (1990)

Berkemer v. McCarty, 468 U.S. 442 (1984)

Bram v. United States, 168 U.S. 532 (1897)

Breithaupt v. Abram, 352 U.S. 432 (1957)

Brown v. Mississippi, 297 U.S. 278, 56 S. Ct. 461 (1936)

Bruton v. United States, 391 U.S. 123 (1968)

Edwards v. Arizona, 451 U.S. 477 (1981)

Escobedo v. Illinois, 378 U.S. 478 (1964)

Fong Foo v. United States, 369 U.S. 141 (1962)

Foster v. California, 394 U.S. 440 (1969)

Gagnon v. Scarpelli, 411 U.S. 778, (1973)

Garrity v. New Jersey, 385 U.S. 493 (1967)

Gideon v. Wainwright, 372 U.S. 335 (1963)

Griffin v. California, 380 U.S. 609 (1965)

Hoffa v. United States, 385 U.S. 293 (1966)

In re Gault, 387 U.S. 1 (1967)

Johnson v. Zerbst, 304 U.S. 458 (1938)

Kirby v. Illinois, 406 U.S. 682 (1972)

Lefkowitz v. Turley, 414 U.S. 70 (1973)

Mallory v. United States, 345 U.S. 449 (1957)

Malloy v. Hogan, 378 U.S. 1 (1964)

Michigan v. Jackson, 475 U.S. 625 (1986)

Miranda v. Arizona, 384 U.S. 436 (1966)

Morissey v. Brewer, 408 U.S. 471 (1972)

New York v. Quarles, 467 U.S. 649 (1984)

Pennsylvania v. Muniz, 496 U.S. 582 (1990)

Pointer v. Texas, 380 U.S. 400 (1965)

Powell v. Alabama, 287 U.S. 45 (1932)

Rhode Island v. Innis, 446 U.S. 291 (1980)

Rogers v. Richmond, 365 U.S. 534, 81 S. Ct. 735 (1961)

Schneckloth v. Bustamonte, 412 U.S. 218, 93 S. Ct. 2041

Schmerber v. California, 384 U.S. 757 (1955)

Scott v. Illinois, 440 U.S. 367 (1979)

Slochower v. Board of Higher Education of New York City, 350 U.S. 551 (1956)

Smith v. Illinois, 469 U.S. 91 (1984)

Spevack v. Klein, 385 U.S. 511 (1967)

United States v. Wade, 388 U.S. 218 (1967)

United States v. Brignoni-Ponce, 422 U.S. 873 (1975)

United States v. Halper, 490 U.S. 435 (1989)

United States v. Felix, 503 U.S. 378 (1992)

United States v. Scheffer, 523 U.S. 303 (1998)

Notes

1. Such concepts were also consistent with the civil concept of *res judicata* in which courts were prohibited from issues of repeat litigation and claims that had reached a formal adjudication or conclusion.
2. *U.S. v. Halper*, 490 U.S. 435 (1989)
3. *Fong Foo v. United States*, 369 U.S. 141 (1962)
4. *U.S. v. Felix*, 503 U.S. 378 (1992)
5. Ibid.
6. *Griffin v. California*, 380 U.S. 609 (1965)
7. *Lefkowitz v. Turley*, 414 U.S. 70 (1973)
8. 168 U.S. 532 (1897)
9. Ibid.
10. *Malloy v. Hogan*, 378 U.S. 1 (1964)
11. 332 U.S. 46 (1947)
12. Ibid.
13. *Adamson v. California*, 332 U.S. 46 (1947)
14. *Malloy v. Hogan*, 378 U.S. 1 (1964)
15. 384 U.S. 436 (1966)
16. Ibid.
17. *Edwards v. Arizona*, 451 U.S. 477 (1981)
18. *Smith v. Illinois*, 469 U.S. 91 (1984)
19. *Rhode Island v. Innis*, 446 U.S. 291 (1980)
20. *Miranda v. Arizona*, 384 U.S. 436 (1966)
21. Ibid.
22. *Miranda v. Arizona*, 384 U.S. 436 (1966)
23. *Berkemer v. McCarty*, 468 U.S. 442 (1984)
24. *Pennsylvania v. Muniz*, 496 U.S. 582 (1990)
25. *Berkemer v. McCarty*, 468 U.S. 420 (1984)
26. *United States v. Brignoni-Ponce*, 422 U.S. 873 (1975)
27. 467 U.S. 649 (1984)
28. Ibid.
29. Ibid.
30. Ibid.
31. Ibid.
32. 475 U.S. 625 (1986)
33. *Bruton v. U.S.*, 391 U.S. 123 (1968)
34. Ibid.
35. *Baltimore Department of Social Services v. Bouknight*, 493 U.S. 549 (1990)
36. 352 U.S. 432 (1957)
37. Ibid.
38. 384 U.S. 757 (1955)
39. 388 U.S. 218 (1967)
40. Ibid.
41. *U.S. v. Wade*, 388 U.S. 218 (1967)
42. *Foster v. California*, 394 U.S. 440 (1969)
43. *Kirby v. Illinois*, 406 U.S. 682 (1972)
44. 496 U.S. 582 (1990)
45. *U.S. v. Scheffer*, 523 U.S. 303 (1998)
46. *Miranda v. Arizona*, 384 U.S. 436 (1966)
47. *Garrity v. New Jersey*, 385 U.S. 493 (1967)

THE DECLARATION OF INDEPENDENCE.

8 Qualifications and Impeachment of Witnesses

LEARNING OBJECTIVES

The learner will:

1 *Explain the primary qualifications of witnesses*

2 *Explain the provisions surrounding child witnesses*

3 *Discuss the intricacies of witness credibility*

4 *Distinguish between specific and nonspecific impeachment*

Before the sixteenth century, jurors statutorily acted as the *triers* and the *witnesses* of fact. Often, they were neither compelled, nor in many cases, even allowed to testify.[1] Compulsory processes regarding witnesses were not enacted until the 1562 Statute of Elizabeth—legislation originally designed to protect a witnesses' "right" to appear but which evolved into a statutory obligation to testify (Wigmore, 1942). The modern **witness**—a competent testifier of the truth who must meet certain qualifications before providing testimony and through whom all evidence is introduced—was an unknown entity. Although such obligations were included in the earliest of American legal codes, they expanded to include defendants' rights that now encompass compulsory processes regarding all relevant witnesses. The role of witnesses in American courts is critical, and the importance of witnesses cannot be overstated. Indeed, the contemporary American criminal and civil legal systems could not operate without them.

witness a competent testifier of the truth who meets certain qualifications before providing testimony and through whom all evidence is introduced.

► Qualifications of Witnesses

Generally speaking, witnesses in American courts must meet three primary requirements before testifying. They must: (1) possess personal knowledge of the matter at issue before the court, (2) take an oath or make an affirmation compelling them to be truthful, and (3) express competency in their ability to understand and communicate the facts of the case. The credibility of witnesses is a different matter and will be discussed later in the chapter.

Personal Knowledge

A witness has **personal knowledge** of the matter before the court when he or she has witnessed the criminal act or possesses—through some special circumstance or ability—direct, firsthand, or authoritative knowledge of the facts of the case (such as a police officer or medical expert). When a witness, for one reason or another, does not wish to testify, he or she may be subpoenaed if his or her presence and testimony are deemed necessary by either the prosecution or the defense. A **subpoena** is a formal directive issued from a court commanding a person to appear as a witness under a penalty for failing to do so. Individuals whose personal knowledge of the case is based solely on secondary sources generally do not fall within the requirements of a subpoena.

personal knowledge direct, firsthand, or authoritative knowledge of the facts of the case.

subpoena a formal directive issued from a court commanding a person to appear as a witness under a penalty for failing to do so.

Oath or Affirmation

In addition to having firsthand knowledge of the case, all witnesses must be prepared to issue an oath or make an affirmation before the court. Without truthful

---

FEDERAL RULES OF EVIDENCE

ARTICLE VI - WITNESSES

Rule 602 – Need for Personal Knowledge

Witness may not testify to a matter unless evidence is introduced sufficient to support a finding that the witness has personal knowledge of the matter.

Evidence to prove personal knowledge may, but need not, consist of the witness' own testimony. This rule is subject to the provisions of Rule 703, relating to opinion testimony by expert witnesses.

oath solemn promise to tell the truth, the whole truth, and nothing but the truth in a court of law, traditionally characterized by putting one's right hand on the Bible and committing to veracity in one's testimony under penalty of perjury. Today's courts allow witnesses to forgo the Bible, but still require them to promise to tell the truth.

affirmation solemn promise to tell the truth, the whole truth, and nothing but the truth in a court of law, traditionally characterized by putting one's right hand on the Bible and committing to veracity in one's testimony under penalty of perjury. Today's courts allow witnesses to forgo the Bible, but still require them to promise to tell the truth.

competency the mental capacity of an individual to participate in a legal proceeding. For a witness to be competent, he or she must be able to independently recollect and communicate the events in question, separate fact from fiction, and adhere to legal requirements of accuracy and truthfulness.

voir dire latin for "to speak the truth," the term traditionally referred to the process through which potential jurors were examined. In contemporary parlance, the term also refers to the preliminary examination of potential witness for competency.

witness testimony, legal matters, civil or criminal, could not be adjudicated and the truth of the issue at hand could not be ascertained. Traditionally in American courts, witnesses were required to swear on the Bible; however, growing recognition and acknowledgment of the multicultural and multidenominational nature of American society have resulted in the introduction of an **oath** or **affirmation**. Indeed, Rule 603 of the Federal Rules of Evidence provides that "before testifying, every witness shall be required to declare that the witness will testify truthfully, by oath or affirmation administered in a form calculated to awaken the witness' conscience and impress the witness' mind with the duty to do so." Such a requirement demonstrates the presumption in American society that the swearing of an oath or the giving of an affirmation in open court increases the legitimacy of a witness' testimony.

Competency

The last, and arguably most important, requirement for witnesses is **competency**. The legal competency of any witness must be evaluated on a case-by-case basis and the determination of such hinges on three primary considerations: (1) the ability of the person to independently recollect and communicate the events in question; (2) the ability to separate fact from fiction; and (3) the ability to appreciate and adhere to the veracity requirements safeguarded by the spirit of the U.S. Constitution and the structure of the American judicial system.

Voir Dire in Determining Competency

Literally meaning, "to speak the truth," the French term *voir dire* traditionally has referred to the process through which potential jurors are examined by counsel, the judiciary, or both to evaluate their suitability for jury service. In American courts, **voir dire** also refers to the preliminary examination of potential witnesses, which often includes questioning and filling out forms, to assess the individual's ability to meet the three primary considerations just mentioned and, in turn, determine legal competency. However, the process often varies according to the individual in question. Child witnesses, for example, may be asked numerous questions designed to evaluate their testimonial ability and potential effectiveness on the stand, as well as to elicit their perceptions and memories about certain facts. Expert witnesses, on the other hand, may be asked to demonstrate their professional education, training, pedagogical retention, and competency in their field of expertise as it relates to the case. In American and European courts, voir dire questioning may be conducted by the judge. Some states do not provide for questioning by counsel.

Although most states comply with similar requirements, the Federal Rules of Evidence demonstrate neither consistent nor coherent binders in respect to state contemporaries. To wit,

---

FEDERAL RULES OF EVIDENCE

ARTICLE VI - WITNESSES

Rule 603 – Oath or Affirmation to Testify Truthfully

Before testifying, a witness must give an oath or affirmation to testify truthfully. It must be in a form designed to impress that duty on the witness's conscience.

ARTICLE VI - WITNESSES

Rule 601 – Competency to Testify in General

Every person is competent to be a witness unless these rules provide otherwise. But in a civil case, state law governs the witness's competency regarding a claim or defense for which state law supplies the rule of decision.

Every person is competent to be a witness except as otherwise provided in these rules. However, in civil actions and proceedings, with respect to an element of a claim or defense as to which State law supplies the rule of decision, the competency of a witness shall be determined in accordance with State law. (Federal Rules of Evidence, Rule 601—General Rule of Competency)

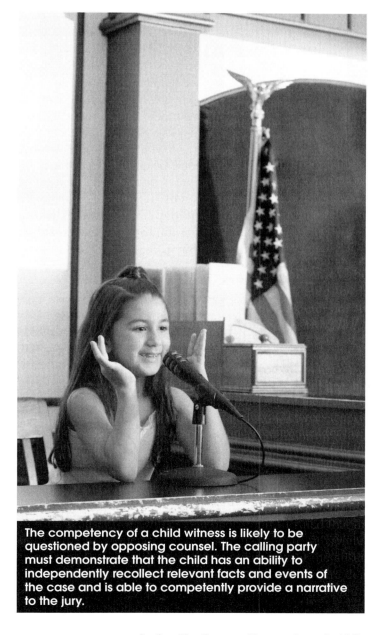

The competency of a child witness is likely to be questioned by opposing counsel. The calling party must demonstrate that the child has an ability to independently recollect relevant facts and events of the case and is able to competently provide a narrative to the jury.

THE LOW COUNTRY RAPIST—A QUESTION OF COMPETENCY

In the early part of the 1990s, women in the low country of South Carolina were terrorized by a serial rapist known as the "Low Country Rapist." One day, the perpetrator was identified by police and, after engaging in a high-speed chase, the man suffered serious head trauma in the ensuing car accident and lingered in a coma for several days afterward. Eventually, Duncan Proctor was convicted of numerous charges, including several rapes. At trial and during subsequent appeals, Proctor's attorneys argued that he was mentally incompetent and incapable of participating in his own defense. Although unsuccessful on appeal, Proctor's case illustrates the elusive nature of the notion of competency within the judicial system.

Thus, competency is defined largely by case law. Irrespective of statutory origination, the burden of proof in demonstrating witness competency rests on the side calling said witness. As a general rule, adults are presumed competent to serve as witnesses and, thus, are seldom challenged.

In some situations, the competency of an adult witness may be at issue. For example, individuals may be ruled incompetent if at the time of the occurrence or at the time of their testimony their mental capacity for observation and knowledge was impaired. Such lack of capacity may be attributed to many different factors, including but not limited to, intoxication, drug use, mental illness, disease, and physical impairment caused by injury. A patient suffering in the later stages of dementia or Alzheimer's disease, for example, may be deemed incompetent to testify about a murder that he or she witnessed decades earlier. In addition, someone under the influence of pain medication or other mind-altering or behavior-modifying substance at the time he or she witnessed an event in question could be deemed legally incompetent.

Witness incompetence is entirely different from witness credibility, which will be discussed later in the chapter. Judges will not allow incompetent witnesses to testify, but they generally do allow testimony from witnesses whose credibility is at issue, thus allowing the jury to ascertain for itself how much credibility to afford the testimony and the witness giving it.

Competency of Child Witnesses

Children usually are not deemed competent with the same ease and clarity typically afforded adults. Although some legislation provides that ". . . all persons, including children, are deemed competent unless otherwise limited by statute," [*Kentucky v. Stincer*, 482 U.S. 730 (1987)], child witnesses are often questioned directly by the trial judge. The necessity for such voir dire questioning derives primarily from the presumption that children may fail to appreciate the consequences of their testimony and the importance of complete and total disclosure

IN SEARCH OF HISTORY: THE *REX* RULE

Traditionally, the presumption that children under the age of 14 were incompetent witnesses could not be rebutted. However, the *Rex* court ruled that a child who was less than seven years old could be qualified "if such infant appears, on strict examination by the court, to possess a sufficient knowledge of the nature and consequences of the oath." [*Rex v. Brasier*, 1 Leach 199, 168 Eng. Rep. 202 (1779)].

In contemporary courts, a child must have the capacity to observe, remember, and narrate the events at issue. In addition, the child must comprehend the duty to tell the truth. Often, the presiding judge evaluates the presence and degree of such abilities by voir dire before any introduction is made in open court. If he or she finds that the witness is not competent, the child's testimony is not admissible.

and **veracity**, or accuracy, regarding their statements. In addition to evaluating the ability of the child to understand the need for truth, the trial judge will also consider the individual's ability to remember and recount the events in question.

Traditionally, children have not been allowed to testify. However, as early as 1895, age in and of itself was deemed not to be an appropriate measure of competency. In its evaluation of the appropriateness of allowing the testimony of a five-year-old child, the court in *Wheeler v. United States* ruled that:

> . . . the boy was not by reason of his youth, as a matter of law, absolutely disqualified as a witness is clear. While no one would think of calling as a witness an infant only two or three years old, there is no precise age which determines the question of competency. This depends on the capacity and intelligence of the child, his appreciation of the difference between truth and falsehood, as well as of his duty to tell the former. The decision of this question rests primarily . . . with the trial judge, who sees the proposed witness, notices his manner, his apparent possession or lack of intelligence, and may resort to any examination which will tend to disclose his capacity and intelligence, as well as his understanding of the obligations of an oath. [*Wheeler v. United States*, 159 U.S. 523 (1895)]

 CASE LAW

OUT-OF-COURT STATEMENTS, CHILD WITNESSES, AND THE CONFRONTATION CLAUSE

In *Ohio v. Clarki*, the Supreme Court considered the appeal of Darius "Dee" Clark. Clark, a small-time pimp, sent his girlfriend hundreds of miles away to engage in prostitution with the assurance that he would care for her two children, ages three and eighteen months. Immediately following, child care providers noticed various injuries to the eldest child's face and torso. Upon subsequent questioning by a supervisor at the facility, the child informed her that "Dee" was responsible. The supervisor promptly called a child abuse hotline to notify authorities of the suspected abuse.

The day following the report, a case worker for social services removed the children from Clark's mother's house and took them to a local hospital where a physician discovered countless injuries on both children. These injuries included, but were not limited to: black eyes, belt marks, bruises, and burns. Two pigtails had also been ripped out of the head of the youngest child.

Neither child testified at the trial. However, out-of-court statements made by the eldest were introduced despite a motion to exclude. Clark was convicted and sentenced to 28 years. His appeal to the Ohio Supreme Court successfully argued that the introduction of the child's out-of-court statements violated the Confrontation Clause. They held that the statements were inadmissible as they were testimonial because the primary purpose of the teacher's questioning "was not to deal with an existing emergency but rather to gather evidence potentially relevant to subsequent criminal prosecution."

In 2015, the U.S. Supreme Court reversed, holding that the introduction of the statements did not violate the Confrontation Clause. To wit:

> The Court has recognized that the Confrontation Clause does not prohibit the introduction of out-of-court statements that would have been admissible in a criminal case at the time of the founding . . . Thus, the primary purpose test is a necessary, but not always sufficient, condition for the exclusion of out-of-court statements under the Confrontation Clause.

> Considering all the relevant circumstances, L. P.'s statements were not testimonial . . . statements to individuals who are not principally charged with uncovering and prosecuting criminal behavior are significantly less likely to be testimonial than those given to law enforcement officers.

> Mandatory reporting obligations do not convert a conversation between a concerned teacher and her student into a law enforcement mission aimed at gathering evidence for prosecution. It is irrelevant that the teachers' questions and their duty to report the matter had the natural tendency to result in Clark's prosecution.

Since that time, courts have continued to recognize the need and the admissibility of the testimonial evidence of children. In fact, every state has enacted statutes that permit witnesses as young as five years of age to testify when judged competent. Some states even allow the qualification of children as young as three, and many have passed legislation to lessen traditional restrictions regarding child witnesses. For example, the introduction of hearsay by child care workers and psychologists is often permitted. Furthermore, many states have enacted legislation that allows the introduction of leading questions.

Special Status of Child Witnesses

maryland v. craig a 1990 decision by the Supreme Court that allowed the use of closed-circuit television (rather than face-to-face testimony) in a child sexual abuse case. In the seminal ruling, the Court determined that the Confrontation Clause did not guarantee defendants an absolute right to a face-to-face meeting with witnesses at trial.

confrontation clause a clause embedded in the Sixth Amendment providing that any accused person has a right to confront any witness testifying against him or her. The clause is also used to refer to the common law rule preventing the admission of hearsay in a criminal trial.

In addition to recognizing the legal competency of child witnesses, the Court has also consistently recognized their special status and particular vulnerability. In the case of **Maryland v. Craig**,[2] the Court evaluated whether the **Confrontation Clause** of the Sixth Amendment includes an absolute right to confront one's accuser face to face. In the case, the Court considered whether the use of closed-circuit television was adequate to satisfy such protections. In a seminal ruling, the Court ruled that the clause did not guarantee defendants an absolute right to a face-to-face meeting with witnesses at trial. While recognizing that the provision for face-to-face confrontation forms the core of the clause's values, the Court determined that such confrontation is not an indispensable element of the confrontation right. The Court further recognized that such a notion "would abrogate virtually every hearsay exception, a result long rejected as unintended and too extreme." In addition, the Court specifically addressed the special nature of childhood victims of sexual assault, recognizing that:

> A State's interest in the physical and psychological wellbeing of child abuse victims may be sufficiently important to outweigh, at least in some cases, a defendant's right to face his or her accusers in court. The fact that most States have enacted similar statutes attests to widespread belief in such a public policy's importance, and this Court has previously recognized that States have a compelling interest in protecting minor victims of sex crimes from further trauma and embarrassment.

In ruling this way, the Court recognized the legitimacy of the state's interest in safeguarding children from the likelihood of harm and trauma associated with being in the presence of the defendant. As a result, many states now allow closed-circuit and videotaped testimony, provided that the defendant's ability and right to cross-examine the witness remain protected. Furthermore, some states allow judges to close the courtroom to all individuals excepting the essential parties. Still others limit the length of time and number of interviews that may be conducted with child witnesses. Finally, many state statutes formally provide for the introduction and use of anatomically correct dolls in child sex abuse cases, making it easier for children to describe events in question.

Special Circumstances Regarding Witness Competency

Mentally infirm and emotionally unstable individuals generally are precluded from testifying because they may be incapable of perceiving the truth or recollecting with veracity the facts and events about which they are called to testify. Whether this is because of a lack of interest in the event at the time of occurrence, general forgetfulness, or simply the passage of time, the interested party may find itself obliged to heighten the witness' recollection. In the recent past, hypnosis has been employed to such ends. In Spokane, Washington, in the 1980s, emotional instability and hypnosis blended to become part of a strange tale involving a mother and her accused son.

▼

HYPNOSIS AND FAMILIAL BONDS

Throughout 1980 and 1981, the residents of Spokane, Washington, had been terrorized by a serial rapist. One of the first victims, an extremely popular radio personality, recounted that her attacker repeatedly beat her, threatened her with a knife, and savagely raped her. She also stated that following the attack, the perpetrator, whom she described as well-groomed and cultured, apologized. Dubbed the "South Hill rapist" by the community, the man continued his reign of terror, preying on female joggers and stalking bus stops. His actions brought many outdoor family and community activities to a stop, and law enforcement seemed powerless to stop him.

Prompted by frustration and impatience, the managing editor of the *Spokane Chronicle*, Gordon Coe, started a criminal hotline to offer monetary rewards for tips leading to the arrest of criminals in the community. The tip line, though effective, did not result in the identification or apprehension of the South Hill rapist. Rather, the distinction for solving the case was attributed in large part to an alert local middle-school custodian who reported that on the morning of the last rape, he had observed a Chevy Citation parked in the bus lane at the school. When police investigated, they traced the car back to Gordon Coe of the *Spokane Chronicle*—the same man who had offered large monetary rewards for information leading to the arrest and prosecution of the perpetrator. The subsequent investigation revealed that the car was driven by his son, Frederick "Kevin" Coe—a former radio announcer in Las Vegas and unsuccessful real estate agent. Installing a tracking device on his car, the police were able to demonstrate Coe's habit of stalking lone female joggers. During the trial, Coe's defense argued that his mother could provide an alibi for each incident charged. She claimed that the pair were active in setting up a mother–son vigilante team to capture the rapist and rid the city of the nuisance themselves. The jury did not find her testimony compelling, and Kevin Coe was convicted and sentenced to life in prison. Several months later, Kevin Coe's socialite mother, Ruth, was caught on tape hiring a hit man to murder the presiding judge and the prosecuting attorney in her son's case. When the tape was played in open court, Mrs. Coe was heard to say that she would prefer that the prosecuting attorney be forced to live in a vegetative state. She was subsequently convicted and imprisoned.

Three years later, the Coe saga continued when an appellate court reversed the rape convictions of Kevin Coe, arguing that the post-hypnotic testimony of three victims was improperly admitted. The court opined that state law prohibited the use of such testimony, and Coe was retried and convicted (though for only one sexual assault this time). The victim in that case had identified Coe without the aid of hypnosis. Although convicted, Coe received a sentence of 25 years minus time served.

In September, 2008, Coe maxed out his sentence and was scheduled for release. At that time, the state transferred him to a Special Commitment Center on McNeil Island, which specialized in the treatment of sexual predators. Under the *Community Protection Act*, Washington authorities then held a civil commitment hearing which evaluated Coe's propensity for violent behavior. The jury decided that the state had proven Coe to be a violent sexual predator beyond a reasonable doubt. He was committed to the facility indefinitely. In 2011, his appeal of his continued commitment was denied.

Hypnosis and Refreshed Memories

Hypnosis, from the name of the Greek god of sleep, *Hypnos*, refers to the induction of an altered state of consciousness. Although such induction has been practiced for centuries, the recognition that altered states may be used for memory enhancement is relatively new. In recent years, many mental health practitioners have incorporated it into patient treatment for purposes of relaxation. Some have even begun to use it to motivate the recovery of *repressed* memories. Based on the theory that the conscious mind can block out unpleasant or harrowing experiences, hypnosis attempts to remove the barriers that were erected as a defense mechanism. Law enforcement has also used hypnotically induced memories as investigative tools to identify suspects and to clarify details. However, critics argue that such memories lack veracity and credibility, primarily because hypnotized individuals are extremely vulnerable and susceptible to suggestive inferences (Scoboria et al., 2002).

In the 1980s, a bizarre case in Spokane, Washington, garnered national interest when a prominent member of the community—the mother of the accused—hired a hit man to kill the judge who presided over the case of her son, Frederick "Kevin" Coe (pictured above), who had become known as the South Hill rapist.

Various studies indicate that hypnotically refreshed memory is often fraught with error (Scoboria et al., 2002). Oddly enough, individuals often have more confidence in these **hypnotically refreshed memories** than in ones that are not—a fact that the Supreme Court recognized as troublesome.

hypnotically refreshed memories recollection of events that is produced under the influence of hypnosis.

> The most common response to hypnosis, however, appears to be an increase in both correct and incorrect recollections. Three general characteristics of hypnosis may lead to the introduction of inaccurate memories: the subject becomes "suggestible" and may try to please the hypnotist with answers [regarding] the subject . . . thinks [answers] will be met with approval; the subject is likely to "confabulate," that is, to fill in details from the imagination in order to make an answer more coherent and complete; and, the subject experiences "memory hardening," which gives him great confidence in both true and false memories, making effective cross-examination more difficult.[3]

However, the Court stopped short of forbidding the introduction of hypnotically refreshed memories and specifically ruled that a per se prohibition of such was a denial of due process for defendants taking the stand in their own defense. Currently, two-thirds of the states maintain a blanket prohibition of testimony based on hypnotically refreshed memories for all witnesses excepting the defendant (Scoboria et al., 2002).

▶ Credibility of Witnesses and The Rights of Defendants

Truthful, competent, and credible witnesses are invaluable to American jurisprudence, and the importance of their role in the legal system is impossible to overstate. To encourage veracity among testifying actors, safeguards have emerged through statute and case law. Such protections, included in the Sixth Amendment

▼

In all criminal prosecutions, the accused shall enjoy the right to a speedy and public trial, by an impartial jury of the state and district wherein the crime shall have been committed, which district shall have been previously ascertained by law, and to be informed of the nature and cause of the accusation; to be confronted with the witnesses against him; to have compulsory process for obtaining witnesses in his favor, and to have the assistance of counsel for his defense.

to the Constitution, for example, grant numerous rights to the defendant regarding all witnesses. These rights include:

- The right to confront and cross-examine any witness
- The right to the compulsory attendance of the witness (e.g., in the courtroom or on closed-circuit television)
- The right to serve as a witness on his or her own behalf
- The right to truthfulness from witnesses and protection from dishonesty in witness testimony (legal ramifications for witnesses engaging in perjury)
- The right to confront his or her accuser in court (however, limitations to the face-to-face expectation have been established, particularly regarding child witnesses in sex abuse cases)

The Sixth Amendment contains specific protections and provisions that exclusively address the rights of defendants regarding witnesses. The following section discusses these rights in detail.

Right to Confront Their Accuser and Cross-Examine Witnesses

The Sixth Amendment provides that "the accused shall enjoy the right . . . to be confronted with the witnesses against him." Evaluated by the Court in several cases, the most succinct explanation of the parameters of the confrontation and cross-examination rights was articulated in *Maryland v. Craig*.[4] To wit,

> . . . the right guaranteed by the Confrontation Clause includes not only a "personal examination," . . . but also "(1) insures[sic] that the witness will give his statements under oath—thus impressing him with . . . the seriousness of the matter and guarding against the lie by the possibility of a penalty for perjury; (2) forces the witness to submit to cross-examination, the "greatest legal engine ever invented for the discovery of truth;" [and] (3) permits the jury that is to decide the defendant's fate to observe the demeanor of the witness in making his statement, thus aiding the jury in assessing his credibility.

In later discussion, the Court addressed whether the clause required the physical presence of the accuser (i.e., witness) in open court. It ruled that the Confrontation Clause of the Sixth Amendment does not include an "absolute" right to a face-to-face confrontation. However, it has recognized that the absence of such can only be permissible in very limited situations or "only where denial of such confrontation is necessary to further an important public policy, and only where the testimony's reliability is otherwise assured."[5]

In short, the Court has ruled that this right includes the right of the accused to confront said witnesses' demeanor. They have also ruled that witnesses cannot shield their faces or otherwise disguise their body language. Although some

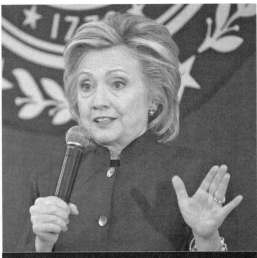

In March 2015, former secretary of state Hillary Clinton was asked by the House Select Committee on Benghazi to turn over all e-mails and correspondence regarding Libya during her tenure. She informed the Committee that despite laws to the contrary, she only used personal e-mail accounts during her time as an appointed official. Later subpoenaed by the Committee to provide access to her personal e-mail server, Clinton wiped the server clean.

exceptions have been established, such as in cases involving child witnesses who may not be forced to testify in open court, adults as a general rule may not be shielded or otherwise hidden from the jury. Witnesses, for example, may be impeached or may not be allowed to testify while intoxicated or otherwise impaired. In short, the importance of evaluating a witness' truthfulness through an analysis of his or her demeanor has been recognized as an important facet of the fact-finding mission.

> It is true that the carriage, behavior, bearing, manner and appearance of a witness—in short, his "demeanor"—is a part of the evidence. The words used are by no means all that we rely on in making up our minds about the truth of a question that arises in our ordinary affairs, and it is abundantly settled that a jury is as little confined to them as we are. They may, and indeed they should, take into consideration the whole nexus of sense impressions which they get from a witness. This we have again and again declared, and have rested our affirmance of findings of fact of a judge, or of a jury, on the hypothesis that this part of the evidence may have turned the scale. Moreover, such evidence may satisfy the tribunal, not only that the witness' testimony is not true, but that the truth is the opposite of his story; for the denial of one, who has a motive to deny, may be uttered with such hesitation, discomfort, arrogance or defiance, as to give assurance that he is fabricating, and that, if he is, there is no alternative but to assume the truth of what he denies.[13]

The American criminal justice system contains numerous provisions that encourage the veracity of witnesses in a criminal trial. As discussed earlier, they include, but are not limited to, mandatory oaths or affirmations, cross-examination of testimony, legal ramifications for dishonesty, and the

PERJURY, FABRICATION OF EVIDENCE, AND THE FBI

Two weeks before the trial of Oklahoma bombing suspect Timothy McVeigh, a supervisor in the explosives residue department of the FBI exposed misconduct dating back to the early 1980s. The allegations included tampering with the evidence that ultimately led to the conviction, sentencing, and execution of Timothy McVeigh. Other high-profile cases that were alleged to have been compromised included the mail bomb assassination of U.S. Circuit Judge Robert Vance and the bombing aboard an Avianca Airlines jet.

While denying most of the allegations, Michael Bromwich (Inspector General of the Department of Justice) stated that:

Our investigation found deficient work in some high-profile cases and also identified policies and practices in need of substantial change. Examples of the types of deficiencies we found include the following: scientifically flawed testimony, inaccurate testimony, testimony beyond the laboratory examiner's expertise, improper preparation of laboratory reports, insufficient documentation of test results, scientifically flawed reports. Inadequate record management and retention and instances in which laboratory managers failed to adequately address and resolve a range of issues. (Public Broadcasting Service, 1997)

mandatory compulsion of personal appearance at trial. However, the jury (or judge in a bench trial) is the absolute trier of fact. His or her decision alone determines the weight to be accorded a particular individual's testimony. Also, he or she decides whether a particular witness lacks credibility. In making such determinations, jurors may consider a range of factors, including demeanor, memory, perception, narration, and potential prejudice or bias. Incredible assertions or allegations that strain the limits of believability may be discounted by the jury entirely. Thus, their importance cannot be overstated—a fact long recognized by various courts who are reluctant to revisit their assessment of credibility.

> The trial court is the arbiter of the credibility of witnesses, and its findings will not be overturned on appeal unless they are inherently or patently incredible, or in conflict with the uniform course of nature or with fully established or conceded facts. See *Chapman v. State*, 69 Wis. 2d 581, 583, 230 N.W.2d 824 (1975). It is for the trial court, not the appellate court, to resolve conflicts in the testimony. See *Fuller v. Riedel*, 159 Wis. 2d 323, 332, 464 N.W.2d 97 (Ct. App. 1990). It is not within the province of an appellate court to choose not to accept an inference drawn by a fact-finder when the inference drawn is reasonable.[14]

Right to Compulsory Process

The Sixth Amendment provides that "the accused shall enjoy the right . . . to have compulsory process for obtaining witnesses in his favor." **Compulsory process**, then, provides the defendant with legal processes to compel the presence and testimony of any material witness. To this end, defendants may request the issuance of a subpoena to any competent witness who possesses personal knowledge of relevant facts. (Subpoenas, however, may not be issued to individuals who lack competency nor may they be used as a delaying tactic). Two types of subpoenas may be issued: (1) a **subpoena *ad testificandum*** requires the individual so named to provide testimony at a specified time and (2) a **subpoena *duces tecum*** requires the individual to produce specified documents or other materials. In either case, subpoenaed individuals are legally required to comply under a specific penalty for failing. Typically, this will

compulsory process a legal provision housed within the Sixth Amendment allowing defendants to compel the presence and testimony of any material witness favorable to his or her case.

subpoena *ad testificandum* a court summons requiring the subpoenaed individual to provide oral testimony at a specified time for use in a hearing or trial.

subpoena *duces tecum* a court summons requiring the subpoenaed individual to appear and present specified documents or other tangible evidence for use in a hearing or trial.

HILLARY CLINTON AND HOUSE SUBPOENAS

On September 11, 2012, an attack on the U.S. Consulate in Benghazi resulted in the deaths of four Americans: Ambassador Christopher Stevens, Information Officer Sean Smith; and, former Navy Seals and current CIA contractors, Scott Strickland and Glen Doherty. Immediately after the attack, various government officials, including President Barack Obama, publicly announced that the attack was an unplanned, spontaneous reaction to an anti-Muslim video. On September 12, 2012, Secretary of State Hillary Clinton delivered a speech at the State Department.

> . . . Some have sought to justify this vicious behavior, along with the protest that took place at our Embassy in Cairo yesterday, as a response to inflammatory material posted on the Internet. America's commitment to religious tolerance goes back to the very beginning of our nation. . . .

More than a week later, Matt Olsen, director of the National Counterterrorism Center, was the first administration official to refer to the events as a terrorist attack during a congressional hearing on September 19, 2012. His comments were followed by an admission by Secretary Clinton on the following day.

An investigation into the events leading up to the death of Ambassador Stevens and three other Americans revealed: (1) a pattern of attacks dating back to December of 2011; and (2) repeated requests for additional security from both Ambassador Stevens and Tripoli lead security officer, RSO Eric Nordstrom.

Despite the violence and the requests for assistance, the U.S. State Department removed the last of three 6-man State Department security teams and a 16-man military SST team from Libya just weeks before the fatal attack.

In a continuing attempt to explain both the lack of security and the subsequent denial of Islamic extremism, U.S. representative Trey Gowdy (R-SC), chairman of the House Select Committee on Benghazi, requested copies of all State Department correspondence concerning Libya. In March 2014, former secretary of state Hillary Clinton informed the Committee that she did not use a government e-mail address during her time in office. She stated that she used a personal e-mail account, which is traced back to a server at the Clintons' private residence in Chappaqua, NY. She indicated that she turned over all relevant information, deleted the rest, and has no intention of granting access to the server.

On March 4, 2015, the Committee issued subpoenas to cover *all communications of former Secretary of State Hillary Clinton related to Libya and to the State Department for other individuals who have information pertinent to the investigation.* They also issued preservation letters to Internet firms informing them of the legal obligation to present relevant documents and ensured that such documents were preserved. On March 27, 2015, Clinton's attorney informed the committee that the server in question was wiped clean by Secretary Clinton.

---

contempt of court
a ruling by a judge against a person who fails to comply with a judicial order or who disrupts the normal process of a court hearing, such as failing to obey a lawful order, showing disrespect of the judge, or publishing material deemed likely to jeopardize a fair trial. Sanctions may involve monetary fines, jail time, or both.

include a **contempt of court** penalty, which can involve monetary fines, jail time, or both.

Right to Serve as a Witness

This right usually is not exercised, but all defendants have the right to testify on their own behalf (see Sixth and Fourteenth Amendments).[6] In the past, defendants who elected to take the stand were required to do so before the introduction of any other testimony presented by the defense. This practice was deeply rooted in the sequestration of witnesses' philosophy, which held that witnesses should be kept separate to ensure the veracity and objectivity of their testimony. In 1972, however, the Supreme Court ruled it unconstitutional because it required the defendant to testify first, which could unfairly burden his or her case.

> Although a defendant will usually have some idea of the strength of his evidence, he cannot be absolutely certain that his witnesses will testify as expected or that they will be effective on the stand. They may collapse under skillful and persistent cross-examination, and through no fault of their own they may fail to impress the jury as honest and reliable witnesses. In addition, a defendant is sometimes compelled to call a hostile prosecution witness as his own. Unless the State provides . . . for discovery

depositions of prosecution witnesses, which Tennessee apparently does not, the defendant is unlikely to know whether this testimony will prove entirely favorable.

Because of these uncertainties, a defendant may not know at the close of the State's case whether his own testimony will be necessary or even helpful to his cause. Rather than risk the dangers of taking the stand, he might prefer to remain silent at that point, putting off his testimony until its value can be realistically assessed. Yet, under the Tennessee rule, he cannot make that choice "in the unfettered exercise of his own will." Section 40-2403 exacts a price for his silence by keeping him off the stand entirely unless he chooses to testify first. This, we think, casts a heavy burden on a defendant's otherwise unconditional right not to take the . . . stand. The rule, in other words, "cuts down on the privilege [to remain silent] by making its assertion costly."[7]

Thus, a defendant's right to testify at any stage of the defense case was firmly established. Such a right, however, does not extend to testimony offered by the defense nor does it entirely protect a defendant from potential pitfalls.

As with other witnesses, defendants who choose to take the stand may be criminally prosecuted for **perjury**, the offering of untruthful testimony. The right to testify does not include the right to commit perjury, and a defendant who "commits a crime and perjures herself in an unlawful attempt to avoid responsibility is more threatening to society and less deserving of leniency than a defendant who does not defy the trial process."[8] Offering false alibis or presenting fraudulent evidence are just two examples of perjurious testimony. Defense attorneys who knowingly allow such testimony may also be subject to punishment, though not by the criminal justice system. Disbarment, fines, and assorted other penalties may be levied at offending attorneys by their respective peer associations and governing boards.

Defendants who choose to take the stand in their own defense may also face the possibility of introducing prejudicial evidence to their own detriment, and the Supreme Court has consistently upheld the admission of a defendant's previous criminal history in such cases.

> It has long been held that a defendant who takes the stand in his own behalf cannot then claim the privilege against cross-examination on matters reasonably related to the subject matter of his direct examination . . . . It is not thought overly harsh in such situations to require that the determination whether to waive the privilege take into account the matters which may be brought out on cross-examination. It is also generally recognized that a defendant who takes the stand in his own behalf may be impeached by

perjury the offering of untruthful testimony by a person sworn to tell the truth. It is punishable when the untruth relates to material facts of the case.

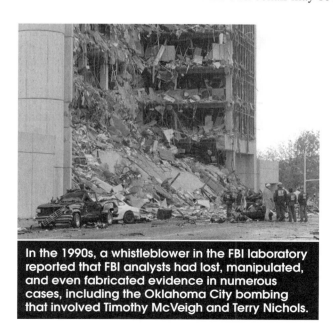

In the 1990s, a whistleblower in the FBI laboratory reported that FBI analysts had lost, manipulated, and even fabricated evidence in numerous cases, including the Oklahoma City bombing that involved Timothy McVeigh and Terry Nichols.

Laws against untruthful testimony did not originate in the United States. Indeed, ancient civilizations imposed significant punishments on those individuals presenting false testimony. For example, some of the earliest laws noted in the Code of Hammurabi address the subject and provide:

- If a man make a false accusation against a man, putting a ban upon him, and cannot prove it, then the accuser shall be put to death.
- If a man [in a case pending judgment] threaten[s] the witnesses, or do[es] not establish that which he has testified, if that case be a case involving life, that man shall be put to death.

proof of prior convictions or the like. . . . Again, it is not thought inconsistent with the enlightened administration of criminal justice to require the defendant to weigh such pros and cons in deciding whether to testify.[9]

Thus, many individuals argue that the defendant is placed in an untenable situation, one that poses hazards on every side. On the one hand, defendants who choose to exercise their right to testify risk the introduction of otherwise inadmissible evidence, which may reveal information before the jury that could imperil them. On the other hand, juries often ignore admonitions that defendants are not required to testify. Indeed, the perception that innocent persons would testify on their own behalf (and guilty person would not) abounds among American juries. In reality, then, defendants may be damned if they do and damned if they don't.

Protection from the Perjury of Witnesses

No witness, including defendants testifying on their own behalf, has the right to introduce perjured or false testimony. In fact, no one, whether testifying for the

VERMONT CODE OF LAWS

TITLE 13—CRIMES AND CRIMINAL PROCEDURE CHAPTER 65—PERJURY

§ 2901. Punishment for Perjury

A person who, being lawfully required to depose the truth in a proceeding in a court of justice, commits perjury shall be imprisoned not more than fifteen years and fined not more than $10,000.00, or both. (Amended 1971, No. 199 (Adj. Sess.), § 15; 1981, No. 223 (Adj. Sess.), § 23; 1983, No. 244 (Adj. Sess.), § 1.)

§ 2901a. Perjury by Inconsistent Statements

A person is also guilty of perjury and may be sentenced under section 2901 of this title if in one or more proceedings before or ancillary to a court or grand jury:

1. he knowingly makes two or more statements under oath or affirmation that are material in the proceedings;

2. the statements are inconsistent to the degree that the person necessarily believed one of them to be false; and

3. both statements were made within the period of the statute of limitations. (Added 1983, No. 244 (Adj. Sess.), § 2.)

§ 2902. Subornation of Perjury

A person who is guilty of subornation of perjury by procuring another person to commit the crime of perjury shall be punished as provided in section 2901 of this title.

§ 2903. Attempt to Suborn

A person who corruptly endeavors to incite or procure a person to commit the crime of perjury, though no perjury is committed, shall be imprisoned not more than five years or fined not more than $500.00, or both. (Amended 1971, No. 199 (Adj. Sess.), § 15; 1981, No. 223 (Adj. Sess.), § 23.)

PHYSICAL FACTS RULE

"The rule has been variously stated: E. G., 'the testimony of a witness which is opposed to the laws of nature, or which is clearly in conflict with principles established by the laws of science, is of no probative value and a jury is not permitted to rest its verdict thereon.' [citation omitted]. 'The testimony of a witness which is positively contradicted by the physical facts cannot be given probative value by the court.' " [*Lovas v. General Motors Corp.*, 212 F.2d 805, 808 (6th Cir. 1954)].

defense or for the state, may knowingly present evidence or testimony that lacks truthfulness. Such prohibitions are deeply rooted in tradition and have been codified in every body of law since Hammurabi. In American society, perjury statutes exist on both the state and federal levels. In criminal cases, perjured testimony may be dismissed from consideration during a trial and may even result in a successful appeal if such evidence were presented by the state.

Although revisited by the Court in several subsequent cases,[10] the Court's ruling in the 1935 case of *Mooney v. Holohan*[11] illustrates the Court's aversion to perjured testimony offered by the government.

> It is a requirement that cannot be deemed to be satisfied by mere notice and hearing if a State has contrived a conviction through the pretense of a trial which in truth is but used as a means of depriving a defendant of liberty through a deliberate deception of court and jury by the presentation of testimony known to be perjured. Such a contrivance by a State to procure the conviction and imprisonment of a defendant is as inconsistent with the rudimentary demands of justice as is the obtaining of a like result by intimidation.[12]

To discourage the government from such practices, the Court has subsequently ruled that the prosecution must reveal to the defense the contents of plea agreements afforded key government witnesses.

▶ Right of Juries to Reject Some Testimony

Just as jurors may assess factors related to the appearance of a testifying witness, they may also independently evaluate the witness' perception of the events in question. Such evaluation might include considerations of physical facts, ability to observe, and the lucidity or state of mind of witness. Unless stipulated to or judicially noted, jurors are not obligated in any situation to accept facts that are contrary to physical facts, laws of nature, common knowledge, or personal experience. In fact, some testimony or evidence on its face may not be considered credible. This **physical facts rule** has been discussed in numerous cases across the judicial landscape. However, the analogies drawn by the Sixth Circuit are quite illustrative:

> Ordinarily, where testimony conflicts, the credibility of witnesses is a matter for the jury. However, in certain instances testimony cannot be considered credible. Where a witness testifies that he looked and listened at a railroad crossing, but neither saw nor heard a train approaching, and the only reasonable conclusion upon the evidence is that there is no doubt that had he looked he must have seen the train, the witness's testimony cannot be considered credible . . . courts have recognized that eye-witnesses' testimony, essential though it may be, is fundamentally "soft" evidence, subject to human failings of perception, memory and rectitude. In law, as in other spheres of human

physical facts rule
legal concept that jurors are not obligated in any situation to accept facts that are contrary to physical facts, laws of nature, or common knowledge.

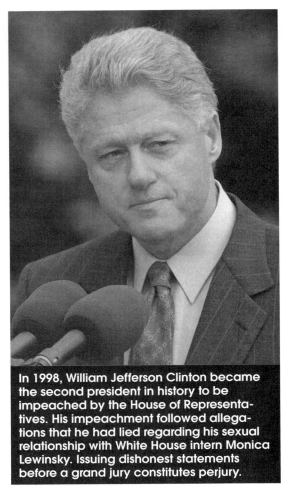

In 1998, William Jefferson Clinton became the second president in history to be impeached by the House of Representatives. His impeachment followed allegations that he had lied regarding his sexual relationship with White House intern Monica Lewinsky. Issuing dishonest statements before a grand jury constitutes perjury.

affairs, simple facts may be far more persuasive than the most learned authorities. As in Dean Prosser's homely example, "there is still no man who would not accept dog tracks in the mud against the sworn testimony of a hundred eye-witnesses that no dog has passed by." *Prosser on Torts* (4 Ed.), 212. . . . Thus, under the physical facts rule, where "the palpable untruthfulness of plaintiff's testimony" is evident because the testimony is "obviously inconsistent with, contradicted by, undisputed physical facts," . . . summary judgment is warranted notwithstanding testimony offered by the plaintiff.[15]

► Impeachment of Witnesses

Just as rules are established to provide for the introduction of testimony into open court, processes for the exclusion, modification, or denial of such are also found within American jurisprudence. In assessing witness credibility, for example, the jury may evaluate the witness' demeanor during the period of cross-examination. During this phase, opposing counsel may attempt to discredit the witness or shed doubt on his or her perception of events. Opposing counsel may also introduce evidence to contradict the sworn testimony of the witness. This process of discrediting and shedding doubt is known as **witness impeachment**. Counsel on both sides may impeach witnesses, and several methods exist for doing so. Although the rules of criminal evidence vary slightly across states in terms of witness impeachment, they generally include the following methods:

witness impeachment the process of calling into question the credibility of an individual who is testifying in a trial.

- Bias or prejudice as motivating factors
- Prior felony convictions

- Character
- Immoral acts, bad reputation, or uncharged crimes
- Prior inconsistent statements
- Inability to observe

Although the parameters and limitations for witness impeachment vary across jurisdiction, the mechanisms tend to remain consistent. As such, the Federal Rules of Evidence provides specific guidance and parameters regarding the impeachment of witnesses by either side. The FRE also specifies methods of impeachment, which may be either nonspecific in nature, such as in a challenge of bias or sensory capacity, or they may be specific, such as through a demonstration of inconsistent statements. Six primary methods of witness impeachment fall under two categories.

Nonspecific methods of impeachment provided for in the FRE include:

- Challenges of bias or prejudice as a motivator
- Challenges to sensory or mental capacity
- Challenges to veracity of witness and testimony
- Challenges of untruthfulness in character

Specific methods of impeachment provided for in the FRE include:

- Challenges involving prior convictions
- Challenges involving inconsistencies in past statements

FEDERAL RULES OF EVIDENCE

Article VI - Witnesses

Rule 607 – Who May Impeach a Witness

Any party, including the party that called the witness, may attack the witness's credibility.

Rule 608 – A Witness's Character for Truthfulness or Untruthfulness

(a) **Reputation or Opinion Evidence.** A witness's credibility may be attacked or supported by testimony about the witness's reputation for having a character for truthfulness or untruthfulness, or by testimony in the form of an opinion about that character. But evidence of truthful character is admissible only after the witness's character for truthfulness has been attacked.

(b) **Specific Instances of Conduct.** Except for a criminal conviction under Rule 609, extrinsic evidence is not admissible to prove specific instances of a witness's conduct in order to attack or support the witness's character for truthfulness. But the court may, on cross-examination, allow them to be inquired into if they are probative of the character for truthfulness or untruthfulness of:

(1) the witness; or

(2) another witness whose character the witness being cross-examined has testified about.

By testifying on another matter, a witness does not waive any privilege against self-incrimination for testimony that relates only to the witness's character for truthfulness.

Rule 609 – Impeachment by Evidence of a Criminal Conviction

(a) **In General.** The following rules apply to attacking a witness's character for truthfulness by evidence of a criminal conviction:

(1) for a crime that, in the convicting jurisdiction, was punishable by death or by imprisonment for more than one year, the evidence:

(A) must be admitted, subject to Rule 403, in a civil case or in a criminal case in which the witness is not a defendant; and

(B) must be admitted in a criminal case in which the witness is a defendant,

(continued)

if the probative value of the evidence outweighs its prejudicial effect to that defendant; and

(2) for any crime regardless of the punishment, the evidence must be admitted if the court can readily determine that establishing the elements of the crime required proving—or the witness's admitting—a dishonest act or false statement.

(b) **Limit on Using the Evidence After 10 Years.** This subdivision (b) applies if more than 10 years have passed since the witness's conviction or release from confinement for it, whichever is later. Evidence of the conviction is admissible only if:

(1) its probative value, supported by specific facts and circumstances, substantially outweighs its prejudicial effect; and

(2) the proponent gives an adverse party reasonable written notice of the intent to use it so that the party has a fair opportunity to contest its use.

(c) **Effect of a Pardon, Annulment, or Certificate of Rehabilitation**. Evidence of a conviction is not admissible if:

(1) the conviction has been the subject of a pardon, annulment, certificate of rehabilitation, or other equivalent procedure based on a finding that the person has been rehabilitated, and the person has not been convicted of a later crime punishable by death or by imprisonment for more than one year; or

(2) the conviction has been the subject of a pardon, annulment, or other equivalent procedure based on a finding of innocence.

(d) **Juvenile Adjudications.** Evidence of a juvenile adjudication is admissible under this rule only if:

(1) it is offered in a criminal case;

(2) the adjudication was of a witness other than the defendant;

(3) an adult's conviction for that offense would be admissible to attack the adult's credibility; and

(4) admitting the evidence is necessary to fairly determine guilt or innocence.

(e) **Pendency of an Appeal.** A conviction that satisfies this rule is admissible even if an appeal is pending. Evidence of the pendency is also admissible.

Nonspecific Methods of Witness Impeachment

Nonspecific methods of impeachment generally are employed to challenge the individual's general capacity for veracity and objectivity. They are designed to cast doubt in the jury's mind about the testimony the witness puts forth.

Challenges of Bias or Prejudice

Although not specifically mentioned in the FRE, impeachment of a witness may be accomplished by a demonstration of bias. For example, if an avowed white supremacist who was a member of the Aryan Nation was called to serve as an alibi witness for a white defendant accused of murdering an African American couple, the prosecuting attorney may introduce evidence of his membership to attack the credibility and general objectivity of the testimony. In a similar case, the Court considered *United States v. Abel*,[16] in which three conspirators and participants in a robbery sought to introduce testimony favorable to each one individually. In each example, the credibility of such testimony was challenged because of the involvement of each party in a recognized prison gang. Both the state and the defense alleged that the veracity of such testimony was questionable because the group encouraged (if not demanded) perjury in defense of members. Although the lower appellate court held that the introduction of testimony as to group affiliation was improper, the Supreme Court disagreed, ruling that such testimony was admissible because it was sufficiently probative to warrant challenges of bias.

While the Federal Rules of Evidence do not by their terms deal with impeachment for "bias," it is clear that the Rules do contemplate such impeachment. It is permissible to impeach a witness by showing his bias under the Rules just as it was permissible to do so before their adoption. . . . A witness' and a party's common membership in an organization, even without proof that the witness or party has personally adopted its tenets, is certainly probative of . . . bias.[17]

Challenges to Sensory or Mental Capacity

A witness may be impeached through challenges to his or her sensory or mental capacity, both at the time of the incident in question and at the time of testimony. As with bias, the purpose of impeaching a witness based on sensory or mental capacity is to cast doubt on the witness' competency and on his or her testimony. Cross-examination of the witness may include questions related to topics such as past or present drug use or history of mental illness. Specifically, such challenges may address the witness' ability to recall information or his or her general perception of the event in question. Challenges may also bring into question the accuracy of the communication about what the witness perceived. For example, counsel might pose a question such as, "When you made the statement that you were coerced into giving testimony, didn't you really mean that the defendant (or prosecutor) asked you for your cooperation?"

Challenges to Veracity

Generally speaking, there are two ways to challenge the truthfulness of a witness. They involve the introduction of (1) uncharged crimes or bad deeds and (2) past convictions in criminal court. Both are specifically addressed in the Federal Rules of Evidence and are available in some form under all state procedures. These two methods attack the competency of the witness through assertions of dishonest or untruthful behavior.

It is important to note that evidence of uncharged crimes or bad reputation is specifically limited to the witness' character of veracity and may not be introduced to attack the person's character outside those parameters. In addition, *assertions to the contrary*, or those that serve to demonstrate or support the witness' credibility, may be introduced only after an attack on his or her character has occurred. Courts have ruled that certain actions by the defendant may speak directly to veracity and thus are probative in an evaluation of credibility. Such actions, for example, might include witness intimidation,[18] receipt of stolen property,[19] failure to file federal income tax returns and bribery,[20] and loss of professional license for deceptive practices.[21]

Challenges to Character

Likewise, demonstration of a character of untruthfulness may be accomplished through the introduction of additional testimony concerning the witness' reputation within the community for veracity and through the testimony of additional witnesses who personally know the defendant and can speak to his or her general honesty and deportment.

Specific Methods of Witness Impeachment

Challenges Regarding Past Convictions

Impeachment may also occur through more specific means, such as the introduction of prior convictions. Courts have recognized that society supports the supposition that convicted criminals are likely to be less credible than the rest of the community. It is well known that a defendant's criminal history may not be introduced if he or she does not take the stand. In addition, the denial of motions seeking to exclude such evidence in the event that the defendant chooses to take the stand are not improper.[22]

▼

The introduction of convictions, however, is not absolute. Federal and state rules establish the parameters within which criminal convictions are admissible. With few exceptions, the Federal Rules of Evidence provides only for the introduction of nonpardoned (or otherwise forgiven) *felony* convictions of adults that occurred within the previous 10 years. In addition, exceptions exist for the introduction of criminal convictions, for false statements, for crimes of dishonesty, and for some juvenile offenses.

Challenges Regarding Inconsistencies in Past Statements

Impeachment of witnesses may also be done on an individual basis. Unlike the introduction of past convictions that generally address the veracity of felons, demonstration of inconsistency or contradictory statements may be employed to discredit an otherwise competent witness. This type of witness impeachment may take many forms and may include, but is not limited to, challenges of inconsistencies in current testimony and contradictory statements made in the past. In all cases, the testifying witness must be given the opportunity to explain or deny purported inconsistencies before the introduction of a prior statement. In addition, the Supreme Court has ruled that the introduction of such statements for the purpose of impeachment may be introduced even when the evidence in question would be otherwise inadmissible under the exclusionary rule or was illegally seized.[23]

► CONCLUSIONS

Because all evidence in contemporary American trials must be introduced through witness testimony, the role of the witness is vital to the integrity of the criminal justice system. Witnesses must be competent and have information relevant to the proceedings. Although competency is generally evaluated on a case-by-case basis, two characteristics must always be present. The first is the ability of the witness to tell the truth under oath and to understand that failing to do so will risk a penalty of perjury. The second is that a witness must be able to independently recollect the events in question and communicate this information competently to the jury.

The jury is the ultimate trier of fact in determining a witness' credibility. When evaluating testimony, jurors can take into account the demeanor of the witness as well the witness' perception of the events in question. Unless judicially stipulated, jurors are not required to accept facts of an account that are contrary to physical facts, laws of nature, common knowledge, or personal experience. This directive is known as the physical facts rule.

The Sixth Amendment grants several rights to defendants, including the right to confront their accuser, require the appearance of witnesses, and serve as a witness on their own behalf. At trial, under the American adversarial system, this right to confront is exercised through cross-examination. Opposing counsel cross-examines (questions) witnesses, and in doing so attempts to shed doubt on witness' recollection or perception of the events. Opposing counsel may even try to discredit the witness by introducing evidence that contradicts past sworn testimony. One important goal of opposing counsel, whether it is the prosecution or the defense, is to *impeach* witnesses who are not favorable to his or her side. Methods of impeachment, whether nonspecific or specific, include, but are not limited to: bias or prejudice, mental capacity, witness veracity and character, prior felony convictions, and inconsistent or inaccurate statements.

Key Terms

Affirmation	*Maryland v. Craig*	Subpoena *ad testificandum*
Competency	Oath	Subpoena *duces tecum*
Compulsory process	Perjury	Veracity
Confrontation Clause	Personal knowledge	Voir dire
Contempt of court	Physical facts rule	Witness
Hypnotically refreshed memories	Subpoena	Witness impeachment

Discussion Questions

1. Discuss the challenges and benefits of using child witnesses. What criteria would you use to evaluate the admissibility of a child witness?
2. Describe the general characteristics you would want in a credible witness if you were his or her legal counsel.
3. Debate the pros and cons of Federal Rule of Evidence Rule 608. Should the personal character of the witness be put on trial, or should this examination be a necessary part of the proceedings to ensure the veracity of court testimony?
4. Discuss the Code of Hammurabi. Do you agree or disagree with its historical law? Would you support its establishment today? Why or why not?

Recommended Resources

Videos

PBS Video. Did Daddy do it? *Frontline*. Available at www.shoppbs.org.

A&E Television. Shattered innocence: The Fells Acres abuse case. *American justice*. This video addresses problems associated with child witnesses. Available at: http://store.aetv.com.

A&E Television. What the girl saw. *American justice*. This case involves a heinous crime—the rape and murder of a man's 54-year-old mother-in-law and rape and attempted murder of his 6-year-old niece—and the problems associated with child witnesses, including the child's mistaken testimony that put an innocent man behind bars. Available at: http://store.aetv.com.

A&E Television. The Central Park jogger case: What went wrong. *American justice*. This documentary covers the notorious gang rape of a young professional jogging in Central Park and new evidence that forced a reexamination of a tragic tale that galvanized a city. Available at: http://store.aetv.com.

Books and Articles

Aron, Roberto, Duffy, Kevin T., and Rosner, Jonathan L. (1990). *Impeachment of witnesses: The cross-examiner's art*. Connecticut: West Group.

Bergman, Barbara and Hollander, Nancy. (1994). *Everytrial criminal defense resource book*. Connecticut: West Group.

Ceci, Stephen J. and Bruck, Maggie. (1999). *Jeopardy in the courtroom: A scientific analysis of children's testimony*. Washington, D.C.: American Psychological Association Books.

Ofshe, Richard and Watters, Ethan. (1996). *Making monsters: False memories, psychotherapy, and sexual hysteria*. California: University of California Press.

Pittman, R. Carter. (1960). *The safeguards of the sixth amendment*. Essay included in the Speaker's Digest of the Bill of Rights Commemoration Committee. Available at: http://rcarterpittman.org/essays/Bill_of_Rights/Sixth_Amendment.html.

Rabinowitz, Dorothy. (2003). *No crueler tyrannies: Accusation, false witness, and other terrors of our times*. New York: Free Press.

Schippers, David P. (2000). *Sellout: The inside story of President Clinton's impeachment*. Washington, D.C.: Regnery Publishing, Inc.

Scoboria, A., Mazzoni, G., Kirsch, I., & Milling, L.S. (2002). Immediate and persisting effects of misleading questions and hypnosis on memory reports. *Journal of Experimental Psychology: Applied*, 8(1), 26–32.

Townsend, Jules A. (1997). The expert witness and the law of evidence. *Forensic Economics*, 9(2): 165–169.

Wigmore, John H. (1942). *Wigmore's code of evidence*. Boston: Little, Brown, and Company.

Wigmore, John H. (1928). *Panorama of the world's legal systems*. Boston: Little, Brown, and Company.

Online Sources

http://www.findlaw.com—Search state and federal case law, statutes, and federal and state constitutions.

http://www.gunstonhall.org/—Official home page for Gunston Hall Plantation (home of George Mason); contains numerous links to online resources and an extensive library of documents relating to the U.S. Constitution and the Bill of Rights.

http://www.landmarkcases.org/gideon/sixth.html—Web site offering a complete discussion of the purpose and application of the Sixth Amendment to the Constitution, including links to relevant case law and answers to important questions.

http://www.house.gov/house/Educate.shtml—Maintained by the House of Representatives, this Web site offers a step-by-step discussion of the passage of law and contains links to major historical documents such as the U.S. Constitution, the Declaration of Independence, and the Federalist Papers.

http://law.onecle.com/constitution/amendment-06/index.html—Web site provides an outline of pivotal cases in the evolution and interpretation of the Sixth Amendment; contains dialogue addressing the rationale of the protections and a full discussion of the rights of the accused as provided by the Bill of Rights.

http://www.crfc.org/americanjury/right_accused.html—Maintained by the Constitutional Rights Foundation of Chicago, this Web page explores the Sixth Amendment from inception to modern day, with a full discussion of the American jury system.

http://www.pbs.org/wgbh/pages/frontline/shows/innocence/etc/other.html—Maintained by PBS, this Web page highlights several well-publicized child abuse cases and discusses the challenges associated with child witnesses. The site also includes complete histories and biographies of relevant participants, along with links to other sites for more information.

Relevant Cases Cited

Alcorta v. Texas, 355 U.S. 28

Brooks v. Tennessee, 406 U.S. 605 (1972)

Chapman v. State, 69 Wis. 2d 581, 583, 230 NW2d 824 (1975)

Dyer v. MacDougall, 201 F.2d 265 (2d Cir. 1952)

Giglio v. United States, 405 U.S. 150 (1972)

Harris v. General Motors, 99–3032, (6th Cir. 2000)

Kentucky v. Stincer, 482 U.S. 730 (1987)—child witnesses

Luce v. United States, 469 U.S. 38 (1984)

Maryland v. Craig, 497 U.S. 836 (1990)

McGautha v. California, 402 U.S. 183 (1971)

Mooney v. Holohan

Napue v. Illinois, 360 U.S. 264

Pyle v. Kansas, 317 U.S. 213

Rock v. Arkansas, 483 U.S. 44 (1987)

United States v. Abel, 469 U.S. 45 (1984)

United States v. Dunnigan, 507 U.S. 87 (1993)

United States v. Fulk, 816 F.2d 1202, 1206 (7th Cir. 1987)

United States v. Havens, 446 U.S. 620 (1980)

United States v. Manske, #98-CR-51–S, (7th Cir. 1999)

United States v. Smith, 80 F.3d 1188, 1193 (7th Cir. 1996)

United States v. Wilson, 985 F.2d 348, 351 (7th Cir. 1993)

United States v. Zizzo, 120 F.3d 1338, 1355 (7th Cir. 1997)

Wheeler v. United States, 159 U.S. 523 (1895)

Notes

1. Originally, the inquisitors or jurors were the only witnesses, and over time, witnesses outside these parameters were included. Eventually, a complete separation developed and individuals having knowledge of the issue before them were dismissed from the jury pool entirely.
2. 497 U.S. 836 (1990)
3. *Rock v. Arkansas*, 483 U.S. 44 (1987)
4. 497 U.S. 836 (1990)
5. Ibid.
6. *Rock v. Arkansas*, 483 U.S. 44 (1987)
7. *Brooks v. Tennessee*, 406 U.S. 60 (1972)
8. *United States v. Dunnigan*, 507 U.S. 87 (1993)
9. *McGautha v. California*, 402 U.S. 183 (1971)
10. More than 30 years ago, this Court held that the Fourteenth Amendment cannot tolerate a state criminal conviction obtained by the knowing use of false evidence. *Mooney v. Holohan*, 294 U.S. 103. There has been no deviation from that established principle. *Napue v. Illinois*, 360 U.S. 264; *Pyle v. Kansas*, 317 U.S. 213; cf. *Alcorta v. Texas*, 355 U.S. 28. There can be no retreat from that principle here.
11. 294 U.S. 103, 112, 55 S. Ct. 340 (1935)
12. *Giglio v. United States*, 405 U.S. 150 (1972)
13. *Dyer v. MacDougall*, 201 F.2d 265 (2d Cir. 1952)
14. *Chapman v. State*, 69 Wis. 2d 581, 583, 230 NW2d 824 (1975)

15. *Harris v. General Motors*, 99–3032, (6th Cir. 2000)
16. 469 U.S. 45 (1984)
17. Ibid.
18. *United States v. Manske*, #98-CR-51–S, (7th Cir. 1999)
19. *United States v. Smith*, 80 F.3d 1188, 1193 (7th Cir. 1996); *United States v. Zizzo*, 120 F.3d 1338, 1355 (7th Cir. 1997)
20. *United States v. Wilson*, 985 F.2d 348, 351 (7th Cir. 1993)
21. *United States v. Fulk*, 816 F.2d 1202, 1206 (7th Cir. 1987)
22. *Luce v. United States*, 469 U.S. 38 (1984)
23. *United States v. Havens*, 446 U.S. 620, 100 S. Ct. 1912 (1980)

THE DECLARATION OF INDEPENDENCE.

9 Examination of Witnesses

LEARNING OBJECTIVES

The learner will:

1   *Explain the uses of lay and expert witnesses*

2   *Recognize the admission standards for scientific and technical evidence*

3   *Discuss the process of direct examination and cross-examination*

4   *Recognize the circumstances under which objections are made*

5   *Discuss the value of objections by counsel*

6   *Discuss the benefits of corroboration*

DISTINGUISHING LAY WITNESS AND EXPERT WITNESSES

There are two types of witnesses that provide testimony in criminal cases. There are *lay witnesses* who possess **firsthand knowledge** of a fact at issue in the case, and *expert witnesses* who possess **specialized knowledge** of a fact at issue in the case. Generally speaking, lay witnesses are limited to those things that are observed by one of their five senses, whereas expert witness may provide opinion and answer hypothetical questions. Expert witnesses are employed to assist jurors in understanding complex issues outside of the boundaries of common knowledge. Areas in which experts are routinely used include, but are not limited to: DNA analysis, fingerprinting, computer forensics, questioned document examination, ballistics, accident reconstruction, psychological disorders, forensic science, crime scene analysis, determinations of point of origin or accelerants in arson investigations, and so on.

As discussed in the previous chapter, witnesses in American courts are required to have firsthand knowledge of the matters at issue and have the capacity to communicate such knowledge to the court. These individuals must not only understand the duty to tell the truth but must also take an oath attesting to such. These qualifications are required of all witnesses regardless of their type—adult or child, expert or lay—and are evaluated by the trial judge before testimony is given.

Generally speaking, two types of witnesses are common in the American criminal court system. These are lay witnesses and expert witnesses. Their respective testimony assists triers of fact in different ways, but both types are absolutely essential to due process and the search for truth. Although there are some common rules governing the questioning of all witnesses, different rules are in place as to the content and scope of lay and expert witness testimony. For the most part, expert witnesses are allocated far more latitude in drawing conclusions, and are able to provide their opinions in situations where lay witnesses may not.

► Lay Witnesses

Lay witnesses are individuals who are privy to an event relevant to the issue at hand. While they are much more common in courtrooms than are expert witness, their testimony is generally limited to actual evidence (i.e., something observed or experienced through one of the five senses) and to material facts of the case. Lay witnesses introduce many different types of evidence when they, for example, are eyewitnesses to the actual crime and are called upon to shed light on some relevant aspect of the case. Although police officers may testify as experts in some cases (to address traffic matters, use of force, police training, etc.), in most instances, they testify as lay witnesses.

As a general rule, lay witnesses present only facts through their testimony, but opinion evidence may be offered as well—if it is based on the perception of the witness and is helpful to the clarification of the witness' testimony or to the determination of the facts. Lay witnesses may offer opinion evidence in the following areas:

lay witnesses any individual with firsthand knowledge who is testifying to the matter at hand and is not providing expert scientific testimony.

- Identification of handwriting
- Statements about a person's emotional state (such as state of the accused)
- Statements about a person's physical condition (such as the condition of the accused at the time of the event in question)
- Voice identification

ARTICLE VII—OPINIONS AND EXPERT TESTIMONY

Rule 701—Opinion Testimony by Lay Witnesses

If a witness is not testifying as an expert, testimony in the form of an opinion is limited to one that is:

(a) rationally based on the witness's perception;

(b) helpful to clearly understanding the witness's testimony or to determining a fact in issue; and

(c) not based on scientific, technical, or other specialized knowledge within the scope of Rule 702.

 APPLICATION OF LAW

EXPERT TESTIMONY IN THE DEATH OF A CASINO MOGUL

Experts may have similar training and education, but they do not always reach the same conclusions. For example, world-renowned forensic pathologists, Cyril Wecht and Michael Baden, offered opposing theories in the death of casino owner, Ted Binion. Wecht, testifying for the defense, argued that the millionaire had simply overdosed on a lethal cocktail of heroin and Xanax. Baden, on the other hand, argued that bruising on the chest and discoloration around the mouth was caused by pressure applied by either Binion's lover and former stripper, Sandy Murphy, or her boyfriend, Rick Tabish.

Such testimony corroborated the prosecution theory that Murphy and Tabish had forced Binion, a known drug addict, to ingest lethal amounts of the drugs so Murphy would inherit a portion of the estate—a financial windfall that she stood to lose if Binion ever broke off the relationship. Baden's testimony, in addition to testimonial evidence that Binion was in the process of changing his will and that Murphy prematurely anticipated his demise, was enough to convict Murphy and Tabish of Binion's murder. Both convictions, however, were eventually overturned on appeal.

- General statements about mental condition (such as whether the accused is a coherent, smart, or impaired person)
- Identity of a person (such as when the accused is recognized from a lineup or photograph)
- General statements about the speed of vehicles (such as whether the car was speeding at the time in question)

► Expert Witnesses

expert witnesses
an individual who possesses specialized knowledge of a subject related to the case because of education, profession, or experience (often proved from authorship in medical journals, for example). Unlike lay (non-expert) witnesses, an expert witness must be deemed "qualified" by the court before testifying.

Unlike lay witnesses who possess firsthand knowledge of a material fact relevant to the matter at hand, **expert witnesses** are individuals called upon to provide expert or specialized testimony related to the facts and events in question based upon his or her special knowledge or training. Expert witnesses may testify only in cases in which aspects of the evidence are beyond the understanding of the average juror (such as DNA evidence and testing protocols). The role of the expert witness, then, is to assist the jury in clarifying meaning, gaining a more complete understanding of the evidence, and grasping how certain conclusions were reached. For example, certain medical procedures may be overly complicated or sophisticated and may need to be explained to jurors. For the most part, expert witnesses are individuals with advanced degrees who have spent years in the study, research, or licensing of issues related to the case. But an expert witness may also be anyone with specialized knowledge. For example, the Supreme Court has ruled that a police officer with many years of specialization in obscenity offenses qualified as

ARTICLE VII — OPINIONS AND EXPERT TESTIMONY

Rule 702—Testimony by Expert Witnesses

A witness who is qualified as an expert by knowledge, skill, experience, training, or education may testify in the form of an opinion or otherwise if:

(a) the expert's scientific, technical, or other specialized knowledge will help the trier of fact to understand the evidence or to determine a fact in issue;

(b) the testimony is based on sufficient facts or data;

(c) the testimony is the product of reliable principles and methods; and

(d) the expert has reliably applied the principles and methods to the facts of the case.

---

an expert witness in "community standards."[1] Regarding expert witnesses, judges must determine whether the proposed individual possesses the adequate qualifications and whether expert testimony exists and will be meaningful. Thus, the court will ask three basic questions:

- Is the area in question one in which expert testimony has been recognized?
- What qualifications must one possess to qualify as an expert witness?
- Does the proposed witness meet the qualifications and possess the appropriate expertise?

It is important to note that although the judge rules on the admissibility and scope of a particular witness' testimony, it is up to the jury to assign weight and importance to it.

As a general rule, the testimony of expert witnesses may not invade issues that the judge or jury is required to decide, such as presumptions, stipulations, and facts that are judicially noted. In fact, experts may testify only within their area of expertise and may not offer professional opinions on issues outside their immediate qualifications. In the case of former NBA star Jayson Williams, for example, the judge disallowed some testimony by Michael Baden, a well-known medical examiner. Williams was charged with aggravated manslaughter in the shooting death of chauffeur Costas Christofi. Williams claimed that the shooting had been accidental and sought to introduce testimony from Baden that would suggest that the shotgun used in the incident accidentally discharged because of a flaw in design. However, the trial judge ruled that Baden's qualifications as a pathologist did not extend to the manufacturing of weapons.

Often, expert witnesses are used in high-profile cases. In fact, many experts make a substantial portion of their livelihood from court appearances and expert opinions. Compensation to expert witnesses for their testimony varies greatly, depending on the nature of the testimony, their reputation as a witness, and their area of expertise. Other factors that may influence the level of compensation include demographic characteristics. For example, an expert who is internationally renowned may demand considerably more to testify in the murder of a politician's wife in Washington D.C. than would a local expert in rural Alabama for the same case. Occasionally, individual experts may choose to testify for a reduced rate when, for example, the case receives great notoriety, he or she feels a sense of injustice, or there exists a desire simply to help. Some experts are in such high demand that they acquire an odd sense of celebrity in their own right. Demand for such experts can be tremendous, so much in fact, that a race can erupt between the prosecutor and the defense to see which one can secure the expert's testimony.

Expert witnesses testify in many different cases, and it is not unusual for two experts to reach entirely different conclusions and provide diametrically opposed testimony. Such was the case in the death of Horseshoe Casino mogul, Ted Binion (pictured above). One forensic pathologist testified that his death had resulted from an accidental drug overdose, while another testified that he had been suffocated.

Often, expert witnesses play an essential role in assisting the trier of fact in the determination of guilt or innocence. They are used in cases in which clarification of facts at issue necessitate the introduction of special testimony or particular expertise, and such testimony is increasingly in demand as technology outpaces the average person's understanding. The introduction of DNA evidence, for example, is becoming so frequent that testimony by expert witnesses is all but required in many murder and sexual assault cases. As such, legislation has been enacted and judicially upheld[2] to provide for the appointment of expert witnesses in cases involving indigent defendants. However, compensation for such witnesses may be

FEDERAL RULES OF EVIDENCE

ARTICLE VII – OPINIONS AND EXPERT TESTIMONY

Rule 704—Opinion on Ultimate Issue

(a) **In General—Not Automatically Objectionable.**

An opinion is not objectionable just because it embraces an ultimate issue.

(b) **Exception.**

In a criminal case, an expert witness must not state an opinion about whether the defendant did or did not have a mental state or condition that constitutes an element of the crime charged or of a defense. Those matters are for the trier of fact alone.

▼

ARTICLE VII—OPINIONS AND EXPERT TESTIMONY

Rule 706—Court Appointed Expert Witnesses

(a) Appointment Process. On a party's motion or on its own, the court may order the parties to show cause why expert witnesses should not be appointed and may ask the parties to submit nominations. The court may appoint any expert that the parties agree on and any of its own choosing. But the court may only appoint someone who consents to act.

(b) Expert's Role. The court must inform the expert of the expert's duties. The court may do so in writing and have a copy filed with the clerk or may do so orally at a conference in which the parties have an opportunity to participate. The expert:

    (1) must advise the parties of any findings the expert makes;

    (2) may be deposed by any party;

    (3) may be called to testify by the court or any party; and

    (4) may be cross-examined by any party, including the party that called the expert.

(c) Compensation. The expert is entitled to a reasonable compensation, as set by the court. The compensation is payable as follows:

    (1) in a criminal case or in a civil case involving just compensation under the Fifth Amendment, from any funds that are provided by law; and

    (2) in any other civil case, by the parties in the proportion and at the time that the court directs—and the compensation is then charged like other costs.

(d) Disclosing the Appointment to the Jury. The court may authorize disclosure to the jury that the court appointed the expert.

(e) Parties' Choice of Their Own Experts. This rule does not limit a party in calling its own experts.

dramatically less than what is necessary to secure the leading experts in a particular field.

Standards Applied to Expert Witness Testimony

Standards for the admissibility of scientific or technical evidence stem from two primary sources: case and statutory law. The courts originally established a legal standard in *Frye v. United States*[3] when they recognized the difficulty in evaluating new technology and science.

> Just when a scientific principle or discovery crosses the line between the experimental and demonstrable stage is difficult to define. Somewhere in this twilight zone the evidential force of the principle must be recognized, and while the courts will go a long way in admitting expert testimony deduced from a well-reasoned scientific principle or discovery, the thing from which the deduction is made must be sufficiently established to have gained general acceptance in the particular field in which it belongs.

The *Frye* **standard**—the concept that the conclusions reached by a given expert were based upon scientifically sound methods which have gained general acceptance in the particular field related to the case—initially was adopted by most courts, but it proved largely unworkable in its burgeoning decade of inception. With technological advancements and scientific breakthroughs occurring at a lightening pace, particularly during the latter part of the twentieth century, a strict application of *Frye* would have prohibited from admission the vast majority of emerging technology and knowledge. Subsequently, many courts modified the standard or completely ignored it. The passage of the Federal Rules of Evidence (FRE) in 1975 attempted to remedy inconsistent application of case law involving witnesses, and it streamlined the introduction of expert testimony. In 1993, the Supreme Court formally recognized the importance of the FRE and criticized the traditional standard

frye **standard** the legal requirement (previous to *Daubert*) that deductions from evidence should be based on methodologies generally accepted by a meaningful segment of the scientific community and specifically by others working in the specific field related to the case. It was replaced by the less restrictive *Daubert* test in 1993.

originally enunciated in *Frye*.[4] Basically, the Court required a preliminary determination that the testimony would assist the trier of fact, through an assessment of the reasoning and methodology behind the technological or scientific evidence and its application to the fact in question. The Court emphasized that the appropriate focus of the inquiry was on the principles and methodology, not on the conclusions, of the scientific evidence. In essence, their ruling emphasized judicial discretion in such matters and cited the following issues for courts to consider:

daubert test a legal precedent requiring trial judges to evaluate the testimony of expert witnesses in order to determine its "relevancy" and "reliability," and thus, admissibility. Daubert is a two-pronged test: (1) relevancy refers to whether or not the expert's evidence "fits" the facts of the case and (2) reliability requires the expert to have derived his or her conclusions from the scientific method.

1. Whether the scientific theory or technique can be and has been tested
2. Whether it has been subject to publication and/or peer review
3. The known or potential rate of error
4. The existence and maintenance of standards controlling the technique's operation
5. General acceptance in the scientific community

The Supreme Court formally recognized that state courts may establish their own measure of inquiry and may use either the *Frye* standard or the **Daubert** test. The Court has since broadened the scope to include all types of expert testimony, not just that which is scientific in nature.

The Daubert "gatekeeping" obligation applies not only to "scientific" testimony, but to all expert testimony. Rule 702 does not distinguish between "scientific" knowledge and "technical" or "other specialized" knowledge, but makes clear that any such knowledge might become the subject of expert testimony. It is the Rule's word "knowledge,"

Jesse Misskelly, Damien Echols, and Jason Baldwin were convicted of the capital murder of three young boys in rural Arkansas. During the trial, several "experts" testified for the prosecution, including an "expert" on satanism. The expert held a mail-order PhD.

not the words (like "scientific") that modify that word that establishes a standard of evidentiary reliability. . . . Daubert referred only to "scientific" knowledge because that was the nature of the expertise there at issue. . . . Neither is the evidentiary rationale underlying Daubert's "gatekeeping" determination limited to "scientific" knowledge. Rules 702 and 703 grant all expert witnesses, not just "scientific" ones, and testimonial latitude unavailable to other witnesses on the assumption that the expert's opinion will have a reliable basis in the knowledge and experience of his discipline. Finally, it would prove difficult, if not impossible, for judges to administer evidentiary rules under which a "gatekeeping" obligation depended upon a distinction between "scientific" knowledge and "technical" or "other specialized" knowledge, since there is no clear line dividing the one from the others and no convincing need to make such distinctions.[5]

As in other areas of criminal law, the identity and background of all expert witnesses must be shared with opposing counsel as provided for in the laws of discovery.

Qualification and Impeachment of Expert Witnesses

Unlike lay witnesses, expert witnesses are qualified outside the presence of the jury to ensure that: (1) their testimony is necessary for clarification, (2) they possess the requisite credentials and qualifications, and (3) the scope of their testimony is within the parameters the court has accepted as scientifically or technologically sound. This process is known as **voir dire**. During this process, the judge will determine whether a particular individual is competent to testify before the jury. As expert testimony is increasingly recognized as necessary in an increasingly complicated world, it is not unusual for opposing counsel to accept the witness without challenge.

Upon qualification, expert witnesses may be called for direct examination. In cases where experts are particularly credentialed or renowned, it is not uncommon for opposing counsel to attempt to stipulate to the witness' expertise or professional reputation so as to limit or prevent a recitation of the witness' accomplishments. However, it is equally advantageous to the calling party for that recitation to occur in the hearing of the jury to increase the weight of their case. Thus, these sorts of stipulations rarely occur.

There are various factors that a jury may consider in evaluating the weight of a particular expert's testimony. While the calling party will use these characteristics to enhance their witness' testimony, opposing counsel will use them to challenge the witness' personal and professional characteristics. These include, but are not limited to:

- Level of education
- Publications or reputation (or lack thereof) in the field of expertise
- Testimony in previous cases
- Level or amount of compensation received by the witness
- Potential bias or conflict of interest

Opposing counsel may also attempt to impeach the expert through challenging the methodological or technical conclusions reached by the expert.

Challenges to the methodology and techniques employed by expert witnesses can result in successful impeachment. Areas open to challenge include:

- Newness of the technology
- Competing technologies
- Opposing theories
- Contradictory findings
- Academic literature

voir dire the preliminary questioning of potential jurors or witnesses to ascertain competency to give or hear evidence. Voir dire is required for jury selection, determinations of competency for children or challenged witnesses, and qualification of expert witnesses.

APPLICATION OF LAW

THE WEST MEMPHIS THREE AND WITNESS IMPEACHMENT

In 1994, three teenagers were arrested and convicted of the mutilation slayings of three 8-year-old boys whose bodies were found in a wooded area of rural Arkansas. During their trial, which was documented on HBO, the prosecution argued that the three teens were involved in the occult and that the gruesome "satanic" slayings were part of their self-styled religious beliefs. Although very little scientific evidence was presented, the prosecution's case heavily relied upon the testimony of "Dr." Dale Griffis. This so-called expert testified that the color of the boys' hair (i.e., black), their preference for the heavy metal music of Metallica, and their fondness for black clothing indicated that they were actively practicing satanic rituals. He also testified that the manner of the killing, the date of the offense, and the draining of the blood had significant occult overtones. Under cross-examination, Griffis was forced to admit that he had never attended a single graduate-level course in

any field and that Columbia Pacific University—from which he received a PhD—was a distance-learning institution. (Ironically, a 1999 court order forced the institution to stop operations in California, in part, because it lacked academic rigor.) Although Griffis lacked the obvious qualifications to testify as an expert, the judge allowed his testimony. It is impossible to determine exactly how much weight the jury gave to Griffis' highly sensationalized testimony, but the defendants were summarily convicted and sentenced to death. Jason Baldwin's death sentence was commuted in 2005 after the Supreme Court ruled that individuals under the age of 18 at the time of the offense could not be subjected to the death penalty. After a successful appeal to the Arkansas Supreme Court, the trio negotiated a plea bargain with prosecutors. On August 19, 2011, they entered Alford pleas and were released. They had served more than 18 years in prison.

CASE LAW

EVIDENTIARY STANDARDS FOR THE ADMISSION OF EXPERT TESTIMONY

In 1923, the federal court first considered the standards that should apply to the admissibility of scientific evidence. Noting that technological developments and scientific discoveries were occurring at a rapid pace, the court cautioned against premature acceptance of emerging methodologies. More specifically, they ruled that the truth of a defendant could not be determined by a mere examination of a rise in their systolic blood pressure. They held that the introduction of scientific or expert testimony must be predicated on a principle or methodology that had gained *general acceptance* in the relevant scientific community. This standard came to be known as the *Frye* standard or the *general acceptance rule*. Unfortunately, this standard did little to delineate a minimum threshold for the admissibility of scientific evidence. The Court remedied this deficit 7 decades later.

- *Daubert v. Merrell Dow Pharmaceuticals, Inc.*, 509 U.S. 579 (1993)—Unlike the criminal case considered in *Frye*, the *Daubert* case involved a lawsuit that had

been filed against Merrell Dow Pharmaceuticals which alleged that Bendectin, a drug marketed by the company, resulted in birth defects of children to pregnant women who had ingested the antinausea medication. In response to the civil filing, company counsel moved for summary judgment—contending that the allegations contained therein were not founded and that the petitioners would be unable to present evidence to the contrary. In support of the motion, the company submitted an affidavit from a world-renowned epidemiologist who reviewed all of the extant literature and studies conducted on the drug. He concluded that maternal use of Bendectin during the first trimester of pregnancy had not been found to be a risk fact for human birth defects. Petitioners, Daubert and Schuller, did not reject this characterization of the published research regarding human births and Bendectin. Rather, they responded with the contradictory testimony of eight experts who were similarly credentialed. These scientists based their conclusions on the results of a number of animal studies evaluating *in vitro* (test tube) and *in vivo* (live) animal studies that found a link between "Bendectin and malformations; pharmacological studies of the chemical structure of Bendectin that purported to show similarities between the structure of the drug and that of other substances known to cause birth defects; and the 'reanalysis' of previously published" epidemiological (human statistical) studies. The District Court did not find this counter evidence admissible under the *Frye* standard. In granting Dow's motion for summary judgment, the court held that the animal-based studies by themselves did not raise a reasonably disputable jury issue regarding causation. The Ninth Circuit affirmed, and the Supreme Court granted *cert* to examine the proper standard for the admission of expert testimony.

Ultimately, the Court ruled that the general acceptance test as established by *Frye* was superseded by the adoption of the FRE.

> . . . There is a specific Rule that speaks to the contested issue . . . Rule 702 . . . Nothing in the text of this Rule establishes "general acceptance" as an absolute prerequisite to admissibility. Nor does respondent present any clear indication that Rule 702, or the Rules as a whole were intended to incorporate a "general acceptance" standard. The drafting history makes no mention of Frye, and a rigid "general acceptance" requirement would be at odds with the "liberal thrust" of the Federal Rules and their "general approach of relaxing the traditional barriers to 'opinion' testimony"

Reminding trial judges of their responsibility to ensure that scientific evidence was both relevant and reliable, the Court specifically noted that their ruling did not suggest that admissibility of purportedly scientific evidence was borderless. Rather, they held that FRE 702 provided trial courts a legal foundation for the introduction of scientific evidence. This standard that provided trial court judges flexibility in determinations of reliability and relevancy became known as the *Daubert test*. Among the factors that trial judges could consider in their determination included: (1) whether the scientific theory or technique can be and has been tested; (2) whether it has been subject to publication and/or peer review; (3) the known or potential rate of error; (4) the existence and maintenance of standards controlling the technique's operation; and (5) general acceptance in the scientific community.

- *Kumho Tire Company v. Carmichael*, 526 U.S. 137 (1999)—In *Kumho*, the Court significantly broadened their findings in *Daubert* to include expert testimony of nonscientists based on technical and other specialized knowledge. In this case, the Court reviewed a case in which a tire blowout was alleged to have been the cause of a fatal accident. The question before the Court was whether the testimony of an expert in tire failure analysis satisfied the requirements articulated in *Daubert*. In holding that the trial court's "gatekeeping" determination could include nonscientific experts, the Court noted that inclusion of such testimony was consistent with the rational employed in *Daubert*, and that there was no convincing need to make such distinctions. In addition, they noted the unworkability of a rule requiring judges to distinguish between "scientific" knowledge and "technical" or "other specialized" knowledge. To wit,

> . . . there is no clear line that divides the one from the others. Disciplines such as engineering rest upon scientific knowledge. Pure scientific theory itself may depend for its development upon observation and properly engineered machinery. And conceptual efforts to distinguish the two are unlikely to produce clear legal lines capable of application in particular cases.

direct examination
interrogation of a
witness by attorneys
by the side that
called him or her to
testify during which
witnesses are asked
open-ended ques-
tions designed to elicit
a narrative response
in which the witness
competently recounts
the events in ques-
tion, such as "Where
were you on the night
of August 25, 2012?"
objections legal
protests made by the
opposing side during
the questioning of a
witness. Rules of crimi-
nal procedure require
objections to be made
contemporaneous
with the alleged viola-
tion of law (i.e., during
the course of the trial,
not at a later date)
and are given for
reasons such as irrele-
vance of material or
improper questioning.
leading questions
questions designed
to guide the respon-
dent's answer or elicit
a certain response—
generally are not
allowed during direct
examination.

▶ Direct Examination of Witnesses

Under the rules of criminal procedure, the government has the responsibility to prove guilt beyond a reasonable doubt. Consequently, it is required to present its case-in-chief before any evidence to the contrary is presented by the defense. As such, witnesses for the prosecution in a criminal case are called to testify first. In most cases, the state's case follows a logical, chronological order in which preliminary witnesses lay the groundwork and timeline for the incident.

Direct examination of a witness occurs when a witness is questioned by the "calling party," or the side that called him or her to testify. During this phase of the trial, witnesses are asked open-ended questions designed to elicit a narrative response in which the witness competently recounts the events in question. This approach is necessary under the American adversarial system to allow for **objections** by opposing counsel—reasons or arguments presented in opposition to a point, approach, or method used by the other side—before the actual testimony. Examples of direct questions often include:

- What did you see or hear between the hours of 1:00 a.m. and 2:00 a.m. on February 14, 2001?

- In response to what you saw or heard, what did you do then?

During direct questioning, interruptions are few as the calling side allows the witness to fully testify as to his or her observations. For the most part, direct examination is not characterized by surprises, since it is familiar practice for both the state and the defense to familiarize themselves with the witnesses and the testimony they intend to present. In fact, both sides often "coach" their witnesses (giving guidance on how to be as effective as possible, for example) before courtroom activities begin. Upon the conclusion of such narration, counsel may then focus on individual areas of the testimony, directing the attention of the fact-finder to specific aspects of same. **Leading questions**—questions designed to guide the respondent's answer or elicit a certain response—generally are not allowed during direct examination. Leading questions are, however, sometimes permissible during the direct examination of children.

FEDERAL RULES OF EVIDENCE

ARTICLE VI—WITNESSES

Rule 611—Mode and Order of Examining Witnesses and Presenting Evidence

(a) **Control by the Court; Purposes.** The court should exercise reasonable control over the mode and order of examining witnesses and presenting evidence so as to:
   (1) make those procedures effective for determining the truth;
   (2) avoid wasting time; and
   (3) protect witnesses from harassment or undue embarrassment.

(b) **Scope of Cross-Examination.** Cross-examination should not go beyond the subject matter of the direct examination and matters affecting the witness's credibility. The court may allow inquiry into additional matters as if on direct examination.

(c) **Leading Questions.** Leading questions should not be used on direct examination except as necessary to develop the witness's testimony. Ordinarily, the court should allow leading questions:
   (1) on cross-examination; and,
   (2) when a party calls a hostile witness, an adverse party, or a witness identified with an adverse party.

► Cross-Examination of Witnesses

Unlike direct examination, in which witnesses are encouraged to use narration as a forum of communication, **cross-examination** is conducted by opposing counsel at the conclusion of direct examination and usually is limited to leading questions. Considered the cornerstone of the adversarial system of American jurisprudence, cross-examination of a witness is designed to ensure the veracity of testifying witnesses, to show the facts in the most favorable light to the cross-examiner's side and, sometimes, to impeach the witness. To wit,

> Cross-examination is the principal means by which the believability of a witness and the truth of his testimony are tested. Subject always to the broad discretion of a trial judge to preclude repetitive and unduly harassing interrogation, the cross-examiner is not only permitted to delve into the witness' story to test the witness' perceptions and memory, but the cross-examiner has traditionally been allowed to impeach, i.e., discredit, the witness. [*Davis v. Alaska*, 415 U.S. 308 (1974)]

In subsequent rulings, the Court has reiterated its earlier estimation in *Davis* and has ruled that the right to cross-examination is firmly rooted in the Bill of Rights:

> It cannot seriously be doubted at this late date that the right of cross-examination is included in the right of an accused in a criminal case to confront the witnesses against him. And probably no one, certainly no one experienced in the trial of lawsuits, would deny the value of cross-examination in exposing falsehood and bringing out the truth in the trial of a criminal case. . . . The fact that this right appears in the Sixth Amendment of our Bill of Rights reflects the belief of the Framers of those liberties and safeguards that confrontation was a fundamental right essential to a fair trial in a criminal prosecution. Moreover, the decisions of this Court and other courts throughout the years have constantly emphasized the necessity for cross-examination as a protection for defendants in criminal cases. This Court . . . referred to the right of confrontation as "[o]ne of the fundamental guarantees of life and liberty," and "a right long deemed so essential for the due protection of life and liberty that it is guarded against legislative and judicial action by provisions in the Constitution of the United States and in the constitutions of most if not of all the States composing the Union." . . . the right of cross-examination is "one of the safeguards essential to a fair trial."[6]

Questions presented during cross-examination are limited to those areas that were originally examined during direct. However, greater latitude is given to attorneys during cross-examination because of the uncertainty of the content of the witness' testimony. Unlike direct examination, cross-examination is exploratory in nature.

> . . . and the rule that the examiner must indicate the purpose of his inquiry does not, in general, apply. It is the essence of a fair trial that reasonable latitude be given the cross-examiner, even though he is unable to state to the court what facts a reasonable cross-examination might develop. Prejudice ensues from a denial of the opportunity to place the witness in his proper setting and put the weight of his testimony and his credibility to a test, without which the jury cannot fairly appraise them.[7]

However, the exploratory nature of cross-examination may also lead to perils unanticipated by the examiner. In some cases, attorneys elicit responses that are explosively damaging to their case. In the 1995 murder trial of O. J. Simpson, for example, the prosecution attempted to place Simpson at the murder scene by introducing gloves that were found there. In a dramatic courtroom exercise, the prosecution forced Simpson to put on the gloves. Unfortunately for the prosecution, it appeared that the gloves were too small, and the defense declared victory.

cross-examination
questioning of a witness by opposing counsel; occurs after direct examination and is designed to ensure the veracity of testifying witnesses, to show the facts in the most favorable light to the cross-examiner's side, and sometimes, to impeach the witness.

The error was so compelling that defense attorney Johnnie Cochran uttered the now infamous phrase "If it doesn't fit, you must acquit." Thus, cross-examination can be extremely risky, a fact that the Supreme Court has recognized but to which it remains unsympathetic.

> . . . counsel often cannot know in advance what pertinent facts may be elicited on cross-examination.
>
> . . . the Confrontation Clause guarantees only 'an opportunity for effective cross-examination, not cross-examination that is effective in whatever way, and to whatever extent, the defense might wish.'[8]

Summarily, cross-examination is often considered the very heart of the adversarial system of criminal justice. It is a fundamental right granted to all defendants and is designed to ensure the veracity of witnesses and to strengthen the case of the cross-examiner. At the same time, it is often the most effective tool for impeachment, a process often necessary to mitigate the testimony of witnesses. As stated in the previous chapter, the FRE provides a range of methods for impeachment purposes, including the introduction of past convictions or uncharged crimes, prior inconsistent statements, and a demonstration of bias or prejudice.

Finally, either side may impeach a witness, as provided for in FRE Rule 607. Impeachment of one's own witness can sometimes become necessary when testimony is inconsistent or unexpected. On the other hand, witness rehabilitation usually is conducted during redirect.

▶ Redirect, Recross, and Rehabilitation of Witnesses

rehabilitation attempt in open court (often during the redirect) by an attorney to reestablish a witness' credibility after the opposing side has brought it into question or has explicitly or implicitly damaged it in the eyes of the jury.

redirect questioning of a witness again after cross-examination; often called the "redirect."

The demonstration of the veracity of a particular witness after impeachment, called **rehabilitation**, is often attempted immediately after cross-examination during a period known as **redirect**. The redirect examination of a witness serves a range of purposes in addition to a bolstering of trustworthiness and a clarification of concerns raised during cross-examination. The redirect is often necessary because the introduction of evidence demonstrating veracity is reserved solely for those instances in which such has been attacked or impeached. The method of rehabilitation is very similar to impeachment, and the redirect examination is limited to those issues raised during cross-examination. So, new evidence independent of issues previously addressed may not be introduced during redirect. For example, if opposing counsel attempted to impeach the witness on grounds of prejudice, then the redirect must specifically address said bias; or, if inconsistent statements were introduced during impeachment, then evidence of prior consistent statements may be introduced. However, none of these practices are exact sciences and neither are failsafe. In the event of prior consistent statements, for example, the jury is still left to determine which inconsistencies are important. Thus, redirect examination may be characterized as the process in which the offering party attempts to qualify potentially damaging testimony made by its witness during cross-examination or in which new evidence addressing issues raised during cross is introduced.

The process of redirect mirrors that found in direct examination. The parameters of the questioning of witnesses and the rules that apply during direct remain intact during redirect. During this time, attorneys are prohibited from being argumentative or overly narrative. Additional witnesses may be called upon to assist in the rehabilitation of a witness who has been impeached or to rebut issues raised during cross-examination.

Recross-examination is the final stage in the examination of witnesses. It immediately follows redirect and is limited to those areas addressed therein. For the most part, questioning is limited during this phase. It is designed to address those issues raised during the redirect examination of the witness, and may not further examine issues addressed during cross-examination.

recross-examination
final stage in the examination of witnesses immediately following redirect and limited to those areas addressed therein.

► Objections by Counsel

Another avenue crucial to the American adversarial system during a criminal trial involves the use of objections. As always, objections are based primarily on procedural law, which delineates rules governing the admissibility of evidence. Substantive objections may be raised for many different reasons and may be categorized into three areas: substance, form, and answer.

- Substantive objections may be made to the substance of a question posed. These objections are raised by opposing counsel and are intended to argue that a solicited answer to an offered question, if given, would be inadmissible. Objections on these grounds typically include, but are not limited to, privileged information, hearsay, incompetence, irrelevance, or immateriality. Usually, these objections are raised before the issuance of an answer. Thus, the jury is not exposed to items determined to be inadmissible.

- Substantive objections may be made to the form of the question. These objections are raised by opposing counsel and are intended to argue that the question is phrased incorrectly or inappropriately. Objections on these grounds typically include, but are not limited to, argumentative, misleading, conclusive, narrative, or leading. Usually, these objections are raised before the issuance of an answer. Thus, the jury is not exposed to items determined to be inadmissible.

- Substantive objections may be made to the answer offered. These objections are raised by opposing counsel and are intended to argue that the answer to the question is not admissible. Objections on these grounds typically include, but are not limited to, the privileged nature of the information or the fact that the answer is based on hearsay or is an unsubstantiated opinion. In addition, these objections may be raised when witnesses exceed the parameter of the original question. This is especially likely during cross-examination when opposing counsel may be looking solely for a yes or no response but the witness initiates a narrative or recitation. Unlike the other types of objections, these are not necessarily given before the issuance of an answer. Thus, fact-finders are exposed to the challenged material after it has been provided. In this case, the remedy generally involves the judge striking the answer from the record and issuing an admonishment to the jury to exclude said material from consideration.

Contemporaneous objection rules are in place in several states. Although they vary, most require that motions to suppress evidence be presented for trial or that objections to the introduction of evidence be made contemporaneous to the admission of same. In other words, objections not made in a timely manner will nullify federal appellate review of the issue in question. To wit,

contemporaneous objection rules
legal requirement that motions to suppress evidence be presented simultaneous to the question asked, the answer given, or the admission of evidence.

> The sweeping language set forth in *Fay v. Noia*, 372 U.S. 391 [433 U.S. 72, 73] which would render a State's contemporaneous-objection rule ineffective to bar review of underlying federal claims in federal habeas corpus proceedings—absent a "knowing waiver" or a "deliberate bypass" of the right to so object—is rejected as according too little respect to the state contemporaneous-objection rule. Such a rule enables the record to be made with respect to a constitutional claim when witnesses' recollections

are freshest; enables the trial judge who observed the demeanor of witnesses to make the factual determinations necessary for properly deciding the federal question; and may, by forcing a trial court decision on the merits of federal constitutional contentions, contribute to the finality of criminal litigation. Conversely, the rule of *Fay v. Noia* may encourage defense lawyers to take their chances on a verdict of not guilty in a state trial court, intending to raise their constitutional claims in a federal habeas corpus court if their initial gamble fails, and detracts from the perception of the trial of a criminal case as a decisive and portentous event.[9]

Thus, it is the absolute responsibility of trial counsel to object contemporaneously with the error in question. It is necessary for such objections to be placed in the trial record to preserve their right to an appeal.

▶ Competency, Relevancy, and Materiality of Witness Testimony

To reiterate important concepts regarding the testimony of witnesses from previous chapters, all evidence must be competent, relevant, and material to the issue at hand. To demonstrate competency, a witness testifying must be an individual with personal knowledge who has the ability to (1) independently recollect and communicate the events in question, (2) competently determine fact from fiction, and (3) appreciate and adhere to the veracity requirements safeguarded by the nature of the U.S. Constitution and the structure of the American judicial system. At the same time, the testimony of the witness must be relevant and material to the issue in question. Relevant evidence is evidence that tends to make a fact in question more or less probable than if the evidence was not introduced. For example, evidence demonstrating that a particular witness has a reputation for lying and deceitful behavior might be relevant in demonstrating his or her general lack of veracity. Finally, all witness testimony must be material to the matter at hand. It should be of such consequence as to have an effect on the trial. In other words, extraneous testimony is not permissible. Thus, eyewitness testimony that included a firsthand account of the defendant fleeing from the scene of the crime would be both relevant and material. It would meet a further test for admissibility if introduced by a witness who was of a mature age and who possessed the ability to narrate. It must be noted, however, that not all competent, relevant, and material evidence is admissible in court.

▶ Corroboration

Examples of inadmissible evidence include evidence that was seized improperly and, as such, may not be introduced against the defendant in court (in most instances). Other examples of inadmissible evidence include confessions or incriminating statements, unless corroborating evidence is available. **Corroborating evidence** refers to supplementary of supporting evidence that tends to strengthen or confirm extant evidence. To avoid the potential for false or coerced confessions, the Court has ruled that:

corroborating evidence refers to supplementary or supporting evidence that tends to strengthen or confirm evidence already supported by other evidence.

> It is a settled principle of the administration of criminal justice in the federal courts that a conviction must rest upon firmer ground than the uncorroborated admission or . . . confession of the accused. We observed in Smith v. United States . . . that the requirement of corroboration is rooted in "a long history of judicial experience with confessions and in the realization that sound law enforcement requires police investigations which extend beyond the words of the accused."[10]

OKLAHOMA STATUTES

TITLE 22—CRIMINAL PROCEDURE

Chapter 10, Section 742—Testimony of Accomplice Requires Corroborating Testimony for Conviction

A conviction cannot be had upon the testimony of an accomplice unless he be corroborated by such other evidence as tends to connect the defendant with the commission of the offense, and the corroboration is not sufficient if it merely show [sic] the commission of the offense or the circumstances thereof.

In addition, many states have created statutes that require the presence of corroborating evidence before the admission of incriminating statements or testimony offered by codefendants.

It must be noted that both parties normally will attempt to provide as much corroborating evidence as possible, even in cases in which it is not required.

▶ CONCLUSIONS

In the American court system, witnesses are required to have firsthand knowledge about the case topic and be able to communicate that experience to the court. There are two types of witnesses: lay and expert. Lay witnesses are individuals who hold direct information regarding the case. Most often, this knowledge is observed or experienced through the senses. Lay witnesses may be used to present relevant facts or to testify as to their opinion regarding general aspects of the case.

Expert witnesses are used when evidence presented in a case is beyond the scope of knowledge of the average juror. These witnesses present testimony based upon their professional experience or academic training as it relates to the facts of the case. Expert witnesses may be impeached through the discrediting of their academic or professional qualifications and of the quality of their research or by demonstrations of their bias.

All witnesses are examined through an established procedure. The justice system is required to prove beyond a reasonable doubt the guilt of the accused. Therefore, the prosecution (the state) most often calls the first witnesses. Direct examination takes place when a witness is questioned by the "calling party" (the side that called them to testify). During this stage, witnesses are asked open-ended questions to provide a general narrative of the case.

Cross-examination, which involves questioning by the opposing side, occurs after direct examination. This segment usually consists of leading questions— questions meant to elicit an expected answer to a specific question. This questioning is meant to create doubt about the veracity of the testimony or to discredit the witness' statements made during direct examination.

Redirect examination provides counsel the opportunity for rehabilitation of their witness. This examination is intended to clarify uncertainties raised through the cross-examination. Recross-examination is the final stage of witness examination. This questioning is limited to topics addressed previously.

Objections may be raised by opposing counsel to oppose the substance of a question, the form of a question, or the answer to a question. Many states apply the contemporaneous objection rule that requires counsel to object formally and immediately to proceedings at the time they take place. Objections given at any other time in the proceedings will not be heard during any appeal.

Finally, corroborating evidence, which is often sought by both the prosecution and the defense, is the supplementary testimony or physical evidence that strengthens or confirms existing evidence. It prevents coerced or inaccurate confessions, and the Supreme Court has ruled that corroboration is necessary before these statements are presented in court proceedings.

Key Terms

Contemporaneous objection rules

Corroborating evidence

Cross-examination

Daubert test

Direct examination

Expert witnesses

Frye standard

Lay witnesses

Leading questions

Objections

Recross-examination

Redirect

Rehabilitation

Voir dire

Discussion Questions

1. In your opinion, when should counsel use expert witness testimony? Discuss the benefits and challenges of using expert witnesses in a trial.
2. In your opinion, did the cross-examination tactic requiring O. J. Simpson to put on the ill-fitting gloves in front of the jury have an effect on the eventual outcome of the trial? Discuss the benefits and challenges of cross-examination.
3. Should religious beliefs or opinions be admitted as witness testimony? Why or why not?

Recommended Resources

Videos

Insight Media. Constitutional law: The right to counsel. Available at: http://www.insight-media.com.

Insight Media. Order in the court. Available at: http://www.insight-media.com.

Insight Media. Eyewitness: Unreliable evidence. Available at: http://www.insight-media.com.

A&E Television. Mistaken identity. *American justice.* This video examines cases that pointed to the unreliability of eyewitness testimony. Available at: http://store.aetv.com.

A&E Television. Lying eyes. *American justice.* This video explores the dangers of relying on eyewitness testimony. Available at: http://store.aetv.com.

Books

Ceci, Stephen J. and Hembrooke, Helene. (1998). *Expert witnesses in child abuse cases: What can and should be said in court.* Washington, D.C.: American Psychological Association Books.

Pope, Kenneth S., Butcher, James N., and Seelen, Joyce. (2006). *The MMPI, MMPI-2, and MMPI-A in court: A practical guide for expert witnesses and attorneys* (3rd Ed.). Washington, D.C.: American Psychological Association Books.

Sales, Bruce D. and Shuman, Daniel W. (2005). *Experts in court: Reconciling law, science, and professional knowledge.* Washington, D.C.: American Psychological Association Books.

Smith, Fred C. and Bace, Rebecca G. (2003). *A guide to forensic testimony: The art and practice of presenting testimony as an expert technical witness.* Boston, MA: Pearson Publishing.

Online Sources

http://www.findlaw.com—Search state and federal case law, statutes, and federal and state constitutions.

http://www.forensic-evidence.com—Forensic Center Web site maintains extensive links to professional organizations involved with expert testimony; provides access to research articles and discussions regarding the differences between lay and expert witnesses.

http://www.aapl.org—Home page of the American Academy of Psychiatry and the Law maintains links to publications and search engines to explore expert testimony.

http://www.aafs.org—Home page of the American Academy of Forensic Sciences maintains links to publications and search engines that explore a plethora of scientific approaches to criminal evidence; allows easy searching of the *Journal of Forensic Science* from 1981 to the present.

http://www.asqde.org—Home page of the American Society of Questioned Document Examiners (ASQDE) with research links, directories, and membership information.

http://www.acfe.com—Home page of the Association of Certified Fraud Examiners provides links and information for training in fraud examination, as well as access to publications and directories.

http://www.tiaft.org//—Home page of The International Association of Forensic Toxicologists (TIAFT) for police officers, medical examiners, pharmacology experts, and even horseracing and sport doping associations to access cutting-edge information, links, database directories, and publications related to toxicology.

Relevant Cases Cited

Alford v. United States, 282 U.S. 687 (1931)

Daubert v. Merrell Dow Pharmaceuticals, 509 U.S. 579 (1993)

Davis v. Alaska, 415 U.S. 308 (1974)

Fay v. Noia, 372 U.S. 391 (1963)

Frye v. United States, 54 App. D.C. 46, 293 F. 1013 (1923)

Kentucky v. Stincer, 482 U.S. 730 (1987)

Kumho Tire Co. v. Carmichael, 526 US 137 (1999)

McKinney v. Anderson, 924 F.2d 1500 (9th Cir. 1991)

Miller v. California, 413 U.S. 15 (1973)

Pointer v. Texas, 380 U.S. 400 (1965)

Wainwright v. Sykes, 433 U.S. 72 (1977)

Wong Sun v. United States, 371 U.S. 471 (1963)

Notes

1. *Miller v. California*, 413 U.S. 15 (1973)
2. *McKinney v. Anderson*, 924 F.2d 1500 (9th Cir. 1991)
3. *Frye v. United States*, 54 App. D.C. 46, 293 F. 1013 (1923)
4. *Daubert v. Merrell Dow Pharmaceuticals*, 509 U.S. 579 (1993)
5. *Kumho Tire Co. v. Carmichael*, 526 US 137 (1999)
6. *Pointer v. Texas*, 380 U.S. 400 (1965)
7. *Alford v. United States* 282 U.S. 687 (1931)
8. *Kentucky v. Stincer*, 482 U.S. 730 (1987)
9. *Wainwright v. Sykes*, 433 U.S. 72 (1977)
10. *Wong Sun v. United States*, 371 U.S. 471 (1963)

THE DECLARATION OF INDEPENDENCE.

10 Hearsay

LEARNING OBJECTIVES

The learner will:

1 *Define hearsay*

2 *Examine the history of hearsay*

3 *Distinguish between assertion-centered and declarant-centered statements*

4 *Identify the hearsay rules regarding admissions by a party-opponent*

5 *Discuss admissions from unavailable witnesses and immaterial witnesses*

6 *Examine the theory and exceptions to the hearsay rule*

Testimonial evidence is an essential part of due process as practiced in American courts. As stated previously, all evidence admitted into a criminal trial must be introduced by a competent witness. Thus, the rules and procedures for the admission of witness testimony are numerous and often lengthy. For the most part, courtroom procedures are designed to ensure the veracity of the testimony by evaluating not only the truthfulness of the witness, but also the witness' perception and recollection of the event in question. As such, witnesses are required to take an oath or affirmation to confirm the truthfulness of their statements and to bind them to penalties for knowingly providing falsehoods. Perhaps most importantly, witnesses are required to be available for cross-examination as guaranteed by the confrontation clause of the Sixth Amendment. The value of witnesses possessing firsthand information about the facts of the case is invaluable to the process. However, secondhand information that is often unreliable, or hearsay, is another thing altogether.

testimonial evidence a written or oral assertion offered as proof of truth in court.

Until the 1600s, English courts allowed the introduction of unverified secondhand evidence as a legitimate part of the proceedings. However, the trial of Sir Walter Raleigh helped English courts recognize once and for all how such evidence could create perilous situations for the accused. The ratification of the Bill of Rights gave American courts a clear definition of the term and ensured that hearsay presented in a court of law would be limited in scope and value.

The precursor to the American hearsay rule originated in the 1600s immediately following the trial of Sir Walter Raleigh. Before this time, English courts traditionally admitted evidence deriving from unreliable, even anonymous, sources. Raleigh's trial is often quoted as an example of the sort of injustice from which the colonials wanted to escape, which they did, in part, through the establishment of a New World. To remedy this, English courts defined *hearsay* as any statement to which neither the Crown nor the defendant was privy. In a general sense, this meant that any statement made outside the court could not be introduced by a third party. This common-law definition continued in the United States until the ratification of the Bill of Rights.

IN SEARCH OF HISTORY: HEARSAY AND SIR WALTER RALEIGH

In 1603, Sir Walter Raleigh was charged with conspiring with Lord Cobham to kill King James I, in an attempt to place Lady Arabella Stuart on the throne of England. Cobham confessed to the plot while being interrogated at the Tower of London. Although he later recanted, Cobham's confession was introduced into evidence at Raleigh's trial for treason. He petitioned the Crown to produce him so that his recantation could be heard.

> Cobham is absolutely in the King's mercy; to excuse me cannot avail him; by accusing me he may hope for favor . . . the proof of the Common Law is by witness and jury . . . let Cobham be here, let him speak it. Call my accuser before my face . . . But it is strange to see how you press me still with my Lord Cobham, and yet will not produce him . . . he is in the house hard by, and may soon be brought hither; let him be produced, and if he

will yet accuse me or avow this confession of his, it shall convict me and ease you of further proof.

The Crown refused his request, and Raleigh was never given the opportunity to cross-examine his primary accuser. The prosecutor then brought forth a boat pilot who testified that a random Portuguese gentleman had told him that ". . . your king [James] shall never be crowned for Don Cobham and Don Raleigh will cut his throat before he come to be crowned." Raleigh vehemently protested the introduction of this "witness"—claiming that it was nothing short of a rumor from a person unknown to him. Unfortunately, the boat pilot's testimony remained in play. Raleigh was never given the opportunity to cross-examine his accuser, and he was found guilty of treason and sentenced to death. He was then released to lead a second expedition to search for El Dorado, the lost city of gold. His quest proved a failure. Upon his return to England, Raleigh was summarily beheaded.

Historically, statements could be introduced against a defendant even when the defendant did not have the opportunity to cross-examine the declarant. With the ratification of the Bill of Rights, however, hearsay rules in the United States helped prevent such treatment—particularly the kind received by Sir Walter Raleigh, who had been convicted largely on non-sworn, non-cross-examined statements made against him.

▶ Defining Hearsay

hearsay statement, other than one made by the declarant while testifying at the trial or hearing, offered in evidence to prove the truth of the matter asserted.

declarant person making a statement in question.

In American courts, **hearsay** is defined as any "statement, other than one made by the declarant while testifying at the trial or hearing, offered in evidence to prove the truth of the matter asserted" (FRE Rule 801). A **declarant** is the person making the statement in question. The American hearsay rule, generally speaking, prohibits the introduction of any hearsay statement, primarily because of the prohibitions in the Sixth Amendment (and elsewhere). However, the Supreme Court has repeatedly argued that while the confrontation clause of the Sixth Amendment and the hearsay rule are designed to safeguard the rights of American citizens, they are not necessarily interdependent. To wit,

> While it may readily be conceded that hearsay rules and the Confrontation Clause are generally designed to protect similar values, it is quite a different thing to suggest that the overlap is complete and that the Confrontation Clause is nothing more or less than a codification of the rules of hearsay and their exceptions as they existed historically at common law. Our decisions have never established [400 U.S. 74, 82] such a congruence; indeed, we have more than once found a violation of confrontation values even though the statements in issue were admitted under an arguably recognized hearsay exception. The converse is equally true: merely because evidence is admitted in violation of a long-established hearsay rule does not lead to the automatic conclusion that confrontation rights have been denied.[1]

ARTICLE VIII—HEARSAY

Rule 801. Definitions That Apply to This Article; Exclusions from Hearsay

(a) Statement. "Statement" means a person's oral assertion, written assertion, or nonverbal conduct, if the person intended it as an assertion.

(b) Declarant. "Declarant" means the person who made the statement.

(c) Hearsay. "Hearsay" means a statement that:

(1) the declarant does not make while testifying at the current trial or hearing; and

(2) a party offers in evidence to prove the truth of the matter asserted in the statement.

(d) Statements That Are Not Hearsay. A statement that meets the following conditions is not hearsay:

(1) *A Declarant-Witness's Prior Statement.* The declarant testifies and is subject to cross-examination about a prior statement, and the statement:

(A) is inconsistent with the declarant's testimony and was given under penalty of perjury at a trial, hearing, or other proceeding or in a deposition;

(B) is consistent with the declarant's testimony and is offered to rebut an express or implied charge that the declarant recently fabricated it or acted from a recent improper influence or motive in so testifying; or

(C) identifies a person as someone the declarant perceived earlier.

(2) *An Opposing Party's Statement.* The statement is offered against an opposing party and:

(A) was made by the party in an individual or representative capacity;

(B) is one the party manifested that it adopted or believed to be true;

(C) was made by a person whom the party authorized to make a statement on the subject;

(D) was made by the party's agent or employee on a matter within the scope of that relationship and while it existed; or

(E) was made by the party's co-conspirator during and in furtherance of the conspiracy.

The statement must be considered but does not by itself establish the declarant's authority under (C); the existence or scope of the relationship under (D); or the existence of the conspiracy or participation in it under (E).

The definition of hearsay, as provided by the Federal Rules of Evidence, is straightforward, but not all out-of-court statements fall into the category of hearsay. For example, verbal and nonverbal statements not intended to be assertive are not considered hearsay and, thus, are admissible in court. Assertive statements are intended to prove that the content of the communication is true and are uttered in an attempt to communicate such an assertion. Two broad categories of hearsay exist: assertion-centered hearsay and declarant-centered hearsay.

Assertion-Centered Statements

Per the FRE, hearsay statements are any oral, written, or nonverbal conduct intended to make an assertion. Statements that must be offered to prove the truth of an assertion are known as **assertion-centered statements**. Examples of such include:

- *Verbal assertions* occur when, for example, a witness testifies that her mother told her that she shot her father seven times in the face while he was sleeping because he had abused her repeatedly. This statement may be admissible under one of the exceptions to the hearsay rule, but it is, by definition, hearsay

assertion-centered statements those statements in which the declarant (person making the statement) intends to communicate his/her thoughts or beliefs.

ARTICLE VIII—HEARSAY

Rule 806—Attacking and Supporting Credibility of Declarant

When a hearsay statement, or a statement defined in FRE Rule 801(d)(2)(C), (D), or (E), has been admitted in evidence, the credibility of the declarant may be attacked, and if attacked may be supported, by any evidence which would be admissible for those purposes if declarant had testified as a witness. Evidence of a statement or conduct by the declarant at any time, inconsistent with the declarant's hearsay statement, is not subject to any requirement that the declarant may have been afforded an opportunity to deny or explain. If the party against whom a hearsay statement has been admitted calls the declarant as a witness, the party is entitled to examine the declarant on the statement as if under cross-examination.

because the witness' mother intended to communicate her intention to shoot her husband because of the abuse she had suffered.

- *Nonverbal assertions* occur when, for example, the witness testifies that when she asked where her father was, the mother pointed to a closet in which the body of her murdered father lay.

Declarant-Centered Statements

declarant-centered statements hearsay statements made by lay or expert witnesses that often involve an evaluation as to the declarant's credibility.

Declarant-centered statements are hearsay statements made by either lay or expert witnesses that often involve an evaluation as to the declarant's credibility.

▶ Defining Nonhearsay Statements

In addition to the different categories of hearsay, it is important to remember that the hearsay rule prohibits only those statements that are "offered in evidence to prove the truth of the matter asserted" (FRE Rule 801). Thus, statements may be introduced for a variety of purposes other than to prove the truth of the matter. Generally speaking, these statements may be offered to demonstrate the state of mind, knowledge of facts, or the sanity of the declarant. In addition, statements may be introduced in an attempt to demonstrate the impact on the witness to the statement.

Prior Statements

prior statements hearsay statements that were made by the declarant prior to the proceeding at hand.

According to FRE Rule 801 (d)(1), **prior statements** by witnesses are not considered hearsay if the declarant testifies at the trial or hearing and is subject to cross-examination regarding the statement. This is true *if* one of the following qualifications is present:

- The statement is inconsistent with the declarant's testimony and was given under oath at a trial, hearing, or deposition in which perjured testimony could be subjected to punishment.

   Example: Witness John Doe testifies that he did not witness the crime because he was in another state at the time. In an earlier sworn statement, however, he testified that he saw the defendant engage in the rape and murder of a young woman for which the defendant is now charged. Because the prior statement is inconsistent with the current testimony, it is not considered hearsay and may be introduced.

- The statement is consistent with the testimony and is offered in rebuttal to a charge that the recent testimony was recently fabricated or is improperly influenced or motivated.

> Example: Witness John Doe testified that he did not witness the crime because he was in another state at the time. The prosecution argues that this is a fabrication because he is afraid of repercussions for testifying against the defendant. However, his testimony is consistent with an earlier deposition. Thus, it is not considered hearsay and may be introduced.

Admissions by Party-Opponent

According to FRE 801 (d)(2), out-of-court statements made by a party to the case [in criminal cases, the defendant(s)] are not considered hearsay because they are actually made by the defendants themselves. Such statements include verbal and nonverbal acts and normally are offered as circumstantial evidence to infer guilt. As a general rule, they fall into three categories: adoptive admissions, admissions by silence, and admissions by conduct. Examples of admissions by conduct include:

- Flight to avoid prosecution
- Failure to call witnesses or produce evidence
- Refusal to submit to physical examinations
- Actions taken to obstruct justice
- Plea negotiations
- Payment of medical expenses (Strong, 1999)

Generally speaking, an **admission by a party-opponent** is a statement offered against another party that meets one of the following criteria:

1. The party against whom the statement is being offered is also the declarant of that statement either personally or in a representative capacity.
2. The party against whom the statement is being offered manifested an adoption or belief in the statement's truth.
3. The party against whom the statement is being offered authorized the declarant to make the statement.
4. The statement is made by an agent of the party against whom it is being offered and concerns a matter within the scope of the employment and is made during the course of that employment.
5. The declarant was a co-conspirator of the party against whom the statement is being offered and the statement is in furtherance of their conspiracy.

admissions by party-opponent an exception to the hearsay rule that permits the introduction of a statement offered against another party if that person was the declarant; or manifested an adoption or belief in that statement; or authorized the statement; or is within the scope or made during the course of employment; or the declarant was a co-conspirator.

adoptive admission a statement of which the party has manifested an adoption or belief in its truth.

Adoptive Admissions

According to FRE 801(2)(B), an **adoptive admission** is a statement "of which the party has manifested an adoption or belief in its truth." To be admissible, the proponent of said statement must demonstrate that an intention to adopt the statement was clearly present. Simply referencing the statement is not sufficient to satisfy this requirement. Rather, it must be demonstrated that the party believed the statement to be true and intended to adopt it with the perception of truthfulness.[2]

Admissions by Silence

It is generally assumed that when confronted by statements that include elements of untruthfulness, listening parties to the communication would deny or otherwise challenge such assertions. Failure to do so may infer an admission by silence by the listening party and may constitute a nonverbal assertion exempted from the hearsay rule. Although authors have noted that such conclusions may be tenuous at best (e.g., Strong, 1999), the Supreme Court has not issued a moratorium on such usage. Other courts, however, have established some guidelines for evaluating such statements. Usually, the following requirements are considered:

- The person to whom the admission by silence is inferred must have heard *and* understood the statement in question, including a demonstration that the listening party had knowledge of the subject matter
- The absence of physical or emotional impediments
- The absence of existing relationships that may lessen the likelihood of confrontation (such as a child and parent, husband and wife, or student and teacher)
- The statement itself must be of such a nature that if untrue would demand a denial (Strong, 1999)

Circumstantial Admissions

circumstantial admission of guilt *statement or conduct of a criminal defendant suggestive of guilt.*

Under the system of criminal law in the United States, the burden of proof as to guilt or innocence rests firmly with the state. As such, the defense is not required to actively present a defense when it perceives that the prosecutor's burden has not been met. However, failure to do so, such as call witnesses or submit to a physical examination, is often viewed by jurors as a **circumstantial admission of guilt**. Thus, most defendants in criminal trials will present evidence and call witnesses to counter assertions by the state. The Supreme Court has recognized such inferences:

> If a party has it peculiarly within his power to produce witnesses whose testimony would elucidate the transaction, the fact that he does not do it creates the presumption that the testimony, if produced would be unfavorable.[3]

Although comment on such may result in a mistrial, the inference itself is exempted from the hearsay rule because it may be construed as an admission by conduct. Similarly, a defendant's refusal to submit to a physical examination (such as a blood or DNA test) may be used to infer guilt.

Actions Taken to Obstruct Justice

Defendants and other parties to the case can obstruct justice in numerous ways, including but not limited to, threatening witnesses, fleeing the scene, and concealing evidence. The introduction of testimony regarding such actions, although circumstantial, is admissible under the hearsay rule. In the Rae Carruth case, for example, testimony that Carruth was hiding in the trunk of car in another state was permitted. Such nonverbal acts are admissible under the hearsay rule because they are considered admissions by a party to the case (in this case, the defendant). However, not all acts by defendants are admissible; only those that demonstrate bad faith may be introduced.

Plea Negotiations

As noted in Chapter 2, FRE Rule 410 precludes the introduction of withdrawn guilty pleas, nolo contendere pleas, or statements made during unsuccessful plea negotiations. However, such may be introduced in perjury proceedings and in cases in which another statement issued during the plea bargaining process was introduced. Thus, in limited situations, some elements of plea negotiations are admissible under the hearsay rule because they are considered verbal admissions by a party to the case (the defendant, for example).

SECTION 1360

(a) In a criminal prosecution where the victim is a minor, a statement made by the victim when under the age of 12 describing any act of child abuse or neglect performed with or on the child by another, or describing any attempted act of child abuse or neglect with or on the child by another, is not made inadmissible by the hearsay rule if all of the following apply:

　(1) The statement is not otherwise admissible by statute or court rule.

　(2) The court finds, in a hearing conducted outside the presence of the jury, that the time, content, and circumstances of the statement provide sufficient indicia of reliability.

　(3) The child either:

　　(A) Testifies at the proceedings.

　　(B) Is unavailable as a witness, in which case the statement may be admitted only if there is evidence of the child abuse or neglect that corroborates the statement made by the child.

(b) A statement may not be admitted under this section unless the proponent of the statement makes known to the adverse party the intention to offer the statement and the particulars of the statement sufficiently in advance of the proceedings in order to provide the adverse party with a fair opportunity to prepare to meet the statement.

Payment of Medical Expenses

In some cases, evidence that the defendant or his or her representative paid the medical expenses of a victim may be introduced under the hearsay rule. Although circumstantial, such testimony infers that the defendant acknowledged some responsibility for the harm suffered and this may be construed as an admission by the accused.

Co-Conspirator Rule

It must be noted that FRE Rule 801 (d)(2)(E) specifically addresses statements made by co-conspirators during the course and in furtherance of the criminal conspiracy. This provision, known as the **co-conspirator rule**, allows for the introduction of evidence of a co-conspirator's out-of-court statements. This provision has been evaluated in several cases before the Court. Although some authors have reported it as an exception to the hearsay rule, the FRE language specifically categorizes statements made by co-conspirators as nonhearsay statements. Thus, such statements are not admissible as an exception but as an exemption from the hearsay rule. For the most part, the primary distinction lies in the perceived veracity of the statement in question. For example, co-conspirator statements are admissible because they have prima facie indicia of reliability. In addition, the Court has reasoned that the statements of co-conspirators are indistinguishable, because the conspiracy itself makes them one.[4] To wit,

co-conspirator rule a legal ruling establishing that the confession of a co-conspirator that identifies or otherwise implicates the defendant can only be used when the individual who confesses takes the witness stand and is subject to cross-examination.

> When men enter into an agreement for an unlawful end, they become ad hoc agents for one another, and have made a "partnership in crime." What one does pursuant to their common purpose, all do, and, as declarations may be such acts, they are competent against all. (*Van Riper v. United States*, 13 F.2d 961, 967)

▶ Exceptions to the Hearsay Rule

Generally speaking, the hearsay rule precluded the admissibility of any statements determined to be hearsay. Such statements included any that were uttered by persons other than the declarant testifying at the trial or hearing and that were offered into evidence to prove the truth of the matter asserted. This definition encompasses various types and methods of communication, including oral, written, recorded, and nonverbal admissions, as well as body language—which were intended to be truthful and assertive. Exclusion of such from judicial proceedings was primarily rooted in the notion that unsworn statements were unreliable. In the United States, such perception was incorporated into the Sixth Amendment in which defendants were granted the right to confront their accuser.

Originally, the exclusion of all statements determined to be hearsay had a chilling effect on the judicial statement (imagine a legal system in which only firsthand accounts were admissible). Thus, American jurists soon recognized the need to introduce exceptions to the hearsay rule. Primarily, such exceptions were based upon the notion that certain statements were reliable on their face and upon a gradual recognition that a dismissal of all nonsworn statements did not serve the interest of justice. For example, society was prepared to accept that while the swearing of an oath necessarily increased the veracity of witnesses, other nonsworn statements might be equally reliable. Statements issued by those declarants preparing to meet their god or those that were unprovoked and made during the excitement of an incident were held to be reliable. Over time, this recognition gradually resulted in various codified exceptions to the hearsay rule. Irrespective of date of inception, these exceptions are based on the notion that certain

Nearly 20 years after Lita Sullivan was gunned down in the doorway of her Buckhead home, her millionaire husband was found guilty of murder-for-hire. Sullivan, a wealthy businessman, had fled the country and was apprehended in Thailand. Due to the length of time between the murder and the trial, many of the witnesses were legally "unavailable", and heresay evidence was introduced.

situations and characteristics create an *indicia of reliability* (i.e., sufficient reliability and trustworthiness). Thus, in certain situations they may be introduced without the benefit of cross-examination, which is a requirement of the confrontation clause of the Sixth Amendment.

> The decisions of this Court make it clear that the mission of the Confrontation Clause is to advance a practical concern for the accuracy of the truth-determining process in criminal trials by assuring that "the trier of fact [has] a satisfactory basis for evaluating the truth of the prior statement."
>
> These circumstances . . . are indicia of reliability which have been widely viewed as determinative of whether a statement may be placed before the jury though there is no confrontation of the declarant.[5]

Witness Unavailability

In many cases, the Court has ruled that some statements are admissible as exceptions to the hearsay rule because the witness is unavailable. The confrontation clause of the Sixth Amendment requires the presence of adverse witnesses so that they may be cross-examined by the accused, and American courts have recognized that such processes are necessary to ensure the veracity of the testimony as presented. However, the Supreme Court and the FRE have acknowledged that statements uttered by a declarant who is currently unavailable may be introduced in certain situations *if* said statements possess an indicia of reliability. Such statements include:

- Former testimony
- Dying declarations
- Declarations against interest
- Statements of personal or family history

Although the parameters of these federally recognized exceptions vary in application across the states, each requires the absence or "unavailability" of the declarant. Under FRE Rule 804, a declarant is not considered "unavailable" for purposes of an exception to the hearsay rule if an exemption, refusal, inability, absence, or claim of lack of memory is attributable to the bad act of the proponent of said statement for the purpose of preventing the witness from attending or testifying. Thus, if a witness to a mob murder is kidnapped by an organized crime family to prevent the witness' testimony at a current trial, his or her previous sworn testimony would be admissible.

Under FRE 804(a), a declarant is considered unavailable when he or she:

1. is exempted by ruling of the court on the ground of privilege from testifying concerning the subject matter of the declarant's statement; or
2. persists in refusing to testify concerning the subject matter of the declarant's statement despite an order of the court to do so; or
3. testifies to a lack of memory of the subject matter of the declarant's statement; or
4. is unable to be present or to testify at the hearing because of death or then existing physical or mental illness or infirmity; or
5. is absent from the hearing and the proponent of a statement has been unable to procure the declarant's attendance (or in the case of a hearsay exception under subdivision (b)(2), (3), or (4), the declarant's attendance or testimony) by process or other reasonable means.

As discussed previously, the confrontation clause of the Sixth Amendment requires a thorough consideration of the status of the witness before a pronouncement of unavailability. It is important to note that the term "unavailability" refers exclusively to the witness' testimony, *not* to his or her physical presence. Some situations evoke a declaration of unavailability because of the absence; others do not. Irrespective of physical presence, however, the calling party must fully demonstrate the elements of each situation just listed. For a witness to be declared "unavailable" because of testimonial privilege, for example, he or she must first present a legal justification for such unavailability.

Insufficient Memory

In cases in which a witness claims to have insufficient memory to testify to particular facts, a demonstration of such is needed. In such cases, opposing counsel may cross-examine the witness to challenge the claims. Upon determination of falsehood, the court may subject the witness to contempt proceedings.

Absence

A simple declaration by counsel that a particular witness is absent may not satisfy the legal requirement for the introduction of a hearsay statement resulting from unavailability unless proof is demonstrated that legal processes and other reasonable measures have been taken to procure his or her attendance. Although state statutes vary as to the parameters of such measures, most include the issuance of a subpoena or a writ of habeas corpus. In addition, most states require a demonstration of other reasonable means. In *Barber v. Page*,[6] for example, the Court ruled that:

> While there is a traditional exception to the confrontation requirement where a witness is unavailable and has given testimony at previous judicial proceedings against the same defendant which was subject to cross-examination by that defendant, the witness is not "unavailable" for the purposes of that exception unless the prosecutorial authorities have made a good-faith effort to obtain his presence at trial.

Former Testimony

Under FRE 804 (b)(1), the former testimony of a witness is admissible when a demonstration of unavailability is successful. This may include testimony that was offered at a hearing (or in a deposition) or testimony offered by the unavailable witness that was taken during the same, or even different, proceeding if the party against whom the testimony is currently offered was able to explore the testimony through direct examination, cross-examination, or redirect. This exception hinges primarily on the belief that a high degree of reliability exists when sworn (by oath or affirmation) testimony is given and cross-examination is conducted.

 CLARIFICATION OF CONCEPTS

DYING DECLARATIONS

A dying declaration is a statement regarding the cause or circumstance of the declarant's impending death made at a time when the declarant believed that death was imminent. While some states only allow the statement in cases where the death was realized, other states and the FRE do not have this requirement. However, there is concurrence across jurisdictions regarding the perception of imminent death. The following statements would not be admissible in either federal or state courts under the dying declaration exception to the hearsay rule:

- Battered wife statements, such as "He tried to beat me to death, I am going to divorce that bastard when I get out of the hospital."

- Dying criminal statements, such as "I want to confess to that bank robbery I did last year and get it off my chest before this cancer kills me."

Former testimony that does not meet the unavailability requirement may also be admitted when such introduction is intended for nonhearsay purposes. For example, former testimony given by a currently available witness is admissible when its purpose is to impeach by demonstrating inconsistency in statements, seeking to refresh recollection, or showing that the statement constitutes an act of perjury.

Dying Declarations

Under FRE 804(b)(2), a **dying declaration** is a statement made by a declarant regarding the cause or circumstances of his or her impending death and is admissible only when the declarant believed that death was imminent. Traditionally, such exceptions could be used only in homicide cases. However, the rule has now been expanded to include both nonhomicide criminal cases and civil cases. In addition, traditional statutes required the death of the declarant. Although the FRE discarded this common-law requirement, it is still found in some state statutes. Other state statutes are somewhat ambiguous regarding it. For example, the California Code of Evidence 1242 provides:

> Evidence of a statement made by a dying person respecting the cause and circumstances of his death is not made inadmissible by the hearsay rule if the statement was made upon his personal knowledge and under a sense of immediately impending death.

As with the other exceptions to the hearsay rule, the dying declaration exception is grounded in the theory that some statements are inherently trustworthy. Thus, the perception remains that individuals who believe that their death is imminent are predisposed to making truthful statements. It is important to note, however, that all state and federal courts require a demonstration that the declarant believed himself or herself to be dying and that all hope is lost. Such demonstration can include statements from doctors or family members.

Dying declarations do not have to be spontaneous and may be solicited by private persons or law enforcement authorities. In addition, the introduction of dying declarations is not limited to the prosecution. In some cases, dying declarations may even tend to be exculpatory in nature, although they are always limited to the circumstances involving the impending death. Evidence of past crimes may not be introduced under this exception. Thus, the deathbed confession of a career criminal cannot be introduced against his former partners in crime unless the circumstances of his current grievous injuries are a result of such association. An example of the defense introducing a dying declaration might be a woman saying "I don't know who did this. I've never seen him before in my life." Such a statement may exonerate the woman's husband were he on trial for her murder. In this example, opposing counsel might introduce testimony to mitigate the impact and limit the credibility of such a dying declaration—for example, testimony about the witness being under the influence of heavy pain medication or in extreme pain.

The introduction of dying declarations was formally recognized in the 1700s in England, where it was rationalized that such statements were inherently truthful. As Chief Baron Eyre opined in *Rex v. Woodcock*[7]:

> Now the general principle on which this species of evidence is admitted is, that they are declarations made in extremity, when the party is at the point of death, and when every hope of this world is gone: when every motive to falsehood is silenced, and the mind is induced by the most powerful considerations to speak the truth; a situation so solemn, and so awful, is considered by the law as creating an obligation equal to that which is imposed by a positive oath administered in a Court.

dying declaration
a statement made by a dying person (or a person who believes death is imminent) about the cause or circumstances of the impending death, such as when a dying woman tells police who shot her. Admissibility of such statements is contingent upon the laws of the corresponding jurisdiction.

RAE CARRUTH AND DYING DECLARATIONS

On November 16, 1999, Cherica Adams, the pregnant girl-friend of Rae Carruth, was shot four times in her car while following Carruth home from a movie. She found the strength to call 911 on her cell phone and told the operator that Rae Carruth, a wide receiver for the Carolina Panthers, had stopped in front of her, blocking her in, while someone pulled alongside her car and shot her. She also indicated that Carruth was the father of her unborn child. After being taken to the hospital and rushed into surgery, doctors successfully saved her unborn son, Chancellor Lee, but unfortunately, were unable to save the child's mother. Cherica Adams died almost a month after sustaining her injuries. While in the hospital, though, Ms. Adams wrote notes in which she recounted the events that led to the shooting.

During Carruth's subsequent murder trial, prosecutors argued that Carruth conspired to kill Adams because he did not want to pay child support. To support this theory, the state introduced a variety of testimonial evidence, including testimony from the co-conspirators and the dispatcher, the 911 tape, and Ms. Adams' notes written in the hospital. Although Cherica's death prevented her appearance at trial, both the 911 tape and the notes written by her were admitted into court under the dying declaration exception to the hearsay rule.

None of the statements supported Carruth's claim that the shooter, Van Brett Watkins, shot Cherica in retaliation for Carruth's refusal to finance a drug deal. Consequently, Rae Carruth was found guilty and sentenced to 18 to 24 years in prison. Chancellor Lee, the couple's son, continues to suffer from a range of ailments—many of which were caused by the trauma associated with his birth.

Statement Against Interest

Under FRE 804(b)(3), statements made against the interest of the declarant are admissible when the declarant is currently unavailable to testify. To wit,

> A statement which was at the time of its making so far contrary to the declarant's pecuniary or proprietary interest, or so far tended to subject the declarant to civil or criminal liability, or to render invalid a claim by the declarant against another, that a reasonable person in the declarant's position would not have made the statement unless believing it to be true. A statement tending to expose the declarant to criminal liability and offered to exculpate the accused is not admissible unless corroborating circumstances clearly indicate the trustworthiness of the statement.

declarations against interest statements that are against the pecuniary or proprietary interest of the declarant.

There are two general requirements for the admissibility of statements under the **declarations against interest** exception. The first requires the statement issued to be against the pecuniary or proprietary interest of the declarant. This is based largely on the notion that individuals would not voluntarily subject themselves to negative consequences. Thus, such statements are considered to have an indicia of reliability. Because such truthfulness relies upon the danger of harm to the individual, whether pecuniary or proprietary, it must be contemporaneous with the actual statement. For example, a statement by declarant that he does not own a piece of land whose ownership is currently under arbitration is indicative of truthfulness because it is counter to his interest. This requirement traditionally included only situations involving financial transactions and statements issued by parties to the case. But it has been expanded over time to include criminal acts and statements made by individuals who are not parties to the matter. The second requirement, of course, is that the declarant is currently unavailable.

Statements of Personal or Family History

Under FRE 804(b)(A), statements of personal or family history are admissible when the declarant is inadmissible. To wit,

> A statement concerning the declarant's own birth, adoption, marriage, divorce, legitimacy, relationship by blood, adoption, or marriage, ancestry, or other similar fact of personal or family history, even though declarant had no means of acquiring personal

knowledge of the matter stated; or (B) a statement concerning the foregoing matters, and death also, of another person, if the declarant was related to the other by blood, adoption, or marriage or was so intimately associated with the other's family as to be likely to have accurate information concerning the matter declared.

Other Exceptions

In addition to the exceptions found in FRE 804, other exceptions have emerged through case law and through the introduction of the catchall hearsay rule found under FRE 807. This rule specifically permits the introduction of hearsay testimony in cases that reach the level of inherent trustworthiness discussed in Rules 803 and 804 *if* the statement is:

- Offered as evidence of material fact

- More probative to the matter than any other evidence that may be reasonably procured

- Able to serve the general interest of justice and the purpose of the rules by such admission

spousal testimonial privilege legal protection against compulsory disclosure of communications occurring during a legally binding marital relationship, irrespective of the state of the marital union. The privilege provides the right of one spouse to refuse to testify against the other and the right to automatically render the witness unavailable.

 CASE LAW

HEARSAY AND TESTIMONIAL STATEMENTS: *CRAWFORD V. WASHINGTON*, 541 U.S. 36 (2004)

The Sixth Amendment's confrontation clause is often considered to be the cornerstone of criminal jurisprudence and due process. As such, the hearsay rule generally requires that the declarant be presented for cross-examination. Early case law indicates a strong reluctance on the part of the Court to recognize any category of out-of-court statements admissible under the Sixth Amendment.

> . . . the principal evil at which the Confrontation Clause was directed was the civil-law mode of criminal procedure, and particularly its use of ex parte examinations as evidence against the accused. It was these practices that the Crown deployed in notorious treason cases like Raleigh's . . . Accordingly, we once again reject the view that the Confrontation Clause applies of its own force only to in-court testimony, and that its application to out-of-court statements introduced at trial depends upon "the law of Evidence for the time being." . . . Leaving the regulation of out-of-court statements to the law of evidence would render the Confrontation Clause powerless to prevent even the most flagrant inquisitorial practices.

Decisions in the twentieth century broadly expanded exceptions to the exclusionary rule—recognizing various exceptions to the rule where a witness is unavailable *if* the statement has adequate indicia of reliability. As a result, the Court generally permitted statements that either fell within a "firmly rooted hearsay exception" or bore "particularized guarantees of trustworthiness." However, two recent cases signal that the

Court is returning to a narrower interpretation of the confrontation clause.

In *Crawford v. Washington*, [541 U.S. 36 (2004)], the Court considered whether a tape-recorded statement to police was admissible in court if the declarant was unavailable for cross-examination at the current proceeding. In this case, Michael Crawford had been found guilty of assault and attempted murder of Kenneth Lee. Crawford had stabbed Lee during an altercation when he confronted him about attempting to sexually assault his wife. In the aftermath, police interrogated Sylvia Crawford, the defendant's wife, on tape as she had witnessed the entire event. Over defense objections, prosecuting attorneys presented the tape as evidence via the hearsay exception for statements against penal interest. The tape strongly suggested that the stabbing was not in self-defense, but was, in fact, deliberate and planned.

On appeal, Crawford argued that the introduction of the statement was a violation of the confrontation clause as his wife was unavailable for cross-examination due to the **spousal testimonial privilege** (in Washington, the privilege does not extend to a spouse's out-of-court statements admissible under a hearsay exception). The Court agreed, stating that the confrontation clause applies to uncross-examined statements of unavailable declarants if they were testimonial in nature. Although the Court stopped short of

(continued)

providing a comprehensive delineation of "testimonial statements," they extended the protection of the confrontation clause to statements made to police or government personnel during interrogation. In addition, the Court rejected traditional tests for "reliability" noting that:

> . . . reliability is an amorphous, if not entirely subjective, concept. There are countless factors bearing on whether a statement is reliable . . . to add insult to injury, some of the courts that admit untested testimonial statements find reliability in the very statements that make the statements testimonial. . . . the Framers would be astounded to learn that ex parte testimony could be admitted against a criminal defendant because it was

elicited by "neutral" government officers. But even if the court's assessment of the officer's motives was accurate, it says nothing about Sylvia's perception of her situation. Only cross-examination could reveal that.

In *Davis v. Washington* [547 U.S. 813(2006)], the Court further distinguished testimonial from nontestimonial statements. In this case, the Court held that calls for emergency assistance to 911 were not testimonial. However, such calls could evolve into testimonial statements once the original purpose (i.e., aid) is satisfied. The Court also held that the constitutional right to confrontation is forfeited if the witness' absence is a result of wrongdoing.

However, this rule specifically requires that advance notice of the introduction of such statement is provided to opposing counsel.

Immateriality of Witness Availability

The two broad categories of hearsay exceptions include the witness being unavailable and the presence of the declarant being immaterial. Situations in which hearsay statements of available witnesses may be introduced include, but are not limited to the following:

Present-Sense Impressions and Excited Utterances

present-sense impressions a statement is admissible if it describes or explains any event or condition made while the declarant was perceiving, or immediately after perceiving, such event or condition. These present-sense impressions do not have to be spontaneous and may be solicited from law enforcement authorities or private parties.

Under FRE 803(1), a statement is admissible if it describes or explains any event or condition made while the declarant was perceiving, or immediately after perceiving, such event or condition. These **present-sense impressions** do not have to be spontaneous and may be solicited from law enforcement authorities or private parties. **Excited utterances** may be introduced under FRE 803(2) when they are observations experienced through any of the five senses and are offered spontaneously under the stress or excitement of an event. Such statements are considered trustworthy because they were unsolicited and offered contemporaneously to the excitement of the event. Most states require that such statements also be made against the interest of the defendant. However, this exception is not used as often as some of the others because such statements are more easily admissible under the admissions exception discussed earlier. Excited utterances and spontaneous statements must contain firsthand knowledge of the matter in question, and both must involve evaluation of time elapsed.

excited utterances observations experienced through any of the five senses and are offered spontaneously under the stress or excitement of an event. Such statements are considered trustworthy because they were unsolicited and offered contemporaneously to the excitement of the event.

Traditionally, the introduction of present-sense impressions and excited utterances required the timely issuance of the statement in question. However, an increase has occurred over time in the number of states allowing an extended period of time between the event and the description by victims of sexual assault *if* the statement contains other indicia of reliability. This is especially true when the alleged victim is a child.

Mental, Emotional, or Physical Condition

Under FRE 803(3), statements offered to demonstrate the declarant's state of mind, emotion, sensation, or physical condition may be introduced. Such statements typically include intent, plan, motive, design, mental feeling, pain, and state of physical health. However, they do not include statements of memory or perception to demonstrate the recollected fact unless they relate to the execution, revocation, identification, or terms of declarant's will. Such statements may be introduced to establish motive, intent, state of mind, or mental illness.

Medical Diagnosis or Treatment

Under FRE 803(4), statements made for purposes of "medical diagnosis or treatment and describing medical history, or past or present symptoms, pain, or sensations, or the inception or general character of the cause or external source thereof insofar as reasonably pertinent to diagnosis or treatment" are admissible. Such statements may be made by a patient to a doctor during medical examinations or other procedures to obtain diagnosis or treatment of a medical condition. This exception also includes statements offered to nonphysicians, such as family members, police officers, hospital employees, or emergency medical personnel, when issued to secure treatment. Some states are more restrictive in their interpretation, but most will allow statements issued in these contexts because of a strong indicia of reliability—the theory being that individuals seeking treatment would be candid and honest with the attending physician. As such, many courts have even admitted statements regarding past symptoms. However, courts have denied the admissibility of any statements of culpability (Strong, 1999). For example, only the second portion of the following statement would be admissible: "While hiding from the police, I fell out of a window." All exceptions to the hearsay rule, including statements for the purpose of medical diagnosis or treatment, are evaluated on a case-by-case basis.

Past Recorded Recollections

Under FRE 803(5), recorded statements concerning a fact at issue may be introduced *if* the declarant's present recollection is insufficient to fully and accurately testify and *if* the statement was recorded in a timely manner consistent with a demonstration that such statement was intended to reflect the knowledge correctly. The physical document itself is not admissible unless offered by the adverse party, but a *reading* of the original statement may be introduced into evidence.

For past recollections to be introduced, the proponent of the statement must demonstrate that the declarant had firsthand knowledge of the fact in question and that the statement would be admissible in the current proceeding *if* the declarant was currently available. In addition, the calling party must demonstrate that the record was made while the witness' memory was clear. This does not mean, however, that the statement must have been issued immediately following the event. Time is certainly a consideration in the introduction of such a statement, but only the memory itself is evaluated by the court. Finally, the introduction of **past recorded recollections** requires testimony regarding their validity and veracity. Thus, the original declarant or someone with firsthand knowledge must testify as to the truthfulness and accuracy of the statement. This can be someone who prepared the writing, such as a police officer, attorney, or friend, or someone who read it near the time of its recording.

Regularly Conducted Activity

Under the FRE, a range of exceptions involving regularly kept records exists. For the most part, their introduction requires a demonstration that the records were kept in the regular course of business and that recordkeeping was consistent and accurate to such an extent that the statement contains an indicia of reliability. Thus, the following categories of statements are permissible:

Reputation

Although reputation evidence is generally inadmissible as an exception to the hearsay rule, it is permitted within specific parameters. For example, FRE Rules

past recorded recollections an exception to the hearsay rule that permits the introduction of a recorded statement *if* the declarant's present recollection is insufficient to fully and accurately testify and *if* the statement was recorded in a timely manner consistent with a demonstration that such statement was intended to reflect the knowledge correctly.

ARTICLE VIII—HEARSAY

Rule 803—Exceptions to the Rule Against Hearsay—Regardless of Whether the Declarant Is Available as a Witness

The following are not excluded by the rule against hearsay, regardless of whether the declarant is available as a witness:

(1) *Records of a Regularly Conducted Activity.* A record of an act, event, condition, opinion, or diagnosis if:

(A) the record was made at or near the time by—or from information transmitted by—someone with knowledge;

(B) the record was kept in the course of a regularly conducted activity of a business, organization, occupation, or calling, whether or not for profit;

(C) making the record was a regular practice of that activity;

(D) all these conditions are shown by the testimony of the custodian or another qualified witness, or by a certification that complies with Rule 902(11) or (12) or with a statute permitting certification; and

(E) neither the source of information nor the method or circumstances of preparation indicate a lack of trustworthiness.

(2) *Public Records.* A record or statement of a public office if:

(A) it sets out:

(i) the office's activities;

(ii) a matter observed while under a legal duty to report, but not including, in a criminal case, a matter observed by law-enforcement personnel; or

(iii) in a civil case or against the government in a criminal case, factual findings from a legally authorized investigation; and

(B) neither the source of information nor other circumstances indicate a lack of trustworthiness.

(3) *Public Records of Vital Statistics.* A record of a birth, death, or marriage, if reported to a public office in accordance with a legal duty.

(4) *Absence of a Public Record.* Testimony—or a certification under Rule 902—that a diligent search failed to disclose a public record or statement if the testimony or certification is admitted to prove that:

(A) the record or statement does not exist; or

(B) a matter did not occur or exist, if a public office regularly kept a record or statement for a matter of that kind.

(5) *Records of Religious Organizations Concerning Personal or Family History.* A statement of birth, legitimacy, ancestry, marriage, divorce, death, relationship by blood or marriage, or similar facts of personal or family history, contained in a regularly kept record of a religious organization.

(6) *Certificates of Marriage, Baptism, and Similar Ceremonies.* A statement of fact contained in a certificate:

(A) made by a person who is authorized by a religious organization or by law to perform the act certified;

(B) attesting that the person performed a marriage or similar ceremony or administered a sacrament; and

(C) purporting to have been issued at the time of the act or within a reasonable time after it.

(7) *Family Records.* A statement of fact about personal or family history contained in a family record, such as a Bible, genealogy, chart, engraving on a ring, inscription on a portrait, or engraving on an urn or burial marker.

(8) *Statements in Ancient Documents.* A statement in a document that is at least 20 years old and whose authenticity is established.

(9) *Market Reports and Similar Commercial Publications.* Market quotations, lists, directories, or other compilations that are generally relied on by the public or by persons in particular occupations.

(10) *Statements in Learned Treatises, Periodicals, or Pamphlets.* A statement contained in a treatise, periodical, or pamphlet if:

(A) the statement is called to the attention of an expert witness on cross-examination or relied on by the expert on direct examination; and

(B) the publication is established as a reliable authority by the expert's admission or testimony, by another expert's testimony, or by judicial notice.

If admitted, the statement may be read into evidence but not received as an exhibit.

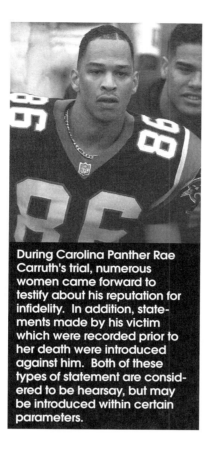

During Carolina Panther Rae Carruth's trial, numerous women came forward to testify about his reputation for infidelity. In addition, statements made by his victim which were recorded prior to her death were introduced against him. Both of these types of statement are considered to be hearsay, but may be introduced within certain parameters.

803 (19) and 803 (20) permit the introduction of reputation evidence concerning personal or family history and general character among associates in the community, respectively. In addition, statements regarding reputation concerning boundaries or general history of land may be admissible under FRE 803 (20).

▶ Hearsay Within Hearsay

The intricacies of the hearsay rule and its various exceptions are further complicated with statements containing **hearsay within hearsay**. By definition, such statements contain multiple levels of hearsay. Under FRE Rule 805, such statements are admissible in court provided that each portion of the combined statements falls within the parameters of an established exception under the FRE. Evaluation of the admissibility of a multiple-hearsay statement begins with a step-by-step analysis of the questioned statement:

> We regard the proper approach to multiple hearsay as nearly identical to that applicable to hearsay itself. The law judge may weigh it, taking into account its remoteness and reliability. Where hearsay within hearsay carries with it sufficient indicia of trustworthiness and the interests of justice will best be served by admission of the statement in evidence, we do not see why it should be deemed inadmissible or insufficient to provide a substantive basis for a decision.[8]

hearsay within hearsay a hearsay statement that includes one or more additional hearsay statements. These statements are admissible in court only when all of the statements conform to the requirements of the hearsay exceptions in the Federal Rules of Evidence.

▶ Impeachment of Hearsay Declarant

The hearsay rule and its relevant exceptions and exemptions found within American criminal codes rely upon the "indicia of reliability." Thus, each court must evaluate the veracity of the statement itself. Many characteristics and circumstances are involved in such analyses, but the credibility of the declarants

More than two decades after teenager Martha Moxley was found dead on her lawn in Greenwich, Connecticut, one of the nation's most exclusive enclaves, Kennedy cousin Michael Skakel was tried for the murder. Various witnesses testified that Skakel had confessed to the crime while a young student at the Elan School. Some individuals relied upon past recorded statements, including the recorded former testimony of a key witness who died before trial.

themselves always requires consideration. As such, FRE Rule 806—Attacking and Supporting Credibility of Declarant—provides a mechanism for opposing counsel to question or otherwise impeach any hearsay witness.

> When a hearsay statement, or a statement defined in Rule 801(d)(2)(C), (D), or (E), has been admitted in evidence, the credibility of the declarant may be attacked, and if attacked may be supported, by any evidence which would be admissible for those purposes if declarant had testified as a witness. Evidence of a statement or conduct by the declarant at any time, inconsistent with the declarant's hearsay statement, is not subject to any requirement that the declarant may have been afforded an opportunity to deny or explain. If the party against whom a hearsay statement has been admitted calls the declarant as a witness, the party is entitled to examine the declarant on the statement as if under cross-examination.

Effectively, such questioning is comparable to the general impeachment of routine witnesses and applies to all statements admitted under the exceptions and exemptions of the hearsay rule, but not to those statements that are not admitted for their truth (Strong, 1999). All means of cross-examination of a declarant taking the stand that would be available for impeachment of witnesses may be explored. At the same time, declarants who have been impeached by opposing counsel may be rehabilitated by the proponent of the hearsay statement through the introduction of additional testimony, including prior consistent statements.

▶ CONCLUSIONS

Under the FRE (Rule 801), *hearsay* is defined as any "statement, other than one made by the declarant while testifying at the trial or hearing, offered in evidence to prove the truth of the matter asserted." Two broad categories of hearsay exist in American law: assertion-centered statements and declarant-centered statements. Assertion-centered statements are those in which the declarant (person making the statement) intends to communicate his or her thoughts or beliefs. Declarant-centered statements, on the other hand, involve evaluating a declarant's credibility (including lay and expert witnesses). Remember, the hearsay rule only refers to statements offered to prove truth. Therefore, statements introduced to prove state of mind, knowledge of facts, or the sanity of the declarant generally are admissible.

Although the Supreme Court has recognized the importance of the confrontation clause of the Sixth Amendment, it has also concluded that requiring all testimony to be the product of firsthand knowledge is too extreme. In addition to several centuries of English jurisprudence, American law delineates exceptions to the hearsay rule. Such exceptions are permitted when a witness is unavailable or when the presence of a declarant is immaterial. For example, when a witness is unavailable, exceptions to the hearsay rule may include former testimony and dying declarations. When the presence of the declarant is determined to be immaterial, exceptions may include excited utterances, statements of a person's reputation, and information found in public records. In sum, it is important to keep in mind that the veracity of all statements is evaluated by the court in light of many factors and very often, the evaluation hinges on the credibility of the declarant.

Witness testimony is the means by which all evidence is presented in court. This requirement renders it one of the most essential elements of the American legal system. Our system requires witnesses to testify in court and under oath, not only to ensure their sincerity but also to safeguard the rights of defendants under the Sixth Amendment, including being able to confront their accuser. Furthermore, observing witness testimony is a powerful tool in a jury's arsenal. Juries often are granted a great deal of discretion when evaluating witness testimony and are permitted to take into account characteristics such as demeanor when weighing evidence. As we have seen in this chapter, hearsay, for many reasons, is usually not admitted in a court of law.

Key Terms

Admissions by party-opponent	Declarant-centered statements	Past recorded recollections
Adoptive admission	Declarations against interest	Present-sense impressions
Assertion-centered statements	Dying declaration	Prior statements
Circumstantial admission of guilt	Excited utterances	Spousal testimonial privilege
Co-conspirator rule	Hearsay	Testimonial evidence
Declarant	Hearsay within hearsay	

Discussion Questions

1. Should dying declarations be admissible in court? What about excited utterances? What are the benefits and consequences from the perspective of both sides?
2. Should statements including hearsay within hearsay be admissible in court? Can these statements truly be reliable? Why or why not?
3. Consider a court system in which only firsthand witness testimony is admissible. How would this rule affect court proceedings?

Recommended Resources

Videos

Insight Media. Fact or fiction: Courtroom myths. Available at http://www.insight-media.com.

Insight Media. Constitutional law: The USA PATRIOT Act. Available at http://www.insight-media.com.

A&E Television. Another man's crime. This DVD presentation involves the case of a police officer wrongfully convicted of the murder of his lover. American justice. Available at: http://store.aetv.com.

A&E Television. Conspiracy to kill: The Rae Carruth story. American justice. Available at: http://store .aetv.com.

Books

Binder, David F. (2001). *Hearsay handbook* (4th ed.). Connecticut. West Publishing.

Broun, Kenneth S., Mosteller, Robert P., and, Bilionis, Louis D. (2001). *Problems in evidence*. Connecticut: West Publishing.

Fenner, G. Michael. (2003). *The hearsay rule*. Durham, NC: Carolina Academic Press.

Kirkpatrick, Laird. (2005). Crawford: A look backward, a look forward. *Criminal Justice Magazine, 20* (2). Available at: http://www.abanet.org/crimjust/ cjmag/20-2/Kirkpatrick.html.

Park, Roger C. (2001). *Trial objections handbook*. (2nd ed.). Connecticut: West Publishing.

Perrick, Tracey L. (2005). *Crawford v. Washington*: Redefining sixth amendment jurisprudence—the impact across the United States and in Maryland. *The University of Baltimore Law Review, 35* (133).

Online Sources

http://www.findlaw.com—Search state and federal case law, statutes, and federal and state constitutions.

http://www.abanet.org—Official home page of the American Bar Association maintains active links to publications and resources regarding various concepts in evidence law, including hearsay and the confrontation clause.

http://www.lexisnexis.com—Powerful search engine providing links and other resources for searching newspapers, periodicals, journals, and the like, along with access to federal and state law, cases, codes, and regulations for use by users to search for law reviews regarding particular areas of interest in the law.

http://caselaw.lp.findlaw.com/data/constitution/ amendment06/—Web site providing comprehensive lists of hyperlinks outlining the Sixth Amendment, including the confrontation clause and rights to a speedy and public trial, impartial jury, assistance of counsel, and compulsory process of witnesses.

Relevant Cases Cited

Barber v. Page, 390 U.S. 719 (1968)

Bourjaily v. U.S., 483 U.S. 171 (1987)

California v. Green, 399 U.S. 149 (1969)

Crawford v. Washington, 541 U.S. 36 (2004)

Davis v. Washington, 547 U.S. 813 (2006)

Dutton v. Evans, 400 U.S. 74 (1970)

Graves v. United States, 150 U.S. 118 (1893)

Idaho v. Wright, 497 U.S. 805 (1990)

Mutual Life Insurance Co. v. Hillmon, 145 U.S. 285 (1892)

Penguin Books USA, Inc. v. New Christian Church of Full Endeavor, Ltd., 262 F. Supp. 2d 251, 261 (S.D.N.Y. 2003)

Rex v. Woodcock, 1 Leach 500, 502, 168 Eng. Rep. 352 (K.B. 1789)

United States v. Salerno, 505 U.S. 317 (1992)

Van Riper v. United States, 13 F.2d 961, 967

Notes

1. *California v. Green*, 399 U.S. 149 (1970)
2. *Penguin Books USA, Inc. v. New Christian Church of Full Endeavor, Ltd.*, 262 F. Supp. 2d 251, 261 (S.D.N.Y. 2003)
3. *Graves v. U.S.*, 150 U.S. 118, 121 (1893), as cited in Strong (1999)
4. *Bourjaily v. U.S.*, 483 U.S. 171 (1987)
5. *Dutton v. Evans*, 400 U.S. 74 (1970)
6. 390 U.S. 719 (1968)
7. *Rex v. Woodcock*, 1 Leach 500, 502, 168 Eng. Rep. 352 (K.B. 1789), as cited in *State of Connecticut v. Ricardo Mills* (AC 23360) (2003)
8. *Administrator v. Repacholi*, NTSB Order No. EA-3888 (served June 21, 1993)

THE DECLARATION OF INDEPENDENCE.

11 Privileged Communications

LEARNING OBJECTIVES

The learner will:

1 *Examine the historical background of privileged communications*

2 *Discuss the parameters of attorney-client privilege and spousal privilege*

3 *Distinguish between physician-patient privilege and psychotherapist-patient privilege*

4 *Explain clergy-communicant, media-source, and governmental privileges*

▶ A Brief History

Historically, societies have been reluctant to recognize the sanctity of certain relationships, and courts have traditionally refused to accommodate privileges against testifying to the contents of communications occurring within such relationships. Indeed, the preeminent legal scholar, John Wigmore, cautioned against such recognition and provided strict parameters for extending such privileges. According to Wigmore (1940),[1] privileges should only be extended in those relationships that meet the following four standards:

1. The communication must be entered into with an expectation of confidentiality.
2. The element of confidentiality must be essential to the maintenance of the relationship.
3. The relationship must be one that, in the opinion of the community, should be sedulously fostered.
4. The injury to the relationship by such disclosure would be greater than the benefit gained for the correct disposal of litigation.

Taking note, the Supreme Court cautiously recognized the right of states to create categories of legally inviolable communication. Thus, jurisprudential recognition occurred long before federal acknowledgment.

Framers of the U.S. Constitution adopted much of the legal rationale from English common law that recognized an assortment of privileged communications. However, the courts have defined such privileges narrowly and expressed reluctance to expand their boundaries or seek their proliferation. In fact, the framers initially characterized the extension of testimonial privileges as reminiscent of the monarchy from which they fled and antithetical to the egalitarianism to which they aspired. However, their reluctance to incorporate large-scale induction of common law privileges did not extend to prohibitions against state governments. Thus, recognition gradually emerged that compulsory disclosure of confidential communications deriving from sacred or trust-based relationships violated the basic tenants of American society. Consequently, state governments were the first to recognize that relationships grounded in socially valued intimacies, particularly those in which secrets are exchanged, must be protected against governmental invasion.[2]

Statutorily, the notion of testimonial privileges in American courts emerged at the same time as compulsory witness testimony. This consequent bilateral evolution ensured that the exemptions and privileges previously recognized as common law were not superseded by the emerging notion of compulsory process (Catz et al., 1987). In 1972 when the Federal Rules of Evidence were originally drafted, nine distinct, Supreme Court-recognized testimonial privileges were proposed. All nine included provisions for exceptions, waivers, compulsions, comments, and inferences,[3] and included:

- Proposed Rule 502—Privilege covering reports and returns required by law
- Proposed Rule 503—Privilege protecting attorney-client confidential communications
- Proposed Rule 504—Privilege protecting psychotherapist-patient confidential communications
- Proposed Rule 505—Privilege allowing one spouse to prevent the other from testifying against him or her in a criminal proceeding
- Proposed Rule 506—Privilege protecting confidential communications between clergy and communicant

ARTICLE V: PRIVILEGES

Rule 501 – Privileges in General

The following are not excluded by the rule against hearsay, regardless of whether the declarant is available as a witness:

The common law—as interpreted by U.S. courts in the light of reason and experience—governs a claim of privilege unless any of the following provides otherwise:

- the U.S. Constitution;
- a federal statute; or
- rules prescribed by the Supreme Court.

But in a civil case, state law governs privilege regarding a claim or defense for which state law supplies the rule of decision.

- Proposed Rule 507—Privilege protecting the secrecy of political votes
- Proposed Rule 508—Privilege protecting trade secrets
- Proposed Rule 509—Privilege protecting state secrets and official information
- Proposed Rule 510—Privilege protecting the identity of informers

However, Congress largely rejected the notion of federal privileges and failed to codify the proposed privileges. Instead, Congress included only one general statement regarding testimonial privileges in the ratified document (i.e., Article V, Rule 501). As a result, the law of privileges that has evolved is varied and inconsistent and areas of communication considered sacrosanct in federal court may not be considered inviolable in some state courts, and vice versa.

As in other areas of the law in which federal statutes are absent or provide little guidance, legislation by varying state governments regarding privileges is often inconsistent. While some give weight to federal case law, others rely more heavily on political platforms or community pressures. Federal courts, on the other hand, largely recognize new evidentiary privileges or expand the scope of existing ones after analysis of four independent factors:

1. Whether federal policy supports the privilege
2. Whether states recognize the privilege
3. Whether recognizing the privilege serves the same policy goals that traditionally have informed the development of privilege law
4. Whether legal scholars have championed the adoption of the privilege[4]

 CLARIFICATION OF CONCEPTS

RATIONALE FOR PRIVILEGES

The common-law principles underlying the recognition of testimonial privileges can be stated simply.

For more than three centuries it has now been recognized as a fundamental maxim that the public . . . has a right to every man's evidence. When we come to examine the various claims of exemption, we start with the primary assumption that there is a general duty to give what testimony one is capable of giving, and that any exemptions which may exist are distinctly exceptional, being so many derogations from a positive general rule [*United States v. Bryan*, 339 U.S. 323, 331 (1950)] (quoting J. Wigmore, Evidence Section(s) 2192, p. 64 [3d Ed. 1940]).

Exceptions from the general rule disfavoring testimonial privileges may be justified, however, by a "public good transcending the normally predominant principle of utilizing all rational means for ascertaining the truth" [Trammel, 445 U.S., at 50, quoting *Elkins v. United States*, 364 U.S. 206, 234 (1960); (Frankfurter, J., dissenting)].

In any event, the recognition of privileged communications varies across jurisdictions, and it is important to remember that no absolute standard exists for their admission. For the most part, invocation of any privilege requires:

- Requisite relationship—It must be demonstrated that the relationship in which the privilege resides is present and that the relationship as entered into was conducted in a manner not suggestive of intentional fraud or attempt to pervert the criminal justice system.

- Expectation of **confidentiality**—It must be demonstrated that the communications were intended to be confidential (secret). Voluntary disclosure to third parties generally will waive the privilege.

confidentiality
legal protection against compulsory disclosure of secret communications, such as between an attorney and his or her client.

requisite relationship a privileged relationship present and entered into without taint of intentional fraud or attempt to pervert the criminal justice system, such as attorney-client privilege.

attorney-client privilege legal protection against compulsory disclosure in open court of communications between client and attorney when such communications were confidential and were undertaken under the auspices of a legal relationship.

▶ Attorney-Client Privilege

Generally speaking, evidentiary privileges are applicable to sworn testimony in formal proceedings. Such privileges may also apply to physical (i.e., documentary) evidence and are exclusionary in nature. Thus, once the **requisite relationship**—a privileged relationship that is present and entered into without taint of intentional fraud or attempt to pervert the criminal justice system—has been demonstrated, communications made therein may be excluded from consideration in the fact-finding mission and are not admissible. **Attorney-client privilege**—a legal concept that provides protection for communications between a client and his or her attorney and allows the parties to keep those communications confidential—is perhaps the oldest recognized privilege under common law.

As with many areas of American jurisprudence, the attorney-client privilege may be traced back to early England. Before the Elizabethan era (1558–1603), there was no legal mechanism for compulsory testimony. In fact, defendants were not even allowed to testify in their own defense. The emergence of compulsory processes fostered a recognition and acknowledgment that attorneys, judges, and jurors, in the interest of objectivity, should be excluded from them.[5] Initially, the privilege belonged to the attorney and not to the client. Today, it resides with the client. If he or she does not object to or even desires disclosure, then counsel must disclose. Contemporary interpretations of the privilege are increasingly important as society becomes more complex and laws become more sophisticated. In the absence of assurances of confidentiality, clients might be dissuaded from completely and totally disclosing facts that may be pertinent to the case. This would significantly hamper the ability of defendants to secure competent counsel and would prevent them from participating in their own defense. As the Court observed:

> The attorney-client privilege is the oldest of the privileges for confidential communications known to the common law. [J. Wigmore, Evidence 2290 (McNaughton rev. 1961)]. Its purpose is to encourage full and frank communication between attorneys and their clients and thereby promote broader public interests in the observance of law and administration of justice. The privilege recognizes that sound legal advice or advocacy serves public ends and that such advice or advocacy depends upon the lawyer's being fully informed by the client. As we stated last Term in *Trammel v. United States*, [445 U.S. 40, 51[(1980)]: "The lawyer-client privilege rests on the need for the advocate and counselor to know all that relates to the client's reasons for seeking representation if the professional mission is to be carried out." And in *Fisher v. United States*, [425 U.S. 391, 403] (1976), we recognized the purpose of the privilege to be "to encourage clients to make full disclosure to their attorneys." This rationale for the privilege has long been recognized by the Court, see *Hunt v. Blackburn*, [128 U.S.464, 470 (1888)] (privilege "is founded upon the necessity, in the interest and

administration of justice, of the aid of persons having knowledge of the law and skilled in its practice, which assistance can only be safely and readily availed of when free from the consequences or the apprehension of disclosure").[6]

Parameters and Limitations

In federal and state systems alike, statutory guidelines exist for the invocation of the attorney-client privilege. First, the client must have sought out the professional services of an individual they reasonably believed was authorized or licensed to practice law with the intention of establishing an attorney-client relationship.[7] Informal conversations in which free legal advice is sought or those that occur in casual or social settings are not considered sufficient to satisfy the requirements of the attorney-client privilege. Second, it must be demonstrated that the communication in question was undertaken in a manner designed to ensure confidentiality. Thus, conversations with an attorney at a crowded train station would not be considered privileged. This is not to suggest, however, that the presence of any third party nullifies the protection. Attendance by individuals under the employ of the attorney, for example, would not generally erode the expectation of confidentiality. The courts have recognized that office workers are both necessary and essential in law practices. So, the presence of law clerks, administrative assistants, or investigators during a communication between an attorney and client does not eliminate the privilege. In addition, the presence of individuals accompanying the client for support, such as a spouse or parent, may not eradicate the protections housed within the privilege. However, most state statutes do not specifically attach to such a circumstance. For example, in California, the inference does not necessarily extend to family members or to those not in the employ of the attorney.

In addition to nonconfidential communications, the attorney-client privilege does not preclude the introduction of all other attorney-client communications. It does not, for example, protect communications that include future criminal activities, especially those that might cause physical harm or death. In addition, it does not attach when the services were retained to enable or aid in the commission or the planning of criminal or fraudulent activity. Some state codes contain provisions that specifically require the production of physical evidence upon receipt by counsel.[8]

Finally, the courts have generally ruled that the identity of the client and fee information is not protected. For the most part, such information is sought in three types of cases: (1) *benefactor* cases, in which the identity of a person paying a co-conspirator's legal fees is sought; (2) *Good Samaritan* cases, in which the identity of an anonymous donor is sought because of the government's interest in contacting or questioning them; and (3) *tax* cases, in which the government seeks the pay arrangements as evidence of unexplained wealth.[9] Thus, the attorney-client privilege does not extend to those cases in which it is suspected that some level of complicity between the attorney and the client exists or in those cases in which tax evasion or questions of financial impropriety abound. In most states, the attorney-client privilege continues after the death of the client. This notion was upheld by the Supreme Court in *Swidler and Berlin and James Hamilton v. United States*,[10] which emerged after the suicide of top White House counsel, Vincent W. Foster Jr.

Work-Product Doctrine. As discussed in Chapter 2, counsel may formally request (through the use of subpoena) the production of documents and other evidence from the adverse party. Such material may include any evidence relevant to the matter at hand except privileged communications. This limitation clearly includes all confidential communications between an attorney and his or her client, but it also includes all material developed in preparation for trial or

work-product doctrine protects materials prepared in anticipation of a legal proceeding. Rooted in *Hickman v. Taylor*, 329 U.S. 495 (1947).

SECTIONS 950–954

950. As used in this article, "lawyer" means a person authorized, or reasonably believed by the client to be authorized, to practice law in any state or nation.

951. As used in this article, "client" means a person who, directly or through an authorized representative, consults a lawyer for the purpose of retaining the lawyer or securing legal service or advice from him in his professional capacity, and includes an incompetent (a) who himself so consults the lawyer or (b) whose guardian or conservator so consults the lawyer in behalf of the incompetent.

952. As used in this article, "confidential communication between client and lawyer" means information transmitted between a client and his or her lawyer in the course of that relationship and in confidence by a means which, so far as the client is aware, discloses the information to no third persons other than those who are present to further the interest of the client in the consultation or those to whom disclosure is reasonably necessary for the transmission of the information or the accomplishment of the purpose for which the lawyer is consulted, and includes a legal opinion formed and the advice given by the lawyer in the course of that relationship.

953. As used in this article, "holder of the privilege" means:

(a) The client when he has no guardian or conservator;
(b) A guardian or conservator of the client when the client has a guardian or conservator;
(c) The personal representative of the client if the client is dead;
(d) A successor, assignee, trustee in dissolution, or any similar representative of a firm, association, organization, partnership, business trust, corporation, or public entity that is no longer in existence.

954. Subject to Section 912 and except as otherwise provided in this article, the client, whether or not a party, has a privilege to refuse to disclose, and to prevent another from disclosing, a confidential communication between client and lawyer if the privilege is claimed by:

(a) The holder of the privilege;
(b) A person who is authorized to claim the privilege by the holder of the privilege; or
(c) The person who was the lawyer at the time of the confidential communication, but such person may not claim the privilege if there is no holder of the privilege in existence or if he is otherwise instructed by a person authorized to permit disclosure.

plea bargaining. In expanding the traditional attorney-client privilege, the Court extended much of the original philosophy to this area, arguing:

> Were such materials open to opposing counsel on mere demand, much of what is now put down in writing would remain unwritten. An attorney's thoughts, heretofore inviolate, would not be his own. Inefficiency, unfairness and sharp practices would inevitably develop in the giving of legal advice and in the preparation of cases for trial. The effect on the legal profession would be demoralizing. And the interests of the clients and the cause of justice would be poorly served. . . . Under ordinary conditions, forcing an attorney to repeat or write out all that witnesses have told him and to deliver the account [329 U.S. 495, 513] to his adversary gives rise to grave dangers of inaccuracy and untrustworthiness. No legitimate purpose is served by such production. The practice forces the attorney to testify as to what he remembers or what he saw fit to write down regarding witnesses' remarks. Such testimony could not qualify as evidence; and to use it for impeachment or corroborative purposes would make the attorney much less an officer of the court and much more an ordinary witness. The standards of the profession would thereby suffer.[11]

However, the Court argued against blanket prohibitions, stating that facts essential to the preparation of one's case may be requested through the proper use of the discovery process. In addition, the Court clarified the parameters in which such

SPECIFIC RATIONALE FOR ATTORNEY-CLIENT PRIVILEGE

Scholars have posited different arguments as to the justification of excluding relevant evidence that may be contained within attorney-client communications. Some argue that the privilege is embedded within the wording of the Sixth Amendment, and others argue that the privilege is to be found within the confines of the Fifth—a legal necessity to protect an individual from self-incrimination. Indeed, if the American criminal process is properly characterized as an adversarial system, it would appear that the privilege is all but mandated; otherwise, defendants would have no voice if they were unable to speak freely with their chosen advocate. Without the assurance of confidentiality, defendants would surely not express any potentially incriminating information with their attorney, thus denying them the right to counsel guaranteed in the Sixth Amendment.

requests would be found meritorious and identified the bearer of the burden of proof. To wit,

> Such written statements and documents might, under certain circumstances, be admissible in evidence or give clues as to the existence or location of relevant facts. Or they might be useful for purposes of impeachment or corroboration. And production might be justified where the witnesses are no longer available or can be reached only with difficulty. Were production of written statements and documents to be precluded under . . . such circumstances, the liberal ideals of the deposition-discovery portions of the Federal Rules of Civil Procedure would be stripped of much of their meaning. But the general policy against invading the privacy of an attorney's course of preparation is so well recognized and so essential to an orderly working of our system of legal procedure that a burden rests on the one who would invade that privacy to establish adequate reasons to justify production through a subpoena or court order. That burden, we believe, is necessarily implicit in the rules as now constituted.[12]

▶ Spousal Privileges

Historically, the recognition of the legal sanctity of the marital union of husband and wife has deep roots in Anglo-Saxon jurisprudence. As such, communications made within the marital bond traditionally were protected from compulsory disclosure in the common law. The U.S. Supreme Court formally noted the existence of such protection as early as 1934, arguing in *Wolfle v. United States* [291 U.S. 7 (1934)] that:

> . . . (t)his rule is founded upon the deepest and soundest principles of our nature. Principles which have grown out of those domestic relations, that constitute the basis of civil society; and which are essential to the enjoyment of that confidence which should subsist between those who are connected by the nearest and dearest relations of life. To break down or impair the great principles which protect the sanctities of husband and wife, would be to destroy the best solace of human existence.

Repeatedly, such recognition has been reaffirmed by the Court.[13] However, the spousal privilege has changed markedly since its inception.

Initially, two types of privileges extended to the marital relationship. The **marital communications privilege** protected spousal communications made in confidence. The **spousal testimonial privilege** gave witnesses (1) the right to refuse to testify against their spouses, (2) the right of the accused to prevent testimony by that spouse, and (3) the right to automatically render the witness

marital communications privilege legal protection against compulsory disclosure of spousal communications made in confidence, regardless of the state of the marriage at the time.

spousal testimonial privilege legal protection against compulsory disclosure of communications occurring during a legally binding marital relationship, irrespective of the state of the marital union. The privilege provides the right of one spouse to refuse to testify against the other and the right to automatically render the witness unavailable.

MARITAL PRIVILEGES

Marital Communications Privilege

- Protects spousal communications made in confidence. In most states, the privilege survives both death and divorce.

Spousal Testimonial Privilege

- Generally gives witnesses the right to testify against their spouse. (Traditionally, it also gave defendant spouses the right to prevent their spouse from bearing witness against them.) Unlike the marital communications privilege, it does not survive death or divorce in most states.

It is important to note that neither privilege extends to crimes committed against family members. Children, in particular, are protected because children are incapable of defending themselves and are thus entitled to greater protection. In that, "society has a stronger interest in protecting such children than in preserving marital autonomy and privacy."[14]

unavailable. Generally speaking, the marital communications privilege requires that the communication occur during a legally binding marital relationship, irrespective of current state of the marital union; the spousal testimonial privilege applies only when such a legal relationship is still in place. (Remember, the philosophy of the privilege is to protect the marital union.) In addition, it is generally assumed that all communications made within the confines of the marital relationship and without the presence of a third party are confidential. However, the recognition and the application of martial privileges vary from state to state.

As stated, the original justification for the protection of confidential communications made during a marital union was to promote harmony in relationships, which the community considered righteous and necessary for the preservation of the society as a whole. The Court first recognized a distinction between the two marital privileges in *Wolfle v. United States* (1934) where they noted that:

> The basis of the immunity given to communications between husband and wife is the protection of marital confidences, regarded as so essential to the preservation of the marriage relationship as to outweigh the disadvantages to the administration of justice,

EXAMPLES OF CODIFIED MARITAL PRIVILEGES

Spousal Testimonial Privilege

Arizona Revised Statute §12-2231—In a civil action, a husband shall not be examined for or against his wife without her consent, nor a wife for or against her husband without his consent.

Marital Communications Privilege

South Dakota Codified Law Annotated §19-13-12—A communication is confidential if it is made privately by any person to his or her spouse during their marriage and is not intended for disclosure to any other person.

Incorporated

Code of Virginia §8.01-398—In any civil proceeding, a person has a privilege to refuse to disclose, and to prevent anyone else from disclosing, any confidential communication between his spouse and him[self] during their marriage, regardless of whether he is married to that spouse at the time he objects to disclosure. This privilege may not be asserted in any proceeding in which the spouses are adverse parties, or in which either spouse is charged with a crime or tort against the person or property of the other or against the minor child of either spouse. For the purposes of this section, "confidential communication" means a communication made privately by a person to his spouse that is not intended for disclosure to any other person.

which the privilege entails. . . . Hence it is that the privilege with respect to communications extends to the testimony of husband or wife even though the different privilege, excluding the testimony of one against the other, is not involved.[15]

However, recent decisions by the Court have tended to reflect a less restrictive interpretation of marital bonds in keeping with the generational perception. Thus, in the 1980 case of *Trammell v. United States*, the Court held:

> The ancient foundations for so sweeping a privilege—whereby a woman was regarded as a chattel and denied a separate legal identity—have long since disappeared, and the contemporary justification for affording an accused such a privilege is unpersuasive. When one spouse is willing to testify against the other in a criminal proceeding—whatever the motivation—there is probably little in the way of marital harmony for the privilege to preserve. In these circumstances, a rule of evidence that permits an accused to prevent adverse spousal testimony seems more likely to frustrate justice than to foster family peace. . . . It hardly seems conducive to the preservation of the marital relation to place a wife in jeopardy solely by virtue of her husband's control over her testimony.[16]

As a result, most state rules grant the ownership of the privilege not to the accused but to the one called to testify. More specifically,

> . . . the witness-spouse alone has a privilege to refuse to testify adversely; the witness may be neither compelled to testify nor foreclosed from testifying. This modification—vesting the privilege in the witness spouse—furthers the important public interest in marital harmony without unduly burdening legitimate law enforcement needs. . . . Here, petitioner's spouse chose to testify against him. That she did so after a grant of immunity and assurances of lenient treatment does not render her testimony involuntary.

As with all privileges, communications disclosed to third parties generally are not protected.

Parameters and Limitations

As with the other privileges, the scope of protection under the marital or spousal privilege is not boundless. It does not extend, for example, to communications that involve criminal activities in which the husband and wife are conspirators. It also does not include crimes committed against anyone in the family unit. Such crimes may include, but are not limited to, abuse, abandonment, and neglect of the victim spouse or children. Thus, the court can compel the testimony of a victim spouse or the spouse of an individual who is physically abusive toward the children of the house. In addition, the privilege usually is limited to criminal cases. It does not apply in most civil proceedings, including divorce or custody proceedings in which the relationship is already severed and is in no need of judicial protection.

 CLARIFICATION OF CONCEPTS

SPOUSAL PRIVILEGE AND THE CHILD EXCEPTION

The spousal privilege does not protect information concerning crimes committed against the spouse or the children. Children, in particular, are protected because children are incapable of defending themselves and are thus entitled to greater protection. In that, "society has a stronger interest in protecting such children than in preserving marital autonomy and privacy."

▶ Physician-Patient Privilege

Unlike the attorney-client privilege that existed in common law, the physician-patient privilege has evolved statutorily. The **physician-patient privilege** typically protects (from compulsory disclosure) communications between a physician and a patient, such as patient statements and physician observations, made in the course of their professional relationship unless consent is given by the patient. In 1828, New York became the first jurisdiction to formally recognize this privilege [N.Y.Rev.Stat. 1828, 406 (pt. 3, ch. 7, Tit. 3, Art. 9, §73)].[17] Since that time, most states have enacted similar statutes. However, this particular privilege has been much debated by legal scholars and no consensus among the community has been achieved. As a result, more than 40 states have adopted a general physician-patient privilege, yet federal courts have neglected to do so (Leonard, 2004).

Generally speaking, the physician-patient privilege has been rationalized in much the same manner as other protections covered in the chapter. Some jurisdictions have deemed it necessary to protect the relationship as it has been argued that adequate medical treatment would not be available in cases in which individuals were not guaranteed confidentiality. It has also been recognized that professional ethics largely preclude the sharing of such information. However, because of the lack of federal consensus, the privilege tends to be more limited than the attorney-client privilege and others. Ethics notwithstanding, physicians are bound by the prevailing legal standard in their particular jurisdiction. In all geographic locations in which such a protection exists, the privilege rests solely with the patient and physicians must disclose any information as requested by the patient. In some states, the privilege extends beyond the death of the patient and may be waived only by a representative of the deceased. In others, the privilege ends with the cessation of life. In most instances, the result of an autopsy is not considered privileged.

Parameters and Limitations

As with the attorney-client privilege, the physician-patient privilege requires a formal, professional relationship between the parties. In addition, such protections attach only when confidentiality is sought. Casual conversations or solicitations of free medical advice and those communications voluntarily divulged to third parties by the patient generally are not protected. Legally ordered medical examinations, such as those demanded by law enforcement authorities, prosecuting attorneys, or judges, are not granted the privilege nor are the dates and names of patients. Finally, many states have explicitly precluded particular instances in which the protection does not attach. Although limitations vary by state statute, the following list shows common examples of situations in which physicians may be required to divulge information:

UPON RECEIPT OF KNOWLEDGE
- Gunshot wounds
- Child abuse
- Spousal abuse
- Fetal death
- Venereal disease
- Unnatural death

UPON SUBPOENA
- Yearly physicals required by occupation
- Blood and urine tests requested in DUI cases

§8.01-399—COMMUNICATIONS BETWEEN PHYSICIANS AND PATIENTS

(a) Except at the request or with the consent of the patient, or as provided in this section, no duly licensed practitioner of any branch of the healing arts shall be required to testify in any civil action, respecting any information that he may have acquired in attending, examining, or treating the patient in a professional capacity.

(b) If the physical or mental condition of the patient is at issue in a civil action, the diagnoses, signs and symptoms, observations, evaluations, histories, or treatment plan of the practitioner, obtained or formulated as contemporaneously documented during the course of the practitioner's treatment, together with the facts communicated to, or otherwise learned by, such practitioner in connection with such attendance, examination or treatment shall be disclosed but only in discovery pursuant to the Rules of Court or through testimony at the trial of the action. In addition, disclosure may be ordered when a court, in the exercise of sound discretion, deems it necessary to the proper administration of justice. However, no order shall be entered compelling a party to sign a release for medical records from a health care provider unless the health care provider is not located in the Commonwealth or is a federal facility. If an order is issued pursuant to this section, it shall be restricted to the medical records that relate to the physical or mental conditions at issue in the case. No disclosure of diagnosis or treatment plan facts communicated to, or otherwise learned by, such practitioner shall occur if the court determines, upon the request of the patient, that such facts are not relevant to the subject matter involved in the pending action or do not appear to be reasonably calculated to lead to the discovery of admissible evidence. Only diagnosis offered to a reasonable degree of medical probability shall be admissible at trial.

- Blood tests for marriage
- Physical examinations conducted for insurance purposes
- Court-ordered physical or mental examinations
- Examinations requested by an attorney for purposes of expert testimony

▶ Psychotherapist-Patient Privilege

Similar to the older physician-patient privilege, the **psychotherapist-patient privilege** has quickly overtaken its predecessor in both application and recognition by the Court. It protects communications between therapist and patient (including oral statements made by the patient and visual observations made by the physician) in the course of their professional relationship unless consent is given by the patient. Formally recognized in the 1996 case of *Jaffee v. Redmond*,[18] this privilege is largely based on the concept that psychoanalysis requires complete disclosure for effective treatment. Indeed, the Court recognized that in the interest of treatment, a patient must be:

> . . . willing to make a frank and complete disclosure of facts, emotions, memories, and fears. Because of the sensitive nature of the problems for which individuals consult psychotherapists, disclosure of confidential communications made during counseling sessions may cause embarrassment or disgrace. For this reason, the mere possibility of disclosure may impede development of the confidential relationship necessary for successful treatment.

Thus, the Court rejected a balancing test that would weigh the "interests of justice" against the patient's privacy interests. Instead, it argued that (1) a privilege

psychotherapist-patient privilege
legal protection from compulsory disclosure of communications between therapist and patient, such as oral statements made by the patient and visual observations made by the psychotherapist, in the course of their professional relationship in the absence of consent given by the patient. Protection does not cover allegations of child sexual abuse, in cases where a patient poses a risk of serious harm to themself or others, or future crimes.

The Supreme Court formally recognized a range of privileges, including the clergy-communicant (formerly priest-penitent) privilege, in *Totten v. United States*, 92 U.S. 105 (1875):

> . . . public policy forbids the maintenance of any suit in a court of justice, the trial of which would inevitably lead to the disclosure of matters which the law itself regards as confidential, and respecting which it will not allow the confidence to be violated. On this principle, suits cannot be maintained which would require disclosure of the confidences of the confessional, or those between husband and wife, or of communications by a client to his counsel for professional advice or for a patient to his physician for a similar purpose.

that included such a balancing act would "eviscerate the effectiveness of the privilege" and (2) the absence of patient confidence would have a "chilling" effect on the treatment process. The Court also expanded the privilege to include social workers because these professionals often served as mental health providers to the economically disadvantaged. Since that time, the Court has recognized in numerous cases that effective mental health treatment hinges upon a culture of confidence and trust that would be obliterated completely if a privilege were situationally extended. Indeed, the mere possibility of disclosure would all but guarantee the collapse of an effective treatment strategy. As with the physician-patient privilege, the ownership rests squarely with the patient/client.

Parameters and Limitations

"dangerous patient" exception removal of legal protection from forced disclosure in open court of a patient's communications with a psychotherapist when the patient—through actions or words—presents a likely threat to the community.

As with other privileges discussed herein, the psychotherapist-patient privilege has a limited scope. For example, it does not cover the planning, commission, or concealment of criminal activity. Also, it does not cover allegations of child sexual abuse or when a patient poses a threat of serious harm to self or others. This **"dangerous patient" exception**, which would remove protection of the patient's communications with a therapist from forced disclosure in open court, stems from the legal notion that psychotherapists have a "duty to protect" the community as well as the patients they serve. In fact, many states have codified this "dangerous patient" exception into law. While the Supreme Court formally recognized this exception in *Jaffee*,[19] it failed to provide the parameters and scope

Lyle and Eric Menendez were convicted of the double murder of their parents inside their Beverly Hills mansion based largely on tapes of their communications with a psychotherapist. Currently some states recognize a psychotherapist-client privilege, whereas others do not.

49.213—EXCEPTIONS TO THE PSYCHOLOGIST-PATIENT PRIVILEGE

1. For communications relevant to an issue in a proceeding to hospitalize the patient for mental illness, if the psychologist in the course of diagnosis or treatment has determined that the patient requires hospitalization.

2. For communications relevant to an issue of the treatment of the patient in any proceeding in which the treatment is an element of a claim or defense.

3. If disclosure is otherwise required by state or federal law.

4. For communications relevant to an issue in a proceeding to determine the validity of a will of the patient.

5. If there is an immediate threat that the patient will harm himself or other persons.

6. For communications made in the course of a court-ordered examination of the condition of a patient with respect to the specific purpose of the examination unless the court orders otherwise.

7. For communications relevant to an issue in an investigation or hearing conducted by the Board of Psychological Examiners if the treatment of the patient is an element of that investigation or hearing.

8. For communications relevant to an issue in a proceeding relating to the abuse or neglect of a disabled or legally incompetent person.

of the exception. Thus, federal courts have alternatively developed typologies and testing for those individual patients suspected of being "dangerous."[20]

Since the *Jaffee* decision, divergent views of the parameters of the "dangerous patient" exception have emerged. In *United States v. Glass*,[21] the Tenth Circuit held that disclosure of confidential communications was permissible only in those cases in which no alternative for revealing threats to third persons existed. In that case, the court had to consider the actions of a psychotherapist who revealed that a patient had threatened harm to President Clinton and the First Lady. The court ruled that the introduction of such evidence was appropriate because of the seriousness of the threat and the absence of alternative means for averting harm to the victims.

 APPLICATION OF LAW

THE PSYCHOTHERAPIST-PATIENT PRIVILEGE AND A MURDER IN BEVERLY HILLS

On August 20, 1989, the silence of a warm summer evening in Beverly Hills was shattered by a series of shotgun blasts. For a brief period afterward, silence returned while the killers returned to their car to reload. Then, more shotgun blasts pierced the stillness surrounding the mansion at 722 Elm Drive. Summoned to the house by the victims' sons, law enforcement authorities discovered the bodies of Jose and Kitty Menendez. Both victims had been shot numerous times, and both had suffered massive shotgun blasts to the head. The initial investigation revealed no signs of burglary or forced entry. Although the brothers were questioned by the police, they were not considered suspects and no gunshot-residue tests were conducted on their hands or clothing. The sons of the victims, Lyle and Eric, suggested that their parents had been the victims of a mob hit—a theory that initially seemed plausible in the absence of any other motive. Shortly thereafter, however, the brothers' behavior caught the attention of the police. It seemed that the brothers could not spend their inheritance fast enough. Designer clothes, fancy sports cars, apartments, rock concerts, even a private tennis coach—nothing was too good or too expensive for the Menendez brothers.

Six months after the murders in Beverly Hills, Eric and Lyle Menendez were arrested and charged with the murder of their parents. During the ensuing trial, the brothers asserted that they murdered their parents after suffering years of sexual abuse at the hands of their father. Their high-priced attorneys brought in several experts who suggested that Eric and Lyle were in fear of their lives from their father. Apparently, the testimony caused some concern for jurors who were unable to reach a verdict.

(continued)

In the second trial, audiotapes and transcripts from the boys' sessions with their therapist were disclosed in open court. These tapes, which were recorded without the knowledge of the brothers, were brought to the attention of authorities by the ex-lover of the therapist who had treated them. Defense counsels' efforts to exclude the evidence on the grounds of patient-therapist privilege were unsuccessful. The court argued that "all therapy records contributing to a determination of dangerousness and the necessity to disclose to prevent any harm are compellable, even if they pertain to the period after a confession."[23] At this second trial, the pair was summarily convicted.

In a ruling contrary to *Glass*, the Sixth Circuit ruled that creating a "dangerous patient" exception to the psychotherapist-patient privilege would create a chilling effect on communications between individuals suffering from mental illness and the only individuals who could help them. In *United States v. Hayes*, the Sixth Circuit heard a case in which a counselor revealed to a targeted victim those threats issued by a patient under his care. Consequently, the patient was arrested and charged with threatening to murder a federal employee based largely on those threats. Upon review, the court ruled that although a counselor or psychotherapist might bear an ethical duty to warn a potential target, such information would not rise to the level to be excluded from the protections of the psychotherapist-patient privilege. Thus, warnings could be issued out of court, but psychotherapists could be prevented from disclosing such information through testimony in court.[22]

► Clergy-Communicant Privilege

clergy-communicant privilege legal protection against compulsory disclosure of the often personal and sensitive communications between a member of the clergy and his or her penitent (formerly known as the priest–penitent privilege).

Originally known as the priest-penitent privilege, the **clergy-communicant privilege** grants legal protection against compulsory disclosure of the often personal and sensitive communications between a member of the clergy and his or her penitent. This privilege was recognized as early as the fifth century in medieval Christianity. The granting of such protection was primarily in response to the traditional "Seal of Confession." The Seal was considered necessary to ensure complete and total disclosure of all sinful activity committed by penitents belonging to the Catholic Church. Sacramental responsibility was necessary for eternal salvation, thus it was rationalized that communications housed within the confines of the confessional were above the boundaries of the judicial process. Such recognition existed in English law for a millennium before its abolition by the Anglican Church after the Protestant Reformation.[24] Because of its abolishment from English law before the American Revolution, the clergy-communicant privilege was not incorporated formally into American law. However, case law since then reveals that the privilege remained an ideal recognized by American jurists. First recognized in a state court in the 1800s, all 50 states and the federal judiciary have recognized some level of privilege in the relationship between members of the clergy and the flock to which they minister.

Perhaps the best known case involving this privilege was heard in 1813. In *People v. Philips*, the Court of General Sessions in the City of New York considered whether a Catholic priest could be compelled to reveal the contents of a penitent's confession or face capital punishment. It stated:

> It is essential to the free exercise of a religion, that its ordinances should be administered—that its ceremonies as well as its essentials should be protected. The sacraments of a religion are its most important elements. We have but two in the Protestant Church—Baptism and the Lord's Supper—and they are considered the seals of the covenant of grace. Suppose that a decision of this court, or a law of the state should prevent the administration of one or both of these sacraments, would not the constitution be violated, and the freedom of religion be infringed? . . . Will not the same result

CODE OF VIRGINIA

§8.01-400—Communications Between Ministers of Religion and Persons They Counsel or Advise

No regular minister, priest, rabbi, or accredited practitioner over the age of eighteen years, of any religious organization or denomination usually referred to as a church, shall be required to give testimony as a witness or to relinquish notes, records or any written documentation made by such person, or disclose the contents of any such notes, records or written documentation, in discovery proceedings in any civil action that would disclose any information communicated to him in a confidential manner, properly entrusted to him in his professional capacity and necessary to enable him to discharge the functions of his office according to the usual course of his practice or discipline, wherein such person so communicating such information about himself or another is seeking spiritual counsel and advice relative to and growing out of the information so imparted. (Code 1950, §8-289.2; 1962, c. 466; 1977, c. 617; 1979, c. 3; 1994, c. 198.)

follow, if we deprive the Roman catholic [*sic*] of one of these ordinances? Secrecy is of the essence of penance. The sinner will not confess, nor will the priest receive his confession, if the veil of secrecy is removed: To decide that the minister shall promulgate what he receives in confession, is to declare that there shall be no penance; and this important branch of the Roman catholic [*sic*] religion would be thus annihilated.[25]

Parameters and Limitations

As with the other privileges, the clergy-communicant privilege is not without limitation. Only conversations designed to be confidential can enjoy the protections afforded under the statutory privilege. Such communications must be housed within the confines of a relationship that has been entered into for the purpose of seeking spiritual guidance. Casual conversations or communications not conducted specifically for such purpose are not included. Thus, the privilege does not

Generally speaking, communications between a priest and a penitent within the confines of a confessional, as pictured here, are considered privileged.

attach to information contained within marriage counseling, religious education classes, and the like. In addition, the privilege includes all levels of clergy, including those with extensive formal education and training and those without. It also may be extended to individuals engaged in spiritual counseling only part-time, such as part-time ministers. In contrast to the privileges discussed earlier, the ownership of the clergy-communicant privilege belongs to both parties—the clergy is extended the privilege so that he or she may not be forced to sacrifice or compromise denominational rules.

▶ Media-Source Privilege

media-source privilege a privilege allowing a reporter or other media representative to withhold disclosure of a source's identity. This privilege does not have the legal standing of other similar privileges such as the attorney-client privilege.

Many of the privileges discussed in this chapter involve relationships generally considered sacred by society. However, the **media-source privilege**—a legal privilege allowing a reporter or other media representative to withhold disclosure of a source's identity—has not found the same level of support. This privilege, unheard of before the turbulence of the 1960s and 1970s, surfaced during a period in which a polarizing climate created a chasm between law enforcement and the communities it policed. At the same time that many residents were communicating their dissatisfaction with and suspicion of the government through the press, representatives of the media took the opportunity to test the parameters of the First Amendment. In *Branzburg v. Hayes* (1972), the Supreme Court firmly decried the notion that media sources were entitled to any special protection from compulsory testimony and opined:

> The First Amendment does not relieve a newspaper reporter of the obligation that all citizens have to respond to a grand jury subpoena and answer questions relevant to a criminal investigation, and therefore the Amendment does not afford him a constitutional testimonial privilege for an agreement he makes to conceal facts relevant to a grand jury's investigation of a crime or to conceal the criminal conduct of his source or evidence thereof.
>
> A number of States have provided newsmen a statutory privilege of varying breadth, but the majority has not done so, and none has been provided by federal statute. Until now the only testimonial privilege for unofficial witnesses that is rooted in the Federal Constitution [408 U.S. 665, 690] is the Fifth Amendment privilege against compelled self-incrimination. We are asked to create another by interpreting the First Amendment to grant newsmen a testimonial privilege that other citizens do not enjoy. This we decline to do. Fair and effective law enforcement aimed at providing security for the person and property of the individual is a fundamental function of government, and the grand jury plays an important, constitutionally mandated role in this process. On the records now before us, we perceive no basis for holding that the public interest in law enforcement and in ensuring effective grand jury proceedings is insufficient to override the consequential, but uncertain, burden on news gathering that is said to result from insisting that reporters, like other citizens, respond to relevant [408 U.S. 665, 691] questions put to them in the course of a valid grand jury investigation or criminal trial.[26]

In *Branzburg*, however, the Court did recognize some First Amendment protection in its acknowledgment that Congress and state legislatures may pass statutes to protect certain categories of journalist they felt were deserving of such protection. The Court ruled further that grand juries that were not held in good faith and those that are designed to harass journalists may be exempt from compulsory testimony of same. However, the application of *Branzburg* has varied. All federal courts excepting the Sixth and Seventh Circuits have recognized a qualified First Amendment journalist privilege prohibiting forced disclosure. Since *Branzburg*, 40 states and the District of Columbia have recognized limited protections afforded

SECTION 19-11-100—QUALIFIED PRIVILEGE AGAINST DISCLOSURE FOR NEWS MEDIA WAIVER

(B) The person, company, or other entity may not be compelled to disclose any information or document or produce any item obtained or prepared in the gathering or dissemination of news unless the party seeking to compel the production or testimony establishes by clear and convincing evidence that this privilege has been knowingly waived or that the testimony or production sought:

1. is material and relevant to the controversy for which the testimony or production is sought;

2. cannot be reasonably obtained by alternative means; and

3. is necessary to the proper preparation or presentation of the case of a party seeking the information, document, or item.

© Publication of any information, document, or item obtained in the gathering and dissemination of news does not constitute a waiver of the qualified privilege against compelled disclosure provided for in this section.

to journalists known as "shield laws." Similar to other privileges, the media-source privilege includes only confidential communications and has various exceptions. For the most part, information considered probative and information that cannot be obtained through alternative means will not be protected and will be evaluated independently by the presiding judge outside the presence of the jury.

▶ Government Privileges

In a general sense, state and federal governments have recognized that certain relationships exist among government actors that are essential to the maintenance of a free society. Thus, in several situations, legislation has been enacted or observation of case law has occurred in which a formal recognition of such situations has evolved. Generally speaking, the protection from compulsory disclosure of information contained within the confines of those relations extends only when the preservation of confidentiality outweighs the necessity for disclosure in the interest of justice.

Police-Informant Privilege

It is a well-documented fact that the law enforcement mission could not be so easily accomplished without the use of confidential informants. Such individuals are essential, especially when few, if any, other witnesses exist because of intimidation or fear of retaliation. In such cases, it is imperative for individuals to be assured of their safety, in general, and the concern of the law enforcement community, more specifically. To create an environment conducive to knowledge-sharing, such individuals must be confident that their identities will remain secret. Thus, many states have formally codified a **police-informant privilege** to give legal protection against the compulsory disclosure of the identity of an informant, including narcotics investigators and corporate whistleblowers.

police-informant privilege legal protection against compulsory disclosure of the identity of an informant, such as narcotics investigators and corporate whistleblowers.

An informant's privilege has been recognized since common law. Generally, such privilege is granted to all confidential informants, regardless of their motivation for disclosing the information, which may include fear, retaliation, financial need, and the like. The Court, in the 1957 case of *Roviaro v. United States*, noted that the privilege actually belonged to the government and not the informant. To wit,

What is usually referred to as the informer's privilege is in reality the Government's privilege to withhold from disclosure the identity of persons who furnish information

Informants often are integral parts of law enforcement investigations. Whenever possible, the authorities shield the identities of informants in order to continue collecting information from them. However, the protections afforded under the police-informant privilege are limited in scope.

of violations of law to officers charged with enforcement of that law. . . . The purpose of the privilege is the furtherance and protection of the public interest in effective law enforcement. The privilege recognizes the obligation of citizens to communicate their knowledge of the commission of crimes to law-enforcement officials and, by preserving their anonymity, encourages them to perform that obligation.

As with others, the informant's privilege is not absolute. Many different exceptions exist. For example, the police-informant privilege does not apply after the identity of the informant is revealed or becomes known to persons who might be displeased with such information. It also does not attach in situations that are not designed to be confidential. In *U.S. Department of Justice, et al. v. Landano*,[27] the Court held that the government is not entitled to a presumption that all sources supplying information automatically meet the requirements for confidentiality. In fact, the Court ruled that the only individuals entitled to such protection are those who give information to the government with the expectation of nondisclosure of their identity excepting law enforcement purposes. Characteristics that might be considered in the evaluation of a reasonable expectation of confidentiality might include: character of the crime, interpersonal relationships between the informant and the target, and their relationship to law enforcement (i.e., paid informants usually enjoy a presumption of nondisclosure). Generally speaking, the identity of an informant largely will be protected if disclosure of such is not important to the defense. In the interest of fairness, however, certain case characteristics will necessarily result in disclosure. For example, eyewitnesses to or victims of a criminal act may not expect any level of confidentiality to be recognized. (This is not to suggest, however, that individuals calling tip lines and such may remain anonymous to both the police and the defendant.) In those cases in which the information is deemed essential to the preparation and presentment of a defense, the government may either disclose the identity or choose to drop the proceedings.

A further limitation on the applicability of the privilege arises from the fundamental requirements of fairness. Where the disclosure of an informer's identity, or of the contents of his communication, is relevant and helpful [353 U.S. 53, 61] to the defense of an accused, or is essential to a fair determination of a cause, the privilege must give way. In these situations the trial court may require disclosure and, if the Government withholds the information, dismiss the action. Most of the federal cases involving

WIKILEAKS AND JOURNALISTIC FREEDOM

In 2006, WikiLeaks.com made its Internet debut. Branding itself as an international, nonprofit, journalistic organization, the group created a depository of millions of classified (or otherwise private or secret) documents. Ostensibly, the site was developed as an avenue to expose government malfeasance. Focusing almost exclusively on the United States, leaks have included, but have not been limited to:

- Documentation of equipment expenditures and real estate holdings in the war in Afghanistan.

- Gunsight footage from the 2007 Baghdad airstrikes in which Iraqi journalists were among the fatalities shot from Apache helicopters (the video became known as *Collateral Murder*)

- A compilation of nearly 80,000 previously unpublished documents about the war in Afghanistan (known as *Afghan War Diary*)

- Hundreds of secret files on detainees at Guantanamo Bay

In November 2010, WikiLeaks collaborated with the global media and released diplomatic cables in redacted format sent by the U.S. State department. Several months later, the unredacted documents became publicly available on BitTorrent. WikiLeaks denied responsibility, but various sources suggested that mistakes by the group had created the untenable situation.

Many of the documents counter to the interest of the United States were given to WikiLeaks by Bradley Manning, an intelligence analyst for the U.S. Army. This material included the Baghdad airstrikes and a quarter million U.S. diplomatic cables. Upon discovery of his treasonous actions, Manning was ultimately charged with more than 20 offenses, including aiding the enemy, which carried the potential for the death penalty. In 2013, Manning was convicted of various charges but was acquitted of the most serious. He is currently serving a 35-year sentence at Fort Leavenworth, where he is currently transitioning into a woman.

this limitation on the scope of the informer's privilege have arisen where the legality of a search without a warrant is in issue and the communications of an informer are claimed to establish probable cause. In these cases the Government has been required to disclose the identity of the informant unless there was sufficient evidence apart from his confidential communication.[28]

Military, Diplomatic, and National Security Privileges

Traditionally, American society and others have recognized the need to safeguard information that may be necessary for the protection of the community at large and, in particular, the government. As such, case law and legislation have been introduced in various manners that protect military, diplomatic, and national security secrets. One of the first cases to test the boundaries of the common law privilege was a civil lawsuit filed by the families of civilians killed in the crash of a United States Air Force (USAF) plane. In its justification, the Supreme Court recognized that the national defense mandated the secreting of certain information. At the same time, the Court recognized that such concealment may even extend to the judiciary even if the most circumspect and secure atmosphere of disclosure is observed. To wit,

> Regardless of how it is articulated, some like formula of compromise must be applied here. Judicial control over the evidence in a case cannot be abdicated to the caprice of executive officers. Yet we will not go so far as to say that the court may automatically require a complete disclosure to the judge before the claim of privilege will be accepted in any case. It may be possible to satisfy the court, from all the circumstances of the case, that there is a reasonable danger that compulsion of the evidence will expose military matters which, in the interest of national security, should not be divulged. When this is the case, the occasion for the privilege is appropriate, and the court should not jeopardize the security which the privilege is meant to protect by insisting upon an examination of the evidence, even by the judge alone, in chambers.[29]

In this particular case, the Secretary of the Air Force claimed that the accident report requested by the plaintiffs contained information of emerging technology (i.e., secret electronic devices) and that disclosure would be detrimental to the security of the United States. In considering his argument, the Court noted recent history and declared:

> In the instant case we cannot escape judicial notice that this is a time of vigorous preparation for national defense. Experience in the past war has made it common knowledge that air power is one of the most potent weapons in our scheme of defense, and that newly developing electronic devices have greatly enhanced the effective use of air power. It is equally apparent that these electronic devices must be kept secret if their full military advantage is to be exploited in the national interests. On the record before the trial court it appeared that this accident occurred to a military plane which had gone aloft to test secret electronic equipment. Certainly there was a reasonable danger that the accident investigation report would contain references to the secret electronic equipment which was the primary concern of the mission.[30]

Since *Reynolds*, the United States Congress has enacted several pieces of legislation to codify government privileges that address the protection of military, diplomatic, and national security secrets. Such acts include the Classified Information Procedures Act (CIPA), the Foreign Intelligence Surveillance Act (FISA), and the United States Patriot Act of 2001. Of them all, only CIPA specifically addresses the procedures for the evaluation of classified or protected information. In a general sense, CIPA allows the court to consider whether classified information should be deemed inadmissible in part or in whole. It also includes provisions for the maintenance of such evaluation in such a manner that neither the appellate process nor the security interest of the information is compromised. Theoretically speaking, it is designed to be procedural in nature and should not interfere with either the substantive rights of the accused nor the discovery obligations shouldered by the government.

Presidential Privilege

In addition to recognizing the need of the government to protect secrets that may affect national security or compromise military or diplomatic missions, the Court has recognized that the president of the United States enjoys a qualified privilege regarding confidential communications that occur between the president and the president's immediate advisors. In justifying such a protection, the Court argued that:

> The expectation of a President to the confidentiality of his conversations and correspondence, like the claim of confidentiality of judicial deliberations, for example, has all the values to which we accord deference for the privacy of all citizens and, added to those values, is the necessity for protection of the public interest in candid, objective, and even blunt or harsh opinions in Presidential decision-making. A President and those who assist him must be free to explore alternatives in the process of shaping policies and making decisions and to do so in a way many would be unwilling to express except privately. These are the considerations justifying a presumptive privilege for Presidential communications. The privilege is fundamental to the operation of Government and inextricably rooted in the separation of powers under the Constitution . . . such Presidential communications are "presumptively privileged," "[i]n no case of this kind would a court be required to proceed against the president as against an ordinary individual."[31]

However, the Court refused to extend a general presumptive privilege to all confidential communications entered into by the president because such a policy would virtually negate the concept of the U.S. government.

Neither the doctrine of separation of powers nor the generalized need for confidentiality of high-level communications, without more, can sustain an absolute, unqualified Presidential privilege of immunity from judicial process under all circumstances. . . . Absent a claim of need to protect military, diplomatic, or sensitive national security secrets, the confidentiality of. . . . Presidential communications is not significantly diminished by producing material for a criminal trial under the protected conditions of in camera inspection, and any absolute executive privilege under Art. II of the Constitution would plainly conflict with the function of the courts under the Constitution.[32]

► Miscellaneous Privileges

For the most part, the privileges discussed so far in this chapter are accepted across the country, with slight variation. It appears that society is willing to accept the sanctity of the attorney-client, clergy-communicant, and husband-wife relationships. But, several new privileges are emerging that may require court opinion. For example, some states are considering extending the husband-wife privilege to domestic partners. Additional privileges have already been enacted including interpreter-deaf privilege (e.g., Code of Virginia §8.01-400.1) and sexual assault counselor-victim (e.g., California Evidence Code §1035-1036.2), to name just two. Privileges that are becoming more recognized include the parent-child privilege and the accountant-client privilege.

Parent-Child Privilege

Although federal courts have refused steadfastly to recognize a parent-child privilege, some states have adopted the privilege by statute. Similar to the rationale for the spousal privilege, the parent-child privilege is designed to foster open communication within the family unit. For the most part, the privilege, where available, protects only those communications between a parent and a minor child and does not attach to conversations between adults. For example, under Idaho's Rule of Evidence 514, "a child or ward has a privilege in a civil or criminal action or proceeding to which the child or ward is a party to refuse to disclose and to prevent the child's or ward's parent, guardian or legal custodian from disclosing any confidential communication made by the child or ward to the parent, guardian or legal custodian of the child or ward."

Accountant-Client Privilege

Although federal courts in the United States have refused to recognize a privilege between a professional accountant or certified public accountant (CPA) and his or her client, some states have incorporated such a privilege into their rules of

---

EXAMPLE OF STATE ACCOUNTANT-CLIENT PRIVILEGE NEVADA REVISED STATUTE

GENERAL RULE OF PRIVILEGE

A client has a privilege to refuse to disclose, and to prevent any other person from disclosing, confidential communications:

1. Between himself or his representative and his accountant or his accountant's representative.

2. Between his accountant and the accountant's representative.

3. Made for the purpose of facilitating the rendition of professional accounting services to the client, by him or his accountant to an accountant representing another in a matter of common interest.

---

evidence. For the most part, states have granted the ownership of said privilege to the client, his or her guardian, his or her personal representative if deceased, or a trustee of a corporation. As with the more traditionally recognized privileges, relationships entered into for the purpose of planning and perpetuating a fraud or other crime are not protected. In addition, communications that involve matters of common interest among clients and those that involve allegations of a breach of fiduciary trust are not included within the parameters of the privilege.

▶ CONCLUSIONS

Generally speaking, law in the United States is characterized by compulsory processes. The legal compulsion to testify is no exception. However, there are some situations in which the expectation of disclosure is all but negated. Such situations are known as testimonial privileges. The rationale for such exclusion derives in part from statutory law developed from state and federal legislatures, as well as from constitutional provisions of same. In addition, case law derived from judicial interpretations of common law provides some measure of explanation as to the exclusion of relevant evidence in particular circumstances. Characterizing some relationships, interests, or rights as legally inviolable protects and sanctifies those situations in which society has a vested interest. Such situations or relationships include, but are not limited to, husband-wife, attorney-client, clergy-communicant, physician-patient, and law enforcement agent-informant (including protections against disclosure of government secrets or matters of national security). Unfortunately, the Federal Rules of Evidence provide little guidance as to the nature and scope of such privileges, allowing the courts to interpret common law and the states to develop the boundaries to wit testimonial privileges apply. In fact, Congress intentionally deleted references to particular privileges in Rule 501, choosing instead to use a generic approach that relied upon federal courts' case-by-case interpretation. Taking their lead, the Supreme Court has narrowly defined privileged communications, noting that testimonial privileges "are not lightly created nor expansively construed, for they are in derogation of the search for truth."[33]

Privileges are distinct from other protections afforded to individuals under rules of evidence:

1. They not only prevent compulsory testimony of individuals at trial but also protect the contents of particular communications from adverse parties even when those contents are relevant.
2. They are not intended to assist in the fact-finding mission of the court by excluding evidence that is inherently unreliable or unduly prejudicial.

In fact, privileges have been characterized as inhibitive to the illumination of the truth. They are designed to protect other interests that have been determined to be significant enough to limit access to otherwise relevant evidence.

Key Terms

Attorney-client privilege	Marital communications privilege	Psychotherapist-patient privilege
Clergy-communicant privilege	Media-source privilege	Requisite relationship
Confidentiality	Physician-patient privilege	Spousal testimonial privilege
"Dangerous patient" exception	Police-informant privilege	Work-product doctrine

Discussion Questions

1. Should spousal privileges be extended to domestic partners? Discuss the advantages and disadvantages.
2. Discuss the extent of presidential privileges. Are the limitations too few? Is the privilege necessary?
3. What are the advantages and disadvantages to the media-source privilege?
4. Under what circumstances do you think privilege should be extended? Should any of the privileges be revoked? Should other relationships (besides those mentioned in the chapter) be extended privileges?

Recommended Resources

A&E Television. A family secret: The death of Lisa Steinberg. *American justice*. Available at: http://store.aetv.com.

A&E Television. The Menendez murders. *American justice*. Available at: http://store.aetv.com.

Books

Beard, Glenn A. (1997). Congress v. the attorney-client privilege: A "full and frank" discussion. *American Criminal Law Review*, *35*(1): 119–135.

Cassidy, R. Michael. (2003). Sharing sacred secrets: Is it (past) time for a dangerous person exception to the clergy-penitent privilege. *William and May Law Review*, *44*(4): 1627.

Edwards, Deborah C. (2006). Duty-to-warn—Even if it may be hearsay? The implications of a psychotherapist's duty-to-warn a third person when information is obtained from someone other than his patient. *Indiana Health Law Review*, *3*(171). Accessed at: http://www.lexisnexis.com.

Karin, Marcy Lynn. (2002). Out of sight, but not out of mind: How Executive Order 13,233 expands executive privilege while simultaneously preventing access to presidential records. *Stanford Law Review*, *55*(2): 529–571.

Montgomery, Bruce P. (2002). Source material: Nixon's ghost haunts the presidential records act. *Presidential Studies Quarterly*, *32*(4): 789–795.

Oppenheimer, Tamara; Bankim, Thanki; Goodall, Patrick; King, Henry; Phelps, Rosalind; Cutress, James; Yeo, Nik; and Carpenter, Chloe. (2006). *The law of privilege (in the UK)*. England: Oxford University Press.

Rozell, Mike. (1998). Executive privilege in the Lewinsky scandal: Giving a good doctrine a bad name. *Presidential Studies Quarterly*, *28*(4): 816–821.

Swinton, Nathan. (2006). Privileging a privilege: Should the reporter's privilege enjoy the same respect as the attorney-client privilege? *Georgetown Journal of Legal Ethics*, *19*(979). Accessed at: http://www.lexisnexis.com.

Wigmore, J. H. (1940). *A Treatise on the Anglo-American System of Evidence in Trial at Common Law* (3rd ed.). Boston: Little Brown and Company.

Online Sources

http://www.findlaw.com—Search state and federal case law, statutes, and federal and state constitutions.

http://www.abanet.org—Official home page of the American Bar Association maintains active links to publications and resources regarding various concepts in evidence law, including hearsay, professional ethics, and the confrontation clause.

http://www.lexisnexis.com—Powerful search engine providing links and other resources for searching newspapers, periodicals, journals, and the like, along with access to federal and state law, cases, codes, and regulations for use by users to search for law reviews regarding particular areas of interest in the law.

http://www.eff.org—Official home page of the Electronic Frontier Foundation, an organization that seeks to secure the privacy of individuals while using technology, provides access to articles and resources to evaluate the sanctity of confidential informants.

http://www.aallnet.org—Official home page of the American Association of Law Libraries; includes a useful search function for researching publications on numerous topics.

http://www.uscourts.gov—Official Web site of the Federal Judiciary; search feature allows electronic access to courts and enables users to research federal cases, constitutional evolutions, and judicial structure.

http://www.fjc.gov—Official home page of the Federal Judicial Center, the education and research agency for the federal courts. The site provides links and access to publications, videos, educational materials, and federal history, including the results of research sponsored by the Center.

Relevant Cases Cited

Branzburg v. Hayes, 408 U.S. 665 (1972)

Department of Justice v. Landano, 508 U.S. 165 (1993)

Hawkins v. United States, 358 U.S. 74 (1958)

Hickman v. Taylor, 329 U.S. 495 (1947)

Jaffee v. Redmond, 518 U.S. 1 (1996)

Roviaro v. United States, 353 U.S. 53 (1957)

Swidler and Berlin and James Hamilton v. U.S., 524 U.S. 399 (1998)

Trammel v. United States, 445 U.S. 40 (1980)

Upjohn Co. v. United States, 449 U.S. 383 (1981)

United States v. Hayes, 227 F.3d. 578 (2000)

United States v. Nixon, 418 U.S. 683 (1974)

United States v. Reynolds, 345 U.S. 1 (1953)

United States Department of Justice, et al. v. Landano, 508 U.S. 165 (1993)

Wolfle v. United States, 291 U.S. 7 (1934)

Notes

1. Wigmore, J. H. (1940). *A treatise on the Anglo-American system of evidence in trial at common law* (3rd ed.). Boston: Little Brown.
2. Lombardo, P. (2005). The newest federal privilege: Jaffee v. Redmond and the protection of psychotherapeutic confidentiality. *Developments in Mental Health Law*. http://www.ilppp.virginia.edu/dhml/issues/jaffeev16n2.html.
3. Leonard, D. (2004). Federal privileges in the 21st century: An introduction. *Loyola of Los Angeles Law Review*, *38*(515). www.lexisnexis.com.
4. Penfil, E. (2005). In the light of reason and experience: Should federal evidence law protect confidential communications between same-sex partners? *Marquette Law Review*, *88*(815). www.lexisnexis.com.
5. Weinstein, J. B., Mansfield, J. H., Abrams, N., & Berger, M. A. (1997). *Evidence: Cases and materials* (9th ed.). New York: Foundation Press.
6. *Upjohn Co. v. U.S.*, 449 U.S. 383 (1981)
7. Ibid.
8. Weinstein et al., 1997.
9. Ibid.
10. *Swidler and Berlin and James Hamilton v. U.S.*, 524 U.S. 399 (1998)
11. *Hickman v. Taylor*, 329 U.S. 495 (1947)
12. Ibid.
13. *Trammel v. United States*, 445 U.S. 40 (1980)
14. *U.S. v. Martinez*, 44 F.Supp.2d 835, 836 (W.D. Tex. 1999)
15. *Wolfle v. U.S.*, 291 U.S. 7 (1934)
16. *Trammel v. U.S.*, 445 U.S. 40 (1980)
17. *United States ex rel. Edney v. Smith*, 425 F.Supp. 1038, 1976 Dist. Lexist 12131 (1976)
18. *Jaffee v. Redmond*, 518 U.S. 1 (1996)
19. *Jaffee v. Redmond*, 518 U.S. 1 (1996)
20. McKeever, B. P. (2004). Contours and chaos: A proposal for courts to apply the "dangerous patient" exception to the psychotherapist-patient privilege. *New Mexico Law Review*, *34*(109). www.lexisnexis.com.
21. *United States v. Glass*, 133 F. 3d 1356
22. McKeever, 2004.
23. Glancy, G. D., Regehr, C., & Bryant, A. G. (1998). Confidentiality in crisis: Part II—Confidentiality of treatment records. *Canadian Journal of Psychiatry*, *43*, 1001–1005.
24. Lombardo, 2005.
25. Sampson, W. (1813). *The Catholic Question in America*. New York: Edward Gillespy.
26. *Branzburg v. Hayes*, 408 U.S. 665 (1972)
27. 508 U.S. 165 (1993)
28. *Roviaro v. United States*, 353 U.S. 53 (1957)
29. *United States v. Reynolds*, 345 U.S. 1 (1953)
30. Ibid.
31. *United States v. Nixon*, 418 U.S. 683 (1974)
32. Ibid.
33. Ibid.

THE DECLARATION OF INDEPENDENCE.

12 Documentary and Scientific Evidence

LEARNING OBJECTIVES

The learner will:

1 *Distinguish between motions and objections*

2 *Explain the process of submitting evidence*

▶ Exclusion of Evidence

I think it a less evil that some criminals should escape than that the government should play an ignoble part. (Oliver Wendall Holmes, 1928)

Although the law governing the admissibility of criminal evidence is adjudicated within the confines of a courtroom, the process of evidence collection begins much earlier. As discussed exhaustively in previous chapters, police actions may result in situations in which pertinent information is excluded from consideration. This may occur for various reasons, in various venues. Such exclusions are governed by a broad spectrum of legislative mandates and case law, including, but not limited to, state and federal rules of evidence and criminal procedure, state and federal case law, and the exclusionary rule. Such legal provisions have primarily been established to uphold constitutional protections, ensure judicial integrity, and discourage unlawful actions by agents of the government, and include bad acts by police officers, prosecutors, magistrates, and others. Challenges to the admissibility of a particular item are initiated by the proponent of the exclusion and take one of two forms—motions or objections.

motion to strike
request made to the court to eliminate a legal pleading, either in part or in entirety.

 CLARIFICATION OF CONCEPTS

COMMON MOTIONS ASSOCIATED WITH SCIENTIFIC EVIDENCE

Motion in limine are requests made at the beginning of a trial for certain pieces of evidence to be ruled inadmissible. Motions in limine are always discussed outside the presence of the jury. Example: John Doe is charged with the murder of a police officer during an armed robbery. Prior to the trial, the prosecuting attorney furnishes the defense with a list of the witnesses they intend to call. Among them is Jane Doe, the defendant's wife, who will be called to testify that the defendant had previously told her in confidence that he intended to rob a bank. The defense files a motion in limine, invoking the marital privilege.

Daubert motions are special types of motions in limine which request the preclusion or exclusion of the testimony of an expert witness who lacks the requisite qualifications or who employs questionable methods to reach his/her conclusions. Example: Among the other witnesses listed by the prosecuting attorney is Ivan Seer, a psychic who will be called to testify that he had a vision of the events as they unfolded.

The defense files a *Daubert motion*, arguing that psychic visions lack scientific acceptance, principles, and empiricism.

Motions to strike also request the exclusion of evidence from jury consideration through the removal of such evidence from the court record. Unlike the motions above, motions to strike are not prophylactic in nature and are made after the evidence has been heard in open court and are often necessary in cases involving overeager witnesses. (Although objections are usually the remedy during the proffering of evidence and are made before a response by the witness, some witnesses may blurt out an answer before the court's ruling.) Successful motions to strike result in deletion of the testimony in the court record and a jury instruction from the judge to disregard the stricken information. Example: During the trial, Mickey Marble, a witness for the prosecution, testifies that he had always thought that John Doe would murder a police officer. The defense files a motion to strike, arguing that a lay witness' opinion regarding defendant's propensity for violence is inadmissible to prove guilt.

Motions

A **motion** may be defined as a formal request submitted to the court that a specific judgment or order to be made. Under rules of criminal procedure, motions are filed generally through written petitions that state the action desired and the legal rationale for it and are decided by a hearing before the judge in which opposing counsel may argue against such order. Attorneys may file motions throughout the trial, but many motions to exclude or suppress are heard before opening statements. Motions are filed for various reasons, including, but not limited to, the postponement of legal proceedings, case dismissal, rehearing, and, most important for our purposes, the exclusion of evidence. Such motions, known as **motions in limine**, request that certain pieces of evidence be ruled inadmissible. Motions in limine may argue that the evidence in question would unfairly prejudice the jury or that constitutional violations occurred. In any event, judges maintain wide discretion in their evaluations. Arguments supporting unsuccessful motions may be readdressed by their proponent in the form of timely objections during the trial—thereby preserving the issue for appeal.

As stated, considerations of the admissibility of evidence occur throughout the judicial process and may be made before or immediately following the formal proffering of evidence. Although they take many forms, many objections are based on constitutional violations and may cite the exclusionary rule as their foundation. As the name implies, the **exclusionary rule** is a legal mandate that requires the exclusion of any evidence that was collected by law enforcement personnel in a manner that violates any provision in the Bill of Rights. The rationale for such exclusion is to discourage improper police conduct and illegal collection of evidence—the result of which may be the dismissal of said evidence. For example, absent exigent circumstances, police searches of private residences require that a search warrant be obtained. This warrant must state, with specificity, the place and time of execution, the items to be seized, and the probable cause justifying a search. When officers aggressively and without regard to due process search a home absent exigent circumstances or a search warrant, evidence collected therein may be excluded from later consideration. However, the Court has opined that such exclusion is limited to circumstances in which the deterrence of future misconduct is desired and anticipated. To wit,

> "The question whether the exclusionary rule's remedy is appropriate in a particular context has long been regarded as an issue separate from the question whether the Fourth Amendment rights of the party seeking to invoke the rule were violated by police conduct." *Illinois v. Gates*, 462 U.S. 213, 223 (1983); see also *United States v. Havens*, 446 U.S. 620, 627–628 (1980); *Stone v. Powell*, 428 U.S. 465, 486–487 (1976); *Calandra*, supra, at 348. The exclusionary rule operates as a judicially created remedy designed to safeguard against future violations of Fourth Amendment rights through the rule's general deterrent effect. *Leon*, supra, at 906; *Calandra*, supra, at 348. As with any remedial device, the rule's application has been restricted to those instances where its remedial objectives are thought most efficaciously served. *Leon*, supra, at 908; *Calandra*, supra, at 348. Where "the exclusionary rule does not result in appreciable deterrence, then, clearly, its use . . . is unwarranted."[1]

As discussed in earlier chapters, several circumstances exist that may allow the introduction of evidence collected by officers absent the benefit of a warrant. These include, but are not limited to, searches involving automobiles, field interrogations, incident to arrest, consent, and plain view. In addition, evidence collected

motion a formal request submitted to the court that a specific judgment or order be made.

motions in limine requests made at the beginning of a trial for certain pieces of evidence to be ruled inadmissible. Motions in limine are always discussed outside the presence of the jury.

exclusionary rule legal mandate requiring the exclusion of any evidence collected by law enforcement personnel in a manner that violates any provision in the Bill of Rights. This judge-made rule is designed to discourage law enforcement from circumventing the protections offered in the Fourth and Fifth Amendments.

▼

in violation of the exclusionary rule may still be admissible when there exists a threat to public safety, an inevitability of discovery of evidence, or good faith by law enforcement personnel.

Objections

Unlike motions that may be filed before or after a formal proffering of evidence, **objections** are made during the questioning of witnesses. Rules of criminal procedure require objections to be contemporaneous with the alleged violation of law. They may be extended for various reasons including, but not limited to, irrelevance of material, improper questioning, speculative inquiry, hearsay, or lack of response. All objections must be based on specific rules of law.

Demonstrating Materiality, Competency, and Relevancy

Once it has been established that the offered evidence should not be excluded because of constitutional violations or improper collection procedures, the proponent of the evidence must demonstrate the materiality, competency, and relevancy of same. As discussed in Chapter 1, evidence is considered *material* if it will affect the outcome of the legal proceeding at hand and *competent* if it appears truthful and reliable. The *relevancy* of an item in question, on the other hand, evaluates the materiality of the item and its probative value.

Although the trial judge conducts the evaluation of the competency of evidence, the jury as trier of fact may decide independently that a particular item or witness lacks credibility, thereby refusing to consider it during jury deliberation. Simply put, the competency of evidence is determined by the credibility of the item in question. There are numerous situations and circumstances—from the credibility of the witness, reliability of the science employed, and consistency of evidence collection and preservation—that may render evidence legally incompetent or unworthy of consideration in the jury's estimation.

As stated in Rule 401 of the Federal Rules of Evidence (FRE), relevant evidence is evidence "having any tendency to make the existence of any fact that is of consequence to the determination of the action more probable or less probable than it would be without the evidence." However, not all relevant evidence is necessarily admissible. In fact, the admissibility of such is determined largely by the judge who evaluates the probity of the evidence versus potential hazards posed by its admission. Evaluation of the probity of the fact or item in question includes consideration of the weight of the evidence versus the expediency of its introduction (i.e., does it add to the case or is it more cumulative). Potential hazards, on the other hand, include potential bias or prejudice, confusion of issues, and misleading the jury.

FEDERAL RULES OF EVIDENCE

TITLE IV: RELEVANCE AND ITS LIMITS

Rule 403—Excluding Relevant Evidence for Prejudice, Confusion, Waste of Time, or Other Reasons

The court may exclude relevant evidence if its probative value is substantially outweighed by a danger of one or more of the following: unfair prejudice, confusing the issues, misleading the jury, undue delay, wasting time, or needlessly presenting cumulative evidence.

Potential for Unfair Prejudice

According to FRE Rule 403, relevant evidence may be excluded if its probative value is substantially outweighed by the potential for unfair prejudice. Simply put, **unfair or undue prejudice** refers to anything that could encourage a fact finder (e.g., jury member) to develop an adverse opinion before having sufficient knowledge of relevant facts. This does not mean damage to the opponent's case because probative information from opposing counsel is necessarily designed to cast doubt on the other's, nor does it infer that information that evokes an emotional response is to be discarded. Rather, unfair prejudice:

> . . . speaks to the capacity of some concededly relevant evidence to lure the fact finder into declaring guilt on an improper basis rather than on proof specific to the offense charged.[2]

Items that tend to invoke prejudice or bias include the introduction of past crimes or bad acts by the defendant or gruesome photographs of the crime scene. The presiding judge determines the admissibility of potentially prejudicial evidence after considering the probative value of the item and the potential for bias.

> Such improper grounds certainly include generalizing from a past bad act that a defendant is by propensity the probable perpetrator of the current crime. Thus, Rule 403 requires that the relative probative value of prior-conviction evidence be balanced against its prejudicial risk of misuse. A judge should balance these factors not only for the item in question but also for any actually available substitutes. If an alternative were found to have substantially the same or greater probative value but a lower danger of unfair prejudice, sound judicial discretion would discount the value of the item first offered and exclude it if its discounted probative value were substantially outweighed by unfairly prejudicial risk.[3]

unfair or undue prejudice refers to anything that could encourage a fact finder (e.g., jury member) to develop an adverse opinion before having sufficient knowledge of relevant facts.

⚖ CASE LAW

PREJUDICE AND CHANGE OF VENUE: *SKILLING V. UNITED STATES*, 561 U.S. 358 (2010)

In the dawn of the new millennium, investors were financially devastated when the seventh highest revenue grossing company in America crashed into bankruptcy. An investigation by a Department of Justice taskforce into the collapse revealed an elaborate conspiracy to increase Enron's stock price by falsely inflating the company's financial well-being. Dozens of employees were subsequently prosecuted and convicted of numerous charges. In 2004, a trio of Enron's top executives were finally forced to face the music that they had created. The three defendants were: Kenneth Lay, the company's founder; Richard Causey, former chief accounting officer; and, Jeffrey Skilling, former chief executive officer.

During the trial, Skilling moved to transfer the trial out of Houston, arguing that extensive pretrial publicity had poisoned any potential jury pool. In support of this motion, Skilling submitted hundreds of news reports about the energy giant's collapse and affidavits from media experts, which compared community attitudes about the case to other potential venues. The motion was denied by the U.S. District Court for the Southern District of Texas. Three weeks prior to the scheduled trial date, Skilling's co-defendant, Richard Causey, pled guilty. Skilling again requested a change of venue arguing that Causey's admission would further prejudice potential jurors. He was once again denied. During the subsequent trial, the District Court emphasized the importance of impartiality and provided a comprehensive explanation of both the presumption of innocence and the Government's burden of proof. After a four-month trial, Skilling was convicted on 19 counts. He was sentenced to 292 months imprisonment, 3 years of supervised release, and ordered to pay $45 million in restitution.

Granting certiorari, the Court considered whether Skilling's right to a fair trial was violated. Specifically differentiating earlier decisions [i.e., *Sheppard v. Maxwell*, 384 U.S. 333 (1966) and *(continued)*

Estes v. Texas, 381 U.S. 532 (1965)] in which the Court ruled that media involvement had "utterly corrupted" the trial, the Court held that those decisions "cannot be made to stand for the proposition that juror exposure to . . . news accounts of the crime . . . alone presumptively deprives the defendant of due process" [citing *Murphy v. Florida*, 421 U.S. 794 (1975)]. The Court further noted that prejudice is particularized.

> Prominence does not necessarily produce prejudice, and juror impartiality, we have reiterated, does not require ignorance . . . every case of public interest is almost, as a matter of necessity, brought to the attention of all the intelligent people in the vicinity, brought to the attention of all the intelligent people in the vicinity, and scarcely any one can be found among those best fitted for jurors who has not read or heard of it, and who has not some impression or some opinion in respect to

its merits" [citing *Reynolds v. United States*, 98 U.S. 145 (1879)].

The *Skilling* Court firmly established a significant threshold in demarking cases for changes of venue based on media-induced prejudice. Under this standard, a defendant must demonstrate that publicity has entirely displaced the judicial process or that courtroom proceedings resemble a circus or lynch mob. Factors that may be considered by trial court judges include:

- media interference with courtroom proceedings;
- the magnitude and tone of the coverage;
- the size and characteristics of the community in which the crime was committed;
- amount of time between the crime and the trial;
- the impact of the crime on the community.

Although the Supreme Court has traditionally recognized that the introduction of prior crimes and gruesome photographs has a prima facie potential for prejudice,[4] it has not issued a blanket prohibition against it. As a result, state courts have established their own standards, usually placing the responsibility with the trial judge to consider a range of factors in making the determination.

> When photographs are helpful to explain testimony, they are ordinarily admissible; the mere fact that a photograph is inflammatory or is cumulative is not, standing alone, sufficient reason to exclude it; even the most gruesome photographs may be admissible if they assist the trier of fact in any of the following ways: by shedding light on some issue, by proving a necessary element of the case, by enabling a witness to testify more effectively, by corroborating testimony, or by enabling jurors to better understand the testimony; other acceptable purposes are to show the condition of the victims' bodies, the probable type or location of the injuries, and the position in which the bodies were discovered; absent an abuse of discretion, the supreme court will not reverse a trial court for admitting photographs into evidence.[5]

▶ Proffering of Physical Evidence

Any discussion of the reasons for exclusion of evidence must also include the process through which evidence is proffered to the court. It is important to remember that the American system of criminal justice is governed by strict rules and regulations regarding the introduction of evidence. Thus, the adversarial approach to criminal proceedings extends to the creation of the record of evidence and is designed to foster a legal atmosphere in which expectations are firmly established and consistently applied to the opposing parties. Generally speaking, specific provisions may vary slightly, but the process is remarkably similar across jurisdictions.

For evidence to be introduced, it must be demonstrated that said evidence is both relevant and competent. In addition, the evidence must be more probative than prejudicial. Gruesome crime scene photographs must be evaluated on a case-by-case basis. In the trial of O. J. Simpson, color photographs of Nicole Brown Simpson's nearly severed head may not only be considered shocking but also prejudicial to jury members. However, long distance shots like the one here may lessen the prejudicial factor.

Laying the Foundation

The first step in the introduction of evidence involves the proponent making a request for a marking by the clerk, who then assigns a number for purposes of identification. Generally speaking, the numbers are sequential and are specific to the side of the calling party. Once identified, the item in question is presented to opposing counsel for inspection. If no objections are raised at this point, the item is presented to the witness for identification and authentication purposes. This is known as **laying the foundation**. Although foundational requirements will vary across jurisdiction, this process is generally satisfied after a demonstration of sufficient evidence regarding the authenticity and relevance of the proffered item. Failure to properly lay the foundation may result in an objection by opposing counsel. Once the exhibit has been authenticated, the proponent will tender the item to the judge and request its introduction with a formal statement, such as "The defense offers this videotape marked Defense Exhibit #2 for identification as Defense exhibit 2."

Documenting the Chain of Custody

For physical evidence to be authenticated, the proponent of the evidence must demonstrate that it is what it is claimed to be and that it has not been altered. This necessarily includes documentation of the **chain of custody**, a description and explanation as to

laying the foundation demonstration of the authenticity and relevance of a proffered item of evidence. Failure to properly lay the foundation may result in an objection by opposing counsel.

chain of custody a description and explanation as to where and how the proffered item was found, collected, and preserved before courtroom introduction. This demonstration of evidentiary integrity also includes a chronological history of all individuals who have had access to or possession of the item from initial seizure to courtroom introduction.

ARTICLE IX. AUTHENTICATION AND IDENTIFICATION

Rule 901—Authenticating or Identifying Evidence

(a) In General. To satisfy the requirement of authenticating or identifying an item of evidence, the proponent must produce evidence sufficient to support a finding that the item is what the proponent claims it is.

(b) Examples. The following are examples only—not a complete list—of evidence that satisfies the requirement:

(1) *Testimony of a Witness with Knowledge.* Testimony that an item is what it is claimed to be.

(2) *Nonexpert Opinion About Handwriting.* A nonexpert's opinion that handwriting is genuine, based on a familiarity with it that was not acquired for the current litigation.

(3) *Comparison by an Expert Witness or the Trier of Fact.* A comparison with an authenticated specimen by an expert witness or the trier of fact.

(4) *Distinctive Characteristics and the Like.* The appearance, contents, substance, internal patterns, or other distinctive characteristics of the item, taken together with all the circumstances.

(5) *Opinion About a Voice.* An opinion identifying a person's voice—whether heard firsthand or through mechanical or electronic transmission or recording—based on hearing the voice at any time under circumstances that connect it with the alleged speaker.

(6) *Evidence About a Telephone Conversation.* For a telephone conversation, evidence that a call was made to the number assigned at the time to:

(A) a particular person, if circumstances, including self-identification, show that the person answering was the one called; or

(B) a particular business, if the call was made to a business and the call related to business reasonably transacted over the telephone.

(7) *Evidence About Public Records.* Evidence that:

(A) a document was recorded or filed in a public office as authorized by law; or

(B) a purported public record or statement is from the office where items of this kind are kept.

(8) *Evidence About Ancient Documents or Data Compilations.* For a document or data compilation, evidence that it:

(A) is in a condition that creates no suspicion about its authenticity;

(B) was in a place where, if authentic, it would likely be; and

(C) is at least 20 years old when offered.

(9) *Evidence About a Process or System.* Evidence describing a process or system and showing that it produces an accurate result.

(10) *Methods Provided by a Statute or Rule.* Any method of authentication or identification allowed by a federal statute or a rule prescribed by the Supreme Court.

where and how the proffered item was found, collected, and preserved before courtroom introduction. This demonstration of evidentiary integrity also includes a chronological history of all individuals who have had access to or possession of the item.

The chain of custody is initiated upon the discovery of physical evidence. In the case of nonvolatile physical evidence, normal practice involves the receiving officer marking the item itself with his or her identification and the date. In cases of volatile or corrosive evidence, evidence tags are usually used. To further prevent challenges to the integrity of the evidence, law enforcement agencies maintain official paper logs of the physical custody of the evidence. This includes every individual having possession of the item, the reason and duration for such possession, the process of the transfer of the item to subsequent custodians, and the procedures for the handling and storage of the item. Thus, the chain of custody requirement also includes testimony as to the proper handling of the evidence in question. For example, discussions of bloodstained articles should include a description as to the manner of drying the evidence before packaging it to prevent the development of mold or mildew.

Although theoretically important in all matters of evidence, the chain of custody is especially so when the introduction of fungible evidence is sought. **Fungible evidence**, or evidence that can be manipulated, altered, substituted, or contaminated, includes several categories—biological, chemical, digital, and other trace evidence. All of the following examples require demonstration of chain of custody:

- Biological evidence—DNA found in body fluids, entomological materials, hair, etc.
- Chemical evidence—Narcotics, accelerants, poisons (or other chemical compounds), liquids, gases, etc.

fungible evidence
evidence that can be manipulated, altered, substituted, or contaminated, includes several categories—biological, chemical, digital, and other trace evidence.

Front of Sample Chain-of-Custody form

Anywhere Police Department
EVIDENCE CHAIN OF CUSTODY TRACKING FORM

Case Number: _____ Offense: _____

Submitting Officer: (Name/ID#)
_____

Victim: _____

Suspect: _____

Date/Time Seized: _____ Location of Seizure: _____
_____

Description of Evidence		
Item #	Quantity	Description of Item (Model, Serial #, Condition, Marks, Scratches)

Chain of Custody				
Item #	Date/Time	Released by (Signature & ID#)	Received by (Signature & ID#)	Comments/Location

APD_Form_#PE003_v.1 (12/2012)   Page 1 of 2 pages (See back)

EVICENCE CHAIN-OF-CUSTODY TRACKING FORM
(Continued)

Chain of Custody

Item #	Date/Time	Released by (Signature & ID#)	Received by (Signature & ID#)	Comments/Location

Final Disposal Authority

Authorization for Disposal

Item(s) #: _____ on this document pertaining to (suspect): _____
is(are) no longer needed as evidence and is/are authorized for disposal by (check appropriate disposal method)
☐ Return to Owner   ☐ Auction/Destroy/Divert
Name & ID# of Authorizing Officer: _____ Signature: _____ Date:
_____

Witness to Destruction of Evidence

Item(s) #: _____ on this document were destroyed by Evidence Custodian
_____ ID#:_____
in my presence on (date) _____.
Name & ID# of Witness to destruction: _____ Signature: _____ Date:
_____

Release to Lawful Owner

Item(s) #: _____ on this document was/were released by Evidence Custodian
_____ ID#:_____ to
Name _____
Address: _____ City: _____ State: _____ Zip Code:
____
Telephone Number: (____) _____
Under penalty of law, I certify that I am the lawful owner of the above item(s).

Signature: _____ Date: _____

Copy of Government-issued photo identification is attached. ☐ Yes ☐ No

This Evidence Chain-of-Custody form is to be retained as a permanent record by the Anywhere Police Department.

APD_Form_#PE003_v.1 (12/2012)   Page 2 of 2 pages (See front)

Source: Technical Working Group on Biological Evidence Preservation. The Biological Evidence Preservation Handbook: Best Practices for Evidence Handlers. National Institute of Standards and Technology. 2013 U.S. Department of Commerce.

- Digital evidence—Data contained within computer storage media, such as desktop computers, laptops, and personal digital assistants (PDAs); video and audio recordings; cell phones, etc.
- Other trace evidence—Glass fragments, fibers, fingerprints, etc.

Exceptions

Although the chain of custody attaches to items that are fungible in nature, incomplete chains of custody do not necessarily result in the exclusion of such evidence.[6] Conversely, the chain of custody requirement is satisfied

CHAIN OF CUSTODY, REASONABLE DOUBT, AND O. J. SIMPSON

At approximately 10:15 p.m. on June 12, 1994, residents of an upscale Los Angeles suburb were disturbed by the barking and whining of a white Akita. A concerned neighbor recognized the animal's distress and approached the animal, at which point he observed red stains on the paws and underbelly of the dog. A second neighbor and his partner agreed to care for the dog, but allowed it to lead them to 875 South Bundy Drive. There in the shadows of the walkway, they noticed what appeared to be a body and they notified police. They had unwittingly placed themselves squarely in what would soon prove to be the trial of the century.

Without question, the slayings of Nicole Brown Simpson and Ron Goldman were horrific. Both victims received multiple stab wounds, and Nicole Brown Simpson sustained a cut to the throat that resulted in near decapitation. Massive amounts of blood were present throughout the crime scene. By all accounts, it was a vicious attack. However, no one has ever been convicted for the murders largely because of the haphazard work of the Los Angeles Police Department and questions regarding the chain of custody.

The crime scene attracted dozens of investigative personnel—more than 20 were representatives of the LAPD that included crime scene technicians, patrol officers, and investigators. As would be noted later, the actions of four lead detectives in the case tainted the evidence beyond repair.

Detectives Ron Philips, Mark Fuhrman, Tom Lange, and Phil Vannatter were present at the residence on South Bundy Drive. In addition to observing the general state of the bodies, they all noted a bloodstained glove in proximity to the victims. Ostensibly intending to make arrangements for the care of the Simpson children, all four left the crime scene and descended upon the Rockingham residence of O. J. Simpson. Noticing a drop of blood on a white Bronco parked at the scene, the detectives entered the property arguing that the residents might need emergency attention. Soon thereafter, Detective Mark Fuhrman discovered a bloodstained glove that appeared to match the one discovered at the murder scene. Soon thereafter, Fuhrman and Philips left the Rockingham estate and returned to the crime scene. This was the first of many trips the men would make between the two residences.

During the trial, the defense argued that the movements of the detectives could have resulted in transference of evidence from the crime scene to the Simpson residence. They further suggested that evidence was planted intentionally by Mark Fuhrman, an individual they characterized throughout the trial as a liar and a racist. Consequently, O. J. Simpson was acquitted of the murders of his ex-wife Nicole Brown Simpson and her friend, Ron Goldman.

---

when it is demonstrated by the proponent of the evidence that the item is what it is intended to be. As the Fourth Circuit recognized in *United States v. Ricco*:[7]

> This testimony sufficed to establish the requisite chain of custody. As we have pointed out, the "chain of custody" is not an iron-clad requirement, and the fact of a 'missing link' does not prevent the admission of real evidence, so long as there is sufficient proof that the evidence is what it purports to be and has not been altered in any material respect." . . . Even if the chain of custody established by the government may not have been unbroken, we find that the government satisfied its burden under Rule 901.

Not all physical evidence requires documentation of a chain of custody—only physical evidence that can be manipulated, altered, substituted, or contaminated. In fact, many courts have specifically differentiated between evidence that is "fungible" (alterable) and items that are more concrete (unalterable). For example,

> The purpose of the chain-of-custody rule is to ensure that the physical evidence against the accused has not been tampered with or altered. *Contu v. State*, 553 P.2d 1000 (Okl. Cr. 1975). However, this burden does not require that all possibility of alteration, however slight, must be negated by the party offering the evidence. *Trantham v. State*, 508 P.2d 1104 (Okl.Cr. 1973). There must be sufficient evidence of the chain of custody to reduce the mere speculation that tampering occurred. . . . Furthermore, cases have distinguished the need for strict application of the chain of custody rule in contraband cases from evidence which is not susceptible to tampering and alteration.

The chain of custody in criminal cases is essential to the entire process—from the collection of evidence to its presentation in court. Computer crime cases are no exception. To prevent charges to validity and reliability of the collected evidence, investigators should take photographs of the entire scene, including the back of the computer that shows identification and equipment configuration and functionality.

See *Hays v. State*, supra; *Ervin v. State*, 580 P.2d 1002 (Okl.Cr. 1978); *Brown v. State*, 518 P.2d 898 (Okl.Cr. 1974).[8]

State's Exhibit 3 is of such a character that only the barest speculation would permit one to conclude the jack had been altered or exchanged during the time it was outside the custody of the police officer. Consequently, although the chain of custody was broken, the break does not provide a ground for reversal of the above conviction. However, we note a caveat in the application of this opinion. In dealing with contraband or substances wherein a chemical analysis is necessary, and a layman would be unable to identify the substance as the same substance taken under a particular set of circumstances, a break in the chain of custody similar to the instant case would be of grave concern.[9]

Thus, various courts have admitted an array of items irrespective of the satisfaction of the chain of custody requirement, including a firearm and ammunition,[10] a pair of handcuffs,[11] a black watch,[12] the contents of a purse,[13] photographs of the deceased,[14] and shotgun pellets and wadding found in a victim's skull.[15]

▶ Types of Documentary Evidence

As the name implies, documentary evidence generally refers to documents. However, the category encompasses a range of communications that includes any medium in which data is collected or information is stored. Examples are video or audio recordings, digital media, printed e-mails, transcripts, and personal writings. The information contained within such media range from incriminating statements recorded in a personal diary to copies of fraudulent checks and from ransom notes to betting records. As with physical evidence, proponents of documentary evidence must demonstrate the chain of custody of the item in question. In addition, the calling party must further demonstrate the authenticity of the item in question. In the most basic sense, authentication of documentary evidence requires witness testimony as to the manner of the production of the document and its ownership, as well as a demonstration of its relevancy and materiality to the case at hand.

Some forms of documentary evidence may also be considered real evidence. For example, if a bloodstained ransom note is admitted into evidence, the contents of the message would be considered documentary evidence while the serological matter would be considered real evidence. The distinction is quite important because one may be admissible but the other would not in certain cases. For example, if the writing of Mr. Kid Napper could not be authenticated by witnesses, the content of the document would not be admissible, but the blood found upon it would. Generally speaking, four areas of interest relate to considerations of documentary evidence: parol evidence, best evidence, authentication, and hearsay.

Parol Evidence Rule

By definition, the **parol evidence rule** hinges upon the assumption that a written agreement or contract is the final expression of that agreement and may not be modified, contradicted, or otherwise considered by outside statements whether oral or written. For the most part, the parol evidence rule is used most often in civil court. However, it may be used in criminal courts when the evidence in question pertains to the legality of a contract.

Best Evidence Rule

In the most basic sense, the **best evidence rule** provides that secondary evidence, such as copies or facsimiles, are not admissible when the original is available. The first official record of such a notion dates back to the eighteenth century in a ruling stating that no evidence could be admissible unless a demonstration showed it to

parol evidence rule
legal assumption that a written agreement or contract is the final expression of that agreement and may not be modified, contradicted, or otherwise considered by outside statements, whether oral or written.

best evidence rule
legal concept that the best evidence is the original version, rather than a copy of the original version. The rule provides that secondary evidence, such as photocopies or facsimiles, are not admissible when the original is available.

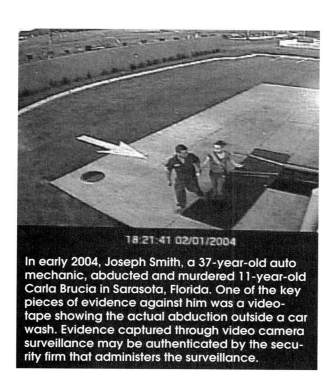

18:21:41 02/01/2004

In early 2004, Joseph Smith, a 37-year-old auto mechanic, abducted and murdered 11-year-old Carla Brucia in Sarasota, Florida. One of the key pieces of evidence against him was a videotape showing the actual abduction outside a car wash. Evidence captured through video camera surveillance may be authenticated by the security firm that administers the surveillance.

ARTICLE X. CONTENTS OF WRITINGS, RECORDINGS, AND PHOTOGRAPHS

Rule 1002—Requirement of the Original

An original writing, recording, or photograph is required in order to prove its content unless these rules or a federal statute provides otherwise.

Rule 1003—Admissibility of Duplicates

A duplicate is admissible to the same extent as the original unless a genuine question is raised about the original's authenticity or the circumstances make it unfair to admit the duplicate.

Rule 1004—Admissibility of Other Evidence of Content

An original is not required and other evidence of the content of a writing, recording, or photograph is admissible if:

(a) all the originals are lost or destroyed, and not by the proponent acting in bad faith;

(b) an original cannot be obtained by any available judicial process;

(c) the party against whom the original would be offered had control of the original; was at that time put on notice, by pleadings or otherwise, that the original would be a subject of proof at the trial or hearing; and fails to produce it at the trial or hearing; or

(d) the writing, recording, or photograph is not closely related to a controlling issue.

Rule 1005—Copies of Public Records to Prove Content

The proponent may use a copy to prove the content of an official record—or of a document that was recorded or filed in a public office as authorized by law—if these conditions are met: the record or document is otherwise admissible; and the copy is certified as correct in accordance with Rule 902(4) or is testified to be correct by a witness who has compared it with the original. If no such copy can be obtained by reasonable diligence, then the proponent may use other evidence to prove the content.

Rule 1006—Summaries to Prove Content

The proponent may use a summary, chart, or calculation to prove the content of voluminous writings, recordings, or photographs that cannot be conveniently examined in court. The proponent must make the originals or duplicates available for examination or copying, or both, by other parties at a reasonable time and place. And the court may order the proponent to produce them in court.

Rule 1007—Testimony or Statement of a Party to Prove Content

The proponent may prove the content of a writing, recording, or photograph by the testimony, deposition, or written statement of the party against whom the evidence is offered. The proponent need not account for the original.

be "the best that the nature of the case will allow."[16] The use of the best evidence requirement remains a fundamental premise in American law and is codified in the FRE (Article X).

The best evidence rule recognizes that the duplication of writings or communication may be fraught with errors and mistakes. Coupled with the realization that the exact wording of a document is essential to its interpretation, courts and legislatures across the globe have recognized this premise. In light of the manner in which duplicates were made historically (i.e., hand copied), governments rationalized that the potential for error was elevated so as to render the admission of secondary evidence most suspect. In addition, it is well known that contextual considerations may be as important as the verbiage employed. Thus, introduction of the original evidence assures the fact finder that the material to be evaluated is a representation of the complete communication and that its intended meaning or content has not been modified, altered, or erased. Finally, the best evidence rule prevents allegations of fraud in that it allows the fact finder to examine the original document for visible signs of alteration or modification, such as erasures, strikes, or editing marks.

The "best evidence" or "original document" rule is codified under the FRE from sections 1002 to 1007 (see the previous section). Generally speaking, an **original document** is any writing, recording, or photograph itself or that is intended to have the same effect, such as documents that have been handwritten, typewritten, photocopied, photographed, magnetically impulsed, mechanically or electronically recorded, or otherwise compiled—also included are photographs, radiographs (x-rays), videotapes, and motion pictures.

To prove the content of a document (i.e., writing, recording, or photograph), the original must be introduced, except in the following situations:

- The original is lost or destroyed (unless the proponent of said evidence acted in bad faith)
- The original is not obtainable
- The original is in the possession of the opponent
- The document is not closed related to a controlling issue

Generally speaking, a "duplicate" of the original is admissible to the same extent as the original unless the authenticity of the original is questioned or if the circumstances are such that the introduction of a duplicate rather than the original would be unfair. A duplicate is defined by FRE Rule 1001 as:

> . . . a counterpart produced by a mechanical, photographic, chemical, electronic, or other equivalent process or technique that accurately reproduces the original.

Duplicates are often used when introduction of the original would prove problematic or too cumbersome, such as in the case of public records or voluminous documents. In cases involving public records, duplicates that are certified or witnessed by someone familiar with the original may be introduced under FRE Rule 1005.

original document
any writing, recording, or photograph itself or that is intended to have the same effect, such as documents that have been handwritten, typewritten, photocopied, photographed, magnetically impulsed, mechanically or electronically recorded, or otherwise compiled—also included are photographs, radiographs (x-rays), videotapes, and motion pictures.

 CASE LAW

BANK DEPOSITS AND PRIVACY: *UNITED STATES V. MILLER*, 425 U.S. 435 (1976)

Most people might assume that personal banking transactions are confidential and legally protected from disclosure, but the Supreme Court has firmly placed such documents outside the areas recognized as private. In the 1976 case of *United States v. Miller*, 425 U.S. 435 (1976), the Court ruled:

> Even if we direct our attention to the original checks and deposit slips, rather than to the microfilm copies actually viewed and obtained by means of the subpoena, we perceive no legitimate "expectation of privacy" in their contents. The checks are not confidential communications but negotiable instruments to be used in commercial transactions. All of the documents obtained, including financial statements and deposit slips, contain only information voluntarily conveyed to the banks and exposed to their employees in the ordinary

course of business. The lack of any legitimate expectation of privacy concerning the information kept in bank records was assumed by Congress in enacting the Bank Secrecy Act, the expressed purpose of which is to require records . . . to be maintained because they "have a high degree of usefulness in criminal, tax, and regulatory investigations and proceedings."

The depositor takes the risk, in revealing his affairs to another, that the information will be conveyed by that person to the Government. . . . This Court has held repeatedly that the Fourth Amendment does not prohibit the obtaining of information revealed to a third party and conveyed by him to Government authorities, even if the information is revealed on the assumption that it will be used only for a limited purpose and the confidence placed in the third party will not be betrayed.[17]

Finally, summaries, charts, or calculations may be employed in cases involving voluminous writings, recordings, or photographs *if* originals or duplicates of the information in question are available for examination or copying.

Summarily, the best evidence rule applies to all documentary evidence, including radiographs (x-rays), photographs, computer documents, printed e-mails, and digitally produced documents. Although it may be argued that the escalation of technology has exponentially increased the potential for fraudulent documents, the use of hashing tools in computer forensics has mitigated attacks on the authenticity of a computer document in question. As with other areas in criminal evidence, allegations of misconduct or bad faith on the part of the proponent of the evidence may negate the admissibility of the item in question. Thus, if the original document is currently "unavailable" because of bad acts by the calling party, secondary evidence may be introduced.

▶ Authentication of Documentary Evidence

As indicated previously, documentary evidence is only admissible upon a showing by the proponent that the evidence is what it is claimed to be. Known as **authentication**, this process takes various forms depending on the nature of the proposed document. Small variations may be found across jurisdictions, but the general parameters set forth in the FRE are illustrative.

authentication a demonstration of the truthfulness (validity) of an item in order for the item to be admissible as evidence.

- **Testimony of witness with knowledge**—Documents may be authenticated by a witness who has firsthand knowledge that the matter in question is what it is proposed to be. For example, this could include the testimony of a person who is in charge of the family Bible in which records of births, marriages, and deaths are inscribed if the Bible is introduced to show the existence of the birth of a child to a particular couple.

- **Nonexpert opinion on handwriting**—Documents may be authenticated by a witness who testifies to the genuineness of handwriting. Based upon the witness' familiarity with the writing in question, this could include, for example, testimony as to the authenticity of a signature or writing on a proposed document. It is generally recognized that an individual can identify the handwriting of his or her spouse.

- **Comparison by trier or expert witness**—Documents may be authenticated through the testimony of expert witnesses. Such testimony includes discussion of the methods employed to compare the questioned document with a known (i.e., exemplar) writing. It might include testimony as to age, authorship, and manner of publication. (Questioned documents are discussed in greater detail later in the chapter).

- **Distinctive characteristics**—Documents may be authenticated through the testimony of a witness that includes discussions of patterns and the like. For example, a witness may testify that the markings on the back of a photograph are consistent with the manner in which a particular individual catalogued memorabilia.

- **Voice identification**—Authentication of a voice, whether heard firsthand or through some other medium, is possible through the testimony of an individual in the form of opinion. For example, a dispatcher may testify that the voice on a recorded transmission of an emergency call to 911 is his or her own.

- **Telephone conversations**—Telephone conversations may be authenticated through evidence that a call was made to a particular number at a particular time.

- **Public records or reports**—A document may be authenticated through the introduction of evidence that the proposed document is from a public office in which items of this nature are kept. For example, an employee from the public library may identify an application for a library card.

- **Ancient documents**—A document may be authenticated through evidence that: (1) the document is in such a condition that no suspicion concerning its authenticity is present, (2) the document was physically located in a place where authentic documents of its kind would likely be, and (3) the document is at least 20 years old. For example, an individual may testify that an alleged copy of a decedent's will dated April 11, 1952, was found in a personal safe in a file folder marked "Wills and Contracts" along with a copy of newspaper clippings from the same date.

- **Process or system**—A document may be authenticated through the introduction of evidence detailing processes or systems routinely used to produce a result that is demonstrated to be accurate. For example, a carnival operator could testify as to the process by which a photograph is taken via a remote camera triggered by the weight of a car on the track and time and date stamped for the purpose of sales to consumers.

FEDERAL RULES OF EVIDENCE

ARTICLE IX. AUTHENTICATION AND IDENTIFICATION

Rule 902—Evidence That Is Self-Authenticating

The following items of evidence are self-authenticating; they require no extrinsic evidence of authenticity in order to be admitted:

(1) *Domestic Public Documents That Are Sealed and Signed.* A document that bears:

   (A) a seal purporting to be that of the United States; any state, district, commonwealth, territory, or insular possession of the United States; the former Panama Canal Zone; the Trust Territory of the Pacific Islands; a political subdivision of any of these entities; or a department, agency, or officer of any entity named above; and,

   (B) a signature purporting to be an execution or attestation.

(2) *Domestic Public Documents That Are Not Sealed but Are Signed and Certified.* A document that bears no seal if:

   (A) it bears the signature of an officer or employee of an entity named in Rule 902(1)(A); and,

   (B) another public officer who has a seal and official duties within that same entity certifies under seal—or its equivalent—that the signer has the official capacity and that the signature is genuine.

(3) *Foreign Public Documents.* A document that purports to be signed or attested by a person who is authorized by a foreign country's law to do so. The document must be accompanied by a final certification that certifies the genuineness of the signature and official position of the signer or attester—or of any foreign official whose certificate of genuineness relates to the signature or attestation or is in a chain of certificates of genuineness relating to the signature or attestation. The certification may be made by a secretary of a United States embassy or legation; by a consul general, vice consul, or consular agent of the United States; or by a diplomatic or consular official of the foreign country assigned or accredited to the United States. If all parties have been given a reasonable opportunity to investigate the document's authenticity and accuracy, the court may, for good cause, either:

   (A) order that it be treated as presumptively authentic without final certification; or

   (B) allow it to be evidenced by an attested summary with or without final certification.

(4) *Certified Copies of Public Records.* A copy of an official record—or a copy of a document

(continued)

▼

that was recorded or filed in a public office as authorized by law—if the copy is certified as correct by:

   (A) the custodian or another person authorized to make the certification; or

   (B) a certificate that complies with Rule 902 (1), (2), or (3), a federal statute, or a rule prescribed by the Supreme Court.

(5) ***Official Publications.*** A book, pamphlet, or other publication purporting to be issued by a public authority.

(6) ***Newspapers and Periodicals.*** Printed material purporting to be a newspaper or periodical.

(7) ***Trade Inscriptions and the Like.*** An inscription, sign, tag, or label purporting to have been affixed in the course of business and indicating origin, ownership, or control.

(8) ***Acknowledged Documents.*** A document accompanied by a certificate of acknowledgment that is lawfully executed by a notary public or another officer who is authorized to take acknowledgments.

(9) ***Commercial Paper and Related Documents.*** Commercial paper, a signature on it, and related documents, to the extent allowed by general commercial law.

(10) ***Presumptions Under a Federal Statute.*** A signature, document, or anything else that a federal statute declares to be presumptively or prima facie genuine or authentic.

(11) ***Certified Domestic Records of a Regularly Conducted Activity.*** The original or a copy of a domestic record that meets the requirements of Rule 803 (6)(A)-(C), as shown by a certification of the custodian or another qualified person that complies with a federal statute or a rule prescribed by the Supreme Court. Before the trial or hearing, the proponent must give an adverse party reasonable written notice of the intent to offer the record—and must make the record and certification available for inspection—so that the party has a fair opportunity to challenge them.

(12) ***Certified Foreign Records of a Regularly Conducted Activity.*** In a civil case, the original or a copy of a foreign record that meets the requirements of Rule 902 (11), modified as follows: the certification, rather than complying with a federal statute or Supreme Court rule, must be signed in a manner that, if falsely made, would subject the maker to a criminal penalty in the country where the certification is signed. The proponent must also meet the notice requirements of Rule 902 (11).

Self-Authenticating Documents

These methods of authentication are necessary for certain examples of documentary evidence, but they are not required in others. In fact, some documents are accepted on their face. These are commonly referred to as **self-authenticating documents**. These are defined in FRE 902 and fall into one of the following categories:

- Certified copies of public records
- Official publications of government agencies
- Newspaper articles or periodicals
- Trade inscriptions
- Business records
- Acknowledged documents
- Commercial paper

self-authenticating documents documents accepted on their face without demonstration of their authenticity, such as certified public documents, newspaper articles, photographs, radiographs (x-rays), and videos.

Certified Copies of Public Records

Under the FRE, certified copies of public records are assumed to be what they are purported to be primarily because of the manner in which government documents are created and maintained. These include any copies of documents that are officially reported or recorded and are certified by a person with authority to verify the accuracy of said document (e.g., certified copies of birth or death certificates).

Thus, the following types of documents are accepted without the need for extrinsic evidence of authenticity:

- **Domestic public documents under seal**—These include any document that bears a seal from a recognized government entity (including federal and state governments and their subdivisions, the Commonwealth, and American territories) and a signature attesting to the execution of the document in question.

- **Domestic public documents not under seal**—These include any document that bears a signature in an official capacity of any recognized government entity.

- **Foreign public documents**—These include:

 . . . document[s] purporting to be executed or attested in an official capacity by a person authorized by the laws of a foreign country to make the execution or attestation, and accompanied by a final certification as to the genuineness of the signature and official position (A) of the executing or attesting person, or (B) of any foreign official whose certificate of genuineness of signature and official position relates to the execution or attestation or is in a chain of certificates of genuineness of signature and official position relating to the execution or attestation. A final certification may be made by a secretary of an embassy or legation, consul general, consul, vice consul, or consular agent of the United States, or a diplomatic or consular official of the foreign country assigned or accredited to the United States. If reasonable opportunity has been given to all parties to investigate the authenticity and accuracy of official documents, the court may, for good cause shown, order that they be treated as presumptively authentic without final certification or permit them to be evidenced by an attested summary with or without final certification.

Official Publications of Government Agencies

Official publications of government agencies do not require authentication through extrinsic evidence and are authenticated on their face. These include documents disseminated for public consumption by government agencies. Information distributed by the Federal Register or the National Archives and Records Administration would be considered self-authenticating. These and other government publications are maintained by the U.S. Government Printing Office and may be found at http://www.gpo.gov.

Newspaper Articles and Periodicals

Newspaper articles and periodicals are considered self-authenticating because of the manner in which they are created and distributed. However, this status only refers to the newspaper or periodical itself and does not suggest that the content of the publication is accurate or even truthful.

Trade Inscriptions

Inscriptions, signs, tags, and labels affixed to a product in the normal course of business and that indicate ownership, control, or origin are considered self-authenticating. For example, it would not be necessary for a store employee to testify as to the authenticity of price tags located on 50 articles of clothing in a major shoplifting case. It would be necessary to prove that the articles were actually stolen, but the tags demonstrating retailer ownership would be self-authenticating.

Other Forms of Self-Authenticating Documents

Other forms of self-authenticating documents include acknowledged documents, commercial paper, business records, and certified domestic and foreign records of routine activity. Also, documents accompanied by a certificate of acknowledgment

Mark Hoffman is one of the most prolific forgers in American history. He successfully passed on forged documents purported to be the writings of Abraham Lincoln, Emily Dickinson, and Mark Twain. However, his forgeries of documents purported to be authored by Joseph Smith eventually resulted in his trial for the murder of two prominent members of the Mormon Church (Church of Jesus Christ of Latter-Day Saints).

 CASE LAW

CONTEMPORARY STANDARD FOR SCIENTIFIC EVIDENCE: *DAUBERT V. MERRELL DOW PHARMACEUTICALS, INC.* 509 U.S. 579 (1993)

In 1993, the traditional "general acceptance" standard in which scientific evidence was evaluated was replaced by one that emphasized relevancy and reliability.

The reliability standard is established by Rule 702's requirement that an expert's testimony pertain to "scientific . . . knowledge," since the adjective "scientific" implies a grounding in science's methods and procedures, while the word "knowledge" connotes a body of known facts or of ideas inferred from such facts or accepted as true on good grounds. The Rule's requirement that the testimony "assist the trier of fact to understand the evidence or to determine a fact in issue" goes primarily to relevance by demanding a valid scientific connection to the pertinent inquiry as a precondition to admissibility.

Faced with a proffer of expert scientific testimony under Rule 702, the trial judge, pursuant to Rule 104(a), must make a preliminary assessment of whether the underlying reasoning or methodology of the testimony is scientifically valid and can be applied properly to the facts at issue. Many considerations will bear on the inquiry, including whether the theory or technique in question can be (and has been) tested, whether it has been subjected to peer review and publication, whether its potential error rate and the existence and maintenance of standards controlling its operation are known, and whether it has attracted widespread acceptance within a relevant scientific community. The inquiry is flexible and focused solely on principles and methodology, not on the conclusions they may generate.[18]

and executed as provided by statute are generally admissible. Examples of acknowledged documents include, but are not limited to, notarized statements and medallion-guaranteed signatures necessary for stock transfers. Records that are routinely created and established during the general course of business or through domestic or foreign practices are considered self-authenticating if the custodian or other qualified individual can testify that such documents were made at or near the time of the occurrence contained therein and kept in the course of regularly conducted activity. Similarly, commercial paper, affixed signatures, and documents provided by general commercial law are admissible. A final example of a self-authenticating document is any signature, document, or other matter declared by or through congressional legislation to be presumptively or prima facie authentic.

▶ Authentication of Scientific Evidence

The introduction of documentary evidence, such as writings, photographs, and videos, is contingent upon a demonstration of the authenticity of the article in question. Such authentication is accomplished through witness testimony. Some documents may be introduced on their face or through opinion testimony by lay witnesses, but others require analysis by a trained professional or "expert." Expert testimony is often required in cases in which the evidence proffered is not incontrovertible. As a result, the term **scientific evidence** has come to encompass a wide array of items and may be defined loosely as any physical evidence that involves theories, processes, experiments, empirical analyses, or results and requires the testimony of a qualified expert. Thus, some documentary evidence is discussed appropriately as scientific evidence. Historically, the admissibility of scientific evidence was only possible once the process or theory had received "general acceptance" in the scientific community.[19] This was known as the *Frye test*. More recently, however, the Court has applied a relevancy test that allows the trial judge to permit any expert testimony deemed germane to the matter at hand.[20] This standard, known as the *Daubert* standard, is used by the federal court and most state courts. Thus, the proliferation of scientific evidence being introduced is growing. The introduction of new technologies and the increasing reliance upon them will continue to produce new lines of scientific inquiry.[21] (See Chapter 9 for a complete discussion.)

scientific evidence has come to encompass a wide array of items and may be defined loosely as any physical evidence that involves theories, processes, experiments, empirical analyses, or results and requires the testimony of a qualified expert. Thus, some documentary evidence is discussed appropriately as scientific evidence.

Questioned Document Examination

As discussed earlier, the authentication of documentary evidence must be completed before a jury may consider it. While some documents are self-authenticating or accepted on their face, others require corroboration to demonstrate the genuineness of the questioned item. In the latter case, such documents may be referred to as "questioned documents." Such items, when examined by a document examiner, may be found to be genuine after a handwriting or signature analysis. Other analyses utilized to demonstrate authenticity include, but are not limited to:

- Ink or paper
- Watermarks
- Duplication processes
- Impressions
- Alterations, obliterations, or erasures
- Damaged or charred documents
- Consistency of content issues (i.e., linguistics)

The scientific examination of questioned documents dates back as early as 1870 when such analyses were performed largely through comparisons of handwriting and signatures via photographic enlargements (Hilton, 1979; Hilton, 1982). Since this inception, the science of document analysis gradually evolved to become extremely sophisticated currently. Generally speaking, a **questioned document** is any type of object with graphic markings whose authenticity is in question. Such documentation may include articles ranging from a personal diary to an international newspaper to neighborhood graffiti. In addition, the authentication of such articles may range from comparisons of handwriting to linguistic analysis.

questioned document any object with graphic markings whose authenticity is in question, such as a personal diary, international newspaper, or even neighborhood graffiti. Authentication often involves handwriting, ink, or content analysis.

Handwriting and Signature Comparisons

The oldest and most common testimony regarding questioned documents involves the authentication of an individual's handwriting or signature. This is accomplished through a comparison of writings of known origin (commonly referred to as *standards* or *exemplars*) with the document in question. The science is based on the premise that individuals subconsciously inject their individuality into any writing even when they are attempting to circumvent or otherwise manipulate the fact-finding mission. It is theorized that the most reliable standards or exemplars are both lengthy in nature and completed within a specified time period, because individuals are more likely to revert to patterning through repetition. Factors that are evaluated in such comparisons include the slope, slant, scale, speed, pressure, and spatial patterning of markings.

 CASE LAW

THE FIFTH AMENDMENT AND HANDWRITING: *GILBERT V. CALIFORNIA*, 388 U.S. 263 (1967)

In 1967, the Supreme Court considered whether the compulsion of writing exemplars was a violation of the Fifth Amendment prohibition against self-incrimination. In the case in question, the petitioner had been convicted of armed robbery and of the murder of a police officer after being compelled by law enforcement authorities to produce samples of his handwriting. On appeal, the petitioner argued that such compulsion, made without the assistance of counsel, was unconstitutional. However, the Court disagreed and reasoned thus:

First. The taking of the exemplars did not violate petitioner's Fifth Amendment privilege against self-incrimination. The privilege reaches only compulsion of "an accused's communications, whatever form they might take, and the compulsion of responses which are also communications, for example, compliance with a subpoena to produce one's papers," and not "compulsion which makes a suspect or accused the source of 'real or physical evidence'. . . ." One's voice and handwriting are, of course, means of communication. It by no means follows, however, that every compulsion of an accused to use his voice or write compels a communication within the cover

of the privilege. A mere handwriting exemplar, in contrast to the content of what is . . . written, like the voice or body itself, is an identifying physical characteristic outside its protection. . . . No claim is made that the content of the exemplars was testimonial or communicative matter.

Second. The taking of the exemplars was not a "critical" stage of the criminal proceedings entitling petitioner to the assistance of counsel. Putting aside the fact that the exemplars were taken before the indictment and appointment of counsel, there is minimal risk that the absence of counsel might derogate from his right to a fair trial. . . . If, for some reason, an unrepresentative exemplar is taken, this can be brought out and corrected through the adversary process at trial since the accused can make an unlimited number of additional exemplars for analysis and comparison by government and defense handwriting experts. Thus, "the accused has the opportunity for a meaningful confrontation of the [State's] case at trial through the ordinary processes of cross-examination of the [State's] expert [handwriting] witnesses and the presentation of the evidence of his own [handwriting] experts."[22]

▼

Perhaps the most contested case in the annals of American criminal jurisprudence involved the trial of Bruno Richard Hauptmann for the kidnapping and murder of the infant son of American hero, Charles Lindbergh. Hauptmann was convicted almost exclusively on the testimony of document examiners who testified as to his authorship. Serious questions about the guilt of Hauptmann remain, and some believe that anti-immigrant sentiment resulted in the execution of an innocent man.

Examination of handwriting and signatures considers the similarities and dissimilarities and tends to focus on lowercase letters rather than capitalized ones, because they are more numerous and thereby harder to intentionally disguise. Peculiarities in handwriting are learned behaviors and are the product of childhood teaching and external stimuli. There is no universally accepted standard or proven number of similarities or dissimilarities that must be noted before authentication is declared, but there are also very few areas of disagreement among qualified document examiners.[23] All eight document examiners in the Lindbergh baby kidnapping case, for example, agreed that the ransom letters had been authored by Bruno Hauptmann. In a rare contrast, however, experts who evaluated the last will and testament of mogul Howard Hughes reached varying conclusions as to the authenticity of the document. With billions at stake and in light of the curious bequests, the will was contested. One particularly interested individual claimed that he had once given a ride to a bum (whom he named as Howard Hughes) and claimed to inherit a significant amount of money. Other significant beneficiaries included the Mormon Church. However, a consensus was reached, the will was thrown out, and Hughes was declared to have died intestate. In a more recent case, questioned document examiners were called to verify the signature of Saddam Hussein on execution orders.

Ink Analysis

Traditionally, questioned documents examiners were called to verify that a questioned document was produced on a particular typewriter (possible only when the suspect machine was available for testing). Examiners visually compared the peculiarities produced by the machine and the questioned document. Individual comparisons included analysis of spacing, text alignment, broken or damaged font, pressure, and ink density. The advent and increasing sophistication of computer printers has complicated the once-simple landscape, and comparisons are often difficult to replicate (i.e., levels of toner and such). However, advances have been made in the following areas:

- Identification of photocopying toners
- Classification of ink-jet printers and ink and laser printers
- Development of electronic databases containing class characteristics of computer printers
- Detection of laser printer defects for individual identification

Despite these developments, most experts agree that these areas pose significant challenges in determining authenticity.[24]

Another area of inquiry by questioned documents examiners involves the differentiation of writing inks and their age for ink-dating purposes. Techniques for such comparisons vary widely and have become increasingly sophisticated. According to Pfefferli (2001),[25] traditional methods of analysis include:

- Thin Layer Chromatography
- RAMAN and RAMAN-SERRS Spectroscopy
- High-Pressure Liquid Chromatography
- Ink Identification (by diode array) spectrophotometry
- SEM-EDX for the examination of pencil marks
- High-Performance Capillary Electrophoresis
- Field Desorption Mass Spectrometry
- Fourier Transform IR Spectrometry
- Micro ATR technology
- Solid Phase Micro Extraction (SPME)

Emerging technologies in the field of forensic ink analysis are increasingly reliant upon automated or computer-generated comparisons, which can include three-dimensional analysis.

Document Content Evaluation

Even when the document is determined to be written by a particular individual at a particular time, questions may arise as to the content of the writing. Documents, for example, may have missing pages, may be burnt, or may be otherwise altered. To resolve such issues, document examiners are tasked with authenticating the contents. Common tools used in such analysis include photography, digital image processing, infrared or ultraviolet light, and photography.

Indentations or impressions made on paper may also be important in criminal cases. Indentations occur when something is written with a firm hand on a stack

---

IN SEARCH OF HISTORY: QUESTIONED DOCUMENTS AND THE HOLY BIBLE

Authenticity of the Apocrypha, or "hidden" books from the Old and New Testament, has been disputed among Christians for centuries. These are the 14 books, known as deuterocanonical books, found in all Catholic and Protestant Bibles until the nineteenth century when the British Bible Society ended their inclusion in English Bibles. (They had previously been "officially removed" from the English Bible by the Archbishop of Canterbury in the *Westminster Confession of Faith* around 1647, but continued to appear in some texts until the nineteenth century.) To this day, divergent views exist among Protestants and Roman Catholics regarding the authenticity of the Apocrypha. These books are currently included in Catholic Bibles, and are recognized by the Church as inspired by God. Contemporary protestant faiths, on the other hand, have deemed the books as heretical, and many contemporary protestants do not know that they even exist.

of papers. Although no ink is present, examiners may be able to reveal the writing using a process known as Electrostatic Detection Apparatus (ESDA). In the most basic sense, ESDA involves applying an electrostatic charge and toner to a questioned document and has been used in various instances, including on impressions made by pencil. In fact, ESDA was used in the case of serial killer, Larry Gene Bell.

In 1985, police in Lexington County, South Carolina, were called by the distraught parents of 17-year-old Sherry Smith. They reported that their daughter's car had been left running and the car door open at the mailbox at the end of their driveway. Responding immediately, South Carolina law enforcement learned quickly that they had few leads. Soon, however, the family received a telephone call from an anonymous caller who reported that Sherry was alive and that a letter would soon be coming. In time, the family received Sherry's last will and testament, in which the young girl, with unparalleled courage and maturity, told them that she loved them and asked them not to be angry with God. Examination of the document revealed the indentation of a phone number. Through forensic analysis, investigators were able to trace the call to a cabin in Michigan and with dedicated police work, the investigators soon identified Larry Gene Bell as the suspect in the case. After murdering Sherry Smith, Bell continued to contact the family to threaten their remaining daughter. Fortunately, he was arrested and convicted based on a mountain of evidence, including the will of Ms. Smith. He was executed by electrocution in 1996.

Electronic Document Authentication

As discussed throughout the text, computer technology is changing the legal landscape. With the emergence of e-mail and instant messaging, the production of physical documents has decreased significantly. This is dramatically different from traditional documentation. The challenges in evaluating the authenticity of a particular document increase as the proliferation of high-end printers, text messaging, e-mails, and instant messaging continues. Forensic computer analysis has become quite commonplace, but it has presented various dilemmas for state and federal judges. Traditional comparisons of ink and paper increasingly have become secondary to computer time-stamping.

Although some suggest that forensic computer science is a new field, it actually has been around for several decades. Recognized in courts and academia alike, the increasing sophistication of forensic computer science makes it possible to uncover document origination and alteration. However, the Supreme Court has steadfastly refused to formally recognize the discipline, denying certiorari (cert) on virtually every case that has come before it.[26]

Computer forensics is the field of science in which computer evidence is identified, preserved, analyzed, and documented for legal purposes. Evidence that may be analyzed using computer forensics includes electronic mail, instant messaging, spreadsheets, word processing documents, images and photographs, and the history of a person's Web site activity. It also includes analysis of software applications. Computer forensic examiners are often able to recover deleted files and intentionally altered data. In some cases, files may be recovered in their entirety but in others, only fragments or "remnants" are capable of being restored. By evaluating the computer in a binary sense, investigators often uncover information in the slack space and random access memory (RAM) of a particular computer. Traditionally, the process was tedious and could involve a significant amount of time. However, several software packages have emerged over the past few decades that have expedited the process. While the packages are as varied as the vendors that created them, most are designed to be user-friendly and employ a graphical user interface (GUI), commonly known as "point-and-click" technology.

computer forensics
the field of science in which computer evidence is identified, preserved, analyzed, and documented for legal purposes.

FORGERY, RELIGION, AND QUESTIONED DOCUMENTS

FORGERY AND RELIGIOUS DOCUMENTS

Throughout history, religious leaders have attempted to bolster their faith-based claims and demonstrate their divinity and righteousness through tangibility. Historically, these claims have been accepted by the masses largely as a matter of their faith. However, recent developments in the field of document examination have brought into question many foundational documents. Perhaps the first religious forgery discovered to be fraudulent was the Donation of Constantine—a letter purportedly bequeathing "Rome and the provinces, districts, and towns of Italy and all the Western regions" to the Roman Catholic Church. It was invoked repeatedly by the Church to further its territorial power and religious authority. In the fifteenth century, however, close examination revealed that the document was a fabrication (Lewis, 2005). Since that time, various questioned documents have been discovered across the religious landscape and discoveries of "religious artifacts" continue to this day.

Here is a brief list of some of the most sensationalized discoveries of the twentieth and twenty-first centuries:

- The Dead Sea Scrolls were discovered in the 1940s and 1950s on the shore of the Dead Sea approximately 13 miles from Jerusalem. Some 900 documents contain additional gospels, religious teachings, and doctrinal interpretations of interest to Christians and Jews alike (Davies et al., 2002). However, their authenticity remains in question.

- The *Gospel of Judas* was unveiled in Washington, D.C. in the early days of April 2006. First discovered (possibly by Egyptian peasants) in the 1970s, the questioned documents (on papyrus) was decaying rapidly until formally being purchased, preserved, and studied by various twentieth-century scientists. The documents are purportedly the thoughts of the traditional "betrayer" of

Christ, Judas Iscariot. The text portrays Judas as a hero who was acting on the orders of Jesus of Nazareth, and the text details the conflict between Gnostics and the hierarchical church. Although hotly debated, the documents have been subjected to a wide array of sophisticated examinations, including carbon testing that date the documents to A.D. 220–340. Other tests on the ink composition, language, and linguistics reaffirm such findings (Cockburn, 2006). However, the Catholic Church and other Christian institutions have decried the writings as fraudulent.

- The *Mormon Papers*, introduced to American society in the 1980s by Mark William Hofmann (one of America's most prolific forgers), included numerous questioned documents including those that were originally "authored" by various members of Joseph Smith's family. Another Hofman forgery, perhaps his most famous, involved the *Salamander Letter*, which reveals that the *Book of Mormon* was given to church founder Joseph Smith by a magical being who was transformed into a salamander. Declared authentic by various experts, the letter was eventually purchased by a private collector who donated the document to the LDS church. Soon thereafter, the authenticity of the document was called into question as individuals became aware of the numerous documents "discovered" by Hofmann (including those represented as being authored by Emily Dickinson, Mark Twain, and Abraham Lincoln). In an attempt to conceal his crimes, Hofmann used bombs to murder two individuals associated with the Mormon Church. Unfortunately for him, he injured himself when a third bomb went off prematurely. He was subsequently convicted of various charges including murder and forgery. His long run of success hinged primarily on his ability to age ink (Roberts & Sillitoe, 1990).

In addition, software vendors have incorporated recordkeeping and report making capabilities in their platforms. These reports enable investigators to focus on the investigation as opposed to the paper trail associated with the evidence. Finally, these packages have incorporated chain-of-custody logs and tools for authentication and verification. Thus, uncovered documents can provide a time line of computer possession and can verify the authenticity of the evidence.

Fingerprints

Most Americans are aware of the use of fingerprints as a form of identification and that the practice dates back more than 150 years. (It is less known that, in

India, a British colonial civil servant first used fingerprints on contracts to prevent impersonations among natives.) The first textbook on the subject was written in 1892, and England's Scotland Yard adopted the practice officially around the turn of the twentieth century. In the United States, fingerprint identification gained popularity in 1910.[27]

A **fingerprint** may be defined as an impression of the intricate design of friction skin ridges found on the palmar side of a person's fingers or thumb. Such ridges also may be found on the palms of a human hand and on the soles of feet. Impressions of fingerprints occur because of the natural oils and perspiration of an individual, which tend to leave behind residue. As such, the likelihood of leaving fingerprint impressions varies from person to person. Generally speaking, there are three types of fingerprints used in criminal prosecutions.

- **Plastic print**—Lasting visible prints found in candle wax, tar, clay, oil, grease, or putty

- **Visible print**—A volatile impression made in a substance susceptible to decay, such as dust, blood, or powder

- **Invisible (or latent) print**—A volatile impression not visible to the naked eye that is deposited when the ridges make contact with a relatively smooth surface, such as glass, wood, or metal. Various fingerprint powders, chemicals, and processes make identifying invisible prints possible.

Unlike plastic, visible, or latent prints which are collected by investigators at crime scenes, **inked prints**, on the other hand, are collected by arresting officers or jail intake personnel, and are made on identification cards through the process of rolling an individual's fingers in ink and depressing them onto the card surface. Fingerprint cards are used not only for comparison purposes but also for identification of a suspect and criminal history searches, which are made possible through national databases such as Automated Fingerprint Identification System (AFIS).

Fingerprint identification is conducted through analysis of an individual's ridge patterns. These include bifurcations, loops, deltas, enclosures, arches, lines, and whorls. Every individual has a unique fingerprint pattern that is established in the early fetal period, and the pattern remains unchanged throughout the individual's life. Traditionally, fingerprint examiners needed to manually analyze and record each print. Using a mathematical formula, each fingerprint was assigned a number. At that point, investigators visually compared the print to others in an attempt to find a match. Computer technology, however, has greatly enhanced the practice of fingerprint identification. Now, AFIS and other systems can scan, digitize, and create spatial maps of prints through binary coding. The computer employs a searching algorithm and can identify the best possible matches to be analyzed by a fingerprint examiner. Although AFIS computes a mathematical score for potential matches, a human examiner conducts the final identification.

For many years, fingerprint identification was accepted almost universally in American courts. However, the incorporation of *Daubert* into FRE 702 has increased the number of challenges to the science. In what appeared to be a heavy blow to prosecutors, one appellate court found that declaring a "match" in fingerprint analysis was not permissible because it failed to meet the *Daubert* standard.

> Accordingly, this court will permit the government to present testimony by fingerprint examiners who, suitably qualified as "expert" examiners by virtue of training and experience, may (1) describe how the rolled and latent fingerprints at issue in this case were obtained, (2) identify and place before the jury the fingerprints and such magnifications thereof as may be required to show minute details, and (3) point out observed similarities (and differences) between any latent print and any rolled print the

fingerprint an impression of the intricate design of friction skin ridges found on the palmar side of a person's fingers or thumb.

plastic print lasting visible prints found in candle wax, tar, clay, oil, grease, or putty.

visible print a volatile impression made in a substance susceptible to decay, such as dust, blood, or powder.

invisible (or latent) print a volatile impression not visible to the naked eye that is deposited when the ridges make contact with a relatively smooth surface, such as glass, wood, or metal. Various fingerprint powders, chemicals, and processes make identifying invisible prints possible.

inked prints are collected by arresting officers or jail intake personnel, and are made on identification cards through the process of rolling an individual's fingers in ink and depressing them onto the card surface.

WHAT IS TRACE EVIDENCE?

The analysis of **trace evidence** involves examining volatile microscopic or macroscopic evidence located at a crime scene. The catchall phrase encompasses much of the physical evidence previously discussed, including fingerprints, hair and fibers, paint, tire impressions, and glass fragments. Such evidence is critical in criminal investigations and prosecutions. Trace evidence can be used by investigators to identify the perpetrator and by prosecutors to place the defendant at the scene.

trace evidence
physical evidence resulting from the transfer of small quantities of material (e.g., hair, fibers, body fluids, textile samples, paint chips, glass fragments, gunshot residue particles, mud, insects, etc.), which may be collected by the police forensic unit, sexual assault team, or medical examiner.

government contends are attributable to the same person. What such expert witnesses will not be permitted to do is to present "evaluation" testimony as to their "opinion" (Rule 702) that a particular latent print is in fact the print of a particular person. The defendants will be permitted to present their own fingerprint experts to counter the government's fingerprint testimony, but defense experts will also be precluded from presenting "evaluation" testimony. Government counsel and defense counsel will, in closing arguments, be free to argue to the jury that, on the basis of the jury's observation of a particular latent print and a particular rolled print, the jury may find the existence, or the non-existence, of a match between the prints.[28]

This seemed in direct contradiction to previous appellate courts that had generally recognized the discipline. Since that time, the original judge and federal circuit courts have ruled to the contrary.[29] However, the issue remains far from settled. A recent case in Massachusetts revealed that even courts that are able to recognize the foundational science of fingerprint identification are cautionary in spreading its application. To wit,

> Consistent with the decisions of other courts that have considered the issue since *Daubert*, we conclude that the underlying theory and process of latent fingerprint identification, and the ACE-V method, in particular, are sufficiently reliable to admit expert opinion testimony regarding the matching of a latent impression with a full fingerprint. In this case, however, the Commonwealth needed to establish more than the general reliability of latent fingerprint identification. It needed to establish that the theory, process, and method of latent fingerprint identification could be applied reliably to simultaneous impressions not capable of being individually matched to any of the fingers that supposedly made them.[30]

Thus, the universal acceptance of fingerprint identification and the parameters of the testimony surrounding it is far from decided.

Voice Recognition

Traditionally, testimony involving voice recognition was limited to lay witnesses and their opinions. A husband, for example, could testify that the voice he heard on his answering machine was that of his wife, a mother could testify that the voice of a child screaming in pain was hers, and so on. However, in recent years, expert testimony has been presented in which the authentication and verification of a particular aural recording is necessary. Although not accepted as widely as fingerprint identification, voice recognition and the use of **voiceprints** is increasing.[31]

voiceprints an individually distinctive pattern of certain voice characteristics that is spectrographically produced.

Voiceprint identification initially was introduced in American courts in the 1960s. It is based on a theory developed by Alexander Graham Bell that every individual maintains unique characteristics in speech because of their resonators and articulators. Theoretically, *resonators* comprising vocal cavities—throat, nasal and oral cavities—and the shape, length, and tension of the vocal cords determine the sound spectrum of a person, much like the individual design and shape of pipes determine the sound quality of an organ. *Articulators*, on the other hand, include the lips, teeth, tongue, soft palate, and jaw muscles—all of which determine the shape of speech and the patterning of words. As such, experts are able to compare the questioned recording with exemplars of voice. They are limited, however, in that such comparisons must be of the same text. In cases in which surreptitious recordings are taken, investigators must provide the experts with conversational records that include all the words, terms, and phrases included in the questioned recording. Thus, the greatest disadvantage to the employment of voiceprint identification is the sheer volume of recording that is necessary. Even when suspects provide voiceprint samples from a written script, it may be argued that comparisons might be difficult because extraneous factors such as physical and mental condition of the subject and intentional manipulation of the voice might alter patterning.

Once adequate samples of speech are available, experts may begin the analysis of the evidence using a twofold process: *aural* comparisons of two recorded voices and *visual* comparisons of graphic representations, such as spectrograms. Visual comparison includes an evaluation of like sounds in terms of time, amplitude, and frequency as represented on the spectrograph. (This includes evaluation of factors such as nasal resonance, pauses, trajectory of vowel formants, and distribution of formant energy.) Aural comparisons evaluate resonance quality, inflection, dialect, manner of articulation, breath pattern, syllable grouping, and pitch. Once the evaluation is complete, the voiceprint examiner will make a decision as to whether the voice on the questioned recording and the samples are the same. At the current time, there is no nationally recognized number of consistencies required to draw an affirmative conclusion.

The admissibility of voiceprint identification is not altogether predetermined. Early courts were inconsistent on the issue (e.g., *People v. King*, 266 Cal.App.2d 437, 72 Cal.Rptr. 478 [1968]; *State Ex Rel Timble v. Hedman*, 192 N.W.2d 432 [Minn. 1971]). Since that time, there appears to be a general lack of consensus in

Stippling patterns are one method of determining distance from target in gunshot wounds. Stippling is caused by burning powder and indicates a close-range discharge.

the courts and in the scientific community. The Federal Bureau of Investigation, for example, refuses to recognize the practice for courtroom introduction and does not provide expert analysis in the area. On the other hand, the Internal Revenue Service actively embraces the technology and maintains a contingent of experts for testimony. Although voiceprint identification may be accepted in many states within specific parameters,[32] others have not followed.

Firearm Identification and Ballistics Evaluation

The rifling of firearms in the commission of crimes has occurred for at least five centuries, but the recognition that evidence resulting from such rifling could be employed for identification purposes did not emerge until the nineteenth century. At that time, in 1835, a mold mark was employed to identify the weapon used in the killing of a British police officer. Early identification attempts were quite rudimentary, but in 1929, the Scientific Crime Detection Laboratory (SCDL) was initiated at Northwestern University after public outcry following the St. Valentine's Day massacre in Chicago. Four years later, in 1932, the FBI Laboratory was formed.[33] By 1980, most states had created similar laboratories. Their efforts were enhanced greatly when the FBI began to distribute the General Rifling Characteristic (GRC) file via the National Criminal Information Center (NCIC). This file originally provided more than 18,000 rifling characteristic measurements, but it is updated on an annual basis.

As with fingerprint and voiceprint identification, the science of firearm identification is based on the premise that projectiles may be matched to the weapon that fired them because of unique characteristics. Generally speaking, two types of characteristics are useful for comparison. *Class* characteristics are common to a select group, and *individual* characteristics are unique to a particular item. Class characteristics are often useful in determining the make, model, and caliber of a particular weapon from an expended projectile, such as a .357 Smith & Wesson, and are useful in cases in which a suspect weapon has not been recovered. They are also used as a screening device when a suspect weapon is recovered. For

Forensic experts may be called to testify as to the distance between the firearm and the victim. Stippling or stellate patterns may be important when individuals argue self-defense. In this photo, the wound inflicted is considered a good illustration of a stellate pattern gunshot. Stellate patterns are created when exploding gunpowder cannot expand or when they cannot penetrate deeply into the tissue. This indicates close contact and may negate claims of self-defense.

RIFLED VERSUS NONRIFLED BARRELS AND FIREARM IDENTIFICATION

With the exception of smooth-barreled shotguns, all firearms have rifled barrels to enhance velocity and accuracy. "Rifling," or the drilling-out process, results in the creation of lands and grooves. The "caliber" of the weapon is the distance between lands on opposite sides of the barrel. Different manufacturers employ different rifling techniques and patterns. Expended projectiles bear the markings of the rifled barrels and extractor and ejector marks (if fired by semiautomatic firearms), and may be used to identify the make, model, and caliber of the weapon. Individual characteristics, known as striations, may be employed for comparison purposes between those projectiles found at the crime scene and those fired by the suspect weapon at the laboratory. In smooth-barreled weapons, comparisons are based on markings from expended cartridges. These include firing pin impressions and extractor and ejector marks.

example, a .22 caliber gun recovered from the suspect's home may be excluded as the murder weapon in a homicide in which the shell casings at the scene and the wounds on the victim are consistent with a .44 Magnum. Individual characteristics, on the other hand, are useful in matching a projectile with a specific weapon because of the unique markings on the projectile caused by random imperfections such as corrosion, use, damage, and the like. These markings, known as *striations*, may be employed to match a bullet to the gun from which it was shot. This is basically done by shooting the same type of ammunition into a pool of water and comparing the expended projectiles with those in question.[34]

In addition to firearm identification, forensic experts may also be called to testify as to firing distance. Generally speaking, gunshot wounds are divided into three broad categories: contact, close range, and distant. The distance between the muzzle and the target may be calculated through the analysis of the gunpowder residue. Such residue is caused because gunpowder is not always burned, resulting in an important maxim—the greater the residue, the shorter the distance. Over the years, common patterns of gunshot residue have emerged. The determination of distance can be extremely important when the suspect's intention is being questioned, such as in an accidental shooting or self-defense claim. It can also be important in determining suicide.[35] Gunpowder is released in a cloud, and the residue is often found on the hands of suspects. Thus, investigators may perform tests that reveal the presence of antimony, barium, and the like. Although circumstantial, such tests may be introduced as evidence that the suspect fired a weapon.

Finally, forensic experts may be called to testify as to the trajectory of the projectile. Such determination, known as **ballistics**, involves the evaluation and identification of the path of a spent bullet. This may be calculated based on the shape and velocity of the bullet. As with distance from target, the path of the bullet may be useful information when the defendant claims that he or she acted in self-defense or accidentally fired the weapon. **Ballistic fingerprints** are also useful for the identification and verification of a suspect weapon. Ballistic fingerprints may be defined as those unique identifying marks made on bullets and cartridge casings that are particular to an individual firearm.

ballistics evaluation and identification of the trajectory of a spent bullet.

ballistic fingerprints ballistic fingerprints may be defined as those unique identifying marks made on bullets and cartridge casings that are particular to an individual firearm.

DNA Analysis and Identification

Since the 1980s, the science of genetic fingerprinting has been used in countless criminal trials. Based on the premise that every individual has a unique genetic makeup, testimony regarding DNA (deoxyribonucleic acid) has been widely accepted in civil and criminal courts. Although civil courts tend to stop short of allowing positive identification of an individual, they generally allow testimony regarding statistical likelihood of a random match of DNA and that a particular individual cannot be excluded as the secretor of a particular sample. DNA found in blood, semen, saliva, or hair has also been used in criminal courts as circumstantial evidence.

Forensic comparisons of DNA can be accomplished in several different ways. The oldest (and least reliable) forensic test, known as Restriction Fragment Length Polymorphisms (RFLP), required a large quantity of DNA, was susceptible to extraneous environmental factors, and involved comparisons of restriction fragments of suspect and known DNA samples. Polymerase chain reaction (PCR), a newer method of DNA analysis, allows the replication of DNA without altering the original sample, much like a copy machine (DOJ, 2002). PCR only requires a small sample of DNA and may even be conducted on skin cells found on ligatures. However, it is more susceptible to contamination. Thus, extra care is needed in the preservation of the sample. The most recent DNA forensic test, and one advocated by the Department of Justice and the Federal Bureau of Investigation, is short tandem repeat (STR) analysis. According to the DOJ,

> Short tandem repeat (STR) technology is a forensic analysis that evaluates specific regions (loci) that are found on nuclear DNA. The variable (polymorphic) nature of the STR regions that are analyzed for forensic testing intensifies the discrimination between one DNA profile and another. For example, the likelihood that any two individuals (except identical twins) will have the same 13-loci DNA profile can be as high as 1 in 1 billion or greater. The Federal Bureau of Investigation (FBI) has chosen 13 specific STR loci to serve as the standard for CODIS. The purpose of establishing a core set of STR loci is to ensure that all forensic laboratories can establish uniform DNA databases and, more importantly, share valuable forensic information. If the forensic or convicted offender CODIS index is to be used in the investigative stages of unsolved cases, DNA profiles must be generated by using STR technology and the specific 13 core STR loci selected by the FBI.[36]

Finally, mtDNA (mitochondrial DNA) and Y-chromosome analysis may be used in cases of unidentified remains. However, the current trend emphasizes STR, because such results may be indexed in a national DNA database.[37]

Expert testimony on DNA has been accepted in most states throughout the country, and the science itself has been validated. However, challenges to the admissibility of testing results may be issued for reasons outside the science field itself. These may include, but are not limited to, contamination, improper collection of specimen, improper preservation of sample, reputation of the individual analyst, and chain of custody.

▶ CONCLUSIONS

As with other forms of evidence previously discussed, documentary and scientific evidence require the testimony of witnesses for authentication and verification purposes. Documentary evidence may be authenticated in various ways, ranging from the opinion of lay witnesses to the testimony of experts. Authentication of physical evidence involves a demonstration of the reliability of the method employed. Since the *Daubert* ruling, trial judges must consider the testing and validation of the method, peer review, rate of error, and the general acceptance of the technology in the field.

Key Terms

Authentication

Ballistics

Ballistic fingerprints

Best evidence rule

Chain of custody

Computer forensics

Exclusionary rule

Fingerprint

Fungible evidence

Inked prints

Invisible (or latent) print

Laying the foundation

Motion

Motions in limine

Motion to strike

Motion to suppress

Objections

Original document

Parol evidence rule

Plastic print

Questioned document

Scientific evidence

Self-authenticating documents

Trace evidence

Unfair or undue prejudice

Visible print

Voiceprints

Discussion Questions

1. What requirements for the introduction of scientific evidence were established in *Daubert*? How did this differ from the previous *Frye* ruling?

2. Should judges be able to exclude relevant evidence that may incite bias? Why or why not? Give examples of unfair prejudice.

3. Should any type of document be considered private and, therefore, inadmissible in court?

Consider bank statements, medical records, and such. What are the benefits and setbacks to each position?

4. Should handwriting and signature comparisons be admissible in court? Discuss why or why not.

5. How has the science of DNA identification changed over the years? On what grounds might the introduction of DNA evidence be challenged?

Recommended Resources

Videos

The History Channel. Dead reckoning. This set of four DVDs thoroughly discusses various fields in forensic science. Available at: http://store.aetv.com.

PBS. The Viking deception. *Nova*. Available at: http://www.pbs.org/wgbh/nova/vinland/shop.html.

A&E Television. Faith and foul play in Salt Lake City. *City Confidential*. Available at: http://store.aetv.com.

Books

Byers, Steven (2005). *Introduction to Forensic Anthropology*. New Jersey: Allyn & Bacon.

Lewis, Susan (2005). *The Viking deception*. PBS: NOVA. Retrieved April 18, 2006 from http://www.pbs.org/wgbh/nova/vinland/fakes.html.

Miller, Hugh (1999). *What the corpse revealed: Murder and the science of forensic detection*. New York: St. Martins Press.

Paulsen, Derek J. and Robinson, Matthew B. (2003). *Spatial aspects of crime: Theory and practice*. New Jersey: Allyn & Bacon.

Roberts, Allen Dale and Sillitoe, Linda (1990). *Salamander: The story of the Mormon forgery murders* (2nd ed.). New York: Signature Books.

Saferstein, Richard (2005). *Forensic Science Handbook, Volumes I and II*. New Jersey: Prentice-Hall Publishing.

Worrall, Simon. (2002). *The poet and the murderer: A true story of literary crime and the art of forgery*. New York: Dutton Publishing.

Online Sources

http://www.lib.msu.edu/harris23/crimjust/forsci.htm—Supported by the Michigan State University library, this Web site contains an exhaustive list of forensic science resources, including links to all major professional associations and research publications.

www.aafs.org—Home page of the American Academy of Forensic Science contains links to various resources in the field and provides online access to various publications.

http://www.ojp.usdoj.gov/—Home page of the Office of Justice Programs at the United States Department of Justice provides links to publications and other resources concerning criminal justice, criminal evidence, and forensic science.

http://www.asqde.org/—Home page of the American Society of Questioned Document Examiners contains information and links to forensic Web sites, online tools and publications, and abstracts of articles published in the Society's scholarly journal.

http://www.thename.org—Home page of the National Association of Medical Examiners contains links to other forensic sites and NAME publications, including several interesting articles regarding forensic pathology in the news.

http://www.ncjrs.gov—Home page of the National Criminal Justice Reference Service provides information and links to various publications and resources in criminal justice, including search function for online articles on forensic science.

http://www.pbs.org/wgbh/nova/vinland/fakes.html—Sponsored by the Public Broadcasting System (PBS), this site details various forgeries throughout history.

Relevant Cases Cited

Alaska v. Coon, 974 P.2d 386 (Alaska Supreme Court, 1999)

Arizona v. Evans, 514 U.S. 1 (1995)

Baker v. The State, 250 Ga. 671, 300 SE2d 511 (1983)

Brown v. State, Okl.Cr., 518 P.2d 898 (1974)

Daubert v. Merrell Dow Pharmaceuticals, Inc. 509 U.S. 579 (1993)

Floyd v. State, 27 FLW S697, Florida Supreme Court (2002)

Frye v. United States, 54 App. D.C. 46, 293 F. 1013 (1923)

Gilbert v. California, 388 U.S. 263 (1967)

Henderson v. State, 463 So.2d 196 (Fla. 1985)

Mosby v. Arkansas, CR 01-784 _____ S.W.3d _____, (2002)

Nelson v. State, Okl Cr., 687 P.2d 744 (1984)

Old Chief v. United States, 519 U.S. 172 (1997)

Olmstead v. U.S., 277 U.S. 438 (1928)

Omychund v. Barker, 1 Akt. 21, 49; 26 ER 15, 33 (1745)

Skilling v. United States, 561 U.S. 358 (2010)

Spencer v. Texas, 385 U. S. 554, 560 (1967)

Thompson v. State, Okl Cr., 567 P.2d 999 (1977)

United States v. Humphrey, 208 F.3d 1190 (10th Cir. 2000)

U.S. v. Llera Plaza, et al., 188 F.Supp.2d 549 (E.D.Pa. 2002)

United States v. Miller, 425 U.S. 435 (1976)

United States. v. Ricco, 52 F.3d 58,61-62 (4th Cir. 1995)

Notes

1. *Arizona v. Evans*, 514 U.S. 1 (1995)
2. *Old Chief v. U.S.*, 519 U.S. 172 (1997)
3. Ibid.
4. *Spencer v. Texas*, 385 U. S. 554, 560 (1967)
5. *Mosby v. Arkansas*, CR 01-784 _____ S.W.3d _____, (2002)
6. *Floyd v. State*, 27 FLW S697, Florida Supreme Court (2002)
7. *United States. v. Ricco*, 52 F.3d 58,61-62 (4th Cir. 1995)
8. *Nelson v. State*, Okl Cr., 687 P.2d 744 (1984)
9. *Brown v. State*, Okl.Cr., 518 P.2d 898 (1974)
10. *Nelson v. State*, Okl Cr., 687 P.2d 744 (1984)
11. *Thompson v. State*, Okl Cr., 567 P.2d 999 (1977)
12. *North Carolina v. Fleming*, Supreme Court of North Carolina, 175A97 (1999)
13. *United States v. Humphrey*, 208 F.3d 1190 (10th Cir. 2000)
14. *Baker v. The State*, 250 Ga. 671, 300 SE2d 511 (1983)
15. Ibid.
16. *Omychund v. Barker*, 1 Akt. 21, 49; 26 ER 15, 33 (1745)
17. *United States v. Miller*, 425 U.S. 435 (1976)
18. *Daubert v. Merrell Dow Pharmaceuticals, Inc.* 509 U.S. 579 (1993)
19. *Frye v. U.S.*, 54 App. D.C. 46, 293 F. 1013 (1923)
20. *Daubert v. Merrell Dow Pharmaceuticals*, 509 U.S. 579 (1993)
21. Because of space and time constraints, a comprehensive undertaking of all categories of scientific evidence will not be included in this text. For a discussion of same, explore forensic science and digital evidence in Saferstein's *Handbook of Forensic Science* (Volumes I and II) and Britz's *Computer Forensics and Cybercrime: An Introduction*.
22. *Gilbert v. California*, 388 U.S. 263 (1967)
23. Moenssens, Andre A.; Starrs, James E.; Henderson, Carol E.; and Inbau, Fred E. (1995). *Scientific Evidence in Civil and Criminal Cases*. Westbury, NY: The Foundational Press, Inc.
24. Pfefferli, Peter, W. (2001). Review 1998–2001 from the Coordinating Laboratory on: Questioned Documents (Other than Handwriting). Presented at the 13th Annual INTERPOL Forensic Science Symposium, Lyon, France, October 16–19, 2001. http://www.interpol.int/Public/Forensic/IFSS/meeting13/Reviews/QDnoHw.pdf.

25. Ibid.
26. Britz, Marjie T. (2013). *Computer forensics and cyber crime: An introduction* (3rd ed.). Prentice Hall: New Jersey.
27. Moenssens et al., 1995
28. *United States v. Llera Plaza*, et al., 188 F.Supp.2d 549 (E.D.Pa. 2002)
29. e.g., *U.S. v. Mitchell*, 365 F.3d 215 (3rd Cir., 2004); *U.S. v. Crisp*, 324 F. 3d 261 (4th Cir., 2003)
30. *Commonwealth v. Patterson*, 445 Mass. 626 (2005)
31. Moenssens et al., 1995
32. *Alaska v. Coon*, 974 P.2d 386 (Alaska Supreme Court, 1999)
33. For a complete discussion of the history of ballistics, please see Hamby, James E. and Thorpe, James W. (1999). The history of firearm and toolmark identification. Association of Firearm and Tool Mark Examiners Journal, 20th Anniversary Issue, *31*(3). http://www.firearmsid.com/A_historyoffirearmsID.htm.
34. For a more detailed discussion of firearms identification, see Saferstein, Richard E. (2005). *Forensic Science Handbook, Volume II* (2nd ed.). Upper Saddle River, NJ: Prentice-Hall.
35. Saferstein, 2005
36. Department of Justice (2002). Using DNA to solve cold cases. *NIJ Special Report* (July, 2002) from http://www.ncjrs.gov/pdffiles1/nij/194197.pdf.
37. Ibid.

THE DECLARATION OF INDEPENDENCE.

13 Cyber Evidence and Demonstrative Evidence in the Pursuit of Justice

LEARNING OBJECTIVES

The learner will:

❶ *Define demonstrative evidence*

❷ *Explore the challenges associated with computer crime and cyber evidence*

❸ *Explain the traditional protections of privacy and the emerging changes in light of emergent technology*

4 *Identify the traditional challenges associated with the investigation and prosecution of computer crime*

5 *Discuss the controversies associated with the USA PATRIOT Act*

6 *Explore the ways in which technology has affected demonstrative evidence*

7 *Distinguish between demonstrative and real evidence*

In previous chapters, we have discussed a wide range of evidence in criminal cases. However, two types of evidence are unique in that they involve digital technology. **Cyber evidence** exists in electronic form and is accessed solely through electronic means. Examples include text from e-mails and the history of Web sites a person accesses. **Demonstrative evidence** illustrates or clarifies oral testimony in a criminal proceeding and often uses computer-generated images and animations to recreate a tangible object (or experiment) or to reenact an event. Examples include computerized diagrams, maps, animated simulations, and three-dimensional models.

The emergence of the Internet and the increasing globalization of commerce and communication have dramatically affected all areas of American life, and it provides new challenges to the pursuit of justice in American courts. Advancements in technology have brought innumerable advantages and created vast opportunities throughout the world. Accessibility to art, culture, even knowledge itself, has exponentially broadened commercial enterprise, and accessibility to information regarding public health and social issues has created a virtual plethora of self-empowerment opportunities. At the same time, this globalization of commerce and accessibility of knowledge has resulted in new forms of criminal deviance and an emergence of a more sophisticated criminal class.

Experts agree that cyberspace provides attractive opportunities to those with felonious intent. Fraud, theft, and misappropriation of funds via digital media are much less expensive for the criminal and pose far less of a physical threat than traditional methods. Such activities do not require the same attention to logistical details, such as securing a method of transportation (e.g., getaway car), storage of the contraband (from drugs to fruit), and exposure to discovery while escaping (e.g., faking a passport). In addition, unlawful activities perpetrated online require little if any additional personnel to affect them. Whereas a bank robbery may require a mask, the presence of a stickup person, a lookout, and a driver, online fund misappropriation requires only a personal computer with a single central processing unit (CPU) and a plan. The fact that a perpetrator can maintain a distance of potentially thousands of miles from the physical "crime scene" is an extremely attractive proposition. Unfortunately, traditional stereotypes and a general lack of law enforcement resources have hampered efforts to combat the problem successfully. Difficulties in prosecuting plague even those rare communities that have adequate resources. Even when law enforcement agents are well-equipped, challenges abound in many instances.

cyber evidence evidence that exists primarily in electronic form and is accessed solely through electronic means, such as text from e-mails and the history of Web sites a person accesses.

demonstrative evidence evidence that illustrates or clarifies oral testimony in a criminal proceeding, such as computer-generated charts, images, and models.

▶ Cyber Evidence and Its Challenges

Several factors have contributed to a general failure in the enforcement of computer-crime laws, the investigation of cyber evidence, and the prosecution of computer-related deviance. Some of these factors are directly related to the nature

PROBLEMS WITH PROSECUTING COMPUTER CRIME

The introduction of computer technology and the explosion of Internet-facilitated communication, commerce, information dissemination, and social media have been accompanied by a plethora of advancements in medicine, scholarship, education, science, and globalization. At the same time, these technological developments have resulted in a marked increase in criminal sophistication. Unfortunately, law enforcement and criminal legislatures have not always kept pace with their criminal counterparts, and criminal prosecutions have often been confounded by factors unique to computer crime. These include, but are not limited to:

- Inadequate resources
- Lack of reporting
- Stereotypes of perpetrators and perceived insignificance
- Dearth of legislation and criminal statutes
- Intangibility and volatility of evidence
- Prosecutorial reluctance
- Judicial ignorance
- Jurisprudential inconsistency[1]

of current criminal law and the U.S. Constitution as they apply to "digital" crime; others are byproducts of traditional systemic deficiencies. Perhaps the most obvious of these is the lack of resources (particularly in the law enforcement community), but other issues certainly exist. For the purpose of this discussion, concerns related to effective enforcement on the street and consistent jurisprudence in the courtroom can be categorized as: nonevidentiary, evidentiary, and legislative.

Nonevidentiary Concerns

Inadequate Police Resources

Law enforcement agencies across the country have always had scarce, or at least limited, resources. There are several reasons for this, including public apathy and strained government budgets. As a result, police departments are notoriously tight-fisted with expenditures and chronically underbudgeted. Administrators, among others, may consider the acquisition of up-to-date forensic computer equipment a recurring expense and therefore display great hesitation toward the purchase of often extremely expensive machinery. Forensic software packages alone can cost thousands of dollars and the requisite hardware costs even more. Apart from the initial investment, the maintenance and upgrading of the hardware and software programs require a continuous flow of monetary support—not to mention the quickness with which they often become outdated and obsolete. In addition, expenses include:

- Physical housing environments to store volatile (i.e., quickly moving and easily corrupted) digital evidence
- Additional personnel (e.g., repair technicians, technical support personnel, etc.)
- Extensive training for computer investigators (e.g., detectives), noninvestigatory personnel (e.g., emergency medical technicians), and patrol officers

Training the right people in the right way is extremely effective, but a lack of appropriate and timely training can be problematic. Because of the intangibility of digital evidence, for example, first responders may not appropriately recognize evidence or use appropriate methods for the preservation of

Digital evidence must be identified, collected, and preserved with utmost caution because of its volatile nature. Fortunately for law enforcement, perpetrators are often not successful in destroying digital evidence. Unfortunately for the public at large, that doesn't stop them from trying.

same. In addition, too many police executives, along with the general public, often perceive computer crime and the individuals associated with it as being relatively harmless and less of an immediate or dangerous threat to their communities.

Lack of Reporting

Although estimates vary, most experts agree that the vast majority of Fortune 500 companies have had their assets electronically compromised at least once—at a cost of more than 10 billion dollars per year.[2] From February 15, 2005, through December 31, 2005, more than 52 million records containing personal information were lost or stolen. However, a remarkably low number of victimized companies report such intrusions to law enforcement authorities, leaving an unclear picture as to the actual state of information theft. Such lack of reporting undermines the efforts of computer forensic investigators, primarily because it lessens the perception of the significance and prevalence of computer crime. Unfortunately, leaders of private and public entities remain reluctant to disclose their victimization often for one or more of the following reasons[3]:

- Fear of erosion of consumer confidence
- Fear of losing control to law enforcement agents (i.e., loss of secrecy)
- Perception that reporting will not result in the capture or identification of a suspect
- Jurisdictional uncertainty

Many corporate executives indicate that the potential loss of consumer confidence is the number one reason for not reporting. They argue that (1) the benefits associated with the successful identification and prosecution of the perpetrator are far outweighed by the economic losses that would occur in the wake of the disclosure of breached security; (2) the potential loss of consumer confidence is too high of a risk; and (3) the likelihood of irreparable (and expensive) damage to their corporate image and reputation is unacceptable. In the current climate of heightened consumer awareness regarding identity theft, the fear of it posed by compromised data from a given company can be an irresistible stimulus for consumer infidelity toward said company. In addition, corporate executives may express reservations about the competency of law enforcement personnel or prosecutorial staff and may perceive that the effectiveness of enforcement and prosecution would be minimal.

Even when corporate executives are inclined to seek law enforcement assistance, many indicate that jurisdictional uncertainly discourages the pursuit. Consider this: In a local office of an international conglomerate, a system administrator discovers that an unauthorized employee has accessed personal information about other corporate personnel. To whom should such malfeasance be reported? Without a clear sense of the potential criminality or understanding of appropriate jurisdiction, should the administrator report it to the Federal Bureau of Investigation, Interpol, the local sheriff's department, the municipal police? Unfortunately, no easy answer exists because each case likely will result in a very different answer. In fact, the determination of jurisdiction may not be immediately clear even to law enforcement authorities. Finally, corporate executives are often reluctant to relinquish control of an investigation to law enforcement authorities. Instead, many of them express the desire to control both the level of access and the scope of the investigation. Once assured that the discovery of criminal activity necessarily requires relinquishment of corporate information, they tend to abandon further cooperation.[4]

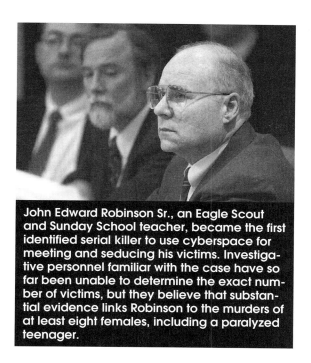

John Edward Robinson Sr., an Eagle Scout and Sunday School teacher, became the first identified serial killer to use cyberspace for meeting and seducing his victims. Investigative personnel familiar with the case have so far been unable to determine the exact number of victims, but they believe that substantial evidence links Robinson to the murders of at least eight females, including a paralyzed teenager.

Stereotypes and Apathy in Law Enforcement and the Community

As the stereotype goes, computer criminals are socially isolated and intellectually challenged individuals who find solace in the anonymity of cyberspace. While this characterization may hold true in some cases, the reality of others is often far more sinister. The general perception among investigators and the public is that child pornography and the exploitation of children are the most prevalent and biggest concerns for law enforcement. Certainly, online technology and the globalization of communication stemming from it have significantly affected the proliferation of such deviance. As a result, available funds tend to be allocated toward investigative and legislative efforts against it, but often at the expense of attention and resources needed in the investigation of other sorts of online criminality.

In addition to the general apathy exhibited by law enforcement and the community, prosecuting attorneys have displayed great reluctance in

APPLICATION OF LAW

JOHN EDWARD ROBINSON, SR.—THE FIRST IDENTIFIED ONLINE SERIAL KILLER

In the summer of 2000, investigators in rural Kansas and Missouri discovered the decomposing remains of five women. Both discovery sites were owned by John Edward Robinson Sr., a married man and father of two, who apparently had lured his victims to their death by soliciting sadomasochistic relationships on the Internet and promising substantial financial incentives. His online screen name was "Slavemaster." The bodies were discovered after several women filed complaints with law enforcement authorities claiming that Robinson was far more brutal than they expected and much more than he had advertised.

Ensuing investigations brought about Robinson's conviction and death sentence for the killing of three women in Kansas. Eventually, Robinson pled guilty to five more killings in the state of Missouri, including teenagers Debbie Faith (a paraplegic) and Lisa Stasi (whose body has never been found). Faith was the daughter of one of Robinson's other victims, Sheila Faith, and Stasi was a young woman fleeing an abusive husband (who apparently found someone much worse). Ironically, the adoption of Stasi's infant daughter by his brother and sister-in-law was coordinated by Robinson.[3]

pursuing computer-related criminals. They often cite a lack of concern among their constituents as a major reason for same, but other reasons exist as well, including: (1) a lack of cooperation associated with extradition requests when the crime is computer-related, (2) victims who often display a reluctance to cooperate, (3) an obvious dearth of offender-tracking capabilities, and (4) the labor-intensive nature of case preparation and execution that can discourage even the most ardent prosecutor.[5]

Evidentiary Concerns

cybercrime any criminal activity involving a computer or computer system that results in a direct or concomitant loss.

Just as the proliferation of online deviance has created additional workloads and backlogs for law enforcement personnel, the multijurisdictional nature of **cybercrime** activities has created a virtual plethora of legal conundrums. Without exception, the Supreme Court has denied cert (certiorari) on virtually every case involving the collection of evidence and questions of vicinage (the statutory jurisdiction of a particular court). Such actions have resulted in a patchwork of law across the United States, providing little guidance to the lower courts. Thus, the enforcement, prosecution, and conviction of computer-related offenses vary widely across jurisdictions.

Issues with Physicality of Evidence

The nature of American law is such that the physicality of the evidence, in substance and in location, is necessary for introduction into a criminal court proceeding. The intangibility of activity and the absence of physical location are simply not provided for by traditional statutes, case law, or even the U.S. Constitution and Bill of Rights. In fact, the legal element of vicinage has traditionally required the specification of a physical, not virtual, crime scene. This is necessary for determining the point at which the crime actually occurred and the particular agency responsible for the investigation of the particular incident. Consider the following case:

The tendency to be dismissive toward the potential criminality illustrated in this example is common, largely because gambling is decriminalized in most of the United States and perhaps because Ima is just a "college kid" in the harmless pursuit of some needed cash. The fact is that proliferation of online banks and money transfer companies has enabled virtually anyone to purchase anything without leaving the comforts of home. Although most exchanges of funds are entirely legitimate, online banking and money transfers have greatly enhanced the possibilities available to the criminally minded. Now, apply the same questions in the example to any case of child pornography, solicitation of murder, embezzlement of funds, and so on.

In addition to the lack of clarity regarding appropriate vicinage, law enforcement agencies are hampered further by the inconsistency of applicable laws and community standards. Based on community standards, definitions of obscenity and criminality in the United States have long varied across jurisdiction. The confusion has been compounded on the international level where some societies tolerate, even condone, certain behaviors. Regarding the practice of gambling, for example, Antigua, Caracas, and the Dominican Republic, have recently challenged American sovereignty over wagers placed by Americans through online casinos and sports books. Finally, the traditional lack of collaboration among agencies in the United States makes the issue of vicinage and jurisdictional sovereignty even murkier. The introduction of entities located internationally has only exacerbated the investigative, enforcement, judicial, and legislative problems.

▼

Facts of the Case—Clemson student Ima Gambler logs on to an online gaming site to play a little poker with some friends she met in her previous foray into online gambling. One is from London, England, another from Buffalo, New York, and the other is from Charleston, South Carolina. Ima uses her debit card to transfer money from her South Carolina account to her PayMe account, whose American headquarters is located in Los Angeles. She then transfers the money from her PayMe account in Los Angeles to the gambling site, which is located in the Dominican Republic. She proceeds to play poker with her friends and wagers $500 on the next Clemson versus South Carolina football game. Although she loses at poker, she wins her bet on the football game. As a result, the gaming site deposits money into her PayMe account, which she promptly transfers to her checking account.

Applicable Law—Gambling in the state of South Carolina is specifically forbidden as provided for in S.C. Code of Laws, specifically, Title 19, Section 16. In addition, her wagering constitutes a violation of several federal statutes, including the Wire Act and the Transmission of Bets, Wagers, and Related Information Act, Pub. L. No. 87-216, §2, 75 Stat. 491, 552–553 (1961).

Questions

1. Which agency has primary jurisdiction (vicinage) over Ima's criminal action? Is it the Clemson University Police, the City of Clemson, Pickens County, the South Carolina State Law Enforcement Division, or the FBI?
2. Where did the crime of illegal wagering actually occur? Did it occur where she physically placed the wager (her South Carolina dorm room)? Or did it occur where the wager was actually received (in the Dominican Republic)?
3. Was there a secondary crime upon receipt of her winnings? If so, in which jurisdiction was the crime committed? In California, where the money was initially deposited (Los Angeles)? Or in South Carolina, where she physically removed the money from her account?

 CLARIFICATION OF CONCEPTS

TERMS AND DEFINITIONS OF COMPUTER CRIME

An additional problem associated with the enforcement and prosecution of computer crime is the definitional inconsistency associated with the phenomenon. Largely a result of the relative novelty of the activity, legal and social definitions regarding computer crime have further complicated the issue. The terms computer crime, computer-related crime, and cybercrime are used interchangeably in the literature, but they are generally defined as any criminal activity involving a computer or computer systems that results in a direct or concomitant loss.

Issues with Existing and Emerging Legislation

The first formal recognition of the need for computer-specific statutes can be traced back to 1977, when Senator Abraham Ribicoff (late congressman and former Connecticut governor) introduced the Federal Computer Systems Protection Act (FSCPA). Although eventually defeated, the bill introduced the notion that computer-specific statutes were necessary in the emerging Internet arena. Before that time, the only laws available to law enforcement were federal statutes within **Title 18** of the U.S. Codes. Some of these statutes could be applied to computer-related crime without modification. They included:

• Fraud and Embezzlement	18 U.S.C. §2314; 641; 2071; 1005; and 1006.
• Terrorism or Espionage	18 U.S.C. §793–795; 1905
• Child Seduction	18 U.S.C. §2421
• Child Exploitation	18 U.S.C. §2251

title 18 portion of the United States Code which constitutes the criminal and penal code of the federal government of the United States.

- Stalking   18 U.S.C. §2261
- Forgery and Counterfeiting   18 U.S.C. §471–509
- Extortion   18 U.S.C. §1951
- RICO   18 U.S.C. §1961–1968

In fact, many of these statutes are still being employed in the identification and prosecution of computer ne'er-do-wells. However, an assortment of federal and state legislation has since been created to specifically address crimes related to and committed through computers and technology. The first of these was the Computer Fraud and Abuse Act of 1986. Known as the "hacking statute," the original language has been modified over the years but is still employed against individuals who have either gained unauthorized access to computer systems or have created and distributed malicious programs. Some of the notables convicted under the act include Kevin Mitnick; Herbert "Shadowhawk" Zinn; and Robert Morris, creator of the Morris Worm that crippled 6,000 computer systems and cost millions in repairs. Morris is the son of the former chief scientist at the National Computer Security Center.[6]

Other provisions addressing computer-related activity have been incorporated into the U.S. Code under Title 18 (the Criminal Code) and Title 17 (Copyrights, Patents, and Trademarks). Most address the specific manner in which electronic surveillance of computer systems can be monitored and provides for the prosecution of hackers, including:

- 18 U.S.C. §1029—Fraud and Related Activity in Connection with Access Devices
- 18 U.S.C. §1030—Fraud and Related Activity in Connection with Computer
- 18 U.S.C. §1362—Communication Lines, Stations, or Systems
- 18 U.S.C. §2510 et seq.—Wire and Electronic Communications Interception and Interception of Oral Communications
- 18 U.S.C. §2710 et seq.—Stored Wire and Electronic Communications and Transactional Records Access
- 18 U.S.C. §3121 et seq.—Recording of Dialing, Routing, Addressing, and Signaling Information

 CASE LAW

DIGITAL FINGERPRINTS AND THE *DAUBERT* STANDARD

In recent years, the field of computer forensics has exploded in size, skill advancement, and efficacy. Professional organizations and congressional panels have increasingly recognized the necessity and validity of the discipline. Unfortunately, federal courts have lagged behind and have consistently failed to validate practices employed by computer forensic examiners. State appellate courts, however, have been less reticent. In fact, many have officially recognized "digital" fingerprints. As an appellate court in Texas opined:

[The examiner] explained that when he takes a hard drive from a computer, he uses a program like EnCase to automate the task of searching and finding the file on it. An image of the drive is taken; the files are copied, and

EnCase validates the copy by an "MD5 hash," a 128-bit algorithm that verifies the image. The MD5 hash is essentially a "digital fingerprint" of a drive, and if the hash values match, Lee said that "basically there's no chance" that an error occurred in making an exact duplicate of the original computer file. Lee used EnCase on computer files taken from Sanders's computer. EnCase indexed the files, and Sanders was able to retrieve deleted files containing child pornography from Sanders's computer. We find that the trial court did not abuse its discretion in admitting Lee's testimony and the evidence from Sanders's computer in the punishment phase. (See *Williford v. State*, 127 S.W.3d 309, 312–13 [Tex.App.—Eastland 2004, pet. ref'd] finding similar testimony about EnCase reliable in child pornography cases.)

▼

In addition to the modifications to Title 18, to the Electronic Communications Privacy Act, and to the Privacy Protection Act, antiterrorist legislation passed in the wake of the 9/11 attacks has provided significant guidance to local officials while increasing the scope and authority afforded to law enforcement.

The introduction of the USA PATRIOT Act in the fall of 2001 heralded significant changes to the manner in which electronic evidence is collected. Generally speaking, such changes greatly enhance the authority of law enforcement and erode privacy expectations that have developed over the past several decades and that have been incorporated into the earlier Privacy Protection Act (PPA) and Electronic Communications Privacy Act (ECPA). In addition, it provides for "sneak and peak" warrants in which contemporaneous notification is eliminated, and lowers traditional standards for collection and surveillance from probable cause to reasonable suspicion. As a result, the act has been criticized greatly by privacy advocates. Despite this, many of the original provisions have been extended indefinitely.

Despite the concerns of privacy advocates, the law enforcement community has championed many key concepts in the legislation. In particular, the introduction of national search warrants and roving wiretaps, as well as the application of pen register provisions to Internet communications have been deemed necessary in the fight against real and perceived terrorist threats. To wit, digital evidence of computer crime is no longer protected by its inherent lack of physicality. This enables law enforcement to seek judicial approval only once.

 CLARIFICATION OF CONCEPTS

PRIVACY IN THE DIGITAL AGE

Once it was recognized that traditional legislation did not provide for the interception of nontelephonic communications, Congress attempted to develop guidelines that would specifically address bulletin boards and e-mail.

- **Privacy Protection Act (PPA) of 1980—** 42 U.S.C. §2000—Specifically precluded the search or seizure of materials that may be publishable unless a demonstration of probable cause exists. By design, it attempted to apply traditional wiretap regulations to electronic bulletin boards while protecting the freedom of press provisions housed within the First Amendment. At the same time, it recognized that no expectation of privacy existed in posted messages to bulletin boards.
- **Electronic Communications Privacy Act (ECPA) of 1986—**Expanded provisions found with the PPA and applied the wiretap provisions originally articulated in Title III of the Omnibus Crime Control and Safe Streets Acts of 1968. In the most basic sense, ECPA applied Title III to nonaural electronic communications, including e-mail. The language also applied such to

wireless communications. Theoretically, it was designed to enhance privacy interests of citizens. Although it provided for the punishment of individuals illegally gaining access to computers, it did not exclude evidence collected in violation of same.

- **USA PATRIOT Act of 2001** (Uniting and Strengthening America by Providing Appropriate Tools Required to Intercept and Obstruct Terrorism)—Reduced or eliminated privacy expectations articulated in both the PPA and the ECPA. Unlike its predecessors, the USA PATRIOT Act was designed to increase the authority of law enforcement agencies and to decrease traditional standards of probable cause. Because of the breadth of its provisions, a termination date was incorporated into specific sections. However, major portions of the USA PATRIOT Act remain intact and continue to be extended.

Ironically, none of this legislation includes provisions for the exclusion of evidence collected in violation of the sections contained therein. At the same time, they all include sections that specify punishments and civil remedies for violators whether they are private or public.

Without question, the most common judicial challenges confronting the prosecution of computer crime involve the First and Fourth Amendments to the U.S. Constitution. Although the First Amendment has traditionally not been synonymous with criminal evidence, the nature of computer crime and the proliferation of child pornography, to name a few, make any discussion of computer crime and criminal evidence incomplete without comparable dialogue regarding the First Amendment. Additional First Amendment issues that have been considered by the courts include the inviolability of electronically published materials, the necessary level of particularity and specificity in emerging legislative acts, the inviolability of electronically published materials, the sanctity of electronic communications, and the intersection of obscenity and community standards.

The First Amendment and Child Pornography

Throughout American history, the freedom of speech provision in the First Amendment has been fundamental to understanding liberty and democracy. As such, the Supreme Court has guarded it zealously and has been reluctant to place blanket prohibitions on any categories of speech. Rather, the Court created a three-pronged test for analyzing questioned material. Under *Miller v. California*, a material may be considered obscene and prohibited by law, if: (1) an average person who is capable of applying contemporary community standards (2) determines that a work "depicts or describes, in a patently offensive way, sexual conduct specifically defined by the applicable state law"; then (3) "taken as a whole, [the work] lacks serious literary, artistic, political, or scientific value."[7] Case law following *Miller* specifically addressed the issue of child pornography. As a general rule, images that depict children in a sexually exploitive manner have been deemed prima facially obscene and, therefore, are illegal to create, distribute, or even possess. In making such determinations, the Court recognized that the sheer presence of such images creates an unacceptable risk to all children and encourages pedophilia.[8] This generalized threat was upheld consistently by the Court and cited as justification for blanket prohibitions against child pornography. Case law and emergent legislation have reflected this ideology. This included the Child Pornography Prevention Act (CPPA) of 1996 that attempted to apply traditional notions of indecency and child pornography to computer technology. To wit, the law specifically forbade "any visual depiction, including any photography, film, video, picture, or computer or computer-generated image or picture, whether made or produced by electronic, mechanical, or other means, of sexually explicit conduct."[9]

The introduction of the CPPA of 1996 was met with little fanfare. In fact, it seemed consistent with societal expectations. Unfortunately, the crafters of the document were too ambitious and included the potential for virtual, computer-generated, or otherwise manipulated images. This characteristic proved to be the act's undoing, and in *Ashcroft v. Free Speech Coalition* (2002), the Supreme Court struck it down. In its opinion, the Court argued that:

> Virtual child pornography is not "intrinsically related" to the sexual abuse of children. While the Government asserts that the images can lead to actual instances of child abuse, the causal link is contingent and indirect. The harm does not necessarily follow from the speech, but depends upon some unquantified potential for subsequent criminal acts. The Government's argument that these indirect harms are sufficient because, as Ferber acknowledged, child pornography rarely can be valuable speech . . . suffers from two flaws. First, Ferber's judgment about child pornography was based upon how it was made, not on what it communicated. The case reaffirmed that where the speech is neither obscene nor the product of sexual abuse, it does not fall outside the First Amendment's protection. . . . Second, Ferber did not hold that child pornography

SEX, LIES, AND MURDER ONLINE

In late 1998, a 48-year-old man was murdered while on the phone in the office of his auto salvage shop. The victim, Bruce Miller, was known to carry large amounts of cash in his pocket, and the homicide was investigated initially as a botched robbery attempt. His young widow, Sharee, appeared devastated and readily pointed a finger at former employee and former lover named John Hutchinson. However, the case took a dramatic turn when investigators in Missouri discovered the body of ex-police officer Jerry Cassaday. Dead of a self-inflicted bullet to the head, Cassaday had written a detailed suicide note for his family and left a printout of an instant message (IM) and a videotape. The rambling suicide note explained in detail how he murdered Bruce Miller. It also told a tale of star-crossed lovers.

Cassaday had met Sharee Miller at a casino in Reno. At the beginning of the affair, she claimed to be a successful business owner who lived with a disabled man and his brother. Upon her return to Flint, Michigan, the couple continued their affair via technology, which included electronic exchanges of pornographic photographs and a videotape recording of Miller masturbating. The couple did manage to find time together during several long weekends, and over the course of time, Miller revealed that she was married and that her husband was abusive. In addition, Miller told Cassaday that on two separate occasions she had become pregnant during their trysts but had miscarried after physical abuse by her husband. Cassaday had no

way of knowing that Miller was incapable of having children and that Sharee had actually shown him a friend's pregnancy test, along with photos of herself that were several years old. Miller, posing as Bruce, also contacted Cassaday via computer and took credit for causing the miscarriages. It was then that the lovers hatched a plan to kill Bruce Miller. Sharee provided maps and logistical information, including the victim's schedule and where the money was located. She also called Miller on the telephone to distract him, providing Cassaday with the element of surprise.

After the murder, Sharee changed her AOL account information, including her screen name, and cut off all contact with Cassaday. Realizing that he had been had, Cassaday wrote the notes to his family, printed out the IMs, and shot himself. When confronted with the overwhelming evidence, Sharee Miller claimed that she was being set up by Cassaday because she had spurned his advances. She further claimed that the IMs and the seminude photographs were manufactured by Cassaday. From Sharee's computer, computer forensic examiners were able to recover additional communications between the couple. Along with the AOL logs maintained by the service provider, the evidence was sufficient for the jury to find her guilty of second-degree murder and conspiracy to commit murder. Her attorneys have indicated their intention to appeal the verdict based on the grounds that the statements of Jerry Cassaday should not have been introduced because the defense could not cross-examine them.

is by definition without value. It recognized some works in this category might have significant value . . . but relied on virtual images—the very images prohibited by the CPPA—as an alternative and permissible means of expression. . . . Because Ferber relied on the distinction between actual and virtual child pornography as supporting its holding, it provides no support for a statute that eliminates the distinction and makes the alternative mode criminal as well.[10]

In later comments, the Court specifically ruled that the wording of the original act was too vague and ambiguous to withstand legal scrutiny. Although state laws that are similar in content, substance, and verbiage are still available to authorities, federal legislation to replace the CPPA has not emerged.

State laws regarding child pornography vary in several significant ways. The most important of these is the issue of age. Under federal law, a "minor" is any individual under the age of 18. However, in some states, the age of majority is lower. In Georgia, for example, the demarcation for the exploitation of children is 16 years of age. Such disparity makes it extremely difficult to accurately identify the age of the actors depicted. As scienter (i.e., knowledge) is a necessary element to establish guilt, prosecutors must demonstrate that the possessor of a questionable image knew that the individuals depicted were below the age of majority. In addition, prosecutors must demonstrate that the actors themselves are minors.

COMPUTER PORNOGRAPHY AND CHILD EXPLOITATION PREVENTION ACT OF 1999

(a) This Code section shall be known and may be cited as the "Computer Pornography and Child Exploitation Prevention Act of 1999."

(b) As used in this Code section, the term:

(1) "Child" means any person under the age of 16 years.

(2) "Identifiable child" means a person:

(A) Who was a child at the time the visual depiction was created, adapted, or modified or whose image as a child was used in creating, adapting, or modifying the visual depiction; and

(B) Who is recognizable as an actual person by the person's face, likeness, or other distinguishing characteristic, such as a unique birthmark or other recognizable feature or by electronic or scientific means as may be available.

The term shall not be construed to require proof of the actual identity of the child.

(c) (1) A person commits the offense of computer pornography if such person intentionally or willfully:

(A) Compiles, enters into, or transmits by means of computer;

(B) Makes, prints, publishes, or reproduces by other computerized means;

(C) Causes or allows to be entered into or transmitted by means of computer; or

(D) Buys, sells, receives, exchanges, or disseminates any notice, statement, or advertisement, or any child's name, telephone number, place of residence, physical characteristics, or other descriptive or identifying information for the purpose of offering or soliciting sexual conduct of or with an identifiable child or the visual depiction of such conduct.

(2) Any person convicted of violating paragraph (1) of this subsection shall be punished by a fine of not more than $10,000.00 and by imprisonment for not less than one nor more than 20 years.

(h) A person is subject to prosecution in this state pursuant to Code Section 17-2-1, relating to jurisdiction over crimes and persons charged with commission of crimes generally, for any conduct made unlawful by this Code section which the person engages in while either within or outside of this state if, by such conduct, the person commits a violation of this Code section which involves a child who resides in this state or another person believed by such person to be a child residing in this state.

(i) Any violation of this Code section shall constitute a separate offense.

This can prove extremely difficult. Consider whether you could positively determine if a particular person was 15, 16, or 17 years of age?

The Fourth Amendment and Computer Forensics

Unlike the First Amendment, which often has been overlooked as important to the law enforcement mission, the Fourth Amendment has always been the cornerstone of police procedure and activity. As mentioned previously, the exclusionary rule is predicated largely on police searches and seizures and considerations of the "expectation of privacy." Although not specifically articulated in the Amendment, the application of the exclusionary rule largely has involved the actions of police and the seizure of evidence. The Fourth Amendment clearly provides:

> The right of the people to be secure in their persons, houses, papers, and effects, against unreasonable searches and seizures, shall not be violated, and no Warrants shall issue, but upon probable cause, supported by Oath or affirmation, and particularly describing the place to be searched, and the persons or things to be seized.

In computer forensic investigations, certain elements of the Amendment have not been fully adjudicated by the Court, and the application by lower courts has proved to be anything but consistent. As with warrants that are unrelated to technology, computer searches are subject to judicial scrutiny of particularity, overbreadth, and third-party origination. In addition, the admissibility of evidence collected in the absence of a warrant is contingent upon a complete demonstration of satisfaction to traditional exceptions.

Particularity, Overbreadth, and Third-Party Origination

In the most basic sense, the Fourth Amendment to the Constitution requires that all warrants specifically describe the place to be searched, the items to be seized, and applicable justification to prevent "general, exploratory rummaging in a person's belongings."[11] Such specificity or **particularity** exists to ensure that investigating officers maintain a proper understanding of parameters and boundaries and that reasonable persons would understand the limitations of the resulting search. Thus, items unrelated to the specific boundaries remain immune from scrutiny. Traditionally, the inclusion of particularity did not present significant problems for LE officials, in part because the requirement of time, place, and items were tied specifically to a physical location. However, the vast and spatially ambiguous nature of the World Wide Web has complicated jurisdictional concerns and muddied the waters of government sovereignty and the lack of physicality has proved problematic to investigators.

Unlike traditional cases that are necessarily limited to the amount of physical evidence sought, computer searches involve potentially voluminous amounts of criminal evidence. At the same time, the possibility exists that evidence is miniscule or carefully hidden inside mountains of material. Unfortunately, the circuit courts have been divided on the level of specificity required in searches of computer files, and the Supreme Court has not entered the melee. Thus, while many courts have allowed broad searches of computer drives, others have likened them to searches of file cabinets—prohibiting exploration of nonassociated files.[12] The nature of computer forensics largely overlooks file names and folder designations, and this can prove problematic to investigators. As a general rule, courts have recognized a broader scope of exploration in computer searches. However, it is recommended strongly that officers seek secondary warrants when material unrelated to the initial investigation is uncovered. Thus, if an officer investigating financial fraud inadvertently stumbles upon a computerized cache of child pornography, it is to the officer's advantage to halt further investigative activity and obtain a secondary warrant that includes evidence of child pornography.

Unlike traditional criminal cases, computer crimes are often discovered by third parties, such as employers or system administrators. In order for the discovery of such criminal activity to be admissible in a criminal court, it must be demonstrated that the third party was not acting under the direction of law enforcement. Once again, the lower courts have applied this differently and rendered inconsistent verdicts. In one case, for example, the government informed a telecommunications company that it was being victimized. Subsequently, the criminal evidence discovered by company employees was deemed admissible because the employees were acting primarily in their own interest.[13] On the other hand, images of child pornography that had been copied by a computer technician at the state's request were not.[14]

Warrantless Searches and Computer Evidence

As mentioned in previous chapters, the Court has recognized and consistently upheld the warrant requirement found within the Fourth Amendment. In fact, the five general categories of searches that do not require the presence of a warrant are (1) automobiles, (2) field interrogation, (3) incident to arrest, (4) consent, and (5) plain view. The first three do not generally lend themselves to computer searches, but the latter two have been applied in several cases.

particularity in search warrants, the specificity of place, time, and actual items to be searched or seized. With particularity, items unrelated to the specific boundaries remain immune from scrutiny.

Consent

Law enforcement authorities may conduct searches of computer files when given consent by a competent person. The fruits of such searches are admissible if the consent was given voluntarily by an individual who had the proper authority of the area to be searched and was legally capable of granting such access.[15] In computer searches, this means that the person granting consent must have a common interest in or ownership of the computer in question. When shared computers are to be searched, the search is limited to that area of the consenting third party's common authority.[16] The presence of encryption or other security measures may negate the concept of common authority, unless the parties are privy to the necessary unlocking mechanisms. As a result, networked computers are largely immune from consent searches, because even system administrators may not have access to all files. Thus, the most important characteristics in determining the validity of common authority are physical control and limited access. Courts must measure these characteristics (including age, maturity, intelligence, education, and the physical and mental condition of the consenter) and evaluate the totality of the circumstances when considering consent searches.

Consideration of the totality of the circumstances is also important in determining the scope of the consent, because consent is rarely absolute or all-encompassing. Generally speaking, the scope of the consent is not without parameters and is limited to what a reasonable person would expect. As several courts have noted, such searches are intended to be direct and not exploratory. To wit, "government

 CASE LAW

REASONABLENESS AND CONSENT SEARCHES OF COMPUTERS

In 1998, a young woman awoke to find a masked intruder in her bedroom armed with a knife. In the ensuing struggle, she received cuts on her hands. After the intruder fled, the young woman's neighbor, Daniel Turner, phoned the police stating that he had been at his computer when he observed the offender fleeing the scene. The following day, detectives observed blood smears on window screens of both the victim and Turner. They then received written consent from Turner to search his apartment for signs of the intruder or evidence of the assault.

While Turner was being questioned downstairs, a detective noticed a screensaver of a young woman whose physical appearance resembled the victim's. Subsequently, the detective looked through the last documents accessed and found images of adult females in bondage. Copying those files to a diskette, the detective extended his search to the remainder of the hard drive and opened files with titles suggestive of child pornography. As a result, Turner was arrested and charged with one count of child pornography.

At his trial, Turner moved to suppress the images, arguing that they were outside the scope of the consent. The district court agreed, and the issue was explored further by the circuit court that identified the following issues relating to the scope of the consent:

- Although Turner voluntarily agreed to a general search of the premises for evidence of the assault, it was not reasonable to assume that the investigators would explore areas in which evidence could not reside (i.e., the computer hard drive). The court stated that "it obviously would have been impossible to abandon physical evidence of this sort in a personal computer hard drive, and bizarre to suppose—nor has the government suggested—that the suspected intruder stopped to enter incriminating evidence into the Turner computer."
- The preconsent exchange of dialogue between Turner and the detectives was such that a reasonable person would assume that the evidence for which the officers were looking was physical evidence linked to the crime, rather than documentary or photographic evidence.[17]

agents may not obtain consent to search on the representation that they intend to look only for certain specified items and subsequently use that consent as a license to conduct a general exploratory search."[18]

Plain View

In some situations, items may be seized without the issuance of a warrant or consent of the owner. Criminal contraband and criminal evidence, for example, may be seized when observed by an officer acting in a lawful manner, when unobstructed, and when obvious in their evidentiary value. For example, officers acting under the authority of a valid search warrant for narcotics may seize printouts of child pornography that were lying in the open and unobstructed. However, investigators cannot broaden the scope of the original search based on new evidence. Rather, investigators in similar situations should immediately obtain a secondary warrant before investigating further,[19] as courts have upheld the original rationale found in Coolidge. To wit, "the plain view doctrine may not be used to extend a general exploratory search from one object to another until something incriminating at last emerges."[20]

Although the Supreme Court has not specifically issued a ruling on the limitations of plain view searches of computer files, many lower courts have tackled the issue. In *Carey*,[21] an investigator looking for evidence of narcotics trafficking noticed an assortment of images with sexually explicit names. He subsequently opened them, identified them as child pornography, and changed the focus of his search. The court rejected the government's argument that computer searches were similar to searches of file cabinets. Instead, the court ruled that the contents of the file were not in plain view. Other courts have ruled in a similar manner, requiring officers to maintain the focus of the original warrant. At the same time, they have permitted the introduction of evidence that was discovered inadvertently.

Emergency Situations or Exigent Circumstances

The Court has upheld the admissibility of evidence that was discovered in the absence of a warrant in emergency situations.[22] Thus, officers may make a warrantless entry of a premises if they reasonably believe that an individual is in need of immediate aid. In such a situation, they are not precluded from seizing evidence that is in plain view. This does not suggest, however, that such seizures automatically warrant a search of the item's content. Indeed, officers are strongly encouraged to seek secondary warrants before undertaking a search of the contents of a seized computer. Consider the example of officers responding to a cry for help. Upon entry, they are unable to locate any person in distress but they do notice that the screensaver on the computer is an image of child pornography. Because possession of the image is illegal and the photo itself is considered criminal contraband, officers have no choice but to seize the computer. In order to search the contents of the CPU, however, a search warrant predicated on the probable cause established by the screensaver is required.

Courts have also upheld the seizure of computers when there is a sufficient demonstration of exigent circumstances. Because of the volatility of digital evidence, investigators may seize equipment vulnerable to manipulation or destruction. A consideration of the totality of the circumstances may include:

- Degree of urgency involved
- Amount of time necessary to obtain a warrant
- Whether the evidence is susceptible to removal or destruction
- Indications that the possessor of said material and/or equipment are aware of law enforcement's intention to seize it[23]

As with seizures in emergency situations, the activity of searching the contents requires a search warrant.

▼

▶ Demonstrative Evidence and Its Challenges

Unlike real evidence, demonstrative evidence may be loosely defined as those visual or aural aids that are created for the purpose of illustration and clarification of oral testimony or that are designed to recreate or reenact a tangible object, event, or experiment. For example, diagrams or sketches from an autopsy report are admissible in court as evidence in lieu of the body itself. The admissibility of demonstrative evidence is contingent upon numerous factors including:

- The need for illustration of tangible evidence that has met the legal requirement for introduction
- Satisfaction of the foundational requirements
- A demonstration of relevancy, materiality, and competency
- A demonstration that the item is more probative than prejudicial

First, the admissibility of demonstrative evidence hinges upon the reliability and authenticity of the tangible evidence it is intended to represent. Thus, visual depictions of the results of a polygraph examination would not be admissible because the exam itself does not meet the standards for admissibility. Second, foundational requirements of the demonstrative evidence itself must be satisfied. Such foundational requirements include demonstrating the authentication and accuracy of representation and answering questions such as: Does the diagram accurately represent the tangible object? Is such representation accurately scaled? Is it distorted in any way?

To demonstrate that an illustration, photograph, or other form of demonstrative evidence is relevant, material, and competent, the proponent of the evidence must show that it is intended to speak to a matter at issue, that it is intended to be illustrative, and that it is within the bounds of appropriate matter for jury consumption. The final hurdle in the admissibility of a particular item involves the evaluation of the probity of it versus any potential prejudice that may arise as a result of its introduction. For example, an 8" × 10" color photograph of a dismembered child might incite a blinding rage in the minds of jurors. Because evidence of the murder and dismemberment may be introduced in alternative form (i.e., a medical examiner's report or witness testimony), the potential prejudice arising from the introduction of the picture probably outweighs the probative value of the item. However, the trial judge has great discretion in evaluating such matters.

Summarily, demonstrative evidence may be viewed as a substitute for real evidence in matters involving the necessity of illustrations or visual presentations for clarification. Not all demonstrative evidence is admissible and may be excluded from consideration as provided by Federal Rules of Evidence, Rule 403. Demonstrative evidence may take various forms, including:

- Experiments
- Blackboards
- Maps and models
- Writing samples
- Photographic evidence and displays
- Videotapes and motion pictures
- Radiographs (x-rays)
- Police composites or mug shots
- Charts, illustrations, and other drawings
- Computer graphics, simulations, and animation
- Other assorted depictions or displays

Arguably, Dr. Henry Lee is one of the most flamboyant expert witnesses to ever testify in an American criminal trial. He has appeared as an expert witness in dozens of high-profile cases, including many discussed in this book. He is known for conducting innovative experiments in the courtroom.

Issues with Experiments

Experts called to testify regarding a particular matter will often conduct out-of-court experiments to validate and illustrate a point they are trying to make. As a general rule, the method and the results of such experiments, whether in the form of a report or video recording, are admissible only when the circumstances of the experiment are "substantially similar" and not distorted in any way.[24] A demonstration of such substantial similarity rests solely on the shoulders of the proponent of the evidence. Generally speaking, the trial judge will determine whether such a burden has been met and courts have urged judges to use care in making such determinations. To wit,

> Evidence of this kind should be received with caution, and only be admitted when it is obvious to the court, from the nature of the experiments, that the jury will be enlightened, rather than confused. In many instances, a slight change in the conditions under which the experiment is made will so distort the result as to wholly destroy its value as evidence, and make it harmful, rather than helpful. [*Navajo Freight Lines v. Mahaffy*, supra at 310][25]

Out-of-court experiments vary widely according to the particular circumstances of the case, but they can include testing of brakes in rainy conditions, nature of a fall, trajectory of a projectile, or visibility at the scene of an incident. When deemed admissible, the experiment may be introduced via diagram, chart, report, or videotape.

Experiments conducted in front of the jury must also meet the standards for admissibility. Thus, they must be relevant, material, and competent and not constitute a waste of time or be more prejudicial than probative. Such experiments often may be limited by the size and shape of the courtroom; a wide range of experiments have been introduced in numerous trials.

Issues with Photographs

Photographs and video recordings can be extremely powerful in criminal cases because they recreate a moment in time that has since passed. Such graphic representation is often more compelling than simple testimonial evidence. For example, the sheer brutality of a triple homicide is communicated best through color

DR. HENRY LEE AND HIS EXPERIMENTS

Many experts have conducted experiments in courtrooms across the country, but Dr. Henry Lee is particularly noteworthy because of his levity and entertaining behavior. Currently a professor at the University of New Haven, Lee is well known for his courtroom antics and general likeability. He is in high demand as an expert witness and is a regular guest analyst on CourtTV. He has testified in numerous high-profile trials, including those of O. J. Simpson, Rae Carruth, and Scott Peterson—all of whom were charged with the murder of female partners.

In the trial of Michael Peterson, a journalist on trial for the bludgeoning death of his wife, Lee spat watered-down ketchup onto cardboard to illustrate his theory that the massive quantities of blood in the stairwell were actually the result of coughing and aspiration by Kathleen Peterson. He also squirted red ink from a dropper to demonstrate basic concepts of blood spatter evidence. In one experiment, he accidentally sprayed the defense attorney with the mixture. Highly theatrical, Dr. Lee's antics continue to receive national attention.

photographs or video recordings of the actual crime scene. Testimony that the victims were stabbed numerous times in the face pales beside a color photograph of blood spatter, broken teeth, and a missing eye. At the same time, the latter form of evidence may be so powerful that it evokes tremendous passion and anger, making it almost impossible for a juror to engage in circumspect, cautious, and fair deliberation of all of the evidence. Because of such risks, photographic or video-recorded evidence may only be admitted when the probity of the item is deemed by the trial judge to outweigh the potential prejudice it may evoke.

In addition to considerations of potential bias, trial judges must also determine whether the photograph or recording satisfies the traditional legal requirements of relevancy, materiality, and competency. The jury in a homicide case may find a picture of the brick façade of a three-story manor where the crime occurred interesting, but the image is irrelevant if it does not depict additional evidence. In fact, such photographs lack any sort of probative value. However, if the prosecution theorizes that the perpetrators entered through a broken window at the front of the house, then the photograph would immediately be probative.

Photographs and recordings may be admitted only when the particular item in question satisfies the parameters articulated by the "best evidence rule." Thus, the negative of the original photograph or the original tape itself is preferred. However, trial judges may admit duplicates or derivatives whenever the original negative is not available. In any event, photographs and recordings must be authenticated through witness testimony. Such authentication normally includes testimony that determines (1) whether the item accurately represents the scene or

 CLARIFICATION OF CONCEPTS

WHEN TO USE PHOTOGRAPHIC EVIDENCE

- When it has a reasonable tendency to prove some material fact at issue
- When it appears competent for a courtroom actor to have viewed or examined the subject of the pictures when they were taken
- When it assists a courtroom actor in understanding the case
- When it corroborates other evidence
- When it tends to disprove the testimony of a witness (i.e., impeachment)
- When it helps illustrate or explain witness testimony

object in question, (2) whether it was taken at or reasonably near the time of the discovery or the incident in question, (3) whether it was developed in a manner consistent with common practices, and (4) whether the chain of custody of the item is documented and available for review.

Although a particular photograph or video recording may be deemed relevant, material, and competent, it may be excluded from evidence on other legal grounds. The most obvious reason for exclusion, of course, is that the item is "unduly prejudicial." This is especially relevant when photos or recordings contain gruesome images, when they lack probative value, when they are not material, or when they are repetitive. As a general rule, gruesome photographs and graphic video or audio recordings should be excluded if the value of the evidence in its entirety can be introduced in an alternative manner. However, this does not suggest that most graphic representations are excluded. To the contrary, appellate courts have consistently held that gruesome photographs are admissible when they are material to the case. With few exceptions, appellate courts have refused to reverse decisions by trial court judges on this particular issue, arguing that such reversal is inappropriate unless it is demonstrated that an abuse of discretion occurred. They have also recognized that such evidence is generally admissible because "the prosecution bears the burden of proof regarding all the elements of the crime regardless of whether the defendant concedes the cause of death."[26] Consequently, photographs depicting the nature, extent, and number of wounds are generally relevant in a murder case. In addition, several courts have specifically noted that because the nature of homicide itself is often gruesome, the

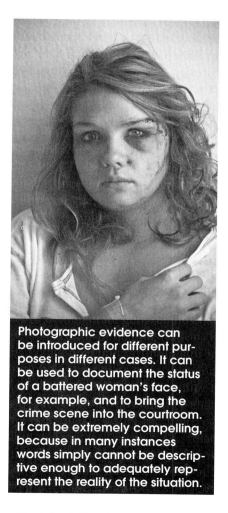

Photographic evidence can be introduced for different purposes in different cases. It can be used to document the status of a battered woman's face, for example, and to bring the crime scene into the courtroom. It can be extremely compelling, because in many instances words simply cannot be descriptive enough to adequately represent the reality of the situation.

introduction of evidence to prove the act may consequently shock and be repugnant to the finders of fact.

> Persons accused of crimes can generally expect that any relevant evidence against them will be presented in court. The test of admissibility is relevancy. Those whose work products are murdered human beings should expect to be confronted by photographs of their accomplishments.[27]

Automatic Photographs

In recent years, emerging new technology has brought American society into the era of surveillance. In fact, cameras seem to be everywhere—ATMs, convenience stores, parking lots—even on interstate overpasses. As such, images depicting robberies, assaults, and murders have become more common. However, the introduction of such evidence has not come without challenges. Because of the lack of witnesses to authenticate, courts have generally required other types of testimony before admitting automatic photographs. This testimony includes information regarding the maintenance of the equipment employed and the nature of the equipment's functionality (i.e., "How does it work?" or "Is it time delayed or triggered by motion?"). In addition, testimony or evidence must be introduced that validates the time, date, and location of the photograph in question. This may be done through operational mechanisms installed on the device or the use of a clock or calendar placed within the scope of the lens.

Digital Photography

Just as technology has resulted in a proliferation of surveillance equipment in the private and public sectors, the use of digital imagery has increased exponentially. Digital photography has entered all facets of American life and is used for personal and commercial uses. In fact, many law enforcement agencies across the country are moving toward a reduction in paperwork with film-based imaging systems and increased use of digital crime scene photography. As a general rule, digitally captured images taken by crime scene photographers are admissible within the same parameters as film-based photographs. Thus, images that accurately represent the item or location at issue, that are not distorted, and that are appropriately scaled, are generally admissible. To prevent allegations of manipulation or alteration, some police departments employ software with verification platforms. However, because the nature of digital photography provides for such allegations, the chain of custody of digital photographs is especially important. Password protection, encryption of files, or other access restrictions help to prevent such challenges.

As stated earlier, many photographs are introduced in court as a substitute for the real evidence they depict. A posed photograph of a battered woman's face that is properly authenticated, for example, demonstrates her injuries at a specific

 CLARIFICATION OF CONCEPTS

GENERAL REQUIREMENTS FOR ADMISSIBILITY OF PHOTOGRAPHS

- Relevancy, materiality, and competency
- Accurate representation of the scene or object in question, including scale, dimensions, and state
- Timeliness of item (i.e., it must have been taken at or reasonably near the time of the discovery or the incident in question)
- Introduction and authentication by witness
- Unbroken chain of custody
- Satisfaction of the "best evidence rule"

GRUESOME PHOTOGRAPHS—RELEVANCY AND MATERIALITY

American courts consistently have held that gruesome photographs may be admitted whenever the potential prejudice is outweighed by the probative value. Justifications for their introduction may be to:

- **Explain a medical examiner's testimony**—*Floyd v. State*, 808 So. 2d 175, 184 (Fla. 2002)

- **Demonstrate the manner of death or the location of wounds**—*Pope v. State*, 679 So. 2d 710, 714 (Fla. 1996); *Larkins v. State*, 655 So. 2d 95, 98 (Fla. 1995); *State v. Carr*, 265 Kan. 608, 623, 963 P.2d 421 (1998)

- **Show the criminal intent of the accused**

- **Show the identity of the victim**—*Larkins v. State*, 655 So. 2d 95, 98 (Fla. 1995)

- **Demonstrate that the perpetrator returned to the scene to administer a killing shot**— *Glidewell v. State*, 1981 OK CR 39, 626 P.2d 1351 (1981)

---

moment in time. Yet, some photographs cannot be classified properly as demonstrative evidence. Images and videos depicting the sexual exploitation of children, for example, are categorized more appropriately as real or physical evidence, because the images themselves represent the element of child pornography. When computers are seized or processed for criminal evidence, allegations of tampering or protestations of innocence are much more likely. Excuses for digital child pornography range from arguments that a virus was responsible for them; that someone else put them there using a back door or a Trojan; that they were unsolicited; and that law enforcement officers were responsible for the images. However, computer forensic software packages enable investigators to: (1) identify viruses, back doors, and Trojan horses; (2) view photographs in the same manner that the suspect did and identify the physical location of the data on the drive; and (3) image verification tools that create a digital fingerprint of the drive. As such, challenges to the authenticity of the image in question may be readily addressed. Although state appellate courts have upheld the admissibility of deleted data and photographs recovered using forensic software,[28] the Supreme Court has not issued a *Daubert* ruling on such packages.

Issues with Video Recordings

In recent years, personal video recorders have become increasingly popular. In the spirit of a free market and capitalism, competition between manufacturers has resulted in an explosion of consumer sales. Consequently, actions and images that may constitute evidence have been submitted in criminal courts, including video footage taken by surveillance cameras or crime scene investigators and dash-mounted cameras—and footage shot by private individuals. The content of such recordings may be extremely varied and may include:

The proponent of the evidence, irrespective of source or content, must lay the proper foundation for its admission, and the evidence must be verified and authenticated by witness testimony. This process includes demonstration and verification regarding:

- The capability and mechanical soundness of the recording device—This may be demonstrated with a recitation of the make, model, age, and general competency and reputation in the field. Verification may also include a demonstration of the device's competency through the introduction of previously accepted recordings.

- The competency of the operator of the recording device—This may be demonstrated with a recitation of the applicable training and experience of the operator.
- The authenticity and accuracy of the recording—This may be demonstrated through witness testimony.
- The method of preservation of the recording—A demonstration of the chain of custody may include a discussion of precautions taken to diminish volatility of evidence (i.e., temperature, humidity, corrosive elements, etc.).
- The identification of the speakers—This may be demonstrated with lay witness identification or testimony of expert on voice analysis.
- The voluntariness of the testimony—This may be demonstrated through analysis of body language, speech patterns, etc.
- The uncorrupted state of the recording—This may be demonstrated through frame-by-frame analysis and totality of the recording.

In addition to videotapes used as substitutes for real evidence, summary videos are often deemed admissible by trial courts within certain parameters. Because summary tapes by their very nature exclude segments of testimony and (occasionally) potential evidence, the proponent of the recording must meet additional requirements.

The admission of videotaped evidence can be cumbersome and time-consuming. Trial courts may allow the introduction of tapes that more succinctly demonstrate the content of the evidence contained therein. Consider the effect on the judicial system if judges required the introduction of every second of every surveillance tape created during a 6-month investigation of a mafia boss. The admissibility of summary tapes requires that opposing counsel has an advance opportunity to review the underlying tapes (in their entirety) demonstrating that:

- The underlying tapes are voluminous.
- The summary tape created is a fair representation/depiction of the original evidence and the subject matter.
- The totality of the original tapes would be admissible.

 APPLICATION OF LAW

PORN STAR JOHN HOLMES AND THE WONDERLAND MURDERS

In the summer of 1981, a mover stumbled upon one of the most grisly crime scenes in Los Angeles history. Inside a house located at 8763 Wonderland, police officers found four individuals bludgeoned to death, their injuries so horrific that blood and brain matter covered the ceiling and walls of the residence. A fifth victim, the estranged wife of one of the corpses, was injured so badly that a portion of her skull was later removed. The prime suspect in the crime was porn king, John C. Holmes. It was theorized that the residents of the home were slaughtered in retaliation for a robbery that two of the men committed. Holmes, suffering from a downslide in his popularity and coping with drug addiction, was a participant in the robbery, and later claimed that he was forced to disclose the identity of his co-conspirators to the victimized drug kingpin. Investigators, on the other hand, believed that Holmes was an active participant in the quadruple homicide. Because of the savagery of the crime, members of the LAPD videotaped the crime scene. The recording, subsequently introduced into evidence against prime suspect John C. Holmes, was the first time that a crime scene videotape had been admitted into court. However, neither the videotape nor the testimony of his former wife (to whom he confessed) was enough to convict Holmes. After his acquittal, Holmes' career deteriorated further. Keeping his 1985 AIDS diagnosis a secret, Holmes remained active in the porn industry and infected an assortment of individuals. After his death, several books were published on his life. In 2003, a star-studded cast recreated the murders in the aptly named Wonderland. The DVD of the same name includes the original crime scene footage.

EXAMPLES OF ADMISSIBLE VIDEOTAPE EVIDENCE

- **Law Enforcement**—Roadside sobriety tests, high-speed pursuits, traffic accidents, interrogation of witnesses or suspects, confessions, crime scene processing, booking process, surveillance, etc.

- **Courtroom Actors**—Depositions of child witnesses, unavailable witnesses, or dying persons, reenactments, "day in the life" films, etc.

- **Experts**—Experiments, reenactments, etc.

- **Civilians**—Riot footage, police actions, neighborhood watch surveillance, etc.

Issues with Computer-Generated Content

Just as the face of commerce has been dramatically altered by the advent of computer technology, courtroom demonstrations and illustrations have become increasingly sophisticated. In fact, computer-generated evidence has been admitted into criminal courts as substantive and demonstrative evidence. The use of computer-generated forensic recreations and simulations may prove to be extremely persuasive to jurors and jurists alike. In the United States, the use of visual aids and technologically assisted learning have become almost universally expected because of the growing importance of computers in education, commerce, and communication. Thus, the use of such has become commonplace in American courtrooms.

Animations and Simulations

Computer animation and computer simulations are completely different entities and may, in fact, be diametrically opposed. At its core, **computer animations** are simply graphic representations of static objects, such as knives or guns. Such

computer animations are simply graphic representations of static objects, such as knives or guns. Such representation does not require suppositions or conjecture.

COMPUTER GRAPHICS AND ANIMATIONS VERSUS COMPUTER SIMULATIONS

Computer simulations generate conclusions based on data input, mathematical formulas, and the laws of science. By their very nature, they are scientific, and require the testimony of an expert who is trained to analyze and conclude. Computer animations, on the other hand, are simply graphic representations of an expert's opinion based on his or her analysis of the facts. Thus, animations merely illustrate an expert opinion as to a particular fact. Although such illustrations may give the image of motion, they actually are frame-by-frame creations based on the expert's own computations and conclusions.

The introduction of computer graphics and animation has become increasingly popular in American courts over the past decade. Accordingly, precedents and the laws of evidence govern the admissibility of such. For the most part,

computer graphics and animation have been treated in much the same manner as photographs (images and depictions that are less probative than prejudicial will continue to be inadmissible). As a general rule, computer graphics and animation must: (1) depict a relevant fact, (2) be introduced by a witness, (3) be authenticated as an accurate representation of the fact at issue, and (4) not be considered hearsay unless such falls within the parameters of an exception to the hearsay rule.

Computer simulations, on the other hand, must meet additional requirements because their purpose is to draw conclusions. Driven by scientific formulas, simulations suggest possibilities based on the information provided. As such, computer simulations that are designed to be substantive must be based on accepted scientific standards and must satisfy *Daubert* or *Frye* requirements.

representation does not require suppositions or conjecture. Computer animations and graphic representations include visual depictions of charts, graphs, and maps. They also involve computer programs designed for presentations such as Microsoft PowerPoint, TurboDemo, and Adobe creative products. **Computer simulations**, on the other hand, involve conclusions or deductions reported by a computer and are contingent largely upon proper data entry and analysis. Current computer simulation packages are limited only by specific case characteristics. Software programs are available for things such as homicide reenactment, traffic accident reconstruction, airplane trajectory and flight consistency, and detonation of explosives. Computer simulations may be either substantive or demonstrative in nature. When offered as proof of a fact in question, qualification of the method employed and the task manager is necessary. When offered for the sole purposes of illustration, however, *Daubert/Frye* requirements do not necessarily apply.

Computer-generated demonstrative evidence has been used in civil courts more often and far longer than in criminal courts. (Illustrations of traffic accidents, for example, have become so sophisticated that three-dimensional demonstrations of car and occupant movement is possible; see CARAT, MADYMO, and CASIMIR.) Recently, however, well-publicized trials have incorporated computer-generated aids. Some have proved more effectively than others. Consider these trials and their use of computer-generated content:

- *O. J. Simpson*—Graphic representations were introduced to demonstrate the theory that the murders could have been committed only by multiple assailants. Simpson, a former NFL star and Heisman trophy winner, was acquitted of the murders of his ex-wife and her friend.

- *Michael Peterson*—Graphic representations were introduced to demonstrate the theory that the injuries sustained by Kathleen Peterson could have been sustained during an accidental fall down the staircase. Peterson, a best-selling author, was convicted and sentenced to death.

- *Dany Heatley*—Graphic representations were introduced to demonstrate the theory that the injuries sustained by Dan Snyder were caused by excessive speeding by Heatley in a Ferrari. Heatley, an MVP for the Atlanta Thrashers, was convicted of vehicular manslaughter and sentenced to three years' probation.

In many of today's courtrooms, traditional hand-drawn representations of maps and charts have been replaced by three-dimensional computer-generated images. Chalkboards and easels have become all but obsolete as courtrooms increasingly equip themselves with overhead projectors, pull-down screens, and computer monitors. However, a discussion of demonstrative evidence cannot be complete without the inclusion of traditional practices and noncomputer representations.

Issues with Noncomputer-Generated Content

It has long been recognized by scholars that retention of learning can be significantly enhanced through the use of visual stimulation. Traditionally, court actors used chalkboards and easels to communicate important points for jurors. During opening and closing arguments, for example, prosecutors would list their most persuasive evidence as bulleted items—encouraging jurors to remember particular facts to the exclusion of others, or they might highlight the viciousness of the crime or the innocence of the victim. On the other hand, the defense might list the flaws in the state's case or outline its alternative theory of events. These practices, long in existence, continue to be employed. However, American lawyers are increasingly using software packages rather than writing instruments and hard surfaces.

The increase in technology has been accompanied by more sophisticated mechanisms to create demonstrative evidence. 21st Century Forensic Animations, as well as other companies, specialize in the preparation of computer-generated demonstrative evidence for criminal proceedings and insurance investigations. Computer-generated graphics are increasingly popular in criminal cases. Images such as this one, created by 21st Century Forensic Animations, are useful for creating a visual representation of particular facts. (Image provided by 21st Century Forensic Animations, Fort Worth, TX).

Just as blackboards are being replaced by computer screens and presentation software, the handcrafting of forensic models is being replaced by sophisticated computer modeling and graphics software. Models may be employed to assist jurors in understanding the physicality of a given crime scene, proximity of objects to victims, and scientific testing. They are extremely useful in displaying the totality of the crime scene in one glance and providing a sense of the physical location of the event in question. For example, an attorney arguing self-defense in a homicide case might introduce a scaled physical model of the crime scene to demonstrate that the accused had no avenue of retreat. On the other hand, a prosecutor might introduce a model of a skull to demonstrate the severity of the victim's head injuries. Forensic modeling, however, can be quite costly and time-consuming. Coupled with the increasing familiarity of computer technology among jurors, the use of physical modeling is becoming less prevalent.

Maps are another way to demonstrate geographic characteristics of events in question. They are especially useful in demonstrations of the closeness of two addresses or the physicality and proximity of points of interest. In other words, they provide the jury with important points of reference necessary to understand the spatial characteristics of the evidence. Community maps and such are still used by many attorneys because of their availability and affordability, but computer-generated mapping is unquestionably the more popular option. The primary advantage to computer-generated maps is the relative ease involved with altering and the potential for the customization of evidence. For example, a prosecutor in a child abduction/murder case might want to emphasize that the accused, a known pedophile, resided within viewing distance of a playground and was within walking distance of the crime scene. Thus, the prosecutor could create a map that displayed those points without the distraction of miscellaneous information.

One type of demonstrative evidence that has not been as heavily influenced by the introduction of technology involves crime scene sketches. These drawings are created by police personnel as they process the crime scene. Rudimentary in nature, such illustrations are the first available record of the scene itself and they provide jurors a firsthand account of the responding officer's perception of the crime scene. Under law, all notes and sketches taken by officers at a crime scene are discoverable and may be subpoenaed. Thus, while some officers recreate the initial sketch once the evidence is processed and the activity has subsided, their initial sketch may still be subpoenaed. As such, the practice of using a graphics program has not caught on.

► CONCLUSIONS

Generally speaking, demonstrative evidence may be defined as that evidence that either recreates a physical object, event, or experiment or that illustrates or serves to clarify matters brought forth in oral testimony. Unlike real evidence that stands on its own, demonstrative evidence requires more than mere authentication by a witness. Without it, jurors would be forced to draw conclusions based on incomplete information. Historically, examples of demonstrative evidence included things like maps, diagrams, sketches, and rudimentary experiments. However, exponential advances in technology have often granted jurors a retro box seat to events in question. Digital photography and video recordings have allowed jurors to visit remote crime scenes without ever leaving the courtroom. In-court demonstrations have further enabled them to visualize blood trajectory and spatter patterns, and computer-generated slide shows have captured their attention and encapsulated arguments.

Perhaps no area of evidence collection, analysis, and presentation has been as dramatically enhanced as cyber evidence. Computer forensics programs have been created which uncover hidden evidence and secrets. The restoration of deleted files has effectively provided a plethora of evidentiary items, including documents or photographs, which uncover motive, means, or opportunity. Analysis of Internet activity and online communications has further enhanced jurors' ability to evaluate timelines, alibis, and other essential elements. In fact, it is expected that the boundaries of demonstrative evidence will continue to expand and further support the pursuit of justice in criminal courts.

Key Terms

Computer animations	Cyber evidence	Particularity
Computer simulations	Demonstrative evidence	Title 18
Cybercrime		

Discussion Questions

1. What are some of the traditional problems associated with the prosecution of computer crime? What suggestions can you think of that might diminish them?
2. What is the current state of privacy regarding electronic mail? How would you compare it to the level of privacy traditionally associated with postal mail?
3. Is the use of computer-generated graphics a positive step in the interest of justice? Why or why not?
4. What Fourth Amendment issues are most salient to the investigation of computer crime?
5. What does vicinage mean? How do we determine vicinage in computer crime?

▼

Recommended Resources

Videos

Insight Media. Crime fighting into the 21st century. Available at http://www.insight-media.com.

Insight Media. Cyber law—Cyber court: The court of next resort. Available at http://www.insight-media.com.

Books

Britz, Marjie T. (2008). *Computer forensics and cyber-crime: An introduction* (2nd ed.). New Jersey: Prentice-Hall Publishing.

Casey, Eoghan (2002). *Using case-based reasoning and cognitive apprenticeship to teach criminal profiling and Internet crime investigation*. Retrieved at: http://www.corpus-delicti.com/case_based.html.

Casey, Eoghan (2004). *Digital evidence and computer crime: Forensic science, computers and the Internet* (2nd ed.). New York: Academic Press.

Online Sources

http://www.justice.gov—Web site of the Department of Justice (Computer Records and the Federal Rules of Evidence) that includes articles on cybercrime and the rules of evidence.

http://www.htcia.org—Official Web site of the High Technology Crime Investigation Association (HTCIA) to encourage, promote, aid, and effect the voluntary interchange of data, experience, ideas, and knowledge about methods, processes, and techniques relating to investigations and security in advanced technologies among its membership.

http://www.infosecinstitute.com—Official Web site of the Infosec Institute provides information on topical issues related to computer forensics, including ethical hacking and computer forensics.

http://www.technosecurity.us/—Official Web site of the Training Company's TechnoSecurity conference which is devoted to the training and education of private companies and public agencies; contains links to various resources in computer crime and forensics.

http://www.iacis.org—Official Web site of the International Association of Computer Investigative Specialists "providing a forum for interpersonal networking and the sharing of research, teaching, and technical information." ACIS is an international, volunteer, nonprofit corporation composed of law enforcement professionals representing federal and state law enforcement professionals dedicated to education in the field of forensic computer science.

http://journals.law.stanford.edu/stanford-technology-law-review—Web site with links to the Stanford Technology Law Review

http://www.cftt.nist.gov/—Home page of the Computer Forensics Tool Testing at the National Institute of Standards and Technology

http://www.call21st.com/—Home page of 21st Century Forensic Animation Company. The Web site displays forensic animations for cases ranging from motor vehicle accidents, homicides, OSHA infractions, fires, and more.

Relevant Cases Cited

Ashcroft v. Free Speech Coalition, 535 U.S. 234 (2002)

Coolidge v. New Hampshire, 403 U.S. 443 (1971)

Floyd v. State, 808 So. 2d 175, 184 (Fla. 2002)

Glidewell v. State, 1981 OK CR 39, 626 P.2d 1351 (1981)

Henderson v. State, 463 So.2d 196 (Fla. 1985)

Jackson v. Fletcher, 647 F.2d 1020 (1979)

Larkins v. State, 655 So. 2d 95, 98 (Fla. 1995)

Miller v. California, 413 U.S. 15 (1973)

Mincey v. Arizona, 437 U.S. 385 (1978)

New York v. Ferber, 458 U.S. 747 (1982)

Osborne v. Ohio, 495 U.S. 13 (1990)

Schneckloth v. Bustamonte, 412 U.S. 218 (1973)

State v. Pennington, 89 KS SC 129 (2003)

United States v. Carey, 172 F.3d 1268 (10th Cir. 1999)

United States v. Dichiarinte, 445 F.2d 126 (7th Cir. 1971)

United States v. Hall [142 F. 3d 988 (7th Cir. 1998)]

United States v. Matlock, 415 U.S. 164 (1974)

United States v. Pervaz [118 F.3d 1 (1st Cir. 1997)]

United States. v. Turner, 169 F.3d 84 (1st Cir. 1999)

Notes

1. For a more complete discussion of computer-related crime and computer forensics, see Britz, Marjie T. (2013). *Computer forensics and cybercrime: An introduction* (3rd ed.). Upper Saddle River, New Jersey: Prentice-Hall Publishing.

2. Ibid.
3. Ibid.
4. Ibid.
5. Ibid.
6. Ibid.

▼

7. *Miller v. California*, 413 U.S. 15 (1973)
8. *New York v. Ferber*, 458 U.S. 747 (1982); *Osborne v. Ohio*, 495 U.S. 13 (1990)
9. Child Pornography Prevention Act, 18 U.S.C. §2256 (2000)
10. *Ashcroft v. Free Speech Coalition*, 535 U.S. 234 (2002)
11. *Coolidge v. New Hampshire*, 403 U.S. 443 (1971)
12. Britz, 2013
13. *United States v. Pervaz* [118 F.3d 1 (1st Cir. 1997)
14. *United States v. Hall* [142 F. 3d 988 (7th Cir. 1998)
15. *Schneckloth v. Bustamonte*, 412 U.S. 218 (1973)
16. *United States v. Matlock*, 415 U.S. 164 (1974)
17. *United States v. Turner*, 169 F.3d 84 (1st Cir. 1999)
18. *United States v. Dichiarinte*, 445 F.2d 126 (7th Cir. 1971)
19. *United States v. Carey*, 172 F.3d 1268 (10th Cir. 1999)
20. *Coolidge v. New Hampshire*, 403 U.S. 443 (1971)
21. *U.S. v. Carey*, 172 F.3d 1268 (10th Cir. 1999)
22. *Mincey v. Arizona*, 437 U.S. 385 (1978)
23. Britz, 2013
24. *Collins v. B. F. Goodrich Company*, 558 F.2d 908 (8th Cir. 1977); *Ramseyer v. General Motors Corp.*, 417 F.2d [*1027] 859 (8th Cir. 1969); *Drake v. Tims*, 287 P.2d 215 (Okl.1955)
25. *Jackson v. Fletcher*, 647 F.2d 1020 (1979)
26. *State v. Pennington*, 89 KS SC 129 (2003)
27. *Henderson v. State*, 463 So.2d 196 (Fla. 1985)
28. *Washington v. Leavell*, (2000) 00-1-0026-8. (Washington Court of Appeals, 2000); *State v. Hayden* (90 Washington Court of Appeals, 100: 950 P.2d 1024)
29. Case SCR28424. California Superior Court, Sonoma County. *People v. Rodreguez*. (Pretrial hearing 1/11/2001)

A   Bills of Rights

Ratified 1791

▶ Amendment I

Congress shall make no law respecting an establishment of religion, or prohibiting the free exercise thereof; or abridging the freedom of speech or of the press; or the rights of the people peaceably to assemble and to petition the Government for a redress of grievances.

IMPORTANT RIGHTS AND CLAUSES: Establishment Clause; Free Exercise Clause; freedom of speech; freedom of the press; right to assembly; and, right to petition

▶ Amendment II

A well-regulated Militia, being necessary to the security of a free State, the right of the people to keep and bear Arms, shall not be infringed.

IMPORTANT RIGHTS AND CLAUSES: Right to keep and bear arms; Right to form a militia

▶ Amendment III

No Soldier shall, in time of peace be quartered in any house, without the consent of the Owner, or in time of war, but in a manner to be prescribed by law.

IMPORTANT RIGHTS AND CLAUSES: Prohibition of the quartering of troops within private homes

► Amendment IV

The right of the people to be secure in their persons, houses, papers, and effects, against unreasonable searches and seizures, shall not be violated, and no Warrants shall issue, but upon probable cause, supported by Oath or affirmation, and particularly describing the place to be searched, and the persons or things to be seized.

IMPORTANT RIGHTS AND CLAUSES: Warrant Clause; protection from unreasonable search and seizures

► Amendment V

No person shall be held to answer for a capital, or otherwise infamous crime, unless on a presentment or indictment of a Grand Jury, except in cases arising in the land or naval forces, or in the Militia, when in actual service in time of War or public danger, nor shall nay person be subject for the same offence to be twice put in jeopardy of life or limb; nor shall be compelled in any criminal case to be a witness against himself, nor be deprived of life, liberty, or property, without due process of law; or shall private property be taken for public use, without just compensation.

IMPORTANT RIGHTS AND CLAUSES: Due Process Clause; right to a grand jury; protection from double jeopardy; protection from self-incrimination through compulsory testimony

► Amendment VI

In all criminal prosecutions, the accused shall enjoy the right to a speedy and public trial, by an impartial jury of the State and district wherein the crime shall have been committed, which district shall have been previously ascertained by law, and to be informed of the nature and cause of the accusation; to be confronted with the witnesses against him. To have compulsory process for obtaining witnesses in his favor, and to have the Assistance of Counsel for his defense.

IMPORTANT RIGHTS AND CLAUSES: right to a speedy and public trial; right to an impartial jury of one's peers; right to be informed of the charges; the Confrontation Clause; right to counsel; and, subpoena powers

► Amendment VII

In suits at common law, where the value in controversy shall exceed twenty dollars, the right of trial by jury shall be preserved, and no fact tried by a jury, shall be otherwise re-examined in any court of the United States, than according to the rules of the common law.

IMPORTANT RIGHTS AND CLAUSES: the right to a jury trial in certain civil trials; the Re-Examination Clause

► Amendment VIII

Excessive bail shall not be required, nor excessive fines imposed, nor cruel and unusual punishments inflicted.

IMPORTANT RIGHTS AND CLAUSES: prohibition of excessive bail and fines; Cruel and Unusual Punishment Clause

► Amendment IX

The enumeration in the Constitution, of certain rights, shall not be construed to deny or disparage others retained by the people.

IMPORTANT RIGHTS AND CLAUSES: general statement, which recognizes that other rights which are not specifically articulated in the Constitution may exist

► Amendment X

The powers not delegated to the United States by the Constitution, nor prohibited by it to the States, are reserved to the States respectively of the people.

IMPORTANT RIGHTS AND CLAUSES: Prior to the passage of the 14th Amendment, the 10th Amendment reserved much power for the states.

Source: Charters of Freedom, National Archives and Records Administration.

THE DECLARATION OF INDEPENDENCE.

B The Magna Carta (1215)

John, by the grace of God King of England, Lord of Ireland, Duke of Normandy and Aquitaine, and Count of Anjou, to his archbishops, bishops, abbots, earls, barons, justices, foresters, sheriffs, stewards, servants, and to all his officials and loyal subjects, greeting.

Know that before God, for the health of our soul and those of our ancestors and heirs, to the honour of God, the exaltation of the holy Church, and the better ordering of our kingdom, at the advice of our reverend fathers Stephen, archbishop of Canterbury, primate of all England, and cardinal of the holy Roman Church, Henry archbishop of Dublin, William bishop of London, Peter bishop of Winchester, Jocelin bishop of Bath and Glastonbury, Hugh bishop of Lincoln, Walter Bishop of Worcester, William bishop of Coventry, Benedict bishop of Rochester, Master Pandulf subdeacon and member of the papal household, Brother Aymeric master of the Knights of the Temple in England, William Marshal, earl of Pembroke, William earl of Salisbury, William earl of Warren, William earl of Arundel, Alan de Galloway constable of Scotland, Warin Fitz Gerald, Peter Fitz Herbert, Hubert de Burgh seneschal of Poitou, Hugh de Neville, Matthew Fitz Herbert, Thomas Basset, Alan Basset, Philip Daubeny, Robert de Roppeley, John Marshal, John Fitz Hugh, and other loyal subjects:

1. First, that we have granted to God, and by this present charter have confirmed for us and our heirs in perpetuity, that the English Church shall be free, and shall have its rights undiminished, and its liberties unimpaired. That we wish this so to be observed, appears from the fact that of our own free will, before the outbreak of the present dispute between us and our barons, we granted and confirmed by charter the freedom of the Church's

elections—a right reckoned to be of the greatest necessity and importance to it—and caused this to be confirmed by Pope Innocent III. This freedom we shall observe ourselves, and desire to be observed in good faith by our heirs in perpetuity. We have also granted to all free men of our realm, for us and our heirs for ever, all the liberties written out below, to have and to keep for them and their heirs, of us and our heirs:

2. If any earl, baron, or other person that holds lands directly of the Crown, for military service, shall die, and at his death his heir shall be of full age and owe a "relief," the heir shall have his inheritance on payment of the ancient scale of "relief." That is to say, the heir or heirs of an earl shall pay £100 for the entire earl's barony, the heir or heirs of a knight 100 schillings at most for the entire knight's "fee," and any man that owes less shall pay less, in accordance with the ancient usage of "fees."

3. But if the heir of such a person is under age and a ward, when he comes of age he shall have his inheritance without "relief" or fine.

4. The guardian of the land of an heir who is under age shall take from it only reasonable revenues, customary dues, and feudal services. He shall do this without destruction or damage to men or property. If we have given the guardianship of the land to a sheriff, or to any person answerable to us for the revenues, and he commits destruction or damage, we will exact compensation from him, and the land shall be entrusted to two worthy and prudent men of the same "fee," who shall be answerable to us for the revenues, or to the person to whom we have assigned them. If we have given or sold to anyone the guardianship of such land, and he causes destruction or damage, he shall lose the guardianship of it, and it shall be handed over to two worthy and prudent men of the same "fee," who shall be similarly answerable to us.

5. For so long as a guardian has guardianship of such land, he shall maintain the houses, parks, fish preserves, ponds, mills, and everything else pertaining to it, from the revenues of the land itself. When the heir comes of age, he shall restore the whole land to him, stocked with plough teams and such implements of husbandry as the season demands and the revenues from the land can reasonably bear.

6. Heirs may be given in marriage, but not to someone of lower social standing. Before a marriage takes place, it shall be' made known to the heir's next-of-kin.

7. At her husband's death, a widow may have her marriage portion and inheritance at once and without trouble. She shall pay nothing for her dower, marriage portion, or any inheritance that she and her husband held jointly on the day of his death. She may remain in her husband's house for forty days after his death, and within this period her dower shall be assigned to her.

8. No widow shall be compelled to marry, so long as she wishes to remain without a husband. But she must give security that she will not marry without royal consent, if she holds her lands of the Crown, or without the consent of whatever other lord she may hold them of.

9. Neither we nor our officials will seize any land or rent in payment of a debt, so long as the debtor has movable goods sufficient to discharge the debt. A debtor's sureties shall not be distrained upon so long as the debtor himself can discharge his debt. If, for lack of means, the debtor is unable to discharge his debt, his sureties shall be answerable for it. If they so desire, they may have the debtor's lands and rents until they have received satisfaction for the debt that they paid for him, unless the debtor can show that he has settled his obligations to them.

10. If anyone who has borrowed a sum of money from Jews dies before the debt has been repaid, his heir shall pay no interest on the debt for so long as he

remains under age, irrespective of whom he holds his lands. If such a debt falls into the hands of the Crown, it will take nothing except the principal sum specified in the bond.

11. If a man dies owing money to Jews, his wife may have her dower and pay nothing towards the debt from it. If he leaves children that are under age, their needs may also be provided for on a scale appropriate to the size of his holding of lands. The debt is to be paid out of the residue, reserving the service due to his feudal lords. Debts owed to persons other than Jews are to be dealt with similarly.

12. No "scutage" or "aid" may be levied in our kingdom without its general consent, unless it is for the ransom of our person, to make our eldest son a knight, and (once) to marry our eldest daughter. For these purposes only a reasonable "aid" may be levied. "Aids" from the city of London are to be treated similarly.

13. The city of London shall enjoy all its ancient liberties and free customs, both by land and by water. We also will and grant that all other cities, boroughs, towns, and ports shall enjoy all their liberties and free customs.

14. To obtain the general consent of the realm for the assessment of an "aid"—except in the three cases specified above—or a "scutage," we will cause the archbishops, bishops, abbots, earls, and greater barons to be summoned individually by letter. To those who hold lands directly of us we will cause a general summons to be issued, through the sheriffs and other officials, to come together on a fixed day (of which at least forty days notice shall be given) and at a fixed place. In all letters of summons, the cause of the summons will be stated. When a summons has been issued, the business appointed for the day shall go forward in accordance with the resolution of those present, even if not all those who were summoned have appeared.

15. In future we will allow no one to levy an "aid" from his free men, except to ransom his person, to make his eldest son a knight, and (once) to marry his eldest daughter. For these purposes only a reasonable "aid" may be levied.

16. No man shall be forced to perform more service for a knight's "fee," or other free holding of land, than is due from it.

17. Ordinary lawsuits shall not follow the royal court around, but shall be held in a fixed place.

18. Inquests of *novel disseisin*, *mort d'ancestor*, and *darrein presentment* shall be taken only in their proper county court. We ourselves, or in our absence abroad our chief justice, will send two justices to each county four times a year, and these justices, with four knights of the county elected by the county itself, shall hold the assizes in the county court, on the day and in the place where the court meets.

19. If any assizes cannot be taken on the day of the county court, as many knights and freeholders shall afterwards remain behind, of those who have attended the court, as will suffice for the administration of justice, having regard to the volume of business to be done.

20. For a trivial offence, a free man shall be fined only in proportion to the degree of his offence, and for a serious offence correspondingly, but not so heavily as to deprive him of his livelihood. In the same way, a merchant shall be spared his merchandise, and a husbandman the implements of his husbandry, if they fall upon the mercy of a royal court. None of these fines shall be imposed except by the assessment on oath of reputable men of the neighbourhood.

21. Earls and barons shall not be amerced save through their peers, and only according to the measure of the offence.

22. No clerk shall be amerced for his lay tenement ecept according to the manner of the other persons aforesaid; and not according to the amount of his ecclesiastical benefice.

23. Neither a town nor a man shall be forced to make bridges over the rivers, with the exception of those who, from of old and of right ought to do it.

24. No sheriff, constable, coroners, or other bailiffs of ours shall hold the pleas of our crown.

25. All counties, hundreds, wapentakes, and trithings—our demesne manors being excepted—shall continue according to the old farms, without any increase at all.

26. If any one holding from us a lay fee shall die, and our sheriff or bailiff can show our letters patent containing our summons for the debt which the dead man owed to us, our sheriff or bailiff may be allowed to attach and enroll the chattels of the dead man to the value of that debt, through view of lawful men; in such way, however, that nothing shall be removed thence until the debt is paid which was plainly owed to us. And the residue shall be left to the executors that they may carry out the will of the dead man. And if nothing is owed to us by him, all the chattels shall go to the use prescribed by the deceased, saving their reasonable portions to his wife and children.

27. If any freeman shall have died intestate his chattels shall be distributed through the hands of his near relatives and friends, by view of the church; saving to any one the debts which the dead man owed him.

28. No constable or other bailiff of ours shall take the corn or other chattels of any one except he straightway give money for them, or can be allowed a respite in that regard by the will of the seller.

29. No constable shall force any knight to pay money for castleward if he be willing to perform that ward in person, or—he for a reasonable cause not being able to perform it himself—through another proper man. And if we shall have led or sent him on a military expedition, he shall be quit of ward according to the amount of time during which, through us, he shall have been in military service.

30. No sheriff nor bailiff of ours, nor any one else, shall take the horses or carts of any freeman for transport, unless by the will of that freeman.

31. Neither we nor our bailiffs shall take another's wood for castles or for other private uses, unless by the will of him to whom the wood belongs.

32. We shall not hold the lands of those convicted of felony longer than a year and a day; and then the lands shall be restored to the lords of the fiefs.

33. Henceforth all the weirs in the Thames and Medway, and throughout all England, save on the sea-coast, shall be done away with entirely.

34. Henceforth the writ which is called Praecipe shall not be to served on any one for any holding so as to cause a free man to lose his court.

35. There shall be one measure of wine throughout our whole realm, and one measure of ale and one measure of corn—namely, the London quart—and one width of dyed and russet and hauberk cloths—namely, two ells below the selvage. And with weights, moreover, it shall be as with measures.

36. Henceforth nothing shall be given or taken for a writ of inquest in a matter concerning life or limb; but it shall be conceded gratis, and shall not be denied.

37. If any one hold of us in fee-farm, or in socage, or in burkage, and hold land of another by military service, we shall not, by reason of that fee-farm, or socage, or burkage, have the wardship of his heir or of his land which is held in fee from another. Nor shall we have the wardship of that fee-farm, or socage, or burkage unless that fee-farm owe military service. We shall not,

by reason of some petit-serjeanty which some one holds of us through the service of giving us knives or arrows or the like, have the wardship of his heir or of the land which he holds of another by military service.

38. No bailiff, on his own simple assertion, shall henceforth any one to his law, without producing faithful witnesses in evidence.

39. No freeman shall be taken, or imprisoned, or disseized, or outlawed, or exiled, or in any way harmed—nor will we go upon or send upon him—save by the lawful judgment of his peers or by the law of the land.

40. To none will we sell, to none deny or delay, right or justice.

41. All merchants may safely and securely go out of England, and come into England, and delay and pass through England, as well by land as by water, for the purpose of buying and selling, free from all evil taxes, subject to the ancient and right customs—save in time of war, and if they are of the land at war against us. And if such be found in our land at the beginning of the war, they shall be held, without harm to their bodies and goods, until it shall be known to us or our chief justice how the merchants of our land are to be treated who shall, at that time, be found in the land at war against us. And if ours shall be safe there, the others shall be safe in our land.

42. Henceforth any person, saving fealty to us, may go out of our realm and return to it, safely and securely, by land and by water, except perhaps for a brief period in time of war, for the common good of the realm. But prisoners and outlaws are excepted according to the law of the realm; also people of a land at war against us, and the merchants, with regard to whom shall be done as we have said.

43. If a man holds lands of any "escheat"—such as from the honour of Walingford, Nottingham, Boloin, Lancaster, or the other escheats which are in our hands and are baronies—and shall die, his heir shall not give another relief, nor shall he perform for us other service than he would perform for a baron if that barony were in the hand of a baron; and we shall hold it in the same way in which the baron has held it.

44. Persons dwelling without the forest shall not henceforth come before the forest justices, through common summonses, unless they are impleaded or are the sponsors of some person or persons attached for matters concerning the forest.

45. We will not make men justices, constables, sheriffs, or bailiffs unless they are such as know the law of the realm, and are minded to observe it rightly.

46. All barons who have founded abbeys for which they have charters of the King of England, or ancient right of tenure, shall have, as they ought to have, their custody when vacant.

47. All forests constituted as such in our time shall straightway be annulled; and the same shall be done for river banks made into places of defence by us in our time.

48. All evil customs concerning forests and warrens, and concerning foresters and warreners, sheriffs and their servants, river banks and their guardians, shall straightway be inquired into each county, through twelve sworn knights from that county, and shall be eradicated by them, entirely, so that they shall never be renewed, within forty days after the inquest has been made; in such manner that we shall first know about them, or our justice if we be not in England.

49. We shall straightway return all hostages and charters which were delivered to us by Englishmen as a surety for peace or faithful service.

50. We shall entirey remove from their bailwicks the relatives of Gerard de Athyes, so that they shall henceforth have no bailwick in England: Engelard

de Cygnes, Andrew Peter and Gyon de Chanceles, Gyon de Cygnes, Geoffrey de Martin and his brothers, Philip Mark and his brothers, and Geoffrey his nephew, and the whole following of them.

51. And straightway after peace is restored we shall remove from the realm all the foreign soldiers, crossbowmen, servants, hirelings, who may have come with horses and arms to the harm of the realm.

52. If any one shall have been disseized by us, or removed, without a legal sentence of his peers, from his lands, castles, liberties or lawful right, we shall straightway restore them to him. And if a dispute shall arise concerning this matter it shall be settled according to the judgment of the twenty-five barons who are mentioned below as sureties for the peace. But with regard to all those things of which any one was, by King Henry our father or King Richard our brother, disseized or dispossessed without legal judgment of his peers, which we have in our hand or which others hold, and for which we ought to give a guarantee: We shall have respite until the common term for crusaders. Except with regard to those concerning which a plea was moved, or an inquest made by our order, before we took the cross. But when we return from our pilgrimage, or if, by chance, we desist from our pilgrimage, we shall straightway then show full justice regarding them.

53. We shall have the same respite, moreover, and in the same manner, in the matter of showing justice with regard to forests to be annulled and forests to remain, which Henry our father or Richard our brother constituted; and in the matter of wardships of lands which belong to the fee of another—wardships of which kind we have hitherto enjoyed by reason of the fee which some one held from us in military service—and in the matter of abbeys founded in the fee of another than ourselves—in which the lord of the fee may say that he has jurisdiction. And when we return, or if we desist from our pilgrimage, we shall straightway exhibit full justice to those complaining with regard to these matters.

54. No one shall be taken or imprisoned on account of the appeal of a woman concerning the death of another than her husband.

55. All fines imposed by us unjustly and contrary to the law of the land, and all amerciaments made unjustly and contrary to the law of the land, shall be altogether remitted, or it shall be done with regard to them according to the judgment of the twenty five barons mentioned below as sureties for the peace, or according to the judgment of the majority of them together with the aforesaid Stephen archbishop of Canterbury, if he can be present, and with others whom he may wish to associate with himself for this purpose. And if he cannot be present, the affair shall nevertheless proceed without him; in such way that, if one or more of the said twenty five barons shall be concerned in a similar complaint, they shall be removed as to this particular decision, and, in their place, for this purpose alone, others shall be substituted who shall be chosen and sworn by the remainder of those twenty five.

56. If we have disseized or dispossessed Welshmen of their lands or liberties or other things without legal judgment of their peers, in England or in Wales, they shall straightway be restored to them. And if a dispute shall arise concerning this, then action shall be taken upon it in the March through judgment of their peers—concerning English holdings according to the law of England, concerning Welsh holdings according to the law of Wales, concerning holdings in the March according to the law of the March. The Welsh shall do likewise with regard to us and our subjects.

57. But with regard to all those things of which any one of the Welsh by King Henry our father or King Richard our brother, disseized or dispossessed

without legal judgment of his peers, which we have in our hand or which others hold, and for which we ought to give a guarantee: we shall have respite until the common term for crusaders. Except with regard to those concerning which a plea was moved, or an inquest made by our order, before we took the cross. But when we return from our pilgrimage, or if, by chance, we desist from our pilgrimage, we shall straightway then show full justice regarding them, according to the laws of Wales and the aforesaid districts.

58. We shall straightway return the son of Llewelin and all the Welsh hostages, and the charters delivered to us as surety for the peace.

59. We shall act towards Alexander King of the Scots regarding the restoration of his sisters, and his hostages, and his liberties and his lawful right, as we shall act towards our other barons of England; unless it ought to be otherwise according to the charters which we hold from William, his father, the former King of the Scots. And this shall be done through judgment of his peers in our court.

60. Moreover all the subjects of our realm, clergy as well as laity, shall, as far as pertains to them, observe, with regard to their vassals, all these aforesaid customs and liberties which we have decreed shall, as far as pertains to us, be observed in our realm with regard to our own.

61. Inasmuch as, for the sake of God, and for the bettering of our realm, and for the more ready healing of the discord which has arisen between us and our barons, we have made all these aforesaid concessions, wishing them to enjoy for ever entire and firm stability, we make and grant to them the following security: that the baron, namely, may elect at their pleaure twenty five barons from the realm, who ought, with all their strength, to observe, maintain and cause to be observed, the peace and privileges which we have granted to them and confirmed by this our present charter. In such wise, namely, that if we, or our justice, or our bailiffs, or any one of our servants shall have transgressed against any one in any respect, or shall have broken one of the articles of peace or security, and our transgression shall have been shown to four barons of the aforesaid twenty five: those four barons shall come to us, or, if we are abroad, to our justice, showing to us our error; and they shall ask us to cause that error to be amended without delay. And if we do not amend that error, or, we being abroad, if our justice do not amend it within a term of forty days from the time when it was shown to us or, we being abroad, to our justice: the aforesaid four barons shall refer the matter to the remainder of the twenty five barons, and those twenty five barons, with the whole land in common, shall distrain and oppress us in every way in their power—namely, by taking our castles, lands and possessions, and in every other way that they can, until amends shall have been made according to their judnnent. Saving the persons of ourselves, our queen and our children. And when amends shall have been made they shall be in accord with us as they had been previously. And whoever of the land wishes to do so, shall swear that in carrying out all the aforesaid measures he will obey the mandates of the aforesaid twenty five barons, and that, with them, he will oppress us to the extent of his power. And, to any one who wishes to do so, we publicly and freely give permission to swear; and we will never prevent any one from swearing. Moreover, all those in the land who shall be unwilling, themselves and of their own accord, to swear to the twenty five barons as to distraining and oppressing us with them: such ones we shall make to wear by our mandate, as has been said. And if any one of the twenty five barons shall die, or leave the country, or in any other way be prevented from carrying out the aforesaid measures,—the remainder of the aforesaid twenty five barons shall choose another in his

place, according to their judgment, who shall be sworn in the same way as the others. Moreover, in all things entrusted to those twenty five barons to be carried out, if those twenty five shall be present and chance to disagree among themselves with regard to some matter, or if some of them, having been summoned, shall be unwilling or unable to be present: that which the majority of those present shall decide or decree shall be considered binding and valid, just as if all the twenty five had consented to it. And the aforesaid twenty five shall swear that they will faithfully observe all the foregoing, and will caue them be observed to the extent of their power. And we shall obtain nothing from any one, either through ourselves or through another, by which any of those concessions and liberties may be revoked or diminished. And if any such thing shall have been obtained, it shall be vain and invalid, and we shall never make use of it either through ourselves or through another.

62. And we have fully remitted to all, and pardoned, all the ill-will, anger and rancour which have arisen between us and our subjects, clergy and laity, from the time of the struggle. Moreover have fully remitted to all, clergy and laity, and—as far as pertains to us—have pardoned fully all the transgressions committed, on the occasion of that same struggle, from Easter of the sixteenth year of our reign until the re-establishment of peace. In witness of which, more-over, we have caused to be drawn up for them letters patent of lord Stephen, archbishop of Canterbury, lord Henry, archbishop of Dubland the aforesaid bishops and master Pandulf, regarding that surety and the aforesaid concessions.

63. Wherefore we will and firmly decree that the English church shall be free, and that the subjects of our realm shall have and hold all the aforesaid liberties, rights and concessions, duly and in peace, freely and quietly, fully and entirely, for themselves and their heirs from us and our heirs, in all matters and in all places, forever, as has been said. Moreover it has been sworn, on our part as well as on the part of the barons, that all these above mentioned provisions shall observed with good faith and without evil intent. The witnesses being the above mentioned and many others. Given through our hand, in the plain called Runnymede between Windsor and Stanes, on the fifteenth day of June, in the seventeenth year of our reign.

Source: National Archives and Records Administration.

THE DECLARATION OF INDEPENDENCE.

C Federal Rules of Evidence

▶ Article I. General Provisions

Rule 101. Scope; Definitions

(a) Scope. These rules apply to proceedings in United States courts. The specific courts and proceedings to which the rules apply, along with exceptions, are set out in Rule 1101.

(b) Definitions. In these rules

    (1) "civil case" means a civil action or proceeding;

    (2) "criminal case" includes a criminal proceeding;

    (3) "public office" includes a public agency;

    (4) "record" includes a memorandum, report, or data compilation;

    (5) a "rule prescribed by the Supreme Court" means a rule adopted by the Supreme Court under statutory authority; and

    (6) a reference to any kind of written material or any other medium includes electronically stored information.

Rule 102. Purpose

These rules should be construed so as to administer every proceeding fairly, eliminate unjustifiable expense and delay, and promote the development of evidence law, to the end of ascertaining the truth and securing a just determination.

Rule 103. Rulings on Evidence

(a) Preserving a Claim of Error. A party may claim error in a ruling to admit or exclude evidence only if the error affects a substantial right of the party and:

    (1) if the ruling admits evidence, a party, on the record:

        (A) timely objects or moves to strike; and

        (B) states the specific ground, unless it was apparent from the context; or

    (2) if the ruling excludes evidence, a party informs the court of its substance by an offer of proof, unless the substance was apparent from the context.

(b) Not Needing to Renew an Objection or Offer of Proof. Once the court rules definitively on the record — either before or at trial — a party need not renew an objection or offer of proof to preserve a claim of error for appeal.

(c) Court's Statement About the Ruling; Directing an Offer of Proof. The court may make any statement about the character or form of the evidence, the objection made, and the ruling. The court may direct that an offer of proof be made in question-and-answer form.

(d) Preventing the Jury from Hearing Inadmissible Evidence. To the extent practicable, the court must conduct a jury trial so that inadmissible evidence is not suggested to the jury by any means.

(e) Taking Notice of Plain Error. A court may take notice of a plain error affecting a substantial right, even if the claim of error was not properly preserved.

Rule 104. Preliminary Questions

(a) In General. The court must decide any preliminary question about whether a witness is qualified, a privilege exists, or evidence is admissible. In so deciding, the court is not bound by evidence rules, except those on privilege.

(b) Relevance That Depends on a Fact. When the relevance of evidence depends on whether a fact exists, proof must be introduced sufficient to support a finding that the fact does exist. The court may admit the proposed evidence on the condition that the proof be introduced later.

(c) Conducting a Hearing So That the Jury Cannot Hear It. The court must conduct any hearing on a preliminary question so that the jury cannot hear it if

    (1) the hearing involves the admissibility of a confession;

    (2) a defendant in a criminal case is a witness and so requests; or

    (3) justice so requires.

(d) Cross-Examining a Defendant in a Criminal Case. By testifying on a preliminary question, a defendant in a criminal case does not become subject to cross-examination on other issues in the case.

(e) Evidence Relevant to Weight and Credibility. This rule does not limit a party's right to introduce before the jury evidence that is relevant to the weight or credibility of other evidence.

Rule 105. Limiting Evidence That Is Not Admissible Against Other Parties or for Other Purposes

If the court admits evidence that is admissible against a party or for a purpose — but not against another party or for another purpose — the court, on timely request, must restrict the evidence to its proper scope and instruct the jury accordingly.

Rule 106. Remainder of or Related Writings or Recorded Statements

If a party introduces all or part of a writing or recorded statement, an adverse party may require the introduction, at that time, of any other part — or any other writing or recorded statement — that in fairness ought to be considered at the same time.

▶ Article II. Judicial Notice

Rule 201. Judicial Notice of Adjudicative Facts

(a) Scope. This rule governs judicial notice of an adjudicative fact only, not a legislative fact.

(b) Kinds of Facts That May Be Judicially Noticed. The court may judicially notice a fact that is not subject to reasonable dispute because it:

    (1) is generally known within the trial court's territorial jurisdiction; or

    (2) can be accurately and readily determined from sources whose accuracy cannot reasonably be questioned.

(c) Taking Notice. The court:

    (1) may take judicial notice on its own; or

    (2) must take judicial notice if a party requests it and the court is supplied with the necessary information.

(d) Timing. The court may take judicial notice at any stage of the proceeding.

(e) Opportunity to Be Heard. On timely request, a party is entitled to be heard on the propriety of taking judicial notice and the nature of the fact to be noticed. If the court takes judicial notice before notifying a party, the party, on request, is still entitled to be heard.

(f) Instructing the Jury. In a civil case, the court must instruct the jury to accept the noticed fact as conclusive. In a criminal case, the court must instruct the jury that it may or may not accept the noticed fact as conclusive.

▶ Article III. Presumptions in Civil Cases

Rule 301. Presumptions in Civil Actions Generally

In a civil case, unless a federal statute or these rules provide otherwise, the party against whom a presumption is directed has the burden of producing evidence to rebut the presumption. But this rule does not shift the burden of persuasion, which remains on the party who had it originally.

Rule 302. Applying State Law to Presumptions in Civil Cases

In a civil case, state law governs the effect of a presumption regarding a claim or defense for which state law supplies the rule of decision.

▶ Article IV. Relevance and Its Limits

Rule 401. Test for Relevant Evidence

Evidence is relevant if:

(a) it has any tendency to make a fact more or less probable than it would be without the evidence; and

(b) the fact is of consequence in determining the action.

Rule 402. General Admissibility of Relevant Evidence

Relevant evidence is admissible unless any of the following provides otherwise:

- the United States Constitution;
- a federal statute;
- these rules; or
- other rules prescribed by the Supreme Court.
- Irrelevant evidence is not admissible.

Rule 403. Excluding Relevant Evidence for Prejudice, Confusion, Waste of Time, or Other Reasons

The court may exclude relevant evidence if its probative value is substantially out-weighed by a danger of one or more of the following: unfair prejudice, confusing the issues, misleading the jury, undue delay, wasting time, or needlessly present-ing cumulative evidence.

Rule 404. Character Evidence; Crimes or Other Acts

(a) **Character Evidence.**
  (1) *Prohibited Uses.* Evidence of a person's character or character trait is not admissible to prove that on a particular occasion the person acted in accordance with the character or trait.
  (2) *Exceptions for a Defendant or Victim in a Criminal Case.* The following exceptions apply in a criminal case:
    (A) a defendant may offer evidence of the defendant's pertinent trait, and if the evidence is admitted, the prosecutor may offer evidence to rebut it;
    (B) subject to the limitations in Rule 412, a defendant may offer evidence of an alleged victim's pertinent trait, and if the evidence is admitted, the prosecutor may:
      (i) offer evidence to rebut it; and
      (ii) offer evidence of the defendant's same trait; and
    (C) in a homicide case, the prosecutor may offer evidence of the alleged victim's trait of peacefulness to rebut evidence that the victim was the first aggressor.
  (3) *Exceptions for a Witness.* Evidence of a witness's character may be admitted under Rules 607, 608, and 609.
(b) **Crimes, Wrongs, or Other Acts.**
  (1) *Prohibited Uses.* Evidence of a crime, wrong, or other act is not admissible to prove a person's character in order to show that on a particular occasion the person acted in accordance with the character.
  (2) *Permitted Uses; Notice in a Criminal Case.* This evidence may be admis-sible for another purpose, such as proving motive, opportunity, intent, preparation, plan, knowledge, identity, absence of mistake, or lack of acci-dent. On request by a defendant in a criminal case, the prosecutor must:
    (A) provide reasonable notice of the general nature of any such evidence that the prosecutor intends to offer at trial; and
    (B) do so before trial — or during trial if the court, for good cause, excuses lack of pretrial notice.

Rule 405. Methods of Proving Character

(a) **By Reputation or Opinion.** When evidence of a person's character or char-acter trait is admissible, it may be proved by testimony about the person's reputation or by testimony in the form of an opinion. On cross-examination of the character witness, the court may allow an inquiry into relevant specific instances of the person's conduct.

(b) By Specific Instances of Conduct. When a person's character or character trait is an essential element of a charge, claim, or defense, the character or trait may also be proved by relevant specific instances of the person's conduct.

Rule 406. Habit; Routine Practice

Evidence of a person's habit or an organization's routine practice may be admitted to prove that on a particular occasion the person or organization acted in accordance with the habit or routine practice. The court may admit this evidence regardless of whether it is corroborated or whether there was an eyewitness.

Rule 407. Subsequent Remedial Measures

When measures are taken that would have made an earlier injury or harm less likely to occur, evidence of the subsequent measures is not admissible to prove:

- negligence;
- culpable conduct;
- a defect in a product or its design; or
- a need for a warning or instruction.

But the court may admit this evidence for another purpose, such as impeachment or — if disputed — proving ownership, control, or the feasibility of precautionary measures.

Rule 408. Compromise Offers and Negotiations

(a) Prohibited uses. Evidence of the following is not admissible — on behalf of any party — either to prove or disprove the validity or amount of a disputed claim or to impeach by a prior inconsistent statement or a contradiction:

(1) furnishing, promising, or offering — or accepting, promising to accept, or offering to accept — a valuable consideration in compromising or attempting to compromise the claim; and

(2) conduct or a statement made during compromise negotiations about the claim — except when offered in a criminal case and when the negotiations related to a claim by a public office in the exercise of its regulatory, investigative, or enforcement authority.

(b) Exceptions. The court may admit this evidence for another purpose, such as proving a witness's bias or prejudice, negating a contention of undue delay, or proving an effort to obstruct a criminal investigation or prosecution.

Rule 409. Offers to Pay Medical and Similar Expenses

Evidence of furnishing, promising to pay, or offering to pay medical, hospital, or similar expenses resulting from an injury is not admissible to prove liability for the injury.

Rule 410. Pleas, Plea Discussions, and Related Statements

(a) Prohibited Uses. In a civil or criminal case, evidence of the following is not admissible against the defendant who made the plea or participated in the plea discussions:

(1) a guilty plea that was later withdrawn;

(2) a nolo contendere plea;

(3) a statement made during a proceeding on either of those pleas under Federal Rule of Criminal Procedure 11 or a comparable state procedure; or

(4) a statement made during plea discussions with an attorney for the prosecuting authority if the discussions did not result in a guilty plea or they resulted in a later-withdrawn guilty plea.

(b) Exceptions. The court may admit a statement described in Rule 410(a)(3) or (4):

(1) in any proceeding in which another statement made during the same plea or plea discussions has been introduced, if in fairness the statements ought to be considered together; or

(2) in a criminal proceeding for perjury or false statement, if the defendant made the statement under oath, on the record, and with counsel present.

Rule 411. Liability Insurance

Evidence that a person was or was not insured against liability is not admissible to prove whether the person acted negligently or otherwise wrongfully. But the court may admit this evidence for another purpose, such as proving a witness's bias or prejudice or proving agency, ownership, or control.

Rule 412. Sex-Offense Cases: The Victim's Sexual Behavior or Predisposition

(a) Prohibited Uses. The following evidence is not admissible in a civil or criminal proceeding involving alleged sexual misconduct:

(1) evidence offered to prove that a victim engaged in other sexual behavior; or

(2) evidence offered to prove a victim's sexual predisposition.

(b) Exceptions.

(1) *Criminal Cases.* The court may admit the following evidence in a criminal case:

(A) evidence of specific instances of a victim's sexual behavior, if offered to prove that someone other than the defendant was the source of semen, injury, or other physical evidence;

(B) evidence of specific instances of a victim's sexual behavior with respect to the person accused of the sexual misconduct, if offered by the defendant to prove consent or if offered by the prosecutor; and

(C) evidence whose exclusion would violate the defendant's constitutional rights.

(2) *Civil Cases.* In a civil case, the court may admit evidence offered to prove a victim's sexual behavior or sexual predisposition if its probative value substantially outweighs the danger of harm to any victim and of unfair prejudice to any party. The court may admit evidence of a victim's reputation only if the victim has placed it in controversy.

(c) Procedure To Determine Admissibility.

(1) *Motion.* If a party intends to offer evidence under Rule 412(b), the party must:

(A) file a motion that specifically describes the evidence and states the purpose for which it is to be offered;

(B) do so at least 14 days before trial unless the court, for good cause, sets a different time;

     (C) serve the motion on all parties; and

     (D) notify the victim or, when appropriate, the victim's guardian or representative.

  (2) *Hearing.* Before admitting evidence under this rule, the court must conduct an in camera hearing and give the victim and parties a right to attend and be heard. Unless the court orders otherwise, the motion, related materials, and the record of the hearing must be and remain sealed.

(d) Definition of "Victim." In this rule, "victim" includes an alleged victim.

Rule 413. Similar Crimes in Sexual-Assault Cases

(a) Permitted Uses. In a criminal case in which a defendant is accused of a sexual assault, the court may admit evidence that the defendant committed any other sexual assault. The evidence may be considered on any matter to which it is relevant.

(b) Disclosure to the Defendant. If the prosecutor intends to offer this evidence, the prosecutor must disclose it to the defendant, including witnesses' statements or a summary of the expected testimony. The prosecutor must do so at least 15 days before trial or at a later time that the court allows for good cause.

(c) Effect on Other Rules. This rule does not limit the admission or consideration of evidence under any other rule.

(d) Definition of "Sexual Assault." In this rule and Rule 415, "sexual assault" means a crime under federal law or under state law (as "state" is defined in 18 U.S.C. § 513) involving:

  (1) any conduct prohibited by 18 U.S.C. chapter 109A;

  (2) contact, without consent, between any part of the defendant's body — or an object — and another person's genitals or anus;

  (3) contact, without consent, between the defendant's genitals or anus and any part of another person's body;

  (4) deriving sexual pleasure or gratification from inflicting death, bodily injury, or physical pain on another person; or

  (5) an attempt or conspiracy to engage in conduct described in subparagraphs (1)-(4).

Rule 414. Similar Crimes in Child-Molestation Cases

(a) Permitted Uses. In a criminal case in which a defendant is accused of child molestation, the court may admit evidence that the defendant committed any other child molestation. The evidence may be considered on any matter to which it is relevant.

(b) Disclosure to the Defendant. If the prosecutor intends to offer this evidence, the prosecutor must disclose it to the defendant, including witnesses' statements or a summary of the expected testimony. The prosecutor must do so at least 15 days before trial or at a later time that the court allows for good cause.

(c) Effect on Other Rules. This rule does not limit the admission or consideration of evidence under any other rule.

(d) Definition of "Child" and "Child Molestation." In this rule and Rule 415:

  (1) "child" means a person below the age of 14; and

  (2) "child molestation" means a crime under federal law or under state law (as "state" is defined in 18 U.S.C. § 513) involving:

     (A) any conduct prohibited by 18 U.S.C. chapter 109A and committed with a child;

     (B) any conduct prohibited by 18 U.S.C. chapter 110;

(C) contact between any part of the defendant's body — or an object — and a child's genitals or anus;

(D) contact between the defendant's genitals or anus and any part of a child's body;

(E) deriving sexual pleasure or gratification from inflicting death, bodily injury, or physical pain on a child; or

(F) an attempt or conspiracy to engage in conduct described in subparagraphs (A)–(E).

Rule 415. Similar Acts in Civil Cases Involving Sexual Assault or Child Molestation

(a) **Permitted Uses.** (a) In a civil case involving a claim for relief based on a party's alleged sexual assault or child molestation, the court may admit evidence that the party committed any other sexual assault or child molestation. The evidence may be considered as provided in Rules 413 and 414.

(b) **Disclosure to the Opponent.** If a party intends to offer this evidence, the party must disclose it to the party against whom it will be offered, including witnesses' statements or a summary of the expected testimony. The party must do so at least 15 days before trial or at a later time that the court allows for good cause.

(c) **Effect on Other Rules.** This rule does not limit the admission or consideration of evidence under any other rule.

▶ Article V. Privileges

Rule 501. Privileges in General

The common law — as interpreted by United States courts in the light of reason and experience — governs a claim of privilege unless any of the following provides otherwise:

- the United States Constitution;
- a federal statute; or
- rules prescribed by the Supreme Court.

But in a civil case, state law governs privilege regarding a claim or defense for which state law supplies the rule of decision.

Rule 502. Attorney-Client Privilege and Work Product; Limitations on Waiver

The following provisions apply, in the circumstances set out, to disclosure of a communication or information covered by the attorney-client privilege or work-product protection.

(a) **Disclosure Made in a Federal Proceeding or to a Federal Office or Agency; Scope of a Waiver.** When the disclosure is made in a federal proceeding or to a federal office or agency and waives the attorney-client privilege or work-product protection, the waiver extends to an undisclosed communication or information in a federal or state proceeding only if:

(1) the waiver is intentional;

(2) the disclosed and undisclosed communications or information concern the same subject matter; and

(3) they ought in fairness to be considered together.

(b) Inadvertent Disclosure. When made in a federal proceeding or to a federal office or agency, the disclosure does not operate as a waiver in a federal or state proceeding if:

(1) the disclosure is inadvertent;

(2) the holder of the privilege or protection took reasonable steps to prevent disclosure; and

(3) the holder promptly took reasonable steps to rectify the error, including (if applicable) following Federal Rule of Civil Procedure 26(b)(5)(B).

(c) Disclosure Made in a State Proceeding. When the disclosure is made in a state proceeding and is not the subject of a state-court order concerning waiver, the disclosure does not operate as a waiver in a federal proceeding if the disclosure:

(1) would not be a waiver under this rule if it had been made in a federal proceeding; or

(2) is not a waiver under the law of the State where the disclosure occurred.

(d) Controlling Effect of a Court Order. A federal court may order that the privilege or protection is not waived by disclosure connected with the litigation pending before the court — in which event the disclosure is also not a waiver in any other federal or state proceeding.

(e) Controlling Effect of a Party Agreement. An agreement on the effect of disclosure in a federal proceeding is binding only on the parties to the agreement, unless it is incorporated into a court order.

(f) Controlling Effect of This Rule. Notwithstanding Rules 101 and 1101, this rule applies to state proceedings and to federal court-annexed and federal court-mandated arbitration proceedings, in the circumstances set out in the rule. And notwithstanding Rule 501, this rule applies even if State law provides the rule of decision.

(g) Definitions. In this rule:

(1) "attorney-client privilege" means the protection that applicable law provides for confidential attorney-client communications; and

(2) "work-product protection" means the protection that applicable law provides for tangible material (or its intangible equivalent) prepared in anticipation of litigation or for trial."

▶ Article VI. Witnesses

Rule 601. Competency to Testify in General

Every person is competent to be a witness unless these rules provide otherwise. But in a civil case, state law governs the witness's competency regarding a claim or defense for which state law supplies the rule of decision.

Rule 602. Need for Personal Knowledge

A witness may not testify to a matter unless evidence is introduced sufficient to support a finding that the witness has personal knowledge of the matter. Evidence to prove personal knowledge may, but need not, consist of the witness' own testimony. This rule is subject to the provisions of Rule 703, relating to opinion testimony by expert witnesses.

Rule 603. Oath or Affirmation to Testify Truthfully

Before testifying, a witness must give an oath or affirmation to testify truthfully. It must be in a form designed to impress that duty on the witness's conscience.

Rule 604. Interpreter

An interpreter must be qualified and must give an oath or affirmation to make a true translation.

Rule 605. Judge's Competency as a Witness

The presiding judge may not testify as a witness at the trial. A party need not object to preserve the issue.

Rule 606. Juror's Competency as a Witness

(a) **At the Trial.** A juror may not testify as a witness before the other jurors at the trial. If a juror is called to testify, the court must give a party an opportunity to object outside the jury's presence.

(b) **During an Inquiry into the Validity of a Verdict or Indictment.**

    (1) *Prohibited Testimony or Other Evidence.* During an inquiry into the validity of a verdict or indictment, a juror may not testify about any statement made or incident that occurred during the jury's deliberations; the effect of anything on that juror's or another juror's vote; or any juror's mental processes concerning the verdict or indictment. The court may not receive a juror's affidavit or evidence of a juror's statement on these matters.

    (2) *Exceptions.* A juror may testify about whether:

        (A) extraneous prejudicial information was improperly brought to the jury's attention;

        (B) an outside influence was improperly brought to bear on any juror; or

        (C) a mistake was made in entering the verdict on the verdict form.

Rule 607. Who May Impeach a Witness

Any party, including the party that called the witness, may attack the witness's credibility.

Rule 608. A Witness's Character for Truthfulness or Untruthfulness

(a) **Reputation or Opinion Evidence.** A witness's credibility may be attacked or supported by testimony about the witness's reputation for having a character for truthfulness or untruthfulness, or by testimony in the form of an opinion about that character. But evidence of truthful character is admissible only after the witness's character for truthfulness has been attacked.

(b) **Specific Instances of Conduct.** Except for a criminal conviction under Rule 609, extrinsic evidence is not admissible to prove specific instances of a witness's conduct in order to attack or support the witness's character for truthfulness. But the court may, on cross-examination, allow them to be inquired into if they are probative of the character for truthfulness or untruthfulness of:

    (1) the witness; or

    (2) another witness whose character the witness being cross-examined has testified about.

By testifying on another matter, a witness does not waive any privilege against self-incrimination for testimony that relates only to the witness's character for truthfulness.

Rule 609. Impeachment by Evidence of a Criminal Conviction

(a) In General. The following rules apply to attacking a witness's character for truthfulness by evidence of a criminal conviction:

    (1) for a crime that, in the convicting jurisdiction, was punishable by death or by imprisonment for more than one year, the evidence:

        (A) must be admitted, subject to Rule 403, in a civil case or in a criminal case in which the witness is not a defendant; and

        (B) must be admitted in a criminal case in which the witness is a defendant, if the probative value of the evidence outweighs its prejudicial effect to that defendant; and

    (2) for any crime regardless of the punishment, the evidence must be admitted if the court can readily determine that establishing the elements of the crime required proving — or the witness's admitting — a dishonest act or false statement.

(b) Limit on Using the Evidence After 10 Years. This subdivision (b) applies if more than 10 years have passed since the witness's conviction or release from confinement for it, whichever is later. Evidence of the conviction is admissible only if:

    (1) its probative value, supported by specific facts and circumstances, substantially outweighs its prejudicial effect; and

    (2) the proponent gives an adverse party reasonable written notice of the intent to use it so that the party has a fair opportunity to contest its use.

(c) Effect of a Pardon, Annulment, or Certificate of Rehabilitation. Evidence of a conviction is not admissible if:

    (1) the conviction has been the subject of a pardon, annulment, certificate of rehabilitation, or other equivalent procedure based on a finding that the person has been rehabilitated, and the person has not been convicted of a later crime punishable by death or by imprisonment for more than one year; or

    (2) the conviction has been the subject of a pardon, annulment, or other equivalent procedure based on a finding of innocence.

(d) Juvenile Adjudications.

Evidence of a juvenile adjudication is admissible under this rule only if:

    (1) it is offered in a criminal case;

    (2) the adjudication was of a witness other than the defendant;

    (3) an adult's conviction for that offense would be admissible to attack the adult's credibility; and

    (4) admitting the evidence is necessary to fairly determine guilt or innocence.

(e) Pendency of an Appeal. A conviction that satisfies this rule is admissible even if an appeal is pending. Evidence of the pendency is also admissible.

Rule 610. Religious Beliefs or Opinions

Evidence of a witness's religious beliefs or opinions is not admissible to attack or support the witness's credibility.

Rule 611. Mode and Order of Examining Witnesses and Presenting Evidence

(a) Control by the Court; Purposes. The court should exercise reasonable control over the mode and order of examining witnesses and presenting evidence so as to:

(1) make those procedures effective for determining the truth;

(2) avoid wasting time; and

(3) protect witnesses from harassment or undue embarrassment.

(b) Scope of Cross-Examination. Cross-examination should not go beyond the subject matter of the direct examination and matters affecting the witness's credibility. The court may allow inquiry into additional matters as if on direct examination.

(c) Leading Questions. Leading questions should not be used on direct examination except as necessary to develop the witness's testimony. Ordinarily, the court should allow leading questions:

(1) on cross-examination; and

(2) when a party calls a hostile witness, an adverse party, or a witness identified with an adverse party.

Rule 612. Writing Used to Refresh a Witness's Memory

(a) Scope. This rule gives an adverse party certain options when a witness uses a writing to refresh memory:

(1) while testifying; or

(2) before testifying, if the court decides that justice requires the party to have those options.

(b) Adverse Party's Options; Deleting Unrelated Matter. Unless 18 U.S.C. § 3500 provides otherwise in a criminal case, an adverse party is entitled to have the writing produced at the hearing, to inspect it, to cross-examine the witness about it, and to introduce in evidence any portion that relates to the witness's testimony. If the producing party claims that the writing includes unrelated matter, the court must examine the writing in camera, delete any unrelated portion, and order that the rest be delivered to the adverse party. Any portion deleted over objection must be preserved for the record.

(c) Failure to Produce or Deliver the Writing. If a writing is not produced or is not delivered as ordered, the court may issue any appropriate order. But if the prosecution does not comply in a criminal case, the court must strike the witness's testimony or — if justice so requires — declare a mistrial.

Rule 613. Witness's Prior Statement

(a) Showing or Disclosing the Statement During Examination. When examining a witness about the witness's prior statement, a party need not show it or disclose its contents to the witness. But the party must, on request, show it or disclose its contents to an adverse party's attorney.

(b) Extrinsic Evidence of a Prior Inconsistent Statement. Extrinsic evidence of a witness's prior inconsistent statement is admissible only if the witness is given an opportunity to explain or deny the statement and an adverse party is given an opportunity to examine the witness about it, or if justice so requires. This subdivision (b) does not apply to an opposing party's statement under Rule 801 (d)(2).

Rule 614. Court's Calling or Examining a Witness

(a) Calling. The court may call a witness on its own or at a party's request. Each party is entitled to cross-examine the witness.

(b) Examining. The court may examine a witness regardless of who calls the witness.

(c) Objections. A party may object to the court's calling or examining a witness either at that time or at the next opportunity when the jury is not present.

Rule 615. Excluding Witnesses

At a party's request, the court must order witnesses excluded so that they cannot hear other witnesses' testimony. Or the court may do so on its own. But this rule does not authorize excluding:

(a) a party who is a natural person;

(b) an officer or employee of a party that is not a natural person, after being designated as the party's representative by its attorney;

(c) a person whose presence a party shows to be essential to presenting the party's claim or defense; or

(d) a person authorized by statute to be present.

▶ VII. Opinions and Expert Testimony

Rule 701. Opinion Testimony by Lay Witnesses

If a witness is not testifying as an expert, testimony in the form of an opinion is limited to one that is:

(a) rationally based on the witness's perception;

(b) helpful to clearly understanding the witness's testimony or to determining a fact in issue; and

(c) not based on scientific, technical, or other specialized knowledge within the scope of Rule 702.

Rule 702. Testimony by Expert Witnesses

A witness who is qualified as an expert by knowledge, skill, experience, training, or education may testify in the form of an opinion or otherwise if:

(a) the expert's scientific, technical, or other specialized knowledge will help the trier of fact to understand the evidence or to determine a fact in issue;

(b) the testimony is based on sufficient facts or data;

(c) the testimony is the product of reliable principles and methods; and

(d) the expert has reliably applied the principles and methods to the facts of the case.

Rule 703. Bases of an Expert's Opinion Testimony

An expert may base an opinion on facts or data in the case that the expert has been made aware of or personally observed. If experts in the particular field would reasonably rely on those kinds of facts or data in forming an opinion on the subject, they need not be admissible for the opinion to be admitted. But if the facts or data would otherwise be inadmissible, the proponent of the opinion may disclose them to the jury only if their probative value in helping the jury evaluate the opinion substantially outweighs their prejudicial effect.

Rule 704. Opinion on an Ultimate Issue

(a) **In General — Not Automatically Objectionable.** An opinion is not objectionable just because it embraces an ultimate issue.

(b) **Exception.** In a criminal case, an expert witness must not state an opinion about whether the defendant did or did not have a mental state or condition that constitutes an element of the crime charged or of a defense. Those matters are for the trier of fact alone.

Rule 705. Disclosing the Facts or Data Underlying an Expert's Opinion

Unless the court orders otherwise, an expert may state an opinion — and give the reasons for it — without first testifying to the underlying facts or data. But the expert may be required to disclose those facts or data on cross-examination.

Rule 706. Court-Appointed Expert Witnesses

(a) Appointment Process. On a party's motion or on its own, the court may order the parties to show cause why expert witnesses should not be appointed and may ask the parties to submit nominations. The court may appoint any expert that the parties agree on and any of its own choosing. But the court may only appoint someone who consents to act.

(b) Expert's Role. The court must inform the expert of the expert's duties. The court may do so in writing and have a copy filed with the clerk or may do so orally at a conference in which the parties have an opportunity to participate. The expert:

(1) must advise the parties of any findings the expert makes;

(2) may be deposed by any party;

(3) may be called to testify by the court or any party; and

(4) may be cross-examined by any party, including the party that called the expert.

(c) Compensation. The expert is entitled to a reasonable compensation, as set by the court. The compensation is payable as follows:

(1) in a criminal case or in a civil case involving just compensation under the Fifth Amendment, from any funds that are provided by law; and

(2) in any other civil case, by the parties in the proportion and at the time that the court direct — and the compensation is then charged like other costs.

(d) Disclosing the Appointment to the Jury. The court may authorize disclosure to the jury that the court appointed the expert.

(e) Parties' Choice of Their Own Experts. This rule does not limit a party in calling its own experts.

▶ Article VIII. Hearsay

Rule 801. Definitions That Apply to This Article; Exclusions from Hearsay

(a) Statement. "Statement" means a person's oral assertion, written assertion, or nonverbal conduct, if the person intended it as an assertion.

(b) Declarant. "Declarant" means the person who made the statement.

(c) Hearsay. "Hearsay" means a statement that:

(1) the declarant does not make while testifying at the current trial or hearing; and

(2) a party offers in evidence to prove the truth of the matter asserted in the statement.

(d) Statements That Are Not Hearsay. A statement that meets the following conditions is not hearsay:

(1) *A Declarant-Witness's Prior Statement.* The declarant testifies and is subject to cross-examination about a prior statement, and the statement:

(A) is inconsistent with the declarant's testimony and was given under penalty of perjury at a trial, hearing, or other proceeding or in a deposition;

▼

    (B) is consistent with the declarant's testimony and is offered to rebut an express or implied charge that the declarant recently fabricated it or acted from a recent improper influence or motive in so testifying; or

    (C) identifies a person as someone the declarant perceived earlier.

  (2) *An Opposing Party's Statement.* The statement is offered against an opposing party and:

    (A) was made by the party in an individual or representative capacity;

    (B) is one the party manifested that it adopted or believed to be true;

    (C) was made by a person whom the party authorized to make a statement on the subject;

    (D) was made by the party's agent or employee on a matter within the scope of that relationship and while it existed; or

    (E) was made by the party's coconspirator during and in furtherance of the conspiracy.

The statement must be considered but does not by itself establish the declarant's authority under (C); the existence or scope of the relationship under (D); or the existence of the conspiracy or participation in it under (E).

Rule 802. The Rule Against Hearsay

Hearsay is not admissible unless any of the following provides otherwise:

- a federal statute;
- these rules; or
- other rules prescribed by the Supreme Court.

Rule 803. Exceptions to the Rule Against Hearsay — Regardless of Whether the Declarant Is Available as a Witness

The following are not excluded by the rule against hearsay, regardless of whether the declarant is available as a witness:

(1) *Present Sense Impression.* A statement describing or explaining an event or condition, made while or immediately after the declarant perceived it.

(2) *Excited Utterance.* A statement relating to a startling event or condition, made while the declarant was under the stress of excitement that it caused.

(3) *Then-Existing Mental, Emotional, or Physical Condition.* A statement of the declarant's then-existing state of mind (such as motive, intent, or plan) or emotional, sensory, or physical condition (such as mental feeling, pain, or bodily health), but not including a statement of memory or belief to prove the fact remembered or believed unless it relates to the validity or terms of the declarant's will.

(4) *Statement Made for Medical Diagnosis or Treatment.* A statement that:

    (A) is made for — and is reasonably pertinent to — medical diagnosis or treatment; and

    (B) describes medical history; past or present symptoms or sensations; their inception; or their general cause.

(5) *Recorded Recollection.* A record that:

    (A) is on a matter the witness once knew about but now cannot recall well enough to testify fully and accurately;

    (B) was made or adopted by the witness when the matter was fresh in the witness's memory; and

    (C) accurately reflects the witness's knowledge.

If admitted, the record may be read into evidence but may be received as an exhibit only if offered by an adverse party.

(6) *Records of a Regularly Conducted Activity.* A record of an act, event, condition, opinion, or diagnosis if:

    (A) the record was made at or near the time by — or from information transmitted by — someone with knowledge;

    (B) the record was kept in the course of a regularly conducted activity of a business, organization, occupation, or calling, whether or not for profit;

    (C) making the record was a regular practice of that activity;

    (D) all these conditions are shown by the testimony of the custodian or another qualified witness, or by a certification that complies with Rule 902(11) or (12) or with a statute permitting certification; and

    (E) neither the source of information nor the method or circumstances of preparation indicate a lack of trustworthiness.

(7) *Absence of a Record of a Regularly Conducted Activity.* Evidence that a matter is not included in a record described in paragraph (6) if:

    (A) the evidence is admitted to prove that the matter did not occur or exist;

    (B) a record was regularly kept for a matter of that kind; and

    (C) neither the possible source of the information nor other circumstances indicate a lack of trustworthiness.

(8) *Public Records.* A record or statement of a public office if:

    (A) it sets out:

        (i) the office's activities;

        (ii) a matter observed while under a legal duty to report, but not including, in a criminal case, a matter observed by law-enforcement personnel; or

        (iii) in a civil case or against the government in a criminal case, factual findings from a legally authorized investigation; and

    (B) neither the source of information nor other circumstances indicate a lack of trustworthiness.

(9) *Public Records of Vital Statistics.* A record of a birth, death, or marriage, if reported to a public office in accordance with a legal duty.

(10) *Absence of a Public Record.* Testimony — or a certification under Rule 902 — that a diligent search failed to disclose a public record or statement if the testimony or certification is admitted to prove that:

    (A) the record or statement does not exist; or

    (B) a matter did not occur or exist, if a public office regularly kept a record or statement for a matter of that kind.

(11) *Records of Religious Organizations Concerning Personal or Family History.* A statement of birth, legitimacy, ancestry, marriage, divorce, death, relationship by blood or marriage, or similar facts of personal or family history, contained in a regularly kept record of a religious organization.

(12) *Certificates of Marriage, Baptism, and Similar Ceremonies.* A statement of fact contained in a certificate:

    (A) made by a person who is authorized by a religious organization or by law to perform the act certified;

    (B) attesting that the person performed a marriage or similar ceremony or administered a sacrament; and

    (C) purporting to have been issued at the time of the act or within a reasonable time after it.

(13) *Family Records.* A statement of fact about personal or family history contained in a family record, such as a Bible, genealogy, chart, engraving on a ring, inscription on a portrait, or engraving on an urn or burial marker.

(14) *Records of Documents That Affect an Interest in Property.* The record of a document that purports to establish or affect an interest in property if:

(A) the record is admitted to prove the content of the original recorded document, along with its signing and its delivery by each person who purports to have signed it;

(B) the record is kept in a public office; and

(C) a statute authorizes recording documents of that kind in that office.

(15) *Statements in Documents That Affect an Interest in Property.* A statement contained in a document that purports to establish or affect an interest in property if the matter stated was relevant to the document's purpose — unless later dealings with the property are inconsistent with the truth of the statement or the purport of the document.

(16) *Statements in Ancient Documents.* A statement in a document that is at least 20 years old and whose authenticity is established.

(17) *Market Reports and Similar Commercial Publications.* Market quotations, lists, directories, or other compilations that are generally relied on by the public or by persons in particular occupations.

(18) *Statements in Learned Treatises, Periodicals, or Pamphlets.* A statement contained in a treatise, periodical, or pamphlet if:

(A) the statement is called to the attention of an expert witness on cross-examination or relied on by the expert on direct examination; and

(B) the publication is established as a reliable authority by the expert's admission or testimony, by another expert's testimony, or by judicial notice.

If admitted, the statement may be read into evidence but not received as an exhibit.

(19) *Reputation Concerning Personal or Family History.* A reputation among a person's family by blood, adoption, or marriage — or among a person's associates or in the community — concerning the person's birth, adoption, legitimacy, ancestry, marriage, divorce, death, relationship by blood, adoption, or marriage, or similar facts of personal or family history.

(20) *Reputation Concerning Boundaries or General History.* A reputation in a community — arising before the controversy — concerning boundaries of land in the community or customs that affect the land, or concerning general historical events important to that community, state, or nation.

(21) *Reputation Concerning Character.* A reputation among a person's associates or in the community concerning the person's character.

(22) *Judgment of a Previous Conviction.* Evidence of a final judgment of conviction if:

(A) the judgment was entered after a trial or guilty plea, but not a nolo contendere plea;

(B) the conviction was for a crime punishable by death or by imprisonment for more than a year;

(C) the evidence is admitted to prove any fact essential to the judgment; and

(D) when offered by the prosecutor in a criminal case for a purpose other than impeachment, the judgment was against the defendant.

The pendency of an appeal may be shown but does not affect admissibility.

(23) *Judgments Involving Personal, Family, or General History, or a Boundary.* A judgment that is admitted to prove a matter of personal, family, or general history, or boundaries, if the matter:

(A) was essential to the judgment; and

(B) could be proved by evidence of reputation.

(24) *[Other Exceptions.]* [Transferred to Rule 807.]

Rule 804. Exceptions to the Rule Against Hearsay — When the Declarant Is Unavailable as a Witness

(a) Criteria for Being Unavailable. A declarant is considered to be unavailable as a witness if the declarant:

(1) is exempted from testifying about the subject matter of the declarant's statement because the court rules that a privilege applies;

(2) refuses to testify about the subject matter despite a court order to do so;

(3) testifies to not remembering the subject matter;

(4) cannot be present or testify at the trial or hearing because of death or a then-existing infirmity, physical illness, or mental illness; or

(5) is absent from the trial or hearing and the statement's proponent has not been able, by process or other reasonable means, to procure:

(A) the declarant's attendance, in the case of a hearsay exception under Rule 804(b)(1) or (6); or

(B) the declarant's attendance or testimony, in the case of a hearsay exception under Rule 804(b)(2), (3), or (4).

But this subdivision (a) does not apply if the statement's proponent procured or wrongfully caused the declarant's unavailability as a witness in order to prevent the declarant from attending or testifying.

(b) The Exceptions. The following are not excluded by the rule against hearsay if the declarant is unavailable as a witness:

(1) *Former Testimony.* Testimony that:

(A) was given as a witness at a trial, hearing, or lawful deposition, whether given during the current proceeding or a different one; and

(B) is now offered against a party who had — or, in a civil case, whose predecessor in interest had — an opportunity and similar motive to develop it by direct, cross-, or redirect examination.

(2) *Statement Under the Belief of Imminent Death.* In a prosecution for homicide or in a civil case, a statement that the declarant, while believing the declarant's death to be imminent, made about its cause or circumstances.

(3) *Statement Against Interest.* A statement that:

(A) a reasonable person in the declarant's position would have made only if the person believed it to be true because, when made, it was so contrary to the declarant's proprietary or pecuniary interest or had so great a tendency to invalidate the declarant's claim against someone else or to expose the declarant to civil or criminal liability; and

(B) is supported by corroborating circumstances that clearly indicate its trustworthiness, if it is offered in a criminal case as one that tends to expose the declarant to criminal liability.

(4) *Statement of Personal or Family History.* A statement about:

(A) the declarant's own birth, adoption, legitimacy, ancestry, marriage, divorce, relationship by blood, adoption, or marriage, or similar facts of personal or family history, even though the declarant had no way of acquiring personal knowledge about that fact; or

(B) another person concerning any of these facts, as well as death, if the declarant was related to the person by blood, adoption, or marriage or was so intimately associated with the person's family that the declarant's information is likely to be accurate.

(5) *[Other Exceptions.]* [Transferred to Rule 807.]

(6) ***Statement Offered Against a Party That Wrongfully Caused the Declarant's Unavailability.*** A statement offered against a party that wrongfully caused — or acquiesced in wrongfully causing — the declarant's unavailability as a witness, and did so intending that result.

Rule 805. Hearsay Within Hearsay

Hearsay within hearsay is not excluded by the rule against hearsay if each part of the combined statements conforms with an exception to the rule.

Rule 806. Attacking and Supporting the Declarant's Credibility

When a hearsay statement — or a statement described in Rule 801(d)(2)(C), (D), or (E) — has been admitted in evidence, the declarant's credibility may be attacked, and then supported, by any evidence that would be admissible for those purposes if the declarant had testified as a witness. The court may admit evidence of the declarant's inconsistent statement or conduct, regardless of when it occurred or whether the declarant had an opportunity to explain or deny it. If the party against whom the statement was admitted calls the declarant as a witness, the party may examine the declarant on the statement as if on cross-examination.

Rule 807. Residual Exception

(a) **In General.** Under the following circumstances, a hearsay statement is not excluded by the rule against hearsay even if the statement is not specifically covered by a hearsay exception in Rule 803 or 804:

(1) the statement has equivalent circumstantial guarantees of trustworthiness;

(2) it is offered as evidence of a material fact;

(3) it is more probative on the point for which it is offered than any other evidence that the proponent can obtain through reasonable efforts; and

(4) admitting it will best serve the purposes of these rules and the interests of justice.

(b) **Notice.** The statement is admissible only if, before the trial or hearing, the proponent gives an adverse party reasonable notice of the intent to offer the statement and its particulars, including the declarant's name and address, so that the party has a fair opportunity to meet it.

► Article IX. Authentication And Identification

Rule 901. Authenticating or Identifying Evidence

(a) **In General.** To satisfy the requirement of authenticating or identifying an item of evidence, the proponent must produce evidence sufficient to support a finding that the item is what the proponent claims it is.

(b) **Examples.** The following are examples only — not a complete list — of evidence that satisfies the requirement:

(1) ***Testimony of a Witness with Knowledge.*** Testimony that an item is what it is claimed to be.

(2) ***Nonexpert Opinion About Handwriting.*** A nonexpert's opinion that handwriting is genuine, based on a familiarity with it that was not acquired for the current litigation.

(3) Comparison by an Expert Witness or the Trier of Fact. A comparison with an authenticated specimen by an expert witness or the trier of fact.

(4) Distinctive Characteristics and the Like. The appearance, contents, substance, internal patterns, or other distinctive characteristics of the item, taken together with all the circumstances.

(5) Opinion About a Voice. An opinion identifying a person's voice — whether heard firsthand or through mechanical or electronic transmission or recording — based on hearing the voice at any time under circumstances that connect it with the alleged speaker.

(6) Evidence About a Telephone Conversation. For a telephone conversation, evidence that a call was made to the number assigned at the time to:

   (A) a particular person, if circumstances, including self-identification, show that the person answering was the one called; or

   (B) a particular business, if the call was made to a business and the call related to business reasonably transacted over the telephone.

(7) Evidence About Public Records. Evidence that:

   (A) a document was recorded or filed in a public office as authorized by law; or

   (B) a purported public record or statement is from the office where items of this kind are kept.

(8) Evidence About Ancient Documents or Data Compilations. For a document or data compilation, evidence that it:

   (A) is in a condition that creates no suspicion about its authenticity;

   (B) was in a place where, if authentic, it would likely be; and

   (C) is at least 20 years old when offered.

(9) Evidence About a Process or System. Evidence describing a process or system and showing that it produces an accurate result.

(10) Methods Provided by a Statute or Rule. Any method of authentication or identification allowed by a federal statute or a rule prescribed by the Supreme Court.

Rule 902. Evidence That Is Self-Authenticating

The following items of evidence are self-authenticating; they require no extrinsic evidence of authenticity in order to be admitted:

(1) Domestic Public Documents That Are Sealed and Signed. A document that bears:

   (A) a seal purporting to be that of the United States; any state, district, commonwealth, territory, or insular possession of the United States; the former Panama Canal Zone; the Trust Territory of the Pacific Islands; a political subdivision of any of these entities; or a department, agency, or officer of any entity named above; and

   (B) a signature purporting to be an execution or attestation.

(2) Domestic Public Documents That Are Not Sealed But Are Signed and Certified. A document that bears no seal if:

   (A) it bears the signature of an officer or employee of an entity named in Rule 902(1)(A); and

   (B) another public officer who has a seal and official duties within that same entity certifies under seal — or its equivalent — that the signer has the official capacity and that the signature is genuine.

(3) Foreign Public Documents. A document that purports to be signed or attested by a person who is authorized by a foreign country's law to do so. The document must be accompanied by a final certification that certifies the genuineness of the signature and official position of the signer or attester — or of any foreign official whose certificate of genuineness relates to the signature or attestation or is in a chain of certificates of genuineness relating to the signature or attestation. The certification may be made by a secretary of a United States embassy or legation; by a consul general, vice consul, or consular agent of the United States; or by a diplomatic or consular official of the foreign country assigned or accredited to the United States. If all parties have been given a reasonable opportunity to investigate the document's authenticity and accuracy, the court may, for good cause, either:

(A) order that it be treated as presumptively authentic without final certification; or

(B) allow it to be evidenced by an attested summary with or without final certification.

(4) ***Certified Copies of Public Records.*** A copy of an official record — or a copy of a document that was recorded or filed in a public office as authorized by law — if the copy is certified as correct by:

(A) the custodian or another person authorized to make the certification; or

(B) a certificate that complies with Rule 902(1), (2), or (3), a federal statute, or a rule prescribed by the Supreme Court.

(5) ***Official Publications.*** A book, pamphlet, or other publication purporting to be issued by a public authority.

(6) ***Newspapers and Periodicals.*** Printed material purporting to be a newspaper or periodical.

(7) ***Trade Inscriptions and the Like.*** An inscription, sign, tag, or label purporting to have been affixed in the course of business and indicating origin, ownership, or control.

(8) ***Acknowledged Documents.*** A document accompanied by a certificate of acknowledgment that is lawfully executed by a notary public or another officer who is authorized to take acknowledgments.

(9) ***Commercial Paper and Related Documents.*** Commercial paper, a signature on it, and related documents, to the extent allowed by general commercial law.

(10) ***Presumptions Under a Federal Statute.*** A signature, document, or anything else that a federal statute declares to be presumptively or prima facie genuine or authentic.

(11) ***Certified Domestic Records of a Regularly Conducted Activity.*** The original or a copy of a domestic record that meets the requirements of Rule 803 (6) (A)-(C), as shown by a certification of the custodian or another qualified person that complies with a federal statute or a rule prescribed by the Supreme Court. Before the trial or hearing, the proponent must give an adverse party reasonable written notice of the intent to offer the record — and must make the record and certification available for inspection — so that the party has a fair opportunity to challenge them.

(12) ***Certified Foreign Records of a Regularly Conducted Activity.*** In a civil case, the original or a copy of a foreign record that meets the requirements of Rule 902 (11), modified as follows: the certification, rather than complying with a federal statute or Supreme Court rule, must be signed in a manner that, if falsely made, would subject the maker to a criminal penalty in the country where the certification is signed. The proponent must also meet the notice requirements of Rule 902 (11).

Rule 903. Subscribing Witness's Testimony

A subscribing witness's testimony is necessary to authenticate a writing only if required by the law of the jurisdiction that governs its validity.

► Article X. Contents of Writings, Recordings, and Photographs

Rule 1001. Definitions That Apply to This Article

In this article:

(a) A "writing" consists of letters, words, numbers, or their equivalent set down in any form.

(b) A "recording" consists of letters, words, numbers, or their equivalent recorded in any manner.

(c) A "photograph" means a photographic image or its equivalent stored in any form.

(d) An "original" of a writing or recording means the writing or recording itself or any counterpart intended to have the same effect by the person who executed or issued it. For electronically stored information, "original" means any printout — or other output readable by sight — if it accurately reflects the information. An "original" of a photograph includes the negative or a print from it.

(e) A "duplicate" means a counterpart produced by a mechanical, photographic, chemical, electronic, or other equivalent process or technique that accurately reproduces the original.

Rule 1002. Requirement of the Original

An original writing, recording, or photograph is required in order to prove its content unless these rules or a federal statute provides otherwise.

Rule 1003. Admissibility of Duplicates

A duplicate is admissible to the same extent as the original unless a genuine question is raised about the original's authenticity or the circumstances make it unfair to admit the duplicate.

Rule 1004. Admissibility of Other Evidence of Content

An original is not required and other evidence of the content of a writing, recording, or photograph is admissible if:

(a) all the originals are lost or destroyed, and not by the proponent acting in bad faith;

(b) an original cannot be obtained by any available judicial process;

(c) the party against whom the original would be offered had control of the original; was at that time put on notice, by pleadings or otherwise, that the original would be a subject of proof at the trial or hearing; and fails to produce it at the trial or hearing; or

(d) the writing, recording, or photograph is not closely related to a controlling issue.

Rule 1005. Copies of Public Records to Prove Content

The proponent may use a copy to prove the content of an official record — or of a document that was recorded or filed in a public office as authorized by law — if these conditions are met: the record or document is otherwise admissible; and the copy is certified as correct in accordance with Rule 902(4) or is testified to be correct by a witness who has compared it with the original. If no such copy can be obtained by reasonable diligence, then the proponent may use other evidence to prove the content.

Rule 1006. Summaries to Prove Content

The proponent may use a summary, chart, or calculation to prove the content of voluminous writings, recordings, or photographs that cannot be conveniently examined in court. The proponent must make the originals or duplicates available for examination or copying, or both, by other parties at a reasonable time and place. And the court may order the proponent to produce them in court.

Rule 1007. Testimony or Statement of a Party to Prove Content

The proponent may prove the content of a writing, recording, or photograph by the testimony, deposition, or written statement of the party against whom the evidence is offered. The proponent need not account for the original.

Rule 1008. Functions of the Court and Jury

Ordinarily, the court determines whether the proponent has fulfilled the factual conditions for admitting other evidence of the content of a writing, recording, or photograph under Rule 1004 or 1005. But in a jury trial, the jury determines — in accordance with Rule 104(b) — any issue about whether:
(a) an asserted writing, recording, or photograph ever existed
(b) another one produced at the trial or hearing is the original; or
(c) other evidence of content accurately reflects the content.

▶ Article XI. Miscellaneous Rules

Rule 1101. Applicability of the Rules

(a) **To Courts and Judges.** These rules apply to proceedings before:

- United States district courts;
- United States bankruptcy and magistrate judges;
- United States courts of appeals;
- the United States Court of Federal Claims; and
- the district courts of Guam, the Virgin Islands, and the Northern Mariana Islands.

(b) **To Cases and Proceedings.** These rules apply in:

- civil cases and proceedings, including bankruptcy, admiralty, and maritime cases;
- criminal cases and proceedings; and
- contempt proceedings, except those in which the court may act summarily.

(c) **Rules on Privilege.** The rules on privilege apply to all stages of a case or proceeding.
(d) **Exceptions.** These rules — except for those on privilege — do not apply to the following:
(1) the court's determination, under Rule 104(a), on a preliminary question of fact governing admissibility;

(2) grand-jury proceedings; and

(3) miscellaneous proceedings such as:

- extradition or rendition;
- issuing an arrest warrant, criminal summons, or search warrant;
- a preliminary examination in a criminal case;
- sentencing;
- granting or revoking probation or supervised release; and
- considering whether to release on bail or otherwise.

(e) Other Statutes and Rules. A federal statute or a rule prescribed by the Supreme Court may provide for admitting or excluding evidence independently from these rules.

Rule 1102. Amendments

These rules may be amended as provided in 28 U.S.C. § 2072.

Rule 1103. Title

These rules may be cited as the Federal Rules of Evidence.

Source: United States Courts, U.S. Government Printing Office.

abandoned property items or premises that have been intentionally discarded, such as drugs tossed away by a suspect during a foot chase by police.

actual possession a consideration in the evaluation of an individual's possessory interest in an object which is demonstrated when that individual is physically holding or grasping the object.

acquittal a finding of not guilty in a criminal trial.

adjudicative facts facts that would require proof if not judicially noticed, such as chemical symbols and common definitions and pronunciations.

admissibility approval by the trial judge that evidence is both probative and relevant, as well as competent and material to the matter at hand.

admissions by party-opponent an exception to the Hearsay Rule which permits the introduction of a statement offered against another party if that person: was the declarant; or manifested an adoption or belief in that statement; or authorized the statement; or is within the scope or made during the course of employment; or the declarant was a co-conspirator.

admissions by silence an exception to the Hearsay Rule, it means the failure by a party, in whose presence, hearing, or observation of an act or declaration is made, to assert that such act or declaration is untrue.

administrative justification a judicially created measure of justification which provides for the limited search of an area in cases where the safety of society outweighs an individual's interest in privacy. Most often used to justify health inspections, intrusions into government workers involved with mass transportation, or school searches.

adoptive admission a statement of which the party has manifested an adoption or belief in its truth.

adversary system a system of law that relies on the skills and attributes of advocates for opposing parties, rather than on a neutral party such as a judge, to ascertain the truth of a case.

affidavit a formal, sworn (often notarized), written claim of a truth or truths confirmed by the signer.

affirmation declaration or promise by a witness to be truthful. An affirmation has exactly the same legal effect as an oath and is an option afforded to those who conscientiously object to the religious implications of an oath (i.e., putting one's right hand on the Bible).

affirmative defense a legal justification for an individual's actions, such as insanity, entrapment, coercion or duress, necessity, and self-defense. Those asserting affirmative defense do not deny the action in question, just the culpability associated with it.

aggravating factors case characteristics that tend to increase the defendant's culpability and subsequent sentence. They include, but are not limited to, past criminal history, dismemberment of body, and flight from prosecution.

Aguilar-Spinelli test a two-prong test for the issuance of probable cause, requiring a demonstration of veracity on the part of the defendant and a showing of the underlying circumstances of the information itself for a magistrate to make a decision regarding probable cause.

Alford plea a plea in criminal court that allows a defendant to assert his or her innocence but admit or acknowledge the existence of sufficient evidence to find the person guilty. Judges may then find the person guilty or put aside a finding for a later dismissal—the prospect of a later dismissal engenders interest in this type of plea.

alibi proof of whereabouts; literally, "another place."

ancient document rule legal concept that provides for a document to be considered valid when it is at least 20 years old, free from suspicious circumstances, and found in a circumstance or area in which such writings are likely to be kept.

anticipatory search warrants legal documentation giving search and seizure authority before the evidence has arrived, such as a large shipment of narcotics.

appellate court a court of appeal or superior court that has the power to hear appeals regarding questions of law deriving from decisions made by a lower court.

Arraignment or initial appearance formal proceeding which follows booking in state systems or the indictment or information in the federal system. During this time, the accused is informed of the charges, bail is set, a plea is given, and the next court appearance is scheduled.) Also, the judge ensures that the accused is aware of his or her right to an attorney and, in the case of an indigent defendant, appointment of counsel is made.

arrest the physical taking or holding of a suspect into custody effected under the authority of a warrant of probable cause or upon witness by a law enforcement officer that a crime has been committed by the individual in question.

arrest inventories personal inventories, or inventories of an individual's personal effects, which are taken during routine booking procedures.

assertion-centered statements those statements in which the declarant (person making the statement) intends to communicate his or her thoughts or beliefs.

attorney-client privilege legal protection against compulsory disclosure in open court of communications between client and attorney when such communications were confidential and were undertaken under the auspices of a legal relationship.

authentication a demonstration of the truthfulness (validity) of an item in order for the item to be admissible as evidence.

bail security (usually an amount of money) pledged to the court that allows for an individual's release with the understanding that the person will return for trial. Bail generally is refunded at the end of the trial, regardless of the verdict.

ballistic fingerprints unique identifying marks made on bullets and cartridge casings that are particular to an individual firearm.

ballistics evaluation and identification of the trajectory of a spent bullet.

***Belton* rule** evidence rule established by the U.S. Supreme Court which permitted officers to make a contemporaneous search of a passenger compartment of an automobile incident to a lawful arrest. (It was overturned in *Arizona v. Gant* (2009)).

best evidence rule legal concept that the best evidence is the original version, rather than a copy of the original version. The rule provides that secondary evidence, such as photocopies or facsimiles, are not admissible when the original is available.

beyond a reasonable doubt the highest legal standard of proof, it is the standard that demonstrates a finding of guilt or proof by triers of fact (jurors or judges) in a criminal proceeding. Reasonable doubt requires a demonstration that no reasonable doubt exists

Bill of rights the first 10 amendments to the U.S. Constitution enumerating several important basic rights and privileges regarding the criminal justice process. Protections include freedom from unreasonable searches and seizures, self-incrimination, double jeopardy, and cruel and unusual punishments. Guarantees include

a speedy trial, compulsory process, a warrant based on probable cause, and assessment of fair and reasonable bail.

booking administrative procedure during which a suspect is formally entered into the criminal justice system through the process of photographing, fingerprinting, and documenting the offense charged.

***Boykin* waiver** a waiver required of all criminal defendants entering guilty pleas in which it must be demonstrated that they are intelligently and voluntarily waiving three important Constitutional rights: the privilege against self-incrimination; the right to a trial by jury; and, the right to confront one's accuser.

***Brady* rule** judicial ruling requiring prosecutors to share all exculpatory evidence with the defense, including any information that may tend to lessen culpability or mitigate subsequent punishment.

brief a written legal argument that summarizes the case and includes a statement of relevant facts and issues of law.

bright line rule a rule established by the Court in *Edwards v. Arizona* which states that individuals invoking their rights may not be subjected to further interrogation in the absence of counsel unless the suspect initiates the dialogue with the authorities.

Bruton rule a legal ruling establishing that the confession of a co-conspirator which identifies or otherwise implicates the defendant can only be used when the individual who confesses takes the witness stand and is subject to cross-examination.

burden of production legal requirement referring to the affirmative duty of a party to produce an item in question, such as a questioned document.

burden of proof legal requirement referring to the affirmative duty of a party to establish that all elements of the issue in question are true and valid as alleged. In criminal trials, the burden of proof lies with the state.

case-in-chief portion of a trial in which the party with the burden of proof presents its case by calling witnesses and presenting all manner of evidence to prove its case, including direct (eye witness testimony), circumstantial, demonstrative, real, testimonial, and scientific (expert).

castle laws or the castle doctrine portion of a self-defense statute, which removes the duty to retreat before employing deadly force when one is in his or her home.

chain of custody a description and explanation as to where and how the proffered item was found, collected, and preserved before courtroom introduction. This demonstration of evidentiary integrity also includes a chronological history of all individuals who have had access to or possession of the item from initial seizure to courtroom introduction.

challenge for cause a request that a prospective juror be dismissed due to a specific and significant reason to believe that the individual is incapable of serving as a juror.

circumstantial admission statement or conduct of a criminal defendant suggestive of guilt.

circumstantial evidence matter, material, or information that requires a presumption; or evidence that indirectly proves or disproves a fact.

case citation it is the unique identifier of a particular legal document which references where the full text of the opinion can be found.

civil law a legal system derived from Roman law (Corpus Juris Civilis, circa 529–534); also the body of law (common law) of a state or nation dealing with the rights of private citizens.

clear and convincing evidence intermediate standard of proof (between the lower standard of a "preponderance of evidence" and the higher standard of "beyond a reasonable doubt") that requires the party bearing the burden of proof to demonstrate that the matter asserted is substantially more probable than not.

clergy-communicant privilege legal protection against compulsory disclosure of the often personal and sensitive communications between a member of the clergy and his or her penitent (formerly known as the priest-penitent privilege).

closing argument the concluding statement of each party's counsel which reiterates the important arguments and evidence most favorable to their case. Occurring after the presentment of evidence, closing arguments may not contain new information.

co-conspirator rule a legal ruling establishing that the confession of a co-conspirator which identifies or otherwise implicates the defendant can only be used when the individual who confesses takes the witness stand and is subject to cross-examination

code of Hammurabi oldest and best-preserved example of commercial custom and law. The Mesopotamian code, discovered in 1902, contains provisions for marital relationships and guidance for prosecution of crimes. Characterized by the burden of proof resting solely with the accused, the code carried severe sanctions, including death, for failure to meet this burden.

common law body of law based on the concept that legitimate legal authority derives from the consent of the people and is based on customs and traditions embodied in case law. It is also known as the law precedent.

competency the mental capacity of an individual to participate in a legal proceeding. For a witness to be competent, he or she must be able to independently recollect and communicate the events in question, separate fact from fiction, and adhere to legal requirements of accuracy and truthfulness.

competent evidence evidence which is both relevant and material which has no impediment to its admissibility.

complaint a legal document describing the offense charged; time, date, and place of occurrence; and identity of suspected offender that is filed with the appropriate judicial authority to initiate prosecution.

compulsory process a legal provision housed within the Sixth Amendment allowing defendants to compel the presence and testimony of any material witness favorable to his or her case.

computer animations computer-generated graphical representations of two- or three-dimensional objects.

computer forensics the field of science in which computer (digital) evidence is identified, preserved, analyzed, and documented for legal purposes. Such evidence may include electronic mail, instant messages, images and photographs, and history of a person's Web site activity. Computer forensics examiners investigate and recover deleted and often intentionally altered data.

computer simulations computer-generated representations that may be substantive or demonstrative in nature (often used for homicide reenactments, traffic accident reconstruction, airplane trajectory and flight patterns, and detonation of explosives). Unlike computer animations, simulations are largely contingent upon proper data entry and analysis.

concealment fraudulent commission or omission of relevant facts, such as disposing of the murder weapon, hiding stolen property, or burning incriminating statements.

conclusive presumptions irrefutable conclusions that must be drawn by a fact-finder.

confession a voluntary, self-incriminating statement of events made to the police by an individual who admits agency or participation in a criminal offense.

confidentiality legal protection against compulsory disclosure of secret communications, such as between an attorney and his or her client.

confrontation clause a clause embedded in the Sixth Amendment providing that any accused person has a right to confront any witness testifying against him or her. The clause is also used to refer to the common law rule preventing the admission of hearsay in a criminal trial.

consciousness of guilt inferred through the introduction of circumstantial evidence which demonstrates uncustomary behavior, statements, or demeanor by the defendant.

consent searches searches conducted in the absence of a warrant, which are predicated on the permission of the homeowner or other competent party but which are limited to the scope of said permission. Original assent is where withdrawal of same reduces all expectation of permission by law enforcement, and immediately ceases any search activities. In the most general sense, the concept of consent as adjudicated by the Court may be divided into three broad concerns: scope, voluntary, and third party.

conspiracy a criminal act in which an actor agrees with one or more persons to engage in or cause the commission of a future crime.

constructive possession a consideration in the evaluation of an individual's possessory interest in an object which is demonstrated when that individuals possess it but are not physically touching it, such as when the item is located in the individual's car.

contemporaneous objection rule legal requirement that motions to suppress evidence be presented simultaneous to the question asked, the answer given, or the admission of evidence.

contempt of court a ruling by a judge against a person who fails to comply with a judicial order or who disrupts the normal process of a court hearing, such as failing to obey a lawful order, showing disrespect of the judge, or publishing material deemed likely to jeopardize a fair trial. Sanctions may involve monetary fines, jail time, or both.

corpus delecti literally "body of the crime," the term loosely refers to the physical evidence associated with a charged offense.

corroborating evidence refers to supplementary or supporting evidence that tends to strengthen or confirm evidence already supported by other evidence.

court of appeals found throughout the federal system and within the majority of state systems, this type of court has the authority of first review.

court of general jurisdiction a court which has legal authority to hear cases involving civil and criminal matters within the geographical area over which it presides. (Depending on jurisdiction, such courts may also be known as trial courts, district courts, circuit courts, or superior courts.

court of last resort a court from which there is no further appeal of a judgment rendered by it in review of a decision by a lower court

court of original jurisdiction the court which has the authority to hear a case first. In criminal cases, trial courts have original jurisdiction.

court of last resort the final appellate court in a jurisdiction or a court from which there is no further appeal of a judgment rendered by it in review of a decision by a lower court

crime scene the physical location of a criminal offense in which evidence of a crime may be found. Some crimes may include multiple scenes, such as a case of murder in which the body is moved after death.

criminal complaint a legal document, filed with the appropriate judicial authority, that initiates prosecution of an alleged offense. Criminal complaints must include the specifics of the incident in question, including, but not limited to the offense charged; the time, date, and place of occurrence; and the name of the suspected offender.

criminal intent a necessary element of a crime involving a conscious decision on the part of an individual to engage in an unlawful act.

cross-examination questioning of a witness by opposing counsel; occurs after direct examination and is designed to ensure the veracity of testifying witnesses, to show the facts in the most favorable light to the cross-examiner's side, and sometimes, to impeach the witness.

cruel and unusual punishment prohibited by the Eighth Amendment, the phrase is roughly defined as any punishment in excess of that which is fair and conscionable in contemporary society, such as torture, execution of mentally retarded or minor offenders, and disproportionate terms of imprisonment. Ambiguity regarding its definition continues to exist, with Justice Clifford defining only one specific example: "(D)ifficulty would attend the effort to define with exactness the extent of the constitution provision . . . but it is safe to affirm that punishments of torture are forbidden."

curtilage the enclosed area of land surrounding a dwelling, distinct from the residence itself (because no roof exists over it).

custody police custody—the physical holding of an individual by law enforcement beginning with arrest; child custody—having control of and responsibility for children under the age of eighteen.

cyber evidence evidence that exists primarily in electronic form and is accessed solely through electronic means, such as text from e-mails and the history of Web sites a person accesses.

cybercrime criminal activity involving a computer or computer systems that results in a direct or concomitant loss; also computer crime and computer-related crime.

"dangerous patient" exception removal of legal protection from forced disclosure in open court of a patient's communications with a psychotherapist when the patient—through actions or words—presents a likely threat to the community.

Daubert **test** a legal precedent requiring trial judges to evaluate the testimony of expert witnesses in order to determine its "relevancy" and "reliability," and thus, admissibility. *Daubert* is a two-pronged test: (1) relevancy refers to whether or not the expert's evidence "fits" the facts of the case and (2) reliability requires the expert to have derived his or her conclusions from the scientific method.

declarant the individual who issues an oral or written assertion or who engages in nonverbal conduct if it was intended to be an assertion

declarant-centered statements hearsay statements made by lay or expert witnesses that often involve an evaluation as to the declarant's credibility.

declarations against interest statements that are against the pecuniary or proprietary interest of the declarant.

defense attorney adversarial counterpart to the prosecutor whose responsibility is to serve as counsel and advocate for the accused. In criminal cases, the defense attorney attempts to create reasonable doubt in the minds of the jury.

demonstrative evidence evidence that illustrates or clarifies oral testimony in a criminal proceeding, such as computer-generated charts, images, and models.

denied powers those powers that are expressly forbidden to a sovereign in a federalist system.

derivative evidence rule an extension of the Exclusionary Rule. Suppresses any evidence that was predicated or derived from evidence deemed inadmissible due to unconstitutional actions by the state. Also known as the Fruits of the Poisonous Tree Doctrine, it includes the suppression of evidence in the following areas: additional evidence that would not have been discovered; witnesses who might have remained unknown; and, confessions or admissions made under the presentment of illegally obtained evidence.

direct evidence information, material, or matter that proves or disproves a fact without the need for inference or presumption

direct examination interrogation of a witness by attorneys by the side that called him or her to testify during which witnesses are asked open-ended questions designed to elicit a narrative response in which the witness competently recounts the events in question, such as "Where were you on the night of August 25, 2012?"

directed verdict a verdict of acquittal which results in cases where a judge instructs the jury to acquit the defendant due to the prosecution's failure to meet the required standard of proof.

discovery the pretrial process by which information is exchanged between the opposing parties. By law, the state must disclose all exculpatory evidence to the defense, even if it may tend to exonerate or mitigate punishment.

documentary evidence documents or other media, such as video or audio recordings, digital content, printed e-mails, transcripts, and personal writings in which incriminating statements are recorded, ranging from personal diaries, fraudulent checks, ransom notes, and even betting records.

double jeopardy Fifth Amendment protection against an individual being tried for a criminal offense more than once in the same jurisdiction. Double jeopardy protection does not preclude prosecution of individuals for the same set of circumstances in different jurisdictions, which explains why some individuals have been acquitted in a federal court but found at fault in a state court.

dual sovereignty or separate sovereigns doctrine an exception to the double jeopardy clause of the Fifth Amendment; protects the interests of both state and federal authorities in cases in which a single act violates the laws of both sovereigns

due process a highly valued guarantee of the Fifth Amendment that protects citizens from the potential of an oppressive government and grants them equal protection and judicial fairness under the law (and explicitly prohibits deprivation of life, liberty, property, and other rights granted by statute).

duress a mitigating factor that may justify the actions of an individual claiming to have been forced to commit a crime, such as murder, against his or her will.

duty to retreat clause portion of a self-defense statute which requires individuals to retreat, if possible, from.

dying declaration a statement made by a dying person (or a person who believes death is imminent) about the cause or circumstances of the impending death, such as when a dying woman tells police who shot her. Admissibility of such statements is contingent upon the laws of the corresponding jurisdiction.

electronic surveillance observation and other practices by law enforcement to gather information in a secretive manner through the use of electronic devices, such as audio or video recorders, cameras, and microphones.

en banc a session where the entire membership of the court participates in the decision as opposed to the regular quorum.

enumerated powers those areas of authority specifically articulated in Article I, Section 8 of the U.S. Constitution.

establishment clause as stated in the First Amendment: "Congress shall make no law respecting an establishment of religion," the clause formally separates the church and state and prevents the federal government from declaring or financially supporting a national religion. In addition, it prohibits preferential treatment by the government to any particular faith.

evidence the demonstration of truth or untruth of allegations in a court of law through the consideration of information that is relevant, competent, material, and probative

excessive bail any bail in excess of that which is necessary to ensure the appearance of the defendant at the action in question.

excessive fine any monetary penalty that is disproportionate to the offense.

excited utterances observations experienced through any of the five senses and are offered spontaneously under the stress or excitement of an event. Such statements are considered trustworthy because they were unsolicited and offered contemporaneously to the excitement of the event. Such statements are considered trustworthy because they were offered unsolicited at the moment (e.g., "Look out! We're going to crash!" or "That crazy man is shooting at us!").

exclusionary rule legal mandate requiring the exclusion of any evidence collected by law enforcement personnel in a manner that violates any provision in the Bill of Rights. This judge-made rule is designed to discourage law enforcement from circumventing the protections offered in the Fourth and Fifth Amendments.

exclusive powers those powers in a federalist system that belong exclusively to the specified sovereign which may not be infringed upon by another exculpatory material information or circumstances favorable to a defendant in a criminal case. Failure by the prosecution to disclose exculpatory evidence can be grounds for dismissal of the case.

executive privilege assertion by the President of the United States (or ranking executive officer) to deny disclosure of information based on the separation of governmental powers (executive, legislative, and judicial).

exigent circumstances facts or situational characteristics that necessitate immediate action, such as threat to human life, escape of a suspect, or imminent destruction of evidence.

expectation of privacy protection against government-sponsored searches, seizures, and unlawful entry (including unauthorized disclosure of personal belongings) without probable cause and due process into areas deemed private. Although not specifically discussed in the Constitution, the "right to be left alone" (Justice Louis Brandeis) has developed into a liberty of personal autonomy valued by all Americans. It is protected by (and narrowly defined in) the First, Fourth, Fifth, and Fourteenth Amendments.

expert witness an individual who possesses specialized knowledge of a subject related to the case because of education, profession, or experience (often proved from authorship in medical journals, for example). Unlike lay (nonexpert) witnesses, an expert witness must be deemed "qualified" by the court before testifying.

federal circuit court an intermediate appellate court of the U.S. federal court system which decides appeals from the district court within its particular judicial circuit.

federal district courts federal trial courts or courts of general jurisdiction.

Federal rules of evidence rules governing the introduction of evidence in criminal and civil proceedings in federal courts (also FRE). Although they are not binding on state proceedings, many states have adopted similar rules.

federalism a system of government of constitutionally divided sovereignty in which power is vested in a central governing body and constituent political units (such as states or provinces).

fingerprint an impression of the intricate design of friction skin ridges found on the palmar side of a person's fingers or thumb

forensic dentistry/odontology the application of dental and paradental knowledge to the analysis of legal questions in civil and criminal matters, including analysis of bite mark evidence and identification of human remains.

forensic entomology the application of scientific knowledge regarding insects and arthropods in the analysis of decomposing human remains and food contamination caused by insects.

forensic pathology the application of scientific knowledge regarding the types and causes of death, including analysis of medical records and toxicology samples. Forensic pathologists may testify to both the cause and manner of death (whether homicide, suicide, accident, or natural).

forensic psychology/psychiatry the scientific analysis of a criminal's mind.

forensic science the application of scientific concepts and methods to the analysis of legal questions or evidence; also forensics.

former testimony sworn statements offered previously in a legal proceeding.

four corners rule legal requirement preventing judges from seeking probable cause beyond the information contained within the specific parameters ("four corners") of the supporting affidavit and preventing law enforcement officers from going beyond the "four corners" of the warrant itself.

fruit of the poisonous tree legal doctrine denying admissibility of evidence collected in an illegal manner, such as from information gathered illegally, with the logic being that if the source of the evidence (tree) is tainted, all evidence gathered from it (fruit) will be tainted as well.

***Frye* standard** the legal requirement (previous to *Daubert*) that deductions from evidence should be based on methodologies generally accepted by a meaningful segment of the scientific community and specifically by others working in the specific field related to the case. It was replaced by the less restrictive *Daubert test* in 1993.

fungible evidence any biological, chemical, digital, or other evidence that can be manipulated, altered, substituted or contaminated.

good faith exception an exception to the exclusionary rule that permits the admission of evidence that was collected in an unconstitutional manner if the law enforcement officers involved in the collection reasonably believed that their actions were legally permissible, as in cases in which officers were executing a warrant later found to be defective.

grand jury an investigative body of impartial citizens selected to hear evidence of criminal allegations presented by the state to determine whether sufficient probable cause exists to pursue trial. Grand juries may compel witnesses to appear at the hearings, which may be held in secret and generally are not attended by the defendant.

grand jury system an alternative to the preliminary hearing system. The system is characterized as a panel of citizens selected to hear evidence of criminal allegations presented by the state to determine whether sufficient probable cause exists to return a true bill (i.e., finding of truth in the allegations).

gruesome photographs images or depictions, often of a brutal nature, that are especially graphic and may tend to incite unfair prejudice. For admissibility, the probative nature of the image must outweigh any potential prejudice; many courts have determined that such evidence should not be excluded from trial.

habeas corpus literally "you have the body" (see writ of habeas corpus).

harmless error an error which is not significantly related to the final disposition of the case.

hearsay any statement, other than one made by the declarant while testifying at the trial or hearing, offered in evidence to prove the truth of the matter asserted

hearsay within hearsay a hearsay statement that includes one or more additional hearsay statements. These statements are admissible in court only when all of the statements conform to the requirements of the hearsay exceptions in the Federal Rules of Evidence.

hostile witness a witness who testifies for the opposing party or a witness who offers adverse testimony to the calling party during direct examination.

hung jury a jury that is unable to reach a verdict with the requisite degree of unanimity, the result of which may be the declaration of a mistrial.

imaging creation of an exact replica of an original piece of evidence, generally for the purpose of leaving the original evidence untouched, untainted, and free from accidental or intentional manipulation or destruction.

hypnotically refreshed memories recollection of events which is produced under the influence of hypnosis.

immediate apparency a term used exclusively in consideration of the constitutionality of a particular "plain view" search. The term refers to the instant recognizability of a particular item's evidentiary value.

immunity a formally issued agreement disallowing prosecution of an individual, generally in exchange for his or her cooperation in an investigation or for testimony implicating another.

impermissible inferences any inference, presumption, or conclusion that is not permissible under law without the presence of corroboration.

implied consent legal term referring to the notion that individuals exercising a privilege are aware of their rights concerning said privilege and have inferred their consent to a search of either their persons or property.

implied powers those powers exercised by Congress which are not explicitly defined in the Constitution, but are "necessary and proper" to execute the powers that are.

impoundment action of formally taking a physical item into government custody.

impressment seizure and inducement of property or people into public use or service.

impressment of private property the confiscation and utilization of privately owned property for state use.

inadvertent discovery an accidental or unplanned detection. The term is usually restricted to discussions or considerations of "plain view" searches.

incident to arrest legal concept allowing an officer to perform a warrantless search during or immediately after a lawful arrest in which only the person arrested and the area immediately surrounding the person may be searched, such as for a weapon.

incompetency legal condition referring to the mental capacity of an individual to participate in a legal proceeding.

incriminating statements statements made that do not necessarily acknowledge guilt but tend to implicate the accused; statements made against the interest of the declarant.

independent source doctrine legal concept that permits the introduction of evidence that initially was discovered during, or as a consequence of, an unlawful search but later obtained independently from lawful activities untainted by the initial illegality.

indicia of reliability legal concept referring to the notion that some facts or circumstances result in a determination of veracity on their face because of their circumstances.

indictment a formal charge against a defendant that initiates a criminal proceeding based upon a formal, written accusation of a criminal offense presented to a judicial official (often upon affirmation of a grand jury).

indigent individuals determined to be financially incapable of providing their own defense.

inevitability of discovery exception an exception to the Exclusionary Rule that allows for the admissibility of evidence collected in an unconstitutional manner if the prosecution can show that the evidence would have been inevitably discovered, through other means.

inference a logical or deductive conclusion drawn from evidence, generally the conclusion that something is more probable than not.

informant an individual who discreetly provides incriminating information to law enforcement authorities.

information a formal accusation of a criminal offense made by a public official following a demonstration of probable cause in a preliminary hearing.

initial appearance or arraignment the formal proceeding which follows booking in state systems or the indictment or information in the federal system. During this time, the accused is informed of the charges, bail is set, a plea is given, and the next court appearance is scheduled. Also, the judge ensures that the accused is aware of his or her right to an attorney and, in the case of an indigent defendant, appointment of counsel is made.

inked prints are collected by arresting officers or jail intake personnel, and are made on identification cards through the process of rolling an individual's fingers in ink and depressing them onto the card surface.

Insanity plea an affirmative defense used by defendants who intend to argue that they should not be held criminally liable for committing the crime in question because they had a mental illness, disease, or defect at the time of the alleged criminal actions.

Intent a necessary element of a crime which involves a conscious decision on the part of an individual to engage in an unlawful act.

intermediate appellate courts found throughout the federal system and within the majority of state systems, these courts are the court of first review.

interrogation as interpreted by the Court, the term for purposes of *Miranda* refers not only to express questioning by the police, but also to any words or actions on the part of the police which are likely to elicit an incriminating response.

inventory search legal term referring to the warrantless search of a person or physical object by law enforcement authorities conducted upon the arrest of an individual or impoundment of property which documents all items contained within.

judge adversarial referee between prosecutors and defense attorneys whose responsibilities are to ensure fairness, adherence to the rule of law, and good sportsmanship between the parties during a trial.

judgment N.O.V. an acronym for the Latin term "non obstante veredicto," literally "notwithstanding the verdict;" legal term referring to the decision by a judicial authority to set aside a verdict, recognizing that a directed verdict should have been asserted.

judicial notice an action taken by the court to make a determination of fact without the formality or examination by a jury; or, an order by a judicial authority to recognize a particular issue as fact.

Judiciary act of 1789 legislation establishing the U.S. Marshals Service, the office of Attorney General, a strong federal court system, a Supreme Court, and jurisdictional responsibilities granting citizens the right to be heard in federal court when issues of constitutional concern were rejected by the highest state appellate court.

jury instructions instructions given to the jury by the presiding judge concerning the elements of the crime, the burden of proof, the standard of proof, and admonitions to avoid external influences.

latent fingerprint A volatile impression not visible to the naked eye that is deposited when the ridges make contact with a relatively smooth surface, such as glass, wood, or metal. Various fingerprint powders, chemicals, and processes make identifying invisible prints possible.

law the codification of social norms and expectations which are deemed necessary for the maintenance of a society.

law of evidence the rules which dictate the admissibility of information into a court of law.

lay witness any individual with first-hand knowledge who is testifying to the matter at hand and is not providing expert scientific testimony.

laying the foundation demonstration of the authenticity and relevance of a proffered item of evidence. Failure to properly lay the foundation may result in an objection by opposing counsel.

leading questions questions designed to guide the respondent's answer or elicit a certain response.

legislative facts factual information regarding the interpretation of a statute or constitutional provision, creation or modification of a common law rule, legislative history of a relevant statute, or information about the impact of extant law.

lineup a procedure in which law enforcement authorities line up several potential suspects and ask the victim or an eyewitness to identify the perpetrator.

magistrate a lower court judge or judicial official who has restricted authority generally limited to preliminary proceedings or lesser criminal cases.

Magna Carta An agreement between King John and his Barons in 1215 which provided the foundations of due process and constitutional law in countries across the globe

mala in se criminal behaviors that are inherently wrong or immoral in and of themselves irrespective of the prevailing law. Most societies would consider the rape of a child or the eating of one's offspring to be exemplars of such behaviors.

mala prohibita criminal behaviors that are not naturally immoral but whose wrongness lies in their legal prohibition. Such crimes in the United States include gambling, drug use, and vagrancy.

marital communications privilege legal protection against compulsory disclosure of spousal communications made in confidence, regardless of the state of the marriage at the time.

Maryland v. Craig a 1990 decision by the Supreme Court that allowed the use of closed-circuit television (rather than face-to-face testimony) in a child sexual abuse case. In the seminal ruling, the Court determined that the confrontation clause did not guarantee defendants an absolute right to a face-to-face meeting with witnesses at trial.

material witness an individual possessing information about the matter at hand of such significance that the outcome of the case or trial may be affected by its inclusion.

materiality a requirement for admissibility, it refers to evidence that is logically connected to a fact at issue and includes a consideration of the germaneness of information or testimony and a determination as to its impact on the trial.

means the ability to commit an offense which is often demonstrated through evidence of special knowledge, physical prowess, or the like.

media-source privilege a privilege allowing a reporter or other media representative to withhold disclosure of a source's identity. This privilege does not have the legal standing of other similar privileges such as the attorney-client privilege.

mens rea literally from the Latin for "guilty mind," the term refers to the criminal intent that is necessary as an element to sustain a guilty verdict in a criminal case. There are four general categories of mens rea that are incorporated into criminal codes. These categories are: intentionally (or purposely), knowingly, recklessly, and negligently.

mitigating factors case characteristics that tend to reduce the culpability of the defendant and the applicable sentence. Some common mitigating factors include, but are not limited to, age of the defendant, intoxication level, absence of criminal history, childhood victimization, and cooperation with authorities.

Miranda **warnings** legally required warnings issued by law enforcement officials to individuals taken into custody. Warnings involve notification that (1) they have the right to remain silent, (2) that anything they say may be used against them, (3) they have the right to an attorney during the interrogation process, and (4) that an attorney will be appointed if they cannot afford to hire one.

mistrial a trial that ends without a final disposition of guilt being established.

M'Naghten standard the "right/wrong test" used to determine whether an individual did not know the nature of an act or that it was wrong and thus may employ the insanity defense.

modus operandi the "way of operating" used to prove that a defendant has exhibited a pattern in behavior or methodology during the commission of criminal acts.

motion a formal request submitted to the court that a specific judgment or order be made.

motion to discover a request to the court to order the opposing party to produce.

motions in limine requests made at the beginning of a trial for certain pieces of evidence to be ruled inadmissible. *Motions in limine* are always discussed outside the presence of the jury.

motion to dismiss request made to the court for an order to cease and dismiss the judicial proceedings based on a lack of evidence.

motion to strike request made to the court to eliminate a legal pleading, either in part or in entirety.

motion to suppress requests by counsel to prevent the introduction of a specific piece of evidence (usually based on allegations of unconstitutional process).

motive reason or circumstance that compels an individual to act. In a criminal case, it is the primary reason or rationale for a defendant's criminal actions (e.g., revenge, jealousy, or the need for money).

negligence a crime characterized by failure to exercise due care toward another.

negligence per se negligence resulting from the violation of a public duty.

nighttime search warrants a legal authorization issued by a judicial officer which grans law enforcement to enter premises at night.

no-knock warrant a legal authorization issued by a judicial officer that grants law enforcement permission to enter premises without first notifying the occupants or owners. Such warrants are issued only in cases in which there exists a risk of harm to evidence, officers, or the community.

nolo contendere   a plea accepting charges without admitting or denying guilt which subjects the defendant to punishment while allowing denial of the alleged facts in other proceedings.

not guilty by reason of insanity   (1) a plea issued by a criminal defendant in open court in which he or she admits participation in the criminal act but not culpability because the defendant claims to have been insane when the crime was committed; (2) a finding by the jury in the form of a verdict of not guilty stating that the defendant lacked the mental capacity to form criminal intent.

not guilty plea   plea issued by a criminal defendant in open court in which he or she denies participation in the criminal act as charged.

not guilty verdict   a finding by the jury that the prosecution failed to prove its case beyond a reasonable doubt.

NOV.   acronym for the Latin phrase non obstante veredicto (literally "notwithstanding the verdict") referring to a decision by the court to set aside or reverse a jury's verdict on the grounds that such was not reasonably based on the facts or the law of the case.

oath or affirmation   a solemn promise to tell the truth, the whole truth, and nothing but the truth in a court of law, characterized by putting one's right hand on the Bible and committing to veracity in one's testimony under penalty of perjury. Today's courts allow witnesses to forego the Bible, but still require them to promise to tell the truth.

objections   legal protests made by the opposing side during the questioning of a witness. Rules of criminal procedure require objections to be made contemporaneously with the alleged violation of law (i.e., during the course of the trial, not at a later date) and are given for reasons such as irrelevance of material or improper questioning.

offer of proof   explanation to a judge made by counsel to overcome an objection, such as a demonstration as to why the question is necessary.

open fields doctrine   refers to the legal concept in which the courts have consistently ruled that no expectation of privacy can be created in an open field. Thus, the Fourth Amendment does not apply to such areas.

opening statement   initial presentation made by counsel in a criminal trial regarding material things that will be introduced during the trial. Such statements do not constitute evidence, and conjecture is generally not allowed.

opinion   explanation of a court's judgment.

opportunity   a set of circumstances that make the offense possible. In a criminal case, this is demonstrated through time that is unaccounted for during the period that the offense occurred.

order   formal mandate by the court directing that a certain action be taken.

original document   any writing, recording, or photograph itself or that is intended to have the same effect, such as a handwritten diary, typewritten photographed, magnetically impulsed, mechanically or electronically recorded, or otherwise compiled—also included are photographs l, radiographs (x-rays), videotapes, and motion pictures.

original jurisdiction   term used to refer to trial courts that maintain jurisdiction and authority over a particular matter, as distinct from appellate courts that hear cases originating in a lower court.

overrule   a judicial rejection of an attorney's objection.

pardon   formal forgiveness of a crime resulting in the individual's conviction being removed from criminal records through the application of the executive power of a governor or the President. Pardons remove all penalties and punishments and prevent any further prosecution of the individual for that particular crime.

parol evidence rule   legal assumption that a written agreement or contract is the final expression of that agreement and may not be modified, contradicted, or otherwise considered by outside statements, whether oral or written.

partial verdict   a jury verdict(s) of guilty regarding some, but not all, charges.

particularity   in search warrants, the specificity of place, time, and actual items to be searched or seized. With particularity, items unrelated to the specific boundaries remain immune from scrutiny.

past recorded recollections   an exception to the hearsay rule which permits the introduction of a recorded statement *if* the declarant's present recollection is insufficient to fully and accurately testify and *if* the statement was recorded in a timely manner consistent with a demonstration that such statement was intended to reflect he knowledge correctly.

per curiam   literally "by the court," a decision by an appellate court presented as being authored by a whole body (no specific authorship is noted).

peremptory challenge   a challenge used by counsel to remove a potential juror without explanation.

perjury   the offering of untruthful testimony by a person sworn to tell the truth considered punishable when the untruth relates to material facts of the case.

permissible inference   a deductive conclusion based on facts that is admissible in court.

personal knowledge   direct, firsthand, or authoritative knowledge of the facts of the case.

petit jury   a panel of individuals who are tasked with determination of fact and the rendering of a verdict in a trial (a "small" jury, as opposed to a "grand" jury). In civil cases, the petit jury helps determine fiduciary responsibility.

petition a formal written request to a court, such as for a continuance, case dismissal, or reduction of bail.

physical evidence evidence that can be experienced through any of the five senses; also called "real evidence."

physical facts rule legal concept that jurors are not obligated in any situation to accept facts that are contrary to physical facts, laws of nature, or common knowledge.

physician-patient privilege legal protection from compulsory disclosure of communications between physician and patient, including patient statements and physician observations, that are made in the course of their professional relationship in the absence of consent given by the patient.

plain error mistake by the trial court identified by an appellate court that is both obvious ("plain") and sufficient to warrant reversal of the original decision; also known as "reversible error."

plain feel doctrine legal authority that provides for the collection of items when such items are inadvertently discovered on an individual's person during legitimate police actions.

plain view doctrine legal authority allowing collection of criminal evidence when the item in question is unobstructed, the officer or authority is in a lawful position, and the evidentiary value of the item is immediately apparent.

plastic print lasting visible prints found in candle wax, tar, clay, oil, grease, or putty.

plea a claim of guilty, not guilty, not guilty by reason of affirmative defense, or nolo contendere (no contest) made by an individual in response to charges against him or her.

plea bargaining process by which a defendant pleads guilty or no contest in a criminal case in exchange for some agreement with the prosecutor as to the punishment generally, the prospect of a lighter sentence for the defendant and avoidance of a trial for the prosecutor engenders mutual interest in such bargaining.

police-informant privilege legal protection against compulsory disclosure of the identity of an informant, such as narcotics investigators and corporate whistleblowers.

polygraph examination a measure of deception or dishonesty by which an instrument records a person's physiological variations through skin conductivity (respiration, heart rate, and blood pressure) as he or she responds to questioning; also known as a psychophysiological detection of deception examination or, less accurately, a lie detector test.

precedents prior opinions of appellate courts that establish the legal authority or rule for future cases dealing with the same legal question.

preliminary hearing

preponderance of the evidence lowest standard of proof, required in most civil cases, that simply requires that a matter asserted is more probable than not.

present sense impression a statement is admissible if it describes or explains any event or condition made while the declarant was perceiving, or immediately after perceiving, such event or condition. These present-sense impressions do not have to be spontaneous and may be solicited from law enforcement authorities or private parties.

peremptory challenge challenge used by counsel to remove a potential juror without explanation.

presentment juries precursors to American grand juries; panels of private citizens who were empowered by the Assize of Clarendon to report crime and criminals in their community at a ratio of 12 per 100 and 4 per township.

presumption a conclusion made as to the existence or nonexistence of a fact that must be drawn from other evidence that is admitted and proven to be true. Conclusive presumptions are irrefutable; rebuttable presumptions may be challenged to disprove presumed fact.

presumption of innocence a rebuttable presumption required in criminal courts that the accused is innocent until evidence presented by the state sufficiently demonstrates guilt beyond a reasonable doubt.

prima facie evidence in a criminal case that "stands on its face," stands alone, or speaks for itself, such as a videotape showing the criminal act being committed and the person or persons involved; sufficient enough to prove the case in the absence of substantial evidence to the contrary.

privilege a special benefit enjoyed by a person or persons; immunity from compulsory testimony in any legal proceeding without the risk of legal consequences.

privilege against self-incrimination the benefit of not being forced to testify against oneself in court as guaranteed by the Fifth Amendment; also "taking the Fifth."

probable cause situated between reasonable suspicion and beyond a reasonable doubt, it is the standard required for an arrest, issuance of a warrant, and affectation of physical detainment. It requires a demonstration that a reasonable person could conclude that the accused has committed a crime or that evidence of such crime exists

probable cause requirement a provision housed within the Fourth Amendment, which limits the attainment of warrants to situations in which probable cause is established.

probity having a potentially major impact upon a jury.

pro bono literally "for the public good," legal work performed by defense attorneys generally without pay to assist the indigent or others with legal problems and limited funds; also may involve legal work performed for charities and social causes.

procedural defense an argument that seeks to negate the criminal charges through the assertion that the criminal justice process in the specific case was violated.

procedural law defines the process of adjudicating social behaviors prohibited by substantive law.

proof confirmation of a fact by presentment of evidence.

prosecuting attorney or prosecutor or solicitor adversarial counterpart to the defense attorney whose responsibility is to serve not only as an advocate for the government but to pursue procedural justice and a finding of guilt in cases in which sufficient evidence exists. In criminal cases, the prosecuting attorney has the burden of proof for demonstrating guilt beyond a reasonable doubt.

protective searches searches conducted by law enforcement authorities, which are designed to safeguard the safety of police officers and the community.

psychotherapist-patient privilege legal protection from compulsory disclosure of communications between therapist and patient, such as oral statements made by the patient and visual observations made by the psychotherapist, in the course of their professional relationship in the absence of consent given by the patient. Protection does not cover allegations of child sexual abuse, in cases where a patient poses a risk of serious harm to themself or others, or future crimes.

public defenders salaried public attorneys assigned by the courts to defend individuals who cannot afford a private attorney.

public safety exception one of several exceptions to the Exclusionary Rule that provides for the admission of illegally collected evidence if the items were collected in a situation where the interests of community safety outweighed the interests of personal liberty.

question of fact an issue of fact for which determination of veracity is evaluated by the trier of fact (i.e., jury member).

question of law an issue of fact determined solely by the court (i.e., judge), involving determinations of definition and application of the law.

questioned document any object with graphic markings whose authenticity is in question, such as a personal diary, international newspaper, or even neighborhood graffiti. Authentication often involves handwriting, ink, or content analysis.

real evidence any evidence that can be perceived with one of the five senses. It is the object itself, not a representation, testimonial impression, viewpoint, or expert opinion.

reasonable doubt a state in which a criminal defendant's guilt has not been proven to a moral certainty.

reasonable suspicion the lowest of all legal standards of justification, is less than probable cause but is that which is necessary to authorize an investigative detention. It requires a demonstration that a reasonable perception exists that a crime has been, is being, or will be committed.

rebuttal an attempt to disprove or contradict other evidence or presumptions through the offering of countervailing proof or argument.

rebuttable presumption a legal conclusion that may be challenged and overcome by the presentment of strong evidence by opposing counsel.

reconstruction amendments the Thirteenth, Fourteenth, and Fifteenth Amendments to the U.S. Constitution which were ratified between 1865–1870, which were intended to free and grant civil rights to former slaves.

recross-examination final stage in the examination of witnesses immediately following redirect and limited to those areas addressed therein.

redirect examination questioning of a witness again after cross-examination; often called the "redirect."

rehabilitation attempt in open court (often during the redirect) by an attorney to reestablish a witness' credibility after the opposing side has brought it into question or has explicitly or implicitly damaged it in the eyes of the jury.

rejoinder a defendant's response to a prosecution claim during rebuttal.

relevancy or relevant evidence refers to any material fact or information which tends to make the existence of any fact that is of consequence to the determination of the action more probable or less probable than it would be without the evidence.

requisite relationship a privileged relationship present and entered into without taint of intentional fraud or attempt to pervert the criminal justice system, such as attorney-client privilege.

reversible error an error of such magnitude that is related to the final disposition of the case.

right to privacy an expectation of protection against government-sponsored searches, seizures, and unlawful entry (including unauthorized disclosure of personal belongings) without probable cause and due process. Although not specifically discussed in the Constitution, the "right to be left alone" (Justice Louis Brandeis) has developed into a liberty of personal autonomy valued by all Americans. It is protected by (and narrowly defined in) the First, Fourth, Fifth, and Fourteenth Amendments.

rule of four to be placed on the docket, a case must receive at least four affirmative votes from Supreme Court justices for certiorari (in which the Supreme Court agrees to hear the case).

scientific evidence any physical evidence that involves theories, processes, experiments, empirical analyses, or results and requires the testimony of a qualified expert.

search an examination of an individual's person, property or other area in which they have a reasonable expectation of privacy by law enforcement.

search incident to arrest a search of a criminal suspect and his or her immediate area prior to or following an arrest conducted for the purpose of securing officer safety, preventing the destruction of criminal evidence, and/or discovering criminal contraband.

seizure a government action which meaningfully interferes with an individual's possessory interests in that property.

self-authenticating documents documents accepted on their face without demonstration of their authenticity, such as certified public documents, newspaper articles, photographs, radiographs (x-rays), and videos.

self-incrimination statements or communications that may expose the declarant to criminal prosecution.

"separate sovereigns" or "dual sovereignty" exception an exception to the double jeopardy clause of the Fifth Amendment which protects the interests of both state and federal authorities in cases in which a single act violates the laws of both sovereigns.

sequestration the isolation of a jury from the public or the separation of witnesses to ensure the integrity of testimony.

shared powers those powers which are delegated to both sovereigns in a federalist system.

silver platter doctrine the doctrine that allows state authorities to serve up illegally obtained evidence to federal agents to be used in federal court. The practice was ruled unconstitutional in *Elkins v. United States*

sneak-and-peak warrants legal authorization for law enforcement officials to gain surreptitious entry into premises or areas, such as residences and offices, upon determination that evidence is likely to be present. Significantly criticized by privacy advocates, the constitutionality of these warrants has been upheld by the Supreme Court as early as 1979.

spousal testimonial privilege legal protection against compulsory disclosure of communications occurring during a legally binding marital relationship, irrespective of the state of the marital union. The privilege provides the right of one spouse to refuse to testify against the other and the right to automatically render the witness unavailable .

staleness one of several considerations in search warrants, this is an often intangible concept that hinges upon a variety of factors, including, but not limited to: the timeliness of the probable cause (varies by offense) or the period between the precipitating factor and the execution of the warrant.

standard of proof that quantum of evidence which is required to demonstrate the truth of the matter in a court of law.

Stand Your Ground Laws laws which authorize the use of force by citizens when they are presented with force in any area outside the home where they have the legal authority to be. Such laws are generally accompanied with a legal presumption of reasonable fear which must be overcome in legal proceedings.

stare decisis literally "to stand by that which is decided"; the legal doctrine requiring courts to adhere to precedent law decided by an earlier high court and applicable when the same legal question is being considered.

statute of limitations *a type of federal or state law that restricts the time within which legal proceedings may be brought or offenses charged.*

statutory immunity a legal prohibition against the introduction of compelled testimony in a criminal prosecution against the speaker.

stipulation a product of an agreement between opposing counsels regarding specific facts of the case.

stop-and-frisk a "patdown" or search of a person's outer clothing or visual search of a vehicle for contraband; also called a "Terry stop."

subpoena a formal directive from a court that requires the named individual to appear at a particular place and time and to provide testimony or evidence under a penalty for failing to do so.

subpoena *ad testificandum* a court summons requiring the subpoenaed individual to provide oral testimony at a specified time for use in a hearing or trial.

subpoena *duces tecum* a court summons requiring the subpoenaed individual to appear and present specified documents or other tangible evidence for use in a hearing or trial.

substantive law law that defines the parameters of social behaviors.

sudden wealth the sudden and uncharacteristic purchasing of expensive items, such as the paying off of bills and the giving of charitable donations, which may indicate that a defendant has experienced a financial windfall and, in the absence of a reasonable explanation regarding the source of such sudden wealth, juries tend to consider it a motive.

take the Fifth the Fifth Amendment protection against compulsory testimony against oneself in which a defendant may refuse to testify against his or her interests on the grounds that the information may be incriminating.

Terry stop legal authority for a law enforcement official to conduct a "patdown" or search of a person's outer clothing or visual search of a vehicle for contraband. Although the Terry stop is not an arrest, the person is not free to leave; also called a "stop-and-frisk."

testimonial evidence written or oral assertion offered as proof of truth in court.

third-party consent usually used to refer to permission to search an area, granted by a non-owner or an individual without a proprietary interest of said area. Determinations of the admissibility of items collected in such searches involves consideration of common authority and competency.

throw-away evidence items collected by the police that have been discarded, thrown down, or similarly abandoned by an individual.

Title 18 the Crimes and Criminal Procedure section of the U.S. Criminal Code.

trace evidence Physical evidence resulting from the transfer of small quantities of material (e.g., hair, fibres, body fluids, textile samples, paint chips, glass fragments, gunshot residue particles, mud, insects, etc.) which may be collected by the police forensic unit, sexual assault team or medical examiner.

trial by battle an ancient dispute resolution method where those in dispute would fight one another until submission or death.

trial by ordeal medieval method of fact-finding which involved torture and which was predicated on the notion that divine illumination would indicate guilt or innocence.

trial de novo a form of appeal in which an appellate court conducts an entirely new trial of a matter. Unlike traditional appeals that review the court record for legal error, a trial de novo is a completely separate and independent hearing.

true bill a grand jury finding that sufficient evidence exists to support the claim that a person more likely than not committed a crime and should be indicted and prosecuted.

Unfair or undue prejudice refers to anything that could encourage a fact finder (e.g., jury member) to develop an adverse opinion before having sufficient knowledge of relevant facts.

U.S. Constitution the supreme law of the United of States of America; a document designed to create a strong central government while protecting the rights of individual citizens and sovereign states.

veracity the notion that something is accurate, truthful, and in accord with facts and reality.

vicinage the statutory jurisdiction of a particular court.

visible print a volatile impression made in a substance susceptible to decay, such as dust, blood, or powder

voiceprints an individually distinctive pattern of certain voice characteristics that is spectrographically produced.

voir dire the preliminary questioning of potential jurors or witnesses to ascertain competency to give or hear evidence.

wages of law or compurgation a medieval means of fact-finding in feudal courts in which the accused could choose to make a statement, take an oath, and provide individuals to swear to his veracity.

warrant requirement a provision found within the Fourth Amendment that mandates the attainment of a warrant by police prior to the execution of a search or an arrest.

warrant a legal directive showing probable cause that is issued by magistrates or judicial officials authorizing law enforcement officers to conduct arrests, seizures, or searches of persons or specified items at particular times and places.

warrantless search a law enforcement search of a person or a place conducted in the absence of a warrant; or, a category of search in which the U.S. Supreme Court has recognized an exception to the Warrant Clause of the Fourth Amendment in situations where the interests of society outweigh the invasiveness of government action.

witness a competent testifier of the truth who meets certain qualifications before providing testimony and through whom all evidence is introduced.

witness impeachment the process of calling into question the credibility of an individual who is testifying in a trial.

work-product doctrine protects materials prepared in anticipation of a legal proceeding. Rooted in *Hickman v. Taylor*, 329 U.S. 495 (1947)

writ formal written order issued by a body with judicial or administrative jurisdiction over a lower court or government official directing them to perform a certain action. In criminal proceedings, writs are issued by courts and include warrants, subpoenas, and such.

writ of certiorari a formal request to a superior court for legal review of potential legal error regarding a lower court's decision.

writ of habeas corpus an order in writing, issued in the name of the government by a judge of competent jurisdiction, and directed to a person who has another in his or her custody or detains him or her in confinement which commands him or her to bring such person so detained before the judge, at the time and place appointed, and to state the reasons for which he or she has imprisoned or otherwise deprived him or her of liberty.

CASES	ISSUES
Adams v. Williams, 407 U.S. 143 1903 (1972)	Warrantless Searches; *Terry* extension
Adamson v. California, 332 U.S. 46, 67 S. Ct. 1672, 91 L.Ed. 1903 (1947)	Self-incrimination
Administrator v. Repacholi, NTSB Order No. EA-3888 (served June 21, 1993)	Multiple hearsay
Alaska v. Coon, 974 P.2d 386, (Alaska Supreme Court, 1999)	Voiceprint identification
Alcorta v. Texas, 355 U.S. 28	Due Process
Alford v. United States, 282 U.S. 687 (1931)	Cross-examination
Anderson v. Creighton, 483 U.S. 635 (1987)	Warrantless searches
Apodaca v. Oregon, 406 U.S. 404 (1972)	Unanimity of verdicts
Arizona v. Evans, 514 U.S. 1 (1995)	Good faith exception to the exclusionary rule
Arizona v. Hicks, 480 U.S. 321 (1987)	"Plain view" exception
Arizona v. Youngblood, 488 U.S. 51 (1988)	Lost or misplaced evidence
Arkansas v. Sanders, 442 U.S. 753 (1979)	Automobile searches
Ashcraft v. State of Tennessee, 322 U.S. 143 (1944)	Consent and repeated questioning
Ashcroft v. Free Speech Coalition, 535 U.S. Amendment 234 (2002)	Child pornography and the First
Baker v. The State, 250 Ga. 671, 300 S.E. 2d 511 (1983)	Chain of custody
Baltimore Department of Social Services v. Bouknight, 493 U.S. 549 (1990)	Noncriminal proceedings and the Fifth Amendment
Barber v. Page, 390 U.S. 719 (1968)	Unavailability and hearsay
Batson v. Kentucky, 476 U.S. 79 (1986)	Jury selection & racial discrimination
Barnes v. United States, 412 U.S. 837 (1973)	Permissive inferences
Benton v. Maryland, 395 U.S. 784, 794 (1969)	Overruled *Palko*
Berkemer v. McCarty, 468 U.S. 442	Defining custody and *Miranda*
Betts v. Brady, 316 U.S. 455 (1942)	Right to counsel
Blackburn v. Alabama, 361 U.S. 199 (1960)	Mental competence to stand trial
Blau v. United States, 340 U.S. 332 (1951)	Spousal privilege
Bond v. United States, 131 S. Ct. 2355 (2011)	
Bourjaily v. United States, 483 U.S. 171 (1987)	Co-conspirator exemption to hearsay rule
Boykin v. Alabama, 395 U.S. 238 (1969)	Guilty pleas
Brady v. Maryland, 373 U.S. 83	Exculpatory evidence
Bram v. UnitedStates, 168 U.S. 532 (1897)	Self-incrimination
Branzburg v. Hayes, 408 U.S. 665 (1972)	Media privilege
Breithaupt v. Abram, 352 U.S. 432 (1957)	Blood tests and due process
Brinegar v. United States, 338 U.S. 160 (1949)	Probable cause
Brooks v. Tennessee, 406 U.S. 605, (1972)	Sixth and Fourteenth Amendments' right to testify on one's own behalf
Brown v. Illinois, 422 U.S. 590 (1975)	Purged taint exception to the exclusionary rule
Brown v. Mississippi, 297 U.S. 278, 56 S. Ct. 461, 80 L.Ed. 682 (1936)	Confessions through torture
Brown v. State, Okl.Cr. 518 P.2d 898 (1974)	Chain of custody
Bruton v. United States, 391 U.S. 123, 88 S. Ct. 1620 (1968)	Co-conspirator's testimony
Bumper v. North Carolina, 391 U.S. 543, 88 S. Ct. 1788, 20 L.Ed. 2d 797 (1968)	Consent
Burdeau v. McDowell, 256 U.S. 465 (1921)	Private party searches

CASES	ISSUES
Burnham v. Superior Court of California, Marin County, 495 U.S. 604 (1990)	Vicinage
California v. Acevedo, 500 U.S. 565, 111 S. Ct. 1982, 114 L.Ed. 2d 619 (1991)	Automobile searches
California v. Carney, 471 U.S. 386 (1985)	Motor home and automobile search
California v. Ciraolo, 476 U.S. 207 (1986)	Expectation of privacy
California v. Green, 399 U.S. 149 (1969)	Hearsay rule and the Confrontation Clause
California v. Greenwood, 486 U.S. 35, 108 S. Ct. 1625, 100 L.Ed.2d 30 (1988)	Curtilage and the Fourth Amendment
California v. Trombetta, 467 U.S. 479, 104 S. Ct. 2528 (1984)	Lost or misplaced evidence
Camara v. Municipal Court, 387 U.S. 523 (1967)	Home inspections and regulatory searches
Carnley v. Cochran, 369 U.S. 506	Waiver of right to plead guilty
Carroll v. United States, 267 U.S. 132, 45 S. Ct. 280 (1925)	Probable cause
Carter v. Kentucky, 450 U.S. 288 (1981)	Jury instructions
Chambers v. Maroney, 399 U.S. 42, 90 S. Ct. 1975, 26 L.Ed. 2d 419 (1970)	Inventory searches
Chambers v. Florida, 309 U.S. 227 (1940)	Consent and length of detention
Chapman v. State, 69 Wis. 2d 581, 583, 230 NW2d 824 (1975)	Jury's determination of credibility
Chavez v. Martinez, 270 F. 3d 852, 01-1444	Fifth Amendment
Chimel v. California, 395 U.S. 752, 89 S. Ct. 2034, 23 L.Ed.2d 685 (1969)	Incident to arrest
City of Indianapolis v. Edmond, 531 U.S. 32 (2000)	Narcotics checkpoints
Collins v. B. F. Goodrich Company, 558 F.2d 908 (8th Cir. 1977)	Out-of-court experiments
Colonnade Corp. v. United States, 397 U.S. 72 (1970)	Warrantless business inspections
Colorado v. Bertine, 479 U.S. 367 (1987)	Inventory searches
Colorado v. Connelly, 479 U.S. 157, 107 S. Ct. 515, 93 L.Ed.2d 473 (1986)	Confessions
Commonwealth v. Patterson, 445 Mass. 626 (2005)	*Daubert* and fingerprinting
Coolidge v. New Hampshire, 403 U.S. 443 (1971)	"Plain view" and particularity of warrants
County of Riverside v. McLaughlin, 500 U.S. 44 (1991)	
Cupp v. Murphy, 412 U.S. 291 (1973)	Fingernail scrapings
Dalia v. United States, 441 U.S. 238 (1979)	Due process
Daubert V. Merrell Dow Pharmaceuticals, Inc., 509 U.S. 579 (1993)	Introduction of scientific evidence
Davis v. Alaska, 415 U.S. 308 (1974)	Confrontation Clause and cross-examination
Davis v. North Carolina, 384 U.S. 737 (1966)	Consent and lack of information of constitutional rights
Delaware v. Prouse, 440 U.S. 648 (1979)	Warrantless roadblocks for licensing and registration
Donovan v. Dewey, 452 U.S. 494 (1981)	Closely regulated business exception to the warrant requirement
Douglas v. California, 372 U.S. 353 (1963)	Right to counsel
Doyle v. Ohio, 426 U.S. 610 (1976)	Post-arrest silence
Drake v. Tims, 287 P.2d 215 (Okl.1955)	Out-of-court experiments
Draper v. United States, 358 U.S. 307 (1959)	Probable cause
Duncan v. Louisiana, 391 U.S. 145 (1968)	Trial by jury
Durham v. United States (1954)	Insanity
Dutton v. Evans, 400 U.S. 74 (1970)	Hearsay and indicia of reliability
Dyer v. MacDougall, 201 F.2d 265, 268–69 (2d Cir. 1952)	Witness demeanor
Edwards v. Arizona, 451 U.S. 477 (1981)	Right to remain silent
Elkins v. United States, 364 U.S. 206 (1960)	Exclusionary rule
Escobedo v. Illinois, 378 U.S. 478 (1964)	Right to remain silent
Estelle v. McGuire, 502 U.S. 62, 112 S. Ct. 475 (1991)	Circumstantial evidence of past abuse
Fahy v. Connecticut, 375 U.S. 85 (1963)	Exclusionary rule
Faretta v. California, 422 U.S. 806, 95 S. Ct. 2525 (1975)	Self-representation
Fikes v. Alabama, 352 U.S. 191 (1957)	Low intelligence and consent
Florida v. Bostick, 501 U.S. 429, 111 S. Ct. 2382, 115 L.Ed.2d 389 (1991)	Custody
Florida v. Jimeno, 500 U.S. 248 (1991)	Scope of consent

CASES	ISSUES
Florida v. Royer, 460 U.S. 491 (1983)	Freedom from restraint and consent
Florida v. Wells, 495 U.S. 1 (1990)	Closed containers
Floyd v. State, 27 FLW S697, Florida Supreme Court (2002)	Chain of custody
Floyd v. State, 808 So. 2d 175, 184 (Fla. 2002)	Gruesome photographs
Fong Foo v. United States, 369 U.S. 141 (1962)	Double jeopardy and new evidence
Foster v. California, 394 U.S. 440 (1969)	Suggestive lineups
Frank v. Maryland, 359 U.S. 360 (1959)	Writs of assistance and search warrants
Frye v. United States, 54 App. D.C. 46, 293 F. 1013 (1923)	Scientific evidence
Garrity v. New Jersey, 385 U.S. 493, 87 S. Ct. 616 (1967)	Fifth Amendment and employment
Georgia v. McCollum, 505 U.S. 42 (1992)	Peremptory challenges and race
Gideon v. Wainwright, 372 U.S. 335, 83 S. Ct. 792, 9 L.Ed.2d 799 (1963)	Right to counsel
Giglio v. United States, 405 U.S. 150 (1972)	Revealing contents of plea agreements of key government witnesses to defense
Gilbert v. California, 388 U.S. 263 (1967)	Handwriting exemplars and Fifth Amendment
Glasser v. United States, 315 U.S. 60 (1942)	Jury's role in determining credibility and weight of evidence
Glidewell v. State, 1981 OK CR 39, 626 P.2d 1351(1981)	Gruesome photographs
Gooding v. United States, 416 U.S. 430, 94 S. Ct. 1780 (1974)	Nighttime searches
Graves v. United States, 150 U.S. 118, 121 (1893)	Failure to call witnesses
Griffin v. California, 380 U.S. 609 (1965)	Fifth Amendment
Griffin v. Wisconsin, 483 U.S. 868 (1987)	Warrantless searches and special needs
Groh v. Ramirez, 540 U.S. 551 (2004)	Exclusionary rule and particularity
Guy v. Wisconsin, 509 U.S. 914, 113 S. Ct. 3020 (1993)	Plain touch
Haley v. Ohio, 332 U.S. 596 (1948)	Consent and age of defendant
Hamling v. United States, 418 U.S. 87, 94 S. Ct. 2887	Cumulative evidence
Harris v. General Motors, 99-3092 (6th Cir. 2000). Argued: December 15, 1999—Decided and Filed: January 31, 2000	Physical facts rule
Hawkins v. United States, 358 U.S. 74 (1958)	Spousal privilege
Heath v. Alabama, 474 U.S. 82, 106 S. Ct. 433 (1985)	State sovereignty and dual jeopardy
Henderson v. State, 463 So.2d 196 (Fla. 1985)	Gruesome photographs
Henry v. United States, 361 U.S. 98 (1959)	Probable cause (first case!)
Herring v. United States, 555 U.S. 135 (2009)	Exclusionary Rule
Hester v. United States, 265 U.S. 57 (1924)	Open Fields Doctrine
Hickman v. Taylor, 329 U.S. 495 (1947)	"Work-product" doctrine and attorney-client privilege
Hiibel v. Sixth Judicial District Court of Nevada, Humboldt County, 542 U.S. 177; 124 S. Ct. 2451 (2004)	Right to remain silent and *Terry*
Hoffa v. United States, 385 U.S. 293 (1966)	Incriminating statements made to undercover officers
Holbrook v. Flynn, 475 U.S. 560, 106 S. Ct. 1340 (1986)	Reliable evidence
Holland v. United States, 348 U.S. 121, 75 S. Ct. 127 (1954)	Guilt through circumstantial evidence alone
Horton v. California, 496 U.S. 128 (1990)	Plain view
Hudson v. Michigan, 547 U.S. 586(2006)	Exclusionary rule
Idaho v. Wright, 497 U.S. 805 (1990)	Unavailable child witness and hearsay
Idaho v. Wright, 497 U.S. 805 (1990)	Confrontation Clause
Illinois v. Caballes, 543 U.S. 405 (2005)	Plain sniff and drug-sniffing dogs
Illinois v. Gates, 462 U.S. 213, (1987)	Probable cause
Illinois v. Krull, 480 U.S. 340 (1987)	Good faith exception to exclusionary rule
Illinois v. Lafayette, 462 U.S. 640 (1983)	Custodial arrests and purses
Illinois v. Lafayette, 462 U.S. 640 (1983)	Inventory searches (nonautomobile)
Illinois v. Rodriguez, 497 U.S. 177 (1990)	Consent and third-party authority
In re Winship, 397 U.S. 358 (1970)	Beyond a reasonable doubt
Iowa v. Tovar, 541 U.S. 77 (2004)	
Jackson v. Fletcher, 647 F.2d 1020 (1979)	Out-of-court experiments
Jaffee v. Redmond, 518 U.S. 1. (1996)	Psychotherapist-patient privilege
Johnson v. Louisiana, 406 U.S. 356 (1972)	Unanimity of verdicts
Johnson v. United States, 333 U.S. 10, (1948)	Neutral magistrate requirement

CASES	ISSUES
Jones v. United States, 362 U.S. 257 (1960)	Expectation of privacy and possession
Katz v. United States, 389 U.S. 347 (1967)	Electronic surveillance; expectation of privacy
Kentucky v. Stincer, 482 U.S. 730 (1987)	Competency of child witnesses
Kirby v. Illinois, 406 U.S. 682 (1972)	Preindictment lineups and suggestive police practices
Knowles v. Iowa, 525 U.S. 113 (1998)	Incident to arrest in non-arrest situations
Kyles v. Whitley, 514 U.S. 419 (1995)	
Larkins v. State, 655 So. 2d 95, 98 (Fla. 1995)	Gruesome photographs
Lefkowitz v. Turley, 414 U.S. 70 (1973)	Self-incrimination
Leland v. Oregon, 343 U.S. 790, 72 S. Ct. 1002 (1952)	Insanity and burden of proof of affirmative defenses
Lewis v. United States, 385 U.S. 206, 87 S. Ct. 424, 17 L.Ed.2d 312 (1966)	Entrapment
Luce v. United States, 469 U.S. 38 (1984)	Introduction of prior convictions of defendant to impeach his testimony
Lynumn v. Illinois, 372 U.S. 528 (1963)	Threats and coercion
Malloy v. Hogan, 378 U.S. 1 (1964)	Made the Fifth Amendment applicable to the states through the Fourteenth
Mapp v. Ohio, 367 U.S. 643, 81 S. Ct. 1684 (1961)	Exclusionary rule applied to the states
Martin v. Ohio, 480 U.S. 228	Affirmative defenses
Maryland v. Buie, 494 U.S. 325, 110 S. Ct. 1093, 108 L.Ed.2d 276 (1990)	Protective sweeps
Maryland v. Craig, 497 U.S. 836 (1990)	Confrontation clause and child witnesses
Massachusetts v. Sheppard, 468 U.S. 981 (1984)	Good faith exception to the exclusionary rule
McCulloch v. Maryland, 17 U.S. 316 (1819)	
McGautha v. California, 402 U.S. 183 (1971)	Introduction of criminal convictions of defendants who take the stand
McKinney v. Anderson, 924 F.2d 1500 (9th Cir. 1991)	Appointment of expert witnesses for indigent defendants
Medina v. California, 505 U.S. 437 (1992)	Affirmative defense
Michigan Department of State Police v. Sitz, 496 U.S. 444, 110 S. Ct. 2481 (1990)	Sobriety checkpoints/Fourth Amendment
Michigan v. Chesternut, 486 U.S. 567 (1988)	Exclusionary Rule
Michigan v. Jackson, 475 U.S. 625 (1986)	Sequential interrogations and Miranda
Michigan v. Long, 463 U.S. 1032 (1983)	Expansion of Terry
Miller v. California, 413 U.S. 15 (1973)	Qualifications of expert witness and three-prong test for obscenity
Miller v. Pate, 386 U.S. 1, 87 S. Ct. 785 (1967)	Perjured testimony
Mincey v. Arizona, 437 U.S. 385 (1978)	Emergency situations and warrantless searches
Minnesota v. Carter, 525 U.S. 23 (1998)	Exclusionary rule
Minnesota v. Dickerson, 508 U.S. 366 (1993)	"Plain feel" doctrine (extension of *Terry*)
Minnesota v. Olson, 495 U.S. 91, 110 S. Ct. 1684, 109 L.Ed.2d 85 (1990)	Overnight guests' right to privacy
Miranda v. Arizona, 384 U.S. 436, 86 S. Ct. 1602 (1966)	Right to remain silent
Mooney v. Holohan, 294 U.S. 103, 55 S. Ct. 340 (1935)	Perjured testimony
Moran v. Ohio, 469 U.S. 948 (1984)	Affirmative defense and burden of proof
Mosby v. Arkansas, CR 01-784 ___S.W.3d___, (2002)	Gruesome photographs and prejudice
Murray v. United States, 487 U.S. 533 (1988)	Exclusionary rule
Mutual Life Insurance Co. v. Hillmon, 145 U.S. 285 (1892)	State of mind and hearsay
Napue v. Illinois, 360 U.S. 264	
National Treasury Employee's Union. v. Von Raab, 489 U.S. 656 (1990)	Warrantless searches and special needs
Nelson v. State, Okl Cr., 687 P.2d 744, (1984)	Chain of custody
New Jersey v. T.L.O., 469 U.S. 325, 105 S. Ct. 733 (1985)	Warrantless searches
New York v. Belton, 453 U.S. 454 (1981)	Searches incident to arrest
New York v. Ferber, 458 U.S. 747 (1982)	Child pornography
New York v. Quarles, 467 U.S. 649 (1984)	Public safety exception
Nix v. Williams, 467 U.S. 431 (1984)	Inevitability of discovery
North Carolina v. Alford, 400 U.S. 25 (1970)	Guilty pleas
North Carolina v. Fleming, Supreme Court of North Carolina, 175A97 (1999)	Chain of custody

CASES	ISSUES
O'Connor v. Ortega, 480 U.S. 709 (1987)	Expectation of privacy
Ohio v. Robinette, 519 U.S. 33 (1996)	Automobile searches
Old Chief v. United States, 519 U.S. 172 (1997)	Relevancy
Oliver v. United States, 466 U.S. 170, 104 S. Ct. 1735 (1984)	Expectation of privacy
Olmstead v. United States, 277 U.S. 438, 48 S. Ct. 564, 72 L.Ed. 944 (1928)	Electronic surveillance
Omychund v Barker, 1 Akt. 21, 49; 26 ER 15, 33 (1745)	Best evidence rule
Oregon v. Mathiason, 429 U.S. 492, 97 S. Ct. 711, 50 L.Ed.2d 714 (1977)	Confessions
Ornelas v. United States, 517 U.S. 690, 116 S. Ct. 1657, 134 L.Ed.2d 911 (1996)	Automobile searches
Osborne v. Ohio, 495 U.S. 13 (1990)	Child pornography and definitions of obscenity
Palko v. Connecticut, 302 U.S. 319, 58 S. Ct. 149, 82 L.Ed. 288 (1937)	Fourteenth Amendment as applied to double jeopardy
Payne v. Arkansas, 356 U.S. 560 (1958)	Consent and low level of education
People v. King, 266 Cal.App.2d 437	Voiceprint identification
Penguin Books USA, Inc. v. New Christian Church of Full Endeavor, Ltd., 262 F. Supp. 2d 251, 261 (S.D.N.Y. 2003)	Adoptive admissions and hearsay
Pennsylvania v. Labron, 518 U.S. 938 (1996)	Automobile searches
Pennyslvania v. Mimms, 434 U.S. 106 (1977)	Extension of *Terry*
Pennsylvania v. Muniz, 496 U.S. 582 (1990)	*Miranda* and routine booking questions
Peters v. New York, 392 U.S. 40, 88 S. Ct. 1889 (1968)	Circumstantial evidence flight to avoid prosecution
Pointer v. Texas, 380 U.S. 400, 85 S. Ct. 1065 (1965)	Cross-examination and the Sixth Amendment
Pope v. State, 679 So. 2d 710, 714 (Fla. 1996)	Gruesome photographs
Pyle v. Kansas, 317 U.S. 213	
Rakas v. Illinois, 439 U.S. 128, 99 S. Ct. 421 (1978)	Expectation of privacy
Ramseyer v. General Motors Corp., 417 F.2d [*1027] 859 (8th Cir. 1969)	Out-of-court experiments
Rawlings v. Kentucky, 448 U.S. 98, 100 S. Ct. 2556 (1980)	Expectation of privacy
Reck v. Pate, 367 U.S. 433 (1961)	Sleep and food deprivation and consent
Rex v. Woodcock, 1 Leach 500, 502, 168 Eng. Rep. 352 (K.B. 1789)	Dying declarations
Rhode Island v. Innis, 446 U.S. 291 (1980)	*Miranda* and interrogation
Rice v. Paladin Enterprises, Inc., 128.3d 233 (4th Cir. 11/10/1997)	First Amendment
Rochin v. California, 342 U.S. 165, 72 S. Ct. 205, 96 L. Ed. 183 (1952)	Due process
Rock v. Arkansas, 483 U.S. 44 (1987)	Hypnosis and right to testify
Rogers v. Richmond, 365 U.S. 534, 81 S. Ct. 735 (1961)	Right to remain silent
Roviaro v. United States, 353 U.S. 53 (1957)	Informant's privilege
Sanders v. Texas, 10-05-00030-CR (2006)	Computer forensic science and *Daubert*
Sandstrom v. Montana, 442 U.S. 510 (1979)	Presumptions and inferences
Schmerber v. California, 384 U.S. 757 (1955)	Fifth Amendment and blood
Schneckloth v. Bustamonte, 412 U.S. 218, 93 S. Ct. 2041, 36 L.Ed.2d 854 (1973)	Consent
Shannon v. United States, 512 U.S. 573 (1994)	Relevancy of insanity defense
Sibron v. New York, 392 U.S. 40 (1968)	Companion to *Terry*
Silverthorne Lumber Co. v. United States, 251 U.S. 385 (1952)	Exclusionary rule
Skinner v. Railway Labor Executives Association, 109 S.Ct. 1384 (1990)	Public safety searches
Slochower v. Board of Higher Education of City of New York, 350 U.S. 551 (1956)	Fifth Amendment and school teachers
Smith v. Illinois, 469 U.S. 91 (1984)	Custodial interrogation and request for an attorney
Smith v. O'Grady, 312 U.S. 329 (1941)	
South Dakota v. Neville, 459 U.S. 553, 103 S. Ct. 916 (1983)	Circumstantial evidence interference with police

CASES	ISSUES
South Dakota v. Opperman, 428 U.S. 364 (1976)	Inventory searches
Spano v. New York, 360 U.S. 315, 79 S. Ct. 1202, 3 L.Ed.2d 1265 (1959)	Confessions
Spencer v. Texas, 385 U.S. 554, 560 (1967)	Prior convictions and unfair prejudice
Spevack v. Klein, 385 U.S. 511 (1967)	Fifth Amendment and attorneys
State Ex Rel Timble v. Hedman, 192 N.W.2d 432 (Minn. 1971)	Voiceprint identification
State v. Carr, 265 Kan. 608, 623, 963 P.2d 421 (1998)	Gruesome photographs
State v. Pennington, 89 KS SC 129 (2003)	Gruesome photographs
State v. Washington, 396 N.W.2d 156, 158 (Wis. 1986)	"Plain feel" exception
Stein v. Bowman, 38 U.S. 209 (1839)	Spousal privilege
Steve Jackson Games, Inc. v. United States Secret Service, 816 F. Supp 432 (W.D. Tex., 1993)	Fourth Amendment and ECPA
Stoner v. California, 376 U.S. 483 (1964)	
Strickland v. Washington, 466 U.S. 668, 104 S. Ct. 2052 (1984)	Ineffective counsel
Swidler and Berlin and James Hamilton v. United States, 524 U.S. 399 (1998)	Attorney-client privilege
Taylor v. Kentucky, 436 U.S. 478 (1978)	Reliable evidence
Teban v. United States, 382 U.S. 406, 86 S. Ct. 459 (1966)	Fact-finding nature of trial
Terry v. Ohio, 392 U.S. 1 (1968)	"Stop and frisk" searches
Thompson v. State, Okl. Cr., 567 P.2d 999 (1977)	Chain of custody
Thornton v. United States, 124 S. Ct. 2127 (2004)	Recent occupants of vehicles and incident to arrest
Torres v. Puerto Rico, 442 U.S. 465 (1979)	Border searches
Totten v. United States, 92 U.S 105 (1875)	Priest-penitent privilege
Trammel v. United States, 445 U.S. 40 (1980)	Spousal privilege to prevent testimony of spouse
Trupiano v. United States, 334 U.S. 699 (1948)	Search incident to arrest
Ulster County Court v. Allen, 442 U.S. 140 (1978)	Due process
Union Pacific Railroad Company v. Botsford, 141 U.S. 250 (1891)	
United States Department of Justice et al. v.Landano, 508 U.S. 165 (1993)	Informant's privilege
United States ex rel. Edney v. Smith, 425 F.Supp. 1038, 1976 Dist. Lexist 12131 (1976)	Physician-patient privilege
United States v. Abel, 469 U.S. 45 (1984)	Witness impeachment on grounds of bias or prejudice
United States v. Biswell, 406 U.S. 311 (1972)	Inspections of gun dealerships
United States v. Carey, 172 F.3d 1268 (10th Cir. 1999)	Secondary search warrants and child pornography
United States v. Ceccolini, 435 U.S. 268 (1978)	Exclusionary rule and witness identity
United States v. Chadwick, 433 U.S. 1, 97 S. Ct. 2476, 53 L.Ed.2d 538 (1977)	Expectation of privacy
United States v. Cortez, 449 U.S. 411 (1981)	Automobile stops
United States v. Crews, 445 U.S. 463 (1980)	Exclusionary rule
United States v. Crisp, 324 F. 3d 261 (4th Cir. 2003).	*Daubert* and fingerprinting
United States v. DeLeo, 422 F.2d 487 (1970)	Custodial searches
United States v. Dichiarinte, 445 F.2d 126 (7th Cir. 1971)	Consent searches
United States v. Drayton, 536 U.S. 194	Consent and random request for permission to search
United States v. Dunn, 480 U.S. 294 (1987)	Curtilage
United States v. Dunnigan, 507 U.S. 87, 113 S. Ct. 1111 (1993)	Right to testify does not include the right to commit perjury
United States v. Edwards, 415 U.S. 800, 94 S. Ct. 1234, 39 L.Ed.2d 771 (1974)	Custodial searches
United States v. Felix, 503 U.S. 378 (1992)	Double jeopardy
United States v. Fulk, 816 F.2d 1202, 1206 (7th Cir. 1987)	Impeachment and immoral acts
United States v. Gaudin [515 U.S. 506 (1995)	Materiality
United States v. Glass, 133 F. 3d 1356 (10th Cir. 1998)	"Dangerous patient" exception to psychotherapist-patient privilege
United States v. Hale, 422 U.S. 171 (1975) Jury instructions and inferences	

CASES	ISSUES
United States v. Hall, 142 F.3d 988 (7th Cir. 1998)	Third-party origination
United States v. Halper, 490 U.S. 435 (1989)	Double jeopardy protections
United States v. Havens, 446 U.S. 620, 100 S. Ct. 1912 (1980)	Introduction of evidence illegally seized for impeachment purposes
United States v. Hayes, 227 F.3d. 578 (2000)	"Dangerous patient" exception to psychotherapist-patient privilege
United States v. Humphrey, 208 F.3d. 1190	Chain of custody (10th Cir. 2000)
United States. v. Jackson, 390 U.S. 570, 88 S. Ct. 1209 (1968)	Guilty plea
United States v. Jacobsen, 466 U.S. 109 (1984)	Third-party searches
United States v. Janis, 428 U.S. 433 (1976)	Exclusionary rule and civil cases
United States v. Leon, 468 U.S. 897 (1984)	Good faith exception
United States v. Llera Plaza, et al., 188 F.Supp.2d 549 (E.D.Pa. 2002)	*Daubert* and fingerprinting
United States v. Manske, 98-CR-51-S (7th Cir. 1999)	Parameters of character evidence and impeachment
United States v. Martinez, 44 F. Supp. 2d 835, 836 (W. D. Tex. 1999)	Spousal privilege
United States v. Martinez-Fuerte, 428 U.S. 543 (1976)	Checkpoint searches
United States v. Matlock, 415 U.S. 164, 94 S. Ct. 988, 39 L.Ed. 2d 242 (1974)	Consent
United States v. Mayomi, 873 F. 2d 1049 (7th Cir. 1989)	Third-party origination
United States v. Mejia, 97 F.3d 1391, 1392 (11th Cir.1996)	Inferences
United States v. Mendenhall [1980] 446 U.S. 544 (1980)	Free-to-leave test
United States v. Miller, 425 U.S. 435 (1976)	Fourth Amendment and banking records
United States. v. Mitchell, 365 F. 3d 215 (3rd Cir. 2004)	*Daubert* and fingerprints
United States v. Montoya de Hernandez, 473 U.S. 531 (1985)	Border searches
United States v. Nixon, 418 U.S. 683 (1974)	Presidential privilege
United States v. Nolan, 718 F. 2d 589, 596 (3rd Cir. 1983)	Illegal searches
United States v. Pervaz, 118 F. 3d 1 (1st Cir. 1997)	Third-party origination
United States v. Place, 462 U.S. 696 (1983)	Reasonableness
United States v. Rabinowitz, 339 U.S. 56 (1950)	Incident to Arrest
United States v. Reynolds, 345 U.S. 1 (1953)	Military secrets privilege
United States. v. Ricco, 52 F.3d 58, 61–62 (4th Cir. 1995)	Chain of custody
United States v. Robinson, 414 U.S. 218 (1973)	Searches incident to arrest
United States v. Ross, 456 U.S. 798 (1982)	Automobiles
United States v. Scheffer, 118 S. Ct. 1261 (1998)	Polygraph examinations
United States v. Smith, 80 F.3d 1188, 1193 (7th Cir. 1996)	Impeachment and uncharged crimes
United States v. Spraque et al., 282 U.S. 716 (1931)	
United States v. Turner, 169 F.3d 84 (1st Cir. 1999)	Consent and the exclusion of evidence
United States v. Villamonte-Marques, 462 U.S. 579 (1983)	
United States v. Wade, 388 U.S. 218 (1967)	Lineup identifications and the Fifth Amendment
United States v. Watson, 423 U.S. 411, 96 S. Ct. 820, 46 L.Ed.2d 598 (1976)	Probable cause
United States v. Weinstock, 231 F.2d 699 (D.C. Cir. 1956)	Inferences
United States. v. Williams, 504 U.S. 36 (1992)	Exculpatory evidence
United States v. Williams, 822 F. 2d 1174, 1184 (D.C. Cir. 1987)	"Plain feel" exception
United States v. Wilson, 985 F. 2d 348, 351 (7th Cir. 1993)	Impeachment and uncharged crimes
United States v. Zizzo, 120 F. 3d 1338, 1355 (7th Cir. 1997)	Impeachment and uncharged crimes
United States Department of Justice, et al. v. Landano, 508 U.S. 165 (1993)	Informant privilege
Upjohn Co. v. United States, 449 U.S. 383 (1981)	Attorney-client privilege
Wainwright v. Greenfield, 474 U.S. 284 (1986)	Inference and right to counsel
Wainwright v. Sykes, 433 U.S. 72 (1977)	Contemporaneous objection rule
Warden v. Hayden, 387 U.S. 294, 87 S. Ct. 1642, 18 L.Ed.2d 782 (1967)	Exigent circumstances
Weeks v. United States, 232 U.S. 383 (1914)	Exclusionary rule

CASES	ISSUES
Wheeler v. United States, 159 U.S. 523 (1895)	Competency of children
Whren v. United States, 517 U.S. 806, 116 S. Ct. 1769, 135 L.Ed.2d 89 (1996)	Fourth Amendment
Williams v. Florida, 399 U.S. 78 (1970)	
Wilson v. Arkansas, 514 U.S. 927 (1995)	Fourth Amendment
Wolf v. Colorado, 338 U.S. 25 (1949)	Due process and the exclusionary rule
Wolfle v. United States, 291 U.S. 7 (1934)	Spousal privilege
Wong Sun v. United States, 371 U.S. 471 (1963)	Confessions and incriminating statements
Wyman v. James, 400 U.S. 309 (1971)	Warrantless welfare inspections of private residences

Abraham, Henry J. (1968). *The Judicial Process* (2nd Edition). England: Oxford University Press.

Alschuler, Albert (1994). A Peculiar Privilege in Historical Perspective: The Right to Remain Silent. *Michigan Law Review*, 94(8): 2625–2673.

Amar, Akhil Reed (2000). *The Bill of Rights: Creation and Reconstruction*. New Haven, CT: Yale University Press.

Amar, Akhil Reed (2005). *America's Constitution: A Biography*. New York: Random House.

American Bar Association (2005). Criminal Justice Section: Standards: Defense Functions. http://www.abanet.org/crimjust/standards/dfunc_blk.html#1.1

Aron, Roberto; Duffy, Kevin T.; and Rosner, Jonathan L. (1990). *Impeachment of Witnesses: The Cross-Examiner's Art*. Connecticut: West Group.

Avery, Michael (2003). Confronting Issues in Criminal Justice: Law Enforcement and Criminal Offenders: You Have a Right to Remain Silent. *Fordham Urban Law Journal*, 30: 571–615.

Balazic, Joze; Prebil, Ivan; and Certanc, Niko (2006). Computer Simulation of the Accident with Nine Victims. *Forensic Science International*, 156(2): 161–165.

Beard, Glenn A. (1997). Congress v. the Attorney-Client Privilege: A "Full and Frank" Discussion. *American Criminal Law Review*, 35(1): 119–135.

Bentham, Jeremy (1827). *Rationale of Judicial Evidence*, v. 1. London: Hunt & Clarke.

Berg, Erik C. (2000). Legal Ramifications of Digital Imaging in Law Enforcement. *Forensic Science Communications*, 2(4): http://www.bafo.org.uk/digital.htm.

Bergman, Barbara and Hollander, Nancy (1994). *Everytrial Criminal Defense Resource Book*. Connecticut: West Group.

Bernstein, David W. (2002). Disinterested in Daubert: State Courts Lag Behind in Opposing "Junk Science". *Washington Legal Foundation*, 14(4). http://www.wlf.org/upload/6-21-02Bernstein.pdf. Last accessed on 18 April 2006.

Besselman, John P. (2005). The Knock and Announce Rule: "Knock, Knock, Knocking on the Suspect's Door". www.fletc.gov/legal/qr_articles/knockandannounce.pdf. Last accessed on 14 September 2005.

Binder, David F. (2001). *Hearsay Handbook* (4th Edition). Connecticut: West Publishing.

Blackstone, William (1765–1769). *Commentaries on the Laws of England*. Oxford: Clarendon Press.

Bradley, Craig M. (2006). A Sensible Emergency Doctrine: Probable Cause and Warrantless Entry. *Trial*, 42(8): 60–64.

Breyer, Stephen (2005). *Active Liberty: Interpreting Our Democratic Constitution*. New York: Alfred A. Knopf Publishing.

Britz, Marjie T. (2004). *Computer Forensics and Cybercrime: An Introduction*. Upper Saddle River, NJ: Prentice-Hall.

Britz, Marjie T. (2013). *Computer Forensics and Cyber Crime: An Introduction* (3rd Edition). New Jersey: Prentice Hall.

Broun, Kenneth S.; Mosteller, Robert P.; and Bilionis, Louis D. (2001). *Problems in Evidence*. Connecticut. West Publishing.

Bulzomi, Michael J. (1997). Knock and Announce: A Fourth Amendment Standard. *FBI Law Enforcement Bulletin*, (May).

Bureau of Justice Statistics (2013). *Examining the Work of State Courts*. Accessed at www.bjs.gov on 4 February 2014.

Casey, Eoghan (2004). *Digital Evidence and Computer Crime: Forensic Science, Computers and the Internet* (2nd Edition). New York: Academic Press.

Cassidy, R. Michael (2003). Sharing Sacred Secrets: Is It (Past) Time for a Dangerous Person Exception to the Clergy-Penitent Privilege. *William and May Law Review*, 44(4): 1627.

Catz, Robert S. and Lange, Jill J. (1987). Judicial Privilege. *Georgia Law Review*, 22(89): www.lexisnexis.com.

Ceci, Stephen J. and Bruck, Maggie (1999). *Jeopardy in the Courtroom: A Scientific Anaylsis of Children's Testimony*. Washington, DC: American Psychological Association Books.

Ceci, Stephen J. and Hembrooke, Helene (1998). *Expert Witnesses in Child Abuse Cases: What Can and Should Be Said in Court*. Washington, DC: American Psychological Association Books.

Chatterjee, Neel I. (1995). Admitting Computer Animations: More Caution and New Approach Are Needed. *Defense Counsel Journal*, 62(1): 36–46.

Cockburn, Andrew (2006). The Judas Gospel. http://www9.nationalgeographic.com/ngm/gospel/feature.html. Last accessed 22 April 2006.

Conti, Richard P. (1999). The Psychology of False Confessions. *The Journal of Credibility Assessment and Witness Psychology*, 2(1): 14–36.

Crawford, Kimberly A. (1997). Sneak and Peek Warrants: Legal Issues Regarding Surreptitious Searches. *FBI Law Enforcement Bulletin*, (February).

CSP (2012). *Examining the Work of State Courts: An analysis of 2010 Court Caseloads.* Grant No. 2011-BJ-CX-K062. Washington, DC: Courts Statistics Project.

Davies, Philip R.; Brooke, George J.; and Callaway, Phillip R. (2002). *The Complete World of the Dead Sea Scrolls.* London: Thames and Hudson.

DeClue, Gregory (2005). *Interrogations and Disputed Confessions.* Florida: Professional Resource Press.

Del Carmen, Rolando V. and Walker, Jeffery T. (2004). *Briefs of Leading Cases in Law Enforcement.* New York: Anderson Publishing.

Department of Justice (1999). Trace Evidence Recovery Guidelines. *Forensic Science Communications*, 1(3). http://www.fbi.gov/hq/lab/fsc/backissu/oct1999/traceack.htm.

Department of Justice (2001). Field Guidance on New Authorities that Relate to Computer Crime and Electronic Evidence Enacted in the USA Patriot Act of 2001. Computer Crime and Intellectual Property Section. http://www.usdoj.gov/criminal/cybercrime/PatriotAct.htm

Department of Justice (2002). *Using DNA to Solve Cold Cases.* NIJ Special Report: July, 2002. http://www.ncjrs.gov/pdffiles1/nij/194197.pdf.

Dershowitz, Alan M. (2004). *America on Trial: Inside the Legal Battles that Transformed Our Nation from the Salem Witches to the Guantanamo Detainees.* New York: Time Warner Book Group.

Dressler, Joshua and Thomas, George C. (2003). *Criminal Procedure: Principles, Policies, and Perspectives* (2nd Edition). Minnesota: Thomson-West Publishing.

Durkin, Kevin P. (2004). Demonstrative Evidence. A paper presented at the 2004 ABA Section of Litigation Aviation Litigation. http://www.abanet.org/litigation/committee/aviation/2004/materials/demonstrative.doc.

Edwards, Deborah C. (2006). Duty-to-Warn Even If It May Be Hearsay? The Implications of a Pyschotherapist's Duty-to-Warn a Third Person When Information Is Obtained from Someone Other than His Patient. *Indiana Health Law Review*, 3(171): www.lexisnexis.com.

Fallon, Richard H.; Meltzer, Daniel J.; and Shapiro, David, L. (2004). *Hart and Weschler's: The Federal Courts and the Federal System 2004 Supplement* (5th Edition). New York: Foundation Press.

Fenner, G. Michael (2003). *The Hearsay Rule.* Durham, NC: Carolina Academic Press.

Fisanick, Christian A. (2003). *Vehicle Search Law Deskbook.* St. Paul, MN: Thomson/West Publishing.

Gardner, Thomas J. and Anderson, Terry (1995). *Criminal Evidence: Principles and Cases* (3rd Edition). St. Paul: Thomas/West Publishing.

Gardner, Thomas J. and Anderson, Terry (2004). *Criminal Evidence: Principles and Cases* (5th Edition). Minnesota: West Publishing.

Garner, Bryan A. (2004). *Black's Law Dictionary* (8th Edition). Minnesota: West Publishing.

Glancy, Graham D.; Regehr, Cherly; and Bryant, Anthony G. (1998). Confidentiality in Crisis: Part II—Confidentiality of Treatment Records. *Canadian Journal of Psychiatry*, 43: http://www.cpa-apc.org/Publications/Archives/CJP/1998/Dec/glancy2.htm

Glass, Albert (1933). Historical Aspects of Habeas Corpus. *St. John's Law Review*, 9: 55–70.

Glatt, John (2001). *Internet Slavemaster.* New York: St. Martin's Press.

Glyn, Timothy P. (2002). Federalizing Privilege. *The American University Law Review*, 52(59). www.lexisnexis.com.

Grenig, Jay E. and Gleisner, William C. (2005). *eDiscovery and Digital Evidence* (Vol. 1). Minnesota: West Publishing.

Hagen, Ed and Nissman, David M. (1994). *Law of Confessions* (2nd Edition). St. Paul, MN: Thomson/West Publishing.

Hall, Kermit (1983). The Judiciary on Trial: State Constitutional Reform and the Rise of an Elected Judiciary 1846–1860. *The Historian*, 46: 337–354.

Hamby, James E. and Thorpe, James W. (1999). The History of Firearm and Toolmark Identification. Association of Firearm and Tool Mark Examiners Journal, *20th Anniversary Issue*, 31(3). http://www.firearmsid.com/A_historyoffirearmsID.htm.

Helmholz, R.H. (1983). Crime, Compurgation and the Courts of the Medieval Church. *Law and History Review*, 1(1): 1–26.

Hemmens, Craig; Worrall, John L.; and Thomson, Alan (2004). *Significant Cases in Criminal Procedure.* Los Angeles, CA: Roxbury Publishing Company.

Hendrie, Edward (2002). Inferring Probable Cause: Obtaining a Search Warrant for a Suspect's Home without Direct Information that Evidence Is Inside. *FBI Law Enforcement Bulletin*, 71(2): 23–32.

Hermann, Michele G. (2003). *Search and Seizure Checklists.* St. Paul, MN: Thomson/West Publishing.

Hilton, O. (1979). History of Questioned Document Examination in the United States. *Journal of Forensic Science*, 24(4): 1424–1432.

Hilton, O. (1982). *Scientific Examination of Questioned Documents.* London: Elsevier.

Holliday, Wyatt (2012). The Answer to Criminal Aggression Is Retaliation: Stand-Your-Ground Laws and the Liberalizatio of Self-Defense. *The University of Toledo Law Review*, 43(407): 1–33.

Hunter, Michael J. (2005). The Man on the Stairs Who Wasn't There: What Does a Defendant's Pre-Arrest Silence Have to Do with Miranda, the

Fifth Amendment, or Due Process? *Hamline Law Review*, 28(277): 431–517.

Joseph, Paul R. (2002). *Warrantless Search Law Deskbook*. St. Paul, MN: Thomson/West Publishing.

Joseph, Gregory P. and Saltzburg, Stephen A. (1994). *Evidence in America: The Federal Rules in the States*. Charlottesville, VA: Michie, Co.

Kardell, Robert (2003). Spousal Privileges in the Federal Law. *FBI Law Enforcement Bulletin*, 72(8): www.fbi.gov/publications.

Karin, Marcy Lynn (2002). Out of Sight, but Not Out of Mind: How Executive Order 13,233 Expands Executive Privilege While Simultaneously Preventing Access to Presidential Records. *Stanford Law Review*, 55(2): 529–571.

Kempin, Frederick (1990). *Historical Introduction to Anglo-American Law* (3rd Edition). St. Paul, MN: West Publishing.

Kirkpatrick, Laird (2005). Crawford: A Look Backward, a Look Forward. *Criminal Justice Magazine*, 20(2): http://www.abanet.org/crimjust/cjmag/20-2/kirkpatrick.html.

Kocourek, Albert and Wigmore, John H. (1915). *Sources of Ancient and Primitive Law*. Boston: Little, Brown, and Company.

LaFave, Wayne R. (2004). *Search and Seizure, 4th (Criminal Practice Series)*. New York: Thomson/West Publishing.

Lasseter, Don (2000). *Die for Me: The Terrifying True Story of the Charles Ng & Leonard Lake Torture Murder*. New York: Pinnacle.

Leonard, David (2004). Federal Privileges in the 21st Century: An Introduction. *Loyola of Los Angeles Law Review*, 38(515). www.lexisnexis.com.

Lerner, Craig S. (2003). The Reasonableness of Probable Cause. *Texas Law Review*, 81(4): 951–1029.

Leveritt, Mara (2002). *Devil's Knot: The True Story of the West Memphis Three*. New York: Atria Books.

Levy, Leonard W. (1999). *Origins of the Fifth Amendment*. New York: Ivan R. Dee Publishing.

Levy, Leonard W. (2001). *The Origins of the Bill of Rights*. New Haven, CT: Yale University Press.

Lewis, Anthony (1989). *Gideon's Trumpet*. New York: Vintage.

Lewis, Jason (2005). To Serve and Protect: Thornton v. United States and the Newly Anemic Fourth Amendment. *Mercer Law Review*, 56:1471–1482.

Lewis, Susan (2005). The Viking Deception. PBS: NOVA. http://www.pbs.org/wgbh/nova/vinland/fakes.html - Last accessed on 18 April 2006.

Lombardo, Paul (2005). The Newest Federal Privilege: Jaffee v. Redmond and the Protection of Psychotherapeutic Confidentiality. *Developments in Mental Health Law*. http://www.ilppp.virginia.edu/dhml/issues/jaffeev16n2.html.

Martin, E.X. III (1999). High Tech Demonstrative Evidence: Show Them, Don't Tell Them. CLE Online

Seminar. http://www.cyberbar.net/expaper/demev.html. Last accessed on 12 May 2014.

McDonald, William (1985). *Plea Bargaining: Critical Issues and Common Practices*. Washington, DC: U.S. Government Printing Office.

McIlwain, C.H. (1914). Due Process of Law in Magna Carta. *Columbia Law Review*, 14(1): 27–51.

McInnis, Thomas (2000). *The Christian Burial Case: An Introduction to Criminal and Judicial Procedure*. Connecticut: Praeger Publishing.

McKeever, Brian P. (2004). Contours and Chaos: A Proposal for Courts to Apply the "Dangerous Patient" Exception to the Psychotherapist-Patient Privilege. *New Mexico Law Review*, 34(109). www.lexisnexis.com.

Moenssens, Andre A.; Starrs, James E.; Henderson, Carol E.; and Inbau, Fred E. (1995). *Scientific Evidence in Civil and Criminal Cases*. Westbury, NY: The Foundational Press, Inc.

Molony, Thomas J. (1998). Is the Supreme Court Ready to Recognize Another Privilege? An Examination of the Accountant-Client Privilege in the Aftermath of Jaffee v. Redmond. *Washington and Lee Law Review*, 55: 247–258.

Montgomery, Bruce P. (2002). Source Material: Nixon's Ghost Haunts the Presidential Records Act. *Presidential Studies Quarterly*, 32(4): 789–795.

Moore, Mark H. (2001). Alternative Strategies for Public Defenders and Assigned Counsel. A paper presented at the Executive Session on Public Defense. Cambridge, MA: April.

Mueller, Christopher B. and Kirkpatrick, Laird C. (2004). *Evidence under the Rules* (5th Edition). New York: Aspen Law.

National Center for State Courts (2003). Examining the Work of State Courts. National Center for State Courts.

Ofshe, Richard and Watters, Ethan (1996). *Making Monsters: False Memories, Psychotherapy, and Sexual Hysteria*. California: University of California Press.

Oppenheimer, Tamara; Bankim, Thanki; Goodall, Patrick; King, Henry; Phelps, Rosalind; Cutress, James; Yeo, Nik; and Carpenter, Chloe (2006). *The Law of Privilege (UK)*. England: Oxford University Press.

Pardo, Michael S. (2005). Disentangling the Fourth Amendment and the Self-Incrimination Clause. *Iowa Law Review*, 90: 1857–1905.

Park, Roger C. (2001). *Trial Objections Handbook* (2nd Edition). Connecticut: West Publishing.

Parrish, Matthew S. (1993). The "Plain Feel Exception"—A Fourth Amendment Rendition of the Princess and the Pea. *University of Cincinnati Law Review*, Summer. (62 U. Cin. L. Rev. 321).

Penfil, Elizabeth (2005). In the Light of Reason and Experience: Should Federal Evidence Law Protect Confidential Communications between Same-Sex Partners?. *Marquette Law Review*, 88(815). www.lexisnexis.com

Petegorsky, Michael Nasser (2013). Plea Bargaining in the Dark: The Duty to Disclose Exculpatory Brady Evidence during Plea Bargaining. *Fordham Law Review*, 81(6): 3598–3650.

Pfefferli, Peter W. (2001). Review 1998–2001 from the Coordinating Laboratory on: Questioned Documents (Other than Handwriting). Presented at the 13th Annual INTERPOL Forensic Science Symposium, Lyon, France, 16–19 October 2001. http://www .interpol.int/Public/Forensic/IFSS/meeting13/Reviews /QDnoHw.pdf. Last accessed on 23 April 2014.

Pittman, R. Carter (1960). The Safeguards of the Sixth Amendment. Essay included in the Speaker's Digest of the Bill of Rights Commemoration Committee; http://rcarterpittman.org/essays/Bill_of_Rights /Sixth_Amendment.html.

Pollack, F. and Maitland, F.W. (1968). *History of English Law* (2nd Edition, v. 2). Cambridge: Cambridge University Press.

Pope, Kenneth S.; Butcher, James N.; and Seelen, Joyce (2006). *The MMPI, MMPI-2, and MMPI-A in Court: A Practical Guide for Expert Witnesses and Attorneys* (3rd Edition). Washington, DC: American Psychological Association Books.

Public Broadcasting Service (1997). Online Newshour: Under Fire. FBI: Feeling the Heat. 15 April 1997. http://www.pbs.org/newshour/bb/fedagencies/ april97/fbi_4-15a.html (last accessed 30 December 2005).

Rabinowitz, Dorothy (2003). *No Crueler Tyrannies: Accusation, False Witness, and Other Terror of Our Times*. New York, NY: Free Press.

Rehnquist, William H. (2001). *The Supreme Court: A New Edition of the Chief Justice's Classic History*. New York: Alfred A. Knopf Publishing.

Rehnquist, William H. (2002). *The Supreme Court*. New York: Alfred A. Knopf Publishing.

Rickless, Samuel C. (2005). The Coherence of Orthodox Fourth Amendment Jurisprudence. *George Mason University Civil Rights Law Journal*, 15: 261–296.

Robbins, John B. (1971). The Confederacy and the Writ of Habeas Corpus. *The Georgia Historical Quarterly*, 55(1): 83–101.

Roberts, Allen Dale and Sillitoe Linda (1990). *Salamander: The Story of the Mormon Forgery Murders* (2nd Edition). Utah: Signature Books.

Rosenberg, Irene Merker and Rosenberg, Yale L. (1995). Perhaps What Ye Say Is Based Only on Conjecture: Circumstantial Evidence, Then and Now. *Houston Law Review*, 31: 1391–1427.

Rozell, Mike (1998). Executive Privilege in the Lewinsky Scandal: Giving a Good Doctrine a Bad Name. *Presidential Studies Quarterly*, 28(4): 816–821.

Saferstein, Richard E. (2005). *Forensic Science Handbook, Volume II* (2nd Edition). Upper Saddle River, NJ: Prentice-Hall.

Sager, Lawrence G. (2006). *Justice in Plainclothes: A Theory of American Constitutional Practices*. New Haven, CT: Yale University Press.

Sales, Bruce D. and Shuman, Daniel W. (2005). *Experts in Court: Reconciling Law, Science, and Professional Knowledge*. Washington, DC: American Psychological Association Books.

Sampson, William (1813). *The Catholic Question in America*. New York: Edward Gillespy.

Scalia, Antonin (1997). *A Matter of Interpretation: Federal Courts and the Law*. Princeton, NJ: Princeton University Press.

Schippers, David P. (2000). *Sellout: The Inside Story of President Clinton's Impeachment*. Washington, DC: Regnery Publishing.

Schmid, Karl H. (2002). Journalist's Privilege in Criminal Proceedings: An Analysis of United States Courts of Appeals' Decisions from 1973–1999. *American Criminal Law Review*, 39(1441). www .lexis-nexis.com

Scoboria, Alan; Mazzoni, Giuliana; Kirsch, Irving; and Milling, Leonard S. (2002). Immediate and Persisting Effects of Misleading Questions and Hypnosis on Memory Reports. *Journal of Experimental Psychology: Applied*, 8(1): 26–32.

Sklansky, David Alan (2005). Police and Democracy. *Michigan Law Review*, 103: 1699–1831.

Smith, Fred Chris and Bace, Rebecca Gurley (2003). *A Guide to Forensic Testimony: The Art and Practice of Presenting Testimony as an Expert Technical Witness*. Boston, MA: Pearson Publishing.

Stelzner, Luis G. (1980). The Fourth Amendment: The Reasonableness and Warrant Clauses. *New Mexico Law Review*, 10: 33–49.

Strong, John W.; Brown, Kenneth S.; Dix, George E.; Imwinkelried, Edward J.; Kaye, D.H.; Mosteller, Robert P.; and Roberts, E.F. (1999). *McCormick on Evidence*. St. Paul, Minnesota: West Publishing.

Stuart, Gary L. (2004). *Miranda: The Story of America's Right to Remain Silent*. Arizona: University of Arizona Press.

Swinton, Nathan (2006). Privileging a Privilege: Should the Reporter's Privilege Enjoy the Same Respect as the Attorney-Client Privilege? *Georgetown Journal of Legal Ethics*, 19(979): www.lexisnexis.com.

Tetu, Philip Raoul (1995). *Probable Cause: Between the Police Officer and the Magistrate*. Illinois: Charles C. Thomas.

Townsend, Jules A. (1997). The Expert Witness and the Law of Evidence. *Forensic Economics*, 9(2): 165–169.

Tracy, John Evarts (1952). *Handbook of the Law of Evidence*. New York: Prentice-Hall Publishing.

Vontu (2006). *Data Security Trends*. San Francisco, CA: Vontu, Inc.

Walsh, Walter J. (2005). The Priest-Penitent Privilege: An Hibernocentric Essay in Postcolonial Jurisprudence. *Indiana Law Journal*, 80(1037). www.lexisnexis.com.

Weinstein, Jack B.; Mansfield, John H.; Abrams, Norman; and Berger, Margaret A. (1997). *Evidence: Cases and Materials* (9th Edition). New York: Foundation Press.

Wetterer, Charles M. (1998). *The Fourth Amendment: Search and Seizure*. New Jersey: Enslow Publishers.

Whitehead, John W. and Aden, Steven H. (2002). Forfeiting "Enduring Freedom" for "Homeland Security": A Constitutional Analysis of the USA Patriot Act and the Justice Department's Anti-Terrorism Initiatives. *American University Law Review*, 51(6): 1080–1133.

Wiecek, William M. (1970). The Great Writ and Reconstruction: The Habeas Corpus Act of 1867. *The Journal of Southern History*, 36(4): 530–548.

Wigmore, John H. (March 6, 1914). The Code of Hammurabi. *Northwestern University Bulletin,* XIV(25).

Wigmore, John Henry (1923). *A Treatise on the Anglo-American System of Evidence in Trials at Common Law: Including the Statutes and Judicial Decisions of all Jurisdictions of the United States and Canada* (2nd Edition). Boston: Little, Brown, and Company.

Wigmore, John H. (1936). *Panorama of the World's Legal System* (Library Edition). Washington, DC: Washington Law Book Company.

Wigmore, John H. (1940). *A Treatise on the Anglo-American System of Evidence in Trial at Common Law* (3rd Edition). Boston: Little Brown and Company.

Wigmore, John H. (1942). *Wigmore's Code of Evidence*. Boston: Little, Brown, and Company.

Wills, William (1853). *An Essay on the Principles of Circumstantial Evidence*. Philadelphia, PA: T. & J.W. Johnson Publishing.

Worrall, Simon. (2002). *The Poet and the Murderer: A True Story of Literary Crime and the Art of Forgery*. New York: Dutton Publishing.

Zotti, Priscilla Machado (2005). *Injustice for All: Mapp vs. Ohio and the Fourth Amendment*. New York: Peter Lang Publishing.

Photo Credits

Chapter Opener: Library of Congress Prints and Photographs Division [LC-USZC2-2244].

Icons: Ghen/Fotolia.

Chapter 1 Page 3: Ghen/Fotolia; 5: Jsp/Shutterstock; 11: Library of Congress Prints and Photographs Division [LC-USZ62-57840]; 15: Larry1235/Shutterstock; 21: Bettmann/Corbis; 28: Alan Diaz/AP Images.

Chapter 2 Page 67: Bikeriderlondon/Shutterstock; 69: Handout/MCT/Newscom; 72: Brett Coomer/Pool/epa/Corbis; 76: Janine Wiedel Photolibrary/Alamy; 79: Kevin Seifert/AP Images.

Chapter 3 Page 99: Bettmann/Corbis; 104: John Angelillo/UPI/Newscom; 105: LAPD/AP Images; 108: Reed Saxon/AP Images; 114: Kathy Willens/AP Images; 116: Lucy Nicholson/Reuters/Landov.

Chapter 4 Page 132: Wellphoto/Shutterstock; 135: Bst2012/Fotolia; 138: Caetano Barreira/Reuters; 143: Marjie Britz, 143: Bill Wippert/Rapport Press/Newscom.

Chapter 5 Page 152: Neil DeCrescenzo/Newscom; 167: Karamysh/Shuttesrstock.

Chapter 6 Page 173: Stockbyte/Getty Images; 183: CBP Photo/Alamy; 186: ZUMA Press, Inc./Alamy; 195: Fstop123/E+/Getty Images; 197: Jim West/Alamy.

Chapter 7 Page 205: Mug Shot/Alamy; 209: Marta Lavandier/AP Images; 210: Library of Congress Prints and Photographic Division; 217: ZUMA Press, Inc/Alamy; 222: Lisa F. Young/Shutterstock;

Chapter 8 Page 231: Glow Images/Getty Images; 236: McClatchy-Tribune/Tribune Content Agency LLC/Alamy; 238: Vicki Beaver/Alamy; 241: Karen Stallwood/KRT/Newscom; 244: Richard Ellis/Alamy;

Chapter 9 Page 256: Steve Marcus/Las Vegas Sun/AP Images; 258: Joe Berlinger/Courtesy of Third Eye Motion Picture Company/Marjie Britz.

Chapter 10 Page 272: Library of Congress Prints and Photographic Division; 278: Sakchai Lalit/AP Images; 287: Mike Yelman/Ai Wire Photo Service/Newscom; 288: ZUMA Press, Inc./Alamy.

Chapter 11 Page 302: Los Angeles Daily News/ZUMApress/Newscom; 305: Doin Oakenhelm/Fotolia; 308: Igor/Fotolia

Chapter 12 Page 321: Vince Bucci/AP Images; 326: Marjie Britz; 327: Getty Images; 334: AP Images; 337: Library of Congress Prints and Photographs Division [LC-USZ62-109416]; 343: Marjie Britz; 344: Marjie Britz;

Chapter 13 Page 353: Alfred Schauhuber/ImageBroker/Alamy; 355: Matthew S. Hicks/AP Images; 367: Paul Buck/Newscom; 369: Plougmann/E+/Getty Images; 375: Marjie Britz.

Index

▼

Videotaped bookings, 223
Videotape evidence, 373
Vignera v. New York, 23
Visible print, 341
Vitale, Pamela, 204
Voice identification, 253, 330
Voiceprints, 342
Voice recognition, 342–44
Voir dire, 25, 85, 230–32, 259
Volstead Act, 133
Voluntariness, 190–91, 218–19
Voluntary statements, 208, 210, 212, 224

W

Wager of law or compurgation, 10
Wainwright v. Greenfield, 118
Warrant clause, 137–38
    and reasonableness clause, 16–17
Warrantless entry, 365
Warrantless searches, 144
    administrative justification exceptions,
        193–97
    automobile searches, 184–89
    and computer evidence, 363–65
    and consent, 189–93
    incident to arrest, 175–81
    investigative detentions, 171–79
    overview, 172
    plain feel doctrine,183–84
    plain view doctrine, 181
Warrant requirement, 172, 175, 187, 197
Warrants, 69, 136–42
    defined, 137
    types of, 141–44
Weatherford v. Bursey, 78
Wecht, Cyril, 254
Weeks v. United States, 149, 150, 152, 157, 159, 168
Wells, William, 102
West Memphis Three, 104–5, 260
Westover v. U.S., 23
Wheeler v. United States, 233
Wigmore, John Henry, 3, 97, 98, 292, 293, 294
Wigmore's systems of law, 3–5
WikiLeaks
    and journalistic freedom, 309
Wilder, Mark, 223

Williams, Jayson, 255
Williams, Wayne, 112
Williams Rule, 112
Williford v. State, 358
Winston, Jameis, 103
Witherspoon v. Illinois, 26
Witnesses
    authentication of evidence, 330, 335, 336
    availability of, 284–87
    children as, 119, 230–34
    competence of, 230–32, 234–36
    credibility of, 236–43
    cross-examine, 237–39, 263–64
    defendants and, 236–43
    defined, 229
    expert, 254–57
    impeachment of, 88, 244–47, 260
    incompetence and, 232
    lay, 253–54
    methods of impeachment, 247–48
    protection from perjury of, 242–43
    qualifications of, 229–36
    redirect, recross, and rehabilitation of, 264–65
    right to serve as, 240–42
    special circumstances and, 234–36
    testimony of, 229, 248, 266
    threatening of, 109
    unavailability of, 279–84
Wolfle v. United States, 297, 298
Wolf v. Colorado, 150
Wonderland murders, 372
Wong Sun v. United States, 153–54, 159
Woodward, Louise, 90
Workplace searches, 136
    and school searches, 196–97
Work-product doctrine, 81, 295
Writ of habeas corpus, 40n1, 60
Writs of assistance, 136
Writs of certiorari, 57

Y

Yates, Andrea, 72

Z

Zinn, Herbert "Shadowhawk,", 358